HISTORY

This book provides an accessible introduction to a wide range of concerns that have preoccupied historians over time. Global in scope, it explores historical perspectives not only from historiography itself but from related areas such as literature, sociology, geography and anthropology which have entered into productive dialogues with history.

Clearly written and accessible, this third edition is fully revised with an updated structure and new areas of historical enquiry and themes added, including the history of emotions, video history and global pandemics. In all of this, the authors have attempted to think beyond the boundaries of the West and consider varied approaches to history. They do so by engaging with theoretical perspectives and methodologies that have provided the foundation for good historical practice. The authors analyse how historians can improve their skills by learning about the discipline of historiography, that is, how historians go about the task of exploring the past and determining where the line separating history from other disciplines, such as sociology or geography, runs.

History: An Introduction to Theory and Method is an essential resource for students of historical theory and method working at both an introductory and more advanced level.

Dr Peter Claus is an Access Fellow, Director of OxNet & CredOx at Pembroke College, Oxford. He is currently writing a book on the 'East End Underworld' in the twentieth century co-authored with John Marriott, also for Routledge. The combination of Access activities and historical research has developed an historical interest in the metropolis and a commitment to research on outreach, education theory and practice, public engagement and the democratization of the archive.

Professor John Marriott is Visiting Fellow at Kellogg College, Oxford. His research has focused on London and Empire from the seventeenth century. Among numerous books are *Beyond the Tower: A History of East London* (2011). He is currently editing a major digital resource on the nineteenth-century British Empire and completing a study of the origins of British territorial power in India.

History
An Introduction to Theory and Method
Third Edition

Peter Claus and John Marriott

LONDON AND NEW YORK

Designed cover image: *História, do pintor grego* Nikolaos Gysis (1892)

Third edition published 2023
by Routledge
4 Park Square, Milton Park, Abingdon, Oxon, OX14 4RN

and by Routledge
605 Third Avenue, New York, NY 10158

Routledge is an imprint of the Taylor & Francis Group, an informa business

© 2023 Peter Claus and John Marriott

The right of Peter Claus and John Marriott to be identified as authors of this work has been asserted in accordance with sections 77 and 78 of the Copyright, Designs and Patents Act 1988.

All rights reserved. No part of this book may be reprinted or reproduced or utilised in any form or by any electronic, mechanical, or other means, now known or hereafter invented, including photocopying and recording, or in any information storage or retrieval system, without permission in writing from the publishers.

Trademark notice: Product or corporate names may be trademarks or registered trademarks, and are used only for identification and explanation without intent to infringe.

First edition published by Pearson Education Limited 2012
Second edition published by Routledge 2017

British Library Cataloguing-in-Publication Data
A catalogue record for this book is available from the British Library

Library of Congress Cataloging-in-Publication Data
Names: Claus, Peter (Research fellow in History), author. | Marriott, John, 1944– author.
Title: History : an introduction to theory and method / Peter Claus, and John Marriott.
Description: Third edition. | Abingdon, Oxon ; New York : Routledge, 2023. |
  Includes bibliographical references and index.
Identifiers: LCCN 2022060845 (print) | LCCN 2022060846 (ebook)
Subjects: LCSH: Historiography.
Classification: LCC D13 .C5835 2023 (print) | LCC D13 (ebook) |
  DDC 907.2—dc23/eng/20221220
LC record available at https://lccn.loc.gov/2022060845
LC ebook record available at https://lccn.loc.gov/2022060846

ISBN: 978-0-367-74097-9 (hbk)
ISBN: 978-0-367-74095-5 (pbk)
ISBN: 978-1-003-15608-6 (ebk)

DOI: 10.4324/9781003156086

Typeset in Times New Roman
by Apex CoVantage, LLC

In dedication to the memory of
David Brion Davis (1927–2019)
Yale University

R. G. Collingwood (1889–1943)
Pembroke College, Oxford
'I miglior fabbri.'

Contents

List of Figures   xii
List of Tables   xiv
Prologue   xv

PART 1
Philosophies   1

1 From the Ancients to the Christians   3

1.1 Herodotus and Gold-digging Ants 3
1.2 Thucydides and Reason: an Historian for Our Times? 7
1.3 What Did the Romans Ever Do for history? 9
1.4 Late Antiquity, Christianity and the End of Days 13

2 From the Middle Ages to the Early Modern   17

Introduction 17
2.1 European Christendom and the 'Age of Bede' 18
2.2 Peoples of the Book: Jewish and Islamic Conceptions of History 22
2.3 The Renaissance, Humanism and the Rediscovery of the Classics 28
2.4 The Battle of Books: Camden, Clarendon and English Historical Writing 31

3 Enlightenment and Romanticism   37

Introduction 37
3.1 The English Enlightenment? 37
3.2 Secular Histories 41
3.3 Romanticism, Nationalism and the Hero in History: Sir Walter Scott and Thomas Carlyle 45

4 The English Tradition   54

Introduction 54
4.1 Responses to the Enlightenment: Edmund Burke 54

4.2 Constitutionalism and the Whig Interpretation of History 60
4.3 The 'New Whigs'?: the School of J. H. Plumb 63

5 The North American Tradition   71

Introduction 71
5.1 America and the New Order of the Ages 71
5.2 The Progressive or 'New' Historians 76
5.3 The Consensus Historians 80
5.4 The Other America 83
5.5 Black Lives Matter: a Coda 89

6 Histories of Revolutions; Revolutionary Histories   93

Introduction 93
6.1 Thomas Paine and the Radical Tradition 94
6.2 Contemporary Responses to the American and French Revolutions 98
6.3 Germany, G. W. F. Hegel and the Spirit of History 102
6.4 Karl Marx and 'Historical Materialism' 105
6.5 Marxism in the Twentieth Century 108

7 Postmodernism and Postcolonialism   114

Introduction 114
7.1 Modernity and the Enlightenment 114
7.2 Postmodernism 118
7.3 Postcolonialism and the West 122

PART 2
Varieties   127

8 Political History   129

Introduction 129
8.1 Theories of the State 129
8.2 High and Low Politics: the Case of the British Labour Party 136
8.3 Beyond State and Party: Political Histories and Civil Society 141

9 Economic History   146

Introduction 146
9.1 Economics, Population and Social Change 146
9.2 Economic Historians and the Big Historical Questions 150
9.3 The Business of Business History 155

10 Social History   162

Introduction 162

  10.1 The Emergence of Social History 162
  10.2 Class and Authority 165
  10.3 The Family in History 168
  10.4 The Social History of Faith 173

11 Cultural History 180

 Introduction 180
  11.1 Towards a Definition of Cultural History 180
  11.2 Survival of the Carnival 186
  11.3 Empire and the Cultural Turn 188
  11.4 History of Emotions 192

12 Feminism, Gender and Queer History 198

 Introduction 198
  12.1 Feminism and History 198
  12.2 The Attack on Class 203
  12.3 Gender and Identity 207
  12.4 Sexuality and Identity 211

13 Public History 221

 Introduction 221
  13.1 What Is Public About History? 221
  13.2 Consumption of Public History 227
  13.3 Producing Public History 230
  13.4 Public History as Contested Knowledge 233

14 Visual History 237

 Introduction 237
  14.1 Visual Histories in Film and Television 237
  14.2 Ways of Seeing: Paintings 245
  14.3 Ways of Seeing: Prints and Photographs 250
  14.4 Playing With History: the Rise of the Video Game 256

15 Global History 262

 Introduction 262
  15.1 The Challenge of Global History 262
  15.2 Origins of the Global Imagination 267
  15.3 Enter 'New World History' 273
  15.4 Global Pandemics 277

16 Environmental History 283

 Introduction 283

16.1 The Scope of Environmental History and Historical Precedents 283
16.2 European Colonialism and the Environment 287
16.3 Modern Environmentalism 291

PART 3
Interdisciplinarities   301

17 Archaeology   303

Introduction 303
17.1 The Lure of Archaeology 303
17.2 The Theoretical Turn: Collingwood and Childe 310
17.3 Historical Archaeology 313
17.4 Jerusalem and Its Layers 315

18 Anthropology   322

Introduction 322
18.1 Pens and Pith Helmets: the Influence of Anthropology on History 322
18.2 Functionalism and Structuralism: Understanding the Lord Mayor's Show 326
18.3 Myths and History: Jewish Conspiracies and the 'Blood Libel' 329
18.4 The 'Dying God': Captain Cook and Ethnohistory 331
18.5 Microhistories: Cheese, Worms, Night Battles and Ecstasies 334

19 Literature   338

Introduction 338
19.1 Literature as History 338
19.2 Historicism: Text and Context 344
19.3 Nostalgia and the Graphic Novel 347
19.4 Writing the Metropolis 351

20 Geography   359

Introduction 359
20.1 History, Space and Place 359
20.2 Geographies of Empire 363
20.3 'How to Lie With Maps': Maps, Methodology and the Metropolis 367

PART 4
Methods   375

21 Proof and the Problem of Objectivity   377

Introduction 377

21.1 History: a Science or an Art? 377
21.2 History and the Status of Historical Knowledge 381
21.3 Choosing Evidence, Challenging Interpretations 386
21.4 Causes in History 391

22 Ordering of Time   397

Introduction 397
22.1 Time, History, Modernity 397
22.2 Newton and the 'Time Reckoner' 404
22.3 Time, History and the Shape of Things to Come 408
22.4 Events, People and Periods: What Is 'Victorian'? When were the 'Sixties'? 412

23 Archives in a Digital World   417

Introduction 417
23.1 What Is an Archive? 417
23.2 'When We Return as Human Beings Again': Archives and the Ashes 420
23.3 'Speaking for Ourselves': State and Community Archives 422
23.4 Archives and the Digital Turn 427
23.5 Social Media 434

24 Oral History   441

Introduction 441
24.1 'Anthropologists of Ourselves': Urban, Rural, Foreign 441
24.2 Oral Historiography 448
24.3 Interviewing Techniques and the Limits of Memory: Arthur Harding and the East End Underworld 452
24.4 The Wider Conceptual Problems 454

Bibliography   459
Index   484

Figures

0.1	Calvin the historian	xvi
2.1	Library at Alexandria	20
2.2	Flavius Josephus	24
2.3	Oliver Cromwell at Battle of Marston Moor, 1644	32
3.1	Phillip de Loutherbourg, *Avalanche in Alps*, 1803	46
3.2	Thomas Carlyle	50
4.1	Edmund Burke	57
4.2	David Wilkie, *Chelsea Pensioners Reading the Gazette of the Battle of Waterloo*, 1822	66
5.1	Thomas Cole, *Oxbow*, 1836	72
5.2	Charles Beard	78
5.3	Eric Williams	87
6.1	Tom Paine	95
6.2	Mary Wollstonecraft	97
6.3	Jacques-Louis David, *Death of Marat*, 1793	102
8.1	Ramsay McDonald	138
9.1	Boundary stone at time of Eyam Plague	147
9.2	Interior of Cotton Mill, 1835	154
10.1	Durham Miners Gala	166
10.2	EP Thompson	178
11.1	Carnival, 1532	183
11.2	Rabelais, *Gargantua*, 1537	189
12.1	Women in coal mines	199
12.2	Women's Liberation Movement, Washington, 1970	204
13.1	Mural of Battle of Cable Street	224
13.2	Battle of Fredericksburg, 1863	224
14.1	American Civil War	241
14.2	*Apocalypse Now*, 1979	244
14.3	Darnley Portrait of Elizabeth I, *c.*1575	247
14.4	Joseph Wright, *Blacksmith's Shop*, 1771	249
14.5	James Gillray, 'John Bull and the Sinking Fund', 1807	251
14.6	John Dixon, *The Oracle*, 1774	253
15.1	Ibn Battuta at ruins of Pharaonic Egypt	269
16.1	Alexander von Humboldt, *c.*1800	290
17.1	Amerindian burial mound, *c.*1850	306
18.1	Captain Cook	332

Figures xiii

20.1	Niels Lund, *The Heart of the Empire*, 1904	360
20.2	Strabo map, *c.*25 BCE	366
20.3	'TO' map, *c.*630 CE	367
20.4	Charles Booth, *Descriptive Map of London Poverty*, 1889. Descriptive map of London poverty, 1889 (north-western sheet)	370
21.1	Indian rebels, 1857	382
21.2	Chartist meeting at Kennington Common, 1848	387
22.1	John Harrison's third clock	403

Tables

1.1	Sources used by Romans in thinking about the past	12
3.1	Key words and concepts of Enlightenment and Romanticism	47
4.1	Elements of old Whiggism in the new	64
13.1	Contesting knowledge – a table of binary opposites	234
20.1	Booth's street classification	369

Prologue

What Did History Ever Do for Us?

In the sense of both what happened in the past and the study of that past, history matters. At a personal level, history offers us an unrivalled means of making sense of where we have come from and therefore where we are in the modern world. In this respect, we are all historians by instinct. The extraordinary popularity of history programmes, costume dramas, documentaries, historical novels and heritage sites testifies to the enduring importance of the past in our lives. While literature and the media may tend to produce a consensual view of history, it is well to remember that in practice the interpretation of the past is contested, often with devastating consequences. Different interpretations of the past have provoked and continue to provoke conflict between peoples. When this escalates into war, opposing sides justify their actions by appealing to competing versions of the historical record. And past grievances – real or imaginary – which are fuelled by selective interpretations of the past have often served as powerful stimuli to action.

But can history be a force for good in shaping our thinking about the present and the future? It is fashionable to bemoan the failure of contemporary leaders to learn from the mistakes of the past. Certainly, the atrocities perpetuated in continued conflict around the world have a sickening familiarity. And yet the rise of fascism as a European power or the nuclear bombing of civilian populations thankfully seem remote possibilities. As for the future, well, historians are not astrologers; most of us would contend that since historical change always has unforeseen consequences it would be rash to predict what is likely to happen in the future, except in the broadest terms.

History, This Book and You

The third edition of this book is not intended, any more than earlier editions, to persuade anyone of the importance of history. We anticipate that by the time you read it as a prospective historian or enthusiastic amateur, the case has already been made in your mind that the past and our access to it are matters of great consequence. Rather, we wish to provide an accessible introduction to some of the concerns that have preoccupied historians over time and what history as a discipline – that is, historiography – can contribute to our lives. Instinctive though we may be as historians, we can become better historians if we take the trouble to learn something of how historians go about the task of exploring the past. This seemingly simple project, however, is fraught with difficulties. From the time of Herodotus and Thucydides in the ancient world, the role of the historian and the very nature of history have been contested. For the past 2,000 years, therefore, the boundaries of history have been fluid. Even now, some hundred or so years after the establishment of history as an academic discipline, we are not entirely sure what 'proper' history is or where the line separating history from, say, sociology or geography runs.

The difficulties are further compounded when we broach the question of historical truth. At school we were inclined to believe the claims that history books told us about the past as it actually happened. Much of this derives from the moment in the late nineteenth century when the discipline of history emerged and embarked on what was considered as a realistic mission to retrieve the truth from the past. Prior to this, people who wrote about the past had other objectives in mind, most notably the political imperative to consolidate the authority of the state or peoples they represented. Many historians today are also committed to historical truth, but despite the various methods used to retrieve it, historical truth remains an elusive goal. Some critics go as far as to suggest that the promise is entirely false, for the historical record is always open to different interpretations, and who is in a position to decide which one is the truth?

Thus, while there may have been a perceptible shift away from the further reaches of linguistic theory, where postmodernism and 'deconstruction' methodologies have sought to convince us that there is no such thing as historical truth and where history is merely a 'text' that can be read in endless different ways, historians continue to reflect on their craft. This book seeks to be part of that reflection but is written unapologetically for real tutors and real students, and relates to courses actually being taught in colleges and universities today.

With an increasing emphasis on interdisciplinary approaches, as well as a greater focus on the processes of study and writing history, courses on theory, method and historiographical practice seem to grow in number and significance. Our ambition is to be part of this debate about historiography but also to provide a resource to students working at both an introductory and an advanced level. In doing this, the book enthusiastically engages with theoretical perspectives and methodologies that have provided the foundation for what it recognized as good historical practice but also engages with areas such as literature, sociology, geography and anthropology, which have entered into productive dialogues with history.

Few have displayed the same clarity and insight as the six-year-old Calvin in explaining to his friend Hobbes some of the fundamental problems faced by historians today. Causality, history as fiction, historical truth and interpretation lie at the very heart of the discipline, and if we have been able to discuss these issues with as much good sense as the wonderful Calvin then our time has been well spent.

Figure 0.1 Calvin the historian

Contributors: Bill Watterson, Andrews McMeel Publishing

Why the Book?

The third edition of the book is as timely as its predecessors. Some of the classic introductory texts which foregrounded debates within historiography, such as E. H. Carr's *What is History?* (1961) and G. E. R. Elton's *The Practice of History* (1967), remain decidedly dated in that they do not address the important developments of recent years. John Tosh's popular and admirable *The Pursuit of History* (2021) claims to be an introduction to modern history but is not for the person coming to history for the first time. We felt the need for a textbook that encompasses the broad range of historical inquiry in ways which were accessible to the non-specialist. We have assumed no previous knowledge of the discipline, eliminated the use of jargon as far as possible, and drawn upon historical examples which we anticipate will be of interest to a modern readership. Above all, in writing the book we had in mind readers who were about to embark on a serious study of history and therefore needed to know more about the nature of the discipline from examples of studies undertaken by some of its leading figures. We hope too that it may be of interest in some of the areas it touches upon to postgraduates eager to consolidate their knowledge and to take that knowledge up to another level. Although this is a textbook, we are anxious not to imply that closure is either likely or desirable in history; in all areas of our discipline we would want to treat history as very much open to dispute. Indeed, we would like to encourage debate and dispute among students and general readers alike.

The book is not designed to be read sequentially; rather, we consider it as a handbook and prefer that you simply dip into individual chapters when the need arises to know more about particular aspects of the discipline. The book is, however, organized in a way to help you make sense of the material. In Part I, *Philosophies*, we begin mapping out the theoretical precepts and broad trajectory of modern historical practice, the origins of which can be traced to ancient Greece and Rome, but which were fundamentally reshaped during the Enlightenment, developed during the nineteenth and twentieth centuries, and challenged in recent times by the critiques launched by postmodernism and postcolonialism. In Part II, *Varieties*, we describe some of the more influential strands of history that have emerged in the postwar period as a challenge to traditional approaches. Their boundaries may be defined only imprecisely, but historians working in the fields of, say, cultural, global or public history have greatly extended the scope of historical inquiry and at the same time placed on the agenda new ways of thinking about who and what are legitimate subjects and objects of study and, indeed, who might be regarded as a bona fide historian. Part III, *Interdisciplinarities*, investigates the often-troubled relationships between history and disciplines within the social sciences, including geography and anthropology. Given that the boundaries of history are fluid and permeable, it comes as no surprise to learn that historians have tended to borrow freely from other disciplines. By breaking down what are often artificially constructed barriers between disciplines, this too has opened exciting new avenues of historical inquiry talking through issues that have been seen as the defining elements of history. Finally, in Part IV, *Methods*, we address questions such as truth, objectivity and the ordering of time which implicitly or otherwise define the scope and limits of the historical enterprise and finish by providing practical guidance on some of the problems encountered by an historian embarking on an exciting venture of research. The focus here is on evidence – what forms it takes, how it is gathered and stored, the opportunities provided by digital archives – and some of the problems this presents for us.

It will come as no comfort to know that these fundamental features of historical inquiry raise complex issues which continue to be hotly debated, but we take you carefully on the first steps of the journey. We have attempted to make the material accessible not only by avoiding overly complex theoretical discussion but also through various pedagogical devices. Each chapter therefore begins with a short introduction which elaborates on the themes in the context of the study of history. At the end of the chapters, there is a brief section entitled 'Postscript' which explains why the issues raised remain important to the study of history and why they should be taken seriously by practising historians. Finally, the 'Further Reading' section provides a selection of books and articles that we have found useful and hope will extend and deepen your awareness of the overarching themes.

History, the Book and Us

Both of us are modern historians. Peter Claus has researched histories of the metropolis and education and has been committed to widening participation and the democratization of the archive, while John Marriott is a cultural and intellectual historian with a long-standing interest in London and Empire during the nineteenth and twentieth centuries. In writing this book we have understandably drawn upon knowledge of our particular specialisms, but at the same time we have attempted to widen the geographical and temporal scope of the book by including discussions of historical episodes in ancient and medieval periods, from both European and non-European worlds.

As this is the third edition of the book, we have eagerly grasped the opportunity to substantially revise its structure, content and approach. We have provided the structure with a stronger chronological narrative and have written new chapters on important areas of historical inquiry such as advances in digital history, social media, the role of pandemics in history and the history of emotions. Equally, we have extended the spread of historical examples and now give much greater emphasis to experience beyond Europe, most notably American and imperial histories.

Finally, we are ever more conscious of the diverse and hugely popular ways in which historical knowledge is created and disseminated. And so we have moved outside the academy to reflect on the production of history in the broadcast, cinematic, literary and digital worlds. Though often dismissed by historians as inaccurate, naïve and fanciful, these genres are worthy of consideration in their own right. Historical fiction, documentaries, films and even video games are some of the most powerful sources of historical knowledge and can be neither ignored nor accepted uncritically.

We stated at the outset that our primary intent was not to persuade anyone of the relevance and excitement of history, but we share a passion for the subject which we hope comes over in the writing. If some of this happens to rub off onto potential historians then perhaps that is no bad thing, for at least one of our unstated goals will have been met.

It would seem an act of madness in this age of research assessment exercises, focused subject specialisms and narrow periodizations to embark on a textbook that roams across periods, disciplines and geographical boundaries with little apparent regard for the particular expertise of its authors. Hence our thanks are due to those colleagues and readers of the book who have helped us enormously to convey historical ideas and concepts familiar to us as experienced tutors but often by using examples less familiar, say from the early modern or medieval periods or from the ancient world. If we have not always pulled this off, it is our responsibility and not theirs.

Colleagues include Paul Sinclair at St Clare's College in Oxford, a medieval scholar; Dr Roy Edwards, University of Southampton, who was instrumental for the section on business history; Avichag Valk (all things Tudor) and Jonathan Valk (all things ancient); Samuel Claus in Oxford for his deep and encyclopaedic knowledge of video games; Xavière Hassan, The Open University; Dr Abigail Green, Brasenose College, Oxford; Brian Smith (Shetland Archive) with his deep and wide knowledge, especially, in this case, archaeology; Ken Warman (BSix College, Hackney) and Felix Slade, plus our colleagues at Pembroke Stephen Tuck (America) and Nicholas Cole (America and digital archives where he is transforming the field); Adrian Gregory (twentieth century and the First World War); Yasmin Khan at Kellogg College; Isabel Holowaty, history librarian at the Bodleian and Laura Cracknell at Pembroke library.

The Master and Fellows of Pembroke College, Oxford, provided both Peter Claus and John Marriott with a convivial academic home, which was later extended through the kindness of the President and Fellows of Kellogg College to John. Thanks also, from Peter, to the OxNet team, particularly Morgan Lewis, the student body, whether those coming through our Access programmes, undergraduates or postgraduates, who make membership of these scholarly communities a pleasure and a privilege.

The late Raphael Samuel has been a point of contact for both Peter and John. While Raph may have resisted the notion of a textbook, seemingly fixed in a point of time, he may well have appreciated the attempt to create a cross-disciplinary narrative that falls outside any special focus on period or subject and that may have utility for students of history.

At Routledge, the History Editor Dr Eve Setch has eased the passage of the book with good sense and humour. Finally, we thank our families. For Peter: Xavière Hassan; Samuel Claus; Avichag and Jonathan Valk and their beautiful children now living in Helsinki; Aya; Nava and (never forgetting Jonah), along with Sequoia and now the youngest of the 'Peskies', Zenobia. Since the last edition, Peter has lost his father, Malcolm Claus, who is much missed, but June in her nineties continues with hardly a grey hair. For John: Kanta and the twins Kabir and Karishma.

Part 1
Philosophies

1 From the Ancients to the Christians

This chapter takes us across centuries, mapping the developments in historical writing from the time of the ancient Greeks to late antiquity. This timeline covers the decline of the Roman Empire to the rise of Christianity. The opening section, therefore, examines the emergence of historical writing in ancient Greece with the contributions of Herodotus and Thucydides. A distinction is made between mythical writing about the past (such as *The Iliad* and *The Odyssey*) and the ethnographical histories of Herodotus and of the more systematic Thucydides. The next section covers the development of historical writing in the Hellenic and Roman periods. Roman historians are seen to be in many ways much less ambitious in approach and scope than the Greeks whom they had succeeded. Finally, we explore the differences in approaches to historical theory, method and practice introduced by Christianity in Europe. This shift in power and influence leads directly to histories which not only seek to understand the past in the present but also to suggest a millennial concern with the future. In this narrow sense, these early interventions from Christian historians set up a later predominance of history writing that (unlike, say, Thucydides) is concerned with prophecy and portents.

1.1 Herodotus and Gold-digging Ants

Why study ancient history and ancient historians? Surely, our approaches to and methods of history in the modern period are far superior to the histories that were written in the centuries either side of the Common Era (CE). (BCE and CE are secular terms that indicate the period before or after the Christian Era, that is, the birth of Jesus Christ.) And being superior in sophistication, methodology, scope and erudition, can we say more about the ancients than they could possibly have said about themselves? Perhaps this is broadly true. Perhaps, however, these historians should be studied for two reasons which make them an invaluable resource to historians today. First, our political systems, science, medicine, philosophy, architecture and built environment would not exist in their current forms if it were not for the influence of the Greeks and Romans. Second, Western morals and ethics, our sense that history has a forward trajectory, the impetus to live under a rule of law and to maintain the rights of the human being, are all shaped by the astonishing influence of that other product of the ancient world: Judeo-Christianity.

The word 'history', meaning investigation or inquiry, comes from the Greek. It is in the second half of the nineteenth century, according to the philosopher and historian R.G. Collingwood (1889–1943) in his *Idea of History* (1994), that history became scientific, that is, was no longer simply recounting something that was already known to an audience but was based on original research using the tools of intellectual inquiry. This history was humanistic in that it put 'Man' at the centre of its concerns, rational in that it applied enquiring questions to evidence and derived conclusions accordingly. It was 'self-revelatory' in that it defined 'Man' through past actions.

4   Philosophies

So, what, by these criteria, are we to make of the Greek Herodotus who first applied the title 'Histories' to a work solely dedicated to verifiable events that occurred in the past? Before looking at him, we need to go back to the earliest Greek stories to seek out the origins of historical writing. The most renowned of these early stories were of course *The Iliad* and *The Odyssey*, written by Homer in the eighth century BCE. *The Iliad* recounted the adventures and tribulations of the hero Achilles against the backdrop of the Trojan Wars between the Athenians and the Persians around 1200 BCE, while *The Odyssey* told of the adventures of the hero Odysseus on his journey home from the war. Given that they recount stories of a war that actually took place, why then do we not consider them history? The stories unfold in a mythological time rather than in the continuous time of human societies. The events – the death of Achilles with his vulnerable heel or Odysseus's encounter with the one-eyed Cyclops – all happen in an order, but the timeframe of the myth pertains only to the myth itself and not against the real world of real people. This is because Homer's aim was not to explain the past but to elucidate moral lessons from a tale in which events were moved solely by the passions of heroes and the caprice of the gods. Thus, Collingwood saw these tales as lacking the standards of history because they were theocratic or mythical – theocratic in that they dealt with gods or supernatural rulers of human societies, mythical in that they were predominately located outside human events (such as the Creation story or the story of the Flood) in some dateless time in the past.

Despite the continued popularity of Homer, between his time in the eighth century and that of Herodotus in the fifth century BCE, Greek writers began to develop what Collingwood identified as three elements of a 'scientific' history:

- Understanding the ways and means of signifying the passage of time in relation to human events.
- Finding ways of relating the passage of time in one society to that in another society.
- Developing ways of periodizing time that allows eras and epochs to be described.

The first advance comes with the poet Hesiod (of whom very little is known, save that he seems to have been from farming stock and was a near contemporary of Homer) who in his book *Theogony*, written sometime during the 700s BCE, accounted for the creation of the universe out of a primal chaos and then the establishment of the pantheon of Greek gods, sired by Zeus, father of the gods. But then Hesiod outlined a societal past after this period of the gods that offered a rudimentary explanation for why things were. He divided human history into five successive periods, ages or, as he put it, 'races' of men:

- An age of peace, harmony and plenty when humans lived among the gods and did not have to work, known as the Golden Age.
- A period of rebellion against the gods, characterized by war and cruelty, known as the Silver Age.
- An age when people had amazing physical strength and vitality, which ended through incessant warfare, known as the Bronze Age.
- A time filled with heroes when men were half gods, such as those who fought in the Trojan War, known as the Heroic Age.
- A contemporary period characterized by suffering, sickness, evil and meanness, known as the Iron Age.

More sophisticated notions of historical time followed. Hecataeus of Miletus (550–c.490 BCE) produced works of geography that attempted to demarcate the world in spatial terms but then in *Genealogies* tried to bridge the centuries between his time and the time of gods and heroes by describing the successive generations of people, tracking a human history back to the mythical age. This chronological method was augmented later in the fifth century by Hellanicus of Lesbos (terminal dates unsure), whose *Attic History* marked the passage of history by compiling lists of state officials and priests recorded by cities and temples.

If Homer had produced myths of gods and heroes because his age needed explanations about origins and causes but was unprepared for a more 'scientific' or systematic approach, what changes had taken place in Greek society which required a new way of thinking about the past? Between c.800 and c.500 BCE the Greek world altered dramatically. The *polis* emerged as the city-state, governing itself and a rural hinterland and became the characteristic political unit over the area. Cities like Athens and Sparta provided the context for energetic social, economic and political development. Greek traders, adventurers and colonists spread across the Mediterranean world, bringing Greeks into contact with a wide range of non-Greeks, or, to use their term, 'barbarians' (a word that merely meant 'non-Greek speaker' and does not have the pejorative element that it has today). This awareness of others sharpened their own sense of their identity as Greeks, not just as citizens of their particular city-state but as part of a Hellenic, Greek-speaking world. Awareness of these differences, often coupled with a sense of their own cultural superiority, fed into their art, poetry and, most critically for our purposes, philosophy, thereby encouraging a more critical sense that there were different trajectories of historical change.

The reputation of Herodotus (c.484–c.430/420 BCE) has varied greatly over the years, but he has richly deserved the title first given to him by Marcus Tullius Cicero (106–43 BCE) of 'the Father of History'. In his great work, known simply as *The Histories*, we can find accounts of gold-digging ants bigger than foxes, Indian men who secrete black semen, men with goats' feet and others who can swim ten miles under water, and armies that drink rivers dry and have soldiers who are carried over the sea on the backs of dolphins. All this is incredible to us but Herodotus' approach to the past was original. Unlike other Greek historians, he was not interested in chronicling local stories and mythologies preserved by the official interpreters of religious orthodoxy but rather attempted to understand folklores, cultures and mythologies in a historical context as part of a vision of the past that embraced geography, natural history and ethnography.

Herodotus employed a coherent framework within which to describe relationships among the many events and developments that he identified. The affairs of the Lydians under King Croesus, of the Persians, the Egyptians and the Greeks were understood in chronological terms, although there was little attempt to relate events to one another within a cohesive historical framework. However, Herodotus wished to understand histories across a wider geographical landscape and to record the cultural differences of people that occupied these strange and faraway lands, thus providing a record much broader than anything attempted by earlier writers.

We know little about the life of Herodotus. We do know that he was born around 490 BCE in Halicarnassus, on the north-west coast of Asia Minor. What set him apart as an historian, however, were his travels throughout the Mediterranean world, including Egypt, Africa, areas around the Black Sea and throughout many Greek city-states. Having won his way across the vastness of the landscape he did not merely tell of the deeds and conquests of the people he found but also of their habits, customs and folklores. Across the Mediterranean to the mouth of the Nile, for example, he not only recounted the glory of the Pharaohs but also related the natural history of their remarkable river. He stood on the high ground and was amazed by the great flood of the Nile, each year rising, at first gradually and then growing into a succession of torrents one eddying into another as dried up wadis became lakes and then rivers in their own right. Simultaneously a catastrophe and a miracle, the floodwaters had for millennia inundated the landscape, drowning all in its path but had also left in their wake layer upon layer of fertile silt. Out of this soil grew the origins of a civilization, already ancient by the time Herodotus witnessed it. This amazed him, the Greeks and all other societies with an awareness of it. It was this determination to locate these origins that makes him so important to us but also that to measure his surroundings – taking a tape measure to the pyramids, for example – or as a pioneer of oral history, to consider folklore and local mythologies as evidence to be recorded and examined.

While there is a debate about the real extent of his travels, most historians now agree that Herodotus stood at the edge of his known world and looked beyond. He reported the world of the Scythians and their neighbours the Cimmerians, ancient nomadic peoples living to the north and east of the Black Sea from the third to sixth centuries BCE, our only knowledge of them coming from Herodotus and subsequent archaeological evidence. Often when he reported things that might be far-fetched, it was with the caveat that he has been told this, leaving the reader to judge their veracity. He used indirect speech ('they say') as a device to distance himself from the flimsiness of the evidence to hand and sometimes offered alternative explanations to those passed on to him:

> About the feathers which the Scythians say fill the air, and make it impossible to traverse, or even to see, the more northerly parts of the continent – I think myself that it must be always snowing in these northerly regions, though less, probably, in summer than in winter. Anyone who has seen heavy snow at close quarters will know what I mean – it is very like feathers; and it is because of the severity of these northern winters that the country is uninhabited. No doubt the Scythians and their neighbours when they talk of the feathers really mean snow – because of the likeness between the two. I have now related the utmost which can be gathered from the report.
>
> (Herodotus, 2002, p. 250)

He also wrote about the Hyperboreans mentioned earlier in a mythological context by Homer and Hesiod, in an account which displayed a taste for the fantastic. The Hyperboreans, according to Herodotus, lived in an ideal society at the edge of the known world to the north of the Greeks. Critics have insisted that in such cases he was prepared to accept hearsay and mythology as historical evidence, yet in the case of the Hyperboreans he makes it clear that he could gather no direct evidence about them and therefore cited only mythological sources. Such an admission suggests that Herodotus considered his own role as an historian and was aware of the need to deploy evidence in a way that was both convincing and plausible.

Herodotus did not seek to speculate beyond the limits of the evidence at hand. He did occasionally cite the will of the gods as causal factors in history, more than his successors but much less frequently and with less force than earlier mythologists such as Homer. Certainly, he instinctively realized that human beings are 'culture-bound' and act 'in accordance with their traditions and upbringing'. He also, by the way that he reported his travels, believed that histories that come from a particular culture should be considered on their merits. We might therefore consider Herodotus less as the 'Father of History' and more as the founding spirit of cultural history (see Chapter 11). And yet it is impossible fully to appreciate the contribution of Herodotus without consideration of the mutual influence that existed with Thucydides, his contemporary and the other great Greek historian of the age.

1.2 Thucydides and Reason: an Historian for Our Times?

The writings of Thucydides (460–c.400/405 BCE) lacked the diversity and (at least to the present writers) the sheer excitement of Herodotus. Fact-gathering, awareness of change and continuity, causation of factors, thesis, synthesis, summary and conclusion are all words associated with Thucydides, who has tended to be more attractive than Herodotus to historians in the modern period – historians who prefer their histories without seasoning or spice, wrapped in the more insipid flavours of profession-based methodologies. But he also favoured history as performance – both the Greeks and Romans read aloud regardless of whether they were in private or public, alone or in a group – and perhaps this emphasis on performance has also attracted the more thespian-inclined lecturer. It almost certainly influenced later historians such as Edward Gibbon who chronicled the fall of Rome (Chapter 4).

This approach was nurtured by Thucydides' attachment to the Sophistic movement. Sophists were practitioners of rhetoric, argument and debate and confident in the mental powers of humanity and the effectiveness of the force of persuasion. Every dispute, for instance, was thought to have two viewpoints. This would extend, presumably, to disputes over historical interpretation and this, the argument might run, formed the basis of his historical methodology. Second, he was also attached to the then growing 'science' of medicine, which involved the close observation of symptoms, diagnosis, prognosis, conditions of environment and so on. Thus for Thucydides, truth was a goal of history. While absolute truth was unobtainable and approximate, historical truth could be observed and effectively conveyed. For these reasons, historians today tend to describe the work of Thucydides as 'full', 'perceptive', 'neutral', 'austere' and 'objective'. Herodotus, by comparison, hardly cuts the rational mustard.

Who was Thucydides? Like Herodotus, little is known of his life. He is thought to have been born around 460 BCE to a well-off and aristocratic Greek family. As a general in the Athenian army, he was well placed to write about warfare and political intrigue, and this formed the basis of his great work *The Peloponnesian War*. He was out of favour, however, when in 423 he was exiled from Athens as a punishment for losing the strategically important Amphipolis to the Spartans. He died in mysterious circumstances around 400 and many sources suggest that, like Cicero, he was murdered. His unfinished *Peloponnesian War* was continued by Xenophon (444/430–357/354 BCE) but in a radically different style.

While Thucydides was remembered for his rational approach, especially during the Renaissance (as we shall see in the next chapter), he was not above piling on the 'literary artistry'. The use of rhetoric in his accounts of political speeches and of the oratory of generals to their soldiers before battles, coverage of historic debates and most famously his reproduction of Pericles' Funeral Oration added up to more than minimalist reportage. His use of the speech, however, was not merely a literary flourish, as he explained:

> As to the speeches of the participants, either when they were about to enter the war or after they were already in it, it has been difficult for me and for those who reported to me to remember exactly what was said. I have, therefore, written what I thought the speakers needed to say given the situations they were in, while keeping as close as possible to the gist of what was actually said. As to the events of the war, I have not written them down as I heard them from just anybody, nor as I thought they must have occurred, but have consistently described what I myself have or have been able to learn from others after going over each event in as much detail as possible. I have found this task to be extremely arduous, since those who were present at these actions gave varying reports on the same events, depending on their sympathies and their memories.

(Thucydides, 1998, p. 11)

8 Philosophies

This was sophisticated stuff. Here we find Thucydides displaying an advanced and acute awareness of the nature of evidence, the vagaries of memory (both that of his witnesses and of his own as an historian), reliability of witnesses and the need for the historian to make a judgement about such evidence given that it depended upon the 'sympathies and memories' of the reporters. On the other hand, Thucydides took licence with evidence, reporting what the speakers 'needed to say', but he was quite open about his processes and kept to the 'gist' of the *actualité*.

This sophistication also explains, perhaps, why he has been preferred to Herodotus by historians writing in the last century or so. Thucydides ignored the supernatural, preferring to focus on the earthbound forces of politics. He may have squeezed the moment for all its dramatic juices, but his approach was still rooted in the notion of historical phenomena as rational and explicable by the human senses. There was not a 'gold-digging ant' in sight, and none of his historical players were goat-footed or performed monumental feats of supernatural strength or endurance. No causal links were drawn between human and natural disasters, man-made war and earthquakes, drought, famines or eclipses; rarely, if at all, were these phenomena raised as a portent of things to come or seen as a direct consequence or punishment for human folly. Most important, the role of supernatural forces was relegated to the mythical. The following list charts the gradual decline of theology and mythology in Greek historiography.

The Role of the Gods in Greek Historiography

Let's start with a rough chronology:

Homer: History of the gods central in the affairs of mortals (8th century BCE).
Hecataetus: Brought the gods down to earth but they remain omnipresent (6th/5th century BCE).
Herodotus: The gods begin to retreat from historical life (5th century BCE).
Thucydides: The gods tend not to interfere with human events (5th century BCE).
Xenophon: Loyalty to the gods is rewarded. Xenophon completed the work of Thucydides (4th century BCE).
Polybius: Emphasis placed on evidence-led history with an absence of the gods as a way of explaining historical phenomena (3rd/2nd century BCE).

In classical times, gods waged wars of favour, taking the side of this people or that particular city. Humans were often at the mercy of gods who ran the affairs of mortals at a collective whim. By the time we get to Thucydides, however, the gods had been more or less expelled from human affairs. Indeed, some have suggested that the originality of Thucydides lies in the very fact that he attempts to gather all human action within the realm of what is humanly possible. In this respect, he has been regarded as the first modern, objective, rational historian who has little time for myths, oracles or gods as prime movers in history.

Taken together Herodotus and Thucydides had much in common. The histories of neither could provide lessons for generations yet to be born – not that the idea of history providing lessons for the future occurred to them. Both were deeply concerned with war and posterity; both have been remembered for the quality, depth and breadth of their histories, although Thucydides always pressed his worth over Herodotus; both contributed hugely to the establishment of history as a genre over, say, rhetoric or other literary approaches and both had the good fortune that their manuscripts survive to be appreciated. In a limited way, both used primary sources dug up from the archives and could distinguish primary sources from secondary sources, although naturally enough with less dexterity and accuracy than would be employed in future centuries but with rather more than that to be mustered by some Roman historians. Both Herodotus and

Thucydides, moreover, were well travelled and used the experience of travel to write their histories, and both could see the viewpoints of those antagonistic to Greece.

Although the work of Herodotus and Thucydides laid the foundations for Greek history, it was not until the lesser-known Polybius (c.200–118 BCE) that the tradition reached its climax. Polybius was born into a distinguished military and land-holding family but in mid-life he was captured and held hostage by the Romans for seventeen years. He was, however, taken into their confidence and became a tutor to Fabius and Scipio Aemilianus, later accompanying the latter on his campaign in Africa, eventually returning to Greece. Living at a time when Roman power expanded dramatically into Egypt, Greece, Africa and Spain, Polybius chose the rise of Rome as a fitting topic with which to write the first universal history. Published in forty volumes (only five of which survive in their entirety), *The Histories* was an ambitious and laborious account written largely for a Greek audience and therefore with a distinctive Greek bias in the use of evidence and interpretation. The events he described were not only within living memory but witnessed by Polybius himself. This was no chronology of events, however, for Polybius strove to analyze them within a much wider historical picture of the rise of Rome.

Probably the greatest of the Greek historians, Polybius hated the idea of history as a branch of entertainment, literary drama or performance. Instead, he emphasized the importance of research in the archives, was very much alive to the basic historical problem of cause and effect and reflected on the problems of forging a more systematic approach to history. In this he identified the attributes of the ideal historian (Mellor, 1999, p. 9):

1 Political experience to understand the actual practice of politics and to evaluate sources.
2 Geographical knowledge, preferably from personal travel.
3 Reliance not only on earlier historians but personal examination of archives, inscriptions and treaties.

More than this, when writing about Alexander the Great, Polybius pondered whether under different circumstances the great man might have successfully marched on Rome, indulging in a device much used by subsequent historians, namely, the counterfactual, asking 'what if' as a way of analyzing the many sides of any historical question. Possessing these attributes, Polybius is now regarded as the successor to Thucydides and the forefather of modern, scholarly historical inquiry. Not only that, but even though his work was not known in Europe until the fifteenth century, its influence can be detected in the writings of Machiavelli and Montesquieu and in the Constitution of the United States.

With the supersession of the Greek empire by that of Rome, the writing of history entered a new phase. While Roman historians and historians of Rome were heirs to the Greek tradition, they tended to be rather more polemical and politically motivated as they sought to come to terms with the now enormous wealth and global reach of Rome. We are about to enter the mighty gates of Imperial Rome in order to find out more.

1.3 What Did the Romans Ever Do for History?

Roman historians, acutely aware of their Greek predecessors, were concerned to locate the place of morality and ethics, especially in the conduct of public life and in the face of the temptations of overwhelming political power. Where Herodotus, Thucydides and Polybius had used philosophy to fathom the moral depths of politics in the past, Roman historians approached history as a way of testing the ethical dimensions in the present. For the Romans, history had civic, intellectual and, to an extent, theological functions, but the past was not deigned to be a space for rumination or philosophical thought; it was more inclined to instruct its readers and to provide cautionary tales about, for example, the results of excesses of the flesh or the wages of Senatorial corruption or conduct on the battlefield.

We shall look more closely in a moment at the best of the Roman historians, but for now, as an example of how Roman history was employed as a way of measuring morality in politics, we shall simply glimpse Tacitus' (c.55–120 CE) description of the licentiousness of Emperor Nero (AD 37–68), a bisexual who was thought by his moral life to have lost all political direction. Here Nero's sexuality and a perceived waywardness in leadership conflate:

> On the banks of the pool stood brothels well filled with women of high rank, while opposite them one could view stark-naked prostitutes. Obscene gestures and motions were under way, and as darkness came on, all of the adjacent grove and surrounding buildings rang with music and blazed with lights. Nero himself, defiled by natural and unnatural pleasures alike, had omitted no vile practice which could add to his depravity, except that he capped all a few days later by actually becoming the bride of one member of that degenerate crew, an individual named Pythagoras, and marrying him in a formal marriage ceremony. The bridal veil was placed over the emperor's head; the regular witnesses were used; the dowry, marriage bed, the nuptial torches were there; in short, they displayed in full view everything which the night conceals even when the bride is a woman.
>
> (Tacitus, 1965, p. 628)

An emphasis on the importance of morality in public life may seem to compromise any approach to the historical record, but on the other hand Roman historians felt a responsibility to be legalistic and publicly minded and meticulous in the recording and preservation of public documents such as decrees (or *annalles*) kept by the Chief Priest, which listed names of officials, military victories and so on. These year-by-year accounts of major officials and important events were meant for posterity, and read beneath the rhetorical liveliness they did provide flashes of incisive analysis; however, the arguments were rarely framed by a coherent analytical framework. (Roman history was not without embellishments and historians would read aloud in the theatre or in the public baths.) Even the more systematic and analytical works tended to retain an *annalist* structure which placed great emphasis on chronology and record.

Here there were continuities with Herodotus and Thucydides, not least of which was the emphasis placed on speeches, drama and the skills associated with rhetoric and apparent in the work of the main historians of the era including Titus Livy (c.59 BCE–17 CE), Sallust (86–35 BCE), Seutonius (c.70–c.160 CE) and Cornelius Tacitus (56–120 CE). But what precisely was the nature of the shift from Hellenistic to Roman approaches to history? The most obvious change was in focus, for all these important historians dealt with the fortunes of the Roman empire, not merely as chronological accounts but also to explore what became the familiar idea of the grandeur and corruption of a mighty empire, in particular, the focus on political, economic and social intrigue promoted by moral laxness.

Tacitus (56–120 CE), a Roman senator, is now generally regarded as the greatest Roman historian. In two major works, the *Annals* and *Histories*, only parts of which survive, he covered the empire from the death of Augustus in 14 CE to the outbreak of the Jewish War in 70 CE, that is, a period in his recent past. Thus in exploring the lives of important emperors including Tiberius, Claudius, Nero and Caligula he was able to draw upon contemporary records, correspondence, speeches and reminiscences. At root, however, he remained an *annalist* historian, albeit with a sophisticated sense of chronological narrative, an avowed impartiality and an adroit form of narration. Furthermore, although he was trained in rhetoric, there was none of the rhetorical invention that informed the writings of previous historians such as Thucydides. When, for example, he reported the funeral of Claudius, he did so by analysing both the funeral itself and by comparing biographical details of former Emperors:

> On the day of the funeral the Emperor started his eulogy. While he was reviewing the ancient history of the family and the consulships and triumphs of his ancestors, both speaker and audience were serious. His references to the deceased's cultural attainments and to the fact that during his reign the nation had suffered no disaster abroad were listened to with favour; but when he turned to Claudius' statesmanship and wisdom, no one could suppress a smile, although the speech, which had been written by Seneca, displayed considerable literary polish, for that writer had a talent well suited to the taste of his day. It was observed by the older men, who have the leisure time to compare past and present, that Nero was Rome's first ruler to need a ghost writer. Caesar the Dictator had rivalled the greatest orators; Augustus had a spontaneous, fluent speaking style, such as was becoming to an emperor; Tiberius also was expert in the art of weighing his words and, besides, was forceful in expressing in meaning, or else deliberately ambiguous; even Gaius Caesar's muddled mind did not ruin his power as a speaker; and Claudius, when delivering a prepared address, showed no want of elegance. Nero, however, had even from boyhood turned his mental energies to interests of a different sort, such as engraving, painting, music, or horsemanship, and in his occasional attempts at writing poetry he showed some degree of training in the fundamentals.
>
> (Tacitus, 1965, p. 628)

He provided genuine insight into the nature of power – in particular the troubled relationship between the Senate and the emperors – and the baneful influence of corruption, hypocrisy, tyranny and decadence as the empire expanded. This emphasis on biography (and autobiography) in the construction of the changing fortunes of the Roman world was very much part of Roman historiography generally, although it is likely that the Romans themselves would have thought this type of literature to be part of the process of recording and understanding history.

Lives of the Twelve Caesars by Suetonius has probably been the most influential study written by a Roman historian. While Suetonius was an important and influential person in his time (he was imperial secretary under Trajan), his antiquarian fascination with the everyday has left rich pickings for our understanding of the details of life in Rome, such as diet, and it provides for the historian raw materials of life in Rome. Here we find him painting a rich portrait of Augustus by pointing out the sources of his evidence:

> In this character sketch I need not omit his eating habits. He was frugal and, as a rule, preferred the food of the common people, especially the coarser sort of bread, small fishes, fresh hard-pressed cheese, and green figs of the second crop; and would not wait for dinner, if he felt hungry, but ate anywhere. The following are verbatim quotations from his letters:
>
> I had a snack of bread and dates while out for my drive today. . . . On the way back in my litter from the Regia, I munched an ounce of bread and a few hard-skinned grapes.
>
> (Suetonius, 2003, pp. 90–1)

Indeed, Suetonius had a sophisticated approach to evidence – even material evidence – and the proper limits of speculation:

> I can prove pretty conclusively that as a child Augustus was called Thurinus ('the Thurian'), perhaps because his ancestors had once lived at Thurii, or because his father had defeated the

slaves in that neighbourhood soon after he was born; my evidence is a bronze statuette which I once owned. It shows him as a boy, and a rusty, almost illegible inscription in iron letters gives him this name. I have presented the statuette to the Emperor Hadrian, who has placed it among the Household gods in his bedroom. Moreover, Augustus was often sneeringly called 'The Thurian' in Antony's correspondence. Augustus answered by confessing himself puzzled: why should his former name be thrown in his face as an insult?

(Suetonius, 2003, p. 47)

It is difficult to say to what extent these historians influenced the historical imagination of the Roman people. Their writings were popular, not least because they were frequently read to audiences, but overall, they formed only part of a complex range of evidence which Romans themselves used as the raw material of the past (Table 1.1). Looking at this list, it is instructive to consider how many still inform a modern historical imagination. The ways in which Romans understood their world and how it might be reinterpreted by historians was not simply the sum of individual histories from this or that historian. Instead, we find popular ideas of what the past meant from a range of sources that were not always considered as sources by historians such as Livi, Sallust or Tacitus. Family records and stories of heroics written by epic poets, architectural traces of the Etruscan people who were the immediate predecessors of the Romans or inscriptions on religious temples helped to shape popular understandings of the past. In the same way, it may be tempting to think that today an understanding of Rome might derive from the novels of Robert Graves, Robert Harris, Tom Holland or the popular television series *Rome* (2005–2007) and before it, *I Claudius* (1976), that seemingly brought alive the ancient world using the skills of our finest Shakespearean actors. Taken together, these public or social ideas of the past gave a sense to *them* about their own past and a sense to *us* that we somehow know Rome, with its gladiators and orgies, its great armies and its political intrigues.

The demise of Tacitus marks the end of historians writing in the language of Rome and the last of the important Pagan historians. (There was, ironically, a return to Greek in history writing after a pause of several hundred years.) Nobody could ever have guessed it, but both the

Table 1.1 Sources used by Romans in thinking about the past

Sources	Functions	Examples
Myth	Explanation of origins	Romulus and Remus suckled by a she-wolf
Legend	Connection with noble antecedents	Exploits attributed to historical figures, like the Tarquin Kings
Language	Preserves otherwise forgotten etymologies	Money, *pecunia* from *pecus*, sheep, showing the early form of wealth
Buildings and urban plans	Civic, military and religious	Etruscan buildings and plans showing previous northern and central Italian civilization from 700 BCE
Objects	Family and community memory	Funeral masks and portrait busts
Religion	Social solidarity	Preservation of rituals
Lists	Continuities in civic life	Names of magistrates
Oral tradition	Family and community memory	Funeral speeches
Inscriptions	Continuities in civic and political life	Early treaties
Written poetry	Community and cultural memory	Lucan, Ovid, Horace
Historical writing	Morality and ethics of the state	Sallust, Livi, Tacitus

Source: Compiled and adapted from Mellor (1999, p. 2)

Greeks and the Romans were about to be displaced by Christian inspired histories and this was to introduce a whole new way of thinking about the past.

1.4 Late Antiquity, Christianity and the End of Days

When in October 312 CE Constantine marched on Rome to confront Emperor Maxentius, he was said to have seen a cross in the sky with a message that read 'In this conquer.' After a famous victory, his 'Edict of Milan' announced freedoms to worship across the empire. As a result, the early Christian church was declared exempt from taxes and duties and became wealthy. Christianity was transformed from the most reviled of religions in the Roman Empire to become the most privileged. It also transformed itself. By the time the Nicene Creed was declared in 325CE, a meeting or synod of the church that declared the divinity of the Son as well as the Father, enthusiastically attended by Constantine himself, Christianity's Jewish and Pagan roots had become half-buried and half-denied. Pagans and Jews were the new outsiders.

The Christianization of Rome progressed falteringly in subsequent years, with only Julian I, when he became Emperor in 360, reverting to Paganism in any serious or meaningful way and then only for a very short time. Thereafter Rome tended to favour Christianity while tolerating Paganism. This Christianization was promoted by the historians of late antiquity.

Rome fell in 476CE, or so most textbooks will tell you. Certainly, this date marks the end of the Emperors, yet the eastern remnant of this once global empire could be said to have survived until 1453 in one recognizable form as the Byzantine Empire. Many reasons are given for the decline and final destruction of Rome: financial mismanagement; invasion by the barbarians in the shape of Vandals, Goths and Huns; civil conflict and war; moral disintegration and so forth. Yet the empire had never been static. Even in the period covered in the previous section, Rome had reinvented itself many times over, not least in the transition of its political systems. There was also the religious crisis that we associate with the early centuries of what today we call the new millennia: the jostle in late antiquity for supremacy among Pagans, Jews and Christians. And here historians played their most active part.

Most notable in this period was the work of Eusebius of Caesarea (*c.*275–339 CE). His histories of the church, works on the Bible and religious dogma, life of Constantine, celebration of early saints and martyrs and demonization of Jews became the measure of history writing over the next few centuries – providing a link between ancient historians and the 'age of Bede' that will be considered in the next chapter. Both Jews and Christians had sought to date their beginnings to Creation, but Christians laid great store in histories that emphasized the birth of Jesus and significant moments in his life, ministry and death. It was from this starting point that Eusebius, historian and first bishop of Caesarea in Palestine, wrote his *Ecclesiastical History* (312–324CE), which covered the history of the church until the eve of the Council of Nicaea, including the life of Jesus and his apostles, martyrs and bishops. For Eusebius, then, historical time began with Creation and would end at the Last Judgement with promises of triumph and victory.

Eusebius was followed by Sozomen (*c.*400–450 CE) and Theodoret (395–437 CE). These figures are not important individually or their histories notable of and for themselves. They are important insomuch as together they developed ecclesiastical or church history as a genre, taking their cue from Eusebius, not only as the historian of the early church but also in his life as a bishop. In the influences from Rome and in their living Christianity, they provided, as Arthur Marwick said of Eusebius, the 'culmination of the ancient tradition and a link to medieval Christian Europe' (Marwick, 2001, p. 54).

Nothing strengthened this link over the centuries when Christianity came to dominate Europe more than the reading of the Bible. From the standpoint of modern scholarship, the stories of the Bible fail to meet most if not all the criteria that would qualify it as history. These stories were not supported by an archive of primary source material which provided some verification for the claims made in the Old and New Testaments. No web of footnotes takes us back to a point of proof that these things actually happened. More than that, they appear to have grown by a process of accretion and syncretism, adding and combining over centuries and centuries, appearing from the mists of time rather than a known historical moment. The idea that the Torah (or Old Testament) is given from heaven and dictated to Moses is based on faith, not something that any historian can verify using modern techniques of evidence. The events described were in any case often explicitly magical or miraculous, defying the laws of physics and biology. This said, the Bible was used by ancient historians and archaeologists as a historical chronology to be proved or falsified, and there was other evidence for the existence of at least some Biblical characters or events.

Historical anthropologists see these stories, and the great narrative that weaves them into a whole, as the foundational myths – or stories of origin and early development – of the religious basis of Jewish, Christian and Muslim societies (see the next chapter). Details and interpretations are contested and debated by believers, but to the social scientist the Bible does not amount to historical description in ways that we would apply to any other sphere of the past. Despite this, the Bible, perhaps the Old Testament in particular, has played a significant part in shaping how Western societies have come to view the past.

The Old Testament shared a great many characteristics with later conceptions of how the process of history has worked; indeed, even the idea that history somehow 'works'. What does this mean? Let's start by looking at some of the major characteristics of the Old Testament narrative. Its overarching story is that of the historical development of the tribes of the Holy Lands of the ancient Middle East. Wars, mass migrations, epidemics, disasters, miracles, heroism and wickedness add up to a majestic grand design in which we can recognize key aspects of our common beginning. Great cities rise and fall; famines bring peoples to the brink of destruction as God's mysterious will is worked out through the course of a mythical past. And there was enough in this story to suggest that, at least in some of its elements, future histories are also mapped out. From this perspective the Bible can be the history of the future as well as the past.

The claim to predict the future would seem to provide another reason to rule out the Bible from the historical canon. On the other hand, the idea that history has a direction and a purpose, a *telos* or teleology, has been a powerful force in shaping later ideas of history and how history 'works'. This is true both in the philosophy of history and in relation to particular moments in history where the idea that history has a trajectory, such as that revealed in the Old Testament, has exerted a decisive influence.

From the perspective of Christianity, this trajectory can be understood in relation to one word: millennium. Around the time of the first millennium CE, movements grew up across the breadth of Christendom, which preached great fear of an impending apocalypse. Based on prophecies, which were in turn rooted in a close study of the Old Testament, they predicted the more or less imminent destruction of the order of things as they then existed and variously predicted the second coming of the Messiah, accompanied by the damnation of the sinners and salvation of the righteous. These millenarian movements may have been wrong in their interpretation of history and certainly wrong in their prophecies, but they were historically influential in their own period and unquestionably saw themselves as trying to apply the sense of historical movement set forth in the Old Testament.

In these ways, the Old Testament structured history and created a sense of history having a direction that might or might not be predictable and had a huge influence in shaping how history was to be conceived in later times. It was of tremendous importance to history written in the

Middle Ages and the Renaissance and then among those historians working up to and beyond the seventeenth century. In the next chapter, we will deal at greater length with this period in Christian historiography.

Postscript

In the writings of these early historians, we can see the beginnings of what we would today recognize as history. The foremost Greek and Roman historians sought to impose order upon their knowledge of past events using the skills of research and critical inquiry that are part of the makeup of the modern historian. By doing so, they distanced themselves from an earlier tradition of storytelling in which myths based largely on the caprices of supernatural beings prevailed. In the best of their writings there is a sophisticated questioning of evidence, use of a variety of written and oral sources of evidence and a desire to think comparatively about cultures on the edge of their known world. So extensive were the travels of Herodotus and so serious his commitment to an understanding of different cultures that he could well be considered not only a pioneering historian but also an anthropologist and archaeologist. Despite the considerable quantity of evidence accumulated, some of which was of questionable value, these historians succeeded in providing a reasonably clear sense of chronology consistent with the historical record.

In other respects, however, their role as historians was compromised by the tasks that they set themselves as public figures. Although Herodotus, Thucydides, Suetonius and Tacitus professed a commitment to the truth, they used the past as a vehicle to explore moral and ethical values or to record historical lineages. Because of a requirement to provide vivid and entertaining accounts – many of which were intended to be read in public – there was also a temptation to embellish what they perceived to be the truth, use anecdotal evidence, and fill in gaps with fictionalized material. None of the historians was averse to the occasional use of folk tales, fables, myths and epic narratives.

The histories of conflict were meant to be instructive, accounts from which lessons could be drawn by present and future generations. In the work of Thucydides, we find attempts to formulate from the past fundamental principles of human action which provide guides for the future. None, however, was concerned with the predictive potential of history. That changed with the emergence of Christian history based largely on the Bible. Both the Old and New Testaments were the products of numerous authors over time, and this led to many contradictory accounts. Amid the confusion, however, are details of historical places, events and people whose existence has been supported by other forms of evidence, including archaeological. Above the historical detail stands an overarching narrative which is teleological and culminates with the realization of God's mission on Earth. In this important respect, Christian historians do attempt to map out a scheme for the future.

All the issues addressed by these early historians are still with us today; indeed, they go to the very heart of history as a mode of intellectual inquiry. Perhaps the answers we can provide are more sophisticated, reliable, and consistent, but one of the great merits of our ancient forebears is that they actually did much to establish the historiographical agenda and set the terms of the debates that continue to challenge us.

Further Reading

Robert Graves and Barry Unsworth (2006) *I Claudius*.
Herodotus (2002) *The Histories*, ed. John Marincola.

Simon Hornblower (ed.) (1994) *Greek Historiography*.
Ronald Mellor (1999) *The Roman Historians*.
Ronald Mellor (ed.) (2004) *The Historians of Ancient Rome*.
G. A. Press (1982) *The Development of the Idea of History in Antiquity*.
David Rohrbacher (2002) *The Historians of Late Antiquity*.
Suetonius (2003) *The Twelve Caesars*.
Thucydides (1998) *The Peloponnesian War*, ed. Walter Blanco and Jennifer Tolbert Roberts.
Stephen Usher (1985) *The Historians of Greece and Rome*.

2 From the Middle Ages to the Early Modern

Introduction

Here we take up the story where the last chapter finished by examining historiographical trends in the period that in the West was known as the Middle Ages. The focus in the opening section is the Venerable Bede who as a seventh-century Christian historian developed a remarkable technique for reading sources. His purpose was better to understand chronology in order that the End of Days might be calculated according to prophecy. Christian notions of the past were predicated on the notion that since history was moved forward by an omnipotent God, there was an urgent need to calculate the timing of the Second Coming. This notion of forward movement was shared by the monotheistic religious traditions, most notably Judaism and Islam. The Jewish tradition believed that history had a forward trajectory but also inhabited a narrative of its own that was provided by a rich tradition of the *Tanakh* representing the canon of the Hebrew Bible and commentaries. Thus, from the first century to the fifteenth century, Jewish historians remained silent in that they tended not to articulate histories outside of their own communities and the narrow concerns of the Hebrew Bible. Islamic scholarship, in contrast, thrived; it was rich in content and voluminous in scale and scope. This innovative tradition in Islam became less dynamic after the end of the Spanish 'Golden Age' in the 1400s and, indeed, gave way to scholarship that was more conservative and inevitably less self-critical of the ways of reading testimony and evidence. The West ended the so-called 'dark ages' (or so it was considered) by a Renaissance of ideas, art and culture. Its importance to the history of historiography was the rediscovery of the classics (not that they completely went away) and all that the Greek and Roman historians were to mean to the discipline in the centuries to follow.

The researching and writing of English history changed fundamentally by the early modern period. When exactly it changed is a matter of dispute but sometime in the late sixteenth century or early seventeenth century seems generally agreed upon by most historians. How it changed is disputed less. The chronicles of the period before about 1580 took their cue from religious concerns and their primary sources from the Bible. The results tended to disregard evidence based on testimony or verifiable fact and instead reproduced narratives of the past that were mythical and fantastic. As we saw in the last section, the writing and research of the national story was influenced largely by the Renaissance and Italian commentators (themselves influenced by the classics) and became the preserve not of monks or churchmen but of the new professional classes who used antiquarian evidence drawn from, say, coins, ruins or landscapes to compose humanist histories.

DOI: 10.4324/9781003156086-3

2.1 European Christendom and the 'Age of Bede'

> And it came to pass, when Moses came down from Mount Sinai with the two tablets of the testimony ... that Moses knew not that the skin of his face sent forth beams while he talked with Him.
>
> (*Exodus*, 34:29)

Pope Julius della Rovere (1443–1513) commissioned Michelangelo (1475–1564) to build a tomb. It was never finished. Yet we know from surviving written sources that this magnificent structure was iconographically designed to represent the Christian world and the world yet to come. The lower level was to be dedicated to Man, the middle level was reserved for prophets and saints and at the top was an unearthly level which would come about at the End of Days. Its summit was to be an embodiment of two angels guiding the Pope out of his tomb on that dreadful day of the Last Judgement. Within this elaborately tiered tomb, the Basilica di San Pietro in Vincoli, can be found statues and icons intimately connected to the symbolism of the age. At its centre is the magisterial figure of Moses: a figure common to the three major monotheistic religious traditions of Judaism, Christianity and Islam, a symbol which straddles ancient and modern times and which has been understood and received by chroniclers and historians in a multiplicity of ways in each of these three major religious traditions.

Overall, this is a stirring setting to place Moses, chosen by God because of his humility and kindness to the sheep that he tended at the rather advanced age of 120, or so the story goes. Sculptured in 1513–1516, the protruding knee of the statue was damaged slightly by the flying chisel of the frustrated artist and the beard is worn thin by the touch of worshippers, apparently in the belief that a statue of Moses could bring relief for their troubles. But what of the horns protruding from his head? As Moses descended from Mount Sinai with the tablets of law, his countenance glowed from a close encounter of the most spiritual kind. He was said to be emitting a 'horn' of light, but this can also be interpreted as meaning 'a ray of light'. (The Hebrew for horn/beam/ray (of light) is in phonetics *keren*; in the Latin or *versio vulgate* reading of the Bible, however, it is translated literally as 'his face sent out horns of light'.) Thus, medieval and Renaissance artists, including Michelangelo, misrepresented Moses with *actual* horns protruding from his forehead. There are other misunderstandings and misinterpretations caused by poor translation, such as the Hebrew word *naara*, which in the context of Mary is translated as virgin (*betulah*) rather than by its former meaning in Hebrew as girl or young woman. This illustrates how different, separated, yet connected the three major monotheistic traditions had become historically. Such difficulties in the transmission of knowledge extended to the understanding of the past and the writing of history in antiquity, the Renaissance and throughout the Middle Ages. This chapter seeks to address these difficulties, explaining why Judeo-Christian and Islamic approaches to the past and the future are so vital to an understanding of historiography throughout the long centuries of the antique and medieval periods right up to the early modern.

Each of the monotheistic traditions did have something besides Moses in common. They struggled in different ways to understand and tell the various stories of exile (in the case of Judaism), incarnation and resurrection (in the case of Christianity), the lives of the prophets (in Judaism and Islam) and creation and the End of Days (in all traditions). And whether we consider Jewish, Christian or Islamic historiography, to be influenced respectively by the Torah or five books of Moses (collectively known in Greek as the *Pentateuch*), or the three gospels of Matthew, Mark and Luke (known as the 'synoptic' gospels) of the New Testament, or the Koran, we find there a single God who is thought to be moving and controlling time, omnipotent and indivisible. One force moved history and could not be rivalled and this unitary God could not be challenged by a rival deity. From this power came all judgements and a single law that would eventually govern all humanity; it could also allow, for the first time in human experience, the possibility of a universal history, but one focused on the unfolding chronology of scripture or prophesies.

The job of the historian in late antiquity and into the medieval period then was to determine providential acts, miracles, portents, prophecies and markers that could reveal exactly where we were on the linear path to the end of history. Thus, the Book of Daniel, for example, was rifled for 'signs' and evidence of history's divine stages. Or, according to Eusebius, introduced in a previous chapter, the reader could be oriented to recognize the 'six ages' of Adam, Abraham, Moses, the building of the Temple, the rebuilding of the Temple and the triumphant birth of Christ. Augustine of Hippo (354–430) was to do something similar with his 'tripartite scheme' of 'world stages': time consisting of 'periods before the law', 'under the law' and 'under God's glory'. It was through the efforts of historians and early figures of the church such as Eusebius, the scholar Saint Jerome (347–419/420), Saint Ambrose bishop of Milan (339–397) and the apologist Lactantius (c.250–c.325), the 'Christian Cicero' as he was known, who looked to the classical texts as a source of public morality. Christianity – with the political clout of that most famous of apostates Constantine the Great – cast off and then denied its formative Jewish influences.

Christian eschatology (the doctrine of the End of Days) in the Middle Ages, however, looked not only to the past but to the future and so connected both the past and the future through the processes of historical change. The question was how to hasten the end of the days and to bring on the onset of Christ's Kingdom. Premillennialists were notoriously pessimistic about human progress and potential. The only way to hasten Christ's Kingdom, they believed, was through divine, not human, intervention. History was biblically prophesied and if studied with care and learning would reveal signs of impending judgement and eventually the Second Coming. In order to separate the moral elect from evil, the sacred and the secular had themselves to be separated: the former venerated, the latter kept at arm's length.

It was from this perspective that early European Christendom understood its history. Through its chroniclers it could chart these signs and portents, celebrate its saints and soothsayers and honour Christ's ministry by honouring God's Holy church, its holy orders and its monasteries or sanctuaries. It is in the writings of the most famous and skilled of these chroniclers and in an important monastery in the north-east of England that we discover more about the development of Christian historical ideas.

Whether the library was concentrated at the monastery of Wearmouth in the far north-east of England, where the Venerable Bede (672/673–735), foremost scholar and historian of the Middle Ages, lived, or at Jarrow, with which he was also associated, is disputed, and it is not known whether it was divided between the two monasteries. What we do know is that the library was big. Containing somewhere between 300 and 600 volumes, it was hardly a store of knowledge to equal the library at Alexandria, but by contemporary standards, at least in the West, it was of huge importance. Within these physical and intellectual walls Bede wrote his magisterial *Ecclesiastical History of the English People* in 731–732, along with voluminous letters, hagiographies, chronologies and essays that provide a precious insight into the period in which he lived, how the past was understood by the early church and how that understanding was first absorbed by Bede and then utterly transformed.

For this unique work, Bede drew freely upon books and manuscripts retrieved from Rome and the furthest corners of medieval Europe. Visitors to Northumberland came from far and wide, adding yet more to the collection. That much of the library was preserved on vellum (quality parchment made of calf-, kid- or lambskin) gives as a real sense of the wealth of the institution and it also tells us something about the importance of those that worked there as teachers or scribes. Bede told of the conversion of England to Christianity while transmitting the Christian

20 *Philosophies*

Figure 2.1 The Library in Alexandria founded *c.*331 BC by Alexander the Great. Originally a small ancient Egyptian town, it became an important centre of Greek until the Muslim conquest of Egypt in AD 641

Contributor: De Luan/Alamy Stock Photo

message. In doing so, he relied on a robust selection of written texts and a determination to find reliable witnesses, yet Bede included 'miracle stories' and, like many medieval Christian chroniclers, he sought to locate the operation of divine providence in events that gave meaning to the fulfilment of God's will.

He recalled, for example, a story of the death of a nun called Hild and the witnesses who anticipated and marked her death in monasteries situated thirteen miles apart. The first account was set in the monastery some distance from the death scene; the second in a remote wing of the monastery where Hild died:

> In this monastery there was a nun called Begu who for thirty or more years had been dedicated to the Lord in virginity and had served Him in the monastic life. As she was resting in

the sisters' dormitory, she suddenly heard in the air the well-known sound of the bell with which they used to be aroused to their prayers or called together when one of them had been summoned from the world. On opening her eyes she seemed to see the roof of the house rolled back, while a light which poured in from above filled the whole place. As she watched the light intently, she saw the soul of the handmaiden of the Lord being borne to Heaven in the midst of that light, attended and guided by angels. . . .

It is also related that, on the same night and in the same monastery in which this servant of God died, her death was seen in a vision by one of the devoted virgins of God, who had been deeply attached to her. She saw Hild's soul ascend to heaven in the company of angels. She related this openly to the servants of Christ who were with her at the very hour it happened and aroused them to pray for her soul, and this before the rest of the congregation knew of her death, for it was only made known to them as soon as they met next morning.

(Sellar, 1907, pp. 276–7)

This example tells us something valuable about the ways in which the medieval chronicle was constructed. Bede was like other medieval chroniclers in that he determined that the task of the historian was to discern God's will, while the task of history was to fulfil providence and determine exactly where we were on the divine journey to the End of Days. Three related elements appear to be common to medieval chronicles: they seek exactitude, the universal and moral application of a factual account and plausibility. They are histories that correspond to comparable truths, albeit 'truths' that we would now probably regard as implausible and far-fetched. On the face of it, Bede's description and explanation for the death of Hild and how it was witnessed by a fellow nun, Begu, is quite simply irrational. Visions, dreams, hearsay are adopted as fact without any secure, evidential basis, but it is an explanation that ought to be set firmly within the context in which it was written. First, the story itself would have originated from a trusted source and would be believable to contemporaries in every detail. In this narrow sense it was neither fanciful or exaggerated nor was it made-up in any way. Second, these contrasting accounts taken from different viewpoints verify a single incident: The foreshadowing of the death of a pious abbess. In this respect it was sound scholarship and good history. It was also well written. Perhaps the narrative itself was difficult to credit, but this is not the point. It made perfect sense to Bede and most of his contemporaries and as such should be treated on its own terms.

Veracity in history is at least to some extent of itself an historical construct, a creature of the time in which a standard of truth is held and the history researched and written. This could also be said about the plausibility of any account set in the past. It needed only to correspond to comparable truths accepted as such by readers contemporary to Bede. We should not, therefore, be surprised that these accepted truths are not accepted as truths by us. This ought not, however, to cloud our judgement about the ultimate worth of histories set within their context, and it should not make us overly judgemental about medieval historical scholarship more generally.

Bede was especially adept at constructing periods, particularly in his attempt to date the religious calendar from historical records. In this respect, his work was analogous to attempts within Islamic historiography to lend veracity to the life and ministry of the Prophet. The difference in this case was that Bede was trying to date, say, Easter in order to calculate – through a comparison of historical events with biblical prophesies – the coming of Christ's Kingdom. In doing this it is quite simply breathtaking how closely he stuck to historical methodology, especially in his ample use of documentation as well as his constructive use of oral accounts and the avoidance of invented speeches – all elements that mark him off from classical historians and quite probably from the bulk of Jewish and Islamic historiography in its infancy. As the medieval historian Given-Wilson (2004) has emphasized, Bede and other chroniclers of the period were seeking to establish continuity between the past and the present. This was because in both the scriptures and the prophecies of the past lay the key to the future; understanding the past provided the key to the gates of heaven. This moved Bede to do nothing less than to locate the origins of Christianity in Britain and to recalculate the age of the world.

Whether it was disagreement about law or faith, the authority of the Prophet or the End of Days, Judaism, Christianity and Islam used history in a variety of ways that would raise the collective eyebrows of many modern historians. Hence Moshe, Moses or the Prophet Moses was a composite as well as a contested figure by the time the tomb of Pope Julius II was constructed in the middle of the Renaissance, but nonetheless he had by this time been effectively claimed by the Catholic Church. Still, Judaism, Christianity and Islam could agree that history was no longer random, a whim of the Almighty. Before we look at how these ideas developed through the writing of history during the period of the Renaissance, we should pause to consider in more detail non-European conceptions of how the past impacted on the present and future, particularly in the traditions of Judaism and Islam.

2.2 Peoples of the Book: Jewish and Islamic Conceptions of History

Switch now from the cold and deserted wastes of north-east England to the warmer lands of Arabia in the East – modern day Saudi Arabia – to the library of the Islamic historian al-Waqidi who, according to the Hijri (Muslim) calendar, died in the year 207 H or 823 CE. What we find is not 600 books that made up Bede's store of knowledge but 600 trunks of books which were only removed upon al-Waqidi's death with the help of two burly men hoisting each container. A similar picture emerges with the essayist al-Jahiz (d. 868) who in old age was crushed to death by his falling books, quite a fate as they totalled some 400 camel loads of theology titles alone. By the late tenth century a library in Cairo hosted hundreds of thousands of books, including many history books. This was far in excess of anything that could be claimed by Bede around the same time and much more than had been accumulated by the ancients. Only China, which traced a historiographical tradition back to Confucius (d. 479 BCE), could rival this burst of historical literature in the Islamic world in the late eighth and early ninth centuries, for the age of Bede and the Abbasid period of Islamic growth were contemporaneous to the T'ang dynasty (618–907), by which time the Chinese had already absorbed centuries of bibliomania. The West would have to wait until the invention of the printing press for the experience to be repeated, most notably the push given to history in Renaissance Europe by the polyglot and printer of books, William Caxton (c.1422–1492). The longer-term consequences of this invention for the uses of the past in the present, for good and ill, we discuss in Chapter 23.

Arnaldo Momigliano (1908–1987) was perhaps the most important commentator on ancient historiographies. In a wide-ranging working life that began in fascist Italy and ended in Chicago, via Oxford and postwar London, Momigliano became increasingly preoccupied with Persian, Greek (how it impacted on Rome) and Jewish historiographies. He helped greatly to establish how these areas related to one another, to a wider antiquarian historical culture and to the genres of biography and prosopography. (Prosopography was first used by historians of Rome and is a study whereby individual biographies could be connected through family ties, career histories, and so on.) In his *Classical Foundations of Modern Historiography* (1990), Momigliano asks three fundamental questions:

1 What have Greek and biblical historiography in common?
2 What are the main differences between Greek and biblical historiography?

3 Why did Greek historiography prove to be so vital while Jewish historiography halted, rather abruptly, in the first century CE?

The first two questions were dealt with in the previous chapter and the last section, but it is the third question that will be addressed now. In the early years of the Common Era and before, Jews tended to write in Greek. Craving respectability and acceptance among majority communities, they had in many cases lost the ability to communicate in Hebrew or Aramaic, a semitic language of the near Middle East which dates from around 1100 BCE, maybe even earlier. Jewish Hellenism, we are told by Momigliano, was openly syncretic – freely mixing Pagan and Jewish elements and working these elements into their own culture and histories. Jewish education was based on the Greek *paideia* of self-knowledge and education for citizenship in the city-state and this fed directly into a wider historical culture. Observant Jews were not unaffected by this wider historical culture that led in turn to increasing levels of assimilation with the wider gentile population.

As part of this assimilative culture in the opening years of the first century CE, Jewish historiography owed much more to classical scholarship and less to visions of the End of Days. Flavius Josephus (37 BCE–c. 101 CE), the first real historian of Judaism and a Jewish historian, drew upon the *Babyloniaca* and the histories of Egypt by Hecataeus of Miletus (whom we met in the last chapter) and Manetho (an Egyptian from the 30th dynasty of whom we know very little) for his reconstructions of the 'Jewish War' against the Romans. His first work was written in Aramaic; his subsequent works in line with Jewish assimilation in the Hellenistic world at this time were composed in Greek. Vastly influential, his histories were to stand the test of time, becoming ubiquitous features, for example, in very many Victorian libraries. Making much of their origins and lineage, he put the Jews at the centre of political and social affairs. Eager to establish the projection of history and the place of the Jews within it, he also made assumptions about the Divine Providence of God and prophecy. Accordingly, his twenty-volume book *Antiquitates Judaicae*, (*Jewish Antiquities*) began at the Garden of Eden from Adam and ended its narrative on the eve of the Jewish revolt against the Romans in 66 CE. As a Jew, educated at a rabbinical school, sometime leader of the Galilee division of Jews that had rebelled against the Romans, he was now valued by the Romans as a seer. His rather changed circumstances allowed him a pension in order that he might devote all his time to writing history.

Flavius Josephus used evidence in a way that was somewhat different from those writing histories before him. Personal knowledge and special access to commentaries from Tacitus (especially his records of military operations) gave him a head start. No doubt this access owed something to his relatively elite situation, and for similar reasons he wrote in the Roman way of establishing annals or yearly accounts. But he also wrote thematically, digressing across pages in the absence of footnotes or appendices, using long speeches and direct quotations from conversations that he could not possibly have been privy to while exaggerating very much in the tradition of the Greeks. Here he is describing the situation in Jerusalem before the destruction of the Second Jewish Temple in Jerusalem:

> As a procurator of Judaea Tiberius sent Pilate, who during the night, secretly and under cover, conveyed to Jerusalem the images of Caesar known as standards. When day dawned this caused great excitement among the Jews; for those who were near were amazed at the sight, which meant that their laws had been trampled on – they do not permit any graven image to be set up in the City – and the angry City mob was joined by a huge influx of people from the country. They rushed off to Pilate in Caesarea, and begged him to remove the

Figure 2.2 Josephus, also known as Flavius Josephus (*c.*37–*c.*100 AD), a first century Jewish historian of priestly and royal ancestry who recorded the Destruction of Jerusalem in AD 70 and later settled in Rome under patronage of Flavius family. Original name Yosef Ben-Matityahu (Matthias in Greek) means Joseph, son of M. Wrote the History of the Jews while in Rome

Contributor: Lebrecht Music & Arts/Alamy Stock Photo

standards from Jerusalem and to respect their ancient customs. When Pilate refused, they fell prone all round his house and remained motionless for five days and nights.

The next day Pilate took his seat on the tribunal in the great stadium and summoned the mob on the pretext that he was ready to give them an answer. Instead he gave a pre-arranged signal to the soldiers to surround the Jews in full armour, and the troops formed a ring, three deep. The Jews were dumbfounded at the unexpected sight, but Pilate, declaring that he would cut them to pieces unless they accepted the images of Caesar, nodded to the soldiers to bare their swords. At this the Jews as though by agreement fell to the ground in a body and bent their necks, shouting that they were ready to be killed rather than transgress the Law. Amazed at the intensity of their religious fervour, Pilate ordered the standards to be removed from Jerusalem forthwith.

(Josephus, 1981, p. 138)

Although Josephus used long, verbatim speeches from his leading historical players, his history is in keeping with the methods of the Romans who were concerned with morality in politics – especially the role of war in historical change – and used annals to construct chronologies. There were elements, however, that singled out Jewish historiography more generally from both its Greek and Roman counterparts: an inclination in Jewish histories to narrate events from the beginning of the world, not simply the beginning of human affairs. There was also a concern with truth, not simply a truth focused on accuracy as we saw with the medieval Chroniclers discussed in the previous section but a truth told under the direct and searing gaze of the unitary and omnipotent God. Indeed, remembrances of God and the miracles purported to have been part of the Hebrew legacy – the escape from Egypt most prominent among them – were (are) ritualistically re-enacted by Jewish families around the *seder* table every Passover. This was only the most famous of remembrances. The religious Jewish year, then and now, recounts and enacts past events with astonishing vividness and monotonous regularity.

Jews perhaps lacked historical method in comparison with the Greeks (or even the Romans) but they did not lack the wherewithal to establish and maintain public records. Some have even described the Jewish archive in the antique period as superior to that of the Greeks. But whereas the Greeks maintained an interest in history through national decline and the rise of the Roman Empire, transmitting this interest through their culture, the Jews just switched off and dropped out.

There was, it appears, no lack of respect for the archive or for the enquiring mind – the Talmud (together made up of the *Mishnah* and the *Gemara*) is a codification of Jewish oral law that was written down between the second and fifth centuries and is a byword for jurisprudence and disputation. Yet even without the Talmud, Jewish books seemingly contained adequate descriptions of historical and 'contemporary' events, or so it appeared. The *Books of Ezra*, *Nehemiah* and the *First Book of Maccabees*, which told the story of heroic resistance against the Persians and Greeks and which, according to Momigliano, stand at the 'crossroads between Jewish and Greek thought', were characterized by fierce rabbinical arguments (Momigliano, 1990). Above all, perhaps, the disappearance of the Jewish state in 66 CE (until its re-emergence in 1948) meant that diasporic Jews (those that left) were in exile from the Promised Land, without a Temple in which to carry out the statutes and ordinances of the Law. This ensured that they retained group solidarity and an historical fascination that centred above all on each other. And, in any case, the Jews had a supreme history book – the Torah. No other history mattered, and it was this, according to Momigliano, that led to an indifference towards other areas of historical research.

In his *The Jew and his History* (1977), Lionel Kochan (1922–2005) confirmed that Jewish historiography was indeed all but non-existent from the antique period until R. Joseph Ha' Cohen (1496–1578) wrote an account of the kings of France and Ottoman Turkey. He rebutted notions that Jews were absorbed by the biblical narrative or that as a people without a state they were less likely to have any kind of conventional historical culture and that this provided a total explanation for centuries of silence. Likewise, he denied that Jews were overly affected by the Christian idea that Jews as a people were part of a redundant covenant that had atrophied after the coming of Jesus and were now no longer relevant – a nation without a future hardly needed a past. Instead, Kochan suggested that the Jews affirmed history by praxis: by 'elaborating the means as opposed to luxuriating in the ends', which he judged to be 'the precise reversal of the utopian thinking common to the Gentile world' (Kochan, 1977, p. 117). While the Talmud does admit to a messianic process in history and even speculates that the world will endure for 6,000 years after the End of Days in a series of eras, it contrasts with the Christian view by rejecting predictions of when, how or by which method the Messiah will appear. These are the 'twists and turns' of history and time that are mentioned by Jonathan Sacks in Chapter 22.

This scepticism about the propriety or efficacy of predicting utopia may explain why the most influential of scholars in the post-biblical era, Rabbi Moses ben Maimon or Maimonides (1138–1204), embraced all other aspects of Aramaic intellectual life such as mathematics, philosophy, medicine and poetry but declared historical books to be a 'waste of time'. Perhaps, however, as has recently been suggested by the historian Kenneth Seeskin, he did have a sense of the past but one that was perfectly in line with the medieval period in which he lived. Above all, the Jews were witnesses to the whole of human history and their solemn duty was to survive (Seeskin, 2004a). Not that Maimonides (the Rambam as he is commonly called) worked in a cultural vacuum. Indeed, this was the 'Golden Age' of toleration among the three Abrahamic traditions, which was prompted by the Moorish conquest of Spain in 711 and did not end until the Jews were expelled by the Christians in 1492. Throughout this period, cultural and intellectual cooperation with Islam was commonplace, although, as we shall now see, there were profound differences in their approaches to history.

Islam had emerged as a military force by 700 but Islamic historiography did not appear in any coherent way until 200 years later. Its emphasis was on the history of dynasties and nations that impacted on the Prophet's genealogy and lineage and on histories of the future, that is, ideas about the end of the world or the Day of Judgement. Like Christianity, histories of the life of Mohammad and Islamic historiography were fixed on the end of the world, and this was anticipated with absolute certainly as if it had already happened. Coverage of events such as the Creation of the world, on the other hand, existed as part of a more general history but remained incidental.

Beginning in earnest around 600 or 700, Islamic historiography was subservient to Muslim law and religion, which was itself fused with Byzantine and Iranian influences. Historians of these trends in Islam have addressed the issues of when exactly this written form of Islamic learning flourished and have sought to assess its effect and impact. Chase Robinson (2003), for example, outlined a formative period of Islamic historiography which spanned from 600 to 900 and a classical period of output that ran from 950 to 1500. Franz Rosenthal (1990), on the other hand, dated Islamic historiography as an independent force from 700. It was a tradition that reflected Muslim ideas and the learned culture of a civilization that had emerged over a very short space of time, coming to prominence in the late eighth and early ninth centuries. It provided an important space for individual self-expression, and only later in the fourteenth and fifteenth centuries did it attract its critics from the 'harder sciences' such as philosophy or medicine.

Whatever the truth about the chronology and the reception of history as a reliable epistemology (a basis of knowledge) within the Islamic world, it is impossible to escape the sheer size of its production and its advanced state. This is especially true when we consider that the Chinese took 500 years to reach the volume and sophistication achieved by Muslim scholars over a period of just five generations. If this creative energy appears to burn out quicker than the Christian fuse that was lit – or at least rekindled – by the historian monk Bede, it was at least partly because this period of historical production within the Islamic world is all but irretrievable. Where European medieval scholars used parchment and animal skin to record their histories, their Islamic counterparts employed paper materials that faded and disintegrated over time, were destroyed by foreign invaders or fell afoul of disputes internal to Islam. Consequently, there is a real problem faced by all present-day scholars of Islam; certainties about the 'formative period' of Islam are difficult to establish, while those seeking to recover the history of pre-Islamic society face an impossible task because there are simply no written records to consult.

After 950, however, we can better scrutinize the Islamic historiography of the so-called classical period. What are its assumptions and methodologies and how should we make judgements about its plausibility and effectiveness? Current scholarship is organized around three broad themes, namely: chronology, biography and prosopography; these distinct approaches have served to establish the contours and peculiarities of Islamic historiography within the wider context of the Arabization of Islam, to provide a more complete record of the Prophet's life and to rescue from oblivion pre-Islamic history before the written record or memory.

The evocation of memory played a crucial role in Islamic traditions but in different guises from that of Judaism or Christianity. Islamic historians used chronology to prove the veracity of prophetic biography and to understand and 'prove' *hadith* or *hadeeth*, the oral tradition within Islam that recounted the teachings and the life of the Prophet, while *Sunnah* sought to learn more about the way of life of the Prophet. The 'science' of *hadeeth* criticism lent method to Islamic historiography. This methodology was immensely complex but at least seven categories of classification have been identified. These classifications were designed to test the reliability of the traditions and sayings that were attributed to the Prophet but where the provenance may be doubtful or where a new issue of jurisprudence has been thrown up by modern circumstances, *hadeeth* criticism looked first for an authoritative chain of evidence. This was called an *isnad*. *Isnad* asked questions about the reliability of witnesses, their links to one another, the chronological integrity of the evidence given or the order of the evidence given.

It is doubtful that *hadeeth* as a legal tradition can be traced directly back to the time of the Prophet, probably dating no earlier than from 200 years or so after his death. While this view is largely a view maintained by Western scholarship, naturally enough Islamic scholars dispute it. In either case, what we discover (and what is critical for historians of Islam in the medieval period) is that the criterion of evidence and reliability of evidence is vastly different between Eastern and Western historiography. Standards of objective judgement and notions of subjectivity wildly differ from each other, at least in periods after what the West calls the Middle Ages (Azzam, 1999).

The main priority of Islamic historiography in the past was to conserve the fragments of the past but it never quite managed to free itself from nostalgia, and it did not adequately press the past into the service of the present. On the cusp of modernity in the 'Golden Age' in Spain, when Islam led the world in science, philosophy and medicine, thereafter it was slow to embrace change. Indeed, the end of the 'Golden Age' in the 1400s coincided with a shutting down of criticism of the Koran while, at precisely the same time, Western science and then biblical criticism would encourage an increasingly open and secularizing society.

28 Philosophies

That said, histories in the Arab world existed in a wider cultural framework than the sayings of the Prophet and broke out somewhat from the constraints of the methodology of the *hadeeth*. Ya'qubi (d. *c*.897) made the first attempt in Arabic to write a world history (while including extracts from the Greeks), and others would later attempt histories that took in natural histories, local histories, dynastical histories, biographies of historical figures and so forth. Histories existed (often in Persian) after the Mongol invasions of the Muslim world in 1219, and by the fourteenth century histories were written in North Africa with a universal aspect and with some theoretical sophistication at that. Islamic histories since, however, have had none of the critical power of their counterparts in the secularizing West, many existing in circumstances where Muslim societies have remained relatively backward and repressive.

2.3 The Renaissance, Humanism and the Rediscovery of the Classics

The preoccupation throughout this chapter has been with the transmission of ideas, particularly, of course, ideas on how to write history. We established in Chapter 1 that ideas of what history meant among the ancients did not rest with the Greeks but continued with the Romans. These ancient writings were often neglected in the Christian years of the Middle Ages until their revival during the period we have come to know as the Renaissance. There was then an extraordinary transmission of Roman influence. It was at work, for example, in the short-lived medieval Roman republic (1347–1354) in Italy which sought to revive the glories of the old Rome and in the Italian communes of the European Renaissance, plus later in both the architecture and politics of the imperial ambitions of twentieth-century Italian fascism and German Nazism. Both these totalitarian systems were informed by the historical might of Rome and the histories of Cornelius Tacitus (*c*.55–117), especially his *Germania*, which when rediscovered in the fifteenth century was seen by Germans as a celebration of national independence and their racially pure beginnings. It was also used during the Reformation as yet more evidence of the alleged venal corruption of (by now) Papal Rome and of the comparative nobility of the Germans in matters of private and public conduct. We also find the influence of Roman historiography at work in the representations of the American and French Revolutions, with figures such as Thomas Jefferson and Napoleon, who were avid readers of the classical masters.

Yet while the Renaissance is conventionally thought to signal the bright new dawn of modernity, a positive gear-shift from the 'dark ages' of the medieval period, it is not entirely clear whether it ought to be regarded as an historical period at all. The provenance of the word *Renaissance* itself is disputed. It has been suggested that the term was coined first in 1550 by Giorgio Vasari (1511–1574) in his *Lives of the Artists*. Others date it much later and credit the French historian Jules Michelet (1798–1874), supporter of the French Revolution and author of the multi-volume *History of France* (1833–1862).

That we do have a sense of the thirteenth, fourteenth and fifteenth centuries as forming a coherent whole is largely due to the intervention of a Swiss Hegelian scholar, Jacob Burckhardt (1818–1897) and his *Civilization of the Renaissance in Italy* (2004). The notion of the Renaissance was thus in many ways a product of the nineteenth century. Here it was imagined that the Renaissance set forth the virtues of truth, reason, art and beauty, free from the superstitious and suffocating constraints of medievalism. The individual was given free reign of expression in the Renaissance period; the modern state (itself conceived as a 'work of art') was found in its purest condition. Burckhardt even went as far as to suggest that individual self-consciousness was awoken through art and cultural expression and led directly to a new secular morality. Corporate identities of guild or church were laid to one side in favour of individualism, a kind of classlessness where merit was favoured before the accident of birth and where even (again according to Burckhardt) gender equality flourished. In some commentaries this movement has been understood as a 'movement' of 'villa' intellectuals based in southern Italy, which eventually spread to the remainder of Italy and then the rest of Europe, or an age which was not so much imagined as an era but experienced as a 'spirit', in line with Hegelian and German Romanticism (see Chapter 6).

Historians since Burckhardt have been more circumspect about this humanist moment when the arts and philosophy of the classical world were rediscovered. A number of serious objections now make his thesis redundant. First, the new individualism that we associate with the Renaissance did not replace the collective solidarities of the medieval world. Both the guilds and the church, for instance, survived well into the modern era proper, as did affinities among a significant body of people of these institutions. Second, Florence or Italy is not given such a prominent place in the history of the Renaissance. Historians are now much more likely to consider economic factors that led to the transformation or 'waning' of the Middle Ages, which in turn ultimately led to the 'renaissance' in culture so brilliantly described by Burckhardt. Finally, many historians would point to earlier phases of cultural renewal and would certainly not reject the Middle Ages as 'dark' and regressive (Woolfson, 2005).

From the sixteenth century, however, we do see the slow rise of humanist approaches to the past, that is, beliefs that the well-being, values and morals of a society were not reliant on the supernatural intervention of God or on the earth-bound rule of the church but instead resided in the characteristics and behaviour of humans themselves. Humanism as a secular and cultural movement grew out of the Renaissance and spread across Europe based on the art and philosophy of ancient Greece and Rome. Above all, humanism and humanist histories focused upon the characteristics of human beings free from any mystical influence, an influence that had characterized medieval historiography. This is vital to understand as it represents a dramatic shift in thinking about the world, producing national histories that were very different in tone and approach from those that had preceded the Renaissance and that simultaneously satisfied a new demand to understand both history and historical origins.

Recent historians have also made important interventions in the field and have been instrumental in improving our understanding of the period. Some, as we have seen, have modified Burckhardt; many have pondered on the proximity (or otherwise) of the Renaissance to modernity and whether we might place it as a period (if distinct period it is) as part of a grand narrative in the Western tradition. Peter Burke in his *European Renaissance* (1998), for example, preferred to decentre the Renaissance experience, making it a global phenomenon involving a discrete network of locales and urban centres that interacted – truly a civic humanism with a republican focus.

All commentaries, however, would agree that this period saw a major and sustained rediscovery of the classics, a renewed enthusiasm for antiquity and the classical tradition, including a *rapprochement* and reassessment of the Greek and Roman historians. Between about 1330 and 1370 a successful attempt to recover Latin texts such as those by Cicero and the historian Livy was witnessed; more than this, knowledge of ancient Greece was introduced into Italy in the last years of the fourteenth century. Above all, however, we saw the first humanist history published by the first of the 'new historians' in Italy, Leonardo Bruni's (*c.*1370–1444) influential *History of Florence*. Bruni acknowledged a debt to Livy but also to Sallust and Tacitus whose *Annals* and *Histories* had been rediscovered in the closing decades of the fourteenth century. He also admitted to being a keen reader of both Thucydides and Polybius, going out of his way to condemn the lack of method and style associated with the medieval chroniclers. Bruni made sophisticated use of comparative sources and his employment of speeches, which were constructed in keeping with the classical approach. What then had changed between the Middle Ages and the high point of the Renaissance?

It is not as if the chroniclers of the Middle Ages were unaware of the ancient historians or, indeed, that the classics remained unread. As Christians, they did not look outside of their tradition for explanations or insights into method and approaches towards the past, any more than the Jews or Muslims had spent much time outside of theirs. Not until, that is, the 'new historians' began to imagine that Florentine's civic virtues were not necessarily specifically derived through Christianity. The 'new history' of the Renaissance took rhetoric seriously (reintroducing the long verbatim speeches associated with Greek historiography) and became more inclined to reject legend or hearsay as solid historical evidence. We also find national histories, such as histories of England and Italy. This is also a continuing civic concern with the history of Florence evident in the writings of Polydore Vergil ($c.$1470–1555), Francesco Guicciardini (1483–1540) and Niccolo Machiavelli (1469–1527).

Most important among these is Machiavelli who has been viewed most often as the personification of political intrigue and as an exponent of a distinctive humanist tradition of classical republicanism (Skinner, 1981, pp. 78–88). Known chiefly for the publication of *The Prince* (1513) and *The Art of War* (1520), we can be forgiven for thinking that Machiavelli's legacy was more important to politics than history. Yet he *is* important for any basic understanding of Renaissance historical thought. The *History of Florence* (1525), which he wrote towards the end of his life, suggested a knowing of and sympathy with classical historiography, as did his *Discourses Upon the First Ten books of Titus Livy* (1517) with its emphasis on public morality that demonstrated his humanist concerns (Skinner, 1981, p. 78). In common with the ancients, Machiavelli was also concerned in his histories with rhetoric and the celebration of ancestry. Here we can see the influence of not only Livy but also Sallust and others. His histories were driven by a character-led narrative that could bend the truth and so were 'dominated by idealized heroes and reprehensible villains' (Bondanella, 1973, p. 17).

Renaissance humanists not only labelled the Middle Ages as the 'dark ages', but they also characterized their own age as immeasurably enlightened by comparison. They celebrated its culture and governance, seeing it as a new period set apart from the past, with any impoverishment in arts and learning a legacy of the stagnation of the Middle Ages. Thus, in 1469, Giovanni Andrea Bussi ($c.$1414–1475) began a process of re-periodizing the history of the West in a way that was to become immensely influential well into the modern period when Burckhardt and other figures such as Jules Michelet and Walter Pater (1839–1894) looked back at the Renaissance as a golden age. This reassessment also had the effect of placing classical antiquity at the foundation of Western civilization, a notion that has become part of a conventional wisdom, although in recent years it has been contested by medievalists such as Marcia Colish (b. 1937), who in recasting the periodization has placed even greater stress on the historical significance of the Middle Ages. While, Burckhardt, Michelet and Pater had argued that the foundations of Western thought were established by classical or Judeo-Christian texts, Colish identifies the importance of the Middle Ages and by so doing presents a challenge to those ideas about the backwardness of the medieval period that had been cultivated by Machiavelli and others:

> [T]he foundations of western intellectual history were laid in the Middle Ages and not in classical Greece and Rome or the Judeo-Christian tradition. In defence of that claim we argue that the thought of Western Europe acquired its particular character not only as a result of the cultural components that flowed into it. Equally important were the attitudes that western thinkers took to their sources and the uses to which they put them. It is certainly true that medieval thinkers expressed concerns, tastes, tolerances, and sensibilities that distinguish this period from other chapters of the western intellectual experience. At the same time, they developed institutions, viewpoints, and methods that mark them as specifically western and

that helps to explain why medieval Europe is the only traditional society known to history to modernize itself from within, intellectually no less than economically and technologically, enabling Europe to impose its cultural as well as political stamp on much of the non-European world as the Middle Ages drew to a close.

(Colish,1997, p. x)

The Renaissance ended, at least according to Peter Burke, in the early seventeenth century when the effects of the scientific revolution were unleashed. It is in this scientific revolution (as well as the waves caused by civil war) that we can locate early English attempts to write national histories and to make sense of an antiquarian engagement with the past. It is, therefore, to the battle in revolutionary England between the 'ancients and the moderns' that we next turn our attention.

2.4 The Battle of Books: Camden, Clarendon and English Historical Writing

That great satirist of the eighteenth century, Jonathan Swift, portrayed the 'Battle of the Books' in his *Tale of a Tub* in 1704 as a war where printed volumes flew across a library in angry pursuit of one another. These were no ordinary books, however, for this was a war between 'ancient' books and 'modern' books. The lines were clearly drawn and the questions stark. Were the Greeks and Romans superior to those that followed them? Or have the 'moderns' equalled or even surpassed them? The battle was thus a confrontation between those that looked to the ancients for their approaches to the writing of history and literature and those that held onto approaches that were nurtured throughout European medieval Christendom but that, in this dispute at least, we must think of as modern. This war in methodology and style, although first mooted in literally circles, was to have a profound influence on history writing.

That the Battle of the Books was fought between the advocates of the ancients and of the 'modern' or Christian-inspired chroniclers is important to us because it was part of the eighteenth-century debate about how histories of England should be written. It might appear that differences between the types of narrative used to describe England were at the heart of the dispute, but we shall discover that the approach to evidence also became important. Certainly, the Battle of the Books illustrated the state of historiography in England at this time and how it had changed in the century between the death of Elizabeth I (1603) until the mid-seventeenth-century Civil War.

By the seventeenth century observers could appreciate the effects of long-term change, the vital importance of national narratives and the attendant changes in manners and sensibilities that turned historical writing from a concern of the local monastic chronicler or civic official into the professional or leisurely pursuit of the university student or lay reader (Woolf, 2000). As a result, English histories drew upon the lessons from the classics by using the evidence of English antiquities and the ruins that marked the landscape, as well as coins, genealogies and maps. But above all else there was a fresh approach prompted by the change in how the church exercised its authority, the rise of commercial considerations of how history might be produced, sold and distributed and the slow growth of a class which had more time and inclination to indulge in historical research that was once the preserve of medieval scribes. So, as it turned out, the ancients were in fact modern, which points to the contradictory nature of these labels.

Swift worked at the time of the controversy for the great advocate of the ancient position, Sir William Temple (1628–1699). Temple had written *An Introduction to the History of England* (1695), which is now seen by historians as limited in scope and range and wildly inaccurate. As

32 Philosophies

Figure 2.3 Oliver Cromwell at the English Civil War Battle of Marston Moor (1644), nineteenth-century engraving after a painting by Abraham Cooper (*Battle of Marston Moor English Civil War 2 July 1644*)

Contributor: Timewatch Images/Alamy Stock Photo

Joseph Levine (1991) argued, it was a history very much written in the style of the classics, in that it:

- Emphasized a good story and is well written.
- Neglected discussion of sources.
- Was without footnotes (like the scrolls used by the ancients).
- Was reliant, like many of the ancient historians, on a 'borrowed' single source (in this case an Elizabethan historian who was not acknowledged in the narrative).

The moderns, by contrast, focused on Anglo-Saxon or biblical narratives about the past, rehabilitating the approach to English history of the medieval chroniclers. Quite often chroniclers had used the *Pentateuch* as both the foundation of their histories and the fountain of all narratives concerned with nations and national consciousness. Accordingly, just as the provenance of Israel could be traced to the exodus from Egypt or to the giving of the Torah at Sinai, so the origins of Albion were told by chroniclers. One such chronicler was the early twelfth-century Benedictine monk, Geoffrey of Monmouth, who made explicit reference to an ancient, mythical past. Albion was a place peopled by giants until Brutus and Curiness came to Britain with the Roman Empire and killed Goemigoy and other giants apparently descended from the biblical figures Noah, Ham, Cain and Enoch who had arrived on these shores sometime before the Flood. Another chronicler was the Benedictine monk from Chester, Ranulf Higden (d. 1364), who wrote *Polychronicon*, which was said to be the first universal history written in England. *Polychronicon* outlined the social customs, religion, social geography and natural history of the British Isles but within the context of a world narrative. Its influence was immense and various editions (different in length) appeared well into the fifteenth century. More generally, the function of these types of chronicles was to narrate the past, present information, commemorate great events, and entertain the reader. Above all else, chronicles emphasized the mythical, only later giving way in the Elizabethan and early Stuart periods to more rational and verifiable histories.

The timing of this apparent revolution in history writing and historical understanding has been the subject of debate among historians. F. S. Smith Fussner (1962) thought these changes in historiography happened somewhere between 1580 and 1640; others such as Arthur Ferguson looked less to the literary changes in writing and more to changes in historical method or, according to Woolf, the slow, 'longer lasting' revolution in social mores as interest grew in literary culture and scholarship along with the ascendency of a commercial society. We could date this moment from the time that the Italian-born Polydore Vergil (whom we have already met) wrote *Anglica Historia* as a humanist-style history in 1512–1513 but waited until 1534 before publishing. It was probably the first of its type in England, a history that discussed the English from the time of the Romans right through to Henry VIII. What made it a 'humanist' history was his use of Renaissance-inspired methodology but also the questioning of some of the more fantastic accounts of English history offered by Geoffrey of Monmouth and others.

That humanist-inspired scholarship was revolutionary has been questioned in recent years. F. J. Levy's *Tudor Historical Thought* (2004) made clear that the changes wrought between Polydore Vergil's arrival in England in 1502 and William Camden's death in 1623 amounted to a fundamentally different approach to historical research and writing but in ways that were essentially gradual. Certainly, William Camden (1551–1623), historian and herald, is a significant figure but not a revolutionary one. His *Britannia* (1586) stuck to the chronology of the traditional annals but made – like the histories of Francis Bacon before him – a sharp distinction between secular and religious history, although he is keen to place blame on the Papists while at the same time steering away from any criticism of Elizabeth I. His history may have been partial, but it was not a history moved by religious sensibilities. (Vergil's history, or at least the first draft, ended at the reign of Henry VIII – he was keen not to offend the monarch.) Considering the use of heraldry and genealogy and the interest this engendered in local as well as national history, Camden's *Britannia* was, in the words of Smith Fussner, 'original, serviceable, and characteristic of the new scholarship' (Smith Fussner, 2010, p. 217).

As historiography was revolutionized (or not) it also fragmented. In addition to antiquarianism, we have memoir and autobiography, local propaganda and satire, which were also concerned with the past. Critically, however, while historians would remain deeply religious and traditional in their own affiliations (Camden wrote in Latin and no translations to the vernacular were permitted in his lifetime), the function of history was no longer simply to 'reveal God's purposes and instruct man in his proper behaviour' (Brownley, 1985, p. 2). This represents a change from the chroniclers who had all but disappeared from public view during the seventeenth century.

Perhaps the most complete demonstration of a humanist history in the seventeenth century came out of the terrible conflict of 1640–1660, which would become a moment when future (Whig) historians thought that England was begun anew. In 1641, Edward Hyde, the First Earl of Clarendon (1609–1674), wrote his *The History of the Rebellion and Civil War in England*, which was to attract huge critical and popular acclaim. In fact, the book was so popular it was erroneously said to have provided the University of Oxford with the Clarendon Building – certainly it hosts a statue of the author. Beyond dispute is that Hyde was to become Chancellor of the University and a major figure in Restoration politics. His prose suggests a fundamentally different approach to evidence and analysis than the medieval chronicles that had preceded it and as such can be categorized as an advanced humanist approach. Unlike the chronicle, it drew differences between past and present, identifying historical anachronism and civil (as opposed to purely religious) morality. Equally, while Camden was an astrologist in his youth, there was no longer need for historians to look for omens and portents in history. Power was more inclined to be earth-bound.

Others who were part of this shift to humanist historiography include Sir Walter Raleigh (1554–1618) who wrote his *History of the World* in 1614 and John Dryden (1631–1700) who became Historiographer Royal in 1670. Second cousin to Jonathan Swift, Dryden was known as a literary figure, having become Poet Laureate in 1668. This is critical to note because history in this time was dominated by antiquarians who utilized the relics of history as the mainstay of evidence while never really elevating history to a literary art. The Society of Antiquaries was founded in 1707 while, both then and now, antiquarianism suggests an approach to the material remains of the past that may include archaeology, works of art, manuscripts and books or the built environment (Sweet, 2004). Indeed, one historian (Brownley, 1985, p. 18) speaks of this period as one of 'arid antiquarian compilation' while suggesting that the 'complete integration of literary art and historical method' would have to wait to the end of the eighteenth century with the work of William Robertson, David Hume and, in particular, Edward Gibbon. These are all historians we associate with the Enlightenment, which will be discussed in the next chapter.

In order to understand the transition from chronicle to humanist history to Whig history it is important to understand how the seventeenth century has been treated by historians. For Clarendon, the conflict that he himself had experienced was a 'Great Rebellion', while for the Whig historian Samuel Rawson Gardiner (1829–1902) it was a 'Puritan Revolution'. His *History of England, 1603–1640* (1863) ran to eighteen volumes. Between 1886 and 1891 another three volumes entitled *The Great Civil War* appeared, taking the story beyond the regicide or execution of Charles I in 1649. Next was *The History of the Commonwealth and Protectorate*, which he completed in 1902. In this body of work, Gardiner displayed some of the characteristic features of Whig history, most notably a narrative approach which prevails over analysis and an empiricism that encourages the collection of facts and a steadfast adherence to chronology and statecraft.

Later, Marxists such as Christopher Hill (1912–2003) would see the events of 1640–1660 as a 'bourgeois' revolution, while later still the so-called Revisionists and then post-Revisionists would in some measure rehabilitate Charles I. Only with the 'New British History' did the Bishop's Wars in Scotland (1639–1641) and the Irish Rebellion (1641) enjoy full coverage, suggesting not a purely English history at all but what seventeenth-century scholars today have labelled a 'War in the Three Kingdoms' or the 'British Civil Wars'. The nature of evidence has changed too. Now there is a good deal more emphasis placed on 'the linguistic turn' (see Chapter 19) and sources that highlight the politics of discourse, symbols or representations of the conflict such as the 'print explosion', which led to the production of the Thomason Tracts, a major source for the English Civil War that Gardiner was one of the first to exploit. As historians have developed this historiography it is in the knowledge that Clarendon made the first, all-important intervention and commented upon the conflict and the political upset while passions were still flaming hot (Walton, 2010, pp. 13–15).

Some see these essentially humanist histories as important moments in the making of the nation and a critical moment too for the fashioning of history in its most up-to-date guise. It was the Exclusion Crisis at the end of the seventeenth century (explaining why Swift made his intervention on the side of the ancients in 1703/1705) that gave birth to the current constitutional settlement that balances Parliament with Monarch. It was as important as the signing of the Magna Carta in 1215, the defeat by the English over the Scots at the Battle of Falkirk in 1298, the expulsion of the Jews in 1290, the Act of Union in 1707, the American Declaration of Independence in 1776 or the British exit from the European Union would become in 2016. History could now tell the story of constitution and country and it was this narrative of unfolding constitutional liberty that defined the Whig interpretation of history.

Postscript

There is a certain orthodoxy which views the Renaissance as a time when the arts underwent a profound transformation. After the darkness and backwardness of the Middle Ages, the argument goes, European thinkers rediscovered the works of ancient Greeks and Romans – in part through translations made by Islamic scholars – and embarked on a new course of intellectual and artistic inquiry which paved the way for the great tradition of Western humanism. The truth behind this rather convenient narrative is more complicated, and we need only to review the fate of historical inquiry to see this was the case.

The legacy of the outstanding classical historians was never lost. Instead, the three traditions of historical inquiry that dominated the medieval period took what lessons they needed about the nature of historical evidence and the ordering of chronological narratives to create new directions for the writing of history. These directions were determined largely by the emergence of the omniscient presence of 'the book' and the perceived need to consolidate its authority by study of the past. Thus, Christian historians who came to dominate Western historiography sought to explain the past and predict the future in ways which were consistent with accounts found in the Bible. Similarly, Jewish historians found inspiration in the Torah, and Islamic scholars looked to the Koran. Despite the differences in emphasis, what united these traditions was a belief in a single God, a universal power which by governing human destiny allowed for the opportunity of a universal history.

In the medieval period, therefore, we find historians such as Bede who drew freely upon classical historiography to write broad historical narratives of events and periods. They used a wide variety of sources, adopted a critical stance to different forms of evidence and determinedly set about recording plausible chronicles which were consistent with the evidence. Despite such promiscuity, the extent to which these traditions entered into a dialogue with one another was limited. Bede, for example, wrote at a time before Islamic scholarship established itself, and after an early flowering, Jewish historical scholarship began a period of protracted silence, only to re-emerge with the Renaissance.

Although the Renaissance was in part made possible by the forgotten works of the classical period newly translated from the Arabic, it signalled a new enthusiasm, particularly among European historians, to look beyond the boundaries of Christian thought and with a return to the concerns of classical historians to think more seriously about the role of human agency in historical processes. This shift towards humanism in turn paved the way for the scientific revolution of the seventeenth century. And yet it should be remembered that the Renaissance did not necessarily signal a sharp break from a stigmatized Middle Ages; rather it brought together the accumulated scholarship of ancient and medieval Europe and the non-European world and reworked it into a new vision of humanism.

This humanism was to reach maturity in the seventeenth century when an age of discovery and bitter civil war promoted approaches which relied less upon the putative influence of unearthly powers and antiquarianism and more upon a sense of real events unfolding over time. This in turn demanded novel approaches to evidence, the adoption of more analytical methodologies to the material and the use of sophisticated narratives to help organize the accounts. This humanism may not have been able to shed completely the legacy of the Middle Ages, but it marked a vital stage in the broad transition to Whig histories, which came to define historiography just as the discipline asserted its self-identity in the second half of the nineteenth century.

Further Reading

Marcia Colish (1997) *Medieval Foundations of the Western Intellectual Tradition, 400–1400*.
Paolo Delogu (2002) *An Introduction to Medieval History*.
Chris Given-Wilson (2004) *Chronicles: The Writing of History in Medieval Britain*.
Lucille Kekewich (ed.) (2000) *The Impact of Humanism: A Cultural Enquiry*.
Arnaldo Momigliano (1990) *Classical Foundations of Modern Historiography*.
Chase F. Robinson (2003) *Islamic Historiography*.
A. M. Sellar (ed.) (1907) *Bede's Ecclesiastical History of England. A Revised Translation*.
Jonathan Woolfson (ed.) (2005) *Renaissance Historiography*.

3 Enlightenment and Romanticism

Introduction

This chapter is concerned with history writing and how the Enlightenment and Romantic movements affected an understanding of the past. New methods of observing phenomena emerged from the seventeenth century in England and in eighteenth-century Scotland and Europe as Enlightenment thinkers attacked the beliefs and assumptions of organized religion. In this respect, the philosopher historians of the eighteenth century, David Hume (1711–1776) and Edward Gibbon (1737–1794), were the most important while the more modern methods of the Scot, William Robertson (1721–1793), pointed us towards historiography as it developed in the nineteenth century. Also, a product of the Scottish Enlightenment, Adam Smith (1723–1790), both constructed a blueprint for capitalist economics and described how societies changed and developed. In contrast to the reason, order, symmetry and harmony that are associated with the Enlightenment, Romantic notions of nationalism and heroism impacted on the writing of history in the modern period. Here, we will explore the significance of freethinking, emotionalism, spiritualism and a profound engagement with nature to the growth in the nineteenth century of Romanticism.

3.1 The English Enlightenment?

Before exploring the intellectual tensions thrown up by the Enlightenment and the consequences for the researching and writing of history, we should ask, as did the German philosopher Immanuel Kant in 1784, 'What is Enlightenment?' While this is a complex, messy and sometimes contradictory historical movement, the term itself suggests several elements:

- A sense that natural and universal laws, the laws of physics, govern both human beings and nature.
- A belief in the ability of reason and human enquiry to penetrate the mysteries of the world and by so doing control it.
- A conviction that the external and physical world could be known by reason and reason alone.

Similarly, the origin of the Enlightenment as a movement or even as a set of ideas is not easy to date or define. There is no single Enlightenment and its central figures are not necessarily in agreement with each other. Some historians see fundamental change occurring in the years 1720–1780, mostly in France and Germany but also in Scotland. Peter Jones concentrates on the 'philosophes' and other figures prominent in Continental Europe and picks out 1759 as a signal year. In that year Handel, the composer, died and the Seven Years War (1756–1763) was at its height. Voltaire published *Candide*, Samuel Johnson *Rasselas* and Adam Smith his *Theory of Moral Sentiments*. The French philosopher Diderot was banned by King Louis XV as he was about to publish the eighth volume of his *Encyclopedie*. And yet, more generally, in 1759 'no one can be said, in a defensible modern sense', to have known anything about:

- Forms of energy other than light and heat.
- The composition of air or water.
- The nature of fire, breathing or procreation.
- The age of the earth or the size of the universe.
- The nature of stars or the origins of life.
- The evolution of animals or genetic inheritance.

Nor could they have known much about history except as a branch of literature and certainly not as a science. Yet the Enlightenment transformed history writing. As history stopped being a literary endeavour, it began to resemble a science, embracing a framework of natural laws that were thought to govern the universe. As science determined, for example, how gravity worked, so history could determine how societal transformation came about. And as French ideas on the laws of motion rested on principles developed by the philosopher René Descartes (1696–1750) from Greco-Roman assumptions that the universe is made up of immovable atoms, so history could begin to comment on the mechanics of change. All physical phenomena, it was thought, could be explained in terms of momentum and velocity, all motion, including historical motion, worked according to *specific* laws.

Cartesian mechanical philosophy (theories taken from the philosophy of Descartes) insisted that motion was restricted as there was no space between particles and thus no vacuum. The universe was full-up and (accordingly) in stasis; precisely because there was no apparent motion, there could be neither historical movement nor progress. This 'law', it was hypothesized, governed the natural world but could extend to a consideration of the 'motion' of societies over time. As a result, societies themselves stood still, not changing with any rapidity. Only when this stasis became dynamic could the study of history (or the study of change) become a distinct discipline and a credible basis of knowledge, plausibly able to explain everything. Only when the laws of motion were seen to work on universal principles could a universal history of the world be contemplated.

Since much of this work took place in France, the Enlightenment is commonly held to have found roots there. Roy Porter (1946–2002), however, suggested that the conditions for enlightened thought based on reason were already apparent in seventeenth-century England with the work of Francis Bacon and Sir Isaac Newton, both of whom insisted that knowledge should be rooted in observable fact and not in 'untestable speculation'. We could look earlier. To the work of William Harvey (1578–1657), for instance, who transported Renaissance science from Italy to the University of Cambridge, describing how circulation in the body worked. From this perspective, the Enlightenment was something made in England, not France, Germany or even Scotland, with its origins found in the seventeenth century, not the eighteenth. Let us run with this supposition for a moment.

English or British empiricism – the understanding of the world through experience rather than abstract theory – informed the methodology of natural science, and the observation of phenomena via the use of the senses, not the construction of untested paradigms based in philosophic speculation, was the first principle of the Enlightenment. Newton was arguably at the origin of this process. Influenced by the work of Bacon and Robert Boyle, he created a methodology that would focus on a hypothesis and the testing of that hypothesis through observation.

His *Principia Mathematica* (1687) was based on observation, not speculation, arguing that the universe conformed to *general* not partial or specific laws:

> I have not as yet been able to deduce from phenomena the reason for these properties of gravity, and I do not feign hypotheses. For whatever is not deduced from the phenomena must be called a hypothesis; and hypotheses, whether metaphysical or physical, or based on occult qualities, or mechanical, have no place in experimental philosophy.
>
> (Newton, 1713, p. 166)

Newton then was not content to speculate in the abstract; a hypothesis must be tested by our God-given senses, hence the well-known and probably untrue story about the apple falling on his head and the 'discovery' of gravity as a testable and falsifiable phenomenon. He hypothesized that the gravity of the Earth must alter the path of the moon, but he could not prove it; thus, when the apple fell, it accelerated using the same force that curved the path of the Moon. In addition, since an empirical phenomenon was true at all times and in all places, it could be repeated. This approach had a massive impact on the way evidence, including historical evidence, was observed and tested. Directly or indirectly, then, it was Newton in seventeenth-century England who had such an influence on historians and 'philosophers' such as David Hume in Scotland (see next section).

Newton's laws of motion and gravity attempted to explain the world by suggesting that the universe is in balance. This metaphor extended to a politics that sought to maximize pleasure and avoid pain. His science then had a tremendous effect on almost all facets of human existence. Too often, historical figures are labelled 'geniuses' but in this case, Alexander Pope's elegy to Newton in 1723 was spot on:

Nature and Nature's laws lay hid in night
God said, 'let Newton be and all was light['].

Although history was considered as a philosophy rather than a science until the nineteenth century, it was profoundly influenced by Newton's theories of force and inertia. These laws of motion – in contrast to Descartes' – envisaged a universe in flux, not in stasis. This allowed change to occur; a discovery that is crucial for our understanding of the impact of Enlightenment thought on historical practice and, indeed, was one factor that allowed history as a discipline to flourish. Another factor, which influenced specifically the relationship between the intellectual culture of both England and Scotland, was the union of 1707. This prompted questions about the role of the nation in history at a time of flux and in part laid the ground for the seismic intervention of Adam Smith (1723–1790) in the affairs of Scotland and upon the development of Western capitalism.

The notion that individual interests and social interests might coalesce and balance, a balance which was thought to occur in natural phenomena, informed Adam Smith's *An Inquiry into the Nature and Causes of Wealth of Nations*, first published in 1776, the year in which David Hume died. Smith, like his friend Hume, was concerned with change. He sketched four phases of development: from the 'lowest and rudest' society based on hunting, without property or government, to the fourth stage that is a commercial, exchange economy. This, however, was not merely an exercise in historiography. Underlying Smith's work was a desire,

- To explain Britain's commercial success.
- To explain the relative poverty of Scotland as compared with England.
- To conduct a general enquiry into trade and economic phenomena.

To do this, he argued against monopolies in home and colonial markets. The restraint on the import of foreign goods caused by the Navigation Acts protected the markets of sugar, tobacco and cotton/wool. Instead of tariffs, trade should be balanced by the maintenance of low taxes and market mechanisms that should be allowed license to do their work. This commercial system had a moral advantage over the old mercantilism that had used naval and military might to maintain markets. Smith also argued, unlike the so-called physiocrats to whom he was opposed, that wealth was not necessarily wholly derived from agriculture but that precious metals and bullion, as well as money, could be the basis of an exchange economy. This adherence to an exchange economy and the wealth it created would come to obviate the views of Thomas Malthus who in the first of very many editions of *An Essay on the Principles of Population* (1798) famously contended that agricultural production could not keep up with population increases without restraining marriage and procreation, war and natural disasters: both checks to population without which the sum of human misery would increase.

Overall, Smith's 'scientific system' was built around the following precepts:

- Existing privileges and anomalies in the mercantile system compromise the principles of a free market.
- Man can imagine or reason a new kind of society, for example, by the construction of a 'system' or blueprint.
- Any monopoly of social or economic power is wrong; instead, there should be a balance of power among the monarchy, the nobility, the landed gentry, merchants, manufacturers, clergy and the labouring poor.

Although Smith saw himself as a moral philosopher rather than an economist, his legacy has been most keenly felt within the economic sphere.

'Classical' economics would encourage free trade and prosperity along with peace where nations would grow. Productivity in manufacturing would rise, costs would fall and hence trade would increase dramatically to the advantage of the country. Using as an example the manufacture of pins, he showed that a vital element in this transformation is an equitable division of labour, allowing the process of production to be separated into discrete tasks, the operation of which could be thus maximized. This level of specialization and the 'separation' between trades will lead, Smith argued, to the further growth of towns and to social intercourse that would in and of itself promote peace. There was then – as Smith was indeed an Enlightenment thinker – a moral dimension to his plan.

Behaviour would inevitably change when individuals were encouraged to make rational economic choices. In his *Theory of Moral Sentiments* (1759), Smith argued that a sophisticated division of labour would lead to a complex society, which in turn would create a limited benevolence among members of society. This is important if we are to understand Smith's contribution to Enlightenment thinking; the self-regarding behaviour apparent in the new capitalist economy meant that self-interest, not just mutual sympathy, would promote the common good.

In order to illustrate these points, Smith used the metaphor of an 'invisible hand' of individual selfishness as the unwitting cause of social benefit when production was organized through a division of labour. That self-interest served the social interest is a notion only challenged in the twentieth century by the development of game theory where it was found that one individual could develop a strategy that can be pursued at the expense of another individual or the social good. Smith's ideas, however, lent significance to Pope's *Essay on Man* when he said earlier in the eighteenth century:

> So too consistent motions act the soul
> And one regards itself, and one the Whole
> Thus God and Nature link'd the gen'ral frame
> And bade Self-love and Social be the same.

This is not to say that reason would triumph totally over religious sentiment. As stated at the beginning of this section, the Enlightenment was messy, complex and contradictory. Hume, for example, pleaded with his friend Adam Smith to become his literary executor upon his death. For all his championing of rational economic man in his new, anti-mercantile, capitalist economy, Smith refused. As a reverend and a Presbyterian, he was unable in conscience to fulfil the dying wish of his atheist friend. Reason then had not triumphed totally over religious sentiment. It is to this theme – reason and religion – and the part it played in the research and writing of history that we shall now turn.

3.2 Secular Histories

After a night of whoring in July 1776, James Boswell, the diarist, paid his friend David Hume a morning visit. Hume, author of the six volumes of the constitutional *History of England*, published between 1754 and 1756, an implacable foe of revealed religion, was dying. Hume shaped the growing secularity of the eighteenth century, and he knew now with an apparent certainly that he was eyeball to eyeball with infinity. According to an account of this meeting between Boswell and Hume in an essay by the political theorist Michael Ignatieff in his *The Needs of Strangers* (1984), Boswell was horrified that Hume when faced with imminent and certain death had not recanted his atheism. And, indeed, Boswell's diary tells us that upon witnessing Hume's nonchalance he was gripped 'with a degree of horror . . . mixed with a sort of wild, strange, hurrying recollection of my mother's pious instructions, of Dr Johnson's noble lessons, and of my religious sentiments and affections during the course of my life' (Weis and Pottle, 1971, quoted in Ignatieff 1994, p. 84). This does not begin, however, to express the conflict Boswell experienced between a rationality of the mind and a spirituality which was not based in reason but which he felt emotionally. Admittedly, he had long rejected the strict piety of his Calvinist mother yet still clung to the promise of an afterlife. Hume would have none of it, of course and was content to give an account of his life and conduct, not to God but to his fellow man. As such, he very much belonged to the Enlightenment.

We associate the Enlightenment with some key words such as reason, order, harmony, symmetry and the restraint of emotion. These words come up repeatedly as the world of science, art, literature, music and architecture changed in ways that reflected Hume's scepticism, but they were changes that were also regretted, a regret that we see in the shock expressed by Boswell at Hume's atheism. Make no mistake that Boswell admired the great rationalists of his day. Nevertheless, his urge to embrace reason and discard superstition was in constant battle with an inner life that seemingly pulled him in an opposite direction. Thus like many contemporaries he was far from reconciled with what the great figures of the Enlightenment were truly saying. Hume's scepticism set down in print was one thing; to see the great man facing death without expectation of an afterlife was quite another. After all, it was only in 1764 that Boswell had engaged in a debate over two days about the truth of Christianity with the French philosopher, poet and sometime historian Voltaire (1694–1778), and he had left his native Edinburgh in March 1760 for the express purpose of converting to Roman Catholicism and becoming a monk.

In the persons of Hume and Boswell then, we can discern countervailing forces – religious sentiment and rational calculation – with each unleashed by a revolution in politics, science and historical thinking. The Enlightenment eventually emancipated women, blacks and religious minorities such as the Jews, and let loose historical writing in the Romantic tradition which focused on national sentiment, the role of the hero, a focus on the universal attributes of human beings and their soluble differences (see next section). Forces that ran counter to the Enlightenment, on the other hand, articulated a deep-seated regret for a world lost to the machine amid a voracious commercialism and for a revolution in thought that affected the credibility of Christian schemes of a teleological history that had as its end or purpose the Kingdom of Christ. Let us have a look at these themes now as evidenced in the seminal writings of Edward Gibbon.

The historian Edward Gibbon at first reflected a similar ambiguity about religion, converting to Roman Catholicism, which he later recanted. Yet his magnificent account of the Roman Empire, *The History of the Decline and Fall of the Roman Empire*, first published in 1776 – the fateful year when Boswell called upon Hume on his deathbed, when Hume's friend Adam Smith published his *Wealth of Nations*, when Thomas Paine published *Common Sense* and when, as we shall see in Chapter 5, American colonialists embarked on their revolution that was to push so much of the world towards democracy – betrayed a deep-seated and emphatic scepticism towards religion, especially towards Christianity. To this extent, he had much in common with Hume who had written 'Of superstition and enthusiasm' in 1741, pejoratively linking religion with priestly power and undue emotional fervour. Gibbon is known as an Augustan historian, that is, an historian who looked back with admiration on a golden age of Roman literature, in particular, the poet Virgil and the historian Livy. He presented history 'candidly' and 'rationally' while writing prose as if it was to be spoken or performed (Lentin and Norman, 1998, pp. vii–xv). This, along with his attack on Christianity as an organized religion, is what makes Gibbon an Enlightenment historian.

Yet it is not so simply stated, for Gibbon's status as an historian has been contested by various critics. Geoffrey Elton, who we meet in Chapter 21, saw little more than literary merit to his work, regarding his scholarship as unconducive to modern scientific methodologies. It lacked objectivity and analytical engagement with primary sources. Gibbon, it was argued, neither assessed the motives of historical actors, nor did he systematically evaluate causality. In response, Roy Porter (1946–2002) set out a convincing defence against charges that Gibbon fell short of technical competence in historical enquiry (Porter, 1988b, p. 164). His Gibbon placed the historian at the centre of the practice of history and as such all history was 'contemporary', 'liberal' and 'useful' with 'every sentence . . . pregnant with the deepest observations and the most lively images':

> I have been suggesting why Gibbon's idea of history was different from the academic formulations of later generations. Gibbon's preoccupations have little to do with the debates about causality, scientific laws, historicism and the philosophical status of explanation in history, which were argued by nineteenth-century idealists, positivists and evolutionists, and which have constituted hard-core 'philosophy of history' ever since. Rather he was fascinated by history as the creation of the historian's mind playing upon the mind of the reader and passionately concerned about its capacity to enlighten, entertain, interest and instruct.
>
> (Porter, 1988, p. xx)

We have no need at this stage to concern ourselves with a precise definition of 'idealists', 'positivists' and 'evolutionists', but it is important to note that Porter suggested that Gibbon was no scientist but was very aware of the nature of evidence, 'contextualizing, interpreting, evaluating, reflecting . . . [with] a degree of detachment'. Above all, he went on, Gibbon understood the historical nature of the exercise of power in past societies and added a precision to historical inquiry that identified him as an Enlightenment historian.

One of the main charges against Gibbon then was his lack of objectivity, especially in his treatment of the part played (as he perceived it) by Christianity in the fall of imperial and pagan Rome. But we can look elsewhere for a more secular turn in his thinking. He was not interested in the accuracy (or otherwise) of biblical chronology, for example, and he displayed little interest in superstition, myths or metaphysics while paying very little respect to the church. Consider this humorous description of a notable Bishop, remembering that Gibbon wrote history as if it was to be performed by an orator from ancient Rome:

> Twenty-two acknowledged concubines, and a library of sixty-two thousand volumes, attested the variety of his inclinations; and from the productions which he had left behind him, it appears that the former as well as the latter were designed for use rather than ostentation.
> (Gibbon, 1998, p. xii)

Indeed, Porter insisted that Gibbon was part of an historiographical trend which took a strongly secular approach, emphasized Man's greatest cultural achievements, transcended traditional Eurocentrism by displaying a sensitivity (for example) to Arabic and Islam and searched for natural causes as well as the social or common experience of humans in history.

Perhaps more than Hume or Gibbon, the real historian of modernity is another figure of the eighteenth-century Scottish Enlightenment, William Robertson. His *History of America* (1777) used modern methods of research and scholarship, comparing what we would now call the American or native Indian with the 'tribes' of Germany. Robertson was an unapologetic Presbyterian, in fact a minister (Smith was himself a member of the Church of Scotland). With his emphasis on the importance of religion and spirituality, Robertson gained fame and fortune from his work and was briefly the official historian of Scotland. And yet his accounts of King Charles V in 1769 and his history of Scotland were cosmopolitan in ways quite unprecedented. Robertson was anxious, for example, to contextualize the history of Scotland by comparing the national experience of the Scots with the experiences of other nations in Europe. He even widened his frame beyond Continental Europe and America to India, coming close to taking in a global perspective.

Above all else, as Enlightenment figures, Smith, Gibbon and Robertson changed Christianity from within, particularly the Protestant strand of Christianity, questioning the truth of the Bible and the interrogation of the scriptures in the light of new discoveries made by natural science. This had vital consequences in the longer term. As the nineteenth century progressed, science became a credible alternative to traditional religious explanations of natural phenomena. Studies in geology, for instance, demonstrated that fossils could date the age of the world, while theories of natural selection and the descent of human beings from primates, outlined by Charles Darwin and others, confounded the Biblical story of creation. German theorists or the 'Higher Critics' such as Friedrich Schleiermacher (1768–1834), David Friedrich Strauss (1808–1874) and Ludwig Feuerbach (1804–1872) ensured that religion was seen merely as a projection of human frailties while Jesus was turned back from a God into a man. The *Critical Essay Upon the Gospel of St Luke* by Schleiermacher in 1825, for example, established that scripture should be considered part of human history and not as a divine text.

Friend and confidant of the poet William Wordsworth (1770–1850), Samuel Taylor Coleridge (1772–1834), helped to bring these ideas to a British public. Inspired by Coleridge, the Young Reformers (notably the novelist George Eliot) led 'Broad Church' opinion by translating Strauss' *The Life of Jesus* in 1846 and, in 1854, Feuerbach's *The Essence of Christianity*. Religious doubt filled the pages of the *Westminster Review*, spilling over to a wider public when a religious census in 1851 identified the 'unconscious secularist' and 'fireside heathen' as chief villains in declining attendance at church. Meanwhile criticism from within the church itself continued to acknowledge the passing of religious certainties. *Essays and Reviews*, published in 1860, recalls this moment precisely when, in his essay on the interpretation of scripture, Benjamin Jowett, later Master of Balliol College, Oxford, famously said that the Bible should be read like any other book. Bishop Colenso (1814–1883), Anglican bishop of Natal, South Africa, also proved to be a distinguished, if dissenting, voice during this period of apparent secularization with his *The Pentateuch and the Book of Joshua Critically Examined* (1863).

But it was Charles Darwin who upset religious orthodoxy by suggesting that Creation and providence were random affairs, which showed little evidence of God's design, since until that point science had been used to provide evidence that demonstrated the divine order of the Universe. At stake here was the status of the discipline itself. As a recent commentator has put it:

> Thus several modern historians have seen the Victorian 'conflict' as not between science and religion, but between a 'religious science' and 'irreligious science'; that is, between a science pursued in the interests of natural theology, that relates its findings to moral and religious values, and a new, professional, 'value free' science. The triumph of this 'new' science in the modern world explains why we have been so ready to accept the science-versus-religion myth of its partisans, such as Huxley.
>
> (Cosslett, 1984, p. 2)

Owen Chadwick, an historian of the church, spoke in *Secularisation of the European Mind* (1975) about the 'unsettlement' in society caused by mechanization, urbanization and the rise of 'irreligious science'. He notes that the word *secularization* had its origins in the notion of anticlericalism, and by the 1860s its 'metaphorical career' had spread to notions of the 'secularization of art' or the 'secularization of politics' and, crucially, the 'secularization of morality'. This was a process that must be taken seriously as we seek to understand how it impacted on historiography.

From at least the revolution in France in 1789 to the rise of Marxism as a secular creed in the twentieth century, the Enlightenment transformed the world and transformed the way historians wrote about the world. The story of the decline of religion and development of science in the nineteenth century fostered a rationalism at the expense of what we might call institutional religion. This shift was evident in a whole range of intellectual concerns and cultural practices:

- The Sabbath gave way to the 'English week-end'.
- Bible reading and daily family prayers were replaced by secular entertainment (professional football and the like).
- Religion retreated to the periphery of individual and national life.
- In public life, by the close of the century, national and local politics became based not on religious domination but on class.
- A system of thought, a way of understanding the world, science was in the vanguard of modern thinking.

- Shifting structures of belief in Britain meant that Christianity moved from being an epistemology (a theory of knowledge, a moral philosophy, a means of understanding the secular world) to becoming a matter of private belief, justified by faith alone.
- Educated theologians were no longer in a 'desperate search for personal salvation' and the daily expectation of the return of Christ.
- By the end of the century the emphasis was less on Christ's sacrificial atonement than 'Jesus as saviour and friend'.
- Concepts of Hell were redefined, and a wider definition of inner belief replaced Christianity as an institution.
- A 'crisis of faith' led to forms of mysticism and non-belief.
- It appeared that there was an increasing gulf between the religious and secular spheres (that is, they were divided or, to put it constitutionally, separated).
- Professional 'brainworkers' and the manual working class practised their secular professions and trades, and although they may have been believers, they did so without reference to religious thought or practice
- Absolute truth and morality no longer took their cue from religion; instead, both were conceived in secular terms without recourse to the Divine.

Jose Harris in her *Private Lives, Public Spirit: A Social History of Britain 1870–1914* (1994) has also argued that while historians have seen the period as one of advancing secularization, they 'have disagreed widely about how and why these changes occurred' (Harris, 1994, p. 150). Harris herself places grave doubt on the broad narrative of secularization and is probably right to do so; indeed, the primary evidence would seem to suggest that secularization was not as linear as many have argued. For example, in *Working Classes and the Church* (1868), Thomas Wright, a skilled artisan and social commentator, argued that church or chapel attendance is not an 'indicator of belief' and therefore simply counting worshippers cannot be used to prove the collapse of religious sentiment. Instead, Wright points to the 'essentials of Christianity' or what the historian Gerald Parsons called an 'effusive Christianity' (1993, p. 28). These included the survival of the attributes of brotherly love, self-sacrifice to assist neighbours, reflection on the hereafter, and optimism about future life, all of which could find a secular expression but which were less tangible than attendees in the established Church of England, at least according to W. Binns who recorded in his *Religious Heresies of the Working Classes* (1862) that unbelief was common. The working class would not respond to aggressive tactics of recruitment, yet secularism was the preserve of only a minority of 'thinking artisans'. If 'over conservatism begets secularism', the encouragement of an 'all or nothing' religion gave rise to a secular society caused by the breakdown of a deferent society, Biblical Criticism, the march of science, and the failure of religious, mainly Christian, institutions to respond to changes within society.

3.3 Romanticism, Nationalism and the Hero in History: Sir Walter Scott and Thomas Carlyle

Tourists to the Highlands of Scotland in the eighteenth century believed that they could only truly appreciate the beauty of its landscape by turning their backs on it. Pitching around a tortuous pass, scrabbling to the summit of a grand peak, they would come across a pre-built booth with a convex, tinted mirror. Walking into the booth, they would view the vista behind them by looking into a mirror or 'Claude glass'. The purpose of turning their backs on nature and looking at it in a manufactured booth was to reproduce the works of the popular landscape painter, Claude Lorrain (1600–1682) who, using a subtle graduation of tones in his paint, lent

46 *Philosophies*

nature a soft, mellow tinge. Drawing upon Enlightenment ideas of the subservient relationship of nature to man, Claude glasses suggested that the only way to appreciate the natural world was mechanically. Romanticism would change all that. Aesthetic tastes began to extend to scenery that was wild and unrestrained, not mastered and controlled, one that did not have to be literally 'framed', transformed for our pleasure. Nature itself became sublime, evoking fear in its vastness and mystery to inspire terror; its colours imagined not in the pastoral tones of Lorrain but rather in gloom and darkness (Figure 3.1). As an expression of extreme emotionalism associated with Romanticism or the counter Enlightenment, *Sturm* and *Drang* (storm and stress) entered the vocabulary. In other words, Romanticism gave vent to unbridled emotion with humanity at the centre of existence against the stifling rationality of Enlightenment thought.

Romanticism then appeared to set its face against objective rationalism and decentred humanity. It emphasized instead subjectivity, the use of imagination, freethinking, emotionalism over logic, spirituality and the naturalness and wildness of nature, as shown in Table 3.1.

One of Romanticisms' greatest proponents, Jean Jacques Rousseau (1712–1778), famously said that 'I felt before I thought'. In a sense, this summarizes Romanticism. This is not to say Romantics somehow abandoned reason. The philosopher Johann Wolfgang von Goethe (1749–1832), who had an enormous influence on eighteenth- and nineteenth-century European thought, was as competent in natural science as he was in poetry and literature. And in 1811 the Romantic poet Percy Bysshe Shelly (1792–1822) was expelled from University College, Oxford for refusing to disavow a notorious book he had co-written with Thomas Jefferson Hogg called *The Necessity of Atheism*. When his room was cleared, scientific equipment was

Figure 3.1 Phillip James De Loutherbourg, *An Avalanche in the Alps*. Painted in 1803, the Alps are depicted as sublime: terrifying and awe-inspiring to the human figures

Contributor: Asar Studios/Alamy Stock Photo

Table 3.1 Key words and concepts of Enlightenment and Romanticism

Enlightenment	Romanticism
Reason	Freethinking, spirituality, passion
Thinking	Feeling
Objectivity	Subjectivity, imagination
Order, symmetry, balance	Irregularity and mystery
(like classical architecture)	(like gothic architecture)
Harmony	Discord
Restraint of emotion	Emotionalism, wildness
Mechanistic	Natural

found – strongly suggesting that the young Shelley was continuing with his scientific experiments. Romanticism, therefore, did not somehow replace Enlightenment thought but as often ran parallel to it.

With this dramatic new describing of nature via the arts came a glossary of terms that have characterized Romantic sensibilities in the face of the stone-cold rationality of reasoned Enlightenment:

Glossary of Romanticism

Pantheism: The belief that God's spirit is present everywhere in creation – in every rock, tree and living creature

Pathetic fallacy: The belief that natural objects – trees, mountains and so on – share or express our ideas and feelings

Subjectivity: The feelings and ideas of an individual mind, rather than specifically proven or objective facts or views influenced by personal feelings

Solipsism: The view that the Self is all that exists or can be known – that is, we can't genuinely know anything outside ourselves

Sublime: Man's response to Nature, particularly responses of awe, terror or fear before the more threatening or dramatic aspects of the Natural World

Romanticism celebrated the intrinsic wisdom of nature and urged the reader to abandon 'our meddling intellect' and the 'full and endless strife' of book learning as impediments to real knowledge. Take, for example, the following stanzas from 'Turning the tables' as part of William Wordsworth's *Lyrical Ballads* (1798):

Books! 'tis a dull and endless strife:
Come, hear the woodland linnet,
How sweet his music! on my life,
There's more of wisdom in it.
Sweet is the lore which Nature brings;
Our meddling intellect
Mis-shapes the beauteous forms of things: –
We murder to dissect.

What else stands out in this extract of the poem is the pinnacle of Romantic sensibility, that is, the emphasis placed on the individual and the sensory perceptions of the individual rather than reason, which would 'murder to dissect' knowledge and then still not truly gain it. Nowhere was this more evident than in the writings of the decades after the 1790s. Whether it is Sir Walter Scott's reaction to nature or the gloom, darkness and grotesque mystery of the gothic or, as we shall see, Thomas Carlyle's emphasis on historical representations of the hero, Romantic sensibilities remained central.

Sir Walter Scott (1771–1832), the novelist who did so much to reinvent Scottish history in the reflection of the Romantic light of the early nineteenth century, grew up between Edinburgh and the Scottish borders in a society increasingly aware of its own changing nature. He had an acute notion of the sublime in nature that was both awe-inspiring and spiritual, applying these ideas to his historical fiction. In the 'Waverley' series of novels, Scott evoked the past by capturing the wildness and beauty of his native Scottish borders. *The Antiquary* (1816), for example, featured the antiquarian Jonathan Oldbuck and used a great many devices that we would associate with the gothic genre, such as the almost overwhelming force and power of weather (nature) and corrupted family lineage or 'bad blood'. Scott conflates the sublime wildness of nature with the horrors meted out to the lost innocents of early, pre-Church, Christianity:

> It was indeed a dreadful evening. The howling of the storm mingled with the shrieks of the sea fowl, and sounded like the dirge of the three devoted beings who, pent between two of the most magnificent yet most dreadful objects of nature – a raging tide and an insurmountable precipice – toiled along their painful and dangerous path, often lashed by the spray of some giant billow which threw itself higher on the beach than those that had preceded it. . . . Here, then, they were to await the sure though slow progress of the raging element, something in the situation of the martyrs of the early church, who, exposed by heathen tyrants to be slain by wild beasts, were compelled for a time to witness the impatience and rage by which the animals were agitated, while awaiting the signal for undoing their grates, and letting them loose upon the victims.
>
> (Scott, 1834, p. 76)

Besides relating the wildness of nature to the wild primitiveness of man's religious past, another element in the relationship between man and his environment was the relationship noted by Scott between life in the new urban core and the equally changing rural periphery. Edinburgh as the capital city of Scotland, a financial centre, a hub of the European Enlightenment and the metropolitan core is just to the north of the still remote and rugged hills of the borderlands. It was this relationship, this proximity, the difference between the city as the heart of commercial and political modernity and the vastness of surrounding rural regions which provided the dynamic context for the emergence of a way of thinking about the past. A part of this process depended upon an emerging identification of the urban with modernity and the rural with tradition, folk-life, superstition and eternal and unchanging values, which are both virtuous and wicked. In this context, the countryside, country people and country folkways and practices could be seen as a world where the past ways still survived and, in a time of great change caused by commerce, industry and urbanization, it was a past that was in danger of disappearing forever.

Scott's view of the past contributed to a growing sense of the need to retrieve and record for posterity important aspects of Scottish life. In most of his Waverley novels, starting with *Waverley* (1814), he recounted key moments in Scottish history and thus revealed a central concern of the Romantic imagination: nationalism. Nationalism, however, had developed in historically different ways. Herder, the German Romantic thinker, saw nationalism as an extension of feeling or sentiment and consequently as a form of identity. Nationalism as it emerged from the chaos of the French Revolution determined that a *citoyen* or citizen could be created by the suppression of social, regional, sexual and racial difference, although we know that regional quirks of language, local currency or non-standard systems of weights and measures nevertheless survived into the twentieth century despite all efforts to fashion a national identity (Weber, 1977). After 1789, the state was not a theocracy or a state run on the dynasty of a family but one based on a notion of popular sovereignty.

This form of nationalism was progressive, even liberal. It explains why great Romantic figures such as Lord Byron went to Greece in 1824 to fight for Greek independence where he ultimately lost his life en route to defend the principle of national self-determination:

> Your efforts to preserve my life will be vain. Die I must: I feel it. Its loss I do not lament; for to terminate my wearisome existence I came to Greece. – My wealth, my abilities I devote to her cause. – Well: there is my life to her.
>
> (Cited in Marchand, 1957, p. 1224)

It is also the 'feeling' of nationalism that made a hero of Lujos Kossuth in Hungary in the 1850s and Giuseppe Maria Garibaldi in Italy a decade later. Only later would nationalism in places such as Germany become illiberal, when the push for territory and the promotion of race combined with terrifying consequences.

For Scott, however, his concern was with the folk elements of national consciousness, such as language and the myths of national origins. But his vision ran even deeper into the undercurrents of society than this. Before he turned to fiction, his poetry had begun to engage with a more popular sense of the national past. *The Minstrelsy of the Scottish Border* (1802–1803) was a three-volume collection of ballads that he had collected in the country around his grandparents' farm at Sandyknowes where he had spent so much of his polio-afflicted childhood. He collected what we would now call folklore both as an end in itself but also as raw material that would not only provide substance for – but also give shape to – his literary endeavours. This is explicit in the case of the *Minstrelsy* and recurs at moments throughout all of the Waverley novels, but is the backbone of books like *Tales of My Landlord* (written variously between 1816 and his death in 1832). What appears to be a literary device, writing fiction as if it were being related by an ancient who is recalling times past, is really a metaphor for how Scott's fiction grew and also for its relationship with history. And central to this relationship with history was the idea that commerce and the urban world were destroying an older world that had to be recorded soon if it were not to be lost to the world entirely.

Perhaps the most enduring element of Romantic and nationalist histories, however, was the role of the hero. Scott was noted for his depiction of heroism for his popular readership. *Rob Roy* (1817), for example, was written in lieu of a history of Scotland that he had promised his publisher. It is a story set during the time of the Jacobite Rebellion of 1715 that aimed to return the crown to the Catholicism of the Old Pretender and as a novel proved to be a huge commercial success. *Ivanhoe* was published two years later in 1819, but this time Scott turned to medieval England for his subject matter. While obviously fictional, *Ivanhoe* may well have been inspired by an 1818 essay on chivalry or by his own growing collection of antique weaponry from the period. In either case, it is a work that drew the reader into the past through a careful and evocative description of man in nature.

Romanticism inspired other literary genres. The first gothic novel, for example, one that helped to promote the themes of Romanticism, was probably the *Castle of Otranto* (1764) by Horace Walpole. Later we have Mary Shelley's *Frankenstein*, subtitled the *Modern Prometheus* (1818), which confronted the power of the forces let loose by industrialization, while a high point in the genre came, arguably, with Bram Stoker's *Dracula* in 1897. Often the gothic dwelt

50 *Philosophies*

Figure 3.2 Thomas Carlyle; 1867 photograph by Julia Margaret Cameron, British, born India, 1815–1879; London, England, Europe; 1867; Albumen silver print

Contributor: Artokoloro/Alamy Stock Photo

on the fear apparent at the time of French invasion (or the fear, perhaps, of Jewish immigration in the 1880s or the rise of the 1890s New Woman in the case of Stoker), a dread of the transformative power of science and an older fear of Republican revolution after the political disruption caused by 1789. Everywhere the untamed landscape, the barbarities of the past (the 'darkness' of Catholicism with its secretive orders a favourite target among artists) was overwhelming.

While Scott was very influential, it was left to another Scot from the borders to take forward themes of heroism and national pasts into the modern age, thereby influencing subsequent historical inquiry. Thomas Carlyle (1795–1881) did much to formulate in the 1830s and 1840s what became known as the 'condition of England question'. He coined the term the 'cash nexus' to describe how social relations had been disastrously transformed by industrialization. Carlyle hated the narrow calculation of his age. Whereas political economy, he surmised, could 'reason' that a ration of precisely 137 ounces of food per workhouse inmate per week was enough to feed a human being, when the church had administered to the poor at least part of the calculation involved compassion and feeling. Now while Carlyle had renounced traditional forms of Christianity, somewhere between 1818 and 1822; having experienced a spiritual crisis, he nonetheless continued to believe in human solidarity. Man was born into society, he wrote in his *Characteristics* (1831), and:

> To understand man . . . we must look beyond the individual man and his actions or interests, and view him in combination with his fellows. It is in Society than man first feels what he

is; first becomes what he can be. In Society an altogether new set of spiritual activities are evolved in him, and the old immeasurably quickened and strengthened. Society is the genial element wherein his nature first lives and grows; the solitary man were but a small portion of himself, and must continue forever folded in, stunted and only half alive.

(Cited in Tennyson, 1984, p. 75)

Carlyle's main objection to modern society was, like many figures of Romanticism, mechanization, of which the factory system is an obvious example but by no means the only example. He extends his critique of the production process to a complaint about the mechanization of the whole of life. Industrialization, he believed, was a symptom of an underlying malaise rather than the root cause of human woes, although human beings would now be tied to the ceaseless rhythm of the machine and beyond doubt this salutary fact threatened our very humanity. 'If we are required to characterise this age of ours', said Carlyle in an essay called *Signs of the Times* (1829), 'by any single epithet, we should be tempted to call it, not an Historical, Devotional, Philosophical, or Moral Age, but above all others, the Mechanical Age'. The base calculations of the schoolteacher Gradgrind (the character created by Dickens who in *Hard Times* wanted only facts) were bound to infuriate Carlyle, who thought of economics as the 'dismal science' that could measure any human output and capacity.

Given Carlyle's implacable opposition to the mechanized and atomized world caused by industrialization, he wanted to argue that this age needed great men to lead and to reinstitute individuality. For this, he turned to the importance of biography in history:

Social Life is the aggregate of all the individual men's Lives who constitute society; History is the essence of innumerable Biographies, nay, our own Biographies. But if one Biography, study and recapitulate it as we may, remains in so many points unintelligible to us; how much more must these million, the very facts of which, to say nothing of the purport of them, we know not, and cannot know! . . . Praying only that increased division of labour do not here, as elsewhere, aggravate our already strong Mechanical tendencies, so that in the manual dexterity for parts we lose command over the whole, and the hope of any Philosophy of History be farther off than ever, – let us all wish her great and greater success.

(Cited in Tennyson, 1984, p. 66)

Where 'men have become mechanical in head and heart', Carlyle sought to use history as a way of understanding this process and to suggest palliatives. G. B. Tennyson recalls how Carlyle gave a lecture in May 1840 on 'Heroes, hero worship and the heroic in history'. His early heroes are from classical mythology. Then came the divine heroes such as Mohammad, poets such as Dante or Shakespeare, priestly heroes such as Luther. Later are the heroes nearer to his own time who were 'men of letters' such as Johnson or Rousseau and finally the heroes who are 'Kings' such as Cromwell or Napoleon. After 1850, his pessimism about the world deepens with his *Latter Day Pamphlets* of that year, *The Life of John Sterling* in 1851 (a friend who he felt had been thwarted by the vulgarities and cruelty of the age) and most famously, perhaps, his life of *Frederic the Great* published in successive volumes (1858, 1863, 1864 and 1865).

Carlyle's work on Chartism in 1839 registered his opposition to liberalism and democracy; his politics confirmed by his support for the appalling behaviour of General Eyre, the Governor of Jamaica, who used undue force against the local population in the Morant Bay rebellion during October 1865. Carlyle defended Eyre in the subsequent controversy, a moment that divided liberal and conservative opinion in Victorian England. Carlyle had already expressed his racist views on the Irish, whom he essentially described as sub-human, and he had infamously written in 1853 about slaves in his *Occasional Discourse on the Nigger Question*. Carlyle fell short of despotic but certainly he revered strong men and found these leaders in the pages of history.

We know from his work before 1850 that Thomas Carlyle was a formidable satirist and commentator on his times. But he also understood the discipline of history and never ceased to argue for its importance. In the 1833 tract *On History Again*, he argues that history 'is the most profitable of all studies', recognizing that in the passing of time all other human interests and activities will fall into its purview. He could write history and write it well. His multi-volume *The French Revolution* (1837) was a balanced attempt to access and judge an event that had bitterly divided intellectual and popular opinion (Chapter 6), while *Sartor Resartus* (1833–1834) contained the ideas that would sustain him until his death. It certainly contained an extraordinary use of language that would be his trademark, not hesitating to make up a word if the existing vocabulary failed him and thus revealing all the subjectivity and creativity we associate with Romanticism as a creative movement.

It is Carlyle's use of prose that reflected his hold on and respect for Romantic literature and German literature in particular – names such as Johann Wolfgang Goethe and Frederich von Schiller who are particularly associated with nationalism, mysticism and spiritual rebirth. Carlyle wanted to make his world (and its past) organic or 'natural' rather than mechanical, moral or hierarchical – certainly not democratic. Duty, work, silence, truth and the hero should be justly revered. In this sense his influences came as much from Continental Europe as his native Scotland.

Postscript

In order to understand the emergence of history as a discipline it is necessary to locate it within the wider contours of intellectual inquiry. Taking a broad paint brush, it could well be argued that if the seventeenth century was the age of science and the eighteenth that of philosophy, then the nineteenth belonged to the historian, before the twentieth seemed to forget the lessons from history at precisely that moment when they were needed most. A sense of the past and the emergence of historiography as a discipline in its own right thus came to prominence in the nineteenth century and suffused virtually all spheres of cultural life. People found that, at a time of unprecedented change, life's complexities could better be understood by thinking back to the past or, if that failed, by seeking refuge therein.

But there was more to it. Historians had a new confidence in what they were doing, and for that they had to thank some of the great thinkers of previous ages, in particular English, French, German and Scottish philosophers of the seventeenth and eighteenth centuries. Whether or not the origins of the intellectual revolution that we know as the Enlightenment can be traced back to seventeenth-century England, it was the work of Francis Bacon, Robert Boyle, William Harvey and Isaac Newton that laid the foundation for an innovative approach to knowledge. No longer built from superstition or religious orthodoxy, knowledge now was seen to derive from the application of a rigorous empirical methodology, the results of which were testable by others. For some, by revealing the mathematics underpinning, say, the movements of the planets, there was no longer a need to acknowledge the works of a divine architect, although many (including Newton) still did. In the social sciences (note the significance of the term), the seventeenth-century philosopher John Locke began to reveal the mechanisms of social cohesion, that is, how societies managed to exist without splitting apart.

Enlightenment thinkers paid due regard to this rational epistemology and considered whether the laws of science could be employed to reveal the hidden structures and processes of human society. This was combined with a powerful desire to know more about the nature of those societies that lay beyond the boundaries of Europe, in particular America, India and China. Limited though this venture was in the hands of writers such as Voltaire and William Robertson, it simultaneously forced onto the intellectual agenda an appreciation of comparative historical development. Different societies were no longer seen to be simply different – as were botanic species – but different by virtue that they occupied different positions on the ladder of societal evolution. Elaborate schemes were drawn up to plot the stages of this evolution, which were recognized to operate with a certain inevitable logic, driving the development of primitive societies such as were found in Africa towards the most advanced, i.e., commercial, societies of Europe. Such profound intellectual transformations often experience a backlash, and so it was that a group of influential nineteenth-century writers, who collectively forged Romanticism, viewed the Enlightenment as a dismal science. In their different ways, therefore, Walter Scott and Thomas Carlyle reacted to what they saw as the cold rationality of Enlightenment dogma and to capitalist industrialization and urbanization (yet other manifestations of inexorable laws) by reclaiming a mythical, organic past, untouched by the ravages of 'civilization'. This required not rational science but those qualities evident in art and poetry but seemingly abandoned by the Enlightenment: imagination, emotion and spirituality.

Most historians working today are heirs to these traditions. The intellectual origins of modern historical inquiry are therefore diverse, and historians tend to draw selectively upon them. This has largely been responsible for the continued tensions that exist among the various approaches to the past, but at the same time this diversity has provided a sense of dynamism for the discipline that underpins its richness and excitement.

Further Reading

Tess Cosslett (ed.) (1984) *Science and Religion in the Nineteenth Century*.
Martin Fitzpatrick, Peter Jones, Christa Knellwolf and Iain McCalman (eds.) (2004) *The Enlightenment World*.
Edward Gibbon (1998) [1776] *The Decline and Fall of the Roman Empire*, ed. and annotated Antony Lentin and Brian Norman.
Anthony Lentin and Brian Norman (1998) *Edmund Gibbon. The History of the Decline and Fall of the Roman Empire*.
Cecilia Miller (1993) *Vico's Imagination and Historical Knowledge*.
Roy Porter (1995) *Enlightenment: Britain and the Creation of the Modern World*.
G. B. Tennyson (1984) *A Carlyle Reader*.
Giambattista Vico (1999) [1744] *Principi di Scienza Nouva*, trans. David March.

4 The English Tradition

Introduction

Edmund Burke is the subject of the opening section. He used all his political skills to oppose the French Revolution of 1779 as it turned into a bloody assize. He became an outspoken critic of the excesses of the revolution and mourned both the death of the queen and the passing of an era. As such, he has been seen as a champion of the counter Enlightenment and a forerunner of conservatism, despite his support for the Whig group associated with Charles Watson-Wentworth, second Marquess of Rockingham, who had supported the American Revolution as a welcome continuity with the 1688 Glorious Revolution.

The second section outlines the Whig inheritance of the accompanying 'revolution' in the understanding of and regard given to history. From the Magna Carta to the culmination of English liberties in the events that led to the Glorious Revolution of 1688, the Protestant ascendency had resulted, it was thought, in a perfect constitution. It was a constitution that compared favourably with that of the French. Whig history approved those historical players who were allies to the perfecting of the constitution and condemned those who stood in its way.

Whig history was, then, present minded in that it judged the past in the light of the present. This led to a school of history practice and outlook that the third section argues can be traced via Macaulay and then Trevelyan to his student Jack Plumb and now to a coterie of 'New Whig' Cambridge historians – Linda Colley, David Cannadine, Simon Schama, Roy Porter and others such as Neil McKendrick and John Vincent – who were taught by or were profoundly influenced by Plumb.

4.1 Responses to the Enlightenment: Edmund Burke

Frank: It's like gardening. Someone once said we was a nation of gardeners, and they weren't far out. Were used to planting things and watching them grow and looking out for changes in the weather.
Ethel: You and your gardening!
Frank: Well it's true – think what a mess there'd be if all the flowers and vegetables and crops came popping up in a minute. That's what all these social reformers are trying to do, trying to alter the way of things all at once. We've got our own way of settling things, it may be slow and it may be a bit dull, but it suits us all right and it always will.

(Noel Coward, *This Happy Breed*, 1944)

While Dublin-born Edmund Burke (1730–1797) was far from the simple Englishman, he would have agreed with the words put into the mouth of Frank Gibbons by the Conservative playwright, composer and raconteur, Noel Coward (1899–1973), in his play *This Happy Breed* (1939). In this everyday saga of urban folk, ideology is scorned; socialists and trade unionists were considered resolutely intemperate and, therefore, un-English. The story juxtaposes – literally – two neighbouring families as the men return from the Great War in 1918. Chipper and doughty, they get through the ravages of the Depression, the General Strike of 1926 and the American imported 'dance crazes' of the 'jazz age' before seeing their offspring go off to another European conflict. It is a people and a country slowly reinvented through experience and renewed by the pleasant association of its inhabitants. The 'flowers, vegetables and crops', mentioned earlier, were a metaphor for the benefits of cautious change while the 'happy breed' of the title was, of course, the English themselves.

Fast rewind back in time and we find the statesman and lawyer Edmund Burke, fearful after the revolution of 1789 that the fate of the French would soon befall all of Europe. Dr Richard Price, the radical Unitarian preacher, speaking to the London Revolution Society on the centenary of the Glorious Revolution (glorious because it was constitutional and bloodless – except in Scotland where it was dubbed the 'killing times'), provided the catalyst that culminated in Burke writing *Reflections on the Revolution in France* (1790), a work which secured his reputation as a founder of modern conservatism (Chapter 6). The section *On Englishness* is a fore echo of Coward. For those who cannot read the more subtle assumptions of what it is to be English (a least as Burke conceived it – a national character that was different from, say, French or German), we have provided squared brackets which act as a rough-and-ready cultural translation:

> Thanks to our sullen resistance to innovation, thanks to the cold sluggishness of our national character, we still bear the stamp of our forefathers **[the English are not hot headed or quick to leap into an unknowable future]**. We have not (as I conceive) lost the generosity and dignity of thinking of the fourteenth century **[an obscure reference to the capture by the English of John II of France]**, nor as yet have we subtilized **[refined – Burke is being ironic]** ourselves into savages **[the noble variety that Rousseau espoused as the chief theorist of the French Revolution]**. We are not the converts of Rousseau; we are not the disciples of Voltaire; Helvetius has made no progress amongst us **[all inspirations for the revolutionaries in France and all theorists – the English are not keen on intellectuals]**. Atheists are not our preachers; madmen are not our lawgivers **[a direct reference to the French revolutionaries themselves]**. We know that we have made no discoveries, and we think that no discoveries are to be made on morality – nor many in the great principles of government, nor in the ideas of liberty which were understood long before we were born, altogether as well as they will be after the grave has heaped its mould upon our presumption, and the silent tomb shall have imposed its law on our pert loquacity **[rights are natural, handed down by our forebears not discovered as part of an abstracted theory]**. In England we have yet been completely embowelled of our natural entrails; we still feel within us, and we cherish and cultivate, those inbred sentiments which are the faithful guardians, the active monitors **[reminders]** of our duty, the true supporters of all liberal and manly **[humane]** morals. We have not been drawn and trussed in order that we may be filled, like stuffed birds in a museum, with chaff and rags and paltry blurred shreds of paper about the rights of man **[our historical selves hollowed out and replaced with contemporary concerns, untested by experience]**. We preserve the whole of our feelings still native and entire, unsophisticated by pedantry and infidelity **[unlike the wretched French who have lost the essence of human sentiment and their 'natural' selves]**. We have real hearts of flesh and blood beating in our bosoms. We fear God. We look with awe to kings, with affection to

parliaments, with duty to magistrates, with reverence to priests, and with respect to nobility **[we really like hierarchy]**. Why? Because when such ideas are brought before our minds, it is natural to be so affected, because all other feelings are false and spurious, and tend to corrupt our minds, to vitiate our primary morals, to render us unfit for rational liberty, and (by teaching us a servile, licentious, and abandoned insolence) to be our low sport for a few holidays, to make us perfectly fit for, and justly deserving of slavery, through the whole course of our lives **[tackling inequality which is anyway natural and God given would be the thin end of the wedge]**.

(Burke, 1790, reproduced in Wu, 1994, pp. 4–5)

Most historians today, although not all, would be very unwilling to go on any serious hunt in the past for 'national character', but even as an Irishman, Burke's approach to history had the English very much in focus. Burke dismissed Prices' interpretation of the constitutional settlement of 1688 and denied any parallels with the French Revolution. For him, the revolution in France was driven by an ideology of natural rights and such rights could never form the basis of a stable society. Radical, secular reform based on notions of rights and reason disassociated from experience was thought to be inherently destabilizing. The 'swinish multitude' (a description Burke famously used of his electors in Bristol) was too susceptible to such projects; stability is predicated only on an experience of continuity provided by custom and tradition – what he termed the 'partnership [or social contract] . . . between those who are living, those who are dead, and those who are about to be born'. The operation of law, for example, was best served by the slow organic development over time characteristic of English common law and not by radical and abrupt change based on arbitrary, metaphysical speculations about rights. For Burke, rights were universal while man as an individual (and an individual player in history) was really nurtured in culture; indeed, born into local cultures that had survived into the present, and having survived, passed the harsh test of time. Burke thus defended culture as a conservative social and political force (Fitzpatrick, 2004, pp. 610–20).

Tradition and reform, however, are not mutually exclusive for Burke. As perhaps his most informed biographer, David Bromwich (2014), emphasized, Burke is often best considered in his own words. Take *Reflections on the Revolution in France*, a tract that was tellingly written as a personal letter to a young Frenchman and not as a book that could be accused of employing the tools of abstracted theory; here Burke passionately defended national interests by promoting a strong sense of custom and tradition:

It is far from impossible to reconcile, if we do not suffer ourselves to be entangled in the mazes of metaphysic sophistry, the use both of a fixed rule and an occasional deviation; the sacredness of an hereditary principle of succession in our government, with a power of change in its application in cases of extreme emergency. Even in that extremity . . . the change is to be confined to . . . the part which produced the necessary deviation; and even then it is to be effected without decomposition of the whole civil and political mass, for the purpose of originating a new civil order out of the first elements of society.

(Burke, 2003, p. 19)

History, that is, lived experience, must then replace idle theory, and with that in mind Burke provided a brief narrative of how English liberties came into being as a result of changes in the constitution that were set in motion by Henry I and have since followed a particular logic – even inevitability – right up to the Glorious Revolution of 1688. 'You will observe', he concludes,

Figure 4.1 Edmund Burke, 1729–1797, Irish-born lawyer, statesmen, author, political theorist and philosopher
Contributor: 19th era/Alamy Stock Photo

that from the Magna Charta, to the Declaration of Right, it has been the uniform policy of our constitution to claim and assert our liberties, as an *entailed inheritance* [emphasis in the original] derived to us from our forefathers, and to be transmitted to our posterity; as an estate especially belonging to the people of this kingdom without any reference whatever to any other more general or prior right. By this means our constitution preserves a unity in so great a diversity of its parts. We have an inheritable crown; an inheritable peerage; and a house of commons and a people inheriting privileges, franchises and liberties, from a long line of ancestors.

(Burke, 2003, p. 29)

Reflections sets out to some extent the tenets of what was to become *conservative* thought and that most certainly informed both aspects of the Whig tradition and modern historiography. In short, these elements comprised:

- Scepticism about the possibility of progress because of the intellectual and moral imperfections of human beings.
- A conviction that society was divinely ordered.
- An assumption that hierarchy was both natural and based on basic human inequalities.
- A political preference for tradition and instinct over reason.
- A commitment to order and authority rather than freedom.

The overall appeal was to family, religion, individual responsibility, the defence of property and the maintenance of the constitution and law and order. The venerable institutions of monarchy and church were to be respected and preserved, not least because

we are afraid to put men to live and trade on each on his own private stock of reason, because we expect that this stock in each man is small, and that the individuals would be better to avail themselves of the general bank and capital of nations and ages.

(Burke, 2003, p. 74)

In this sense, Burke was not only reacting to the French Revolution but reacting within and to some sense against the Enlightenment or what has been termed 'the age of reason'. Thus, Burke would have argued that societies are made up of its natural elites by virtue of birth, wealth and education and that these elites should provide considered leadership. Since community is held together by venerable customs and traditions, gradual changes can be made but only when they have gained wider acceptance.

Progress was to be made by natural processes which emerged out of a time-forged experience rather (as in France) than by conscious human intervention which sought to impose a blueprint on history based on nothing but hope and conjecture. Equilibrium in society and the elimination of social ills such as poverty – if possible at all – could be achieved only by allowing the laws of economics to work uninhibited. Human nature was assumed to be imperfect, which ruled out any notion of a perfect society. Utopian solutions, therefore, would not work because human beings could not be trusted to act with true rationality and to live in harmony with their fellows unless society has been matured in history, tried and tested over centuries. This was an organic view of society and history with society itself seen as a machine that could not be tampered with because each component (individual) of society is tied to the survival and well-being of others as a living and breathing organism. Burke therefore opposed as being despotic equality, popular representation, popular sovereignty, universal franchise or majority rule.

Burke allowed, though, limited government controls in order to moderate economic strife and competition and to avoid wide differences of wealth and poverty. As Member of Parliament (MP) for Bristol from 1774 to 1780, he also defended free trade in Ireland and the repeal of legal disabilities for Catholics. His insistence that an MP should be a representative of the constituency rather than a delegate or puppet of interests prompted him to remind his constituents in one of the speeches for which he was famous that by the exercise of his conscience he had saved his constituents from themselves. He did favour order, co-operation in society, restraints on government and the supremacy of law that could be natural, divine or customary; that is, like seeds in a garden, society would develop slowly with minimal intervention.

Like the gardening metaphor with which we opened, however, affinities to the 'little platoons' of society, to the binds of local affections and sympathies, 'the generous loyalty to rank and sex' should be spontaneous – not forced – and were preferable to loyalties of class or even of nation. Above all, change should be considered and rooted in the sureties of past behaviour. 'You see, sir', addressing Richard Price (1723–1791) again,

> that in this enlightened age I am bold enough to confess that we are generally men of untaught feelings, that instead of casting away all our old prejudices, we cherish them to a considerable degree and, to take some shame to ourselves, we cherish them because they *are* prejudices. And the longer they have lasted, and the more generally they have prevailed, the more we cherish them.
>
> (Burke, 2003, p. 74)

For these reasons, Burke responded to the French Revolution as he did, and it was this framework of thought (ideology?) that governed his approach to history itself:

> It is now sixteen or seventeen years since I saw the queen of France, then the dauphiness, at Versailles; and surely never lighted on this orb, which she hardly seemed to touch, a more delightful vision. I saw her just above the horizon, decorating and cheering the elevated sphere she had just begun to move in, glittering like the morning star full of life and splendour and joy. Oh, what a revolution! and what a heart must I have, to contemplate without emotion that elevation and that fall! Little did I dream, when she added titles of veneration to those of enthusiastic, distant, respectful love, that she should ever be obliged to carry the sharp antidote against disgrace concealed in that bosom; little did I dream that I should have lived to see such disasters fallen upon her, in a nation of gallant men, in a nation of men of honour, and of cavaliers! I thought ten thousand swords must have leaped from their scabbards, to avenge even a look that threatened her with insult.
>
> But the age of chivalry is gone; that of sophisters, economists, and calculators has succeeded, and the glory of Europe is extinguished forever. Never, never more, shall we behold that generous loyalty to rank and sex, that proud submission, that dignified obedience, that subordination of the heart, which kept alive, even in servitude itself, the spirit of an exalted freedom! The unbought grace of life, the cheap defence of nations, the nurse of manly sentiment and heroic enterprise is gone. It is gone, that sensibility of principle, that chastity of honour, which felt a stain like a wound, which inspired courage whilst it mitigated ferocity, which ennobled whatever it touched, and under which vice itself lost half its evil, by losing all its grossness.
>
> (Burke, 2003, p. 65)

If his advocacy of the American Revolution as well as his defence of Irish freedoms inspired Burke to look back at the Glorious Revolution for justification of present events, Price's *A Discourse on the Love of Our Country* (1789) compelled his defence of conservatism in *Reflections* (1790). But it is his 1757 essay, *A Philosophical Enquiry into the Origins of our Ideas of the Sublime and the Beautiful*, that situates Burke in the Romantic tradition, an approach to the understanding and interpretation of the past where the subjective individual could express 'untaught feelings' rather than rely solely on cold and calculated reason. In this sense we can see again the importance Burke placed on the past, particularly in the *Sublime and the Beautiful*, on the literary past.

Equally, in his prosecution of Warren Hastings, a former governor-general of Bengal, Burke used history as a tool to argue against the abuse of power in the treatment by Britain of the

Americans and its empire in India. In 1783 (Lord Rockingham had died the year before) Burke had made unlikely common cause with Lord North (he who had lost America) and delivered his *Speech on Fox's East India Bill*, which set out the unfortunate history of the British in India. While this says something about the man (Bromwich maintains that Burke was especially averse to cruelty), it also says something about Burke's approach to history. While the prosecution of Hastings was to take from 1788 to 1795, leading to acquittal, it is also true to say that Burke construed this exercise as a valued attempt to reform empire itself (Bromwich, 2014, p. 4).

Like Thomas Paine (1737–1809), the great advocate for both the American and French Revolutions whom he indirectly addressed in a 1791 tract, *An Appeal from the New to the Old Whigs*, Burke was a political commentator but also a practitioner, yet his exhortations to the study of history were never realized. His history was at the level of generalization, often ill-informed and organized by narratives designed principally to bolster political lessons he wished to convey (see also Chapter 6). His choice of evidence from the historical record was highly selective, and he was indifferent to the changing modes of historical inquiry (Ankersmit, 2001a). If he did have a legacy for historiography, it was in his ability to ask whether revolution was an aberration or simply a stage in the development of human society.

It was also to act as a very important staging post in the Whig tradition. As J. G. A. Pocock has brilliantly argued in his now classic *Virtue, Commerce and History* (1985), this was a continuity that ran from the First Whigs to the True Whigs and Burke's Old Whigs, from the response to the American Revolution, to the reaction to the French Revolution and on to Thomas Macaulay's *History of England*. It was Macaulay who would mark the transformation of Whig political thought and practice and turn it into the Whig approach to history and part of a significant academic discipline.

4.2 Constitutionalism and the Whig Interpretation of History

Whig history has been an influential current in English historiography. Its nineteenth-century origins can be traced to Thomas Babington Macaulay (1800–1859) who was to become the first of a dynasty of Whig historians. His Whiggish approach to history was to be employed to good effect in his *History of England* (1848) where he argued that history writing must recover from the novelist account or the recording of ordinary lives alongside narratives that deal only with power. His *History* was not a tract for democracy or radical in any conventional sense but his sources reflected the experiences of the common people – routinely using ballads and popular songs as historical evidence. So, despite his broadly empirical approach, he and other Whigs did not regard history as a science or the historian as a scientist.

In 1904, George Macaulay Trevelyan (1876–1962), a great nephew to Macaulay and a worthy successor in the Whig tradition, published his well-received survey called *England under the Stuarts*. In familiar Whig style, his focus was the story of the Civil War and the settlement of 1688 where he located the victory of Protestant religious toleration, winning over Catholic absolutism in a climate of parliamentary freedom that, critically, signalled the beginning of the modern empire. This was accomplished but unremarkable as an argument; the reforms of the Whig ascendency of the 1820s and 1830s were, after all, the origins of the wider franchise. His *History of England* (1926) did something similar: it was concerned with the national story, the development of parliament and the evolution of independent systems of law, freedom and the singularity of empire.

Whig history has attracted its critics, the most influential being Herbert Butterfield (1900–1979), who in his *The Whig Interpretation of History* (1931) launched an assault on an approach to the past which had been dominant – or at least so it was argued – from the seventeenth century to the early twentieth. Butterfield argued that the Whig interpretation carried several mistaken assumptions. Perhaps the most prominent of these is the present-minded nature of Whiggish historical enquiry:

> Real historical understanding is not achieved by the subordination of the past to the present, but rather by our making the past our present and attempting to see life with the eyes of another century than our own. It is not reached by assuming that our own age is the absolute to which Luther and Calvin and their generation are only relative; it is only reached by fully accepting the fact that their generation was as valid as our generation, their issues as momentous as our issues and their day as full and vital to them as our day is to us . . . for both the method and the kind of history that results from it would be impossible if all the facts were told in all their fullness. The theory that is behind the Whig interpretation – the theory that we study the past for the sake of the present – is one that is really introduced for the purpose of facilitating the abridgement of history; and its effect is to provide us with a handy rule of thumb by which we can easily discover what was important in the past.
> (Butterfield, 1931, p. 13)

According to the Whig view of history, the constitutional settlement established in England in the seventeenth century – the Glorious Revolution – was the zenith of political governance, the 'Central Period' as Sellar and Yeatman put it in their spoof of schools' history, *1066 and All That*:

> With the ascension of Charles I to the throne we come at last to the Central Period of English History (not to be confused with the Middle Ages, of course), consisting in the *utterly memorable* struggle *between the Cavaliers (Wrong but Wromantic) the Roundheads (Right but Repulsive)*. Charles I was a Cavalier King and therefore had a small pointed beard, long flowing curls, a large, flat, flowing hat and *gay attire*. The Roundheads, on the other hand, were clean shaven and wore tall, conical hats, white ties and *sombre garments*. Under these circumstances a Civil War was inevitable.
> (Sellar and Yeatman, 1930, p. 75)

As a send-up of late Victorian and Edwardian 'drum and trumpet' school history it remains quite brilliant; put simply it satirizes the tendency for Whig history to pick historical winners while telling the story of nation, constitution and great men.

From that moment all previous and subsequent history could be judged, and the present would be subservient to the past by emphasizing 'certain principles of progress in the past . . . to produce a story which is the ratification if not the glorification of the present' (Butterfield, 1931, p. 2). Those Whigs who facilitated this leap forward in human affairs were heroes; those who opposed it political villains. All history, therefore, was a struggle between Absolutist (usually Royalist or Catholic) power and that of the popular will, most often expressed in Parliament and Protestantism. For Butterfield, this led historians to make false connections across periods and epochs – to 'abridgement' – picking out an event they supported or opposed depending on whether it fitted a narrative of unfolding political freedom. Most seriously, it suggested that the unfolding constitution was as perfect as any in human history and was the main prompt or context for understanding and writing English history as evidenced, say, in Burke.

From this perspective, all history worth retrieving was connected to the history of progress. The Whig interpretation of history skewed the selection of evidence that was important to this narrative and implied a causation between events that may only have existed in the mind of the historian. Butterfield argued instead that historians should reject links in history that lend history a progressive trajectory; instead, they should look for what is unique in any epoch and not for continuities that confirm history as developmental.

These 'fallacies', he proceeded to explain, to 'which all history is liable', include the identification of crucial events or turning points on the road to Protestant constitutional freedoms that we enjoy today. Butterfield then lists historians whom the contemporary historian J. W. Barrow thought belonged to what he described as part of a 'Liberal Descent' or liberal tradition which focused, like William Stubbs' *Constitutional History of England* (1873–8), on constitutional progress or the preservation of the ancient constitution.

Probably the first history in this tradition, however, was the *Constitutional History of England from the Accession of Henry VII to the Death of George II* (1827) by Henry Hallam (1777–1859). Defending the constitution by arguing for Catholic emancipation, which was much debated at the time, Hallam similarly deplored the persecution of Protestant dissidents under the Stuarts and Tudors. Within this tradition also William Lecky (1838–1903) wrote *A History of England in the Eighteenth Century* (1879–1887), which outlined the greatest division within English history, namely, that between the Civil War and the peaceful constitutional settlement of the Glorious Revolution of 1688. Whig historians regarded it as axiomatic that these events were stepping stones to the present, so much so that in 1892, Lecky said revealingly, 'we are Cavaliers or Roundheads before we are Conservatives or Liberals' (Collini, 1999, p. 14).

In a succinct commentary, Peter Ghosh went back to Butterfield's critique that the Whig interpretation of history was invented by sixteenth- and seventeenth-century lawyers (Ghosh, 1999, pp. 1293–4). Yet in the later *The Englishman and his History* (1944), we find Butterfield arguing that while history was based on the notion of unfolding liberty, it was at the very least fortuitous and the result of the English – note 'English' – character. In this respect Butterfield never really escaped from the clutches of the Whig approach himself, and, according to Ghosh, he could not accept (as a Christian) a non-Christian or secular teleology (that is, history has an end or purpose). In fact, Butterfield's analysis of Whig history drew upon a longer current of criticism. Historians such as J. R. Green (1837–1883) in his *Short History of the English People* (1878) and Eben William Robertson (1815–1874) in his *Historical Essays in Connection with the Land and Church, etc.* (1872) had said much the same:

> To look upon the past with the eyes of the present, to judge of its events and of its characters by a similar standard, awarding praise or blame to the men who felt and thought and acted in bygone days, as if their conduct had been shaped in accordance with the ideas influencing their remote descendants, – such has, and is, and ever will be the habit of the majority of living men. . . . The present age simply repeats the habit of the past.
>
> (Robertson, 1872, pp. vii, viii)

Perhaps the touchstone of Whig history, however, was seen as the Protestant ascendency of the fifteenth and sixteenth centuries and the changes in religious practice that took place between about 1530 and 1580. 'Popular' and lay religion was thought by Whig historians to be infused with heresy, witchcraft, superstition, Paganism and magic, while the 'elite', Catholic religion was seen to be a separate force, manipulative and controlling the masses. Protestantism, on the other hand, had greater rationality; folk beliefs gave way to the Reformation, and a more diverse Protestant orthodoxy stood against Catholic absolutism which by that time was a decadent religious tradition that had run out of steam.

This narrative is challenged in Eamon Duffy's magisterial and ground-breaking book *The Stripping of the Altars: Traditional Religion in England c.1400–c.1580* (1992), in which he argued against the generations of school essays and undergraduate theses that assumed the Whig view of Protestantism to be an inevitable part of constitutional progress. Unlike the Whig convention that has Protestantism carrying the torch of progress, almost destined to usher in the constitution that emerged from the 'stripping of the altars' leading to the Civil War and the Glorious Revolution when Protestantism ran riot into Puritanism, Duffy sees the Protestant influence as exaggerated. Put simply, 'late Medieval Catholicism exerted an enormously strong, diverse and vigorous hold over the imagination and the loyalty of the people up to the very moment of Reformation' (Duffy, 2005, p. 4). Instead of 'popular' and 'elite' religious structures, Duffy argues for the notion of 'traditional' religion, which as a Catholic himself (the book is dedicated to the Latin Mass) he takes to be, as one reviewer recalled, 'vibrant, popular, unified and flourishing', a vitality he demonstrated by the church use of liturgical books, painted images, saints' lives, devotional treatises, churchwardens' accounts, ecclesiastical court records, personal commonplace books and wills (Ryrie, 2009). Under these circumstances, if Protestantism was to supersede Catholicism, its rise was far from inevitable. Duffy thus, unwittingly perhaps, confronts Whiggish assumptions that Protestantism was an irresistible force and Catholicism a moveable object to be brushed aside by the progress of the Reformation and then by the late-seventeenth-century settlement of the Glorious Revolution.

So, what has happened to Whig history? The 1890s was the critical decade when Whig history was weakened by calls for English historiography to be as scientific as that of France or Germany and by the professional growth of the discipline within the academy (Blaas, 1978). And the critiques of people like Butterfield have been telling. Ghosh goes so far as to argue that there is a limited timeline for Whiggish history. As empire, economic prowess and independence from supranational bodies such as the United Nations or various European bodies did not survive 1940, neither will the Whig approach, save for histories published by that old Whig Winston Churchill in the 1950s. Yet it might be argued that, in a reinvented form, Whig history has survived to the present day in the work of a corpus of prominent historians. Trevelyan's studies not only represented all the attributes, qualities and weaknesses of the Whig historical approach, but he also provided a link to the next generation of English historians. Now the emphasis was democratic, popular, multi-national and multi-cultural. It may be no accident that Trevelyan's Festschrift, *Studies in Social History* (1955), was edited by his first doctoral student and the subject of our next section, the historian J. H. Plumb (1911–2001), who created a fresh school of Whiggish history and a new approach to writing national history and the consideration of national identity.

4.3 The 'New Whigs'?: the School of J. H. Plumb

Sir David Wilkie (1784–1841) was Principal Painter to the Queen. He was a Scot and son of a Reverend from Fife. A friend of the historical novelist Walter Scott and a notable artist in his own right, Wilkie was best known for a history painting *Chelsea Pensioners Reading the Gazette of the Battle of Waterloo, 1822*. It was first exhibited at the Royal Academy in that year when its popular appeal demanded the erection of rails to keep the crowds back in an exhibition which would take record receipts. Dating precisely from Thursday, 2 June 1815 and the first official confirmation of the British victory over the French, it showed for the historian Linda Colley in her major history *Britons* (2005) a perspective on the 'present crisis' of Britishness – a multi-cultural present that raised questions of what it meant to be British in a post-colonial age – and brought to mind nationalist politics in Scotland that envisaged the undoing of the Act of Union of 1707. These are important considerations and take us back to questions that had once been the chief concern of Whig historians. These concerns also explain why Colley and her generation of Cambridge historians that studied under Jack Plumb or are influenced by him are so important to our understanding of postwar English historical writing and suggest continuities with earlier forms.

Like Trevelyan, Plumb advocated social history and was, at least in his early days, progressive in both his politics and in his approach to history. He was a working-class boy who longed for a Cambridge education. His impact on reformulating eighteenth-century politics and his influence on historiography with his book *The Death of the Past* (1969) has been immense. To the professional development of those who were taught by him or counted him as a mentor he was to become very important. He refashioned his Leicester youth as a son of a 'shoe clicker in the boot and shoe industry' (*Oxford DNB*) to become a 'courtier and connoisseur', eventually embracing Thatcherism with (as he apparently put it himself) all the zeal of a convert. His students remember his collection of fine porcelain in his rooms and the fine wine after seminars. He came to wider public attention in 1977 with a BBC television series called *Royal Heritage*, which told the story of the builders and art collectors of the British Royal family, and it was accompanied by a best-selling illustrated book. He was, as we are also told in an introduction by Niall Ferguson to the 2004 edition of *The Death of the Past*, a 'meticulous portraitist' and certainly his life of Walpole and his work on eighteenth-century politics endure (Ferguson, 2004, p. xxvii).

Unlike Macaulay or the nineteenth-century Whigs, Plumb approved of traditional archival research and applied scientific-type methods to questions of the English constitution. While he was no crude positivist, he did believe that history was much closer to a science in that truth could be identified through research and that in some degree we could learn what to do in the future by learning from the past – a belief shared with Geoffrey Elton (see Chapter 21). Ironic then that Elton's bright young boy was David Starkey and Plumb's (or at least one of them) was Simon Schama and that years later Starkey and Schama would be themselves rivals as stars of the small screen, presenting history as an edge-of-the-seat drama in which cliffhanging episodes unfolded on a weekly basis.

The influence of Plumb can be detected in such diverse historians as Roy Porter, Niall Ferguson, David Cannadine, Neil MacKendrick, Simon Schama and John Vincent, as well as Colley, adding up to what this section will suggest is a school of historical thought and practice – a 'new Whig' approach. Insofar as we can find a thread running between these diverse historians and the diverse Whig historians that preceded them, it is an emphasis on certain defining features listed in Table 4.1.

Table 4.1 Elements of old Whiggism in the new

'Old' Whig history	'New' Whig history
Non-scientific; social; political	Non-scientific; cultural; political
Concern with liberty; progress; civilization	Concern with liberty; progress; civilization
Constitution; parliament	Constitution; state
English 'exceptionalism'	English and British 'exceptionalism' within context of national decline
History has a social function	History has a social function
Popular and accessible	Popular and accessible; with emphasis on accessible visual evidence
Emphasis on well-written prose	Emphasis on well-written prose
Biographical approach	Biographical approach
Empire	Post-empire
Narrative driven	Narrative driven

Emphatically, this is not to suggest that the 'new Whigs' believed in a vulgar tautological approach to history, where evidence is read back from the present as a justification for the current constitutional arrangement. Nor did they reflect Plumb's notion of history as science; indeed, any confident notion that history had the ability to inform the future categorically does not run from Trevelyan to Plumb's generation onto the 'new Whigs'. Further, neither should it suggest a slavish agreement with either his approach or his conclusions. Colley has argued against many of his views regarding the eighteenth century and Plumb himself seems to have encouraged her in this. There are, however, continuities.

That these diverse historians may indeed be considered as a coherent school of historical thought and writing, let alone that they have synergy enough to be called 'new Whigs', is not necessarily a view that is widely held by historians. To explore this contention further, we shall concentrate on Colley's *Britons* in an effort to tease out the elements of what might be meant by a 'new Whiggish' approach but then go on to touch on other historians associated with Plumb, in particular Simon Schama.

The first and most obvious feature of Colley's work is that it is present-minded; second, it is popular and public-oriented using the 'poetry and philosophy' of a well-written, well-crafted style and last it tends to be English focused (although Britain is invariably heavily featured). Like many others of the Plumb school of 'new Whigs', Colley is an adherent of biography (she authored a very good biography of one of Plumb's bitter rivals, the historian Lewis Namier (1888–1960). Others who were not students of Plumb such as David Cannadine or perhaps even Peter Mandler, who has no formal or informal connection with Plumb, nevertheless tell a story of the nation and in the case of Mandler support the popular telling of history in books such as *The English National Character* (2006) and *History and National Life* (2002).

Colley's discussion of Wilkie's *Chelsea Pensioners Reading the Gazette after the Battle of Waterloo* revealed much about her approach to historical writing. The home for military 'pensioners' or a veteran of Britain's former wars was the Royal Hospital Chelsea, a retreat for old and disabled soldiers from 1692. Just nearby in the old Jew's Row in Chelsea, the soldiers are shown receiving news of Wellington's victory at Waterloo on that never-to-be-forgotten June day in 1815. They are mostly shown in their uniforms, representing several different regiments and ranks.

Many black men fought in the Napoleonic Wars, and one of the retired soldiers shown here is black. He is wearing an elaborate uniform coat and has a ring in his ear. Sweeping leftwards across the canvas we find that the horseman is from a Welsh regiment, while the gathered soldiers are identified as Scots, Irish and English by their clothes and other symbols. They surround the black soldier whose presence not only reminds us of his contribution in war but that he may also be there, it could be further speculated, to state that (even in 1822) no man is a slave when in England (or Britain?). There are signs and symbols of past victories besides the Chelsea Pensioner reading aloud, a veteran from the battle of Quebec in 1759 who stands at the conceptual middle of the painting. Off-centre we can see that the inn sign is 'The Duke of York', a reminder of a battle with revolutionary France while the other public houses bear the mark of the 'The Snowshoes', a 1758 battle from the American War of Independence and the Marquis of Granby who is a hero both of the Battle of Culloden in 1746 and of the Seven Years' War:

> Explicit in this strictly imaginary scene is the existence of a mass British patriotism transcending the boundaries of class, ethnicity, occupation, sex and age . . . and it is 'one man's very perceptive interpretation of both the variety and the roots of Britishness.
>
> (Colley, 2005, p. 365)

Figure 4.2 David Wilkie, *Chelsea Pensioners Reading the Gazette of the Battle of Waterloo*, 1822
Contributor: Painters/Alamy Stock Photo

It is war (and empire) that brought the diverse nations of Britain together while it was Protestantism that 'first allowed the English, the Welsh and the Scots to become fused together, and to remain so, despite their many cultural divergences' (Colley, 2005, pp. 367–8). To be British was to be against the French; to be Protestant was to be against Catholicism. To be both was to identify with a distinct and 'Chosen People', a providential destiny and with God who had entrusted them with empire, a testimony to their status as the 'Protestant Israel'. Colley again:

> Well into the twentieth century, contact with and domination over manifestly alien peoples nourished Britons' sense of superior difference. They could contrast their law, their treatment of women, their wealth, power, political stability and religion with societies they only imperfectly understood, but usually perceived as inferior.
>
> (Colley, 2005, pp. 368–9)

Telling the story of 'Britain' as opposed to England has long been the cause of tension among historians. 'British history' has been seen as problematic in the sense that Whig history was concerned more with England. The remaining countries of the 'four nations' or 'three kingdoms' – Scotland, Wales and Ireland – tended to be organized around separate historical accounts of their component national identities while the histories of Irish nationalism and Unionism were given priority. Even Roy Porter who wrote a splendid history of Britain and the Enlightenment did so without much reference to examples outside England (Porter, 1995). Unfortunately, he never completed a two-volume *Social History of Britain* that was intended by Penguin to replace the classic *English Social History: A Survey of Six Centuries from Chaucer to Queen Victoria* (1944) by G. M. Trevelyan.

In emphasizing Britain, however, Colley found a new point of origin for the nation. Against the old Whig histories, the founding date is no longer 1215 (the Magna Carta) or 1688 (the

Glorious Revolution) or 1832 (the Great Reform Act) but 1707 and 1800 as the acts of Union with Scotland and Ireland. She also wanted to listen to loyalist and patriotic voices – not unreasonably given her subject matter, but at the expense of E. P. Thompson's workers and radicals and the expressions contained in his work of working class agitation or disquiet. Discussing the Bristol riots of 1831, for example, where there were protests against delays in political reform, Colley insisted that:

> The growing involvement in politics of men and women from the middling and working classes that characterised British society at this time was expressed as much if not more in support of the nation state, as it was in opposition to the men who governed it.
> (Colley, 2005, p. 371)

Historians have accused her (like Burke) of repositioning the working class as nationalistic and conservative. Even when considering the substantive points of her case, it is difficult to see how differences of class within the nations that made up Britain were suppressed to the degree suggested by Colley and, if they were, how fault lines within the component nations of Britain such as nationalisms and local belongings, language, religion, and urban and rural divides could be as equally suppressed as the class allegiances that she underplays. Indeed, after her end date of 1837, we know that they are not.

It does appear, however, that there is indeed a present-minded quality to these 'new Whig' histories and even a desire to appeal to current policymakers in exactly the way envisaged by the 'old Whigs' such as Macaulay. In Colley's more recent book, *Captives: Britain, Empire and the World* (2003), for example, the chapter on Afghanistan compared captives taken in the nineteenth century with the American hostage crisis in Iran in 1979–1981 where a weak country could apparently hold captive the citizens of a strong country with impunity, asking historical questions about the limits to the reach of empire and the consequences for foreign policy in the here and now. In a country where Afghans (or at least Muslims) may live cheek by jowl with the 'indigenous' Britons but may not consider themselves to be primarily British, what is to be done in an environment where there is terrorism and the threat of terrorism is a real issue. In a 2006 newspaper article, Colley had a solution:

> [A] chronological history of Britain should become part of the national curriculum. This history need not be built around the reigns of monarchs. It need not obscure the cultural and political differences between Wales, Scotland, England and Ireland, although it should draw attention to the persistent and powerful connections that have always existed between them. And it certainly does not need to be insular, or remotely reactionary. . . . But most of all, schoolchildren need to learn. For how can they grow up to be British citizens if they haven't a clue how Britain came to be what it is?
> (Colley, *The Guardian*, 18 May 2006)

Above all, it was the constitution that will make good Britons:

> Britain possessed many such iconic constitutional and legal documents in the past. American revolutionaries, for instance, borrowed their bill of rights from the document of the same name that was passed at Westminster in 1689 . . . people here often assumed that Britain has no significant constitutional documents. This is dangerous. The Magna Carta, the Petition of Rights, the Treaty of Union, the Catholic and Jewish emancipation acts of 1829 and 1858, the Parliament Act of 1911, the Scotland and Government of Wales Acts of 1998, and more,

should all be put on show together somewhere. Copies, and explanations of their significance, should be made available online to every school. Not for the purpose of crude patriotic drum-banging, but in order to encourage people, especially young people, to think hard about what the struggle for citizenship has involved, and what it has meant.

(Colley, *The Guardian*, 18 May 2006)

Given this list of British constitutional achievements, it would be surprising if there were not a small roll on the drum and a modest blow on the trumpet or that her proposal for national exhibitions could do anything else but place the unfolding of constitutional progress at the centre of history. Like the call for a return to chronological history, it did not quite take us back to the Whiggish history that Sellar and Yeatman by the 1930s perceived to be on the lips of every schoolchild in Britain, every bit as alive as the children's empire literature in the Edwardian period or as vivid as a globe of the time coloured red by British (or is it English?) conquest, but it did give pause for comparison with some of the features of the new Whig history.

This section suggests, therefore, that Whiggish history has survived, predominantly through the Whig approach of Plumb and his school. It seems that above all else Whiggism saw constitutionalism as worthy of comment and the 'identities' of the British as the subject of extensive histories. After all, what else is Simon Schama's *Citizens* (1989), a history of the French Revolution but a sneer at French millenarianism and an attack on hapless French attempts at statebuilding, argued alongside a soft defence of the British constitutional arrangement? Likewise, his *History of Britain* (2000), written for consumption on television, was popular, narrative-driven and had a Plumb-like social purpose to tell the story of a nation still in the making with more than a hint of celebration. Because of this, perhaps, Schama is as likely to be called in to the television studio as a voiceover to a Royal Wedding or to pontificate as the votes in an American Presidential election are counted.

Schama's work in many ways epitomizes the new Whig position. Read alongside Colley's *Britons*, there is no doubt of the value placed on constitutional stability. One volume of Schama's *History of Britain* recalled his Jewish father and what it meant to be a 'foreigner' in England and how that belonging played itself out amid economic decline, end of empire and the rise of the European dream:

Born and bred in him (for he himself was born in Whitechapel not Botosany) was the sense that being British meant being a European, but also being something else too. Whether that something else extended our sense of place out west into the Atlantic or much further across the world, it was not something, even with the vanishing act of empire, to feel defensive about. Nor should we now. It is true that I argue this as a transatlantic Briton myself, but the increasing compulsion to make the choice which General de Gaulle imposed on us between our European and our extra-European identity, seems to order an impoverishment of our culture. It's precisely the roving, unstable, complicated, pock-marked migratory character of our history which ought to be seen as a gift for Europe. Since it is a past which uniquely in European history combined a passion for social justice with an incorrigible attachment to bloody minded liberty, it is a past designed to subvert, not reinforce the streamlined authority of global bureaucracies and corporations. Our place at the European table ought to make room for our peculiarity or we should not bother showing up for dinner.

(Schama, 2002, pp. 553–4)

After the EU referendum, Britain has no longer 'bother[ed] showing up' to the European dinner, and Linda Colley has called for a federal system in the UK while admitting that constitutions 'are not remotely magic bullets' (*The Guardian* July, 2016). Thus, in Schama's work – extraordinary as so much of it is – we have all the elements of the new Whig approach. Its concerns are political, and its evidence base is cultural with the visual (such as works like *Rembrandt's Eyes* (1999) or *Landscape and Memory* (1995)) ever present and, like Colley, brilliantly accessible in their descriptions. It focuses on liberty and the growth of civilization where it charts state action and reaction, and his concern is both with empire and its disappearance. Plumb valued good historical writing and Schama, like many others of the Plumb School such as David Cannadine and Linda Colley, is a fine exponent of the art.

Postscript

The tradition of history writing discussed in this chapter has been – and continues to be – important and influential. With its origins in the early modern period, the rise of what we refer to as Whig interpretations of the past reflected a growing confidence in the British nation, and today it can in many respects be seen as a celebration of its stability and progress – although with Burke it was also located in the 'national character' of the English. This in part explains the wide popular appeal of books written by its leading proponents. The thing about history is that it is full of good stories, and few contemporary historians can tell a story as well as Simon Schama, David Cannadine, Linda Colley and others inhabiting this tradition. Few can deny that their narratives are often compelling, and we cannot say that of many postmodern studies.

It is, however, the very appeal of Whig interpretations that ought to place us on our guard. Far too easily can we be seduced by their engaging narratives, temporarily abandoning our critical faculties, when we should constantly remind ourselves that these accounts are framed by particular teleologies that tend to articulate notions of progress. Thus, the history of England or Britain is seen variously and reassuringly as the forward march of constitutionalism, liberty, democracy, civilization or Protestantism. This optimistic perspective is not entirely misplaced. The record of British history over the past three centuries has suggested real advances in individual freedoms and in political and religious rights. The problem, it might be argued, is that these advances have often been incomplete and won at considerable cost to others. It is the 'darker side of progress' that is underplayed or ignored completely. Thus, for example, Whig interpretations of the British empire stress its achievements in spreading education, free trade and the rule of law, at the same time giving scant regard to its brutal realities. If the unacceptable face of empire is occasionally admitted, then it is viewed as a price that was worth paying. Similarly, while we may see the eighteenth century as a time when the British state was happily unified, there is little regard for those people living at the margins who were simultaneously being subjected to harsh legal and imperial disciplinary regimes. The English tradition, therefore, despite its avowed objectivity, is somewhat uncritical in its use of sources. Not only are they gathered and employed selectively, but they are rarely interrogated as evidence.

Further Reading

J. W. Barrow (1981) *A Liberal Descent: Victorian Historians and the English Past.*
David Bromwich (2014) *The Intellectual Life of Edmund Burke. From the Sublime and the Beautiful to American Independence.*
Stefan Collini (1999) *English Pasts: Essays in History and Culture.*
Frances Ferguson (2004) 'Burke and the Response to the Enlightenment', in Martin Peter Jones Fitzpatrick, Christa Knellwolf and Ian McCalman (eds.), *The Enlightenment World.*

Frank Smith Fussner (2010) *The Historical Revolution: English Historical Writing and Thought, 1580–1640*.
Peter Ghosh (1999) 'Whig Interpretation of History', in K. Boyd (ed.), *Encyclopaedia of Historians and History Writing*.
J. H. Plumb (1988) *The Making of an Historian: The Collected Essays of J. H. Plumb*.
J. H. Plumb (2004) [1969] *The Death of the Past*.
J. G. A. Pocock (1985) *Virtue, Commerce and History*.
D. R. Woolf (2000) *Reading History in Early Modern England*.
Duncan Wu (ed.) (1994) *Romanticism: An Anthology*.

5 The North American Tradition

Introduction

The one-dollar bill reflects the development of North American approaches to the past. First issued in 1862, its focus has been both the founding constitution and the vicissitudes of the nation. As such, it has altered – as historians in the United States have altered – with the changing political, social and economic weather, and, like the US itself, the bill has been redeemed and reinvented on numerous occasions, often in the teeth of hardship and conflict. The reverse side of the ever-popular 'buck' gives us in narrowly expressive terms the section headers from which changes to North American historiography will be described and analysed during this chapter. Constant is the Great Seal of the United States, which acts for the various arms of the state as the national coat of arms. This has been in use since 1782, although it wasn't added to the dollar bill until 1935. On the back, we can see the object of our opening section: histories that begin with the desolate landscape of the pre-European America and the all-seeing eye of providence. Roman numerals (MDCCLXXVI) spell out the date when the thirteen colonies gained independence from Great Britain (1776). Among other Latin notations, we can spot a banner that shouts *Novus Ordo Seclorum* or the New Order of the Ages which gave notice for the era of *Pax Americanus*. How historians responded to this founding moment of the United States of America is also discussed in the opening section. Of those Latin phrases, 'Out of many states, one nation', until 1956 a motto of the country, probably best sums up the changes in American approaches to the past which are reviewed in Sections 2 and 3, namely, from the progressive historians who moved beyond the so-called 'frontier thesis' to a fundamental questioning of the motivations and interests of the founders, to the consensus historians who shifted from the class-based, social scientific and largely secular viewpoints that had dominated up until the Second World War. It was probably no accident that the context in which these historians lived and wrote was the Cold War and the Age of Affluence. By 1957, 'In God We Trust' was included by law on the one dollar 'greenback'. The final section of the chapter moves the great American story away from the narrow confines of constitution, economic interests and American exceptionalism in order to take into account narratives connected to the experiences of black people, the oppressed and the poor, and encounters with those who were not American.

5.1 America and the New Order of the Ages

The most prominent member of what became known as the Hudson River School of American artists was Thomas Cole (1801–1848). Cole was born in Lancashire in England and had a keen sense of history. His set of paintings called *The Course of Empire* (1833–1836) charted the rise and fall of the powerful, warning of the hubris that comes with power and untrammelled

DOI: 10.4324/9781003156086-6

expansion. His equally famous series *The Voyage of Life* (1840) also sought to present a narrative where time follows an individual, a pilgrim, through the perils that accompanied him from infancy to old age – perhaps acting as a metaphor for the life of a nation. In 1836 he painted *The Oxbow* (Figure 5.1) which, by using conventional techniques of landscape painting, summed up a vision of man in nature that revealed the influence of European Romanticism. In his depiction of the Connecticut River cutting back upon itself in a horseshoe shape, we find on the right of the canvas a landscape that is flat and controlled; on the left, however, we see the darkness of a sky which is wild and menacing, while the advancing brushwood bears witness to the taming and perhaps destruction of this 'new' land. In other paintings by Cole, an American Indian is placed in the scene to suggest unspoilt nobility (the so-called noble savage, perhaps?) or even a train rushing through the wilderness and felled trees that serve as a warning that America may yet go the way of an already corrupted Europe.

This take on the history of a new nation must be read alongside the influence exerted on the school by transcendentalism – a creed that hit Boston on the east coast of America among New England Congregationalists (a Protestant doctrine that placed religious authority in the congregation itself). Prompted by both English and German Romanticism, transcendentalists celebrated individuality and social transformation. By the mid-century they were part of a movement that opposed slavery and social injustices and promoted an ethos of struggle for fundamental change. With this came a belief in an American future which, by abandoning Puritan pessimism, would bring a new millennium to this vast continent. This future was soon to be realized when the 'manifest destiny' of a country that expanded from Atlantic to Pacific coasts

Figure 5.1 Thomas Cole, *Oxbow: View from Mount Holyoke Northampton Massachusetts after Thunderstorm*, painted in 1836

Contributor: Peter Horree/Alamy Stock Photo

would lead, as the Democrat journalist John L. O'Sullivan said in 1839, to a fresh era in human affairs under God. The concept of manifest destiny may have been essentially metaphysical, but as the new Americans claimed the land from 'sea to shining sea' it promised a life that was not only utterly different from the European experience but also promised to sweep all of nature before it.

The religious ideas illustrated by the Hudson River School and others had a profound influence on American historical scholarship as expressed through the work of Harvard educated New Englander George Bancroft (1800–1891; see also Chapter 6). His rethinking of the nature and purpose of the nation changed how people thought about the American past. He asked questions that remain fundamental about the value of history as a form of knowledge and was, in short, the sort of Whig that formed much of our discussion in the last chapter. When Bancroft wrote the introduction to his *History of the United States* in 1885, he penned the following:

> It is the object of the present work to explain how the change in the condition of our land has been brought about; and, as the fortunes of a nation are not under the control of a blind destiny, to follow the steps by which a favouring Providence, calling our institutions into being, has conducted the country to its present happiness and glory.
>
> (Bancroft, 1857, p. 4)

Bancroft's Whiggism adopts a fresh covenant with the New World. Here man strides the land with liberal guarantees shipped over on the Mayflower from England, while a rugged individualism develops organically. This viewpoint saw American exceptionalism (not just 'difference') as a unique gift from God. But if Man (in the abstract) was born free, the environment changed national character. Transcendentalists such as those in the Hudson River School agitated for the abolition of slavery and the promotion of women's rights and thereby adopted the intellectual basis of the European Enlightenment from the very continent they had left.

In fact, the historical sensibilities of the New World can only be understood by reference to the Old J. Hector St. John Crevecoeur, a Frenchman, who asked in 1782, 'What then is the American, this new man who had thrown off all his ancient manners?' Arthur M. Schlesinger (1917–2007) answered this question in his Presidential address to the American Historical Association (AHA), which he delivered on the evening of the annual business meeting in Washington on December 30, 1942: 'This "new man" abounds in courage, creative energy and resourcefulness,' the very 'qualities that made possible the occupying and development of the continent, the building of a democratic society, and the continuing concern for the welfare of the underprivileged' (Schlesinger, 1943, p. 244).

In order to understand how it was imagined that America grew from and then against Europe, the old from the new, we need to look briefly at Johann von Herder, Jules Michelet and Giambattista Vico, the principal theorists who helped to pave the way for an intellectual transformation of American approaches to the past and (it was thought) the re-creation of what it meant to be a 'new man'; that is, an American.

Johann Gottfried von Herder (1744–1803) was a German philosopher and theologian who exercised great influence on the historical imagination. He was part of the Romantic revolt against the Enlightenment belief in scientific method that judged every society by the standards of the most modern. He argued that each period, civilization and historical event was unique, specific to time and place and should be studied as such. History could unlock the special qualities of nationality, national destiny and the life of the *Volksgeist* or spirit of peoples within that nation. The proper focus of history should thus be upon the language, folk-law, myth, literary traditions or 'national character' and culture of the group. His search was not for individual heroes but the *zeitgeist* or mindset of a whole society. Yet this mindset was not in any way innate or eternal, rather it was the specific product of social, historical and cultural forces. This may sound straightforward and rather too obvious a point to make. In the eighteenth century, however, it provided history with a definite task: to find the origin of these forces and allow historians to relive, reconstruct and rethink the past using their own subjectivity, a subjectivity – as we have found in recent chapters – that would become part of the Romantic critique of Enlightenment objectivity.

This subjectivity stood in stark contrast to the objectivity struck by the American Historical Association (AHA) when founded in 1884. Then the thought of Ranke (see Chapter 21) was important, and even Bancroft could write proclaiming the value of objectivity for the historical method following a visit to Berlin in 1867 (Novick, 1988, p. 25). In either case, a powerful academy was born, and we cannot decouple this process of professionalization with the reinvention of America through the past-regarding narratives of the leading members of the AHA. Yet, neither can we place to one side the Romanticism of the early Whiggish approaches. For the French historian, Jules Michelet (1798–1874), for example, the author of the then definitive history of the French Revolution in seven volumes (1847–1853), subjectivity was emphatically associated with Romantic thought, which allowed an inquiry into the past through popular psychologies and beliefs. It also permitted historians to understand their own psychologies. To this end, he pioneered histories of mentalities in the areas of witchcraft, children, labour and the family. His work on the Renaissance is of great moment while a concentration on culture and art revealed new ways of understanding the past. Cathedrals became under his scrutiny 'great historical facts' while tombs and gravestones were evidence of changing attitudes to death (Haskell, 1993, p. 262).

The European influence did not halt there, and we cannot get to the heart of the contributions of Herder and Michelet or understand why they are important to our understanding of American historiography unless we understand the earlier thought of Giambattista Vico (1668–1744), in particular his *Principi di Scienza Nouva* (1744). This was designed to be a new science of humanity but one whose laws could be discerned subjectively. It was an unusual, rich, if repetitive, work – but one that has influenced generations of historians and philosophers including Herder, Michelet, Benedetta Croce (1866–1952), R. G. Collingwood (1889–1943) and Isaiah Berlin (1909–1997). Berlin saw Vico as an important figure in the so-called counter Enlightenment, linking him to the alternatives that sprang up to challenge 'Enlightenment dogma'. Perhaps the greatest of these so-called alternatives was Vico's emphasis on imagination in the process of understanding historical change, the type of imagination that informed the Hudson School and whose approach may well be ultimately traced back to Vico. Vico's case against an Enlightenment scepticism which threatened to kill God and raise the study of the natural world – science – to the status of a popular faith was built on the premises that:

- The quest for knowledge of the external world can never be completed.
- The culture of each society is unique.
- Culture can best be understood through the study of language.
- Forms of language, therefore, shape the present and are worthy of study.
- History (the study of culture such as customs like burial rituals, language, myth, landscape) allows us in turn to understand the laws of social development.

(Burke, 1985, p. xx)

Many of Vico's ideas then tend towards a historical methodology which revealed and reconstructed the mentalities of past peoples. To Herder and the German Romantics, however, national spirit transcended all divisions and a consciousness that, according to the German Georg Wilhelm Friedrich Hegel, transcended history (see Chapter 6). It is this national 'spirit' that justified for the American historian, George Bancroft and the Hudson River School democracy, divine providence and the natural desire of all human beings for liberty and that also provided examples of the historical culture that was one major legacy of the Enlightenment.

It may have been that this intellectual legacy from Europe explains the sense of foreboding expressed by Cole and the Hudson River School and the strident optimism of the American 'new man' articulated by Schlesinger; if so, this sense was anticipated by Frederick Jackson Turner (1861–1932) and his address to the AHA in July 1893. His stated topic was 'Problems in American History', and the paper outlined what was to become known as the 'frontier thesis', which would take centre stage in American historiography for over a century. By the time the applause had finally died down, Turner had moved from the University of Wisconsin to occupy a Harvard Chair (Schlesinger was also to occupy this Chair) and assume the Presidency of the AHA, collecting a Pulitzer Prize and all the public glitter that went with this status.

Turner identified 'Out West' as America's foundational myth and essential identity: the history of the West – 'the meeting point between savagery and civilization' – was what made America, America (Turner, 1920). In the words of American President Woodrow Wilson, who made a rough-and-ready political translation that would pervade the language and thought of American views about the past for generations, 'The Westerner is the type and master of our American life'. Turner developed his thesis in 'The significance of the frontier in American history' where 'the existence of an area of free land . . . and the advance of American settlement westward explain American development' (Turner, 1920). This was an encounter, he argued, which ultimately led America away from European influence:

> In the settlement of America we have to observe how European life entered the continent, and how America modified and developed that life and reacted on Europe. Our early history is the study of European germs developing in an American environment. Too exclusive attention has been paid by institutional students to the Germanic origins, too little to the American factors. The frontier is the line of most rapid and effective Americanization. The wilderness masters the colonist. It finds him a European in dress, industries, tools, modes of travel, and thought. It takes him from the railroad car and puts him in the birch canoe. It strips off the garments of civilization and arrays him in the hunting shirt and the moccasin. It puts him in the log cabin of the Cherokee and Iroquois and runs an Indian palisade around him. Before long he has gone to planting Indian corn and plowing [sic] with a sharp stick, he shouts the war cry and takes the scalp in orthodox Indian fashion. In short, at the frontier the environment is at first too strong for the man. He must accept the conditions which it furnishes, or perish, and so he fits himself into the Indian clearings and follows the Indian trails. Little by little he transforms the wilderness, but the outcome is not the old Europe, not simply the development of Germanic germs, any more than the first phenomenon was a case of reversion to the Germanic mark. The fact is, that here is a new product that is American. At first, the frontier was the Atlantic coast. It was the frontier of Europe in a very real sense. Moving westward, the frontier became more and more American. As successive terminal moraines result from successive glaciations, so each frontier leaves its traces behind it, and when it becomes a settled area the region still partakes of the frontier characteristics. Thus the advance of the frontier has meant a steady movement away from the influence of Europe, a steady growth of independence on American lines. And to study this advance, the men who

76   *Philosophies*

grew up under these conditions, and the political, economic, and social results of it, is to study the really American part of our history.

[www.xroads.virginia.edu/~hyper/turner/chapter1.html]

A nation was crafted, and a national character or 'intellect' developed which was now quite separate from Europe. And so America came into being through its sense of the past. America, Turner said, was to become 'another name for opportunity':

> From the conditions of frontier life came intellectual traits of profound importance. The works of travellers along each frontier from colonial days onward describe certain common traits, and these traits have, while softening down, still persisted as survivals in the place of their origin, even when a higher social organization succeeded. The result is that to the frontier the American intellect owes its striking characteristics. That coarseness and strength combined with acuteness and inquisitiveness; that practical, inventive turn of mind, quick to find expedients; that masterful grasp of material things, lacking in the artistic but powerful to effect great ends; that restless, nervous energy; that dominant individualism, working for good and for evil, and withal that buoyancy and exuberance which comes with freedom -these are traits of the frontier, or traits called out elsewhere because of the existence of the frontier. Since the days when the fleet of Columbus sailed into the waters of the New World, America has been another name for opportunity, and the people of the United States have taken their tone from the incessant expansion which has not only been open but has even been forced upon them. He would be a rash prophet who should assert that the expansive character of American life has now entirely ceased. Movement has been its dominant fact, and, unless this training has no effect upon a people, the American energy will continually demand a wider field for its exercise. But never again will such gifts of free land offer themselves. For a moment, at the frontier, the bonds of custom are broken and unrestraint is triumphant. There is not *tabula rasa* [blank slate]. The stubborn American environment is there with its imperious summons to accept its conditions; the inherited ways of doing things are also there; and yet, in spite of environment, and in spite of custom, each frontier did indeed furnish a new field of opportunity, a gate of escape from the bondage of the past; and freshness, and confidence, and scorn of older society, impatience of its restraints and its ideas, and indifference to its lessons, have accompanied the frontier. What the Mediterranean Sea was to the Greeks, breaking the bond of custom, offering new experiences, calling out new institutions and activities, that, and more, the ever retreating frontier has been to the United States directly, and to the nations of Europe more remotely. And now, four centuries from the discovery of America, at the end of a hundred years of life under the Constitution, the frontier has gone, and with its going has closed the first period of American history.
>
> (www.nationalhumanitiescenter.org/pds/gilded/empire/text1/turner.pdf)

Influential though these arguments were, they came to attract criticism; most notably the so-called new or progressive historians with whom we associate the period 1910–1945 questioned whether America was any longer a land of opportunity for all and asked in whose interests the constitution served. It is to this important group that we now turn.

5.2   The Progressive or 'New' Historians

> The intelligent public continues to accept somewhat archaic ideas of the scope and character of history. . . . The time has now come when [the present] should turn on the past and exploit it in the interests of advance.
>
> (James Harvey Robinson, *The New History*, 1912)

Ruskin Hall in Oxford, England, opened to much fanfare on 22 February 1899. From the beginning it had the support of senior Labour movement figures such as Keir Hardie, the inaugural leader of the Labour Party and a great historical figure of the British Left. The intention was to prepare working-class men (later women) to govern on behalf of industrial communities and organizations such as trade unions, political parties, co-operative societies and working men's institutes. They were to be the leaders of a socialist tomorrow. Oxford Town Hall played host to the ceremony; the building was festooned with a mixture of Union Jacks but also with the Stars and Stripes. The celebration was held on George Washington's birthday; fittingly because Ruskin Hall was largely the creation of Americans: Walter Watkins Vrooman, his wealthy wife Anne L. Grafflin and Charles Austin Beard (1874–1948), then a twenty-four-year-old postgraduate student at the University of Oxford. By the time Beard had written his bestselling and seminal book, *An Economic Interpretation of the Constitution of the United States*, in 1913, Ruskin Hall had become an independently governed college, with a permanent and dedicated building. It was affiliated to the University of Oxford, enabling the college's working-class students to use Oxford's considerable facilities and to take – if not a full degree – the university's Diploma in Economics and Political Science.

Ruskin College was born with an assumption that history was driven by material economic class interests, by the clash of antagonistic class relationships but more centrally by the assumption that capitalism was ugly and wasteful. It continued to nurse these assumptions until the moment it sold its Walton Road site in 2008 to a constituent college of the University of Oxford, Exeter College and in a year when global capitalism appeared to implode in a financial crisis. Even as Ruskin faded in the educational firmament, the notion that politics, culture and ideas were subordinate to the power of wealth was almost made at a stroke by the construction of a new quadrangle on the site dedicated to the major donor that had paid for it, while the remnants of the late-Victorian vision for a world made anew retreated to the Rookery in Headington, a campus towards the outskirts (in every way) of Oxford.

Less than a decade earlier, Ruskin College, Oxford had celebrated its hundredth birthday on 20 February 1999. Bands, feminist songs of protest, notable alumni (the last in a long line of senior Labour politicians and leaders from around the globe) told stories about the old days, and well-wishers sang the Red Flag as the party went well into the night (Thompson, 1999). It turned out to have been a wake. There was no sign at all of the American flag, and none mentioned those Americans without whom there may never have been a college of the Labour Movement that was in Oxford but not of Oxford. £3m of debt later and by August 2021, it is owned lock, stock and barrel by the University of West London, no doubt pleased to have a base among the spires and to continue a proud tradition of adult education.

Charles Beard, a key player in the founding of the working-class college in Oxford, was hugely influential in North American historiography and rose to great heights in the US academy. Along with, notably, Carl Becker (1873–1945), James Harvey Robinson (1863–1936) and V. L. Parrington (1871–1929), Beard led what became known as the progressive or 'new' historians. Their economically inclined and present-minded interpretation of history made a swift impact among historians and soon became an accepted convention. They were not to be wholly displaced until the 1940s and 1950s when simple but effective empirical research had thoroughly undermined their case, namely, that the radical promise of the Revolution that was thought to have been driven by the entrepreneurial capitalist classes had in fact been ultimately crushed by the vested interests of the plantation slave owners and others. A. M. Simons' *Social Forces in American History* (1911) and Gustavus Myers' *History of the Great American Fortunes* and *History of the Supreme* Court, Vol 1–3, (1909–10), for example, argued that 'The constitutional convention . . . was little more than a committee of the merchants, manufacturers, bankers, and planters, [who] met to arrange a government that would promote their interests' (Goldman, 1952, pp. 242–3). This is what Marx might

Figure 5.2 Charles Beard, eminent American historian and historian of the United States

Courtesy of the Library of Congress Prints and Photographs Division Washington, D.C. 20540 USA, George Grantham Bain Collection, LC-USZ62–36755

have called the 'organizing committee of the bourgeoisie', jam packed with slavery-related economic interests.

Carl Becker in many ways anticipated many of these economistic themes in American historical writing for which Beard seems to have taken much of the credit. His *History of Political Parties in the Province of New York, 1760–1776* (1909) argued against the exceptionalism of the American experience. Where Turner saw the Constitution as unique and the encounter with the Western frontier that had distanced Americans from their European antecedents as critical, the progressive historians saw class, power and special interests looming large in the story of America. For Becker there were two revolutions: the first was against European power; the second was to determine the sharing of the homeland spoils. Beard took these assumptions about the founding moment of the United States and ran with them.

What has been labelled the 'Becker-Beard' interpretation of American history was followed by Arthur Schlesinger's *The Colonial Merchants and the American Revolution* (1918) and J. Franklin Jameson's *The American Revolution Considered as a Social Movement* (1926), which 'postulated that the Revolution ushered in an age of democratization . . . [which also involved the] distribution [of land] in small parcels to ordinary farmers'. This argument was discredited by Harry Yoshe whose *The Disposition of Loyalist Estates in the Southern District of New York* (1939) produced data that emphatically proved that the estates of the Hudson Valley were in fact sold to speculators and not to the small farmers. Other research was to follow this lead into the 1950s (McDonald, 1997), by which time American historiography had become more complicated and arguments over the motives of the framers of the constitution more hotly contested. What prevails, however, is the durability of the *economic* interpretation of the Constitution. Economics and class delineation were rooted in the very same soil that nurtured the founding of Ruskin College.

Faced with criticism, Beard protested that he was not overly influenced by liberal Darwinism or Marxism; still less was he slavishly driven by the historical evidence as it sat impassive in the documents. We should believe him. Instead, he was moved by James Madison (as a framer of the Constitution) and the Federalist tradition with its emphasis on the Bill of Rights. 'Well I did read the writings of the Fathers, hundreds of them, hundreds of pages of economic emphasis', he insisted. Beard refused then to be determinist about his histories, especially the 1913 volume that remained popular in American approaches to histories of the founding of America. On the one hand, he insisted that 'history is just a cat dragged by its tail to places it rarely wants to go. Another man, with a different social view, could have used the same materials and written a volume with the opposite effect.' This is sage advice for any historian. On the other, Beard emphasized the context of the times in which he was writing, 'when reformers were filling the air with shouts of "who gets what"' (Goldman, 1952, p. 249). Beard was no revolutionary. E. R. A. Seligman (a colleague of Beard at Columbia in New York) had already emphasized in his 1902 book, *The Economic Interpretation of History*, that 'Wherever we turn in the maze of recent historical investigation, we are confronted by the overwhelming importance attached by the younger and abler scholars to the economic in political and social progress.' This amounted to a social scientific approach which took in sociology, philosophy, history of law and geography, as well as economics, a cross-disciplinary and secular approach that Beard was to make his own.

Looking back on this set of so-called progressive historians, one cannot help but consider again Frederick Jackson Turner's *The Significance of the Frontier in American History*, which was such an influential sounding board. Here we notice continuities as well as historical breaks. Beard, at the very least, was a complex radical and it seems the expression of nationalism promoted by Turner – that the frontier was 'more of a place and a process than an economic setting' – did nonetheless move historians away from political and towards economic approaches. An astute commentator writing from the vantage point of the 1950s declared:

> during the first century of American history, the sectional division between frontier and seaboard corresponded roughly to an economic division between debt-ridden farmers and wealthier planters and merchants. Consequently, the vogue of Turner had the effect of pulling historians away from thinking in terms of political abstractions and of shifting their minds to a concept that approximated economic interpretation.
>
> (Goldman, 1952, p. 240)

The 'Frontier thesis' was not displaced then but challenged in the early years of the twentieth century. Narratives about sectional and economic differences were already part of the great American historical debate. Because of this, the so-called new or progressive historians had already taken a distinctly economic turn by the time Charles Beard had written his infamous book in 1913 and lent his efforts to establish a college for working men in Oxford.

For both 'new' historians and the historians that were to follow them, there was no 'political man' or 'religious man' or 'natural man' but a 'whole man' meaning that historians had to look at it in three dimensions, a point made by the historian Richard Hofstandter (1916–1970).

80 Philosophies

Hofstandter was also an historian at Columbia who was to put his stamp on the postwar period and who was associated with a loose group to be known as the 'consensus historians' (Holfstadter, 1950). As we are about to discover, the 'consensus historians' would emerge in very particular historical circumstances.

5.3 The Consensus Historians

> If there is a single way of characterizing what has happened in our historical writing since the 1950's, it must be, I believe, the rediscovery of complexity in American history.
>
> (Hofstadter, 2012)

In the period after 1945, 'Beardism' appeared to be a busted flush. No longer was economics or class at the stormcentre of historical enquiry but rather a sort of nationalism seen through an international prism, an assumption of American uniqueness arrived at through critical comparison. By the early 1950s, Richard Hofstandter and others (Louis Hartz, Daniel J. Boorstin, David M. Potter, Perry Miller, Clinton Rossiter, Henry Steele Commager, Allan Nevins and Edmund Morganhad) had either moved away from progressivism or had never occupied that ideological ground. American history was without division or internal conflict. America was wealthy and it was successful. America was exceptional in its love of freedom and liberty was a major export. Tyranny was a foreign curse. In what seems even now to be the halcyon days of the 1950s, racial tensions seem at this distance to have been contained while Vietnam and Watergate were beyond imagination.

Consensus history was nothing if not a return to the notion of American exceptionalism, as if it had ever really gone away. The US was unique. Some historians have argued what assumption was implicit among the old 'new' historians and was shouted from the ever-higher rooftops of America's skyline and across an ever-widening global vista with the new consumer economic settlement. Keywords were bandied about with increasing regularity: 'Mobility', 'abundance', 'pragmatism', 'the absence of feudalism'. Suddenly the idea of national 'character' was back in the frame as once it had been – literally – in our opening section. The progressives saw only internal division and class strife; the consensus historians, in contrast, had eyes only for cross-national and cross-cultural difference. Why was America so different and so at peace with itself, asked Higham (Higham, 1989, p. 465)? Peter Novick offered an explanation, quoting the Book of Judges: 'There was no King in Israel . . . and every man did what was right in his own eyes' (Novick, 1988, p. 628). Here, we cannot avoid the immediate context of the international political situation, which was urgent and all-consuming and followed historians around (as everyone else) like a medieval miasma: the United States had emerged from the Second World War as a superpower. The lines of East and West were set for a Cold War that was to envelop the entire globe for a generation while the majority responses to this conflict have been summarized by historians as the 'orthodox view':

> These scholars took a realist view of international affairs: rational decision-makers were acting on national interest. . . . Their central argument was that the Cold War had its origins in a power struggle. They blamed the expansionist urges of the Soviet leader, Josef Stalin, suggesting that he was guided by communist ideology which favoured the spread of the communist message. This outlook united conservatives such as W. H. Chamberlin and liberals such as Arthur Schlesinger, though the conservatives were critical of Presidents Franklin D. Roosevelt and Harry Truman for not adopting sufficiently tough responses to Stalin, while

liberals applauded US policy as a creative response to the Soviet threat and a recognition of America's global responsibilities.

(Hopkins, 2007, p. 914)

Likewise, the consensus historians, living under a secular constitution and threatened constantly by the Bomb, could readily proclaim that it was in God they trusted. The notion of the 'affluent worker' or affluence itself was also a reality for many in the postwar boom, and this too was transforming the American past.

Enter then the political consensus and the consensus historians. Space does not permit a lengthy biographical introduction of these historians, but it is interesting to note the observation by Higham that

[m]any, if not most of the leading consensus historians were secularized, highly assimilated Jews. Themselves the sons of immigrants, they belonged to the first generation of Jewish students who encountered no serious obstacle in rising into the humanistic disciplines. How could they avoid perceiving the United States as an increasingly inclusive society resting on a universalistic value system? And in looking abroad, how could they fail to contrast American success and affluence with the catastrophes of Europe?

(Higham, 1989, pp. 464–465)

This is as may be. Let us try to summarize the views of each of the important players in turn, starting with Daniel Boorstin who in *The Genius of American Politics* (1953) argued tellingly that America did not produce a first-order theorist or a discernible philosophy. Even when Alexis de Tocqueville visited the United States from France to investigate the prison system of the New World and to write *Democracy in America* in 1835, his interest was more in the equality and individualism of this new civilization rather than its history or national identity. He would have looked in vain for an American theory of the world. As such, there was no 'philosophy' or 'theory' to export and no democracy to imitate.

In Louis Hartz's *The Liberal Tradition in America* (1955) individualism and the defence of property rights provided the 'single factor analysis' that unlocked a master narrative that explained American history. The historical engine that made this thesis plausible, according to Hartz, was 'the absence of feudalism and the presence of the liberal idea'. This liberal tradition – its origins were established with John Locke and the idea of a social contract and balance of powers – was accompanied by an absence of either revolution or reaction as a governing strategy or a form of politics. A 2001 retrospective review argued that Hartz had promoted this thesis 'by means of a rhetorical strategy calculated to dazzle his readers' (Kloppenberg, 2001, p. 460).

If these aforementioned histories were concerned with culture, David Potter's *People of Plenty: Economic Abundance and the American Character* (1954b) goes to the heart of the relationship among American culture, capitalism and consumerism. The 'American character' came under scrutiny but from an economic perspective. Natural resources and technological innovation meant that while America had to devote large resources to agriculture, it grew under conditions of abundance. This had a political spinoff: 'Essentially, the difference is that Europe conceived of redistribution of wealth as necessitating the expropriation of some and the corresponding aggrandizement of others; but America has conceived of it as primarily of giving to some without taking from others' (Potter, 1954a, p. 40). Within a context of unprecedented growth and consumption at the time this was written in the 1950s, it made a lot of sense. It also hinted at the absence of a large-scale socialist alternative in American politics – something that we shall address in the next section.

82 Philosophies

Finally, Richard Hofstadter's *The American Political Tradition* (1948) argued influentially that politics and political thought have been limited in American history by the horizons placed on the accepted definitions of property and enterprise. While varying political traditions have clashed over this or that issue, they 'have shared a belief in the rights of property, the philosophy of economic individualism, the value of competition; they have accepted the economic virtues of capitalist culture as necessary qualities of man' (Hofstadter, 1948, p. viii). In a sense, this acknowledges the emphasis placed by the progressives on conflict but ensures that conflict in American history was ring fenced and limited to a defence of property:

> The American nation was born in an age of almost constant stress and crisis that lasted from 1763 to 1788, during which its people experienced a dozen years of agitation over imperial policies; The Union was in some danger of division during 1798–1801; It was in serious trouble during the years 1807–14 and again in 1832 (economic issues as the slave trade was subject to international legislative sanction); It was racked by such grave differences in the 1850s that it finally broke in two (The Civil War); It went through a touchy crisis again in the Reconstruction, climaxed by the events of 1876–7; It was deeply disturbed in the 1890s and again in the 1930s, and now, in the 1960s (economic distress and social revolution).
>
> (Hofstadter, 1968, cf. 437)

Beard and the intellectual legacy of the progressives was not quite banished from the historiographical memory – conflict, economics, culture, power were all subjects of historical discussion. Both the 'new' historians and the consensus historians had to explain how the 'American Eden' was eroded by intolerance and violence, how 'one nation, indivisible, with liberty and justice for all' could produce slavery and the exclusion of so many from the liberal rights of the constitution. In fairness, it could well be that the focus on class by the progressive historians may well have missed some of this important nuance:

> The progressive scheme of polarized conflict has been replaced by a pluralistic vision in which more factors are seriously taken into account. To a degree, the direct impact of economic forces has in some cases been downgraded; but I do not think that the force of the historical writing lies primarily here. Indeed, had the Progressive historians had been saying nothing more than that economic forces were somewhat underestimated, they could be said to have won the day, for few historians now are likely to repeat that neglect of material factors that sometimes characterized their predecessors. What is distinctively new is that ideas and attitudes as forces in history have returned and are now being explored as explanatory categories in a novel way.
>
> (Hofstadter, 1968, p. 443)

By the time Hofstadter wrote these words, the proverbial cat was out of the bag. He went further:

> There are three major areas in which a history of the United States organized around the guiding idea of consensus breaks down: first, I believe it cannot do justice to the genuinely revolutionary aspects of the American Revolution; second, it is quite helpless and irrelevant on the Civil War and the issues related to it; and finally, it disposes us to turn away from one of the most significant facts of American social life – the racial, ethnic, and religious conflict with which our history is saturated.
>
> (Hofstadter, 1968, p. 459)

Also, by the 1960s, consensual America had found an echo in non-consensual America with 'charges of exclusion' being made by labour, blacks and women. What re-emerged was the oldest historiographical question of them all: was America really unique? By the time Michael Harrington wrote *The Other America* in 1963, issues around racial prejudice, urban poverty and the history of the South within the context of the Union had surfaced, and this promoted a move away from histories of the Protestant middle class, whose assumptions of social mobility seemed enshrined as a constitutional right, to histories of America which placed the 'others' centre stage.

5.4 The Other America

We must go beyond consensus (c.1960s–1980s) but first to a simple question: Why no Marxism in America? Eric Foner (b. 1943), the historian of the post-Civil War reconstruction period, said with Louis Hartz in mind, 'Without a feudal tradition, and a sense of class oppression in the present, Americans are simply unable to think in class terms' (Foner, 1984, p. 62). This was just the topic broached by Walter Sombert in 1906, a German contemporary of Max Weber, who ventured to understand why the United States did not appear to play host to a vigorous proletariat when it was the most advanced capitalist country on the face of the planet. In classical Marxist doctrine, history moved in stages with capitalism as an advanced stage that would yield to a socialist and planned economy. The United States showed little sign of moving in that direction. Sombert reasoned, in a section called the 'Political Position of the Worker', that America ought to have given rise to a critique of an economic system which, after all, favoured the few at the expense of the many. Instead, he observed, Americans took pride in the constitution and the political rights that it implied. Workers had been assimilated into the apparatus of capitalism with income, housing and consumer goods on every greater display. This was firmly thought to have improved the lot of the worker. The otherwise facile promise of social mobility in a capitalist economy (the so-called American Dream) appeared to have substance. If this was so, Sombert concluded, it was because of the power of the major political parties to manipulate financial resources which would allow just enough concessions to the proletariat in order to retain a hope that one day riches will one day be realized. Class consciousness was uniformly a middle-class conscience, and almost anyone could become 'Middle Class'. Knowledge that wealth could be derived from the virtues of working hard 'to get on' had led to a strong sense of security and contentment. That is, unless you happened not to part of a non-white and Christian elite.

Dr W. E. B. Du Bois (1868–1963) was one such person, who also happened to be a very notable historian. His *Black Reconstruction* (1935) asked whether democracy extended to all; indeed, he went on, 'The true significance of slavery in the United States to the whole social development of America lay in the ultimate relation of slaves to democracy'. What was the 4th of July to the black slave; what was it to the black worker?

> Above all, we must remember the black worker was the ultimate exploited; that he formed that mass of labor which had neither wish nor power to escape from the labor status, in order to directly exploit other laborers, or indirectly, by alliance with capital, to share in their exploitation. To be sure, the black mass, developed again and again, here and there, capitalistic groups in New Orleans, in Charleston and in Philadelphia; groups willing to join white capital in exploiting labor; but they were driven back into the mass by racial prejudice before they had reached a permanent foothold; and thus became all the more bitter against all organization which by means of race prejudice, or the monopoly of wealth, sought to exclude men from making a living.
>
> (Du Bois, 1935, p. 15)

84   Philosophies

As slavery had been the engine for the eighteenth-century economy, so the black proletariat that had been prevented from joining the American middle class would become the 'founding stone of a new economic system in the nineteenth century and for the modern world' (ibid., p. 15). It was this democratic deficit that caused the civil war in America, Du Bois argued, and it was this fault line in American history that had the most significance, as the subtitle of his book suggested: 'of the Part Which Black Folk Played in the Attempt to Reconstruct Democracy'.

Also published in 1935 was Merle Curti's book, *The Social Ideas of American Educators*. As more than one contemporary scholar has noted, there was no doubt about the importance and scholarship regarding either of these interventions in creating what was a live and difficult debate about the soul of America. Curti took colonial education as an example of religious and ruling class oppression which pitted itself against the underclass. Even servants could be made docile by moral instruction. With religion as a tool of social control, the 'economically dominant class' used the bible and religious schooling as an explanation and justification for slavery while the Christian idea acted as a promise of redemption to the most helpless and hopeless of the black population.

Historians who have attempted to place Du Bois and Curti into the context of twentieth-century historiography have noted the extent to which the combined effect of the consensus historians and the political effects of the Cold War in the postwar period appear to have marginalized radical history after its first flush in the years when Beard dominated. The 1960s would bring forth another type of scholarship. Yet, there is a nuance here that should be understood. In many ways, the suppression of radical approaches to history fit perfectly with a culture-wide intolerance of deviance that 'The Sixties' would succeed in puncturing. Another perspective, however, would acknowledge that the consensus gave permission for radicalism and radical history to exist. Before the 1960s, it has been convincingly argued, by Higham at least, that 'consensus history actually facilitated the rise of radical history instead of standing in its way'. This allows us to situate Du Bois and Curti as historians with a cause but one disastrously before their time:

> Both men wrote their explicitly anticapitalist books at the height of the radical wave of the early 1930s, when they had close at hand the moral and intellectual support of congenial associates. They wrote, one might say, as prospective members of a deviant community-in-the-making, a community of radical scholars. But the community never solidified. After 1935 radicalism receded, particularly among intellectuals. Moreover, the decade turned out to be hostile to the deep social nonconformity that would make possible a radical counter-culture thirty years later. Du Bois, by holding to an increasingly belligerent and outspoken Marxism, cut himself off from other students of Negro history and thus he had no disciples. Curti, by moving back to the eclectic empiricism of his earlier work, retained his base in an anti-Marxist academic community. The two radical books survived as isolated achievements instead of becoming contributions to a school.
>
> (Higham, 1989, p. 462)

Out of time, out of place certainly, stuck in a time when conformity was valued and nonconformity was eschewed, Du Bois was, after all, the very personification of conformity: ordered and mannered to the point that even his closest friend was discouraged from using his first name, but as historians have also suggested, Marxism could never in any case have breached the 'radical' fortress that Becker/Beard et al. had built – brick by brick:

> Paradoxically, Progressive historians disarmed Marxist theory by absorbing its most attractive elements. Marxism's sympathy with the underprivileged and its dynamic of struggle

between opposing social strata resonated with strong native heritage of the Jacksonian-populist ideas. Progressive scholars, following Beard's lead, could therefore give the language of social conflict a distinctly American inflection. By detaching the themes of class and social protest from the specifically Marxist theory of an irreconcilably polarized social system, Progressive history made Marxism seem alien and unnecessarily doctrinaire. Americans would surely have put Marxism to more and better use if Progressivism had not suffused their perceptions of it.

(Ibid.)

Certainly 'perception' or the 'reception' of Marxism was critical. For whatever reason, its message fell on stony ground and this has been critical to the development of American approaches to the writing of history. 'The sharpest difference between the progressive and Marxist scheme, Higham went on, was 'the nationalism of one and the internationalism of the other'. The major social distinction was between what was American and what was not (Higham, 1989, pp. 462–3).

If it was the 'sixties', then this was when the New Left became resurgent. We speak about this period at length in Chapter 22 and so it is enough to say now that the countercultural, iconoclastic and politically radical elements of this historical moment were reproduced among historians in America. One product of the scepticism about the governing liberal ideologies in the US and its mirror opposite in the Soviet Union was the work of the New Left. One flowering of this movement was the publication in 1968 of Barton Bernstein's *Towards a New Past: Dissenting Essays in American History*. This was but a single hint of what was to become a new approach to the American past. A book that illustrates this shift can be found in the still elegant volume by Robert Fogel and Stanley Engerman, *Time on the Cross: The Economics of Negro Slavery* (1974), which sought to undermine the 'traditional interpretation' of the American slave system:

The traditional interpretation suggested that (1) slavery was generally unprofitable, (2) it was economically moribund (3) that slaves led agricultural production (4) that the South felt keenly these economic truths and (5) that slavery as a system uniformly meant that conditions for the slave were harsh.

(Fogel and Engerman, 1974, p. 226)

While the criticism of the system remained trenchant, the overall analysis was optimistic, and for this reason the study proved highly controversial. This is not to say that the New Left and other historians were not writing in this most radical of decades but that there was a sense that historians were discovering experiences which up to this point had remained hidden from history. It was also a time when innovation in the use of sources was at a high point. L. W. Levine's *Black Culture and Consciousness* (1977) paid witness to what looked at first sight to be a world away from the approach taken by consensus historians. Two footnotes to this narrative should be considered, however. The first is that the methodology displayed by Levine was indeed a powerful signal of a fresh approach. The subtitle of *Black Culture* is *African Folk Thought from Slavery to Freedom*, which makes generous and interesting use of folk tales, hymns and secular music and the interesting significance of gospel. The second is that Levine was, in fact, a doctoral student of Hofstadter and so continuity featured in the American historical work of the 1960s as much as breaks in methodology. Yet generally the professional academy remained conservative in approach. This said, non-white minorities began to populate the Organization of American Historians with John Hope Franklin becoming President in 1974, Gerda Lerner in

1981, Darlene Clark Hine in 2005 and, most recently, Erika Lee, who is the granddaughter of Chinese immigrants, in 2022.

In contrasting ways, these studies were part of a seismic shift in the ways in which historians approached the complex and painful experience of American slavery. From its beginnings, American historians were faced with uncomfortable questions. How was it that Thomas Jefferson, when proclaiming in the Declaration of Independence that 'all men are created equal', owned large numbers of slaves? How was it, indeed, that eight of the first twelve presidents of the newly formed United States of America were slave owners (Kolchin, 2003, p. 3)? More widely, how was it that a nation enthusiastically heralded as a new civilization continued to rely so heavily for its economic vitality on a barbaric system of unfree labour?

American historians found these questions difficult to avoid but chose instead obfuscation. George Bancroft's *History of the United States*, published in 1834 when slave plantations still flourished, recognized the horrors of slavery but simultaneously emphasized its ancient lineages and universality to support the idea that the institution could readily be planted in modern nations without compromising their civilizing mission (Davis, 1988, p. 21). And then in a move that was to become part of received wisdom, Bancroft declared that by bringing Christian civilization to Africans, America must be seen as a vital part of a providential plan to redeem the human race.

The nineteenth century witnessed a remarkable transformation in attitudes to slavery. After millennia when the slave trade was almost universally accepted and practised, in the space of a few decades it became so reviled that those Western nations that had been largely responsible for the growth of the trade dedicated themselves to its eradication. In the United States a bitter civil war was fought over abolition. This shift necessarily influenced the historiography of slavery and emancipation but in ways that were less than radical. Thus, although strident pro-slavery rhetoric was in decline by the end of the nineteenth century, many of the older attitudes fostered by slavery refused to go away. In Britain, Reginald Coupland, Beit Professor of Colonial History at Oxford, published *The British Anti-Slavery Movement* (1928), which proved less an indictment of Britain's role in the slave trade than a celebration of the pioneering work of British humanitarians such as William Wilberforce leading to abolition. And in the States, W. E. Woodward's *A New American History* appeared as late as 1936 to considerable popular acclaim. It contained the following verdict:

> The slave system . . . did incalculable harm to the white people of the South, and benefited nobody but the negro, in that it served as a vast training school for African savages. Though the regime of the slave plantation was strict it was, on the whole, a kindly one by comparison with what the imported slave had experienced in his own land. It taught him discipline, cleanliness and a conception of moral standards.
> (Woodward, 1936, p. 412, cited in Davis, 2000, pp. 455–6)

Then in 1944 appeared Eric Williams' seminal *Capitalism and Slavery*. Based on his studies for a DPhil at Oxford, this book effectively changed the historiographical agenda simply by confronting head on those awkward questions around slavery that previous scholars had sedulously avoided. What was the relationship between industrial capitalism and the growth of Atlantic slavery? Was slavery built on or created out of racism? Were British humanitarians really responsible for the abolition of the slave trade? How did the American colonies come to play such a key role in the Western imperial economy? Over seventy years and many shelves of detailed studies later, Williams' theses may appear simplistic, but he launched a ship; on board were the large majority of scholars who contributed significantly to future debates.

Figure 5.3 The historian and politician Eric Williams, whose book *Capitalism and Slavery* led to a paradigm shift in the scholarship on the slave trade and abolition

Contributor: BNA Photographic/Alamy Stock Photo

And the course charted was a sound one, for over the past forty years slavery has attracted brilliant historical scholarship. For reasons that are not entirely clear, most of this work was rooted in the American rather than European academy, but then there were no plantations in Europe. In the space available to us it is impossible to give this corpus of work due regard. Instead, we wish to focus on some of those awkward questions, neglected in the past, that have recently prompted lively debate (for an accessible and yet authoritative survey upon which we have drawn, see Kolchin (2003)).

The relationship between slavery and race was posed early on by Oscar and Mary Handlin (1950) and Carl Degler (1959). Researching the shift from indentured labour to slavery in the Chesapeake region, the Handlins argued that slavery led directly to racism. Degler, on the other hand, contended that racism predated slavery and that racial discourses served as a powerful device to justify its introduction and perpetuation. Later Winthrop Jordan's masterly *White over Black: American Attitudes Toward the Negro* (1968) demonstrated the role racism played in shaping social relationships on plantations, while Douglas Deal's *Race and Class in Colonial Virginia* (1993) explored the complex racial dynamics that operated among English colonists, native Amerindians and African slaves in the seventeenth century. This work has not definitively resolved the question on the causal relationship between slavery and racism. It is incontestable, for example, that negative stereotypes of Africans existed in the European imagination long before the seventeenth century, but whether they were a precondition of the introduction of slavery in the Americas is a much more difficult matter. Ultimately, perhaps the more useful approach is to understand how the dialogue between race and slavery determined social and economic relationships in slave plantations before and after the War of Independence.

The slave trade has attracted the interest of many quantitatively minded historians who have addressed the vexed question of how many slaves were transported to the Americas. Philip Curtin's *The Atlantic Slave Trade: A Census* (1969) put the figure at 9.5 million, which has in subsequent work come to be seen as low. Important studies such as David Eltis, *Economic Growth and the Ending of the Transatlantic Slave Trade* (1987) and Herbert Klein, *The Atlantic Slave Trade* (1999) have gradually pushed up the estimate to approximately 11 million, although, because of deaths during the so-called middle passage, even this grossly underestimates the total actually taken from the shores of Africa. The demographics are of great interest, for it is now generally accepted that while eighty-five per cent of African slaves were transported to Brazil and various Caribbean colonies, the slave population of North America was the one that emerged as by far the largest (Eltis and Richardson, 1997). We do not yet have an entirely satisfactory explanation for this, but diet, climate, work, fertility and disease all affected the demographics of the slave trade.

Finally, the seeming discrepancy between the ideals of the American Revolution and slavery still commands the interest of scholars not least because as a political issue it has continued to reverberate through the ages. Although most would accept that the democratization of American society brought by the Revolution was imperfect, the ideals of egalitarian republicanism laid down are compromised by the presence of the slave population and their descendants. The obvious way out of the conundrum that all are *not* free and equal is to declare that slaves are in every way so different that they are not entitled to the same rights as 'free Americans' (Finkelman, 1996). From this it was one small step to the all-too-familiar injunction that slaves and their descendants were innately inferior and therefore not fit for freedom.

Many of the disputatious questions around the history of American slavery operate in the realm of ideas. Notions of slavery, freedom, property, labour, equality, emancipation and so on were complex and dynamic, and in order to understand how they were constructed and viewed by contemporaries we need to look carefully at their writings and speeches. This is the stuff of intellectual history, and here the sustained work of David Brion Davis has been inspirational. From *The Problem of Slavery in Western Culture* (1966) to *The Problem of Slavery in the Age of Emancipation* (2014) Davis with immense erudition, insight and eloquence revealed the broad contours of thought that since ancient times have underpinned the operation of slavery and its (incomplete) abolition.

Many of these historians are now part of an older generation; only time will tell if their achievements will be taken forward by the next. And the agenda? Here Joseph Miller's *Problems of Slavery as History: A Global Approach* (2012) provides some valuable suggestions. He argues that the treatment of slavery as an 'institution transcending time and space have frozen the dynamics of slaving in most part of the world as a historical process' (ibid., p. 1). The result is that institutionalized slavery is thought of primarily through the lens of abolitionists in the States, with the enslaved as 'one-dimensional victims of similarly one-dimensional brutal masters'. Without masking the violence upon which slavery was built and sustained, we need to recognize that the institution did nothing. Slavery was the outcome of individual and collective decisions taken in specific historical circumstances. These strategies can only be understood in the wider context of the use of bonded and unfree labour. As Miller puts it:

> My method is to contextualize slavers, as they have thrived in specific times and places in enormously varied ways, and also to contextualize the enslaved to sense their meaningful experiences as human beings and to identify their resultant responses. . . . I want to treat slaving not only as the transcending contradiction of dehumanization that it created against the background of modernity but also as a strategy that people in historical positions of

marginality have pursued, since time immemorial, with significant consequences for themselves and for others around them, beyond the sufferings that the practice imposed on the people they enslaved.

(Ibid., pp. 18–19)

Let us hope that there are sufficient historians to take up this demanding challenge.

In the meantime – to return to the broader landscape of American history – we can perhaps discern some continuity and also some modest evolving of method and approach in the American sense of History. Jay Sexton's *The Transnational Turn in American Historical Writing* (2005) takes us to what has become known as a 'transnational turn' in the type and range of histories attempted. Likewise, regionalism, which was a non-starter in the 1950s, has now became popular. 'From its founding', said Peter Onuf and Ed Ayers (1996), 'the new nation was a nation of regions'. It was also indistinguishable from nationalism as a functioning creed. Some themes just kept returning, like the proverbial bad penny. The idea of American exceptionalism was certainly one.

This said, attempts at transnational study take on a distinct comparative and radical air. These are histories that often look at the United States from the outside in. Innovation is not always homegrown either, with scholars such as Stephen Tuck making a real impact:

He joins the new British invasion, which uses not the *Ed Sullivan Show* as its venue of entry but, primarily, university presses. The more recent invasion will not likely rock American culture from a conformist smugness as did the Beatles, Rolling Stones, and even Herman's Hermits, but participants have made important contributions to American civil rights historiography.

(Davis, 2002, pp. 1595–6)

With cries that 'the British are coming', the American past is now under scrutiny from Britain and elsewhere. In *The Night Malcolm X Spoke at the Oxford Union* (Tuck, 2014), we can now see a great figure of the American Civil Rights struggle as a global figure. The reader also becomes gradually aware of a shared struggle for racial equality. The inspiration for ending racist and imperialist societies may have been led by the great American figures of the civil rights movement but the problem itself existed in Britain at the time of Malcolm X's visit and civil rights activism travelled in the opposite direction. This is why the book is subtitled *A Transatlantic Story of Antiracist Protest*. America and Europe then were a shared field of study just as it was for the Hudson River school in our opening section of the chapter.

5.5 Black Lives Matter: a Coda

The murder in 2020 of George Floyd at the hands of a white police officer in Minneapolis has recently reawakened interest in racial justice on both side of the Atlantic, raising it to levels rarely seen since the height of the Civil Rights Movement sixty years ago. The slogan 'Black Lives Matter' has entered into public discourse, tens of thousands have taken to the streets in marches, public figures have conspicuously 'taken the knee' and statues of figures historically implicated in slavery and imperialism have been torn down; together, these acts of defiance have galvanized demands for an end to inequalities based on skin colour. And yet the killing of a black man, woman or child by the police is hardly unprecedented; indeed, it was a spate of killings followed by the acquittal of police officers in the States which first inspired the creation in 2012 of Black Lives Matter (BLM) not only as a political slogan but a grass-roots movement committed to a struggle against police brutality and systemic racism (see also Chapter 23). Since then, as further killings occurred, the movement has grown into a global force with branches in Europe, Australasia, South America and the Far East (Lowery, 2017; Lebron, 2019).

The movement raises important historical questions. How does BLM compare with previous struggles for racial justice? Where are the principal sources of its support? How has the movement adapted to the different circumstances encountered across the world? What progress has been made in eradicating racism? Sadly, we have little space to address such issues in any detail but do feel compelled to think briefly about the origins and distinctive nature of the movement and its challenge to the extant capitalist-racial order.

It is tempting to trace the immediate precedents to the Civil Rights Movement of the 1960s, which heralded, it is claimed, the end of Jim Crow segregation laws. Such a record was built on a strategy of peaceful struggle and resistance, which as far as the BLM is concerned was its most powerful legacy. Indeed, BLM has repeatedly stressed that its protests are overwhelmingly peaceful and that any violence which occurred was committed by the police or counter protesters.

Despite the obvious success of BLM in mobilizing what has arguably been the largest movement in the history of the United States, the strategy of civil disobedience has come under critical scrutiny by historians and political scientists. At the heart of this critique is the notion of civil disobedience itself (Delmas, 2018, 2020; Hooker, 2016, 2020). The rhetoric of civil disobedience, it is argued, became attached to – and in vital ways directed – the course of the Civil Rights Movement. It was attractive to activists *and* observers because it laid stress on the qualities of self-discipline, peace, love and respect that motivated the breaking of laws. Here the debt to Mahatma Gandhi's mantra of *satyagraha*, nonviolent resistance against evil, was clear. According to Gandhi, such resistance was 'gentle, truthful, humble, knowing, wilful yet loving, never criminal and hateful', and these sentiments had a genuine appeal to his ardent admirer Martin Luther King who later contrasted his followers' loving disobedience with the segregationists' hateful defiance of the law (Quoted in Delmas, 2020, p. 18). However, the valorization of civil disobedience has led to a serious misreading of American history; through a romantic narrative the Civil Rights Movement, later struggles of black people, and even the election of Barack Obama are viewed teleologically as steps in the inevitable march towards the end of segregation and the achievement of racial justice. This narrative has masked and rendered illegitimate the more radical aspects of the struggles and the differences among activists on the potential of non-violent protest (Hooker, 2016, p. 457).

A second consequence is that, in peaceful protest, black politics becomes that of democratic sacrifice. In no democracy can individuals do exactly what they want; on the contrary, they are occasionally required to sacrifice their own particular desires in the interest of the common good. This democratic sacrifice should be equitably distributed across the whole of society, but in the pursuit of racial justice the burden of sacrifice has been shouldered disproportionately by black people. In other words, the community that has suffered most from systematic repression and killings is at the same time the one that has to disavow any notions of violent retaliation. Under such circumstances where there is no reciprocity, should blacks refuse to make further sacrifices in order to maintain the status of (American) democracy? Should they instead adopt strategies based on 'uncivil disobedience' (a term of Delmas, 2020)? Many would say yes and point to the stark contrast between the romantic narrative and the history of black writers and activists that we have already mentioned in this chapter but who have advocated for radical forms of action. From Fredrick Douglass to James Baldwin and Malcolm X, prominent black leaders and intellectuals have rejected the 'democratic sacrifice', often at great personal cost. Even the politics of Martin Luther King have been called into question. In his later years, it has been argued, the adherence to peaceful protest was gradually displaced by a recognition that, since racism was endemic to capitalist American society, reform was impossible; the only solution was to reconstruct America in its entirety and this required radical action (Fairclough, 1983).

We wish to close by asking briefly if BLM has any relevance to Europe. BLM has given birth to fledgling movements in Europe, expressing solidarity with the struggles against police brutality in the United States and developing their own forms of anti-racist struggle domestically. And for good reason. In Britain, the number of blacks killed at the hands of the police, while not at the same level as in the United States, remains alarmingly high, while the repression of black communities continues, seemingly as a matter of routine policing. We must be cautious, however, not to push such parallels too far, for the historic engagements with 'blackness' on each side of the Atlantic have been very different, and these have created contrasting contexts within which anti-racist struggles have operated (De Genova, 2018). At the risk of oversimplification, in America racial formations had their origins and were fostered by the enslavement and settlement of Africans and their descendants in the New World, while in Britain, to take one example, 'blackness' was born out of colonialism and reworked in postcolonialism. Britain had no plantations, rather as a colonial power it encountered a heterogeneous population of 'natives' who were constructed as black or non-white. In the postwar period, immigrants from the various corners of the empire were subjected to similar categorizations, as a result of which the idea of blackness became generalized. For many, such racial constructs were entirely novel as people from India, the Caribbean and other former colonies discovered that they were black. The question inevitably follows: when thinking of BLM in Britain, precisely whose lives are we talking of? The answer to this question is likely to define the course and relevance of BLM's struggles in the years to come.

Postscript

One constant thread of this chapter might be the idea that America has always possessed more space than history. The sheer vastness of the land, its merciless weather changes, its time zones that separate forest from desert, small town life and the wonders of its great cities may have dictated American exceptionalism – from sea to shining sea. The historian James Patterson once said that 'history-writing about twentieth-century America . . . is less a field than a thicket', while Joyce Appleby also insisted that we are 'snowed under by an avalanche of information, much of it inassimilable into a coherent national narrative'.

How could it have been otherwise? American historiography has migrated from the nurturing of an academy, independent from yet influenced by the European continent that was left behind because of its ancient rivalries, to the emphasis placed by the progressive historians on economic interests at the founding moment of the Constitution, to the postwar consensus histories that wanted to stress the liberal traditions of America just as it was going head to head with another superpower. Naturally then, there has been a through-going search for synthesis as black history is brought to the fore, or global histories are given their head or the regions given their due. Not that these fragments have in the past been considered without opposition or dissidence. Lynne Cheney (the wife of a Republican vice president but also very much a qualified professional in her own right) wrote to the *Wall Street Journal* in October 1994 to complain that politically correct history had crowded out the full majesty and historical importance of the constitution itself as it was taught in the schools of America. This is as may be. Now the emergence of Black Lives Matters as an American and global movement in recent years has truly foregrounded black history and rendered consciousness of it all but universal. It was the historian Thomas Bender who wrote in 2002, in the wake of 9/11, that 'The field of American history is at a formative (or reformative) moment . . . the quest for new understandings that has undermined established narratives has now, perhaps, prompted new efforts at crystallizing a very unstable body of historical writing'. He added the question, and this will serve as our conclusion, 'Might democracy be the word, the concept, the commitment that will move U.S. in that direction?' (Bender, 2002, p. 133).

Further Reading

Peter Burke (1985) *Vico*.
David Brion Davis (1984) *Slavery and Human Progress*.
Robert Fogel and Stanley Engerman (1974) *Time on the Cross: The Economics of Negro Slavery*.
Eric Foner (1984) 'Why is There no Socialism in the United States?'
Richard Hofstadter (2012) [1968] *The Progressive Historians*.
Wesley Lowery (2017) *The Can't Kill Us All. The Story of Black Lives Matter*.
Peter Novick (1988) 'That Noble Dream', in *The 'Objectivity Question' and the American Historical Profession*.

6 Histories of Revolutions; Revolutionary Histories

Introduction

This chapter explores through the eyes of protagonists the revolutionary impulses that convulsed the Western world in the latter stages of the eighteenth century and their legacy for political activists aspiring to world revolution in the ensuing decades. The American Revolution of 1776, the French Revolution of 1789 and the resurgence of popular radicalism in Britain during the 1790s together point to a massive shift in the world order, the reverberations from which affected every corner of the globe and continue to this day. Signs of change had been apparent for decades to those who cared to look for them. Calls for freedom from the constraints of the ancien régime which found voice in the writings of leading French *philosophes* reached a crescendo in the 1760s. Simultaneously in London, the charismatic John Wilkes orchestrated popular resentment against the monarchy and an aristocratic parliament to press for radical reform. From 1760–1775, pamphlets and newspapers helped foster a radical culture in the American states, which led ultimately to the War of Independence. Widespread protests in the major cities against the imposition of the 1765 Stamp Act forced its repeal in the following year. This about turn may have pre-empted open rebellion against British rule, but the protest had helped to define grievances and in many respects acted as a blueprint for the revolutionary struggles of the next decade.

There were shared ideals which shaped the revolutions, many inherited from Enlightenment thought and recognized by protagonists as having the power to change the world order. Overall, they are perhaps captured best in the slogan 'Liberté, egalité, fraternité', although how they played out differed from one context to another – in America, for example, such ideals did not apply to the large population of slaves. At the core of these ideals were the notions of liberty and equality. Liberty meant self-determination, that is, the right for the citizenry to overthrow oppressive, corrupt and arbitrary forms of rule and so determine and realize its collective will. Equality was based on the idea that all men and women were naturally equal and that this equality entitled us to certain rights which needed to be protected by the law. Enshrined in America's Declaration of Independence (1776) and France's Declaration of the Rights of Man and of the Citizen (1789), these ideals were considered 'self-evident' truths. The Declaration famously advanced the notion, for example, that 'all Men are created equal, that they are endowed by their Creator with certain inalienable Rights, that among these are Life, Liberty, and the pursuit of Happiness'. France's Declaration, which consciously drew upon that of America, declared 'All men are equal by nature and before the law' and set forth a programme of individual and collective rights protected when threatened by any government that seeks to violate them.

How did historians respond to these momentous events? Were they enthusiastically welcomed as harbingers of a more just new world or feared because they overthrew centuries of

6.1 Thomas Paine and the Radical Tradition

His seeming indolence exasperated friends. Routinely, he arose late, had a leisurely breakfast, and took a stroll when he composed a few sentences which were written down on his return. A large lunch was followed by a nap of two or three hours, another walk, a light supper and long conversations in the evening before retiring to bed. And yet in writing *Common Sense*, *The Age of Reason* and *The Rights of Man*, Thomas Paine secured a place in history as one of the most brilliant pamphleteers whose writings shaped the course of the American and French revolutions.

The origins and nature of radicalism are difficult to trace. It emerged as an influential political culture in the last decades of the eighteenth century after a prolonged period of relative calm. Some historians have traced its antecedents to the extraordinary flowering of radical thought during the turmoil of the English Civil War. The Ranters, Levellers, Diggers and other radical movements may have been suppressed during and in the immediate aftermath of the conflict, but their demands for freedom, justice and suffrage were kept alive by the motley ships' crews – which in traversing the Atlantic had laid the foundations for the modern global economy – and by the migrants who sought a new life along the eastern foreshore of North America (Linebaugh and Rediker, 2000). The result was that New England, in particular, (appropriately called!) grew as a significant centre of customs and rituals inherited directly from the carnivalesque plebeian culture of early modern England. From this culture sprang more radical impulses which took strong hold in cities such as Boston and Philadelphia with large populations of artisans, projecting them to the vanguard of the struggle for independence. Here the activists found inspiration in the works of John Milton, John Locke, Algernon Sidney and other leading figures of the English Civil War who had given such voice to the demands for liberty and justice (see Bailyn, 1992, and the essays in Jacob and Jacob, 1991).

Thus, when this political culture resurfaced it was in the context of the Enlightenment and the revolutionary upheavals of America and France. Its prophet was Thomas Paine whose writings at the time attracted unprecedented levels of popular readerships. Born near Norfolk, England, in 1737, Paine had little formal education and various unappealing jobs before sailing to North America at the age of thirty-seven. In Pennsylvania, he found refuge in radical publishing and began to make a name for himself as the editor and principal writer of the *Pennsylvania Magazine*. Like so many radicals at the time, Paine chose the newspaper and the pamphlet to air his political grievances. His first pamphlet, *Common Sense*, published in 1776 at the height of agitation against British rule, was a clarion call for independence from the iniquities of British monarchy and aristocratic rule. 'The cause of America', Paine declared, 'is in great measure the cause of all mankind'. However, his arguments lacked originality and sophistication; they had none of the rigour, say, of those employed by Adam Smith in *Wealth of Nations*, which was published in the same year. What his writing lacked in originality and coherence was made up for in style and courage. The pamphlet came to be the most widely read of the revolution, helping to shape its popular political ideals. After the revolution, Paine's reputation was secure, and for a while he took on important secretarial responsibilities, but he did not stay to help build the foundations for the new nation. Rather, he returned to England in 1787 and occasionally visited Paris where he made contact with radical circles. Incensed by the publication of Edmund Burke's *Reflections on the Revolution in France* (1790), Paine responded with *Rights of Man*, which vigorously defended the rights of each generation to struggle against tyranny and govern its own affairs.

Figure 6.1 A portrait engraving circa 1794 by Laurent Dubos of author, intellectual, revolutionary and US Founding Father Thomas Paine (1737–1809), who in a series of pamphlets did as much as anybody to promote the ideals of the American and French Revolutions

Contributor: Archive Images/Alamy Stock Photo

Worried by the influence that Paine now exerted on radical opinion, the British government drove him into exile in 1792. This had no immediate effect since at the time Paine was serving as an elected albeit critical member of the new National Convention for Calais, but it did tend to hasten his isolation. Anticipating imprisonment and even execution, he turned his attention to religion and in 1793 published *Age of Reason*, a damning attack not on religion as such (he professed a belief in God until the end) but on the ways in which a corrupt and venal church organized Christianity. Paine merely stated openly what much dissenting opinion had argued behind closed doors since the seventeenth century, but the pamphlet was almost immediately banned by the British state as seditious libel. Typical is the following passage:

It is curious to observe how the theory of what is called the Christian church sprung out of the tail of heathen mythology. A direct incorporation took place in the first instance, by making the reputed founder to be celestially begotten. The trinity of Gods that then followed was no other than a reduction of the former plurality, which was about twenty or thirty thousand. The statute of Mary succeeded the statue of Diana of Ephesus. The deification of heroes changed into the canonization of saints. The mythologists had gods for everything; the Christian mythologists had saints for everything. The church became as crowded with the one, as the pantheon had been with the other; and Rome was the place of both. The Christian theory is little else than the idolatry of the ancient mythologists, accommodated to the purposes of power and revenue; and it yet remains to reason and philosophy to abolish the amphibious fraud.

(Paine, 1794, p. 7)

He survived illness and impending execution and continued to compose less well-known pamphlets, but Paine's vulnerability prompted a return to the United States in 1803 where he eventually died in poverty and relative obscurity. Because the links between Paine and the debates about democracy voiced by seventeenth-century radicals are somewhat tenuous, he cannot easily be located within transatlantic radicalism of the late eighteenth century. We, however, are rather more interested in the question: 'How did Paine employ history to put across his message?' The answer is that he didn't. Paine was above all a political propagandist who sought to identify principles that had a universal application, and so rather than attempting to reveal in detail the nature of particular historical moments, he uses history at the broadest levels of generalization with little regard for the sources of evidence. Take, for example, his discussion in *Common Sense* on the origins of inequality, which was not merely crude and ill-informed but displayed more than a hint of antisemitism. According to the authority of the scriptures, he claimed, there were no distinctions in the earliest societies between kings and subjects. Government was a form of republic administered by tribal elders. The 'quiet and rural lives' of these peoples, however, vanished with the emergence of Jewish royalty. The hankering of the Jews for the 'idolatrous customs of the Heathens', he proceeds, promoted demands for kingly authority, which, although initially renounced by Gideon and Samuel, eventually took hold. Thus, the evil of monarchy and hereditary succession came into being, and by exerting a degrading influence on human affairs has since acted as 'an imposition on posterity'.

To be fair, Paine's evasion of history was part of a wider hiatus. It is often said that historians are attracted to the excitement of revolutions, but paradoxically in this supreme age of revolutionary turmoil no historical work of significance was created. We have already noted that *Common Sense* and *Wealth of Nations* were published in 1776, but this annus mirabilis witnessed another milestone when the first edition of Edward Gibbon's *Decline and Fall of the Roman Empire* first appeared. It was the last work of such stature in Britain until Frederick Engel's *The Condition of the English Working Class in England* (1844) and Thomas Macaulay's *History of England* (1848). A large part of the reason for this is that history as a discipline had yet to emerge, and there were simply no writers at the time of revolutionary turmoil who possessed the historical imagination and skills necessary to record and interpret the events as they unfolded. For evidence of changing outlooks over this period, therefore, we have instead to look to the extraordinary flowering of political commentary, poetry and fiction that grew in the 1790s. Often writing under the watchful eye of the censor and real threats of imprisonment – even death – for publishing what were considered seditious texts, William Godwin, William Blake, Mary Wollstonecraft, Anna Barbauld and others were able to sustain a political culture which in its support for revolution displayed contempt for traditional forms of authority.

Nonetheless, political suppression during the 1790s did make an impact, for elements of popular radicalism were forced underground, most notably in London where a small but influential world of irreverent publishing sprang to life. Here a multitude of tiny printers defied the threat of prosecution to publish cheap versions of radical texts including *Rights of Man*, Comte de Volney's *Ruins of Empires*, the American Joel Barlow's *Advice to the Privileged Orders*, and William Godwin's *Political Justice* (McCalman, 1988, p. 24), in addition to the writings of contemporary radicals such as Robert Wedderburn, Thomas Davison and William Benbow. Here also a brilliant tradition of graphic satire was sustained, particularly by the outstanding figures of James Gillray and George Cruickshank and a scurrilous, at times obscene, Grub Street press. Equally importantly, this underground counterculture shared personnel and ideas with the radical communities of America, Ireland and France, and although entering terminal decline from the late 1820s, it successfully laid the foundation for the great urban literature of Victorian Britain (see Section 19.4). Vital also was the growing influence during the 1820s of Romanticism. Driven by the more historically informed works of journalism, drama and fiction, most notably the writings of William Wordsworth, William Hazlitt, Percy Shelley and Sir Walter Scott, this movement sought to capture what was known as the 'spirit of the age' and the unmitigated belief in progress that it represented (Chandler, 1999).

Figure 6.2 Mary Wollstonecraft, *c.*1797. Artist: John Opie.

A prominent member of the radical culture of late eighteenth-century England before her premature death in childbirth, Mary Wollstonecraft is probably best remembered for her struggle for the rights of women.

Contributor: Heritage Image Partnership Ltd/Alamy Stock Photo

Despite – or because of – this, Paine lived on. He did not call for the revolutionary overthrow of the state, deny private property of the rich or condemn the doctrine of laissez faire, but the tradition of secular, radical egalitarianism he did so much to promote had considerable appeal for the ascendant popular urban culture of the nineteenth century. A contempt for the principles of monarchy, aristocracy and hereditary distinctions, a faith in representative government and an undimmed optimism in the power of reason remained at the core of Chartist and later socialist demands for universal suffrage to guarantee a government which would truly serve the needs of the population as a whole.

6.2 Contemporary Responses to the American and French Revolutions

Because of his proximity to the revolutionary events in North America and France, Paine might justifiably claim to be a legitimate expression of the aspirations of their participants. There were others, however, who were prepared to weigh into the debates, and in this section we wish to consider briefly what they brought to the table.

America may not yet have had historians to comment on the significance of 1776, but there were lawyers, writers and ministers, many of whom had been directly involved in the events, who were intent on justifying the revolution as a legitimate, even necessary act of self-determination. The first histories to appear celebrated the contributions of individual states. Thus, Jeremy Belknap's *History of New Hampshire* (1784–1792), David Ramsay's *History of the Revolution of South Carolina* (1785), John Burk's *History of Virginia* (1804–1816) and Hugh Williamson's *History of North Carolina* (1812) recount the relatively brief histories of their states from the time of the first settlements to the close of the eighteenth century, seeing in miniature a history of the nation as a whole (Cheng, 2008, p. 15). Mercy Warren's *History, Rise, Progress, and Termination of the American Revolution* (1805) was exceptional in taking a national perspective, but her task was no different. Like the authors of the Declaration and of regional studies, Warren sought 'to justify the *principles* of the defection and final separation from the parent state'. In so doing she revealed that the broad body of this work had a moral purpose to educate by providing examples of virtue and collective national identity. With the deaths of John Adams and Thomas Jefferson in 1826, signalling to many the passing of the revolutionary generation, the desire to remember the founding of the republic and celebrate its achievements intensified. Disproportionately represented by the intellectual elite of New England, historians in a recognizably modern sense began to move beyond sectional loyalties to take a more measured perspective on the revolution and its aftermath. Influenced by developments in European historiography, in particular the works of Thomas Macaulay and Henry Hallam, American historians also began to display a more rigorous approach to evidence and problems of interpretation.

George Bancroft's *History of the United States, from the Discovery of the American Continent*, written and constantly revised over 1834 to 1874, was a milestone. After graduating from Harvard, Bancroft studied in Germany and while there became acquainted with Goethe, von Humboldt and Hegel. He had a career as a statesman but in later life devoted much energy to historical research. So much we have seen in Chapter 5. His immersion in European culture had helped to provide him not only with the skills of an historian but a moral vision and a belief in progress that underpinned his entire historical project. Bancroft had his critics, however, notably among a small but growing band of professional historians of note. Jared Sparks and William Prescott belittled Bancroft's history, describing it as sketchy and episodic. They spoke with some authority and in the long term had a rather greater influence on the course of American historiography. Sparks was President of Harvard and author of *Life and Writings of George*

Washington (1834–1837); he knew Paris and London well and corresponded regularly with leading European historians, while Prescott, author of classic studies on the Spanish empire and Mesoamerica, was generally regarded as America's first scientific historian and one of its greatest intellectuals.

In late eighteenth-century Britain and France, the protracted historical silence on the revolution stood in sharp contrast to the flood of political commentary. As we have seen, Paine's *Rights of Man* attracted a huge readership on both sides of the channel, but it is instructive to remember that the pamphlet was a direct response to other significant interventions. Toward the end of his life in 1790 Dr Richard Price, a dissenting minister, prominent mathematician and a leading figure in London's radical circles, published a sermon. In *A Discourse on the Love of Our Country*, Price celebrated the achievements of the Glorious Revolution of 1688 not only in overthrowing arbitrary rule but in acting as a catalyst for two other 'glorious' revolutions. The 'ardour for liberty' fostered by the American and French revolutions has displaced the 'dominion of kings' by the 'dominion of laws', the 'dominion of priests' and by the 'dominion of reason and conscience'. |In so doing, it kindled a blaze that lays 'despotism in ashes, and warms and illuminates *Europe*!' (Price, 1789, p. 50; emphasis in the original).

For the statesman and lawyer Edmund Burke, fearful that the fate of the French would soon befall all of Europe, Price provided the catalyst that culminated in his writing *Reflections on the Revolution in France* (1790), a work which secured Burke's reputation as a founder of modern conservatism (Chapter 4). Burke dismissed Price's interpretation of 1688 and denied any parallels with the French Revolution. For him, the revolution may have been driven by an ideology of natural rights, but such rights could never form the basis of a stable society. Radical, secular reform based on notions of rights and reason disassociated from experience is inherently destabilizing for the 'swinish multitude' and is too susceptible to such projects; stability is predicated only on an experience of continuity provided by custom and tradition – what he termed, the 'partnership . . . between those who are living, those who are dead, and those who are about to be born'. The operation of law, for example, is best served by the slow organic development over time characteristic of English common law and not by radical and abrupt change based on arbitrary, metaphysical speculations about rights. Furthermore, tradition and reform are not mutually exclusive:

> It is far from impossible to reconcile, if we do not suffer ourselves to be entangled in the mazes of metaphysic sophistry, the use both of a fixed rule and an occasional deviation; the sacredness of an hereditary principle of succession in our government, with a power of change in its application in cases of extreme emergency. Even in that extremity . . . the change is to be confined to . . . the part which produced the necessary deviation; and even then it is to be effected without decomposition of the whole civil and political mass, for the purpose of originating a new civil order out of the first elements of society.
>
> (Burke, 2003, p. 19)

History must then replace idle theory, and with that in mind Burke provides a brief narrative of how English liberties came into being as a result of changes in the constitution that were set in motion by Henry I and have since followed a particular logic – even an inevitability – right up to the Glorious Revolution of 1688. 'You will observe', he concludes,

> that from the Magna Charta, to the Declaration of Right, it has been the uniform policy of our constitution to claim and assert our liberties, as an *entailed inheritance* derived to us from our forefathers, and to be transmitted to our posterity; as an estate especially belonging to the

people of this kingdom without any reference whatever to any other more general or prior right. By this means our constitution preserves an unity in so great a diversity of its parts. We have an inheritable crown; an inheritable peerage; and an house of commons and a people inheriting privileges, franchises and liberties, from a long line of ancestors.

(Ibid, p. 29)

Like Paine, Burke was a political theorist and commentator; his exhortations to the study of history were never realized. His history was at the level of generalization, often ill-informed and organized by narratives designed principally to bolster political lessons he wished to convey. He choice of evidence from the historical record was highly selective, and he was indifferent to the changing modes of historical inquiry (Ankersmit, 2001a). If he did have a legacy for historiography, it was in his ability to ask whether revolution was an aberration or simply a stage in the development of human society.

The degeneration of the revolution into a reign of terror seemed for many to realize Burke's worst fears, but other writers sprang to the defence of the French. In addition to the articles in journals like the *Annual Register* and *Gentleman's Magazine*, which were keen to publish opinion, more substantial studies started to appear. Mary Wollstonecraft's *A Vindication of the Rights of Men* (1790) – a riposte to Burke – was soon followed by *Vindication of the Rights of Woman* (1792) and *Historical and Moral View of the French Revolution* (1794). The prolific Arthur Young, who had already secured a reputation as the leading commentator on agricultural improvement, published *Travels in France* (1792) and *An Idea of the Present State of France* (1794), which, while revealing the pitiful state of the French peasantry and decrying what he saw as mob rule, remained broadly sympathetic to the ideals of the revolution.

Arguably, the first real history of the revolution in English was John Adolphus' *History of France from 1790 till the Peace of 1802* (1803), which combined a scrupulous regard for the oft conflicting evidence – much of which was in French – and motives of the various participants in the struggle. In showing that the revolution was worthy as an object of historical study in its own right and not merely a terrain of political debate, he pioneered approaches that continue to this day (Ben-Israel, 1968, pp. 21–3). The history of the revolution reached maturity, however, with the publication in 1837 of Thomas Carlyle's classic *The French Revolution: A History*. The book established Carlyle's fame, is still in print and has been a seemingly endless source of debate among historians quarrelling over its putative merits. Influenced principally by Romanticism and the foremost German theorists including Goethe, Herder and von Ranke, Carlyle was compelled by a desire to describe events in ways which were accessible and appealing to the reading public (see Chapter 4). This led to an intricate attention to detail expressed in an ornate literary style at the expense of a mature reflection on the underlying historical dynamics. Take, for example, the following passage recounting the events leading to the assassination in 1793 of the radical republican Jean-Paul Marat by Charlotte Corday, a twenty-four-year-old woman from an impoverished royalist family (an event immortalized by the famous Jacques-Louis David painting):

About eight on the Saturday morning, she purchases a large sheath-knife in the Palais Royal; then straightway, in the Place des Victoires takes a hackney-coach: 'To the Rue de l'Ecole de Medicine, No. 44.' It is the residence of the Citoyen Marat! – The Citoyen Marat is ill, and cannot be seen; which seems to disappoint her much. Her business is with Marat, then? Hapless beautiful Charlotte; hapless squalid Marat.

(Carlyle, 2010, p. 153)

Corday reaches the apartment but Marat, sick and worn, refuses her admittance. But she was determined, and he eventually relents and opens his door:

> Citoyen Marat, I am from Caen the seat of the rebellion, and wish to speak with you. – Be seated, mon enfant. Now what are the Traitors doing at Caen? What Deputies are at Caen? – Charlotte names some Deputies. 'Their heads shall fall within a fortnight', croaks the eager People's-Friend, clutching his tablets to write: Barbaroux, Petion, writes he with bare shrunk arm, turning aside in the bath: Petion, and Louvet, and – Charlotte has drawn her knife from the sheath; plunges it in, with one sure stroke, into the writer's heart. 'A moi, chere amie, Help, dear!' No more could the Death-choked say or shriek. The helpful Washerwoman running in, there is no Friend of the People, or Friend of the Washerwoman, left; but his life with a groan gushes out, indignant, to the shades below.
>
> (Ibid, pp. 154–5)

In his endeavour to get as close as possible to the turmoil of the revolution, convey a vivid sense of what it was like to be there and present the evidence minutely and accurately, Carlyle rightly claimed impartiality; indeed, few have accused him of inventing facts. Nonetheless, the obvious literariness of his writing and his lack of a broader perspective have provoked many questions about his stature as an historian. If he has survived intact, it is perhaps because successors have recognized how difficult it must have been – even in the 1830s – to describe an unprecedented event of such world importance – and, of course, because of the excitement that he is able to transmit through his prose.

It would be remiss of us to finish this section without a brief mention of how the French perceived their own revolution. As in America and Britain, the large bulk of contemporary writing was in effect political commentary rather than history, but this amnesia was broader, for France produced no novels like Dickens' *Tale of Two Cities* or plays like Georg Büchner's *Danton's Death*. It seems that the revolution created a void in French literature, perhaps because the event was still too febrile and too close (Orr, 1990, p. 17). Eventually, however, three historians of note attempted to fill the gap in the remarkable year of 1847: Louis Blanc's *Histoire de la Révolution Français*, Jules Michelet's *Histoire de la Révolution Français* and Alphonse de Lamartine's *Histoire des Girondins*, followed within a decade by Alexis de Tocqueville's *L'Ancien Régime et la Révolution*. Together, these works facilitated a new phase in the study of the revolution. In part, this was because previously unexplored archives were now available, but more importantly, by standing back from the events, historians were able to take longer-term perspectives. Blanc saw the revolution as the natural development of European thought, fuelling anxieties in England that a similar course of events could be witnessed there. Tocqueville also pointed to continuities by stressing that tensions created by changes to the social structure, origins of economic and political grievances and moves towards centralization were already manifest in pre-revolutionary France. When combined, these tendencies precipitated the revolution and were subsequently resolved, albeit imperfectly. In this respect, the revolution did not signal a new history of France but was the flowering of the past (Furet, 1998, p. 81). Furthermore, Tocqueville directed more attention to the specific and exceptional conditions of France and unlike his contemporaries was prepared to condemn aspects of the French character that were responsible for excesses of the revolution, rather than as a natural and inevitable unfolding of processes which had been set in motion.

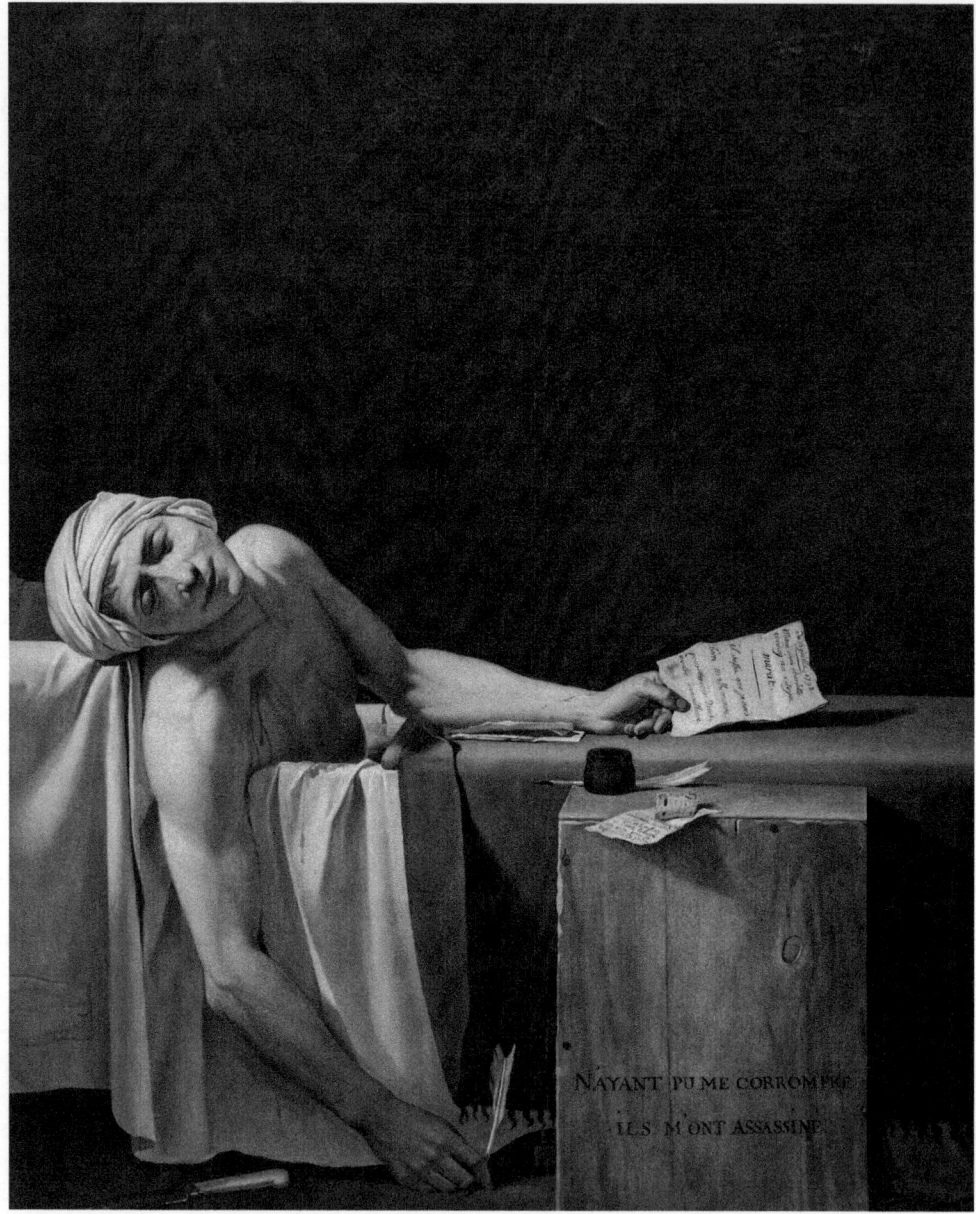

Figure 6.3 Jacque-Louis David's *The Death of Marat* (1793) captures something of the drama evident also in the account of Thomas Carlyle

Contributor: ACTIVE MUSEUM/ACTIVE ART/Alamy Stock Photo

6.3 Germany, G. W. F. Hegel and the Spirit of History

Reverberations from the French Revolution had an immediate and direct impact on Germany (Blanning and Wende, 1999). In 1791, the revolutionary armies began a series of invasions of the numerous, loosely allied states which then made up the region now known as Germany, culminating in a period from 1806–1814 when Napoleon effectively ruled. The intellectual legacy of the revolution was ambiguous, for while suspicion greeted the ideas of a conquering nation, the attendant reform, which was secular and anti-nationalist, had popular appeal. Georg Wilhelm Friedrich Hegel was twenty-one when the invasions began. He lived in Jena, and in 1799 was appointed to the university, which at the time was at the heart of German Romanticism and idealism. Among its intellectual community numbered leading figures including not only Hegel but Friedrich Schiller, Johann Fichte and August Schlegel. Despite active resistance from its students, Jena was conquered in 1806, the university shut down. Displaced, Hegel found a job as a headmaster and began to write works on philosophy, on the back of which he was offered the chair in philosophy, first at Heidelberg and then at Berlin where he remained until his death in 1831.

Hegel's approach to the philosophy of history was first outlined in the *Phenomenology of Spirit* (1807) and followed up with *Philosophy of History*, published posthumously in 1837. These books and the work of Hegel more generally had an enormous influence on nineteenth-century writings, including those of the young Karl Marx. Although they contained a great deal of hard historical information on ancient civilizations and the path of European history from the feudal era to the French Revolution, this is used only as raw material to develop a theory of historical development. His argument was that the essence – or spirit – of human existence is freedom and that the progress of history across civilizations is the realization of that freedom. Thus, history is one in which peoples and constitutions actualize their national 'spirit' and so is the sum of a people, their consciousness or 'mind' and the national cultures that inform this process. Accordingly, history unfolds according to predetermined laws, the end of which is signalled by the realization of that idea or spirit in the institutions of the state – a perfect manifestation of the human will for freedom.

Famously, Hegel's methodology was dialectical, according to which a thesis is challenged by an antithesis, leading to resolution in a synthesis. He saw world history as one great dialectical movement. Take, for example, his interpretation of the ancient Greek world. This was a harmonious society with no active opposition (thesis). At some stage, this customary morality was challenged by philosophers led by Socrates who asserted the importance of independent thought (antithesis), a movement which dismantled the Greek state, subsequently gaining momentum until during the Reformation the supreme right of individual thought was secured. No stable society can be based on individual conscience, however, and so it was finally with nineteenth-century German society that an organic community, rationally organized to preserve individual freedom (synthesis), was attained.

These are complicated ideas but vital to grasp if we are fully to understand the contribution of Hegel to the writing of history and the influence of Hegel on Marx and other post-Enlightenment thinkers. To summarize Hegel's model of historical change:

- History evolves an awareness of and then actualization of the spirit of freedom.
- Each stage of history has a 'world spirit' that is expressed peculiarly in each nation state.
- This spirit has a consciousness that is expressed in the culture of the nation.
- Historical events follow this national consciousness and progress towards the 'absolute idea' or an end state.
- Change occurs in a dialectic with a clash of ideas or consciousness that moves history through stages towards this end state.

The legacy of Hegel was considerable. Most historians today are in his debt. And yet the legacy was diverse and contradictory. One of the most important developments was the founding of history as a practical discipline which had its genesis in a rejection of the philosophical idealism of Hegel. Here the name of Leopold von Ranke (1795–1886) featured prominently. Von Ranke (von after his ennoblement in 1865 by Wilhelm I) was known as the 'father of objectivity' and is well known in our own time for his pursuit of history as a science and for his use of primary sources in his teaching (Chapter 21). This teaching, which stretched across the nineteenth century, was marked by the use of sources and was ultimately a dismissal of Hegel's purely 'philosophical school'. Although Ranke had an abiding interest in a world history determined by abstract principles, he forged the 'historical school' and took Hegelian thought away from philosophy, turning it into 'real' history, that is, a history concerned with 'localized memory' and 'human language and culture' that was 'particular and changing'. With this came a distinctly 'scientific' approach to evidence as part of an historical methodology which most historians would recognize today as valid:

> But from what sources can such a new investigation be made? The basis of the present work, the sources of its material, are memoirs, diaries, letters, ambassadors' reports, and original accounts of eyewitnesses. Other writings were used only if they were immediately derived from such as these, or seemed to be equal to them in some original information. These sources will be noted on every page; the method of investigation and the critical conclusions will be presented in a second volume, to be published concurrently.
>
> Aim and subject shape the form of a book. We cannot expect from the writing of history the same free development as is, at least in theory, to be expected in works of literature; I am not certain that it was right to ascribe this quality to the work of the Greek and Roman masters. A strict presentation of the facts, contingent and unattractive though they may be, is the highest law. A second, for me, is the development of the unity and the progress of the events. Therefore, instead of starting, as might be expected, with a general account of the political situation of Europe, which would have confused if not distracted our attention, I have preferred to discuss in detail each people, each power, and each individual only at the time when each played an importantly active or leading role. I have not been disturbed by the fact that here and there they have had to be mentioned earlier where their existence could not be ignored. But thereby we are better able to grasp the general line of their development, the paths which they followed, and the ideas by which they were motivated.
>
> (von Ranke, 1981, pp. 56–9)

Von Ranke saw history as part of a divine plan in which the state (and like Hegel he meant the Prussian state) was (again like Hegel) unique with a unique history. As we can see from this extract, von Ranke was determined to treat past societies on their own terms. These principles were reflected in his histories of the rivalries of great powers, from the ancient civilizations to the Ottomans.

What has survived of Hegel's influence? Francis Fukuyama achieved a certain notoriety in 1992 with the publication of *The End of History and the Last Man*. Drawing heavily on Hegel, the book argued that with the end of the Cold War and the dismantling of the Berlin Wall, Western liberal democracy emerged triumphant. Taking Hegel's idealization of German society a step further, Fukuyama argued that we had reached the 'final form of human government', and there was nowhere else to go. Predictably, the argument was hotly contested, and we will hear little of it now. It may well be, then, that the work of Karl Marx is the most obvious legacy, and so we turn to the notion of historical materialism that was at the heart of his theory of history.

6.4 Karl Marx and 'Historical Materialism'

Karl Marx was born in Trier, Germany in 1818. He attended the university at Berlin six years after the death of Hegel and initially studied law but then developed an interest in philosophy. Here he was attracted to the writings of Hegel and joined a group of radical intellectuals calling themselves the Young Hegelians. Marx used Hegel's notion of the dialectic but replaced the notion of a 'spirit' running through history with material class relations. This reworked dialectic, therefore, described a clash of classes – bourgeois and proletarian – born out of material relations or the forces of production of capitalism, which then, by overthrowing capitalism produces another kind of society, namely, socialism.

Where Hegel in the *Philosophy of Right* (1820) said that 'the owl of Minerva spreads its wings only with the falling of the dusk'; that is, philosophy only understands history and historical epochs when they are about to pass on, Marx suggested that history (or at least epochs) could be anticipated, hence the well-worn phrase contained in his *Thesis on Feuerbach* in 1845: 'philosophers have only understood the world, the point is to change it'. Finally, Hegel's theory of history, outlined most comprehensively in his lectures on the *Philosophy of History* given between 1822 and 1830, concentrated on the political – on constitutions and states that possess national principles. Marx, in contrast, is concerned with economics and the dynamics of capitalist organization. Without Hegel, there would have been no Marx or the theoretical framework for understanding historical change that has been one of the most important influences on history and historiography in the last century or so.

Whether as a correspondent for the *New York Daily Tribune* or scribbler for one of the many penny pamphlets that mushroomed on the left of Continental politics in his lifetime, Marx was forever reading the runes of what he believed to be the immediate and inevitable collapse of capitalism. So too his erstwhile companion, Frederick Engels, the Manchester-based industrialist who maintained his friend financially and even took up patrimony of a child that belonged to Marx. Engels may have been fonder of the finer things of life – champagne, lobster and even foxhunting – but he shared with Marx a fundamentalist belief in the dialectic as the scientific means of understanding history. Yet neither Marx nor Engels was a historian and little of what Marx wrote can be considered 'real' history. His writings contained no sweeping accounts of historical episodes or movements of the kind we normally think of as history, although his subject is sometimes the role of the individual in the past and the weight of the past on the actions of the living, such as his *Eighteenth Brumaire* published in 1852. In this guise, he tended to use history – often brilliantly – as a means of making sense of current affairs such as the Indian mutiny, the rule of Louis Bonaparte in mid-nineteenth-century France or indeed capitalism as a mode of production.

There is enough here, however, to help us understand something of his approach to history, and we might well begin this venture with one of the most famous passages in his writings. Published in 1859 as a *Preface to a Contribution to the Critique of Political Economy*, it sketched his ideas on how society is constituted and undergoes transformation. Pitched at a high level of abstraction, the extract has given rise to some very heated discussions on what Marx really meant and has unsurprisingly been used by many unsympathetic to historical materialism to launch attacks on its foundations. We have neither the will nor the space to enter into this debate, but it is necessary to draw out some of the salient points from the passage as a means of illustrating how Marx and his followers thought about historical change. Let us therefore consider the following: *Humans in societies enter into relations of production which are independent of their will. The forces and relations of production constitute the economic base upon which the superstructure is erected.* Societies are structured by their relations of production, which therefore largely determine how people behave. Capitalist society, for example, is defined by the fundamental antagonisms between those who own and control the means of production (employers, capitalists, managers – or, in a word, the bourgeoisie) and those who are forced to sell their labour in order to survive (factory workers, plumbers, needlewomen – or, in a word, the proletariat). Such a conflict has nothing to do with how these people think; rather it is the relations of production that determine how people see themselves (as a class consciousness that is for themselves or of themselves, to use an old Marxist adage) and their position in society. This emphasis on the material conditions of life goes to the heart of Marx's methodology. We must start, he argued, with material production and from there reveal how society in its various stages is created by and connected with the mode of production.

This quite deliberate challenge to how Hegel saw the relationship between how people think and live created many problems for Marx and his followers, as we might have anticipated. It is perhaps well to confront notions which gave priority to thoughts or ideas, critics have argued, but to replace them with theories that see productive relations as all-powerful simply substitutes one determining factor with another. In response Marx later claimed that he never meant to suggest that the economic base determined the form of the ideological superstructure, that is, the forms of religion, philosophy and culture in society are mere pale reflections of the economy. Rather, all he suggested was that the way in which people organize themselves to produce in order to survive conditions how they think; for example, people in capitalist societies have very different ways of thinking than those who lived in feudal times. It was a spirited defence, but to this day, Marxist approaches to history have never been able to shrug off the charge of determinism.

Historical change is driven by the contradictions between forces and relations of production. The mode of production comprises the forces, that is, productive power, machinery, skills, technology and use of labour and the social relations within which production is organized. The relations of production therefore support and are broadly consistent with material production, but at definite stages tensions appear between them which threaten to destabilize the mode of production itself. At a particular moment in the past, feudal relations of production, for example, could no longer contain a productive and potentially fast-developing economy within the structure of feudal society; feudal lords were too concerned to retain the status quo, thereby restricting innovation. Eventually, the feudal order was overthrown, releasing production from its fetters and paving the way for industrial capitalism. In turn, Marx argued, the productive power of capitalism would be held back by the repressive class system until irreconcilable antagonisms, say, between the bourgeoisie and proletariat, brought down the capitalist mode of production and a new mode of production within a classless society – socialism – would be introduced, realizing the full potential of society's productive capacity.

This schema of historical change has to be understood in a wider context. As with many thinkers of the Enlightenment (Chapter 3), Marx believed that there was a certain inexorable logic to change, that if we looked closely at the historical record, we can see that from the earliest forms of human society, change has been progressive and unilinear, that is, history runs in a straight line – forward. He identified the following stages, which marked the trajectory of human progress:

1 *Primitive communism*, in which individuals carried out all types of work. There was no specialization and no division of labour; humans were in touch with their true nature. With specialization, for example, the emergence of a labouring population and the creation of a surplus primitive communism was superseded by slave society.

2   *Slave society*, in which divisions opened between those who had property and wealth and those who did not. On the lowest rung of society were slaves who had neither property nor rights. They were treated as domestic animals. Slave society was not efficient, however, so there emerged a new way of production (although slavery did not die out).
3   *Feudalism* is a system based on land in which peasants work on the land of their masters, the rent for which is paid by expropriation of a proportion of the crops which are harvested. The whole is sustained by a landed aristocracy with the backing of private or state militaries. This too proved inefficient over time and so was replaced by capitalism.
4   *Capitalism* is characterized by a system of wage labour, in which the working class is paid only a part of what they produce. The surplus is extracted by the bourgeoisie who come to own most of the property.
5   *Socialism* is predicated on the overthrow of the class system and the introduction of the rule of the proletariat and the withering away of the state.
6   *Communism* is a society of equality and cooperation, in which there are no antagonisms or contradictory interests. Under such circumstances, humans will realize their true nature. There will be no antagonisms between them or between humans and their work.

Critics have rightly pointed out that this schema is teleological and as such is unacceptable. What Marx has done is identify a stages theory of societal evolution, one that operates rather like an iron law. It is as if all human societies are on the same progressive path towards the realization of communism, which becomes the ultimate, necessary and inevitable goal. The historical record suggests otherwise. There is no such law in operation; societal change is not always 'progressive', as we well know from the experience of the twentieth century alone when, for example, Germany, recognized at the time as the most advanced country in Europe, regressed into a genocidal state with the most horrific powers of destruction. And Marx's notion of change tends to understate the power individuals have to promote change – Gandhi, in South Africa or India for example – and that accidents can happen with dramatic consequences. What would have happened if Hitler had done well at art school and become an artist? It is as if individuals are simply conduits for the hopes, fears and desires of the population or accidents have little influence on the broader contours of historical movements.

Marx's theory of history has remained tainted with what critics have seen as tendencies towards economic and teleological determinism, and yet it has attracted some of the most brilliant historical scholars of recent times. It has done so despite flaws which were very much a product of the nineteenth century; yet the theory is an extraordinarily powerful system for understanding the nature of historical change. No other historical theory quite demonstrates the same ability to encompass the economic, cultural, ideological, social and political into an integrated and coherent analytical system and to take account of the role of the proletariat in making history. Thus, for example, C. L. R. James (1901–1989), Eric Williams (1911–1981) and David Brion Davis (1927–2019) have effectively redefined the agenda for studying modern slavery, through a detailed understanding of the relationship between capitalism and slavery and demonstrating the value of a non-reductive and humanitarian approaches to the problem (Chapter 5). Through the work of Christopher Hill (1912–2003) and David Underdown (1925–2009) we know much more about the role of culture and ideology in the seismic struggles of seventeenth-century England, in particular the revolutionary impulses of an emergent capitalist society that underpinned religious conflicts. And Sumit Sarkar, Ranajit Guha and Partha Chatterjee have revealed the ways in which the British bourgeoisie developed their thinking about how to govern India and the nature of the indigenous resistance mounted against this rule. We could go on, but the list is a long one.

Marx has also entered our vocabulary like no other writer: phrases such as 'All history is the history of class struggle', 'Religion is the opiate of the masses' or 'Workers of the world unite, you have nothing to lose but your chains' are freely quoted, often parodied. Such phrases may be great political slogans, but as historical truths they tend to be rather unreliable. Not only do they operate at the highest levels of abstraction, but they are also in fact virtually impossible to test in meaningful ways from the historical record. Marx himself must take some responsibility for this state of affairs; while he devoted much time to an exploration of the workings of capitalism, he said virtually nothing about what would happen when it fell.

So far, we have talked of a unified body of Marxist theory, but this idea has been challenged, most notably by the French political philosopher Louis Althusser in *For Marx* (1962). Althusser argued that Marx had discovered in his allegedly scientific model of historical materialism a whole array of possibilities for understanding and changing the world. But that the corpus of Marxist thought was not a unified one for Marx's approach developed and changed over time. Althusser detected in fact an 'epistemological break' in his writings, signalling a shift from the 'early' Marx of philosophical inquiry evident in the *Economic and Philosophic Manuscripts* of 1844 to the more mature Marx of *Das Kapital* where he is concerned with outlining a revolutionary economics and a science of history. The debate on how Marx should be understood has since raged within Marxist circles with the same fervour that medieval Christian apologetics were once said to have – probably erroneously – disputed the number of angels that could dance on the end of a pinhead, but it is no less important for all that.

In recent years, there has been a move away from Marx, in large part because of the problems identified earlier; many fewer historians would wish to describe themselves as Marxists. Perhaps he is no longer fashionable (we should never understate the role of fashion in historical writing). But it is not necessary to accept all that Marx wrote. If, on the other hand, historians remain who are influenced by his approach to history and the questions he asks of historical change or who, by rejecting a simple economic determinism, have taken Marx in new directions, then Marxist historiography will be with us for many years to come.

With all this conceded, however, what remains if we look back to the influence of Marxism in history is its relation to practical, everyday politics around the world. In many ways if the Berlin Wall crumbled overnight in 1989, its intellectual ramparts were breached decades before. Like the breaching of the Jewish Temple in Jerusalem two millennia ago, it would take time before the citadel would finally fall, and even then, zealots continued to fight among the ruins long after the conquering armies had overrun the city. Marxism, as we are about to discover, has been compared more to an old time religion than a secular theory of history, and its embattled remnants have emerged in different guises, suggesting other ways of understanding the past, in other manifestations – it is these manifestations over recent decades that we shall consider in the next section.

6.5 Marxism in the Twentieth Century

G. D. H. Cole and Raymond Postgate first published *The Common People 1746–1938* in 1938. It was written as a rejoinder to the sort of Whig history that we encountered in Chapter 4 and told the story of nation, constitution and great men. Its opening page took the reader to a remote dirt road east of Inverness, where in 1746 the clans of Scotland were brutally defeated by overwhelming English forces. As socialists, Cole and Postgate presented the Battle of Culloden and the eighteenth-century Jacobean uprising as the conflict between an ancient society and a society much more advanced. As socialism would yet triumph, so the English forces had prevailed precisely because England was a class-based society, not a society based on family, tribe or the individual charisma of this or that leader.

In many ways, Cole and Postgate were anticipated by J. L. and Barbara Hammond, pioneers of 'history from below' who believed that one of the lessons from popular history was the need for institutional reform and by Fabian historians Sidney and Beatrice Webb who felt that 'the people' could be persuaded to forge a socialist commonwealth if only they knew their history. In the first case, 'the people' were invested with liberal sensitivities, and in the second they became historically significant in their collective combinations, especially through their trade unions.

Marxists, such as A. L. Morton and Allen Hutt, took another viewpoint. *A People's History of England* (1938), for example, was written in the belief of the imminent establishment of a workers' state. Here the emphasis was on the economic system, class and historical transition. The Marxist tradition was anxious to establish histories that anticipated the emergence of a class-conscious industrial proletariat; all posited the working class as the unblemished champions of liberty and democracy in line with the principles of historical materialism and all saw 'the people' as the instruments of inevitable social, political and economic transformation.

Cole and Postgate were influenced by all of these strands but differed from them in subtle ways. They lacked the absolute faith in revolutionary transformation that marked the Marxist school – famously Cole styled himself a 'Marxian' – but this made the moral message of their work all the more urgent. Faced by the persistence of unemployment and social division and the growing menace of fascism in the 1930s, they wrote a tract for their times that emphasized both the failings of capitalist society and the hope that the democratic traditions of the masses could remoralize the British state and build a better future. In this, they represent a remarkable anticipation of the wartime urge for social reform.

Since the 1930s and 1940s, liberal, Fabian and Marxist-inspired history 'from below' has blossomed and thrived. The most famous example of this was E. P. Thompson's *The Making of the English Working Class* (1963), which sought to rescue the experiences of ordinary men and women from the 'condescension of posterity'. Like Raymond Williams and Richard Hoggart, who contributed to the 'new social history' of the 1960s, Thompson put class – theorized as a set of relationships both political and economic – centre stage in his narrative of English history. He criticized developmental and progressive accounts of history, as they distorted the past and emphasized only those elements they recognized as harbingers of the future. The victors were celebrated in the Whig accounts that adhered to a developmental model of history, as were the prophets of future electoral victory in the Fabian accounts.

For both Fabians and Marxists, the working classes defeated in the period of the Napoleonic wars and the era of the First Reform Act (and beyond that in Chartism, which is discussed in Chapter 21) ultimately emerged victorious as the agents of socialist transformation, despite the trade unions and political parties that caged their radicalism. It is clear, however, that Thompson's (and indeed Cole and Postgate's) socialist faith has been sorely challenged in recent years. The industrial working class has declined in numbers, and the socialist revolutionary experiment in the Soviet Union and Eastern Europe has conclusively failed. We know, for example, that, far from being a socialist state, the actions of the Soviet Union from Communism's murderous past resulted in famine, purges, war and seventy million unnatural deaths, according to the historian Catherine Merridale in her remarkable book *Night of Stone: Death and Memory in Russia* (2001). Equally significant is the emerging critique of the intellectual roots of socialist historiography. Rather than being understood as an objective and scientific approach to the study of history, Marxism is now being understood as driven by metaphysical and religious concerns. To many, therefore, it seems imperative to challenge the theoretical basis of Marxism and its analysis of class conflict as rooted in economic and social contradictions and to embark on a post-socialist rethinking of a history of 'the people'.

Let us pause here and unpack the origins of this challenge. Mike Savage and Andrew Miles, authors of *The Remaking of the British Working Class 1840–1940* (1994), have a chapter on 'Labour history' that is useful for our purposes. They make the point that leftist histories have always been organized around the notion of agency, either from the point of view of the institutions of the working class (as in Fabian histories) or from the experience of the industrial proletariat within a global context (such as the Marxist histories). The first sought to 'service and celebrate' the Labour movement and underlined its evolutionary development while the second described its membership as being invested with revolutionary potential.

The Communist Party Historians Group most notably promoted this approach to histories of class (Kaye, 1984). From a revolutionary politics grew the *Universities and Left Review* and the New Left. Thompson, along with other notable Marxist historians such as Christopher Hill, Rodney Hilton (1916–2002), Eric Hobsbawm (1917–2012), George Rude (1910–93), Dona Torr (1883–1957), Victor Kiernan (1913–2009), John Saville (1916–2009) and a youthful Raphael Samuel (1934–1996), had been members. Their founding texts were diverse and included *Studies in the Development of Capitalism* (1946) by Maurice Dobb (1900–1976), which inaugurated an important debate on the transition from feudalism to capitalism.

By the 1960s and 1970s, the Communist party was divided along both organizational and ideological lines. After the Soviet invasion of Hungary in 1956, the party lost members. Thompson, disillusioned, founded what was to become an influential journal called the *Reasoner* and then in 1957 the *New Reasoner*. His ill-tempered and ill-judged open letter to Leszek Kolakowski in 1973, published in his *Poverty of Theory* in 1978, sought to expose this former Communist dissident from Poland, who had washed up at All Souls in Oxford, accusing him of succumbing to the hypnotizing charms of capitalism, revealing yet more divisions among former comrades.

The biggest chasm was yet to open up; when it did it would scar the leftist landscape for a generation. This chasm was between Thompson and Perry Anderson. Anderson is known best as author of *Lineages of the Absolutist State* in 1979, *Passages from Antiquity to Feudalism* in 1985 and *Origins of the Present Crisis*, written in the apparent shadow of Britain's economic malaise in 1964, which we shall discuss in Chapter 8. Anderson was committed to demonstrating the continued relevance of critical perspectives on classical Marxist theory. He had arrived from France to edit the *New Reasoner* in 1962 (which was to become the *Universities and New Left Review*) and then promptly sacked Thompson and those others who had been authentic Communist dissidents during the 1950s.

Thompson also distanced himself from crude Marxist approaches, which he felt were determinist and anti-historical. Instead, he wrote histories that emphasized class as experience and the 'peculiarities' of English history. In his work on Blake, William Morris and, indeed, the English working classes, Thompson had argued for a history of England that traced a particular working-class history which, independent from European models, was based on the liberty of the 'Free Born Englishman'. One of his early collaborators on this matter at least was the literary critic and Marxist Raymond Williams, who in his own work laid down the charge of 'cultural nationalism', a charge Thompson rejected with some justification, pleading his internationalist activity in the peace movement and elsewhere.

Later, the rise of the *History Workshop Movement* and feminism widened those divisions (see Chapter 12). The new concern was less for nation or constitution (like the Whig historians) or even for structures of class power but for minorities and outsiders. Like Thompson, they were concerned with the poor and the disenfranchised, but they also turned to the historical plight of women, the colonial victims of imperialism and the sexually excluded. The 'people', thereby, were de-coupled from their representative organizations, whether they be trade union or Labour Party, and because of the new sensitivity to gender and race in history, they were now diverse as well as fragmented.

Sociological studies suggest that the continuing de-radicalization of the working class and its very existence as a class with 'only its labour to sell' (the classic Marxist formulation) has all but disappeared in the Western hemisphere. Culture was no longer thought to have material foundations linked to the rituals of work. Indeed, the view of the primacy of the economic base was replaced by the belief in the autonomy of culture that in turn placed emphasis on discourse or language before experience (associated with postmodern theory, which we will examine in Chapter 7). The spotlight now is less on class and more on the competing identities associated with gender, race, sexuality and national and local belonging. Thus, the past, like the present, is thought to be socially fragmented, making the idea of a homogeneous working class implausible.

Where liberal and Fabian Labour historians saw the working class as part of Britain's democratic and tolerant traditions, Marxists were left asking why there had not been a revolution. Some argued that the institutions of the working class had betrayed a more radical working class; the development of an elite or patrician culture had thwarted revolution. Others, such as Hobsbawm, identified an 'aristocracy of labour' that by possessing skills that could be sold readily in the marketplace and, by their deferent politics, had divided a potentially homogeneous proletariat. Others still, like Perry Anderson and Tom Nairn, argued that as Britain, unlike much of mainland Europe, had never had a bourgeois revolution, it was anti-intellectual and anti-theoretical and ill-placed to accommodate a workers' state. Its institutions and outlook remained that of an ancien régime, which after the First Reform Act in 1832 could accommodate the demands of the industrialist and financial middle class alike. The dialectic of class and the model of historical materialism demanded the movement of history by the contradictory interests of two antagonistic classes – capital and labour. There was little evidence of this in Britain. By maintaining a monarchy and aristocracy, by developing a fluid and open middle class, by its liberal, almost pre-industrial, labour movement that was modest in its demands, by its artisans or labour aristocrats aping their social betters and by the persistence of a lumpen-proletariat or underclass, the country remained stubbornly unwilling to turn to revolution.

In 1993, the *International Review of Social History* asked whether what has been described really amounted to the end of class histories and, by implication, of Marxist history. Contributors suggested several problems at the heart of this malaise which has now affected the social history of labour in the same way as it had once dogged older histories of 'the people':

1 Geographical, spatial and environmental circumstances of labour have been neglected. What are the effects of ecological and locational influences on histories of class?
2 How can we bridge the gap between the objective facts of daily life and work (labour processes, wages, housing and so on) and people's subjective experiences of, say, work, poverty and living in a slum?
3 How can the history of labour admit outside influences, like business, and how can they be treated together?
4 How can we find a consistent approach to the plural identities of the working class? Issues involving gender, race, ethnicity and age are treated as separate subdisciplines, while labour history research no longer appears to focus implicitly on young, white, male workers.
5 Why do we continue to concentrate on the 'core' Western countries at the expense of comparative histories and the histories of labour in the poorer nations?

In April 1997, the same journal published a few tentative responses by the German historian Jurgen Kocka, suggesting that historians needed to:

- Increase efforts to connect gender and class, linking the history of wage labour with the domestic economy of the household.
- Look afresh at the language of the labour movement.
- Include more politics in historical accounts of labour.
- Look again at the relationship between Fabian-style social democracy and Communism and judge whether the two socialist traditions can be divided.
- Ask not why there was no revolution, but why there was still so much radicalism among labour movements.
- Look at trade unions as a part of civil society not as potentially revolutionary state apparatus.

He adds, in hope more than expectation, that as working class and labour history is influenced by present-day concerns, that comparative history will increase, that we will, as he puts it, 'get the economy back in' and even that the 'history of work' will gain a new prominence. Perhaps, he goes on, even Marx will gain new credibility.

As a means of better situating Marxism within the development of intellectual thought rather than a body of theory with universal application, Gareth Stedman Jones began to rethink its importance as a post-Enlightenment ideology. Marxism, according to Stedman Jones, originated in Hegel's theory of history, which derived from reactions to the French Revolution in the 1790s and German philosophical debates of the same decade, attributing to nature a special mystery and energy:

> Where Hegel's theory of history suggested 'innate powers, purposive activity, striving after perfection, a self-sufficient divine impulse at work within man and the world'. . . . Marx by replacing class for Spirit, did not free himself of these elements by focusing in upon the so-called forces of production. The shocking rider to this view, at least for conventional Marxists, was that mankind, whether before or after the revolution would never escape the clutches of ideology.
>
> (Stedman Jones, 2002, p. 165)

Ultimately, Marxist theories were utopian because they were based on metaphysical assumptions about man which are 'scarcely comprehensible outside the quasi-religious context in which they had been conceived'. Marx, it turned out, had not turned Hegel's theory of history on its head by displacing idealism with a materialism rooted in history. In contrast, Marx's theory of history was subjective, contained a religious element and was far from offering a science of history. The consequences of this are telling, for now Marx could be placed back into a more general consideration of Enlightenment thought. By doing this, socialism was seen not as a transcendental or eternal philosophy of new society, a higher civilization, a cooperative system based on rationality that promises the end of division at an 'end state' but as a philosophy bound by time and place. If Marx constructed a new, materialist concept of history, it was as part of a vision to present communist society as an alternative to capitalism. This project has failed, a failure that for some has fatally weakened Marx's theory of history. However, when asked whether he thought that the ideas of Marx are still important today, Stedman Jones responded in a way that nicely summarizes what might be described as a consensus among most historians today: class and class struggle still retain something of their power as a means of understanding historical change and the nature of the contemporary world.

Postscript

Historians tend to enjoy revolutions. Times of radical upheaval provide more exciting fare than the routine exigencies of daily life. Perhaps because of this the term revolution has been somewhat overplayed; too often it is used to describe merely times of rapid change rather than profound disruption. So, when we encounter reference to, say, the revolution in manners or in fashion, a certain degree of caution has to be exercised. There are historical episodes, however, which are of such world-shaking significance that revolution is entirely apt and appropriate; among them are the events of this chapter – the American and French revolutions.

Despite – or perhaps because of – the fact that these revolutions were of such dramatic significance, they had to wait on their histories. Those caught up in the events found it impossible to secure the distance necessary to write anything more than simple narratives or political tracts. Thomas Paine, who did more than any to promote in the popular imagination the virtues of the revolutions, published radical pamphlets which lacked any real sense of historic development. It was not until the beginning of the nineteenth century that holistic accounts of the revolutions began to appear, and another thirty years would pass before such an approach reached maturity. The British experience was somewhat similar. Britain had its revolution in the seventeenth century (Chapter 4) and arguably still awaited its chronicler, but in the aftermath of the American and French revolutions, there arose a powerful radical culture which for a time challenged the state and found its political voice – particularly when mapping the currents of radical thought – but lacked an all-encompassing history.

It was at the moment when histories of the revolutions reached maturity that an alternative approach emerged. Karl Marx and Friedrich Engels were not interested so much in the history of the revolutions as in a quest to understand their underlying dynamics. Drawing upon the work of Hegel, they explored the driving force of revolutionary societal change as a means of mapping the course of present and future revolutions which would culminate in a utopian, communist society. Now largely considered by historians as fatally flawed, this broad theory of revolution has, nonetheless, been credited with inspiring the great revolutions of the twentieth century and fostered some of the outstanding historical accounts of revolutionary change since ancient times. With its decline, it is as if historians have found it necessary to return to the drawing board and rethink their causes, dynamics and legacies.

Further Reading

Bernard Bailyn (1992) *The Ideological Origins of the American Revolution*.
Hedva Ben-Israel (1968) *English Historians on the French Revolution*.
Thomas Carlyle (2010) [1837] *Carlyle's French Revolution*, ed. Ruth Scurr.
Peter Linebaugh and Marcus Rediker (2000) *The Many-Headed Hydra. The Hidden History of the Revolutionary Atlantic*.
Karl Marx and Frederick Engels (2002) [1844] *The Communist Manifesto*.
Iain McCalman (ed.) (1999) *An Oxford Companion to the Romantic Age. British Culture 1776–1832*.

7 Postmodernism and Postcolonialism

Introduction

In many respects, this chapter touches on a debate we introduce in Chapter 21 on the status of historical knowledge. There, we discuss the problem of historical truth and whether it is attainable. In recent years these concerns have intensified, as a result of which the debate has taken some perhaps unexpected twists and turns against the backdrop of a changing world order. The experience of the Second World War and the immediate postwar period in Europe transformed an order based on the possession of colonies by Western powers; instead, this period witnessed the demise of the imperial order as colonies fought successfully for their independence from foreign rule and the rise of new superpowers, and it was these that redefined the balance of power. The new order, it was argued by theoretically driven historians, could not be interpreted by the conventional methods of history. Not only that, the horrors of the experience of colonial rule and the Second World War threw into crisis any belief that the West – and Enlightenment thought upon which it was built – could claim superiority over the non-Western world. Indeed, for some, the distinct historical trajectory that purported to describe an inevitable rise of the West was no longer tenable.

These events forced a fundamental re-examination of the historiographical approaches which had sprung from the Enlightenment to create two new fields of intellectual inquiry – postmodernism and postcolonialism. Although addressing different historical concerns they shared certain suspicions of traditional historiography, in particular those related to the operation of specific types of narratives. By abandoning such narratives, it was argued, history would be released from a straitjacket. This promise, however, posed its own sets of awkward questions, most of which remain unresolved. It is this process that we wish to examine in the chapter.

7.1 Modernity and the Enlightenment

It took a German of Jewish descent to observe that the progressive aims of the Enlightenment had become stuck in the mud of Auschwitz and that to attempt to write something as creative or beautiful as poetry in the knowledge of this atrocity would be an act of barbarism. Theodor Adorno, of the famous Frankfurt School of philosophy, was not alone in this thought. Many historians and other social theorists have detected a profound transformation around the time of the Second World War and its immediate aftermath. Of course, the war itself effectively defined a new world order in which the old European powers found themselves in a sorry state, in no position to challenge the rising strength of the two new superpowers – the United States and the Soviet Union. Soon thereafter, these same European powers were forced to cede control of their empires and grant independence to the fledgling nation states of the continents of Asia and

Africa. And yet, perhaps, contemporary observers witnessed at the same time a dramatic shift in the trajectory of history itself, more specifically the end of ideas of liberty and reason which had underpinned and protected the rise of the West.

This moment signalled the end of what has been referred to as the Enlightenment project – or the demise of modernity – and our entry into a qualitatively new age. In broad terms it is difficult to distinguish between the two ways of defining this moment. In talking of the Enlightenment project, we may well focus on its intellectual formation (as outlined in Chapter 3), while modernity is seen to have a wider remit, encompassing as it does the economic, political, cultural and aesthetic, but in practice, as modernity was so implicated in the Enlightenment project, such a distinction lacks precision. The Enlightenment was modern and to be modern was wrapped up entirely in the Enlightenment.

So let us begin an exploration of these issues by refreshing our thoughts on what the Enlightenment stood for. According to its protagonists, the Enlightenment spread reason like light, so playing a critically important role in the emergence of modern thought. It thus formed the first stage in the forging of a modern conception of society as an entity amenable to the action of human agency, whose underlying workings were in principle open to scientific scrutiny and revelation. These changes were attendant on certain important historical shifts in the West, among which we can include the following:

1. The increased use of secular forms of political power and authority displacing absolutist forms of authority based on religious ideology and the rise of nation states underpinned by conceptions of sovereignty and popular legitimacy.
2. Exchange economies based on the large-scale production and consumption of commodities, the extension of private ownership and new ideas on the worth of private property and the systematic accumulation of capital characteristic of self-sustained growth.
3. A decline in the feudal social order, with its rigid social hierarchies and overlapping allegiances and the appearance of dynamic social and sexual divisions of labour, which in a capitalist society meant new class formations based on antagonisms between the bourgeoisie and proletariat and patriarchal relations between men and women.
4. The displacement of a worldview that was religious, superstitious and insular by a secular and materialist culture promoting individualism and rationality.

What lay at the heart of the project was a belief that it was possible for the first time to know human society and behaviour rather than see them through the ancient lens of religious orthodoxy and superstition. And by knowing them it was thought possible to change them. Part of this project was clearly historical. Within the Scottish and French Enlightenments, for example, there were determined attempts to understand how societies had developed over time, as a result of which there emerged fully fledged ideas about the stages theory of human development, capable of being employed to rank the peoples of the world beneath the 'natural' superiority of Europeans.

Also embracing advances in medical, scientific, technological and other innovations which were seen as integral to the endeavour to improve human life, the Enlightenment has rightly been considered as one of the starting points for modern thought. Critical to this process was the appearance of the secular intellectual within Western society – a figure whose role was intimately bound up with the analysis and critique of society and history. In no area was this more important than that of political modernity. The Enlightenment laid the foundations for rule by the modern institutions of state bureaucracy and capitalist enterprise by developing particular notions of citizenship, human rights, equality before the law, distinctions between the public and the private, democracy and popular sovereignty, all of which bore the imprint of European thought and history.

Notions of the modern have therefore been around for a long time. Arguably, since the latter stages of the eighteenth century people have been sensitive to the fact that they live in modern times, which invariably they find exciting and challenging. It is only in recent years, however, that we have begun to think more carefully about what 'modern' means. There is a danger to think of the modern in purely chronological terms, that is, to be modern is to live in the modern world, in which case the argument becomes tautological. More helpful are those approaches that have tried to think through the question of what is distinct about the modern. Marshall Berman in *All That is Solid Melts into Air* (1983) provides us with an evocative sense of its defining features:

> There is a mode of vital experience – experience of space and time, of the self and others, of life's possibilities and perils – that is shared by men and women all over the world today. I will call this body of experience 'modernity'. To be modern is to find ourselves in an environment that promises adventure, power, joy, growth, transformation of ourselves and the world – and, at the same time, that threatens to destroy everything that we have, everything we know, everything we are. Modern environments and experiences cut across all boundaries of geography and ethnicity, of class and nationality, of religion and ideology; in this case, modernity can be said to unite all mankind. But it is a paradoxical unity; it pours us all into the maelstrom of perpetual disintegration and renewal, of struggle and contradiction, of ambiguity and anguish. To be modern is to be part of a universe in which, as Marx said, 'all that is solid melts into air'.
>
> (Berman, 1983, p. 15)

This conveys nicely the dual-edged nature of modernity. The modern world offers us empowerment and opportunity, but at the same time it has developed unprecedented powers of destruction. What are the changes that have brought about this state of affairs? According to Berman, the modern world has been forged by the following events:

- Great discoveries in the physical sciences, changing our images of the universe and our place in it.
- Industrialization of production, creating new human environments.
- New forms of corporate power.
- Immense demographic upheavals.
- Rapid and often cataclysmic urban growth.
- Systems of mass communications, which are dynamic in their development.
- Increasingly powerful nation states.
- Drastically fluctuating world markets.

The relationship between how people have viewed the Enlightenment and modernity is therefore close, and in practice it is difficult to disentangle them. For many, Enlightenment ideas underscored and promoted the emergence of the modern world. For the more critical, not only have the virtues of the Enlightenment been overstated, but also both it and modernity came to an abrupt end during the Second World War and the years that followed. Largely as a result of changes in production, the increasing dominance of the visual in our lives, the loss of faith in the centrality of the Western individual and growing suspicion of 'grand narratives' or descriptions of the world that can explain everything, modernity was displaced by the condition we know as postmodernity. The Enlightenment project, on the other hand, launched some 200 years previously to bring rational thought and action to human endeavour and so banish superstition, irrationality, hunger and disease from the face of the globe, now floundered in the Nazi death camps and disappeared amid the mushroom clouds of Hiroshima and Nagasaki. How, people now asked, can we talk still of progress and civilization when what were considered the most civilized parts of the world were shown capable of such acts? The fact that these acts of supreme destruction were carried out by the two nations thought to be in the forefront of civilization – Germany and the United States of America – only compounded the sense of a profound rupture between Enlightenment modernity and postmodernity. This was to have profound implications for the writing of history.

The crisis is seen to be one that we associate with the West, but this assumption is based on some awkward presuppositions. When historians talk of modernity and the Enlightenment, they may necessarily privilege the experience of the West in such a way that they become synonymous – the West is modern, and a definition of modern is centred on the West. If the modern can be detected in other parts of the world, then this is probably a result of the effects of colonialism and global capitalism. In response to this reasoning, questions have been raised about precisely whose modernity we are referring to. Surely, we can point to modernizing tendencies in, say, China and Africa which owe little to the West? Should we therefore not speak of different modernities rather than a single Western modernity? Such questions pose theoretical challenges which cannot be pursued here; suffice to say that historians are still squabbling over them.

Yet it is true to say that it was out of the Enlightenment that the vital notion of human progress emerged and took hold of influential sections of European opinion in the second half of the eighteenth century. For the first time in human history it was possible to think that human societies were on the path of perpetual progress. This is nicely illustrated by the simultaneous transformations that took place in British thought on the issues of slavery, colonialism and poverty towards the end of the century, all of which came to be seen as massive barriers to progress. After centuries when slavery was unquestioned – seen as a natural condition of man – a transformation of dramatic proportions occurred. In the space of a few decades, universal acceptance of the slave trade was overturned by opprobrium directed towards it. Much of the impulse for the stirrings of abolition came from Quakers and other non-conformist denominations. But the real driving force was the new breed of political economists such as Adam Smith who argued that slavery confronted the laws of morality, was a barrier to the breaking up of monopoly interests and imposed restraints on free trade.

Poverty had previously been seen as a state of grace – a condition to be borne with pious fortitude. If relief was offered as it had been since the introduction of Elizabethan poor and vagrancy laws, it was as a last desperate resource. The real solution was to be found in the regulation of employment and prices of staples such as bread and the provision of alms. Above all, the merits of labour were extolled – the result of the English revolution and the introduction of the Protestant work ethic. But none of these measures had been successful, and towards the end of the eighteenth century, following displacement from the countryside, large numbers of migrants found their way to the urban centres, in particular to London, where desperate masses of the poor settled in enclaves seen increasingly to harbour criminal activity, threatening the imperial and commercial future of the nation. Simultaneously, levels of relief were beginning to compromise the actuarial stability of the poor law system, and measures were laid down that culminated in the harsh disciplinary regime of the New Poor Law of 1834.

Anxieties also surfaced over the nature and extent of imperial ambition in India. Following the loss of the American colonies in 1776, Britain turned to India, and there under the aegis of the East India Company emerged as an imperial rather than simply a trading power. The Company, however, proved inefficient and profligate and had to be saved from bankruptcy by loans from the government. Then 1776 – an annus horribilis for the British state if ever there was one – saw the publication of Adam Smith's *Wealth of Nations*, Edward Gibbon's *Decline and Fall of the Roman Empire* and, critically, Tom Paine's *Common Sense*, which together mounted a devastating attack on the dangers of imperial endeavour and aristocratic profligacy while supporting the American colonists. The British state drew the appropriate lessons and, determined not to allow the Company a free rein, interceded to take over an increasing responsibility for Indian affairs.

Despite the troubling presence of the poor and occasional setbacks in imperial advance, the British were able to assume the high moral ground on the abolition of slavery, consolidating authority as an imperial nation (particularly after the demise of the East India Company in 1858) and striding forward in the nineteenth century, confident in the knowledge that progress was an integral part of modernization. This profound sense of belief in progress, engendered in part by revolutionary changes in the sciences and arts, also dominated European thought in the nineteenth century, but as we entered the twentieth it began to falter. The mass slaughter of the First World War and the onset of mass culture engendered a profound sense of pessimism among a European intelligentsia worried that elite culture was threatened by the onset of popular forms such as magazines and the cinema. All this impacted on the writing and understanding of history.

The Second World War witnessed barbarities that eclipsed anything seen before. If there was one moment that ended the belief in a law of inexorable progress, then this was it. Whether we see this period as the end of modernity or of the Enlightenment project, the emphasis is on what many considered to be a profound shift in social thought. This is because the supposed passing of modernity created a crisis not merely in the economic, political and cultural spheres of our lives: it was also a crisis in the whole way of understanding the world; a state of being that challenged previously accepted approaches to the past. We now entered, it was argued, a postmodern condition which required an entirely different way of reflecting on our experience, and if this means abandoning the basic tenets of intellectual thought that were founded in the Enlightenment, then so be it. What, then, is this postmodern condition?

7.2 Postmodernism

There is a tale about an academic conference in which one speaker announced that the First World War was nothing but a text, a story or a series of stories, and any historian bent on determining the truth of the conflict needs to examine its discursive appropriation – the ways in which it has been represented – rather than the grim evidence of unfolding events and conditions experienced by the combatants. It is as if the all-too-vivid reality of the killing fields of Ypres and the Somme are reduced to an exercise in the deconstruction of language used to describe the conflict itself, making any assessment among competing discourses – let alone a final judgment regarding its historical significance – simply impossible. That was until another delegate at the same conference reminded colleagues that his grandfather had lost a leg in this 'text', and that its reality can be confirmed by those millions killed or maimed by its 'discourse'. This exchange captures – albeit simplistically – something of the debate between postmodern thought – with its preoccupation with discursive strategies and the operation of narratives – and the certainties about historical evidence that we associate with the Enlightenment project.

As we have seen, the Enlightenment hastened an underlying cluster of assumptions and expectations about the nature of the modern world. Collectively this amounted to Western epistemology, and it is this that has recently come under the critical scrutiny of postmodern theorists intent on reorienting its fundamental categories. The postmodern challenge thus involves either rejecting or at least seriously questioning the pillars of Enlightenment thought. Specifically, this critique denies the following:

1. Our knowledge of society over time was cumulative and broadly progressive in character.
2. We can attain rational knowledge of society.
3. Such knowledge is universal and hence objective.
4. Enlightened knowledge is both different from and superior to distorted forms of thought such as ideology, religion, common sense, prejudice and superstition.
5. Such knowledge leads to the mental liberation and betterment of humanity.

The challenge to the status of knowledge has been the most important and telling. Because Enlightenment thinkers believed that it was possible to attain the truth, they tended to emphasize the objective and scientific basis of knowledge. According to postmodernist critics, however, historical and social truth was also predicated on highly selective discursive strategies – in particular, the recognition of certain grand or overarching narratives (metanarratives) – about the development of societies over time. Thus, for example, European society took the form it did because it was the logical culmination of inevitable processes of historical development including industrialization, democratization and liberalization. More than this, the postmodern position was often seen as 'the death of centres'. Critics such as Keith Jenkins have argued that the 'organizing frameworks' that describe human phenomena privilege various centres – 'Anglo-centric', 'Euro-centric' or even 'gender-centric' – but these are little more than 'temporary fictions' that serve not universal interests (as is implied by the Enlightenment) but instead very particular interests to consolidate Western power. In sum:

> The objects of knowledge seem to be constructed arbitrarily, thrown together in a manner of collage, montage and pastiche. . . . The old centres barely hold, and the old metanarratives no longer resonate with actuality and promise, coming to look incredible from late twentieth-century sceptical perspectives. . . . Post-modernism is the general expression of those circumstances.
>
> (Jenkins, 1991, pp. 59–63)

So let us pause at this moment to consider how one of the most influential postmodern historians approached the Holocaust. Hayden White (1928–2018) has in his various writings addressed the matter of narrative. He argued persuasively that narrative – basically, the ways in which we tell stories about the past – reflected something deep within human culture. So pervasive is it as a device to endow experience with meaning and so accepted and understood across cultures that we can think of narrative as a universal language. While some historical forms such as annals and chronicles cannot be considered narratives, most historical accounts rely on an ability to tell a story. Stories about events do not tell themselves and so stories are imposed by historians – such as that of the First World War – but they do not imply that the event itself did not happen. Because of their very universality, however, there is a danger of simply taking narratives for granted – as seeing them as neutral conveyors of meaning. White rejected this and argued that we must understand how the operation of imaginative narrative fictions such as the epic, folk tale, myth, romance, farce, tragedy and so on that truthfully represented the past.

Of all the narrative genres that are available to historians, humour seems to be singularly inappropriate as an approach to describing the Holocaust. It would be difficult, for example, to apply the comic or pastoral modes to the task since it would be impossible to reconcile them with the factual record. If, however, they are used metaphorically, then they may have validity. White mentions Art Spiegelman's *Maus: A Survivor's Tale*, published in 1986, which uses the medium of the comic book and in true Orwellian fashion depicts Germans as cats, Jews as mice and Poles as pigs. Not, one might think, the most appropriate means of representing the Holocaust, but for White Spiegelman's satire is one of the most moving narrative accounts. In the same way, some may recall the initial bewilderment that greeted Roberto Benigni's award winning *Life is Beautiful* (1997), a cinematic account of life and death in a concentration camp. What was remarkable about this film was that it used slapstick comedy to convey a sense of profound humanity and resilience.

Given White's arguments that historical writing is shaped profoundly by particular narratives that we have been introduced to since early in our lives, how do we decide on the status of historical knowledge? As far as French postmodern philosopher Jean François Lyotard is concerned, this is the job of the philosopher. It is philosophy rather than science that can distinguish between real knowledge and mere narrative. It is philosophy that can inform us of the true story of human progress because it can interrogate all those concepts such as progress, reason, order, civilization, well-being and freedom that have been the underlying precepts of Enlightenment thought but have too often been simply taken for granted.

Having recognized how such narratives have operated, critics such as Lyotard and White have proceeded to argue that historical and social knowledge, even personal knowledge – how we can know ourselves – derives from narratives which, far from being grand, were often an awkward mix of political ideas, moral attitudes, myths and religious sentiment. Modern Britain, for example, was not the child of Enlightenment rationality but retained a contradictory mix of the modern and the ancient. Just think for a moment of how the present-day monarchy operates and is seen. The legacy of the Enlightenment, therefore, is deeply suspect, for all universal narratives are tainted. Instead, we must recognize the contingent nature of historical knowledge.

To take a few examples, the West has tended to believe that the drive to industrial and commercial growth was a precondition for human well-being and civilization. Of course, these processes have led to the improvement of conditions for large numbers of people, but the costs to others have been immense. And here we are talking, it could be argued, not only about the exploitation of large sections of the population and not merely about the division that created the third world but also those cataclysmic events such as the Holocaust and the dropping of atomic bombs on civilian populations.

We cannot leave postmodernism without discussion of one of its most influential and baffling figures. Michel Foucault (1926–1984) was a French philosopher with an abiding interest in systems of thought and how they shape power relations in society. He may have resisted the idea that he was within the pantheon of poststructuralists, but retrospectively he has been seen as such. His rejection of fashionable theories of existentialism in the 1960s, suspicion of the implied certainties of Western rationalism and a commitment to reveal the hidden structures of knowledge meant that he shared many of their concerns. Although a philosopher, Foucault held firmly to the belief that a study of history was essential to an understanding of how power had been and continued to be exercised. Thus, for example, in works such as *Madness and Civilization: A History of Insanity in the Age of Reason* (1965), *The Archaeology of Knowledge* (1972), *The Birth of the Clinic: An Archaeology of Medical Perception* (1973) and *Discipline and Punish: The Birth of the Prison* (1977), he mapped out how the development of the modern practices of dealing with madness, illness and crime were at the same time deeply implicated in their control and in the subjugation of those affected. (Foucault comes back into our reckoning when we discuss historical sexualities in Chapter 12.)

Foucault's approach to history has, however, been a source of some puzzlement. While engaging critically with Marxism, he abandoned any claim to truth in the scientific histories offered by Marx and von Ranke. More telling was the influence of the *Annales* School, in particular Fernand Braudel (1902–1985). Like Braudel, Foucault believed that the task of the historian was not to write a total history that sought to bring the economic, social, political and cultural levels into a unified whole according to a grand scheme but rather to point to the divergences, incongruities, discontinuities and unevenesses which operate among them as part of the historical process. He was interested in the conditions that engendered the development of particular 'archaeologies' of knowledge which came to possess significance. Take, for example, the case of madness. In the medieval period, madness was first identified as a human vice, but it was not outside reason, rather it was part of everyone's imagination. In this sense, madness and reason existed in a state of free exchange. With the 'Age of Reason' beginning in the middle of the seventeenth century, the mad were defined as such by medical discourse and subjected to confinement in asylums. Madness was thus banished from the public gaze and thereby silenced. *Madness and Civilization* is thus a study of why this epistemological break in approaches to madness and reason took place at that moment and what its effects were on the relationships between the state and its citizens.

These relationships went to the heart of Foucault's attempts to understand the modern state. In *Birth of the Clinic*, he demonstrated that from the very beginning it sought to control and administer not only madness but the health of the nation. The clinic therefore arose out of a need systematically to observe and record people's health and assigned the task to the enclosed profession of medicine. This surveillance of – and intervention in – the social domain by state agencies was for Foucault a much more fundamental characteristic of modern societies than their economic forms.

By abandoning familiar historical narratives, the field of postmodernism has thus opened up the possibility of multiple narratives of seemingly equal validity and worth. Professional histories now vie with popular histories, black histories, women's histories, regional histories, television histories and the historical novel (which we shall discuss in Chapter 19) in providing interpretations of the past. Has postmodernism gone too far? Well, the achievements have been real, particularly in identifying the constructed rather than given nature of historical knowledge. But there is a sense in some circles that it has led to a free-for-all, a relativism in which all forms of historical knowledge are considered legitimate and of equal worth. It is wise under these circumstances to remind ourselves of some of the achievements of the Enlightenment and perhaps so guard against the chance that in rejecting its fundamental premises we are throwing out the proverbial baby with the equally proverbial bath water.

It is from the work of the German cultural historian Jürgen Habermas (b. 1929) that we have seen the stoutest defence of the Enlightenment in recent years. Habermas (1972) shared many of the concerns of postmodern thinkers. He admitted that the Enlightenment project was only ever an ideal because from the start there was never one source of Enlightenment knowledge. He also had no faith in the future of an Enlightenment project – the brutalities of the twentieth century had shattered this bland optimism. On the other hand, we must recognize the real gains, few of which are really appreciated by postmodern thinkers. The Enlightenment in its various guises was a massive advance of knowledge when seen in the light of the superstition, bigotry and religious orthodoxy of the pre-Enlightenment era. To abandon it completely would lead not to the liberation of thought but to retrenchment and disillusionment because of an abandonment in the hope of progress. The search for some degree of universality (truth) is a viable one not least because it remains wedded to the hope that it might promote justice, egalitarianism, rationality and even happiness. And we can hold onto this without falling prey to naïve expectations. In any case, the alternative is despair arising out of nihilism. Many historians today, while welcoming the questioning of metanarratives launched by postmodernism, reject the idea that different forms of knowledge have equal status and instead cling onto objective notions such as justice and historical truth as preconditions for a more equal, fair and just world, a world where, for one thing, the chains of imperialism have worked loose. It is to the loosening of these imperial chains that we now turn.

7.3 Postcolonialism and the West

Edward Said (1935–2003) was a Palestinian, raised within a comfortable middle-class family in Egypt. He probably could have been a concert pianist (he was co-founder with Daniel Barenboim of the West-Eastern Divan Orchestra, which brings together musicians from Israel and the Arab world) but migrated to the States to take up a position teaching literary studies at Columbia University. In 1978 he published *Orientalism*, which retrospectively came to be seen as one of the founding texts of postcolonialism. Subtitled *Western Conceptions of the Orient*, the book attempted to demonstrate that from the time of Napoleon's invasion of Egypt in the early nineteenth century, the orientalist project was launched by European powers to represent the East as a primitive, exotic, despotic and irrational culture as evidenced, for example, in the salacious potentate presiding over his harem. Simultaneously, this enterprise helped to valorize the West as being everything that the East was not. In a very real way, the West continues to live with this legacy for the rhetoric, language and ideology used to think about the East today have powerful continuities with the Orientalism described by Said.

Influential though Said was, he has not been without his critics. Some like the post-colonial theorists Homi Bhabha and Robert Young have argued that Said extrapolated from a limited historical experience, that is, Egypt and India in the nineteenth century, to erect an edifice of Orientalism which is too monolithic and homogeneous – like a giant machine manufacturing images according to a blueprint. In practice, Orientalism was more complex and nuanced, depending upon specific historical experiences and regions; indeed, it is from this versatility that it derived its continued authority. There may have been parallels between, say, representations of India and Egypt, but over time there were crucial differences – for example, in the ways religion was viewed – which informed contrasts in British interventions. And these representations cannot necessarily be applied to, say, China and the wider Arab world. Related to this is the thorny issue of just how powerful this machine was. Was it really the case that those subjected to Orientalist stereotyping supinely accepted the images manufactured by the West? Well, given the record of anti-colonial struggles this was clearly not the case, for these struggles were often waged precisely over issues of who had the right to determine the culture, identity and history of indigenous peoples.

Postcolonialism as a body of work explored the crucial relationship between the Enlightenment project and the West. For all the claims to reason, civilization and progress, writers claim, the Enlightenment was the inner conscience and underlying rationale not only of Western industrial capitalism but also of Western imperialism. And here the synchronicity between the emergence of postmodernism and postcolonialism is evident, for it was precisely in the immediate aftermath of the Second World War that European imperialism entered into terminal decline as their colonies waged determined struggles against foreign rule, eventually securing independence. During this period, many nationalist leaders and intellectuals understandably raised fundamental questions about the 'natural' superiority of European powers, the centredness of Western identity, the legitimacy of imperial rule, and the narratives that have justified foreign rule – questions that reach to the very core of postcolonial concerns.

Many of these issues have recently been explored by Priya Satia (2020). In an elegant work which complements well our approach to the theoretical underpinnings of Western historiography since the Enlightenment, she demonstrates that historians played a critical role in building and sustaining British power from the eighteenth century, most notably during the era of the empire. Such was the influence they were able to exert over policy makers and the reading public at large that we can speak of the imperial project as a time when historians ruled. As we have seen, the Enlightenment fuelled the conviction that history was a story of progress; from there it was merely a small step to the acceptance that imperial endeavour, despite the occasional excess, was necessary if the millions of colonial subjects were to be raised from a life of ignorance, heathenism and superstition. As nineteenth-century inheritors of Enlightenment thought, a large body of eminent historians including James and John Stuart Mill, Thomas Macaulay, J. R. Seeley, Thomas Carlyle and Samuel Galton shared a particular historical sensibility that rendered empire not only ethically thinkable but desirable. In so doing, their writings shaped the course of imperial endeavour and legitimized even the worst acts of violence in pursuit of the civilizing mission. In a postcolonial world, they might be thought as an anachronism, except that their legacy is abundantly evident in the widespread belief today that on balance empire was of great benefit to its colonial subjects.

At first sight there appears little in common between postmodernism and postcolonialism. Both have their distinct range of concerns pursued by protagonists such as Said. And yet there are affinities arising from a shared concern to problematize the role of the West in world history. Postmodernism questions those grand narratives, explaining the rise of the West by showing the contingent nature of Enlightenment thought upon which its advance was based. In a related way, postcolonialism exposes ways in which Europe's colonial past was underpinned by the uncritical acceptance of ideas of natural superiority and modernity that masked the brutality and exploitation of its rise to imperial pre-eminence.

The metanarrative that has the West marching triumphantly to a position of world power is self-confirming since its advanced and sophisticated civilization is seen to testify to the 'naturalness' of its ascent. Only the West had the education, skills and authority (both moral and divine) to embark on this task and did it out of a sense of duty, even altruism, since by taking control of the destinies of 'primitive' peoples it was offering them the opportunity to step into the modern world. Only with the humanist vision of Arnold Toynbee, whom we discuss briefly in Chapter 15, did historians first become conscious of the extent to which such narratives were a product of views on the supremacy of the West. We know now how flimsy this 'Eurocentrism' is and how this has changed the ways we think about the past.

And yet for those able to read the signs, this critical consciousness was integral to the Enlightenment project itself. Enlightenment thinkers were fascinated by the non-European world and saw therein lessons about, say, administration and government that could usefully be learnt by the West. Many were therefore highly critical of European imperial endeavour (Muthu, 2003). They rejected imperialism as immoral and unworkable. Jeremy Bentham, Condorcet, Diderot, Herder, Kant and Adam Smith all attacked what they saw as the injustices of European imperialism on the grounds that it was a corrupt and despotic enterprise, that it conflicted with notions of self-determination and that it stood in the way of free trade. For the most part, however, in sharp contrast to its assault on slavery, this critique failed to take root in the broader political culture. Smith's strictures on the monopoly privileges of the East India Company, for example, may have hastened the end of its monopoly trading rights to the East, but the Company continued to operate as an imperial power.

While it is the case that postcolonialism as a body of work emerged in the period when colonialism was ending, it can be traced back rather earlier. Thus, while the postcolonial moment generally refers to a distinct experience centred on the loss of the French and British empires, we can point to other 'postcolonial' moments which might well be considered. The loss, for example, of the Iberian empire in Latin America in the early nineteenth century or even the British loss of the thirteen colonies of North America in the late eighteenth century may be seen as part of a postcolonial moment – a sense in which colonialism has always provoked postcolonial struggle – and that if we examine the history of struggle against European rule we can detect important continuities in the way people have struggled against foreign oppression. In this way, ideas from the Enlightenment shaped the ideals of the American Revolution and underscored the long struggle for Indian independence. For our purpose, however, we intend to follow convention and focus on the important concerns raised principally by intellectuals of the developing world after the Second World War.

At the heart of postcolonialism is a deep commitment to challenge Western historiography, which is seen to be complicit in the European colonial experience. This historiography, it is claimed, is a triumphalist narrative of Western dynamism in which the role of colonized subjects in making their own history is neglected or deliberately understated. India gained independence, to take one familiar argument, because of the generosity of the British rather than through nationalist struggles waged by Indians themselves. Such accounts tend to emphasize the benefits of colonial endeavour – bringing backward indigenous peoples into the modern, civilized world – while dismissing resistance to foreign rule as atavistic treachery and barbarity. In this sense, the history of the West and approaches by Western historians tended to remain sovereign – a model against which all other histories have to be read, including those of resistance. Thus, for example, challenges to British rule mounted by insurgents who were seemingly mobilized by religion, superstition and myth instead of reason and progress were dismissed by historians as evidence of peasant irrationality.

Postcolonial theorists have interrogated every detail of such narratives. They have exposed the changing ideological underpinnings of imperial rule, the complex motives of imperial administrators and agents, the quotidian nature of imperial rule in practice and the diverse and imaginative ways in which indigenous peoples responded to and resisted that rule. The project has attracted a wide range of scholars from disciplines including history, literature, cultural studies, politics, philosophy, psychoanalysis, law and science, some of whom fit a little uncomfortably within the general rubric. Of these, Edward Said (as we have seen), Homi Bhabha, Gayatri Spivak and the Subaltern Studies Collective have been among the more important in mounting the critique.

Formed in the early 1980s, largely under the inspiration of Ranajit Guha and Partha Chatterjee, Subaltern Studies became best known through a series of edited collections. In the first of these published in 1982, Guha laid out what was effectively a manifesto for rethinking the historiography of India under colonial rule, in particular its conscious neglect of the role of subaltern groups in anti-colonial struggles. The historiography of Indian nationalism, argued Guha, has been dominated by a concern to record the activities of colonial and bourgeois nationalist elites, with the result that the making of the Indian nation and nationalism are seen as elite achievements, many of which were driven by expectations of rewards of high office. These perspectives have their merits in helping us to understand processes of collaboration and contestation between colonial and indigenous elites such as Nehru, Gandhi and the Brahmans who dominated the Indian National Congress, but they are fatally flawed by an inability to interpret the contributions made by the mass of the Indian people independently of elite nationalism. Rather, the involvement of millions in anti-colonial struggle was represented as a diversion from the politics of the state – or worse as a problem of law and order, such as in 1919 when mass mobilization took place in opposition to the Rowlatt Act, which was designed to repress forms of popular resistance by banning public meetings and allowing incarceration without trial. To redress the balance, we need to pay due attention to the politics of the people, namely, those forms of mobilization that simply cannot be explained by elite accounts.

These popular mobilizations were manifest most frequently in peasant uprisings but included instances when the working people and petty bourgeoisie in urban areas took up the cause of nationalism, such as in the revolt of 1857. Under these circumstances it was apparent that Indian elites were never able to speak for the nation as a whole; there remained vast areas of Indian life, which were beyond their influence. Subaltern politics, however, was neither powerful enough to organize a struggle for national liberation, nor mature enough to assume and complete the mission for independence that elites had failed to bring about. It is this historic failure, Guha concluded, that should constitute the key question to be addressed by the historiography of India under British rule (Guha, 1982, pp. 1–7).

Although lacking a certain cohesion because of the many different approaches (Guha called for a hundred flowers to bloom), the project initially claimed for its intellectual progenitors the humanistic Marxism of the Italian theorist Antonio Gramsci and the work of the outstanding group of British Marxist historians – Eric Hobsbawm, Christopher Hill and E. P. Thompson – which had influentially captured a history of the people. What followed in the eight edited collections and monographs by individuals were studies of subaltern culture written by members and associates of the Collective (Guha, 1982–9; Pandey and Chatterjee, 1992; Arnold and Hardiman, 1993). Partha Chatterjee's 'Agrarian relations and communalism in Bengal, 1926–1935', David Arnold's 'Rebellious hillmen: the Gudem-Rampa risings, 1839–1924', Gyan Pandey's 'Peasant revolt and Indian nationalism: the peasant movement in Awadh, 1919–1922' and Gautam Bhadra's 'Four rebels of 1857' give a good idea of their scope and nature. Here were explorations of a diverse range of tribal groups and peasant communities which engaged in struggles determined by their own sense of priorities and dynamics and which have to be understood in these terms rather than as the expression of a primitive or undeveloped consciousness.

Important though the work of Subaltern Studies has been, it has attracted its critics. Gayatri Spivak in particular, writing as an insider (she was loosely a member of the group), has asked pointedly: 'Can the subaltern speak?' By this, she questioned whether it is possible to get access to subaltern consciousness from acts of insurgency that are recorded only in colonial historiography, particularly when all we can expect from such texts are representations of peasant rebels as criminals or mutineers (Spivak, 1993). Under such circumstances we should recognize not a single 'peasant consciousness' but a variety of intersecting identities derived from the economic, social, sexual, historical and political structures that peasant communities inhabit. Despite such critiques and the fact that Subaltern Studies no longer operates as a collective, its legacy is still evident in the body of published work and members who have continued to make important contributions.

Postcolonial thought has also been open to the criticism that historians have not been able to extricate themselves from the thrall of Western systems of knowledge, as a consequence of which little encouragement has been offered to explore the potential of alternative ways of thinking about history. Yes, the Enlightenment has rightly been subject to an increasingly critical gaze, but its appeal to universalist ambitions in promoting individual rights has remained powerful. Thus, while a few attempts to theorize, say, different concepts of historical time as a prelude to developing alternatives to Western epistemologies have attracted interest, they have had little lasting impact on postcolonial histories (see, for example, Narayana Rao et al., 2001). In the meantime, the so-called safronization of history promoted by sections of Hindutva nationalism, far from forging alternatives, has led to gross distortions of the historical record in ways to serve their political agendas. Postcolonial scholars have repeatedly stressed the important benefits gained from bringing together the histories of the worlds of colonizer and colonized; perhaps now this should also include dialogues among different approaches to historical understanding (Nigam, 2020).

Postscript

This chapter has sought to develop some of the themes introduced in earlier chapters by looking at how postwar historians have approached unresolved issues about the uncertain status of historical knowledge. As we have seen, conventional historiography had inherited a tradition of inquiry from the nineteenth century. This placed emphasis on the gathering and utilization of evidence – for the most part documentary – as a means of reporting on the past 'as it actually happened'. Implicit in this approach was the idea that historical truth is accessible to those properly trained in the historians' craft. A minority of historians raised dissenting voices, questioning whether it was ever possible to be objective in interpreting the past, but then the Second World War and its aftermath created a climate in which the very foundations of conventional historiography came under close scrutiny.

The horrors experienced during the war persuaded many theorists that narratives of historical change that had emerged from the Enlightenment had no legitimacy. How, for example, could notions of human progress which had underpinned many historical accounts still be retained when the experience of death camps and nuclear bombing of civilian populations seemed to prove that even the most advanced nations were capable of barbarity? When this critique was combined with a sense that the world order was fast changing, that new forms of organizing production and communication had emerged which created a new condition – postmodernity – the critique of grand narratives gathered momentum.

In the meantime, the loss of European empires forced a re-examination of the colonial past. So emerged an influential body of work under the umbrella of what came to be known as postcolonialism. Sharing with postmodernity the same suspicion of narratives such as progress, emancipation and liberalization, postcolonial historians challenged conventional interpretations of imperial rule and brought into sharper focus the role of popular struggles for independence.

Much of the work of postmodern and postcolonial historians has operated at a high level of abstraction, tilting the balance away from evidence to theoretical inquiry and creating works which are often not that readily accessible. At the extremes this has had some unfortunate consequences in promoting the idea that history is a text – that is, something that goes on in the head of the historian – or in arguing for a free-for-all in which varieties of narratives flourish, none of which has privilege over others. So while postmodernism and postcolonialism have been of real benefit in exposing the underpinnings of historical interpretation, the solutions they offer have not always been helpful. What is clear is that the debate continues and will do so for many years to come.

Further Reading

Homi Bhabha (1994) *The Location of Culture*.
Vinayak Chaturvedi (ed.) (2000) *Mapping Subaltern Studies and the Postcolonial*.
Peter Childs and Patrick Williams (1997) *An Introduction to Post-Colonial Theory*.
David Harvey (1989) *The Condition of Postmodernity*.
Keith Jenkins (ed.) (1997) *The Postmodern History Reader*.
Edward Said (1991) *Orientalism: Western Conceptions of the Orient*.
Robert Young (2001) *Postcolonialism: An Historical Introduction*.

Part 2
Varieties

8 Political History

Introduction

Approaches to political history have traditionally been divided. On the one hand, histories of the structures of state and government have relied on high theory and 'long' histories with empirical facts sometimes sparse and thin on the ground. On the other hand, when evidence-driven history has been brought to bear over a long period and across vast spaces, the results have been both impressive and useful to the historian. The theory of 'gentlemanly capitalism', for example, has been used to explain the relative decline of the British economy by focusing on the role of the state and finance capitalism. A discussion on the challenges in finding workable theories of the state comprises the opening section.

High politics and the history of elites has been the preserve of historians who have placed emphasis on the importance of decision making in the political process. Its sources have been specifically concerned with the private motivations of historical actors in critical positions of power and influence. Popular or 'low' political history has focused on structures of power such as political parties. The second section of the chapter, therefore, examines the evolution of the British Labour Party from both perspectives: the high politics of its leaders, plus the role of electoral sociology that determined its development as a political movement.

We return to the City in the final chapter in order to understand how extra-parliamentary pressure in the clubs, societies and associations of the square mile acted as an important political lever in the transformation of radicalism and liberalism in late nineteenth-century Britain.

8.1 Theories of the State

Martin Daunton's work of synthesis on what is now well known as the 'gentlemanly capitalism debate' aimed to challenge orthodox views that industrial 'interests' were subordinated to the 'interests' of the aristocracy or land-owning classes and to question how far this orthodoxy explained Britain's relative economic decline (Daunton, 1989). In setting himself this task he had in mind a City invested with power and importance, informed by a predominant set of cultural codes and assumptions. Central was a particular understanding of the workings of the British state and, perhaps, European states. And for good reason, historians researching and writing at societal level could hardly fail to ignore the state as a structure which influenced political, economic, cultural, and social affairs. An understanding of the state is therefore crucial to historians, as is an historical conception of modernization and how both state formation and modernity were connected to cultural and social assumptions that were historically informed.

All sides of the 'gentlemanly capitalism' debate agreed that there were many industrial revolutions in Britain during the eighteenth and nineteenth centuries which were divided by sector and region. The main divide, from one of these perspectives, was that between a producers' North which was industrial, loyal to free trade and hostile to the Lords and land and a consumers' South which supported the economic protection of markets, especially argued by those landowners who sat as peers in the House of Lords. It was the south of England or the Home Counties (still the stronghold of the Conservative Party up until the present) which incorporated the growing interests of the City as a centre of finance capitalism. This social and economic divide, however, was interrupted in the 1830s by what W. D. Rubinstein called the end of 'Old Corruption' (Rubinstein, 1977). This was a label given to the political alliance of church and state before the so-called Whig reforms of the 1820s and 1830s opened the state to the influence of (in turn) non-Anglican Christians or nonconformists, Catholics, elements of the middle class and eventually to Jews, atheists, working-class men and (and later still) to women. Modernizing the state, Rubinstein insisted, not only led to the separation of landowner interests from the commercial and industrial middle classes, but it also produced fission within the middle classes themselves.

The passing of the First Reform Act in 1832 meant that, as rich financiers rose in importance, the section of the professional middle class that had benefited from the aristocratic state ('Old Corruption') diminished. Equally, as landowners profited from farming, coal royalties and urban ground rents, so the commercial middle class turned away from the British state or at least from domestic markets and towards financing overseas trade. The accumulated result was a 'gentlemanly capitalism' which, according to P. J. Cain and A. G. Hopkins, was the main sponsor of Imperialism (Cain and Hopkins, 2001).

The peculiar nature of this new imperial state was nevertheless shaped by the pre-capitalist character of the aristocracy whose attitudes continued to be moulded by interests in commercial agriculture. This formation emerged as the most important element of the British economy and provided the basis of new investment in finance and capital. Hence, the attendant values of 'gentlemanly capitalism' were easy and rustic living, a sense of paternalism and the cult of the amateur, plus contempt for the everyday world of wealth. These attitudes infected both the industrial *and* financial sectors.

Previous work argued along similar lines. The cultural historian Martin Wiener, for example, had placed particular emphasis on Britain's anti-entrepreneurial spirit and its influence on the composition of the state in order to explain relative economic decline. To Wiener, a culturally determined pre-modern and anti-modern bent had produced a particular type of Englishness, enhancing the role of the 'gentleman' (and all that the term implied socially and culturally) at the expense of industry and the industrious (and all *that* term implied socially and culturally; Wiener, 1981). Likewise, seen through the lens of a wider European history, Arno Mayer had argued in *The Persistence of the Old Regime* (1981) that the European ancien régime had survived to at least 1914, while Britain's rentier aristocratic country and land-orientated capital had maintained a cultural dominance that shaped the industrial bourgeoisie that increasingly eschewed entrepreneurship. With a high concentration of land and wealth, owners were free to maintain tenant farmers, thereby guaranteeing an income stream and leisure time which provided opportunities to engage in politics.

As a result of this type of politics and culture, the state tended to favour the interests of the aristocracy at the expense of the 'me too' bourgeois industrialists who nonetheless busily acquired mock family mottos emblazoned on mock family crests, rode with the hounds and sent their offspring to great, old Public Schools and the ancient universities of Oxford and Cambridge (ancient in that order, it should be hastily emphasized). If Britain's social and economic rulers were made up of the landed aristocracy, merchant bankers in the City were not an open elite, welcoming to rising classes such as the northern industrialists but a closed grouping which created an hegemonic coalition of 'gentleman capitalists' who desperately searched for social acceptance while distancing themselves from an industrial sector and industrialists that were seen to lack gentility, political guile or cultural sophistication, no matter how much they tried (Lisle-Williams, 1984). Hence, in the views of Wiener and Mayer, the British state was essentially firmly established before the onset of industrialization. Indeed, its economic or political power remained unchallenged by industrialization – save for the modest and steady adjustments to the franchise – but was nonetheless singularly incapable of addressing the decline of British capitalism as it began to lose ground to German and American competitors.

This state formation was interrupted in the 1880s as landed incomes fell in the face of imports of foreign food and as the City, the apex of the commercial and financial elite, moved into more formal political alliance with landed interests via the Conservative and Unionist Party committed to land and inherited privilege, church and the institutions of state, City and imperialism. Industry and the industrial remained of second order, certainly in cultural terms. The consequence, so the argument runs, was that status accrued to those who were established aristocrats or 'something in the City' became as important landowners, merchants or bankers, all of whom appeared to distance themselves from industry and the petit bourgeoisie traders that dominated the City of London Corporation, the local government of the square mile. Thus the entrepreneurship and innovation required to renew both the economy and the state was thwarted. Indeed, it might be further argued that this remained the case until the shock and awe of global war in 1914–1918 and 1939–1945 forced change down the gullets of the establishment. Not for nothing did Labour MP Hartley William Shawcross (allegedly) shout across the floor of the House of Commons in 1945 that 'we are the masters now', a phrase rich with irony from this German-born lawyer who was to leave the Labour Party and become a peer when faced with the growing hegemony of the Conservative Party in the 1950s.

We can see then that historical 'arches' were created by historians in order to help us understand long-term structural changes to the composition and objectives of the state which would otherwise be impossible by looking simply at the machinations of day-to-day politics (Barratt Brown, 1988). When this 'helicopter' view of political change is applied to the City of London, we can begin to see the forces and personalities that allowed the City to construct a pathway to modernity.

While evidence-based accounts of state formations have been written in the main by historians, how state formations, economies and cultures work over the long term have attracted the interest of sociologists and political theorists such as Perry Anderson, Charles Tilly, Immanuel Wallerstein and Michael Mann who have provided us with highly theorized grand narratives that concentrate, above all, on power, political authority, capital, conflict, class and state structures. With the example of the City in mind, let us examine the usefulness to political historians of each of these key thinkers and writers.

Perry Anderson is probably best known for his early work, *Passages from Antiquity to Feudalism* (1974) and *Lineages of the Absolutist State* (1975), which influentially attempted to capture continuities in state formations over vast times and geographies. For Anderson, changes to the absolutist state (where power was unchecked) in Western Europe (Spain, France, England, Italy and Sweden) and Eastern Europe (Prussia, Poland, Austria, Russia plus the 'house of Islam' and 'Japanese Feudalism') can best be understood using Marxist theory. However, in singling out the diversity of state formations he produced a landscape of the past which was far from simplistic. Absolutist states fell or dissolved, he contended, at different rates from, say, the Netherlands in the sixteenth century to Russia in the twentieth but without necessarily conforming to the laws of Marxist theory or any 'single temporality'. In this sense, Anderson constructs an historical theory of the state which is flexible enough to be of real use to the historian; that is, the presumptions of Marxist theory do not override the historical evidence.

This firmly stated, there is a grand narrative which tends to be simply assumed by Anderson: the primitive accumulation of capital, religious reformation (albeit in varying forms), the rise of the nation state and the onset of industrialization and with it the push to establish overseas markets via imperialism. This scheme, in other words, follows a linear pattern that looks for all the world like a Marxist theory of history, untroubled by empirical research.

Anderson sought to place the English experience, including the role of the City of London, in the context of what he regarded as the development of an immature state formation. In a bitter and protracted debate conducted in the pages of the *New Left Review* and *The Socialist Register*, E. P. Thompson wrote a razor-sharp essay in 1965 called the 'Peculiarities of the English' in which he summed up some of Anderson's arguments (Thompson, 2008). His narrative, according to Thompson, is deceptively simple and differs little from the chronology set down in the 'gentlemanly capitalism' debate:

1. In the premature, unfulfilled character of the seventeenth-century revolution, and the ensuing compromises of 1688 and 1832, the industrial bourgeoisie failed to attain to an undisputed hegemony and to remake the ruling institutions of society in its own image. Rather, a 'deliberate, systematized symbiosis' took place between the landed aristocracy and the industrial bourgeoisie, in which, however, the aristocracy remained as senior partner.
2. Because the seventeenth-century revolution was 'impure' and the struggle was conducted in religious terms, the bourgeoisie never developed any coherent worldview or self-knowledge and made do with an 'ideology' of 'empiricism' which has characterized English intellectual culture to the present day.
3. A premature bourgeois revolution gave rise to a premature working-class movement, whose heroic struggles during the Industrial Revolution were nullified by the absence of any commensurate theoretical growth: 'Its maximum ardour and insurgency coincided with the minimum availability of socialism as a structured ideology.' When this movement fell apart after Chartism (through 'exhaustion') there followed a 'profound caesura' in English working-class history, and the 'most insurgent working class in Europe became the most numbed and docile'. 'Marxism came too late', whereas in other Countries it swept through the ranks of the working class. Thereafter, the post-1880 Labour movement has nullified its entire existence by expressing only corporative (and not hegemonic) virtues and by becoming subject (with Fabianism) to an ideology which mimics, with impoverished equipment, the banal empiricism of the bourgeoisie.

There is neither time nor space to count the numbers and types of angels dancing on the end of this particular Marxist pinhead, but it is enough to say that, regardless of whether or not the structuralism of Anderson or the humanism of Thompson was the most convincing explanation for the lack of revolution in England or for the nature of its state formation, any concentration on the state as a continuous entity has merit for the historian of any denomination.

Charles Tilly's *Coercion, Capital and European States* (1990) also has use and merit. As a sociologist profoundly interested in social change, Tilly examined European societies over the last millennia and characterized states into three types: tribute-taking empires; city states that had systems of disparate and fragmented sovereignty; and national states as experienced in the modern period. Like Anderson, Tilley associated states with power. More particularly, states were 'coercion-wielding organizations that are distinct from households and kinship groups and exercise clear priority in some respects over all other organizations within substantial territories'

(Tilly, p. 1). Clearly, states from, say, Sweden or Italy had variations of what Tilly calls 'form and activity' which were not always linked to their mode of production. This presents problems for conventional Marxist approaches since state development is unconnected to economic relations. Tilly also rejected the approach of Immanuel Wallerstein's *The Modern World System* (2011), which attempted to explain why states developed out of synch (so to speak) with property relationships, by suggesting that economies working as a world system could determine regional class structures:

> Geopolitical and world system analysis provide stronger guidance, but so far they lack convincing accounts of the *actual mechanisms* [our italics] relating position within the world to the organization and practice of particular states. In particular, they fail to capture the impact of war and the preparation for war on the whole process of state formation. . . . To the extent that great, exploitative landlords survived the transition to intensive cash-crop farming, authoritarian government persisted into the contemporary era. To the extent that the bourgeoisie predominated, some form of democracy existed.
>
> (Tilly, 1992, pp. 11–12)

Here then is the crux of his argument. Historical research had not yet revealed the details of the world system analysis and had not fully articulated the part played in the relations or conflicts *among* states. In making this emphasis, Tilly is clear that he both echoes that work of several scholars such as Lewis Mumford – who explained the growth of the urban by a particular concentration of political and productive power and Barrington Moore, whose *Social Origins of Dictatorship and Democracy* (1966) also sought to provide details of how the behaviour of a state influenced a wider system. The twist that Tilly brought, however, was to take the argument further than Mumford, Barrington Moore and others, 'emphatically in two ways':

> first by placing the organization of coercion and preparation for war squarely in the middle of the analysis, arguing in its rasher moments that state structure appeared chiefly as a by-product of rulers' efforts to acquire the means of war; and second by insisting that relations among states, especially through war and the preparation for war, strongly affected the entire process of state formation.
>
> (Ibid., p. 14)

This compunction by states to prepare for and prosecute war led to the three types of European states identified. Tilly was careful, however, to make clear that there was nothing neat about this process; there was no smooth succession from one type of state to another: 'the long survival and coexistence of all three types argues against any notion of European state formation as a single, unilineal process, or of the national state – which did, indeed, eventually prevail – as an inherently superior form of government' (ibid., p. 21).

Indeed, from the nineteenth century 'all European states involved themselves much more heavily than before in building social infrastructure' (ibid., p. 31). The features of this 'social infrastructure' included:

- Providing public services.
- Regulating economic activity.
- Controlling population movements.
- Assuring citizen welfare.
- Exerting some control over production and distribution.

What form did this take, and how did this conception of the state challenge previous accounts? The modern nation state from about the seventeenth century had proved itself to be efficient in concentrating capital in a war economy and this, in turn, was a compelling model in which to build social infrastructure in peacetime. This for Tilly is the missing element in Anderson's approach, which was anyway too heavily governed by the presumptions of historical materialism. Wallerstein, if anything, was more economically determinist than Anderson (the subtitle of his *The Modern World System* was *Capitalist Agriculture and the Origins of the European World Economy in the Sixteenth Century*). Absolutism, an astute reviewer of Wallerstein's book remarked, 'was engulfed in a more general and specifically economic process which made use of a variety of political formations', not the feudal 'stage' of history or the capitalist stage (Martin, 1976, p. 269). But while Anderson may have baulked at Wallerstein's chronology, which had departed from a linear model of history that moved forward in stages, Tilly thought highly of Wallerstein and his notion of the state operating within a comprehensible world system.

Tilly also noted that Anderson did not attempt to fit the findings of empirical research into neat theoretical boxes, declaring that 'there is merely that which is known – established by historical research – and that which is not known: the latter may be the mechanisms of single events or the *laws of motion* [our italics] of whole structures' (Tilly, 1992, p. 268). Anderson never, Tilly is careful to say, 'resorts to an appeal to what theoretically "must have been" in the absence of data, nor does he reduce data to the status of irrelevant epiphenomena' (ibid.). Anderson may not see history as 'determined' and its outcomes as inevitable, but he does bring up the idea of a law of motion for state formation that does rather take us back to theoretical assumptions that seem more akin to theology than evidence-driven history.

There was a gap then in the mechanical details of how states formed and worked. Tilly managed only partially to fill this gap. Other historians have provided that detail, however. For the eighteenth century, for example, John Brewer (1989) has spoken about the fiscal military state, while David Edgerton (2006) has written convincingly about the twentieth-century 'warfare state'. Both, like Tilly, placed a firm emphasis on the role of war in state formation. Thus, Brewer spoke then of a transformation of the eighteenth-century state as the making of the 'Sinews of War' where increased military commitments were met by a large increase in taxation, the furnishing of public debt and the populating of a substantial public administration:

> [M]ost eighteenth-century commentators were sure that fluctuations in the fortunes of war and the conduct of peace affected the everyday conduct of economic life. Similarly, they argued that the longer-term changes in the nature of government – the emergence of the fiscal-military state – had altered the balance of social forces in Britain by penalizing the landed classes, creating a new class of financier and laying a heavy burden of taxes on the ordinary consumer. For more than a generation the state was seen as one of the major agents of social and economic change.
>
> (Brewer, 1989, p. xxi)

The question to ask (but with no time to answer now) is why Georgian Britain could establish state power and state legitimacy that had the wherewithal to put boots on the ground in times of international conflict but that could simultaneously avoid a despotic state when it came to the administration of its domestic affairs. One way to gauge this dichotomy – if dichotomy it is – would be to go with Brewer to examine that nature of the state prior the eighteenth century. Another is to fast forward in time to the twentieth century when conflict had become brutally industrialized and the state had modernized to facilitate the terrible power that is modern warfare.

By the first decades of the twentieth century, at the very moment that it was acquiring a 'cradle to grave' welfare state, Britain acquired a much larger state than before. David Edgerton looked closely at three elements of the period 1920–1970: state policy and the arms industry; the civil service and the elites of the British state; the economy and the wider understanding of the British state. Sitting behind these facets of the industrial-military complex was the incongruity (as it was perceived by both British and American historiography of the period) of any sort of militarism that could plausibly be seen as significant in the context of decolonialization and the relative economic decline that the gentlemanly capitalism debate addressed. Instead,

> [i]n the first decades of the century this state was created and commanded a military-industrial-scientific complex which was, in the phrase of the time, 'second to none'. For some decades after the Second World War it held a sharply differentiated third place in a bipolar world. It was the pioneer of modern, technologically focused warfare; its naval and air forces long led the world. It was for a very time the leading exporter of arms. It had a state machine operated not just by bureaucrats but also by technicians. It had intimate links with business, and indeed it successfully intervened in the economy, transforming its industrial structure. It saw itself as a global, liberal power, as a world political-economic policeman, an arbiter of the fate of nations.
>
> (Edgerton, 2006, p. 1)

More recently, Daniel Todman (2020, 2021) with both his *Into Battle, 1937–1941* and *Britain's War: A New World, 1942–1947* emphasized how the British state pursued national strategic priorities at a critical time.

If Martin Weiner in the gentlemanly capitalism debate assumed that there was an anti-industrial 'spirit' in nineteenth-century Britain which led to decline, then so did Corelli Barnett in his *Audit of War* (1986) assume that an inefficient postwar state, its face now 'turned to the dank reality of a segregated, subliterate, unskilled, unhealthy and institutionalized proletariat hanging on the nipple of state maternalism', had necessarily turned its back on industrial and technical excellence (Barnett, 1986, p. 304). If Edgerton is correct, then the views of both Barnett in respect to the twentieth century and Weiner in the nineteenth century are little more than impressionistic (Edgerton, 2006, pp. 301–2). At the same time, again according to Edgerton, the debate between Anderson and Thompson in the 1960s was prompted by evidence from the twentieth-century military state which suggested (as historians make histories in their own present) that Anderson had 'reproduced standard technocratic declinist analysis' while Thompson had showed 'an anti-declinist streak' (ibid., p. 4).

Whether (like Anderson or Thompson) these theories of the state are accurate or make up a valuable analysis of the state over time, they are all established to at least some extent in the abstract. Here Marxism has taken a clear and leading role. Yet, for Tilly, class is but one force propelling history. Here the founding work of Max Weber (1864–1920) is as important as the theory of history propounded by Marx. Sometimes states are not always thought to be tied to the forces of production but may be autonomous with very specific powers that are particular to time and place. Where Tilly uses both Marx and Weber to explain the role of the state in making war, Theda Skocpol in her *States and Social Revolutions* (1979) talks about the 'state centred approach' to history, which doesn't discount the history of class but which may not necessarily elevate class analysis to the point where class could become both the chief explanation for change and the only one.

In his wide-sweeping volumes *The Sources of Social Power* (1986–2012), Michael Mann uses the expression 'organizational materialism' to explain how the study of the state as a

136 *Varieties*

fiscal-military capitalist system might be less useful to the historian than the study of individual organizations and the autonomous power of organizations that adopt Weberian notions of how state bureaucracies work. Such state power is not power that originates in conflict but it is a power that is entwined in the economic, ideological and political spheres, so enabling the state to act autonomously from the economic interests that govern or oppose society. The nature of that entwining determines the motives and actions of historical actors, not just their relationship within the material dialectic created and altered purely by economic conditions. Stephen Skowronek's *Building a New American State: the expansion of national administrative capacities, 1877–1920* (1982) is a good example of this so-called organization-analytic approach.

Whether or not one is inclined to prefer the Marxist approach to the Weberian framework, the astute historian may well detect a significant fly in the ointment. This emerges in much political history as a tension: the need among historians of politics to acknowledge the effects of power as an area of study but also to look anew at its opportunities and challenges. To look more closely at those practitioners of 'history from below' or 'People's History' and the political elites is to look at High and Low politics and the differing approaches that these varying mythologies imply.

8.2 High and Low Politics: the Case of the British Labour Party

The British Monarchy has an official website which features '40 facts about Buckingham Palace'. One of these facts concerns the dress codes when visiting the monarch. When the prime minister goes to the Palace after an election supposedly to 'kiss hands' with the head of state, the requirement after every election until the Second World War was to wear formal court evening dress. Except once: after the election of a Labour government in 1924. Then Ramsey James MacDonald (1866–1937) became Prime minister of a minority administration. A photograph shows Labour's first Prime minister leaving the Palace in a suit with a top hat that was almost certainly borrowed.

MacDonald was to lead the 1931 Labour government and was also to be expelled from the party he had been so instrumental in bringing to power. MacDonald was a Scot from an impoverished background who, before meeting his wife of independent means, once almost died for lack of food. He was the first of his kind and almost the last to date: a working-class leader of a governing party of the state; in this case, of the Labour Party. There would not be another working-class leader of any party until James Callaghan (1912–2005) who became Labour prime minister in 1976. (Edward Heath, the Conservative Prime minister who preceded Callaghan in the same decade is said by the *Oxford Dictionary of National Biography* to have been brought up 'on the subtle English borderline between the working and middle classes'). Like MacDonald, Callaghan was raised by his mother in poverty; like MacDonald he used his middle name, not his first (MacDonald was really James, Callaghan was Leonard); like MacDonald he was from a non-conformist Christian background; like MacDonald he served both as Foreign Secretary as well as First Lord of the Treasury and like his predecessor, Callaghan found it difficult to manage power in the face of opposition within his own party.

Politics is about power, and political history is about the history of power (Hoffman and Graham, 2006, p. 3). Or it is concerned with the history of theories about power: it may focus, perhaps, upon issues connected to the central state or local government or histories of democracy or citizenship. While histories of 'high' politics, preoccupied with the biographies and temperaments of leaders, have become rarer in recent years, historians have become more interested in popular politics or 'politics from below' that emphasize electoral sociology, trade unions, the role of pressure groups and the like. While the manoeuvrings of say MacDonald or Callaghan in parliament and in the corridors of the state have not been discounted by historians, there is a greater tendency to study the pressures they faced from outside parliament; the impact of the welfare state on social mobility and voting patterns or the demands for political enfranchisement made, for instance, by women.

One way of illustrating how popular politics has made a real impact in recent years is to sketch one of the central concerns of twentieth-century British politics, the replacement of the Liberal Party as the main party of progress by the Labour Party. In tackling this question of how and why the British Labour Party grew and transformed into a party of government (albeit one spectacularly unsuccessful in winning elections until Tony Blair in 1997), political historians conform to trends that can be found in other sub-disciplines of history. Historians initially looked at sociological factors such as expansion of the franchise, and the make-up of the Labour vote; more recently, in a move away from class-based determinism, the emphasis is on textual approaches and the importance of language used in political debate or the development of policy. There is also now a 'four nations' approach where regional or local variation in the United Kingdom is recognized as contributing to the political processes of the whole.

As well as studies of region and nation, popular political history has also been concerned with the constitution. This has been especially true of the devolution of power from the political centre to the peripheries. Interventions such as Brian Harrison's *The Transformation of British Politics* (1996) and Vernon Bogdanor's *The British Constitution in the Twentieth Century* (2003) are overloaded with details of how the constitution works, with electoral statistics and a labyrinthine civil service placed in context. Party has also been a concern with both the Labour Party and the Conservative Party surveyed over long periods, and as parties of state their conduct in and out of power is related to economic, social, cultural and constitutional development more generally. The latest of these are histories of coalition government in Britain and, the apparent disintegration of the Labour Party in Britain after the Brexit campaign in 2016, the retreat from its 1918 constitution (Clause 1), which committed it to maintain representation in parliament and, as we write, its tentative electoral recovery under a more centrist leadership.

Challenges to the constitution were very much part of the historical story of Liberal and Labour transition. In a book that has become a classic, George Dangerfield in his wonderfully written *The Strange Death of Liberal England*, first published in 1935, argues for the significance of the 'hiatus' of the period 1910–1914 when the House of Lords threatened to rebel and was thwarted by the Parliament Act of 1911, when Ireland revolted, suffragette and suffragist protest was at a fairly violent peak and trade union activity threatened European levels of militancy. While it must be true to say that Liberalism did not die because of these constitutional threats, we know that after 1922 the Liberal Party would never govern again unless we count its resurrection via the Liberal Democratic Party who became the junior partner to the Conservatives in the 2010 Coalition but whose 14 members are now (2023) so few that they could fit into a large taxi.

This brings us to another central concern of popular political history in this period: the *timing* of Labour ascendancy, which Dangerfield places in the period before the First World War (1914–1918). The 1918 extension to the franchise and the socialist and trade union militancy that characterizes the postwar world are well known, but Dangerfield insists that 'the extravagant behaviour of the postwar decade, which most of us thought to be the effect of war, had really begun before the War. The War hastened everything – in politics, economics, in behaviour – but it started nothing' (Dangerfield, 1997, p. 14).

Historians of popular politics dispute this chronology, but they do so from the perspective of understanding the class and sociological makeup of the period. Peter Clarke's *Lancashire and the New Liberalism* (1971) brilliantly uses a local case study to argue that New Liberalism as

138 *Varieties*

Figure 8.1 Ramsay MacDonald, Labour Party pioneer, Prime minister and 'traitor'

Contributor: Courtesy of the Library of Congress Prints and Photographs Division Washington, D.C. 20540 USA, George Grantham Bain Collection, LC-DIG-ggbain-37952

an ideology was committed to collectivist solutions that appealed to a segment of the respectable working class. This enabled the Liberal Party to hold at bay the emergent Labour Party until 1914. Then the war introduced new elements in the way that work and the state were organized – such as compulsory conscription and the constitutional claims of women which divided the party at the parliamentary level.

The picture at the local level, in local government in fact, looked different again. Duncan Tanner famously argued in his *Political Change and the Labour Party* (1990) that Clarke's position was overstated. Clarke was right to emphasize relative Liberal strength until 1914 but that the 'politics of place' offered a different perspective from that of ideology or national political strategies. Others fix on 1918 and the expansion of the franchise to suggest that Labour's rise after the War depended upon the emergence of a working-class constituency, which from a sociological perspective makes perfect sense but which offers little room for explanations of change that was focused on power, leadership and personalities.

Counter to this approach, Maurice Cowling (1926–2005), the foremost historian of the 'high politics' approach to political history, took the view that focusing on decision-making and the wielding of power was the only way to get either a complete historical or satisfactory sociological picture on the rise of the Labour party. In so doing he was concerned more with social scientific models of power rather than a self-conscious and deliberate attempt to follow in the footsteps of the influential historian Lewis Namier (1888–1960). Namier made his name by reconstructing power structures in the eighteenth-century parliaments, painstakingly piecing together the career histories of politicians. While Cowling claimed that he belonged to a different historiographical tradition from that of Namier, he too emphasized the roles of parliament and party.

Cowling argued that the interaction between political leaders and their followers was the essence of politics. In his introduction to the *Impact of Labour* (1971), Cowling said emphatically that:

- It was the high politics of parliamentary politicians that 'mattered'.
- Politicians and political party ties may have had beliefs but their calculations and strategies were not based on these beliefs.
- Parliament was affected by outside pressures from, for example, the media and electorate, but party strategy was decided at the top and this is where the historian should seek evidence.

Politicians from every party had to make strategic decisions in response to the rise of the Labour Party, and they had a clear responsibility to educate the electorate to act moderately. Accordingly, the Conservatives between 1920 and 1924 'made three long time decisions':

1 To remove Lloyd George, the Prime minister of the Coalition government.
2 To take up a role as 'defender of the social order'.
3 To consider the Labour Party as the chief party of opposition and to school the Labour Party to be loyal and responsible in that important constitutional position.

These decisions were not easily made, and they were strongly contested among the leadership, but the Conservatives needed to contain the political upheaval announced by the arrival of the Labour party on the political scene and at the same time to seek electoral advantage. Their consequences were wide ranging, for the next phase of political struggle leading up to the general election of 1924 and, subsequently, the new Tory leader, Stanley Baldwin, would now take up the challenge of opposing 'socialism' as a creed that was essentially un-English.

In his astonishing scholarship and attention to method, Cowling revealed a complex and thoughtful approach to the past and the present but from 'above', that is, from the policy makers and power brokers. Many criticized him for ignoring constituency politics and extra-parliamentary activity in say trade unions or the formation of public opinion more generally. He certainly recognized that power from outside parliament permeated into its chambers and, equally, saw the importance of rhetoric as it related to public opinion. But it is equally certain that Cowling represented the 'high' approach to politics and not the interest in popular politics with which we begun.

He was interested, however, in political language, the motivations for speaking – where and to whom, why and at what moment – than the actual words themselves. This is why he preferred private letters and diaries over public documents because the former was bound to reveal more than the latter. Finally, he utterly rejected notions of historical method as a science. Historical actions were, he thought, without cause and effect like phenomena in the natural world. In this sense, his influences could not be Namierite but were rather closer to the approaches of R. W. Collingwood (1889–1943) and the Conservative Michael Oakeshott (1901–1990) who also rejected notions of the historian as objective fact gatherer. In short, context was all-important and 'the historian himself was part of the context he investigated' (Craig, 2010, p. 468).

Until recently, this overall approach was thought to be part of a so-called Peterhouse School or Cambridge School of Politics and History, which narrowly restricted politics and political endeavour to that which took place within the parliamentary sphere, but the able defenders of Cowling such as Philip Williamson and David Craig have argued that he was also interested in a much wider frame of reference, connecting party politicians who wielded individual power to movements in the political landscape of the nation. Thus, elite politics was not the only politics that 'mattered', and his use of private sources allowed an understanding of the real motives of political elites. Cowling adopted a high politics approach only because he wanted to get beyond the narrow limits of political sociology that he found ultimately inadequate.

Drawing upon electoral statistics, political thought, biography and memoir, as well as official sources, political historians have thus approached the history of the Labour Party in myriad ways. The narrative outlined here has drawn largely upon the popular political histories because it has sought to represent the bulk of histories written in this way over recent years and not because Cowling's approach hardly strayed beyond the specific cultures of the political elite. We should take notice of David Craig, however, when he says that there is now a narrower gap between political histories of elites and histories of popular politics – or Susan Pedersen's equally wise suggestion that 'high' politics and 'low' politics may have converged with a common focus on political language or rhetoric making up what is now called the 'new political history' (Pederson, 2002, p. 42).

'New political history' would cast so-called 'Labour culture' in a somewhat different light. These new histories argue that political parties construct their political constituencies through discourse and vocabulary. Politics from this viewpoint was not built within national party organizations, working within newly equalized constituencies after the mid-1880s, and political preference cannot be simply expressed through the sociological make-up of neighbourhoods. Rather it is the sum of the language used to describe or articulate the centrality of, say, empire or masculinities and the wider culture: E. H. H. Green (ed.), *An Age of Transition: British Politics, 1880–1914* (1997); Jon Lawrence and Miles Taylor, *Party, State and Society: Electoral Behaviour in Britain since 1820* (1997); Jon Lawrence, *Speaking for the People: Party, Language and Popular Politics in England, 1867–1914* (1997). All are concerned with suggesting that the older electoral sociology is outmoded and deterministic and that more attention should be paid to political rhetoric.

We now know from the work of Alex Windscheffel, for instance, in his *Popular Conservatism in Imperial London* (2007), that Conservative Party success at the end of the nineteenth century – a moment when Conservatism in London swept progressive politics aside – was not simply the result of a politics that held a mirror up to the new suburbs. 'Villa Toryism' was not a newly found class identity that somehow found a natural home in Conservative politics and in which the Conservative Party was but a perfect reflection, but rather the Conservative Party invented a new metropolitan politics. By celebrating empire, the new 'denizens of the Little Palaces' in the suburbs could now see London as an imperial metropolis and saw the Conservative Party successfully *describing* their place in the capital. There is now no longer any reason to suppose, however, that simply by virtue of their class or occupation that the dwellers of the suburbs automatically fashioned Conservatives any more than the slums of London or 'the North' robotically manufactured Socialists with flat caps that raced pigeons, attended football matches, drank light ale and were therefore impelled to vote Labour.

8.3 Beyond State and Party: Political Histories and Civil Society

That 'Devil Wilkes' was an English radical, journalist, politician, Member of Parliament and Lord Mayor of London. His meaningful and now notorious activities began in that signal decade of London and British politics – the 1760s. Yet John Wilkes (1725–1797) was most influenced by the American War of Independence and the popular support that it engendered among the American rebels across significant parts of Britain. In this sense he provides a good introduction for historians interested in histories of the constitution and the importance of political structures, but his case also illuminates how to take into account extra-parliamentary or 'unofficial' protest. Having supported Catholic Emancipation and led a militia against the anti-Catholic rioters led by the infamous Lord George Gordon (1751–1793), Wilkes later drifted to the right. Moreover, he had been always a libertine of quite shocking proportions, which may have overshadowed a radical and liberal tradition, but which was also not untypical of radicals who were quite often pornographers and who saw the libertarian basis of free sexual expression but also its profitability. In any case, 'Cry Wilkes and Liberty' was to remain a prominent feature in British, English and City politics and serves to remind us of an 'unofficial' politics that was local and existed alongside recognized structures such as state or party.

At the heart of the Wilkes agitation was a strong sense of a popular politics that was not party based but which nonetheless placed parliament and the processes of law centre stage. If the context for the rise of Wilkes was a demand for local accountability borrowed from the American colonists, it was given impetus by a shrinking electorate and the dissipation of political energy away from Westminster. The occasion may well have been dissatisfaction with the one-party government which had effectively been predominant in Britain since the 1720s.

The debate about taxation and representation was critical both to British parliamentary life and also to British extra-parliamentary activity. This was a point forcibly made by John Brewer in his book *Party Ideology and Popular Politics at the Accession of George III* (1976). In this sense, according to Brewer, Wilkes was at the head of the first extra-parliamentary movement 'devoted to a programme of reform' that was aimed at parliament (Brewer, 1976, p. 21). Wilkes' Society of the Supporters of the Bill of Rights was supplemented by a sophisticated marketing and propaganda campaign that promoted the radical and liberal agenda in a way that had not yet been seen in modern politics:

> Political argument in eighteenth century England was never the exclusive preserve of the parliamentary classes. It could be found expressed in pamphlets, in the columns of almost every provincial paper and, in ideographic form, in political cartoons and caricatures. Much of the ritual behaviour of crowds during political demonstrations was ordered by their view of politics. Ballads, verse, periodicals and squibs, all, with varying degrees of sophistication, touched upon the chief political issues of the day.
>
> (Ibid, p. 35)

This then is a section that deals with politics outside of the party model – say, Tories versus Whigs – but instead examines the make-up of politics where forces were gathered remote from the political centre. Hence, the agitation organized around the person of Wilkes, made possible by the boost to radical opinion that had been received from the American revolutionary wars, took place largely in the streets and meeting houses of London. Similarly, where the French Revolution created domestic revolutionaries so did it provide an extra-parliamentary counterweight in the shape of popular loyalism, leading to state suppression of radicalism in the mid-1790s. As radicalism revived at the conclusion of the French wars (or rose to the surface after decades underground, if E. P. Thompson in his *Making of the English Working Class* (1963) is to be believed), it manifested as Luddism, the political radicalism of William Cobbett and a romantic radicalism that was cut down in the 1819 massacre at Peterloo, near Manchester. Philosophical radicalism and the commentators of political economy (the so-called Benthamites, after Jeremy Bentham (1748–1832), the philosophical radical) began as a politics focused on parliamentary reform and then entered into a certain quiescence in the mid-1820s during a period of relative prosperity before returning to radical activity over religious disabilities by the end of the decade. Next came the agitation for the vote via Chartism, industrialization, the rise of both the middle and working classes and, finally, the conditions that gave rise to the Labour Party.

The varying methods and the divergent aims of protest movements emerged as critical in this rather pared-down and simplified narrative of liberal change. So too was the idea of what could be accepted as legitimate forms of politics. E. P. Thompson wrote in *Whigs and Hunters* (1975) about the eighteenth century and saw the Black Act of 1723 as the occasion for criminal activity against forest officers who protected the plunder of the forests by elites and those that fermented popular discontent as a protest against Robert Walpole and the Whig grandees. Likewise, E. J. Hobsbawm identified Balkan haiduks, Indian dacoits or Brazilian congaceiros as *Bandits* (1969) whose criminality disguised a political intent. Or George Rudé's *The Crowd in History. A Study of Popular Disturbances in France and England, 1730–1848* (1964, 2005), which highlighted the role of popular political pressure at work, as did the Colchester Oyster Feast, which David Cannadine in 1982 argued was an instance of the transformation of politics that could be traced through civic ritual in Britain. What started as an 'obscure private dinner' was to become an event of national significance, albeit with the expressive aspects of its public pageantry declining and retreating into private spaces. Where *The Crowd* articulated what Hobsbawm had called 'collective bargaining by riot', *The Oyster Feast* closely paralleled local political concerns outside of the formal structures of politics.

Historians need to take note of forms of politics that do not necessarily appear obvious or overt. Returning to the example of the City of London from which we started the chapter, a radical liberalism there developed through its relationship with the state in the promotion of technical education and then was matured in the civil society of its associational life after 1867. Individual members of the Corporation (as the local government of the square mile) acted out roles as civic representatives but also as businessmen and representatives of the financial City. These roles were played out in the formal economic relationships of the City but also in the local associational life around the London Chambers of Commerce, some of its Imperialist relations such as the Naval League, as well as organizations including the Liberty and Property Defence League, ratepayer associations, livery companies and various City-based clubs.

The City's politics was re-made then at the end of the nineteenth century. Once the heart of radicalism and radical causes, the place where John Wilkes had been Lord Mayor in the 1770s and Lord Chamberlain for longer, there was a move away from a politics necessarily linked with a resident population, towards one concerned with property interests. This was not caused by the disappearance of a resident community through de-population or because radicalism lost its constituency (the numbers able to vote in municipal and parliamentary elections actually increased in the course of the City's physical changes). This was a constituency that had not been replaced but rather transformed by changing approaches to what constituted the idea of liberty, expressed not in state or party but in extra-parliamentary and local politics.

The emphasis here was on anti-statism but one that tried to apply the classical ideal of equality before the law and non-intervention in the economy, more or less along the lines of John Stuart Mill's *On Liberty* (1859). For example, the 'Vigilance Association for the Defence of Personal Rights and for the Amendment of the Law wherein it is Injurious to Women'; the anti-centralization credentials of this particular pressure group were beyond doubt. In its early days it campaigned against state coercion implicit in the Contagious Diseases Acts of the 1860s as well as arguing against compulsory vaccination laws. Like the later campaigns against legislation in matters of labour contracts that restricted female labour, it believed that state action and personal responsibility were irreconcilable. This attracted some of the early suffragettes like Elizabeth Wolstenholme, older followers of the Italian nationalist and revolutionary Giuseppe Mazzini (1805–1872) and figures such as the co-operator George Holyoake, the radical free-thinker George Howell, the atheist Charles Bradlaugh and Joseph Arch, the agricultural trade unionist. Then Joseph Haim Levy (1838–1913), Professor of Birkbeck College and lecturer at the City of London College, retailored the Vigilance Association into the 'Personal Rights Association'. This meant less concern with the individual rights of women and the collective rights of labour and more preoccupation with the general defence of the citizen from centralizing agencies.

Like the City of London Corporation, the Personal Rights Association was concerned with ascertaining the limits of power, albeit, in the case of the Corporation, from a Whig viewpoint. State action was necessarily class or aristocratic action and as such would have been traditionally linked with the Court party or Tories. The championing of civil and religious liberty and the working of the ward system (the Corporation was made up of twenty-six electoral areas called wards) encouraged the exercise of personal rights and responsibilities in the 1840s and 1850s. However, as the century wore on, the City's liberal stance changed perceptibly. It did not stop talking about liberty but rather altered what it meant by the term. The constitution of the Association stated its intention 'to effect the repeal or amendment of existing laws which directly or indirectly violate the principle of personal right or of perfect equality before the law'. This translated into opposition to the Registration of Births and Deaths Act (1874), Infant Life Protection Act (1874), Teachers Registration Bill (1879), Prison's Act (1879) and, as far as they imposed on women's 'freedom of industry', the Factory and Workshops Act (*Journal of the Vigilance Association for the Defence of Personal Rights*, January 1881). Its members also opposed corporal and capital punishment. The concern was to define the limits of state power and the power of a tyrannical majority in the age of democracy. With the formation of the Liberty and Property Defence League in July 1882, mainly located on the right-wing of the Conservative party, property took the side of Individualism. Given the choice between the rights of property and the claims of democracy, anti-statist politics came down in favour of property – so much so that the Personal Rights Association and the Liberty and Property Defence League shared a common membership by the 1880s.

Now most radical and liberal activists looked less to J. S. Mill and more to the 'prophet' Herbert Spencer for inspiration. His book, *Man versus the State* (1884), attracted many to the Individualist fold. Among them we can count at least four Lord Mayors who were active in the League. By the 1890s the visions of liberty offered by the Personal Rights Association of the 1870s and that of the Liberty and Property Defence League of the 1880s, for the most part, could no longer be said to be competing. From the writings of Spencer came a three-part doctrine: an adherence to laissez-faire economics, a defence of the proprietary right of the individual to self and property and the notion that a competitive society was the key to social progress. This was the text of late nineteenth-century Individualism. Its context was the nation's continuing economic malaise, the resultant social problems and the response to economic decline made manifest by gentlemanly capitalism. Most of those connected with the Liberty and Property Defence League took their liberalism from Adam Smith, the early philosophical radicalism of Bentham, Mill the elder (James, the father of John Stuart) and the free trade theorists Richard Cobden, John Bright and William Molesworth – all 'small-state' radicals and liberals. As M. J. Lyons, one of the members of the Liberty and Property Defence League protested at a meeting of the North London Working Men's Club, and as it was reported in the *Clerkenwell Press*, he and others were 'Let Us Alone' radicals. Looking to the free-trade victory of 1846, to freedom of association and to the removal of burdens from the press, they abhorred the meddling interventionism of New Liberalism in the context of the rise of the Labour Party.

It was concluded that reform such as that suggested by New Liberalism or the Labour Party was both useless and damaging to the given balance of society. It followed, therefore, that legislative action, even on the pretext of a worthy cause, should be resisted. Not only was increased state intervention seen as an unfortunate extension of democracy, but it also posited an opposite: on the one side was property and enterprise and on the other the rights (natural or otherwise) of the majority. Both sides of a divided liberalism shared a Benthamite concern for the extent of government rather than its form. While anti-collectivist and anti-Socialist, the Individualists ensured that they became defenders of not only property and the constitution but also, by doing so, the champions of the status quo. From this concern came the British Constitutional Association (1907) and the Anti Socialist Union (1908).

The City continued to lend support to individualist organizations. After the formation of the London County Council in 1889 and the creation of a Progressive-Socialist coalition, the League began a programme of co-operation with the organization of great ground landlords, the Property Protection Society. On this occasion the Goldsmiths' Company agreed to contribute £100 annually, and in total twenty City Companies enrolled. Likewise, the London Ratepayers' Defence League was formed in 1891 to resist the taxation of land values and to oppose the London County Council as well as the London School Board. It was succeeded in 1894 by the Conservative London Municipal Society in which the Corporation played a full part. This promotion of the state in the bolstering of imperial interests, Herbert Spencer argued, was of a piece with the trend towards collectivism. The preference for state rather than voluntary methods was another step back to Spencian definitions of barbarism. Hence, from the 1880s, the City's link with imperialism, militarism and nationalism and its use of state action to secure markets was simply the reverse side of the same collectivist coin: a social imperialism that at once bound classes together and blunted that other product of the 1880s, the socialist revival (Semmel, 1960, p. 24).

At the centre of both commerce and nation was the City, and enveloping all three was the military-fiscal state, so taking us back to theories of the state by Tilley and Edgerton in the first section. By the time prime minster Gladstone had resigned over naval estimates in 1894, the City and its Corporation would have forsaken the grail of free trade for the nirvana of the gold standard. Its approach to liberty, therefore, was qualified and partial, linking an examination of local politics with an understanding of how the state works within the context of both the 'High' and 'Low' politics of party. Without an understanding of these varying approaches to political history, we would be unable to conclude that the Edwardian City favoured Individualism and licence where once the ideal of mutuality, shared responsibilities and rights and duties had once held sway. Making sense of all this means getting to the hidden roots of the ideology that informed economic behaviour in the City and a comprehensive approach to state, party and extra-parliamentary activity in the City (as a case study) that allows us to conclude that, by the end of the Victorian period, the only thought given to mass democracy in the City was how it might be caged or how it might be tamed.

Postscript

Politics was the stuff of history. As history emerged as an independent, the majority of its practitioners seemed preoccupied with studying how particular constituencies had been able to exercise power over others. In Europe, this meant an almost exclusive focus on party politics. Thus, in Britain where much of the pioneering work was done, the parliamentary system was subjected to prolonged investigation as historians sought to understand how political parties and their leaders manoeuvred themselves into power and how a detailed study of the party system could explain the changing fortunes of the British state. At their best, such studies were authoritative and influential; Lewis Namier's *Structure of Politics at the Accession of George III* (1929) and Norman Gash's *Politics in the Age of Peel: A Study in the Technique of Parliamentary Representation* (1977), for example, have stood the test of time. Indeed, this strand of high politics has endured in the work of historians such as Maurice Cowling whose work focused on the detailed motives behind the decisions taken by political leaders.

Around the mid-twentieth century, this tradition was challenged by new lines of inquiry. If political history was concerned with the history of power, it was argued, then it was necessary to move beyond the confines of the party system in parliament. This opened the door to approaches which, while not ignoring parliamentary politics, located it firmly within wider power relationships. Predictably, perhaps, the remarkable story of the British Labour Party took centre stage, as historians attempted to record how the growth of the party, its distinct regional basis and its changing fortunes sprang not from parliamentary manoeuvrings but from the struggles conducted by trade unions, cooperative parties, women's organizations and other extra-parliamentary groups since the late nineteenth century.

The other challenge came from more theoretically inclined scholars who insisted that the state was not made up exclusively of the formal political system but comprised a rather more powerful, complex and extensive apparatus of political, military, economic and even cultural networks. In order to make sense of the state, it was felt necessary to elaborate theories that would hopefully explain its historic development since ancient times but also draw attention to the comparative development of different forms at different times and in different geopolitical contexts. Such a project has attracted the interest not only of historians but also of sociologists and political scientists who have striven to identify general laws of political development at the level of the state.

Lest we are tempted to see state and parliament existing in a climate of interdependent and mutual self-interest, the nineteenth-century City provides a valuable rejoinder. Here there were constant tensions within the political culture, manifest in the changing relationships between business and finance and between the party system and local associational life. Much of the tension was centred on notions of liberty as the liberal agenda of the eighteenth-century was gradually displaced by Individualism and anti-statism. The legacy of this struggle still informs the politics of the City today.

Further Reading

Perry Anderson (1979) *Lineages of the Absolutist State*.
John Brewer (1976) *Party Ideology and Popular Politics at the Accession of George III*.
John Brewer (1989) *The Sinews of Power*.
M. J. Daunton (1989) 'Gentlemanly Capitalism and British Industry 1820–1914', *Past and Present*.
David Edgerton (2006) *Warfare State. Britain, 1920–1970*.
Charles Tilly (1990) *Coercion, Capital and European States*.
Immanuel Wallerstein (2011) *The Modern World System*.
M. J. Wiener (1981) *English Culture and the Decline of the Industrial Spirit 1850–1980*.
Philip Williamson (2010) *Maurice Cowling and Modern British Political History*.

9 Economic History

Introduction

Economic history has a massive influence on the wider discipline of history, even if it has become a little unfashionable in recent years. Marxist history has particularly benefited from a concentration on what it would call the 'economic base' of historical societies, but more generally economic history has been sufficiently strong in the recent past to have maintained academic departments separate from 'straight' history and a number of dedicated professional journals. Economic history can reasonably claim to explain societies holistically while working on data (often by the application of the most up-to-date technology) which raise fresh questions about past societies. The opening section of the chapter will examine how data about population can unpick the shape of past societies, while the methods of economic history (with help from other disciplines such as archaeology) can add significantly to our historical knowledge. The second section focuses upon the contribution by economic historians to the understanding of wealth and poverty over centuries; in particular, we are concerned with the role of luxury and luxury goods in the modernizing process and the way that historians have dealt with pessimistic and optimistic approaches to industrialization, that is, economic understandings of industrialization that argue whether the Industrial Revolution benefited the economic lives of contemporaries. The final section of the chapter will switch attention to the role that business historians play in understanding past societies, defining and explaining the relationship of business history to economic history.

9.1 Economics, Population and Social Change

On the edge of a remote track, deep wooded until it branches out to reveal a vista of the Derbyshire countryside, is a field that contains a wall-bound graveyard containing just seven weather-beaten gravestones quite unattached to any church. The names on the stones are dated August 1666; all were victims of an outbreak of the bubonic plague in the village of Eyam. At least from the nineteenth century this outbreak has been notorious as the plague village par excellence. Here, after George Viccars, a journeyman tailor, first succumbed to the deadly disease in 1665, huge losses were suffered when the villagers decided in an act of heroic self-sacrifice that the plague would not spread by them beyond the village boundaries. The story goes that the villagers quarantined themselves and thereby saved nearby communities from their own terrible fate. As a result, by the spring of the next year, the present day residents of the secluded graves would be dead too. Not for the plague itself but for the response of the villagers, Eyam has become a cause célèbre for historians and the general public alike.

Economists and economic historians are not, contrary to popular belief, concerned simply with money. If they were, their interest would stop at the boundary to Eyam where villagers

Figure 9.1 The boundary stone at Eyam, the plague village in Derbyshire, where coins were left in vinegar to pay for food from neighbours

Contributor: Rick Edwards/Alamy Stock Photo

collected food and medicines and where coins were left in shallow pools of vinegar to prevent the spread of the contagion. Rather, they are interested more generally with economic resources and, in particular, with their scarcity and distribution. It should be no surprise, therefore, that the impact of plague, pestilence and disease on human populations should be relevant topics for the economic historian as they touch on the elements that affected economic conditions in the past, whether it be the plague that first struck the Greeks in the centuries before Christ, the Great famine of 1315–1317, the Black Death of 1348–1350 or the plagues of the seventeenth century, to which we shall return in a moment. First, a little more should be said about what economic history is, why it is important for those historians working in the modern and medieval periods.

Economic history as a branch of history dates to the social crisis of the 1880s and the need, particularly in London at the heart of the biggest and most important empire of the time, to understand a society where economic want existed for the many in the midst of economic plenty for a few. In order to address this issue and others like it, Arnold Toynbee (1852–1883) flew the flag for economic history while Alfred Marshall (1842–1924) was perhaps the best-known exponent of the craft of modern economics. Around this time, the London School of Economics and Political Science (LSE) was founded and reflected contemporary interest in law, government, statecraft and the origins of the modern economy. In a sense, then, economic history became a way of defining modernity, especially by describing and explaining the roles of the ascendant middle classes. This section will attempt to draw the boundaries of these concerns and to offer some examples of how this approach works in historical practice when seeking to understand, for instance, medieval plagues and epidemics.

The production and distribution of resources in the past are the main concerns of the economic historian. Christopher Dyer goes further, however, for according to him the value of economic history derives not only from its ability to reveal the nature of societal resources, but also all social and cultural endeavours are built upon the economy:

> It is the only branch of history which gives pride of place to the whole population, and through the study of the economy we can understand the everyday lives of working people. The economy was important. All other human endeavours depended on the production of food and other goods, which means that any investigation of non-material things must take into account the material base. Economic history is a unifying subject, not taking us into an obscure byway of the past, but acting as a crossroads from which we gain access to the history of the environment, culture, politics and thought.
>
> (Dyer, 2002, p. 1)

The plague outbreak at Eyam in 1665 has entered popular imagination as an incidence of extraordinary self-sacrifice by a village community. Recent work by economic and demographic historians, however, has provided alternative narratives of the episode. From the work of Leslie Bradley, Philip Race and Patrick Wallis, we now know that the mortality rates in Eyam were less extraordinary than had been believed. Bradley tells us that a 'very few' wealthy villagers fled at the outset of the epidemic, that those with sufficient wealth erected huts in nearby valleys to escape the plague, while some children of the better off were sent away only in June 1666, some eight months after the beginning of the epidemic when the mortality rates began to climb. Quarantine was not heroically self-imposed but enforced by the authorities as had been the case with other villages (Slack, 1985).

It seems, therefore, that circumstances surrounding what should be considered an historical myth must question the altruism of the villagers. (For a discussion on history and myth see Chapter 18.3.) The source that set the tone for histories and commentaries on the plague was Anna Steward's *Poetical Works*, which appeared in 1810, although it dates from 1765. Patrick Wallis argues that this description of the Eyam plague is set within the Romantic tropes of nationalist sentiment (the invention of the stiff-lipped Englishman), the value of strong leadership that partly characterized the Victorian age and the melodrama of romantic love that inculcates Victorian historical fiction and that was represented in various cultural productions such as art. If the history of epidemics and the tragedy of the Eyam plague are located chronologically in the seventeenth century, it was largely forgotten in the eighteenth, only to be reinvented at a moment when cholera stalked Victorian centres of population. In this sense, Eyam is a Victorian creation and is explained in narratives available and familiar to the Victorians.

For Race, self-consciously building on the work of Bradley, the key text in this myth building was that of William Wood, *The History and Antiquities of Eyam* (1865), but then other qualitative 'evidence' accumulated which sought to understand the nature of the plague, its origins and whether the epidemic had travelled from London or was sourced locally. All this evidence is legitimate context for the economic historian, but it is only context. Race, as someone who is concerned with quantitative evidence, looked instead to the newly available parish register of St Lawrence in Eyam, which dates from 1630. This register was especially valuable because it was annotated later in the seventeenth century with the names of the plague victims, giving a baseline from which questions of demography (population), births, mortality and the lasting economic effects of the epidemic could be considered. From it, Race discerned that no more than half of the population died (not the 259 of a total population of 330 suggested by accounts reported immediately after the event). Moreover, there was no serious demographic collapse in subsequent decades. There was severe mortality, however, which itself no doubt contributed to the accumulation of stories about the tragedy in the centuries since, among the last being a 2015 play that was serialized on BBC 4's Woman's Hour and another performed at the Globe Theatre in London in 2018. By understanding approaches to epidemics taken by economic historians we can more readily appreciate the impact of demographics or population change on human societies. To take another example, some estimates of the deaths caused by the Black Death of the 1340s have suggested that half Europe's population was wiped out, others that the figure is nearer to one-fifth. One older historiography argued that the population in 1348 was perhaps 3.75 million but by 1377 it had fallen to 2.2 million because of the Black Death and other epidemics. After 1430, it was further argued, the population began to rise. Data such as these, however, only have value to economic historians at the point when they explain related changes in economic activity. We know, for example, that prices rose as a result of the Black Death and that food shortages ensued. In the longer term, the amount of productive land and labour fell and with it demand for goods and produce, thereby creating an economic downturn.

The relationship between population and economic activity was first investigated by the eighteenth-century political economist, Thomas Malthus (1766–1834), who in *An Essay on the Principles of Population* (1798) argued that population would rise inextricably but the means of maintaining that population would not keep up, which would lead in turn to an economic crisis. Under such circumstances, he continued, population increases should be prevented by powerful checks such as moral restraint, by which he meant sexual abstinence; if these checks fail then economic failure and famine will ensue until a new balance is struck. Economic historians and demographers since Malthus have spent much time and effort investigating the relationship between population checks and economic activity. Perhaps the most dramatic intervention into this area of historical demography came from E. A. Wrigley and R. S. Schofield who in the *The Population History of England, 1541–1871: A Reconstruction* (1989) measured fertility, mortality and migration as the essential components of population change, concluding that population growth led to a fall in real wages over this period.

Influential though the gloomy picture of Malthus has been, there are limits to its explanatory power. While the misery of the Black Death undoubtedly led to social tension, which was linked to the 1381 Peasants' Revolt, for example, we know that there was no economic collapse or Malthusian crisis. Historians might agree with Malthus, however, to the extent that low marriage and fertility rates rather than mortality and migration were indeed the main constraints on population recovery. Undeniably, cultivated land improved in quality and new economic relations were born that culminated in the revolt. Equally, there is also no doubt that the 1348–1350 outbreaks were indescribably severe and had economic ramifications that lasted decades.

To bring us sharply up to date, a long-term effect on the economy might also be associated with the recent global economic crisis. According to Andrew Gamble (2014) there are three alternative explanations for the overall situation since the credit crunch then crash of 2008–2009. The first is that a record slump in production and economic growth is simply a blip. Recovery will come and the upward trajectory of Western growth eventually will be resumed. The second is that the fundamentals of the capitalist and neo-liberal economy have indeed been changed and that 2008–2009 represented a watershed (every bit as transformative as a medieval plague) which will permanently transform the nature of domestic politics while heralding the gradual introduction of a new international order. Gamble prefers the third option, however. Here he suggests that the West (in particular) has reached an impasse. The worst immediate effects of the crisis have been successfully contained but the conditions that caused the crisis may yet be repeated: 'The crisis is not over, because it is structural rather than cyclical. It has been postponed, but will erupt again, if nothing is done. The neo-liberal order has become highly unstable.' He proceeds to argue that although there has been

> relatively little dissent, radicalism or resistance. The absence of alternatives has been marked. Orthodox narratives around debt, retrenchment and austerity have for the most part defined the crisis and determined how it has been perceived, and protest has been muted. No insurgent populist anti-system party of right or left has yet succeeded in breaking the hold of mainstream parties over government in any western state, despite the economic pain inflicted on their citizens.
>
> (Gamble, 2014, pp. 5, 7)

This was in 2014. In a few short years, the decidedly unorthodox politician or party has gained power or has competed for power in (to name a few) the United States, the United Kingdom, France, Austria, Greece, Italy and Spain, with many such leaders trading on a resurgent, anti-immigrant sentiment. Nor could it factor in the economic effects of the global pandemic (Chapter 15.4).

As with the example of Eyam, population change but also migration have had direct impacts on the real economy. It is evident that a healthy supply of labour and the survival rate of the key groups within the economy have been historically vital and that this has been generally true for centuries and applies as much to Eyam as it does to our present economy. In the same way as Wrigley et al. identified migration as one of the main components of population change and economic success or failure, modern economies have compensated for their demographic weaknesses by encouraging immigration from outside their borders. If immigration is not linked to economic success, however, it can also evoke nationalist responses among electorates who are now fully experiencing the instability of free-market neo-liberalism.

If we can draw a straight line from plague in Europe to the Peasants Revolt, we may also assume that 2008–2009 was likely to prompt a political crisis: from Brexit in the UK and the election of Donald Trump in the US (Gamble, 2014, p. 133) to the 2019 global pandemic that is ongoing. Similarly, if we examine the raw numbers of those that died in that small Derbyshire village and join the dots forward to the economy that followed it, we can be satisfied that demographics are an important consideration for the economic historian. Indeed, we would know nothing of this and other related questions without economic history. The next section will underline this point by concentrating on how economic historians have approached important historical questions related to the decline of the Roman Empire and the so-called standard of living debate that arose from attempts to assess the impact of the Industrial Revolution.

9.2 Economic Historians and the Big Historical Questions

N. J. G. Pounds in his *Economic History of Medieval Europe* (1994) explained why the Roman empire declined – a process which is often thought to signify the beginning of the Middle Ages – and how its slow downfall in the East culminated in the fall of Constantinople in 1453 when the Christian Byzantine empire fell to the Muslim Ottomans. Pounds looked in places familiar to the economic historian in order to explain how this came about:

> The facade of Roman civilization in the West, its towns, villas and roads, was created mainly in the first two centuries of the Empire, when the profits of imperialism made it possible to do so. It constituted, however, a superstructure which the later Empire found increasingly difficult to support. The barbarians did not overthrow the Empire in the West; they merely caused

it to expend its scanty *resources* [our emphasis] in ways which it could not really afford. In other words, they made necessary high taxation for military ends.

(Pounds, 1994, p. 37)

Ultimately, Pounds argues that the Western empire was dependent upon its force of arms and that the shortage of recruits to the army explains why it was finally unable to maintain its imperial influence. But why were there shortages of manpower in the army? To answer this question, he looks at demographic explanations that should, after the last section, be familiar. These explanations include a high death rate, low life expectancy (thirty to thirty-five years), and the incidences of disease such as the Black Death in 542–543. Demography was also influenced by taxation. Taxes that had to support the army were paid by four-fifths of the population, a 'venal and oppressive bureaucracy' made the task of collecting taxes more difficult while a shortage of labour in what was an agricultural economy led to the abandonment of productive land when the principal source of state revenue was a land tax on small proprietors. For all the reasons mentioned, the tax take was reduced. As more slaves were used for productive purposes and barbarians recruited to the army had no loyalty to the empire, so the empire weakened.

Pounds also highlighted the role of the 'frivolous and idle rich' in the decline of empire, raising the question of why frivolity, idleness or even decadence should be the business of the economic historian. Socially unequal societies demanded that luxury goods be produced. This alone altered the economy of towns, and in the case of the Roman Empire compounded the problem of maintaining the strength of the army since it was the army that maintained the roads on which these goods were transported. When the strength of the army became compromised, luxury goods, enjoyed at the centre of the empire, could not be distributed to the provinces. The biggest impact on an economy distorted by luxury production and bedevilled by problems of distribution, however, derived from the avoidance of taxes paid by the senatorial class and their determination to abandon their social obligations.

These are economic explanations but they contain unstated assumptions about the role of the barbarians in the loss of the empire and implicitly ask whether barbarian influence constituted an 'overthrow'. That the barbarian or Germanic forces were finally to overrun the glory of Rome and that these forces were to somehow dominate the grandest of empires without the apparent use of undue violence has been perhaps the main unchallenged assumption of histories written on this subject. But Bryan Ward-Perkins in his *The Fall of Rome and the End of Civilization* (2005) overturned decades of established historiography by suggesting that the crisis of the Roman Empire in the West was not the result of gentle transformation or 'accommodation' of an organic and incremental kind but of an invasion.

Ward-Perkins contended that economic explanations for the end of Roman power are not as convincing as those highlighting the economic ramifications caused by the invasion itself. One commentator, Ward-Perkins reminds us, enterprisingly took evidence from written documents but also tree-ring data to suggest that the obscuring of the sun in 536–537, caused by an asteroid strike, had an adverse effect on crops and therefore on the economy. Similarly, as in the analysis of the same problem of Roman decline by Pounds, the Black Plague was cited as a negative impact on the economy and as a factor in the eventual collapse of the Western empire (ibid., p. 134). None of these more piecemeal explanations, however, can be compared to the shockwaves caused by invasion and the collapse of security for a sophisticated economy that required security to function as a coherent whole.

Ward-Perkins agreed that economic factors in the demise of the Roman Empire in the West are indeed important, but he pointed to a fundamental change in the economy of the ancient world which led to significant ruptures in all five of the Roman provinces (ibid., p. 122). Central

North Africa, the islands and coastal provinces of the Aegean, Britain and the Levant, which comprised a region that would include parts of modern-day Egypt, Turkey, Israel and Syria, reacted differently to economic pressures and declined at different rates. For Ward-Perkins, however, the primary reasons for the ultimate decline are twofold: the problems of security hastened by invasion from the Vandels, Sueves and Alans when they crossed the Rhine into Gaul (ibid., p. 2) and the excessively interdependent economic system whose lines of communication became stretched to breaking point under the pressures of conflict and invasion. All the provinces of the empire had relied on a complex and interlocking economy that had facilitated mass production and exchange, but under these new conditions, specialized trades that had once acted as the bedrock of the economy and had enjoined its various parts now stood alone, quite unable to meet local needs. This caused privations in some areas, although in others (the Levant, for instance) prosperity stayed constant or even improved up until the seventh century.

Economic history is thus the study of scarce resources in past societies, a point mentioned in the first section but which is now reinforced. Economic historians have argued that well-being in the past was all about essentials (not luxuries) such as mass-produced soap made of vegetable oils. It was also about cheap, washable cotton, better nutrition, plus, of course, advances in science and technology. All these factors (particularly the industrial use of soap) improved hygiene, transformed mortality rates and boosted demographic growth.

Maintaining population levels and wealth, equality or inequality, diversity or uniformity, conflict or social peace, rested on whether societal needs and expectations could be met. The nature of the relationship between poverty and wealth has long been of interest to thinkers beyond the realm of economic history. It was the radical Thomas Paine (1737–1809) who, as a veteran of both the eighteenth century French and American revolutions, first began to argue that inequality was neither natural nor was it divinely ordained and a result of sin, and in this he was joined by Enlightenment intellectuals. As a result of the ideas unleashed by the eighteenth-century revolutions, poverty and understandings of poverty changed in the modern period, and with this transformation came the recognition that the state had a responsibility to provide welfare support to the disadvantaged (Chapter 6).

The push to understand poverty as a societal problem and not as a problem of the flawed individual corrupting a hierarchy pre-ordained by God continued in the mid-nineteenth century with various forms of social and economic investigation that sought scientifically to ascertain the extent of poverty. These largely private initiatives from Henry Mayhew and Charles Booth to Benjamin Seebohm Rowntree (1871–1954) – and the Institute of Community Studies in the 1960s – thereafter disappear into the corridors of state responsibility. While poverty remains today, Western societies are better off now than we were only sixty years ago, although as we write in 2023 some of the metrics of economic wellbeing are slipping in the UK. Nevertheless, our collective focus has moved away from poverty as the main cause of social conflict. This shift in perception and focus has occurred among economic historians too but may yet come back into view if it is indeed proven that the West is experiencing relative economic decline.

One such shift is from production to consumption. Where once economic historians (and others) focused on histories connected to issues around production and how skills developed in the industrial process promoted productivity, now they are equally concerned with how things were consumed through, say, shopping, advertising or fashion. From histories of production and consumption come questions of how we earned our living in the past and the extent to which the Industrial Revolution improved standards of living. This, as shall be seen, has meant a wider, more holistic, cultural and social view of the Industrial Revolution that has, if anything, challenged the centrality that it once occupied in interpretations of Europe's advance.

Neil McKendrick and John Brewer, for example, have each drawn attention to the 'birth of the consumer society', inhabited by people who have both the desire and the ability to consume.

Advertising and selling, fashion and credit promoted a change of lifestyle (for some). This was to be a new world of 'things', and prosperity would come from self-indulgence. The result of this approach, according to the historian Maxine Berg, was that 'consumption has reshaped the grand narrative of the period, replacing the former narrative of the industrial revolution' (Berg, 2005, p. 27). This new narrative does not tackle the divisions and conflict thrown up by industrial production; indeed, it admits of no inherently antagonistic division.

Perspectives on luxury, like those on poverty, have changed significantly over time. Until Bernard Mandeville wrote his *Fable of the Bees* in 1714, benefits of a life of luxury and idleness derived from 'avarice, prodigality, pride, envy and vanity' were unquestionably immoral. After Mandeville and, for that matter, David Hume's oft-quoted 'ornaments and pleasures of life', set down in his essay *Of Luxury* published in 1752 but acquiring a new name *Of Refinement in the Arts* in 1760, the new consumer society or consumerism would become associated with words such 'ingenuity', 'imitation', 'convenience', 'utility', 'taste and style', 'delight' and the desire for luxury considered necessary for economic growth.

This in a very small nutshell is the narrative within which economic historians have understood luxury, consumption and poverty. What impact has this thinking had on how economic historians have understood industrialization and the standard of living? E. A. Wrigley, among other economic historians, has approached the question by investigating increases on productivity. He demonstrated that industries such as soap and paper manufacture, brewing and ship building grew to a considerable level of sophistication and productivity between say the 1760s and 1770s and the 1830s – the timespan that is normally allotted to the first Industrial Revolution. In addition to this there was, in some regions at least, a qualitative as well as quantitative change in the mode of industrial production – a decisive shift away from the methods and limitations of handicraft production towards larger units of production such as the mills and factories found in the textile producing areas of Lancashire and the West Riding of Yorkshire.

The approaches of economic historians are nicely illustrated by different perspectives on the revolutionary nature of the Industrial Revolution. The idea of an early start for English industrialization is one made by many economic historians. Nick Crafts and C. K. Harley argued that the whole phenomenon was long and drawn out, with growth rates that were too low to be described as 'revolutionary'. Even if cotton has transformative power, the centres of production were too regionally localized, and more importantly the growth of this sector did not make up enough of the aggregate economy to justify the high level of overall growth in the British economy that earlier historians like T. S. Ashton, Phyllis Deane and W. A. Cole had suggested. The growth in the total volume of the economy owed much to agriculture and traditional technologies; for example, there were few steam engines driving anything but water even by the 1840s. Accordingly, Crafts and Harley revised earlier growth figures downwards.

Maxine Berg and Pat Hudson insisted on a radical critique of Crafts and Harley and in so doing reinvested the Industrial Revolution with something of its old significance. They argued that growth and productivity change have been underestimated and that growth rates alone are an inadequate measure of change. They have underestimated growing sections of the labour force such as women (the family economy) and the informal economy, that is, the agrarian/industrial overlap in the countryside where most people were still locked into seasonal employment, low wages and rural deprivation. There has been too much emphasis on finished goods, with the result that the products of some industries were underestimated, while the service sector is all but ignored. Berg and Hudson conclude:

> It is time to move on from the macro accounting framework and to rebuild the national picture of economic and social change from new research at regional and local level. We need

to adopt a broader concept of innovation, to insist on a greater awareness of female and child labour, and to recognize that the economic, social and cultural foundation of an industrial capitalist order rests on much more than conventional measures of industrial or economic performance. If this is done it should not be long before the notion of an industrial revolution, occurring in England in the late eighteenth century and early nineteenth century is fully rehabilitated.

(Berg and Hudson, 1992, p. 44)

What is the importance of this debate to our understanding of economic history? The period under review was a time of economic development – no matter how much or little may be attributed to the Industrial Revolution – and it was also a period of rapid population growth and urbanization. Taking these three things together – economic development, population growth, urbanization – we have the makings of one of the great debates concerning the industrializing period, namely, that of whether the Industrial Revolution improved the standard of living for ordinary people. This debate has been of fundamental importance to economic history and brings together many themes of this section and the last.

Optimists believed that real wages grew as an immediate consequence of economic growth and industrialization, and in so doing they improved the lot of the majority very quickly. Much of their case was based on early work by influential economic historians such as Sir John Clapham (1873–1946) and T. S. Ashton (1889–1968). Clapham's *Economic History of Britain* (1926) looked at wages and prices and concluded that working-class living standards had improved. T.

Figure 9.2 1835 interior of cotton mill: girls and women tend carding, drawing and roving machinery as an active and important part of the economy

Contributor: Chronicle/Alamy Stock Photo

S. Ashton in the 1940s examined population, import and export prices, housing and diet. Poor conditions, he concluded, had existed but were balanced by the increased benefits of industrialization. F. A. Hayek (1899–1992), the liberal economist, reinforced the optimist case when he highlighted the relative merits of improving wages and prices in an industrialized capitalist economy. The pessimists, including E. P. Thompson, Eric Hobsbawm and other members of the Communist Party Historians Group, believed that the rapidity of change, the rapaciousness of capitalism and the pace of urban growth led to desperate suffering at least in the short term. Even if manufacturing wages were good, they were not enjoyed by the majority who worked in dreadful conditions, for long hours and from very young ages (if the evidence and conclusions of the Factory Commission are to be believed).

To an extent the differences between the two camps arose over the nature of the evidence used. Pessimists argued that optimists had measured working life using hard data such as incomes, food expenditure and so on, while the 'moral economy' of customs and culture provided a fuller and more meaningful context for assessing the impact of the Industrial Revolution on people's lives. Pessimism about the effect on the masses could be found in poems, novels and paintings (Chapter 14). Because the pessimists used this more imaginative evidence rather than hard data, it came under the microscope of economic historians such as R. M. Hartwell, W. H. Chaloner and W. W. Henderson who all argued that much of the Marxist or pessimistic viewpoint was biased and ideological – a fruitless search for the missing revolution without due attention to the integrity of the sources.

The ideological divide between pessimists and optimists has recently narrowed and there is recognition that there is 'no single, measurable "standard of living" in history. Indeed, Lindert and Williamson have argued that:

- Real wages rose after 1820, though mostly among 'white-collar' workers.
- Purchasing power increased in real terms – although the unskilled were worse off.
- The rich and the middle class got richer and so did the poor, although the relative difference between social extremes became greater.

Most historians now agree that real wages remained steady over the period 1750–1820 but rose substantially up to 1850. It appears that the increase in the standard of living resulted from falling prices rather than rising wages. However, pessimists have been bolstered by the stature of the population (measured in height), which in the years 1825–1860 declined, reflecting poor diet, environment and disease. Indeed, the relationship among nutrition, height and mortality rates has become a very live area in economic history (A'Hearn et al., 2009; Floud et al., 1990).

Contemporary debates about luxury and poverty and consumption and production have their antecedents in those about the timing, extent and substance of the Industrial Revolution and the standard of living it produced. Much of the recent debate has centred on use of evidence at the micro level of the firm, not at the macro level of national economies. How firms operated, say, in employing particular skills, to source raw materials or to shift had a profound influence on their capacity to produce, and this in turn had implications for the economic fate of countries. The study of this world is the business of the business historian to which we turn next.

9.3 The Business of Business History

Hundreds of historians, artists and authors use the British Library every day, and few give a thought to what stood on the site before the present library building. Just next door in St Pancras Station thousands of people pass through having travelled from all over Europe, perhaps visiting the shops and restaurants in the basement undercroft. Fewer still ponder the existence of such a space, putting it down to clever design and the skill of the architect. However, what stood on both sites was conceived by individuals but built by companies – in particular, a business called the Midland Railway. The Midland built a space under St Pancras for the storage of beer from the Burton Brewery (a company) of Burton on Trent, while the site of the British Library was occupied by an enormous goods yard bringing a huge range of commodities into London for the consumption of its inhabitants and taking commodities away from London destined for the smallest corners of the union and, indeed, the empire.

Let us think about this in more detail: how was bread brought to Manchester? From a farm (family owed business) to a railway (the London North Eastern Railway, joint stock limited liability company) via a road haulier (Carter Paterson, company) onto a miller/baker (the Hovis company), then on to a shop (the Co-operative, a co-operative shop on a corner somewhere in rural or industrial Britain). Think about the variety of transactions involved and how goods were delivered to the consumer. All this involved business, to a varying degree, depending upon the time and location under consideration.

The importance of business, of companies, in the Industrial Revolution should be recognized. This is not to say that business always delivered social goods or goods useful to society – it did not. But no one should deny their important role, alongside stable government, in delivering much higher standards of living across the globe. Equally, we ought not to ignore the enterprise of business history itself; indeed, it might be argued that it is undeservedly neglected.

What is business history and what are its concerns? According to Edwin Hunt and James Murray in *A History of Business in Medieval Europe 1200–1550* (1999), business is 'any activity involving exchange between two or more parties – in country or town, and on a local, regional, or international scale'. Essentially, business history is concerned with how production and the delivery of goods and services was organized in the past, by an individual, a sole trader, a group of individuals, a partnership or a joint stock limited liability concern – the modern company. It is also concerned with understanding the processes underlying decision making. All this makes business history distinct from economic history, although they are clearly allied, and to understand it historians need to engage with a variety of cognate disciplines, notably accounting, finance, law and even engineering.

In Britain, the origins of the company lay in the organization of universities and hospitals via a Charter granted by the Crown, and it was not until the seventeenth century that they expanded into other areas, with joint stock companies (like the East India Company) gaining monopoly access to trading rights around the world, and in return they acquired the national debt from which they could offer shares. The outcome of this particular type of company was the financial collapse known as the South Sea Bubble in 1720, which led to the banning of the corporate firm until 1844 when limited liability was introduced. Accordingly, in order to avoid the misuse of monopoly status, Britain's financial services expanded in more diverse ways, and the railways and canals were organized by private Act of Parliament, as were many of the new utility industries such as gas, telephone, electricity and water. Indeed, most economic activity was concerned with the private firm, whether with limited liability or not.

So the difference between economic and business history is one of emphasis rather than substance. Steve Broadberry's study of British manufacturing productivity, *The Productivity Race: British Manufacturing Performance in International Perspective 1850–1990* (1997), for example, is widely regarded as an economic history but it also engages with the performance of individual businesses and sectors. An important difference for the business historian is the role of the individual case study, whereas the economic historian is usually more concerned with industry-wide analysis of business. Economic history is also concerned with much more than the business sector – after all the company as we know it is itself a relatively recent phenomenon – and covers ancient, medieval and early modern forms of organizing production. There are also more subtle differences. For example, while Broadberry emphasizes productivity, businesses rarely want to maximize productivity. Instead, entrepreneurs, managers and shareholders will look at profitability and perhaps market share as measures of performance. As finance developed as a discipline, increasingly cash flow was used as a basis for assessing how well a business was being managed.

Business history requires the macro theorizing of the economist, sociologist and statistician but is combined with micro knowledge about accounting, finance and commercial/business law. The history of business may not be just about the history of a particular business – often referred to by some economic historians in pejorative terms as an indulgence, an 'antiquarian' study – but may encompass the history of regulation, government business relations, the history of labour, technology and the social history of the workplace.

The development of business history as an academic discipline began in the United States with N. S. B. Gras, *Business and Capitalism: An Introduction to Business History* (1939). This told the story of capitalism's development through the perspective of business organization and its transactions with other producers and customers. Gras's scholarship provided the foundation for business history at the Harvard Business School and was followed later by Alfred Chandler's pioneering work, *Strategy and Structure: Chapters in the History of the American Industrial Enterprise* (1962) and later *The Visible Hand* (1977). These examined instances of business decision-making in a historical context but in a way that was intelligible to those studying organizations and management. Together with the business history curriculum at Harvard Business School, Chandler built on a tradition of case studies for teaching, thereby establishing business history in the United States.

In the United Kingdom, however, the interest in business history developed alongside the growing field of industrial archaeology. 1950s Britain was undergoing a period of change with many Victorian business premises, if not the businesses themselves, closing down, merging or moving to new locations. The preservation of business archives often went alongside the development of the textile or railway museum or the preservation of defunct office equipment now deposited at the London Museum – all offering new opportunities to research varying viewpoints including from the angle of locality, which could give us fresh insights into histories of place.

Business history remained marginalized within economic history until the late 1980s when economic history departments themselves began their long decline, until at the time of writing there are only two dedicated Economic History departments in Britain, that is, at Edinburgh and the London School of Economics (LSE); but more exist throughout the world such as the University of Barcelona and the Stockholm School of Economics, which has an Institute for Research in Economic History. To take Britain as an example, however, in 1978, the Business History Unit at LSE was established as a venue for the writing of histories commissioned by firms themselves and the training of doctorates. Through its existence the unit was headed by two of the most influential business historians – first Les Hannah (b. 1947), author of a commissioned history of Barclays Bank – *Barclays: The Business of Banking 1690–1996* (2001) – and then Terry Gourvish, *British Railways 1948–73. A Business History* (1986) and *The Official History of Britain and the Channel Tunnel* (2006).

Has business/economic history had a massive impact on the wider history profession? Business historians are mainly found in business and management schools, increasingly being replaced by first social and then cultural historians in history departments (Chapter 10). The trend has moved decidedly away from economic and business history departments (there were perhaps twenty dedicated departments in the 1970s), and history departments are not interested in business history. Yet even more recently, business history has struggled to become accepted by both the wider academic community of historians and scholars of management. An editorial piece in the January 2007 edition of *Journal of Business History* reviewed some of the issues faced by the discipline. However, some of the sub-branches have been notably successful. For example, the history of accounting has managed to break into the so-called mainstream accounting journals, with a mix of sophisticated methodology and archival analysis. Trevor Boyns' survey of recent scholarship in this field shows how theory and archival evidence have been used to explore the relationship between accounting and decision-making in the running of business (Boyns, 2007). The relationship between history and management in business history has also been debated in the *Oxford Handbook of Business History* (Jones and Zeitlin, 2008).

What is clear from this escalating interest is that business history uses archival evidence, and for the historian to make sense of this archive there must be an understanding of the documentary material that remains. And to appreciate this material, the business historian needs to understand the variety of processes and procedures involved in management – accounting, law, finance, marketing, human resource management, strategy and technology. The best way to archive this is to do what contemporaries would often have done – read a textbook from the time, consult the technical and trade press associated with an industry or sector. So, for example, to put together data on profitability from internal company accounting information, it is necessary to understand what was meant by depreciation, costs, revenue and so on. The documents assume that the reader understands what they contain – they were written for a well-qualified audience who understood the accounting practices of the day. There is much to learn from engineering texts and trade catalogues. Students interested, for example, in how factories were organized and the relationships among skill, technology and skill acquisition might wish to examine how raw materials were moved to the workplace, around the factory and then distributed to customers.

Two problems arise when using a company archive: either there may be a great deal of information concerning the plant, machinery or organization of work or there might be very little information at all. A text, such as the *Materials Handling Handbook*, published in 1958, provides extensive evidence of best practice material handling. Although this is an American publication, this was the practice that many British firms were aspiring to, and so it is still useful. This might be supplemented by trade catalogues such as that produced by the firm Herbert Morris Ltd of Loughborough. They published in 1933 a trade catalogue cum textbook over an inch thick, full of pictures and technical specifications for a range of handling equipment. Both these would enable an understanding of the language and technical aspects of the processes and render the archive more intelligible. Where there is little evidence, then these texts can fill in the gaps. Of course they may not be representative of specific firms, and like any evidence they should be used with care. Similarly, the trade press is an excellent source of evidence both for the entire industry and for individual firms. *Modern Transport*, for example, first published in 1919 and lasting until 1963, is full of evidence from the shipping, railway and road haulage industries, including reports on financial performance, technical innovation and policy. These are questions and problems with which the historian of business must grapple.

Linked with this need to interrogate documents is an awareness, an appreciation of the events that contextualized how the actors perceived their environment. The development of transportation in the inter-war period offers a good example of this approach. The industry was shaped by a 1921 Railway Act that created the so-called big four railway companies. But this represented something more – the ending of government control after World War I and the formation of the first Ministry of Transport in 1919. These events are linked in a way that was apparent to participants but that is not always clear to later historians. We are reading history backwards, and so we need to be mindful that contemporaries appreciated these points at a time when they were more concerned with both the detail and breadth of haulage operations. The Ministry of Transport and railway management were aware of the impact of the internal combustion engine. Parliamentary records and company documents reveal this concern and the attempts by individuals to adjust the regulatory settlement to reflect a changed reality. By contrast, at the same time, the construction of light railways was being encouraged to supplement main line railways and branch lines. These were built to reduced standards and cost less. We seem to have a contradiction here – but this is easily resolved if we recognize that the economy is multifaceted with various interest groups and agents all seeking to work, manage and live in society. Detailed examination of government reports and the trade press – including newspapers – are critical to this understanding. Using the trade press alerts the historian to debates previous generations of scholars might have thought trivial and so were ignored.

All history reflects the concerns and issues of contemporary society, and economic/business history is no different. The perceived emergence of a knowledge- or information-driven economy has been examined by Joel Mokyr in *The Gifts of Athena: Historical Origins of the Knowledge Economy* (2002). Mokyr examines the increasing role of knowledge in the economy noting the difference between knowledge required for doing (practical application) and that for understanding (learnt theory). In his later work, *The Enlightened Economy: An Economic History of Britain, 1700–1850* (2009) he explores the notion of an industrial enlightenment, examining how scientific method entered the workplace. Business records can be used to see how this worked on a firm-by-firm basis. By using internal company documents it is possible to examine the nature of the technology and the role of the individual in the design and manufacture of products. Josiah Wedgewood, Matthew Boulton and James Watt, for example, were all involved in the industrial enlightenment, and the records of their activity reside in archives. The records of companies such as Cowens and Sheldon, Crane Makers and J & E Hall, Engineers, contain records on production and engineering calculations that reveal how technical decisions were made and production organized. Most scholars would agree that the notion of a modern knowledge economy is overstated and that, to a varying degree, the economy has always had a foundation in knowledge.

Economic history often provides a more aggregated, macro view of how economies and industrial sectors have developed – or not – as the case may be. Business history offers a way into the reality of economic change. Individuals live near, work in and buy the products of businesses. The location of factories and the history of product lines are eulogized on websites and monographs. The heritage sector draws implicitly on business and organizational history from the steam locomotives of defunct railway companies to the warehouses of canal enterprise – all relate to how people organized production. Family historians note the occupations of their ancestors, local historians, the creation of regions and landscapes – all influenced by processes of management control and decision-making within organizations. This makes the use of business and management records an important skill.

On the other hand, this does present a difficulty: the interpretation of accounting, legal and engineering/technical records may require some degree of knowledge to fully understand what the documents are telling us. That said, there is a great deal of material online with enthusiast groups and amateur historians who may have these skills and are ready and willing to offer their help. In a very real sense, business and management history is a public history, largely outside the mainstream of academia since the 1970s with the gradual demise of industrial archaeology as a discipline within universities and the decline of extra-mural education. It should be remembered that EP Thompson's work *The Making of the English Working Class* was written while the author was employed in the Extra-Mural Department at the University of Leeds.

So, business history has carved itself a valuable place within economic history. It has moved from a concern with the individual firm (such as the Midland Railway) to the role of business more generally, say in the so-called knowledge economy. The key to its ascendency, perhaps, may have been a decline in labour history that dominated the field for decades but also surely the increase among a new breed of business historians who have unearthed fresh archives.

Postscript

In recent years there has been something of a reaction against the decisive influence that was once exerted by economics as an explanatory factor of historical change. Political, social and cultural historians have all responded by asserting the vital importance, even primacy, at least in Marxist terms, of 'superstructural' factors. Thus, for example, there are detailed studies of political movements, the role of sex in society, missionary work in the empire and carnival, which pay little if any regard to economics. At face value, this seems sound practice. It would be difficult, say, to explain the nature and chronology of missionary endeavour by relating it to economic change, for missionaries were not evidently motivated by economic considerations.

An historian does not have to be Marxist, however, in order to appreciate the importance of economics to any explanation of historical change. To say that how societies organize to sustain themselves and to distribute their resources, impacts massively upon their structures and behaviours is so self-evident that one wonders how any could question the assertion. Economic historians take it as a given, and in this chapter we have looked at ways in which some have attempted to understand such dramatic events as epidemics, demographic change and the Industrial Revolution primarily as economic phenomena. We would wish to argue that without an awareness of the economic dynamics of such historical phenomena, our understanding of them would be compromised. The nature of human conflict and imperial expansion could just as easily have been investigated, for ultimately these too have been driven by struggles over limited resources.

As an adjunct to economic history, business history has in recent years reached a degree of maturity. Although most of the studies have been about individual companies or sectors of the economy, they have demonstrated the value of company archives to the historian. Such records can reveal a great deal about the nature of economic transactions, improvements in technology and therefore productivity and relationships with other concerns. Together such studies help to build a more nuanced picture of the changing economic fortunes of the nation as a whole.

Having said that, there are perhaps limits to the approach that economic historians take in explaining human behaviour. Like missionaries, people do not always act consciously or unconsciously as economic agents, and they are not driven by economic considerations. It could well be argued, for example, that the Industrial Revolution was made possible by the dramatic shift in bourgeois ideology that took place during the Civil War of the seventeenth century. The ideas about work, profit and private property that emerged were instrumental in encouraging entrepreneurial endeavour and hence industrialization. As historians, therefore, we must remain mindful of the role of economic forces but at the same time recognize that they are not reflected linearly in how people act as historical agents.

Further Reading

Maxine Berg (2005) *Luxury and Pleasure in Eighteenth-Century Britain.*
Alfred Chandler, Jr. (1977) *The Visible Hand: Managerial Revolution in American Business.*
D. C. Coleman (1992) *Myth, History and the Industrial Revolution.*
Christopher Dyer (2002) *Making a Living in the Middle Ages. The People of Britain 850–1520.*
Economic History Society [www.ehs.org.uk/ehs/refresh/default.asp].
Andrew Gamble (2014) *Crisis Without End: The Unravelling of Western Prosperity.*
Andrew Hinde (2003) *England's Population.*
David Landes (1999) *The Wealth and Poverty of Nations.*
N. J. G. Pounds (1994) *Economic History of Medieval Europe.*
Gareth Stedman Jones (2004) *An End to Poverty. An Historical Debate.*
Bryan Ward-Perkins (2005) *The Fall of Rome and the End of Civilization.*
E. A. Wrigley (1990) *Continuity, Chance and Change.*

10 Social History

Introduction

The chapter explores the contribution of social history to historical inquiry. Often thought in the past to be a somewhat marginal interest, devoted for the most part to aspects of the human experience that were trivial when compared with weightier matters such as politics, recent years have witnessed a sharp growth in studies broadly under the umbrella of social history. In addition, the deep-seated suspicion among historians that sociologists are concerned with elaborating universal laws began to recede as they found sociological concepts of value in interpreting historical evidence. The result has been a widening of the historiographical agenda and a flowering of interest in topics such as leisure, language, rituals and customs that have defined our social lives.

No theme has attracted more interest than class, and in the second section we examine the ways in which social historians have found the concept of value in social stratification. The initial interest was provoked by the writings of Marx, who placed class centre-stage. This notion has proved to be extremely fertile, particularly in those historical inquiries concerned with changing societal relationships, but in recent years, largely under the influence of feminist and postcolonial historians, class has been displaced by gender and race.

In the final section, we discuss one of the other organizing concepts of social history, namely, the family. In full recognition of its longevity and near universality, sociologists and social historians have long been interested in the family. There have been diverse approaches, however, which foregrounded different aspects of the family experience, often leading to different conclusions about its role in past and present societies.

10.1 The Emergence of Social History

In recent decades social history has emerged as one of the most vibrant strands of historical inquiry, successfully revealing a wide range of topics previously considered of little interest or value to serious historians. Despite this, historians struggled to provide a satisfactory definition either of social history or of its boundaries. Perhaps, then, we can best approach the topic by considering the scope of social history and something of its development over time. A good place to start is Adrian Wilson, who in *Rethinking Social History* (1993) usefully provided a sense of its endeavour:

> The term 'social history', as used in English historiography, covers three different yet overlapping approaches: first, the history of the people; second, what I call the 'social history paradigm', consisting in the historical application of concepts derived from the social sciences;

and third, the aspiration to a totalising or integrating history, which has been called 'total history' or the 'history of society'.

(Wilson, 1993, p. 9)

What does this involve? Well, first, social history seeks to reveal the historical experiences and expressions of the people rather than, say, those of the great men who until then had dominated historical writing. Auguste Comte, a pioneering French sociologist from the nineteenth century who was attracted to the study of historical processes, encapsulated this idea when he talked of social history as history without the names of individuals. And it was Comte and his successors who did much to develop social theories which later proved valuable to historians attempting to uncover the nature of societal change. This leads to the third broad area of social history, namely, its rejection of narrowly focused study towards a history of society in its totality, not in the sense of an attempt to build a picture which captures every aspect of society but rather a history which is sensitive to the idea that different elements of society are intimately interconnected.

Some of this may become clearer if we look briefly at how social history emerged as a singular, and here the most accessible guide is Peter Burke's *History and Social Theory* (1992). According to Burke, there were no hard and fast distinction between social theorists and historians in the eighteenth century. Works such as Charles de Montesquieu's *Spirit of the Laws* (1748), Adam Ferguson's *Essay on the History of Civil Society* (1767), Edward Gibbon's *Decline and Fall of the Roman Empire* (1776–1788) and Adam Smith's *Wealth of Nations* (1776) were all studies of the 'philosophy of society' (Chapter 3), employing general theories to elaborate the nature of historical change. Over the nineteenth century, however, historians disavowed the use of social theory. In part this was as a means under the influence of von Ranke (Chapter 21) of carving out a separate identity for history, in part of employing it to promote nationalist sentiment at a time when many European states strove to overcome regional diversity. Under such circumstances the inclusion of the social in historical accounts became increasingly criticized as curious and quite inferior when compared with the serious business of politics. The two camps dug in, attitudes hardened and a long period of trench warfare followed. Historians took the view that social theory was little more than a pseudo-science, while sociologists accused them of gathering historical evidence, which in their hands amounted to heaps of stones and bricks; only sociologists had the wherewithal to build edifices out of the rubble.

These antipathies reflected broader differences in the approaches of the disciplines, traceable to their emergence as disciplines during the nineteenth century. The task of historians, it was believed, was to record the past as it happened. The emphasis was therefore very much on the expert use of historical evidence to put together a persuasive account of a particular event, person or period. Sociologists, on the other hand, were not usually concerned with *particular* historical circumstances but wanted instead to explain *general* phenomena such as power relations, the legitimacy of authority, the way bureaucracies and states work and the mechanisms that make modern societies function. As such, sociologists claimed to help historians understand the particular by locating it within wider historical processes that reach across space and time. To summarize:

1 History is concerned with the unique and particular, while sociology is interested in the general (universal).
2 History is preoccupied with the refined use of evidence; sociology with the formulation of theories of society.

3 History is interested in change over time; sociology with questions of stability.
4 History deals with the past; sociology with the present.

Stated like this, the differences are somewhat oversimplified, whereas in practice the approaches can be complementary. This was manifest in the work of Emile Durkheim and Max Weber at the turn of the century. While they did the most to establish sociology as a discipline and exerted a powerful influence on succeeding generations, both had a deep interest in history, even writing historical studies; indeed, Weber, whose work on the Protestant Ethic we come to later in the chapter, viewed himself as a comparative historian. But it would be decades before historians turned to them for inspiration.

In the meantime, a group of French historians known collectively as the *Annales* school also promoted less attention to the simple narration of events, more to the hidden structures underlying all social and economic change. Thus, for Marc Bloch, Lucien Febvre and most importantly Fernand Braudel working in the interwar and immediate postwar periods, history should strive to capture the totality of human experience. Under their influence and in a way that drew upon ideas from social theory, historians for the first time began to debate topics such as food, leisure, language and the family, so laying the foundations for what came to be recognized as social history. By the 1960s this branch of historical inquiry had been born and showed encouraging signs of vigorous growth (Feldman and Lawrence, 2011, p. 1). In America, the *Journal of Social History* was launched in 1967 followed in Britain nine years later by *Social History*. The editors enthusiastically announced a new kind of history which had the potential to transform our understanding of the past by creating a 'total history'. Simultaneously, in a special issue of the American journal *Daedalus* devoted to a critical assessment of where history stood, Eric Hobsbawm provided a timely insight into the popularity and intellectual ambitions of social history (Hobsbawm, 1971). He acknowledged the infancy – and perhaps immaturity – of the new approach. Prior to 1939 there had been a mere handful of creditable studies which could be described as social history, but the past twenty years had witnessed a remarkable growth, stimulated in large part by the turn to history evident in related disciplines and the imperative to address the problems of modernization, colonial struggle and domestic upheaval. Such work had tended to cluster around the following topics:

1 Changes in population and kinship.
2 Urban environments.
3 Classes and other social groupings.
4 History of mentalities or collective consciousness.
5 Societal transformation.
6 Social and protest movements.

While all this, he concludes, is to be welcomed, Hobsbawm ends on a cautionary note. Much of the work remains schematic and tentative, leaving rather more to be done before a history of society is successfully accomplished.

To what extent was this convergence between history and social theory evident in the work of sociologists? The sociologist Philip Abrams' *Historical Sociology* (1982) remains one of the most eloquent statements on the potential of sociology in historical understanding. He argues that the differences between history and sociology have been exaggerated, and in the past decades any perceived differences have narrowed radically. This is hardly surprising since at the heart of both disciplines is a 'common project' to understand how people in structured society behave. It follows that if sociologists adopted more historical approaches to their work, and by extension if historians were more sensitive to the structural properties of society, then many of the problems faced by the disciplines would be resolved. Drawing upon the work of Marx, Durkheim and Weber, as well as contemporary authors such as Barrington Moore who had influentially used social theory to explain the rise of dictatorships, Abrams then imaginatively used historical case studies around industrialization and the formation of states and human agency to persuade us of the intrinsic value of historical sociology.

Although history and sociology continued to enjoy a dialogue and have much in common, there were dissident voices that remained sensitive to the differences. The sociologist John Goldthorpe, although or perhaps because he was first trained as an historian, has argued that sociologists are ill-placed to interpret primary sources or what he seemingly dismisses as 'relics of the past'. Rather, sociologists should concentrate on constructing theoretical models and generating data in the present. Sociology should be 'historically minded' but sociology and history are fundamentally different 'intellectual enterprises' (Goldthorpe, 1991, 1994).

Since the 1960s social historians have applied themselves to the task of overcoming the sorts of criticisms levelled by Hobsbawm, and the branch has continued to flourish. Broadly speaking, the same topics dominate the agenda today, even though forms of the urban, urban mentality, social transformation and social protest have undergone radical revision. We have thus witnessed what amounts to a roll call of some of the most pioneering work: from urban histories, to histories of public health and of the lives of working people. To take a few examples, almost at random: Benedict Anderson, *Imagined Communities* (1983), is a history of how ideas of nationhood have been used in imperial projects; Leonore Davidoff and Catherine Hall's *Family Fortunes* (1987) is a study of the English middle-class family from the late eighteenth to mid-nineteenth centuries; Jack Goody, *The Development of the Family and Marriage in Europe* (1983), is a wider historical study on similar themes; Peter Laslett (ed.), *Household and Family in Past Time* (1972), is a collection edited by one of the most skilled users of social historical data and the works of Harold Perkin, including *The Rise of Professional Society* (1989) and *The Structured Crowd* (1981), have done as much as any to establish the worth of social history. In the remainder of the chapter, we wish to focus on some of the vital themes, starting with the enduring question of class.

10.2 Class and Authority

'And fookin' amen to that' was a riposte from a member of the audience to 'an inordinately long, self-satisfied, godly and officious grace' from the president of the British mineworker's executive. According to the Marxist historian E. P. Thompson, the riposte represented the meeting of two contrasting working-class or plebeian cultures that developed sometime between 1870 and 1926 in the Deerness Valley, County Durham and doubtless elsewhere in the British coalfield (Thompson, 1976). The miner giving the grace was a 'devout Methodist' and as such represented respectability and anti-Communism and an acceptance of the conventions of society. The rather uncouth reply to the toast 'from a veteran class warrior and no respecter of persons' suggested a disputatious working-class culture more to Thompson's taste that was older, rougher, tougher and politically radical. In this sense the exchange may be seen as resonant of a distinct coal mining culture and politics at the end of the nineteenth century. By that time, the North-East of England was dominated by coal mining: it dictated the politics, culture and society of that area and more broadly impacted on the economy of a mighty empire. And yet the political allegiances of miners were complex and dynamic. Represented in this exchange was a class-collaborationist Methodist versus an irreverent plebeian, and in a sense, this determined the course of politics. After 1870 miners had come to express allegiance to a symbiosis of Liberalism and

Figure 10.1 Trade Union banners on Elvet bridge in Durham during 'The Big Meeting' or Durham Miners' Gala, Durham, England, UK

Contributor: AC Images/Alamy Stock Photo

Methodism; but a dissident minority retained a voice. Only with the shedding of this Liberal skin to assume a Labour form could the conformist majority assimilate the minority; intrinsic to this non-revolutionary settlement was Methodism.

How class relationships at work can be understood in all their complexity from this single incident, however, is largely through sociological methodology. Thompson was a sophisticated proponent of the sociological approach and claimed that 'there is no difference whatsoever in the methodology appropriate to the sociologist and to the social historian' but also warned of problems attached to the use of sociological methodology. According to Thompson, there was 'a sociological itch' to generalize, to claim typicality in descriptions of phenomena when historians should be more inclined to find contrast and difference (Thompson,1976, p. 389). To understand the development of miners' attitudes, working-class culture and politics in the modern period, we must differentiate between the old plebeian culture (especially apparent among the radical Primitive Methodists who merged with the Methodists in the 1930s) and those who had taken up positions of authority and trust on behalf of the miners. Drink, gambling, traditional fairs and feasts, sexual licence and profane song in this older culture had given way to sobriety and conformity in the new. Sociology, according to Thompson, can help to understand this transition, but only if deployed by the historian with subtlety and skill. (We are reminded here of Arthur Marwick's passing remark that 'Class . . . is too serious a subject to leave to the social scientists' (Marwick, 2001, p. 15)).

Care needs to be taken first to recognize that the old culture of a radical politics represented by Primitive Methodism had not completely disappeared and that the existence of the drunkard, gambler, fornicator, blasphemer and layabout was worthy of comment. If historians uncritically adopt a sociological classification of people into types which takes no account of historical change, then we will not be able to adequately explain how 'fookin' amen' could have been so utterly offensive to a dominant Methodist respectability yet still represent a continuing or surviving counterculture. It would be just plain rudeness and not historically significant at all. Alternatively, if we say that this is offensive to contemporaries but not representative of them in any way, then we merely parrot Methodism's own self-image, deploying an inflexible sociology to a situation that demands flexibility. Thompson urged us to register that both the 'officious, self-respecting, class-collaborationist Methodist lay preacher' and the 'irreverent blasphemer . . . class-conscious, self-disciplined secularist' are components of a common culture which have co-existed for a long period. By keeping the polar extremes – collaborationist and respectable Methodism and cursing political radical – in *historical* view, we mitigate the tendencies in sociological methodology to favour one element of this common culture as 'typical' of the whole, so encouraging us to tell one half of the story at the expense of the other.

The example of the Durham miners suggested a community where class and culture were influenced by work, income and occupation but also a consciousness among miners that the sum of their existence was, in fact, working class. How then might we describe in sociological terms what it means to be 'working class'? Marxists contend that class location is based objectively in property relations and what Marx called the forces of production. The marketplace thus determined the social standing of the proletariat or bourgeoisie. With class analysis used in this way, it is difficult to account for different cultures *within* the Durham miners, unless we say that one is a genuine expression of the working class and any other an expression of false consciousness. Max Weber, partly in response to Marx, focused on the meaning of social stratification, not merely through relationships unleashed by property relations but also through the roles that individuals performed in society. Status, for example, can account for prestige, lifestyle, aspiration or deference in history. From this perspective, we can understand the deference or conservatism of the so-called blue-coated or newly affluent worker or the uniformed working class, such as railway or postal workers, with their military sense of pride. These groups enjoyed a certain status and for that reason had a certain consciousness about their place in society, leading to a deference towards other status groups that in terms of income were, perhaps, a notch above them.

Thompson, however, rejected the idea of class as simply a structure that could be understood objectively, preferring instead to think of class as a subjective experience. It was not a 'thing' but a 'happening' that was realized in a 'relationship' with other classes, which most certainly cannot be found in passive sociological constructs such as occupation or status. As he argued in the introduction to his classic *The Making of the English Working Class* (1963):

> I do not see class as a 'structure', nor even as a 'category', but as something which in fact happens (and can be shown to have happened) in human relationships. . . . And class happens when some men, as a result of common experiences (inherited or shared), feel and articulate the identity of their interests as between themselves, and as against other men whose interests are different from (and usually opposed to) theirs. The class experience is largely determined by the productive relations into which men are born- or enter involuntarily. Class consciousness is the way in which these experiences are handled in cultural terms: embodied in traditions, value-systems, ideas and institutional forms.
>
> (Thompson, 1976, pp. 10–11)

In becoming receptive of ideas about class, in particular by challenging some of the rigid orthodoxies about class consciousness, these arguments proved to be fertile and influential. For the next twenty years or so, an extensive range of important studies appeared in which class acted as a touchstone for analysis. Geoff Eley and David Blackburn's *The Peculiarities of German History: Bourgeois Society and Politics in Nineteenth-Century Germany* (1985), Gareth Stedman Jones' *Outcast London: a Study in the Relationship between Classes in Victorian London* (1971), John Foster's *Class Struggle and the Industrial Revolution* (1974), François Bédarida's *Social History of Britain, 1851–1975* (1979), Ross McKibbin's *Classes and Cultures: England, 1918–1951* (1998) and Robert Gray's *The Labour Aristocracy in Victorian Edinburgh* (1976) were just a handful of such studies. Importantly, however, such scholars who were critically engaging with what may be described as an Anglo-Marxist tradition were not confined to Britain or even the West. In India, for example, the leading social historian Sumit Sarkar constantly expressed his debt to E. P. Thompson and vigorously defended the continued relevance of his work to the study of late colonial Indian history (Sarkar, 1997). And while Dipesh Chakrabarty's *Rethinking Working-Class History: Bengal, 1890–1940* (1989) is more reticent about the application of Thompson and others to the study of the Indian jute workers of Calcutta, the broad contours of his study are defined by revised notions of class and class consciousness.

During the flowering of social history, historians were not Marxist to a man or woman, but this did not prevent them from approaching the study of societies, communities, even families using the framework of antagonistic class relationships laid down by Marx. As Geoff Eley put it in his autobiographical *A Crooked Line: From Cultural History to the History of Society* (2005), social history saw itself as situated 'within a self-confident materialist paradigm of social totality, grounded in the primacy of class' (p. 89). Part of the reason for this was the sheer versatility of class as an analytical tool in explaining not only the changing nature of social stratification and endemic conflict within society but a host of 'superstructural' features including the nature of law, art, religion, popular culture and politics. Occasionally, perhaps, this versatility was pushed beyond its limits as class was invoked to describe countries and pre-modern periods where capitalist formations had yet to develop, but its value to historians cannot be denied. In more recent years historians have turned away from such foundational concepts as class struggle and revolution (whether industrial and political). This was driven by broad societal change, which in Britain included de-industrialization, the assault on trades unions launched by Margaret Thatcher, the ascent of a consumer culture and large-scale migration of peoples from former colonies; intellectually, it was part also of a wider suspicion of approaches which prioritized material experience. The consequence was a displacement of the 'totality' of class or at the very least its complication by notions of gender, race and sexuality which were seen not through their materiality but via their identities, memories and linguistic categories (see Chapter 12).

Where has this left class? Some historians have argued that with the loss of manufacturing in the West the working class has effectively vanished and that we no longer live in a class-based society. Such obituaries, however, are almost certainly premature for unless we adhere resolutely to the view that the working class is defined by manual labour, the proletarianization of white-collar workers may have actually swollen the ranks of the working class. For the historian Jon Lawrence this may be the time to revisit the language of class politics (Lawrence, 2013). Whether this happens – and whether historians return to class – remains to be seen.

10.3 The Family in History

Given its near universality and existence since the earliest records of human activity, the family has attracted the enthusiastic attention of social historians, sociologists and anthropologists in considerable numbers. The essential problem was to explain this universality and longevity, and in attempting to do so scholars have studied why the family has been found in a such a wide variety of forms in different regions of the world, what functions they served, and what prompted their change over time (Wiesner-Hanks, 2011). It has been evident since the mid-nineteenth century that such approaches necessarily required the application of social theory in identifying familial forms. Thus, *L'organisation de la Famille* (1871), an early and much cited study by the French sociologist Frédéric Le Play, distinguished among patriarchal, unstable and stem families, largely on the basis of the fate of their sons. In the patriarchal family, found in nomadic and herding societies, married sons remained within the household. Here the emphasis was on stability, authority, lineage and tradition. In the unstable family (or nuclear in modern parlance), on the other hand, which is most characteristic of urban manufacturing populations, independence and freedom are stressed with children leaving the parental household on marriage or as soon as they have the means to do so. The third family type, found in European peasant societies, tended to retain patriarchal features but normally allowed only one son and his family to stay (Anderson, 1980, p. 23).

Despite this early work, the interest expressed by Durkheim and Weber – and by subsequent generations of sociologists and social anthropologists – the family did not attract serious work among historians until the rise of social history in the 1960s. Since then, the number of studies has increased exponentially. The volume of this literature renders futile any attempt to provide even a rudimentary assessment of its worth; instead, we wish to outline briefly some of the main approaches to the study of the family with reference to specific examples drawn from the experience of the West.

The most immediate and pressing problem faced by social historians in approaching the Western family is its sheer diversity. Even within the Western experience – let alone that of Africa and Asia – a wide diversity of family forms has been found. Peasant families in premodern France, for example, differed sharply from those in Germany, England and Sweden in terms of their size, patterns of inheritance and structure, and in most modern countries forms existed which seem to challenge any societal norms. French Canadian or religious communities such as the Mormons in North America followed their own distinct rules. Such diversity has tended to frustrate any attempts to identify general historical trends (Anderson, 1980, p. 14). Frustrate but not entirely prevent – for historians have shown little evidence of abandoning the family – and so it is worth devoting attention to what Michael Anderson has identified as the three main approaches to tackling this problem, namely, demographic, sentiment and household economic.

E. A. Wrigley and his colleagues in the Cambridge Group for the History of Population and Social Structure (whom we met in the last chapter) have for the past forty years or so pioneered work on demographic history, particularly in England. They started by rejecting the use of literary sources, which had previously formed the basis of family history on the grounds that it was unreliable and narrowly focused. Instead, they turned on the one hand to parish registers, which since the sixteenth century had been compiled by parish priests and officials and which recorded details of the baptisms, marriages and burials of the parish population and on the other to censuses, which since 1801 had amassed details of individual households. These sources were neither wholly complete nor reliable, and yet they were able to build up a solid database upon which much subsequent work has relied (see, for example, Wrigley and Schofield, 1981; Wrigley et al., 1966; Wrigley et al., 1989). Their work suggested that from medieval times the family forms of Western Europe were almost unique in world history. Among characteristic features we might include:

1 Marriage tended to be late, and this combined with long birth intervals before the late nineteenth century led to smaller family sizes. In England at least, large, extended and complex families had never been the norm for mean household sizes and from the sixteenth century

had remained fairly constant at 4.75 members. From this, Peter Laslett concluded that the nuclear family has been one of the fundamental and enduring aspects of Western society, with profound implications for the role of the family and the dynamics of family relationships (Laslett, 1977).
2 Apart from small variations, comparative rates of premarital pregnancies between, say, England and North America have displayed remarkably similar trends. During the eighteenth and early nineteenth centuries, numbers grew steadily but then halted and, until the Second World War, fell. Since the end of the war there has been a dramatic rise.
3 While systems of inheritance in premodern Western societies have differed in detail, most displayed powerful continuities over time and have had a major bearing on the age of marriage, rates of illegitimacy and family structures (Goody et al., 1976).

Much of this work has been contested on the grounds that demographic characteristics are only part of a complex picture of how the family is positioned within society and that too much should not be read from them. And if the use of parish registers and census data constituted a major advance on previous approaches, these sources – let alone the less complete and reliable sources in other countries – need to be treated with rather more circumspection than they have by family demographers.

Mindful of the limitations of this approach, writers in the 'sentiments tradition' prefer to focus not on the family as a reality but as it has been imagined. A key text here has been Edward Shorter's *The Making of the Modern Family* (1976) in which he argued that changes in family structure and dynamics could be explained better by exploring ways in which attitudes to and within the family have shifted over time. Within the same family structure, he contended, we find many different sentiments across cultures. As far as the nuclear family is concerned, it is a 'state of mind rather than a particular kind of structure', and therefore what distinguishes it is 'a special sense of solidarity that separates the domestic unit from the surrounding community' (Shorter, 1975, p. 205).

Shorter was a sociologist and can perhaps be forgiven for erecting hypotheses from somewhat fragmented bodies of historical evidence gleaned from different periods and regions and so for us a better representative of social history here is Lawrence Stone's influential *The Family, Sex and Marriage in England, 1500–1800* (1990). Stone's central argument is a strong one. Radical shifts in views and value systems occurred in England between 1500 and 1800. If we assume that family relationships reflected these changes, then the family itself was a microcosm and can be used to throw light on the broader landscape of cultural transformation. Thus, Stone launches into an extended study of how family members related to each other in terms of formal arrangements, structure, power, emotion and sex. How did they think about and treat each other and look on their relationship with various levels of societal organization from the family to the state? Examining the evidence, he concludes that in the early modern period there was a change from relationships based on distance, deference and patriarchy to what he terms affective individualism, which was not only fundamental but arguably the most important in social attitudes seen in the last millennium of Western history. Thus, by 1750 families of the middle and upper classes shared features which were recognizably modern. These included enhanced emotional bonding among members of the nucleus at the expense of friends and wider kin, a sense of personal autonomy, belief in freedom to pursue happiness, enjoyment without guilt of sexual pleasure and felt a need for physical privacy. By the end of the nineteenth century, these features had spread to the aristocracy at the one end and the mass of the respectable working-class at the other.

What was distinctive about this approach to the family? Stone starts with demographics, which, he declares, determined many of the basic features of the family, including seemingly independent variables such as emotional commitment. Furthermore, they are necessary in order to distinguish between the social elite and the mass of the population. Using parish registers and the occasional survey, he proceeds to chart changing patterns of marriage, birth and death. Many of the conclusions confirmed earlier findings. Over this period marriage was typically later than in any other known society, and infant mortality rates remained high. Indeed, death was such a part of life that the early modern family was little more than a loose association in which any sense of permanence was constantly broken up by the deaths of its members. Stone denies, however, that there was a direct correlation between demographic trends and what he terms the affective relationships within the family. To take one example, there was no necessary link between levels of infant mortality and the emotional relationships surrounding children. To understand better changes in the family we need to look closer at the cultural norms and expectations of the wider society.

Occupying the large bulk of his study, these cultural features are charted with great care, primarily in their impact on the bourgeois family (much less is known about family life for the mass of the population). In the early modern period high mortality rates placed severe limits on the composition and structure of the family, shaped patterns of inheritance and discouraged material and emotional investment, particularly as far as the children were concerned. There was little sense of domestic privacy, and relationships between husbands and wives on the one hand and parents and children on the other were emotionally and psychologically remote. From the early seventeenth century the rise in the power of the state, the spread of Protestantism and unprecedented levels of social and geographical mobility focused increasing attention on the nuclear family as the basis of order and spiritual worth. Moral theologians began to urge the importance of marital and parental love but paradoxically stressed the need for patriarchal and authoritarian ideologies which installed the husband – acting by proxy as king and priest – as the head of the household. Although the emphasis on the nuclear family remained undiminished, by the eighteenth century the principles of affective individualism gained strength. Marriage partners were now decided largely by free choice, the patriarchal authority declined, there were moves towards greater equality between the sexes and children attracted more care and attention.

What needed explaining, concluded Stone, is not change in the structure or organization of the family but in sentiment. Here the specificity of this historical experience of the English bourgeois family challenges the application of any general sociological theory of modernization. The progressive erosion of a sense of community, authority and deference, social stability and tradition, all of which have been identified as key features, impose a uniformity and linearity on family change which never existed. Likewise, the transition from a traditional 'moral' economy to industrial capitalism, the values of which have been seen by Shorter and others to encourage changes in family sentiment – except that this explains neither the chronology nor the class specificity of such changes. Better explanations may derive from consideration of the rise of the spirit not of industrial capitalism but of capitalism itself: here religious, philosophical and political thought championed the values of democracy, independence and individualism their various manifestations, thereby steering the course of the bourgeois family over the early modern period.

The third main approach to study of the family has focused on the role of economic factors, in particular their role in determining the behaviour of its members. This approach seeks to determine how economic resources were made available to the family, how its members exploited them and how these strategies helped shaped power relations within the family. Much of this work has been comparative, usually looking at the experience of different cultures across the same period, and it has leaned heavily on social science theory and has introduced the use of novel sources including probates, property holdings and family budgets. Among its important themes are the family economy and patterns of inheritance, both of which are worth discussing, albeit briefly.

The transition from a medieval to industrialized economy has provided a useful vehicle with which the mode of production sets limits to the generation of resources. At the heart of challenges faced by peasant families was access to land, thus it is important to understand how law and local customs regulated the ownership of property and how land impacted on the size and structure of the family, particularly in striking a delicate balance between having enough to provide labour but not too many to feed, on the employment of its individual members and on the patterns of inheritance which determined how property was passed on from one generation to another. The early stages of industrialization disrupted these family economies. Increasing numbers of landless labourers together with the proletarianization of factory labour created a large reservoir of male, female and child labour with no rights to land and no inheritance. Families became independent households which acted as units of labour – often working away from the household – the rewards of which were paid to individual members.

The fine study by Tilly and Scott (1989) investigated the changing role of women within English and French families from the beginnings of industrialization in the mid-eighteenth century to the present. Industrialization, they argue, impacted on the economy, demographics and structure of the family in complex ways. In the preindustrial economy the family was typically small and had low productivity. Tasks were differentiated according to age and gender. Fertility was high but effectively controlled by comparable mortality rates, late marriage and enforced celibacy for some members. Industrialization led to an increase in family productive units, members of which moved beyond the confines of the household to the factories and workshops and were paid in wages. High fertility and mortality rates continued, and married women alternated productive and reproductive activities, working for the most part when necessary to supplement the family income.

By the end of the nineteenth century, industrial production and organization had raised productivity and the standard of living for most of the population. The family economy continued to allocate labour to its members, including children after leaving school, but increasingly married women turned away from paid employment and devoted their time to nurturing children and organizing consumption. This process was promoted also by improved infant and maternity care, which resulted in lower levels of infant mortality and restrictions on fertility. Smaller families required investment of more time to the survival of their children. Over the whole of this period, therefore, the changing role of women was the outcome of the shifting relationship between their responsibilities for production and reproduction.

To conclude, we have outlined three broad approaches to the family adopted by social historians. Each has emerged as a response to perceived inadequacies in previous work. Historians developed an interest in sentiments because they felt that the demographic approach failed to take account of the extent to which the family was shaped by perceptions and ideologies, while those exploring the family economy do so because the family is not simply an ideological construct, it is a functioning economic and social unit. But we must be careful not to draw strictly defined boundaries around them; in practice, they draw upon one another, and the future of work in this area depends upon continuation of this constructive interplay.

10.4 The Social History of Faith

Victorians had views about religion. It almost defined them; it was everything they were for and everything that they were against. The cathedral, church and chapel were the landmarks of their lives and the points of navigation for a morality that was encoded in every almost every thought they had, in almost every individual or social act. It moved their souls and offended their reason at one and the same time. As religion or popular faith declined and then transformed, it would remain at the very heart of what social history (old and new) was created to understand. We shall see in this section that as religious attachment was expressed through attending the various houses of worship, the working class was singled out by contemporaries and then by sociologists and historians as lacking religious attachment. Yet neither church nor theology was free-standing, set apart from society or history. Perhaps urbanization and industrialization were structurally incompatible with religion, throwing up rival associations that detracted from the church or chapel.

Social historians have been interested in religion and the structures of religion but have felt compelled to frame some of the more complex questions into theories that allow religion and faith to be examined in more systematic ways. Once again sociology has proved more than useful for historians. Looking at the founders of sociology – Emile Durkheim, Karl Marx and Max Weber – we find that religion has been taken seriously. For Durkheim (1858–1917) religion and belief were key parts of every society. His *Elementary Forms of Religious Life* (1912) recognized the utility of religion to every society and its ability to express a universal or collective consciousness. He theorized the conditions in which the sacred and profane existed with different societies behaving in slightly different ways depending on their varying levels of sophistication. Durkheim thought that demands for justice and new moral demands would diminish the separate space given to things mystical. It is this assumption, that secularization is solely about a retreat from Christianity, that this retreat is progressive and ongoing, that is essentially equated with modernization. Marx (1818–1883) thought religion would fade away as science came to determine contemporary thinking, a process that had begun when the newly powerful bourgeoisie had embraced materialism in the wake of the French Revolution. Atheism was a natural bedfellow of revolution, that is, it was equated with social status and class power. For Marx, religion was an ideology and as such was constructed and subjective. It was part of the ideological state apparatus of the ruling class and was, famously, the 'opium of the masses', a distraction that masked the true nature of class society. Weber (1864–1920) differentiated among different types of religion but this ought not to overly concern us as historians. More interesting is his application of theory in *The Protestant Ethic and the Spirit of Capitalism* (1905). Here Weber argues, controversially, that the theology of Calvinism that emphasized pre-destination and a doctrine of the saved and the damned, a status already decided by God, removed the need to appeal to the mysteries of a priesthood and, as earth-bound material efforts because rational, ordered and directed, coincided with the demands of capitalism. Weber believed religion served a functional purpose in giving meaning and shape to a society that was essentially amorphous and arbitrary; he saw its effect increasingly offset by rationality and bureaucratization that not only had led to the decline of religion but also, in his famous phrase, to the 'disenchantment of the world' (Giddens, 1971, pp. 205–14).

Following Weber, the educationalist, socialist and historian R. H. Tawney (1880–1962) wrote *Religion and the Rise of Capitalism* (1926). He too emphasized the importance of Protestantism but added hard work, individualism and thrift as major attributes of religious life and, by extension, the life of the capitalist economy. Social history then helps us make these types of links. A closer examination of the secularizing process in Britain should emphasize this process and illustrate why and how social history can assist us in understanding the nineteenth-century crisis in religion.

We would like now to begin that quest by looking at the design and building of the Natural History Museum in London and the circumstances in which it was commissioned and finally completed. This will take us closer to an understanding of the relationship between religion and secularization and to the nub of what it is that social historians do in the face of the major challenges that religion and faith have posed historically.

The Natural History Museum had a longer gestation period than some of its exhibits. Finally completed by the Liverpudlian Quaker Alfred Waterhouse (1830–1905) in April 1881, the Museum was an amended design from two rival plans that had been submitted two decades earlier. Professor Richard Owen, superintendent of the Natural History Departments of the British Museum, submitted a plan in 1859 and another in 1862 for a separate and fitting home for natural history. As a Christian and an enemy of evolutionary theory, he was a conservative if brilliant administrator. His original plans were rejected, but since land was now vacant in South Kensington, a competition was launched in order to attract a suitable design. The winner in 1864 was Captain Fowke. When the triumphant architect died the following year, it fell to Waterhouse to continue the project, although his drawings in 1868 proved to be only preliminary and would be developed in the following decades.

Owen had imagined a Baroque or Palladian palace with a classical portico and matching architecture. Fowke, however, 'abandoned the traditional symbolism of a classical temple, entered by a portico, for the symbolism of a Christian church or cathedral, surmounted by a dome' (Girouard, 1999, cf. 26). Waterhouse retained this metaphor but transformed Italian Renaissance into German Romanesque – only faintly echoing his heroes of the Gothic Revival, Pugin, Scott and Ruskin. These competing designs merely reflected contemporary disputes that were religious at root:

> To understand why he did this one has to understand his background. He was still a committed supporter of the Gothic Revival and all Gothic Revivalists were united in the belief that the Renaissance was a disaster. Its roots, they contended, were pagan, not Christian. It had replaced the vitality, freedom and colour of the Middle Ages with the tyranny of the five orders [the classical styles of architecture].
>
> (Ibid.)

The combined effect of governments changing and economies that were forced on the project meant that Waterhouse was unable to switch easily from Fowke's classicism to a more desirable Gothic design. The result in 1881 was a compromise that embraced German (rather than English) Romanesque that was symmetrical in the classical style but adorned by terracotta figures of birds and animals, topped by a figure of Adam at the top of Creation. Adam has long since been toppled from the roof, ironically aided by the German Luftwaffe during the Second World War. Romantic artistry, however, also found expression in the skylines, colourings and staircases. Indeed, as Mark Girouard commented, the Central Hall was a 'brilliantly unlikely combination of cathedral-style Romanesque arcades, and roof and cast-iron columns reminiscent of Victorian railway architecture make it one of the most exiting interiors devised in the nineteenth century' (ibid.). In truth, the Natural History Museum was built as a cathedral to science and evolutionism and that sense was as modern as any railway terminus. As such it reflects the time that it was designed and built, nicely illustrating the effects of secularism and rationalism as they broke against the social history of faith.

Let's look a little more closely at that context and the relationship between religious faith and secularization. The historian Frank Turner, in his *Contesting Cultural Authority: Essays in Victorian Intellectual Life* (1993), argued that there was no clear-cut distinction between the religious and the secular:

> Religious ideologies could cloak secular objectives, just as secular ideologies could be pursued with quasi-religious intensity. [This crisis of faith] was a result not of an attack on Christianity but a reaction against the most fervent religious crusade that the British nation had known since the seventeenth century.
>
> (Turner, 1993, pp. 3–37, 73–100)

The expressive aspects of religion in the modern period may be summed up in the contrast between late Georgian functionality and Victorian aestheticism, an aestheticism that was rooted in the massive church extension that had been in place before the 1830s. This multiplied as industrialization encouraged a pronounced scepticism about God and church. Before 1832 and the widening of the franchise, the unreformed Church of England was largely centred in rural areas of depopulation, the dioceses were large and unmanageable, the finances were poorly balanced and the internal government of the church lacked adequate representation. Many of these problems were addressed and some of them solved by legislation and internal reform. More critical in ways that should alert the social historian was the turn to a more Catholic way of worship and what this shift meant for the wider society. It was this shift that had prompted the argument between Owen and Waterhouse about the architectural style of the Natural History Museum: between the gothic revivalists (those that wished for a return to the 'colour' of the Middle Ages) and those that wanted to retain a traditional classicism. The return to a more Catholic liturgy and form of worship placed an increasing focus on the altar with church décor, furnishings and music fundamentally altering British society and culture by the end of the nineteenth century.

The crisis was compounded by the onset of an ever more plural constitution and the effects of industrialization that encouraged Ritualism or Tractarianism. These were the names given to the outputs of the High Church Oxford Movement, which from the 1830s had led the charge back to a pre-Reformation approach to religion and religious worship. Ritualism also allowed a way of communicating with the working-class city dweller. Slum churches appeared in the industrial areas which reflected the changing styles of Anglican worship and vastly improved acoustics which enabled the priest to celebrate the Eucharist with his back to the Congregation. They were also gloriously decorated and were reckoned to cheer up the grey landscapes of industrial England and bring some absent churchgoers back into the fold.

Low Churchmen and Evangelicals were also deeply concerned about the state of worship in England (Parsons et al., 1988, p. 62). They too made demands for reform: increased congregational participation and improved musical quality, which was one reason for the revolution in hymns during the period. To the Low Churchman, changing services introduced a popular element into the ceremonies; that is a renewed participation in church which mirrored a new participation in the business of the state.

The importance of music and preaching was also a feature of nonconformity or dissent, that is, those religious traditions (Congregationalists, Methodists, Baptists, etc.) that were Protestant groupings but not part of the established Church of England. R. Key on Primitive Methodism in Eastern England during the 1830s; W. Gibson on the Ulster Revival, 1860; C. M. Davies on 'Moody-and-Sankeyism', 1875 (an import from the United States) and W. Booth on 'Darkest England and the Way Out', 1890, a vivid theology from the Salvation Army, all bear witness to the increase in musical performance and preaching conducted outdoors and in great city halls which was rooted in the community and which were as much civic as ecclesiastical.

The nonconformist conscience appeared, as has been suggested by the historian Richard J. Helmstadter, at the same moment that nonconformity began its structural decline (Helmstadter, 1988, pp. 61–95). This phenomenon has been examined in several local studies such as S. J. D. Green's 'social history of the chapel' in Yorkshire, which dealt more generally with religious decline (Green, 1996). Two factors have been especially emphasized as historians have sought to understand the apparent switch from belief to unbelief among the general populace. First, the links between the rise of a secular mass entertainment society and secularism existed in a state of 'bitter hostility' with nonconformity. Second, theological shifts altered from an idea of God as Judge to God as Father, a decline in the belief in everlasting damnation and acceptance of Christ as a minister of the poor. Socialism and organized labour in Britain actively grew out of the rich associational life of the nonconformist chapel and the ethical principles of nonconformity.

For example, W. R. Lambert in his essay *Some Working-Class Attitudes Towards Organised Religion in Nineteenth Century Wales* (Lambert, 1988, pp. 96–111) found a growing alienation and apathy among the working class but also a working-class led organization and a set of moral beliefs. The local chapel (as opposed to the Church of England) was:

- Working-class in character – but respectable.
- The social centre of the community.
- An internal structure that promoted social mobility.
- A place that enjoyed relatively large attendance.
- A voluntarist tradition (hatred of the Truck system, for instance, where payment in kind prevented the giving of cash to charities).
- A place where the minister and Church officers were elected from the congregation (that is, had a democratic structure),
- A doctrine that offered 'an equality of opportunity' for salvation.

There was an assumption that the solutions to the ills of society were collective. If nonconformity would eventually provide the shock troops for radical Liberalism and then the Labour Party and the chapel a model for political organization, the ranks of Christian Socialism were more abstract and were filled by High Church radicals such as Stewart Headlam and Thomas Hancock and only later by people such as Hugh Price Hughes, a Welsh Methodist minister, political campaigner and author in 1890 of a book called *Secular Christianity*.

The Forward Movement (led by Hughes and others) was inspired by the Neo-Hegelianism of T. H. Green to whom Humphrey Ward's controversial novel in 1888, *Robert Elesmere*, was dedicated. This was part of the 'modernist storm' of the 1880s. It was also a time of severe trade depression, a chronic shortage of working-class housing and a revival of socialist and collectivist alternatives to the dominant liberal ideology. It was a crucial decade and one that found many people in a state of intellectual and spiritual confusion. Organized religion had already been buffeted by the attacks of science, Biblical criticism and the resultant waves of 'honest doubt', the 'gospel of freethinking', atheism and even republicanism. History was moving the way of collectivism. Again, the context is of profound interest to the social historian. All of this provides rich pickings for the social historian, encompassing as it does so much human interaction coupled with strong conceptual underpinnings.

Indeed, the historian Raphael Samuel (1934–1996) wrote about the Puritan spirit that was invested in the early Labour movement, such as those we have seen in the chapels of the Welsh valleys. It was a Puritanism that transferred, for instance, from the leaders of metropolitan nonconformity such as Charles Spurgeon and John Clifford, to the cultural politics of 'municipal Puritanism' in the progressive London County Council (Garnett et al., 1993, pp. 201–48). It may be that non-conformity and the socialist revival had much in common: shared ideas of a community of the saved and a moral elect, saving souls and 'making socialists' that may not be stuck in separate historical tramlines. And it was not the only vehicle in which Puritanism travelled. No doubt the spiritual politics of the Guild of St Matthew in 1877 were bolstered by the popularity of the economics of Henry George's *Progress and Poverty* two years later, the moral outrage caused by Andrew Mearn's *Bitter Cry of Outcast London* in 1883 as he described the horrors of metropolitan poverty. In addition, we can look at the minutiae of organizations dedicated to the service of humanity, from the Positivist inspired urban religious settlements to the Fellowship of the New Life in 1882 (to which Labour leader Ramsay Macdonald became secretary), the largely nonconformist, non-doctrinal and ethical Christian Socialist Society in 1886 and later the Christian Socialist Union in 1889 and so on.

An eagerness to join, to save and be saved, to be active in the service of the public, was matched by a tension between an individualism – inherited from an older Evangelical liberalism – and the impulses of the new collective agencies of modernity. The 1880s saw homophobia and the emancipatory movements of feminism emerge. (The latter was not unimportant as the congregations of nonconformity were thought to be mainly made up of women.) This was all part of a Puritan zeitgeist. But if one road led to a vogue for vegetarianism and the New Hygiene Movement, another led to other forms of popular faith such as spiritualism (Yeo, 1977, pp. 5–55). Social historians might also note the diffuse pantheists or nature worshippers on our list or the Unitarian minister John Trevor of the Labour Church and Albert Mansbridge, founder of the Workers' Education Association, who both fell back on mysticism.

Is all this the proper concern of the social historian? It was certainly dismissed by that doyen of social history, E. P. Thompson, as the epiphenomena of 'cosmic mooning'. Yet it is an approach to religion and faith in the past that has been too often overlooked by historians who have been content to register the contemporary influence of the Eastern religions: Annie Besant being the most famous adherent of theosophy; along with 'Menticulture', 'Soul-Culture', 'Higher Health', 'Yogi', and 'The New or Cosmic Consciousness' all based, like Evangelicalism, on personal idealism and on individual reward or salvation. If we are to fully understand the impact of the 1880s using the tools of social history, we also need to know all the resting places of Puritanism, the nonconformist conscience and what Edwardian enthusiasts liked to call the 'New Theology', which was emphatically not individualist at all but collectivist. In that respect, we should be able to see how the social history of faith complies with the definition of social history provided by Adrian Wilson in the opening section – as a history of the people, as the historical application of concepts often borrowed from social science (not least the sociology of Durkheim, Marx and Weber) and as part of an aspiration to construct a history of society.

Postscript

Recent approaches to social history have posed a few important questions for us all to consider. First is the question of theory. Conventionally, historians have not been that much concerned with theory. Working assiduously with the evidence, they tended to see their role as objective chroniclers of historical episodes, leaving the partialities of theoretical abstraction to scholars in the social sciences. That has changed. Historians increasingly recognize that theory has always informed their accounts and that there is much to be learnt from work in such disciplines as sociology, anthropology and geography. The widespread adoption of notions such as class,

Figure 10.2 E. P. Thompson, British historian, writer, socialist and peace campaigner.
Contributor: Trinity Mirror/Mirrorpix/Alamy

structure, consciousness, discourse, identity and ideology has resulted from a welcome dismantling of the rather artificial boundaries that historians have erected around themselves.

The relationship between sociology and history, most evident in the development of social history, is not unlike that between quarrelsome siblings. As recognizable disciplines, they were born and reached maturity at about the same time. And their interests are remarkably close. Social ordering and social order, bureaucracy, leisure, religion, war, the city, the family, electoral behaviour, to name a few, have attracted considerable attention from sociologists and historians. Their respective approaches to these matters have, however, been a source of friction, for the underlying premises contrast sharply. Sociologists are interested in identifying general patterns on the basis of which they can formulate universal laws of human behaviour. Historians, on the other hand, are rather more interested in explanations of the unique and the particular. Take, for example, the important phenomenon of human migration. Sociologists have studied different forms and experiences from which they have laid down laws that enable us to identify and explain their variety. In so doing, they have drawn distinctions between diasporas which have been forced, such as the movement of those escaping persecution (for example, Huguenots, African slaves and Jews) and those impelled by attempts to seek a better life (Asians and many Irish). Historians, on the other hand, look to understand the quite specific features and dynamics of these different diasporic experiences and find the suggestion of any similarity between Huguenots and slaves rather unhelpful.

At times, however, historians have looked with envy on the ability of sociologists to play with theoretical toys. As we have seen, the development of history tended to eschew the idea of theory since it was believed that the use of theory would inevitably distort the historian's ability to deal with evidence objectively. With the recognition that history could never be totally objective because all history was informed consciously or otherwise by theoretical perspectives, historians looked more seriously at what theory had to offer. And there were many historians by now who were interested in going beyond the unique to identify universal or even regionalized patterns of human behaviour in the past on the basis of which laws could be formulated. Their own house had few theoretical toys to offer, and so they looked elsewhere. Anthropologists, economists and political scientists had their own, but the best ones were found in the possession of sociologists. Thus it was that historians enthusiastically took up the task of applying concepts such as class, bureaucracy, identity and social control – all of which had been developed by sociologists – to the historical record.

The results have been encouraging in that the scope of historical study has broadened into exciting new areas. Without this interest in sociology, historical work in areas such as family, crime and popular faith and religion (the subject of the final section) would not have happened. Historians have to ensure that they simply do not take sociological concepts on board in an uncritical fashion. The relevance, meaning and therefore value of concepts can change from one historical period to another, and there is a real danger that universal theoretical categories mask the exceptional or particular in both the past and the present. We must therefore remain vigilant to avoid being too readily seduced by the attractions of our siblings' shiny toys.

Further Reading

François Bédarida (1979) *Social History of Britain, 1851–1975*.
British Journal of Sociology, vol. 27, no. 3, September, 1976, Special Issue: History and Sociology.
Peter Burke (2005) *History and Social Theory*.
Patrick Joyce (ed.) (1995) *Class*.
Gerald Parsons, J. R. Moore and John Wolffe (eds.) (1988) *Religion in Victorian Britain*.
Sumit Sarkar (1997) *Writing Social History*.

11 Cultural History

Introduction

For most of its existence as a distinct discipline, history has tended to neglect culture. Part of the problem was that when compared with the political and economic in human affairs, culture was seen as trivial and inconsequential. How, for example, could songs have had any influence on the important matter of historical change? Another problem has been to define the object of inquiry. Since culture was notoriously difficult to define, it was entirely understandable that historians felt a degree of apprehension in approaching it. We review some of these concerns in Section 1 and proceed to argue that, despite the reticence among historians, there have been pioneering – albeit isolated – studies of what now would be considered cultural history.

All that was to change in the postwar period, when we witnessed a genuine flowering of interest in the cultural sphere. Aided by the questioning of any privileging of the economic and the emergence of poststructuralism, historians turned with enthusiasm to topics such as art, music, language and customs, thus creating a body of exciting and innovative historical work. In Section 2 we take as a case study the carnival and discuss how historians have approached this extraordinary phenomenon. Arising to become the great form of popular entertainment in medieval Europe, carnival suffused the lives of the whole community and, even following its suppression in the early modern age, tended to shape the course of popular culture.

Finally, in Section 3 we explore how an interest in culture has enriched the study of imperialism. It is now widely accepted that colonial authorities did not rule simply through the exercise of political, economic and military power; arguably of equal if not more importance were interventions in the realms of education, religion and popular culture writ large. Not only that, imperial endeavour was driven by and reflected back on metropolitan culture with immense long-term consequences for notions of Britishness.

11.1 Towards a Definition of Cultural History

What is Cultural History? inquired Peter Burke in 2004, and in so doing he conceded that it was easier to say what cultural historians did rather than to try to define what cultural history was (Burke, 2008). Either venture, however, poses a particular range of problems for the approach of historians to the study of culture and has been fraught with difficulty and imprecision. Perhaps because of this, it is only in recent years that cultural history has been recognized as a legitimate strand of historical inquiry. In 1971, to take one indicator, a comprehensive survey entitled 'Historical Studies Today' included articles on political, intellectual, local and social history, but there was no mention of cultural history (SRG, 1971).

Since that time, coincident with the rise of cultural studies, cultural history has blossomed. However, even if we assume for the sake of argument that cultural history exists as a legitimate strand of historical inquiry, it is a brave person who attempts to define its boundaries and hence distinguish it from, say, social or intellectual history. A cursory glance at a current catalogue of books described as cultural history reveals miscellaneous titles on language, travel, disease, crime, consumption, migration and commodities such as sugar, tobacco and wine, many of which could equally have been classified as social history.

A large part of the problem faced by historians stems from the notion of culture itself. Raymond Williams famously claimed that culture was one of the 'two or three most complicated words in the English language' (Williams, 2010, p. 87), with a complex history of shifting meanings, but then he proceeded steadfastly to identify its three main uses:

1 The general process of intellectual, spiritual and aesthetic development from the eighteenth century. What this refers to are the ways in which societies have expressed concerns and aspirations as they entered the modern world, that is, how artistic traditions, political and religious movements and philosophical developments have emerged and have come to define and distinguish particular societies, most notably, the 'West' from the 'East'.
2 A particular way of life of a people, period or group, or humanity writ large. Culture here refers to the whole way of life of a people, how it is organized, how it reproduces and expresses itself.
3 The works and practices of intellectual and artistic activity. This is a variation on 1, but with a rather clearer focus on the specific works of art, literature, scholarship, music, theatre and film.

Now it is not immediately clear which of these areas are of legitimate interest to historians. The study of culture as a whole way of life has been claimed almost exclusively by anthropologists, sociologists and archaeologists, perhaps with good reason. It may well be feasible to grasp the whole way of life of a 'tribal society', a relatively small group such as teenage gang or an ancient society which has left few remnants as evidence – but a large and complex modern society? And surely works of art are best left to scholars of literature, art, film and so on, who can bring to bear their own specialist knowledge to an understanding of these expressive forms?

The other problem confronting historians was to audit precisely what role culture played in historical change. It is clear for many that, say, music or art, let alone popular recreations such as dancing, were mere fripperies when compared to elemental forces such as economic changes, political machinations and war. Happily, however, there were notable exceptions. In 1870 Jacob Burckhardt, whom we first met in Chapter 2, published *Civilization of the Renaissance in Italy*, a study charting the extraordinary flowering of culture at the time. Burckhardt may have done this by linking Renaissance culture to the classical world rather than contemporary developments, but the fact that the book was viewed as the first study of the history of art said something about the acceptance among historians of the legitimacy of inquiries into great cultural movements as indicators of fundamental shifts in human thought and imagination. It is unlikely that a study, say, of the popular festivities of French peasants would have been accorded the same status in the late nineteenth century, although, as we shall see, this is very much the fare of more recent work.

Burckhardt's study was at the same time a celebration of the rise of bourgeois individualism, for this was the trait that underpinned the lives and works of the artists of the time. Implicitly, therefore, he accepted that the social and economic conditions of fifteenth-century Italian society gave rise to particular aspirations among the bourgeois elite that expressed themselves in art. This approach was one that necessarily appealed to twentieth-century historians of Marxist persuasion who were largely responsible for taking on the mantle of cultural history. According to them, art, music, literature and so forth were part of the superstructure of society and as such reflected or expressed changes in the socio-economic base. Thus, Arnold Hauser's *Social History of Art* (1951), to take one influential example, argued like Burckhardt that the art of late fifteenth-century Florence was an expression of bourgeois naturalism which was evident in the deliberate flaunting of artistic skill such as perspective and which was a direct response to nationalist sentiment boosted by momentous contemporary historical developments, including the discovery of America and the invasion of Italy by France in the 1490s.

In recent years, this approach has been undermined by two connected developments (Burke, 2008, pp. 118–20). First, historians have moved away from an exclusive interest in elite cultural forms to embrace popular culture. Second, culture is no longer seen as a passive response to the socio-economic, but it is now viewed as an active force in its own right. Let us consider some examples. As a nice counterpoint to studies of elite Renaissance culture, Peter Burke's *Popular Culture in Early Modern Europe* (1978) studied the popular cultural forms that spanned Europe from the late medieval period (1500) to the beginnings of the Industrial Revolution (1800). From the outset, Burke spelt out what was distinctive about his approach. Borrowing promiscuously from various meanings of the term, he claimed that culture is a system of shared meanings, values and attitudes and the forms (literature, plays, and so on) used to express them. In this sense, culture is in part a whole way of life, but it is not identical with it. Popular culture relates to the subordinate classes, made up mostly of craftsmen, peasants and their families; to understand it, he claimed, we cannot fall back on conventional historical analysis but have to adapt the approach of Burckhardt by borrowing concepts and methods from other disciplines, in particular, literature, folklore and social anthropology. The result was an evocative and insightful account of the origins and structures of popular cultural forms and the extent to which they revealed the nature of the wider societies.

The most significant and lasting of these forms was the carnival, which took place early each year throughout Europe – particularly in the temperate south – and represented a celebration of popular sentiment before the austerities and lean times imposed by Lent. It was therefore a brief time of excessive consumption of food, alcohol and sex, when through transgressive acts of social inversion the 'world was turned upside down'. During carnival symbols of this challenge to the dominant social order were pervasive – the king became the fool, the fool became the king, animals rode on humans, fish flew.

Burke was not alone at the time in seeking to approach history from below. The 1970s witnessed a rich flowering of studies of peasant and plebeian cultures from the pens and typewriters of outstanding radical historians. In France, Emmanuel Le Roy Ladurie, a leading member of the *Annales* School, published *Montaillou: Cathars and Catholics in a French Village 1294–1324* (1975), a vivid and detailed reconstruction of the life of a small medieval village in the early fourteenth century, which he followed shortly after with *Carnival in Romans: Mayhem and Massacre in a French City* (1979), a dazzling account of when celebrations at Romans in south-west France turned into a people's uprising against repressive authority. In Italy, as we will meet in a slightly different context in Chapter 18, Carlo Ginzburg wrote *The Cheese and the Worms*, which used records around the trial of a sixteenth-century miller to shed brilliant light on the Italian peasant culture. In Britain, Edward Thompson (see Chapter 10) wrote a series of pieces on plebeian village culture collected together in *Customs in Common*, while Christopher Hill in *The World Turned Upside Down* (1972) and his student David Underdown in *Pride's Purge: Politics in the Puritan Revolution* (1971) – and then more particularly in *Revel, Riot and Rebellion* (1985) – effectively rewrote the history of the English Civil War by demonstrating the extent to which the conflict was not merely political and religious but at every

Figure 11.1 Scene of social inversion from a European carnival of 1532 in which women act as draught animals driven by men in costumes
Contributor: Sunny Celeste/Alamy Stock Photo

turn cultural. In their eyes, struggles over the status and survival of popular recreations such as sport and theatre exerted a decisive influence on the course of events. This body of historical work compares favourably with any. It has stood the test of time, and is largely responsible for the richness of cultural history today

The second challenge to historical studies of elite culture has come from theorists who are seen collectively to inhabit approaches based on structuralism. Structuralists (as opposed to the culturalists against whom they are pitted) seek to invert the relationship between society and its cultural forms. Whereas previously cultural historians began with economic and social structures as a means of explaining modes of cultural expression such as religion, language, and art, structuralists argue that these forms of expression are actually decisive since they – and not, say, the class structure – create the mindsets through which people interpret their experience. A member of the bourgeoisie, for example, does not think and behave in ways defined by his or her position in society but according to the ideologies they inhabit. Thus, for example, they come to believe that they have a natural right and ability to rule. To state the opposition pithily but hopefully in a helpful manner: for culturalists, experience tends to structure expression, while for structuralists, expression tends to structure experience. Take, for example, literature. Culturalists have argued that literature is the embodiment or expression of societies, classes and communities because it represents their lived realities, while structuralists argue that literature expresses nothing, rather it shapes the way people view these lived realities. The use of the term 'structures' rather than, say, 'determines' is important, for most historians within these camps have no wish to work with crude Marxist visions of base and superstructure, as outlined in Chapter 6. Instead, in their various ways, they see culture as part of the whole fabric of social practices that comprise human activity; the trick is to understand the changing dialogue between cultural forms and social behaviour at particular times.

The origins of structuralism can be traced back to early twentieth-century work on language undertaken by Ferdinand de Saussure (1857–1913) and Roman Jakobson (1896–1982). They perceived that language operates to create meaning not through vocabularies themselves – which are purely arbitrary – but by systems of rules governing structural relationships, which for the most part we are simply not aware of. Thus, for example, there is nothing in the word 'table' which signifies the object being described; it is only when we realize that 'table' does not mean chair or floor and so on that it comes to take on meaning. What this meant was that there was no necessary relationship between the meaning created by the linguistic system and the reality of experience and that the system operated independently of the speaker. There was – to express it bluntly – nothing beyond the text.

After the Second World War, anthropologists, political theorists and sociologists began to understand that this approach to language had a much wider relevance. In the appropriately titled *Structural Anthropology* (1958), the French anthropologist Claude Lévi-Strauss (1909–2009) claimed that cultures were in effect languages and operated according to the same system of rules. Myths, kinship systems and rituals were ordered in specific ways; once we understood the underlying structure through application of the tools of linguistic analysis, we could then reveal how they operate to create meaning and hence patterns of behaviour. An example of such a ritual was the meal, which is highly structured like a language, and even if we are not aware of how the structure works, we act accordingly. The courses are rigidly organized (just think of the confusion if treacle sponge and custard was offered before roast beef and vegetables, finishing with pea soup), and tight protocols of eating them are followed. Levi Strauss hoped, therefore, to identify universal structures which underpin all cultural systems; the increasing awareness of the common features of myths suggests he was travelling broadly in the right direction.

What has this concern with structures meant for historians? When Fernand Braudel wrote his magisterial *The Mediterranean and the Mediterranean World in the Age of Philip II* in a prisoner of war camp, he was probably not aware of the latest work in linguistic theory, and yet it is clear he was thinking along similar and parallel lines. He was concerned above all with downgrading narratives of the individual and event that tended to prevail in previous historical writing by instead focusing on the deep historical structures that produce change. This demanded a total history involving society, culture and the physical environment and not the narrow diplomatic and political histories that had tended to prevail. Fundamental in this approach was his use of time, which can also be understood as language. For Braudel, time was an organizing principle in human societies. In the period and place of his study, it operated at different levels. Fundamental was the *longue durée*, a history of recurring cycles which span centuries, but this was mediated by the medium *durée* – a history of trade cycles and demographic change over decades – and finally *histoire événementielle*, which charts the day-to-day course of historical change. Thus, lives of individuals and events, the normal fare of historical writing, are in fact merely surface manifestations of deeper and more fundamental temporal structures of which we are for the most part ignorant (Gunn, 2006, pp. 14–15). We say more about history and the ordering of time for historians in Chapter 22.

It is generally the case, however, that this approach to history has been less fertile than that of culturalism. Historians have remained suspicious of what they see as the influence of continental philosophers, although there are some notable exceptions whose work deserves mention. Michel Foucault is discussed more fully in Chapter 7, but suffice it to say here that his studies of madness, incarceration and power all start with the premise that histories presenting unified and linear chronicles of events that sustained a sense of stability are not to be trusted. Rather we must look at how knowledge is produced and operates, for it is on the basis of such sources of meaning and identity (or 'discourses' in Foucault's terminology) that people act as historical agents. Thus, people inhabit ordered structured discourses of, say, commerce, economics or bourgeois individualism which impact directly upon how they see themselves and the world around.

There are few historical studies of culture that could be described as purely structural; any such study would probably be quite dull. We have seen in important recent work, however, the incipient influence of structuralism. Simon Schama would resist any tendency to rank him among the structuralists, and yet his *The Embarrassment of Riches* (1987), subtitled *An Interpretation of Dutch Culture in the Golden Age*, clearly owes something to their work. The book is a detailed account of how the burgher world of the Dutch in the seventeenth century constructed a collective sense of identity. The ideology they inhabited determined how they conducted themselves in civic affairs, how they dressed, how they viewed others outside their universe, how they lived within the family and so on. In *Landscape and Memory* (1995), Schama turned his attention to the ways in which representations of the landscape has woven the fabric of Western culture. He wished to understand the richness, antiquity and complexity of the landscape tradition not by gazing at its obvious appearance but by excavating below to reveal the 'veins of myth and memory that lie beneath the surface' (Schama, 1995, p. 14).

Questions of myth and memory have featured prominently in recent cultural history. Myth, like culture, is a complex term. Commonsensically, myth refers to an untruth, usually one that has grown organically over time to be accepted by many; belief in the ancient continuity of the British royal hereditary line serves as an example. And there are, as we have already mentioned, myths of a universal nature involving human struggle against imposing odds. Historians, by contrast, use the term to refer to an interpretation of events which has abstracted from what is a complex picture to convey one that appears cogent, simple and, above all, natural. Myths are profoundly important to the creation of collective identity – just pause to think for a moment of how our senses of Britishness or Americanness are mythological. By unravelling the ways in which such myths are put together, what rhetoric and narrative devices they employ, how, in other words, they are structured, we can better understand their latent power. As examples of recent work, we can do no better than refer to the studies of Alessandro Portelli, an Italian scholar of American literature and culture whom we shall meet briefly in Chapter 24 on the subject of oral history and Luisa Passerini, also an Italian, whom we introduce in the same chapter as an expert on memory and fascism. Portelli's *The Death of Luigi Trastulli and Other Stories* (1991), for example, shows how the death of an Italian worker in a demonstration in 1949 was selectively remembered by subsequent generations. Such remembrances were not, he claimed, the result of wayward memories but emerged from an effort to make sense of what happened. Similarly, Passerini's *Fascism in Popular Memory* (1987) investigated how the experience of fascism in Italy was subsequently appropriated in popular memory, not as a reliable record but as a means retrospectively of incorporating the experience into narratives that were seemingly rational. We investigate the use of myth in history more fully in Chapter 18.

Memory has long been of interest to historians. Most have argued that memory was the fickle product of the subterranean mind, thereby relegating it to the instinctive and intuitional. This helps to explain the hostility of conventional historians to oral testimony, and yet few appreciated that all documentary evidence was in part built on memory simply because the documents were created in part from memory of the events they described. In recent years, there has been a growing recognition in the work of people like Portelli that memory is not a passive store of images from the past but an active and dynamic force in the creation of historical thought – one where the silences and gaps are as important as the presences. We all interpret and act from personal and collective memories of past events, most often in the belief that these memories are reliable and secure. Often the indefensible, irrational and horrific in collective memories are deliberately erased or reworked. Memories are thus not stable and inviolable; they are historically conditioned, altering from generation to generation, from place to place.

In *Theatres of Memory* (1994), Raphael Samuel (1934–1996) took up these arguments by showing how popular memory of the past is not fixed but actively created, most notably by television, which has become the principal source of unofficial knowledge. Drama documentaries, series such as *Timewatch, Who do you think you are?* and *Time Team*, fictional dramas of the past such as *Band of Brothers* and *Madmen*, biographies, anniversaries of events and even the replaying of old films may help satiate our appetite for all things past, but at the same time they construct popular memories of that past even when the images they present conflict with memories based on personal experience (much more on this in Chapter 14). In Britain, this tension was amusingly exploited in *'Allo, 'Allo*, which parodied the ways in which the French resistance to Nazi occupation had been represented in television drama. Under such circumstances it is the role of the historian to provide correctives where necessary, to reveal how historical memory operates and to develop strategies for a more critical popular historical imagination.

11.2 Survival of the Carnival

Despite the manifest problems faced by cultural historians, there is no doubt that they have long been interested in culture and collectively have been responsible for a body of work which in its inventiveness, imagination and importance stands comparison with any. To explore further the promise of cultural history, we wish to return to the carnival. One good reason why carnival has attracted attention is its sheer universality. Think of carnival today and you invoke images of jubilant festivities on the streets of Rio de Janeiro, the mayhem of Mardi Gras in New Orleans and the revellers at Notting Hill carnival in London. Such celebrations seem a world away from the carnival of medieval Europe, held in the cold winter weeks just before Lent, but the links are direct, for it was largely thanks to French, Spanish and Portuguese immigrants that the European carnival was translated to the Americas, there to be reworked, largely through the influence of African cultures (Burke, 1997, p. 150). (Interestingly, in the case of the Notting Hill carnival, traditional festivities of the Caribbean were exported back to the shores of Europe.) And despite this reworking, carnival holds onto certain shared features including music, dancing in the streets, fancy dress, grotesque masks, the mixing of social groups and conspicuous consumption.

Equally important has been the recognition that the course of the carnival reveals much about the nature of its host society. As a popular celebration it acted as a counterculture to elite authority which could on occasion erupt into a violent confrontation, but for the most part carnival was a licensed affair that over time was suppressed. Not that it ever disappeared completely; as we know, in part through exportation various versions have continued to the present, but significantly in Europe carnivalesque elements went underground and continued to shape the literature, music, theatre and rituals more generally of oppositional cultures. It is this underground that has appealed to the interests of many recent historians. Running as a vibrant thread through much of the work of Peter Burke, Christopher Hill, Emmanuel Le Roy Ladurie and E. P. Thompson, carnival has continued significance to an understanding of popular cultural forms. The excessive festivities of medieval Europe may have died out, but recent cultural histories have testified to the survival of the carnivalesque in the plebeian imagination, arguably well into the modern era. Thus, in language, sport, body imagery, music, theatre and literary forms we can detect elements of the carnival as a boisterous celebration of popular identity, acting simultaneously as a counterculture to that of the respectable elite.

Christopher Hill may not have employed the term *carnival*, but the title of his outstanding study of the radical undercurrents of the English revolution gives a good indication of where he is coming from. In *The World Turned Upside Down* (1972) he revealed what he describes as the revolt within the revolution, namely, the attempt by sections of the common people to secure their solutions to the problems thrown up by the turbulent times, often in direct opposition to the elites who had called them to action in the first instance. The revolution against absolute monarchical authority had unleashed, like the sorcerer's apprentice, forces that threatened to become out of control. At a time of profound political flux and excitement, a wave of radical sects which in their different ways offered programmes of continued reform in pursuit of a new society not only challenged older societal values but proposed daringly new ones.

Among these sects were Levellers, Diggers and Ranters who, in vigorously advocating egalitarian ideals, drew upon aspects of the carnivalesque. 'Foolery', Hill argues, had served a social function since the Middle Ages. On certain occasions including Shrove Tuesday, the Feast of Fools and All Fools Day, the 'social hierarchy and the social decencies could be turned upside down' (ibid., p. 16). These transgressive acts, however, were to a large extent licensed, a convenient safety valve to release tensions and thereby make the extant social order appear more tolerable. What changed in the turmoil of seventeenth-century England was the belief expressed in a profusion of published tracts that social inversions could be made permanent and a utopian future secured, which was a 'land of Cokayne, of tipsy topsy-turvydom . . . a revised version of the dream of the medieval peasant' (ibid., p. 340).

This counterculture was suppressed by parliamentary forces, and a large majority of the various sects died out, but some of its ideas fed into and helped sustain the radical political culture of the eighteenth-century Atlantic, especially as evidenced by the writings of John Wilkes and Tom Paine and the American revolutionaries (Chapter 6). Such lineages are not easy to trace, let alone prove, but ironically in one fascinating postscript they may have served at last to throw off the shackles of English rule. *The World is Turned Upside Down*, a broadside ballad from 1646, was a popular song of the eighteenth century, reputedly played when Cornwallis surrendered to American forces at Yorktown in 1781 (ibid., p. 380).

E. P. Thompson has done much to reveal how the carnivalesque survived in the plebeian culture of Britain well into the twentieth century (Thompson, 1991). Like Hill, he eschews the term *carnival*, preferring instead *charivari*, a French word to denote specifically a serenade of rough music, but the similarities are clear. In a British context rough music referred to a din created by loud instruments and the beating of pots and pans, accompanied by raucous laughter and the shouting of obscenities. This noise was part of a ritual enacted by village communities as an expression of hostility against individuals who had transgressed social norms and was often accompanied by various forms of street theatre including the burning of effigies, riding the victim on a donkey while pelting him or her with all matter of filth, and mock trials. Most of the victims subjected to these humiliations had committed misdemeanours such as scolding, husband- or wife-beating, cuckolding, bastardy and petty theft rather than the more serious murder, rape and abduction, but the message was clear – reform or be banished.

The extent to which rough music was a genuine counterculture is open to question. At a time when the moral authority of the church was on the wane, it could be seen as a ready means of community self-regulation. Victims rarely suffered serious physical harm, for the rituals were above all symbolic acts of violence. In this respect, charivari was, like carnival, a licensed affair, and its participants, by adhering to limits in dispensing justice, at the same time endorsed the real source of judicial power. And it is worth noting that charivari (or *shivaree*, as it came to be known), migrated across the Atlantic to resurface in large areas of the South and Midwest (ibid., p. 470).

Before leaving the study of carnival, we wish briefly to consider the issues raised by its intellectual origins. In many respects the founding text was Mikhail Bakhtin's *Rabelais and his World*, first published in English in 1965. The subject of this study, François Rabelais (c.1494–1533), was a Franciscan monk and French satirical writer best remembered for the remarkable characters of Gargantua and Pantagruel who in his hands come to represent the bawdy, irreverent folk culture of the time. Consider, for example, the following extract describing the birth of Gargantua, taken from the first English translation in 1653 (warning: this is not for the faint hearted):

> a little while after she began to groane, lament and cry, then suddenly came the midwives from all quarters, who groping her below, found some *peloderies*, which was a certaine filthy stuffe, and of a taste truly bad enough, this they thought had been the childe, but it was her fundament, that was slipt out with the mollification of her *streight-intrall*, which you call the *bum gut*, and that merely by eating of too many tripes, as we have shewed.
>
> (Rabelais, 1653, p. 31)

This was part of a task to recover aspects of a popular culture which at the time was in decline, in particular the notion of carnival, embodying as it did the spirit of opposition to authority. The weapons chosen were parody, humour and mockery conveyed in a crude and scatological language; with these he railed against official culture, most notably, the scriptures and liturgy of organized religion. Little wonder that the Catholic Church declared the book obscene and banned it, but it is now recognized as a classic which helped to lay the foundations of European writing. For Rabelais, carnival represented a temporary suspension – indeed, an inversion – of authority when the king becomes the clown and old truths a comic monster. And the grotesque realism of body imagery, evidenced in the celebration of the belly and buttocks of Gargantua, comes to stand for the body of the fecund people engaged in creative renewal (Gunn, 2006, p. 68).

Apart from his revival of Rabelais, what was distinctive about Bakhtin's approach to cultural history? Bakhtin was above all a cultural theorist with a particular interest in language, and in early work on the theories of language he set out to distance himself from the structuralist theories of Ferdinand de Saussure (1857–1913). While Saussure had attempted to separate 'text' and 'context' by arguing that language was an abstract and rather static system governed by rules little recognized by speakers, Bakhtin held that language evolves over time just as does the 'speech community'. Individual members are not simply the subjects of the linguistic system; they inhabit a dynamic social situation, which thus provides the context for how language operates in society. 'Text' and 'context', in other words, are inextricably linked in what Bakhtin termed a dialogical relationship (idem, pp. 65–6). Bakhtin's contribution to cultural history therefore goes beyond the carnival. He first became known in the West during the 1960s when his works appeared in translation. Given this was the time at which a fledgling cultural history began to take flight, it was likely that Bakhtin's influence would be welcomed, particularly by those of a culturalist persuasion.

11.3 Empire and the Cultural Turn

Few areas of historical inquiry have been more influenced by the rise of cultural history than that of empire. It may be premature to talk of a new paradigm, but in recent years we have seen an unmistakable shift away from studies of the ascent of European economic, military and political power in their various colonies to a more nuanced picture of imperial authority. We now recognize that imperial rule operated on the terrain of culture as well as in the military, political and economic spheres. Indeed, it could well be argued that intervention in the religious and educational life of, say, India had a profound impact on the course of imperial rule. Such considerations have stood at the heart of the important body of work collectively known as postcolonialism (which we discuss in Chapter 7) and the various studies undertaken by Western scholars. A recent survey of the field, to take one example, has thematic chapters on consumption, crime,

Figure 11.2 Engraved frontispiece to the 1537 edition of Rabelais' *Gargantua* showing the giant with his son Pantagruel

Contributor: Lebrecht Music & Arts/Alamy Stock Photo

race, religion, culture, art, science and modernity, most of which simply would not have figured in the minds of historians of empire a generation ago (Levine and Marriott, 2012).

The founding text of the 'cultural turn' was Edward Said's *Orientalism* (1978), which mapped how over the nineteenth century the British and French colonial projects imagined and hence effectively appropriated India and the Levant in ways that legitimized their rule (Chapter 7). Said's use of the term *culture*, developed further in his *Culture and Imperialism* (1993), tended to foreground the production and interpretation of meaning rather than a whole way of life in an anthropological sense. Thus, he mapped the ways in which an array of British and French poets, novelists, scientists, journalists, missionaries, philosophers and colonial administrators constructed the 'East' and its peoples as culturally, intellectually – even biologically – inferior to the West. This served to define the agenda for subsequent work within the field right up to the present. Broadly speaking, therefore, cultural approaches to empire cohere around three principal concerns:

1. The production of knowledge in building and consolidating notions of colonial otherness.
2. The critical role played by notions of cultural difference and identity in both the ideological underpinnings of empire and the everyday practices of colonial rule.
3. The complex network of global interconnections in which these knowledges circulate.

(Ballantyne, 2010, p. 451)

For evidence of the creative potential deriving from this agenda, do look at the recent edited collections by Nicolas Dirks, *Colonialism and Culture* (1992); Catherine Hall, *Cultures of Empire* (2000) and Kathleen Wilson, *A New Imperial History* (2004).

To investigate these matters further, let us glance at two recent studies within this field that have extended and deepened our knowledge of the nature of British rule in India. Christopher Bayly's *Empire and Information* (1997) is a highly regarded study of how British rule depended not merely upon military power but upon a sophisticated intelligence-gathering network. Bayly draws upon the idea of an information order, originally developed by the cultural geographer Manuel Castells, to show that it operated relatively independently of social and economic change. Information circulated, not through the power exercised by the British state to control the channels and technology of communication but rather through a dialogical relationship between its surveillance agencies and the indigenous networks of social communication.

As British rule spread, so it was increasingly seen as necessary to engage with the information order of indigenous societies. But the control it was able to exercise was weak and superficial. Anxieties were expressed about the seemingly mysterious transmission of indigenous information and the difficulties of translating Indian languages, including Sanskrit, which, while no longer spoken, was that of the ancient fables and moral codes. Accordingly, native informants were recruited who provided a degree of access to this information. From them the British learnt, importantly, about systems of land revenue administration, indigenous codes of law, religious rites and languages, but the British hold remained tenuous, an ignorance that the uprising of 1857 cruelly exposed. This process had a profound impact on the flow of information in North India where the British ruled, for the introduction of the printing press, newspapers, libraries and archives thought important in controlling information simultaneously transformed indigenous publishing and other forms of social and political communication among Indians. Before 1800, to take one example, only a handful of printed material was published by Indian presses; by the end of the nineteenth century, Calcutta was second only to London as a publishing powerhouse. This transformation, argues Bayly, was more thorough and comprehensive than that effected by colonial capitalism on the Indian economy (idem, p. 9).

Colonial dialogue is also the subject of Jyotsna Singh's study on the staging of Shakespeare in the theatres of nineteenth-century Calcutta (Singh, 1996). The re-creation of London's theatrical scene, she argues, was an important feature of the transmission of metropolitan culture. When the first theatres opened in the early years of the century, they not only staged a standard repertoire of English plays but employed many actors who had previously appeared on the London stage. Initially, the audiences also were made up exclusively of members of the colonial elite, but by mid-century successful schemes were being launched to attract the English-educated, Bengali elite, together with rich native merchants. It was all part of a 'civilizing mission' designed to assimilate local indigenous elites into British thought and culture, and what better vehicle than Shakespeare?

Yet this process was not as straightforward as colonial authorities might have wished, for, as was so often the case, the transmission of culture was contested. While approaches to literature in educational institutions maintained a deep reverence for all things Shakespearean, playwrights and producers in Indian theatre were quite prepared to interpret the plays through the optic of their own theatrical traditions. This was apparent soon after 1830 when the first Bengali playhouses opened and started to present adaptations of the canon, as well as English translations of Sanskrit folk dramas. Over time, Bengali translations of the plays appeared. Thus, in the inherently more subversive theatres of Calcutta, Shakespeare underwent a process of 'transculturation'; that is, plays were transformed through strategies of translation and adaptation, thereby disrupting any association that had been forged with metropolitan culture and the civilizing mission (ibid., p. 137). These hybrid forms led to a decline in the appeal of English plays to Bengalis and the emergence of an indigenous repertoire which helped not only to consolidate the sense of Bengali identity but also by the end of the century to lay the foundations of a nascent nationalism.

At a time when the 'linguistic turn' seemed to offer little insight into the diverse nature of imperial experiences, the bringing together of culture and empire has revitalized both fields of historical inquiry. However, important though the cultural turn has been to the study of the imperial experience, a number of issues have been thrown up which await further work (Price, 2006). In the early stages of the rise of cultural history when, for example, class was supplanted as the organizing principle of social change, certain anxieties were expressed that, by erasing references to the social and economic context, the terrain of culture was poorly equipped to explain such change. Those anxieties have if anything intensified, for too often it has seemed that by focusing exclusively on the cultural dynamics of empire the social, economic and political played at most a minor role. In other words, since culture is seen to operate quite independently of the economic and social there is no good reason to take them into account.

Second, the metropolis has attracted a disproportionate level of attention. Admittedly, London was the seat of imperial power, but it is necessary to unravel the truly national dimensions of the urban culture that sustained its expansion. Kathleen Wilson's *The Sense of the People* (1995) is a notable exception to these tendencies, for she skilfully demonstrates that the rise of the provinces in the eighteenth century was vital to the forging of an imperial ethos which in turn was embedded within a wider political culture. The urban culture that grew out the industrial heartlands and service centres of capitalist agriculture, the attendant rise of the middle classes and the emergence of a buoyant print culture gave rise to an extra-parliamentary political culture which promoted distinct senses of citizenship, 'the people', liberty, civilization and the nation within which notions of imperial expansion took root and flourished.

However, the question of precisely how important empire was to British political culture continues to promote debate. Bernard Porter's *The Absent-Minded Imperialists* (2004) poses a challenge to what he considers is the ubiquity of the 'cultural imperialist' reading of modern British history. In particular, he offers a spirited rebuttal of the notion that British nationhood and identity were significantly shaped by imperial sentiment. From an extensive trawl through printed sources, parliamentary archives, memoirs and correspondence and the sorts of cultural transmission found in schools, theatres and literature, Porter concludes that empire was nowhere near as ubiquitous as has been claimed by others, and therefore the relationship between empire and domestic society was rather more complicated. In particular moments of intense anxiety, such as 1857 when the Indian uprising was at its height, empire commanded a great deal of attention in parliament and the press, but routinely British political culture was dominated rather by concerns over such matters as social reform, free trade and religion.

Finally, if we accept that empire was framed by the various discursive practices through which meaning was created, disseminated and consumed, then how was this process translated into the practical realities of colonial rule? There is often the tendency to view the culture of empire as a determining influence on the practicalities of rule when in fact there were manifest difficulties in effecting that translation. There was no coherent ethos of imperial rule, and this created an instability that the colonized were able to exploit. In the British case, for example, governors of the East India Company in London may have dictated policy, but they were aware that servants operating on the ground 3,000 miles away had to deal with problems that were not foreseen or had simply moved on (before the telegraph it took 6 months for a letter from London to reach India and a response to be received). Furthermore, what imperial administrators said and wrote had no necessary connection to what they did; in this respect there was a real disconnect between stated policy and the quotidian reality of colonial rule.

Despite these problems there is no sign that interest in the cultural history of empire is on the wane. Hopefully over time, as some of these issues are addressed more directly, its full potential will be realized. If this means that cultural history loses something of its identity, this is a price worth paying.

11.4 History of Emotions

Until the 1980s, most historians considered emotions as primitive and irrational, hardly worthy of serious study. Not only that, emotions such as anger, joy, disgust, surprise, sorrow, fear and pity, particularly when compared with broader structural factors such as class, were thought to play no essential role in promoting historical change. Since then, however, the history of emotions – or affective history, as it is often but confusingly referred to – has emerged as such a significant branch of social or cultural history that many talk of an emotional turn in historical inquiry (following quickly on from the linguistic, material, spatial and imperial turns – no wonder historians occasionally feel giddy!). In this section, we wish to investigate how this reversal came about and assess the potential of this development.

Let us begin with an example of work within the history of emotions. Following calls from social historians to consider the emotional dimensions of human experience, studies were undertaken to explain why the rituals, beliefs and institutions of medieval and early modern Europe were responses to the prevailing emotional climates. But it was the history of the family that attracted the most attention (Stearns and Stearns, 1985). According to some narrative accounts, the emotional landscape of the family was prone to change. Thus, historical studies on familial relationships in Europe and colonial America have revealed a sharp increase in affection in the late seventeenth and eighteenth centuries, particularly when compared with the cold, detached and instrumental emotional landscape of the premodern Western family. To cite one example, as property relations became less tense in seventeenth-century New England, so greater family affection was displayed towards the elderly. By the time we reach the eighteenth century, we find, as birth and infant mortality rates fell, children giving and receiving greater and more intense levels of affection.

Studies on family demography have also pointed to the role of emotions. Research has shown that reductions in infant mortality are correlated with increases in the emotional investment in children. In other words, the fewer children dying in infancy, the more joy, empathy and affection we feel for them. By a similar logic, reductions in birth rates are almost certainly the result of rational calculations at times of changing economic circumstances, but they may be tied also to emotional shifts such as the ways in which affection is extended to and expected from children.

The latter decades of the premodern era have, therefore, been seen as something of a watershed in the history of emotions. What followed, however, is rather more contested. With the putative rise in familial affection and in toleration of public displays of affection, it has been argued, we witnessed a decline in marriage based on a cold calculus of instrumentality to one embedded in notions of love between couples attached above all romantically. There are, however, many examples from the premodern era of passionate attachments between couples duly celebrated in popular culture, which in general were accompanied by a decline in violence, especially towards women. More importantly, we hit the buffer of the Victorian period with all its contradictions. Somewhat tendentiously, many have seen the bourgeoisie in the vanguard of the romantic revolution, and yet Peter Gay, the meticulous chronicler of that experience, has skilfully captured its contradictions:

> The nineteenth-century bourgeois experience of love was both stylized and spontaneous. Efficient middle-class institutions all the way from the adroitly orchestrated dinner party to the cool treaty between mercantile clans fostered suitable unions. They could not keep the impressionable from falling in love, but they could make sure that young men and women encountered few except eligible partners. . . . Acceptable paths to love were plainly marked and heavily guarded; the penalties annexed to misalliances threatened or consummated – social ostracism, transfer to remote posts, legacies withheld – were extremely harsh. . . . In the age of Victoria perhaps more than any other, the boundaries between erotic expressiveness and reserve were shifting, problematic, almost impossible to map with any sense of finality.
>
> (Gay, 1986, p. 3)

The dialectic between unbridled sexual passion and the fabled repression characteristic of Victorian society, in other words, has and continues to be difficult to grasp. How precisely are we to assess the place of Victorian poets, novelists and diarists in the history of emotions? What is the significance of middle-class slumming around the brothels of East London? Why, and with what effect, did some Victorians find it necessary in the interests of decency to cover the legs of tables? Rather more historical work will need to be undertaken before we have satisfactory answers to such questions.

Before moving on, it is worth discussing briefly another emotion which has attracted attention, namely, fear. From the various investigations, it is evident that there is no universal emotion of fear, rather fear is specific to particular parts of the globe at particular times (Bourke, 2003). Fear, therefore, is mobile and changes over time. The decline in magic and rise of scientific rationalism since medieval times may have led to decline in irrational fears, but the fear of death and the hereafter had remained intact. In Britain and America of the nineteenth century, for example, arguably the greatest fear was of the precariousness of life, the notion that at any time we could be taken by death. And this seemed to be pervasive. True, mortality rates were invariably higher among the poorer sections of society, but cholera, tuberculosis and typhoid knew no barriers and could strike members of the middle and upper classes at any time. With advances in medical science, in particular bacteriology, such fears receded, to be replaced in the postwar years by anxieties about old age and the threat of deterioration in our social status and well-being. The fear of death was no longer centred on pain and the final judgement but the curtailment of 'life, liberty and the pursuit of happiness' and the distressing consequences for those left behind. The recent outbreak of COVID-19 has again raised the spectre of premature and unexpected death.

With these examples in mind, we wish now to turn attention to the ways in which historians have approached emotions and their location within society. Questions such as what is anger or what is fear have not been of interest to historians. The nature of emotion – how it is located within our psyche – is generally considered the province of neuroscientists and psychoanalysts whose work is thought to be of limited value in understanding historical change. Historians, by contrast, inquire into how particular cultural environments give rise to, frame and view emotions at particular historical periods. At the heart of the enterprise are several radical precepts which have driven the work and offered genuine insight into specific historical episodes (Boddice, 2018, pp. 1–2):

1. Because emotions are not universal or innate, they change over time and from one geographical area to another, and therefore they are of interest to historians.
2. Emotions arise from specific historical circumstances but are not merely responses. They actively intervene to create events and therefore need to be taken seriously in theories of causation. Emotions emerge from history but simultaneously make history.
3. Far from being irrational and peripheral, emotions are a vital constituent element of humans as historical subjects and are intimately tied into relations of power. What groups in society promote the emergence of emotions – and subsequently control them by governing the conventions for emotional expression – tend to exercise power.
4. Emotions are therefore at the centre of such subjects as identity, class, gender, race and sexuality, understandings of which are enhanced by thinking through the ways in which they are played out in history.

Early historical scholarship tended to rely on notions that emotion was a universal backdrop to historical action, that the human subject displayed powerful similarities across time and space (Barclay, 2021). More recently, as empirical studies have begun to challenge this approach, historians have been increasingly attracted to the idea that emotion is not universal but varies across time and space and as such is worth investigation. But precisely how is the relation between emotion and society viewed? At this point some of the difficulties arise, for while there seems to be a consensus around the idea that emotions are not innate but the products of cultural environments, the emphasis is less on their cognitive psychological dynamics than on the ways in which emotions are named and framed by humans and how societies value and control them. Historians, then, have not been that much interested in emotions per se but in how they come into being and react back on the societies that created them.

One early and influential school of thought associated above all with the sociologist Peter Stearns and his psychiatrist wife Carol Stearns argued that emotional norms were created and perpetuated by social structures (Stearns and Stearns, 1986). Accordingly, emotions are not universal and natural manifestations shared by humans but are socially constructed. This social constructionism – as it is known – contends that emotional responses to events such as disasters and wars are not given; they are shaped by discourses emanating from particular communities and societies at particular times. Here the distinction between emotion and what they term *emotionology* is crucial. Emotions are a human response; emotionology, on the other hand, refers to the attitudes that a society or community have towards emotions and their expression and the ways in which institutions including schools, families and societies promote or discourage such expression. Here we are less interested in how people felt or displayed their feelings than in how society responded to them. The emergence of affect in marriage that is the rise of familial love was an historical process created and nurtured in the early modern period to meet particular needs, largely through the acceptance and approval of the feelings associated with familial love. Emotional norms therefore surface which are disseminated in novels, manuals on etiquette, diaries, music, art and later the broadcast media that regulate or guide us on how we should respond emotionally or express emotion.

To illustrate this approach, the Stearns investigate changing attitudes towards anger in American history (Stearn and Stearn, 1986). In the first period chosen, 1750–1850, the ideal of an anger-free family was introduced and spread. From 1850–1920, a certain ambivalence towards anger appeared which reached its peak after 1920 when the general condemnation of anger inherited from the earlier period gained strength, leaving the family as the only outlet for the expression of anger.

At a time when the linguistic turn in historical research was beginning to make its mark, social constructionism came under attack from critiques which saw in it too pronounced an emphasis on discourse. It was almost as if, they insisted, language was exclusively responsible for determining societal responses to the expression of emotion and hence how emotion is displayed. As an alternative, new approaches emerged which took rather more seriously the complexities of emotional utterances. An early article of William Reddy (1997) set much of the tone. Proposing an 'historical ethnography of emotions' on the back of an attack on social constructionism, he asserted that any insistence that there is 'nothing to emotion beyond the local discursive structures through which it is figured and practiced' is fundamentally flawed. 'A proper understanding of the dynamic character of emotional gestures and utterances', he continued, 'offers a starting point for a coherent, politically meaningful historical ethnography of emotions'. Recognition of this dynamic character is a necessary first step since it challenges the notions of discourse and essentialism that together form the underlying precepts of social constructionism:

1. Any notion of the pervasive and all-powerful play of discourse accepts the absolute plasticity of individuals and therefore the power of discourse to determine emotion down to the most fleeting impulses. Studying history shows to the contrary that 'discourse' fails to capture the changing and complex nature of emotional expression.
2. Views that humans possess essential, universal characteristics but with every gender identification and orientation that can be used to distinguish them from others and that work against the fluidity of emotions and the specificities of their locations.

In *Navigation of Feeling* (2001), Reddy applies these ideas better to understand the relationship between language and emotion. He surmised, for example, that when we look upon a particular human, we feel a body sensation which we can call love and then align that sensation better to map it onto societal norms of what the emotion of love should feel like. Similarly, we can view a particular episode and respond with a sensation named disgust which is them realigned to conform to common-sense norms of what disgust is. Humans, therefore, attempt with varying degrees of success to match their feelings with conventional modes of emotional expression. The closer the match, the stronger the continuity of the emotional regime; the wider the discrepancy, the greater the emotional suffering and the more likely the chance of historical change (Boddice, 2014).

To investigate the utility of this theory, Reddy turned to French history and offers nothing less than a reinterpretation of the origins of the revolution. Under the absolutism of Louis XIV an aristocratic code of honour was consolidated using new standards of etiquette and comportment. Through the careful wielding of arbitrary force and emotional suffering, Louis was able to tighten his grip on the aristocracy and his authority over the role of the bureaucracy that ruled the country. To escape this code, individuals sought emotional refuge in salons, friendly groups and masonic lodges where a spirit of companionate equality prevailed. Here they found warm companionship, a new confidence in human reason, and natural sentiments which could form the basis for political reform. The feelings of these emotional refuges appeared and were disseminated throughout the arts. Figures such as the caring and benevolent parent, marriages built on affection and representations of natural communities untainted by corruption offered new visions which if thwarted would lead to horrific consequences. When combined with the worst harvest of the century in 1788, high food prices, even famine, this emotion regime fuelled the revolution of the following year.

We hope this brief tour of the some of the work within the field of the history of emotions has given you a sense of its potential. Even though it is located outside the mainstream of historical research, the study of emotions has produced innovative work that has challenged conventional interpretations. Some while ago, Barbara Rosenwein, a medieval historian, confessed she was worried not about emotions themselves but about the ways in which historians had treated them (Rosenwein, 2002). Proceeding to review the record of research and critiquing grand narratives that had proposed a progressive acceptance of (self-) control, she saw instead a plurality of emotional communities which if organized into a coherent narrative could provide a way forward. Since then, historians have successfully embarked on this venture so that now we might all stop worrying about emotions and begin to love and enjoy them.

Whether the history of emotions has established itself as a distinct school within the broader terrain of cultural and social history is open to question. It is the case that there is no consensus on its approach or language, but its potential to link individuals to social structures and negotiate between the quotidian and the larger discourses is undeniable.

Postscript

Although it had tended to defy definition, cultural history has flourished recently and now occupies a special place within the practice of history. Its rise has in part been built on the belated recognition that the terrain of culture is not an incidental sideshow to the economic and political; it rather exercises a profound influence on the nature and course of societal change, and struggles over the legitimacy of culture have often determined the course of that change. Evidence for the new confidence of cultural history comes from the attention now devoted to topics such as consumption, food, play, ritual, manners and fashion which previously would have been thought inconsequential.

If anything brings this field together it is the reliance on cultural theory, virtually all of which derives from associated disciplines. Thus, for example, the anthropological work of Clifford Geertz and Mary Douglas has been employed widely to shed light on popular ritual and custom, and the linguistic theory of Mikhail Bakhtin has been applied to reveal the workings of popular countercultures from the Middle Ages to the present.

Cultural histories have made significant contributions to most areas of historical inquiry. Here we have tended to focus on popular and imperial experiences, but similar arguments could have been made about other areas. Attempts to understand the dynamics of popular culture have been among the most interesting and fruitful lines of inquiry. Drawing upon such notions as the carnivalesque, various historians have explored how vigorous countercultures, with their own distinct senses of memory and custom, have sought symbolically to assert senses of collective identity, simultaneously resisting attempts by dominant authorities to impose control. Within an imperial context, we understand now far more about the processes through which colonial powers were able to exert power. Ultimately, this power derived from a military presence which could be mobilized whenever required, but on a routine basis it relied upon interventions in indigenous literature, language education and religion as a means of disseminating the putative superiority of European thought and values.

As a discipline, history is notoriously prone to changing fashions. With the declining influence of postmodern thought that had done much to promote cultural history, we might have expected the cultural turn to have receded. Fortunately, however, there is little sign that this is the case, as thought-provoking and entertaining studies within the broad field of cultural history continue to appear. One area that has attracted an increasing body of historians is the history of emotions. The term, along with the alternative affective history, is not best chosen, leading as it does to some confusion, but work here has been important in attempting to locate human emotions within the broad contours of historical understanding and consciousness. Given that we all recognize the powerful influence that emotions can be wield on our thinking and behaviour, it may appear uncontentious that they play a part in the historical process. But precisely what emotions are involved and how they are conceptualized are tasks that continue to confound us.

Further Reading

Mikhail Bakhtin (1965) *Rabelais and His World*.
Peter Burke (1997) *Varieties of Cultural History*.
Peter Burke (2008) *What Is Cultural History?*
Nicolas Dirks (ed.) (1992) *Colonialism and Culture*.
Simon Gunn (2006) *History and Cultural Theory*.
Christopher Hill (1972) *The World Turned Upside Down*.
Lynn Hunt (ed.) (1989) *The New Cultural History*.
Kathleen Wilson (1995) *The Sense of the People*.

12 Feminism, Gender and Queer History

Introduction

This chapter describes how historiography has been transformed by the question of gender, both in the ways that the subject is now researched and written but also in how historians have read evidence to include women and gender issues more generally. The opening section tackles the relationship between gender and class in historical analysis and investigates how an interest in female experiences in the past has created a considerable and diverse body of work. Approaches have been variously determined by theoretical perspectives including conservative, liberal and Marxist feminisms, which in their various ways have influenced male-centred histories. It is not merely a question of reasserting women in the historical record but of understanding fully how a concern with gender relationships can provide more satisfying accounts of historical change. In Section 2 we examine how feminist work since the 1980s has effectively challenged the primacy previously placed on class to provide nuanced interpretations of such events as the Industrial Revolution and Italian Renaissance. In Section 3, we explore questions around feminine and masculine identities and the significance of recent work on witchcraft with due consideration of approaches which borrow from psychoanalytical and linguistic theory. Finally, we look at the extraordinary surge in historiography concerned with sexualities and historians that have developed a more comprehensive understanding of the sexual.

12.1 Feminism and History

Betty Wardle, a housewife of Outwood, near Lever in Lancashire, England, recalled her working life in a coalmine in an interview with the Royal Commissioners in 1842. Having worked since the age of six wearing a belt and chain (not uncommon for mineworkers in her day) she had given birth twice underground, bringing the last baby to the surface in her skirts. The reason why she could recollect this, she told her incredulous interviewers, was that the infant had been born the day after her marriage. These were clearly desperate circumstances, and as these interviews are all-too-rare testimonies from female industrial workers during the early-Victorian period, they reveal for the historian a harrowing account of how women balanced work with an almost unimaginable burden of maintaining a family.

'Independent' is a word used frequently by Commissioners sent by an anxious Parliament to describe these women workers. They found girls in Bilston, Staffordshire whose language and conduct they described as unfeminine: riding astride horses, drinking, swearing, fighting, smoking and singing. Yet, like the children who worked in factories and mills, the 'little elves' described by the Scots manufacturer Andrew Ure (1778–1857), these women were also described as happy with their lot and should, it was concluded by the Commissioners, be 'no

Figure 12.1 Women carrying baskets of coal from underground from I. Taylor's book *The Mine* (1829)

objects of pity'. In Darlaston, near Walsall in the West Midlands it was found, for example, that women went into public houses, ordered beer and smoked pipes: all category errors for a Victorian society that in its most evangelical Christian phase in the years before the 1840s saw women as 'helpmeets' or 'angels of the hearth'; the very bedrock of domestic stability. They were, it was thought, the 'chief sufferers' of the industrial process, victims of capitalism which, raw in tooth and claw, extracted an unacceptable toll from the weakest in society. When Parliament heard the verdict of the Royal Commission, it lost little time in banning women from working underground, but not because they were victims of the industrial process. It was because to do otherwise would have upset the established order of relationships between the sexes.

This story about the struggles of women as mothers, daughters and sisters in a harrowing and brutal moment of Britain's industrialization touches on issues of vital importance to feminist history. Some might argue that the history of these women fills a significant gap in our reading of the Industrial Revolution. For most feminist historians, however, it is not merely or principally a matter of providing a more complete picture by the inclusion of women; it is more a question of approaching the past with due regard to the complex and dynamic power relationships between men and women.

What sorts of questions would a feminist historian therefore ask of the experience of these women working underground? That they were forced to work under such conditions was clearly a matter of their class and the logic of capitalist exploitation which underpinned the Industrial Revolution, but did it also have something to do with their gender? There is a tension between approaches which see class and gender as the most important aspect of the historical experience, and feminist historians have attempted to weigh the balance between them with greater accuracy. Given that women had on average less physical strength than men, why were women chosen? Was it because employers could pay them less? If so, why was it that most people accepted the fact that women should be paid less than men, even if the work they were doing was identical? And why was the Commissioners' report so anxious about the state of these women? Were they troubled that the employers, by subjecting these women to such toil, endangered their health and general well-being? Or was it rather that the existence of these seemingly strong and independent women actively challenged male-dominated, patriarchal perspectives that women should be confined to the domestic sphere in subordinate and supporting roles to the male head?

In thinking about the female historical experience, a variety of strands have emerged in feminist historiography over the past hundred years or so. Disparate and somewhat antagonistic though these are, they tend to cohere around three broad approaches, namely, conservative, liberal and Marxist (or socialist). Victorian women such as Mrs C. M. Yonge (1823–1901), Mrs Humphrey Ward (1851–1920), whom we met in Chapter 10 and Octavia Hill (1838–1912) articulated the principles of conservative feminism in the so-called first wave of feminism at the end of the nineteenth century. As prominent campaigners, authors and charity workers, they saw women's true natures as best developed in the home on behalf of the family. These conservative women opposed female political activity (like paid employment) because it took place in the public sphere that they assumed to be competitive and therefore unfeminine.

By the end of the nineteenth century, however, philanthropy and a religious duty to do good works allowed conservative women alarmed by the social dislocation of the new urban centres to go into the slums and courtyards of the poor. Philanthropy was seen as an extension of the domestic sphere and therefore was an activity permitted to women, a world away from the corrupting influences of public discourse, parliament, courts of law and so on. Many of those who occupied private as opposed to public spaces did so in the context of a dominant religious sensibility and clearly thought of themselves as leading moral lives. Despite differences in religious affiliation, wealth and politics, these conservative women wanted to maintain separate roles for men and women in a moment of rapid and destabilizing change. These separate spheres articulated the different meanings of masculinity and femininity at the time. To be a man was to be serious, upright, respectable and honourable. If women were retiring and emotionally vulnerable, men should be brave, honest, self-disciplined and hardworking while also displaying tenderness and care for others. A true gentleman was masculine in every sense.

Liberals had no such reservation about the public role of women. John Stuart Mill in the nineteenth century outlined a humanist case for feminism, that is, he saw human beings as sharing characteristics such as altruism and a desire for social justice regardless of gender or social differences. Mill believed that the unequal treatment of men and women was wrong, that these inequalities offended against reason and conscience and that social or environmental reform could overcome biological differences like motherhood. The emphasis here on overcoming biological differences was important because it suggested that women could not be defined by their natural attributes such as an ability to give birth. Accordingly, liberal feminists such as Mill argued for state intervention in areas such as child welfare that had previously been part of women's domestic preserve and called for the related need for women to enjoy equal participation in the workplace. Women were different but they could be equal.

Both conservative and liberal feminist ideologies have fed into the writing of histories, but Marxist-inspired feminism has probably enjoyed the most influence. Marxists met gendered histories initially with derision, fearing that writing women back into the historical record threatened the primacy of class as a mode of analysis. That fear was well founded. There was a time when historians told big stories about class. These grand narratives are still around, of course, but they no longer for the most part connect to a political project such as Marxism. This is largely because histories sensitive to gender and race have usurped grand narratives about class, using a range of sources which describe the past from the point of view of belongings and identities constructed outside or alongside those of class. That these gendered histories could have been written since the signal year of 1970 (as we shall argue in the next section) is overwhelmingly because we no longer see ourselves as simply members of a social class but feel our identities to be more fluid – accordingly writing sexuality, ethnicity and religious backgrounds, as well as gender, back into history.

For Marxist historians, modern history is shaped profoundly by the sexual division of labour within capitalism. Women in most historical accounts form a largely unskilled, disorganized 'industrial reserve army'. In times of labour shortage, they could be utilized or 'called-up' to maintain employment, job insecurity and low wages. Thus, the economy mirrored social divisions between public and private spheres: the latter located in the home, a domestic economy that supported capitalism through the reproduction of workers. From a traditional Marxist perspective, 'gendered' approaches to the past could add little, as all history was the history of class struggle: gender blind and race neutral.

Some feminist historians who had shared this Marxist perspective soon argued for a 'patriarchy first' model of history. They acknowledged that the capitalist system worked in favour of the propertied but, more significantly, that it worked also to the advantage of men with men wielding power as men, not as capitalists or workers. This more gendered approach to historical research, as we shall see in more detail in Section 2, won considerable support in the 1970s and beyond. More recently, however, an influential study of the lives of working-class women in Burrow, Preston and Lancaster between 1890 and 1940 by Elizabeth Roberts (1996) resisted the 'patriarchy first' approach by arguing that the lot of women in the industrial working class was a result not of patriarchy but of poverty. Gender is given no more priority than 'work' or 'production', and real liberation for women depended upon a struggle against both male domination and the capitalist system of production that sustained it.

One of the most damaging consequences of patriarchy was seen to be the establishment and perpetuation of 'separate spheres' for men and women. According to this notion, men operated almost exclusively in the public sphere, while women were confined to the domestic, where they rightfully assumed the roles of wives and mothers. Some of this discussion around this issue has focused on the role and place of middle-class women within the political and economic milieux of the nineteenth century. *Family Fortunes: Men and Women of the English Middle Class, 1780–1850* (1987) by Leonore Davidoff and Catherine Hall is a prominent example. Davidoff and Hall compared industrial Birmingham with rural Essex and Suffolk, looking at the private and public lives of banking, trading and farming families to conclude that a new sexual division of labour emerged by the mid-nineteenth century based on economic success, domestic happiness and at least some cooperation between the sexes. The home fulfilled the evangelical idea of a 'cottage religion' where women were considered theologically as the helpmeet of men – spiritually equal, if socially and politically unequal. If mid-century women were modelled on the biblical Eve, a mixture of mother and temptress, by the end of the century they began tentatively to enter the public sphere when philanthropic work was thought to match the inherent female qualities of purity, sympathy, gentleness and obedience.

The debate between the importance of capitalist economic relations to the lives of women and the power wielded by individual men has also mounted serious challenges to conventional accounts of industrialization. While the Marxist historian Eric Hobsbawm's *Labouring Men* (1968) tended to focus almost entirely on male paid employment during certain phases of industrialization, Maxine Berg (1994) concentrated on the presence of female labour in the workforce at a time of rapidly changing technologies, thereby questioning any simple binary between public and domestic spheres for the working class as a whole. She especially highlighted the significance of family labour and the family wage, that is, the combined income of men, women and even children, although their precise role has been open to debate. Some Marxist historians see the family wage as a side-effect of the casualization of the workplace inherent in capitalist production, which by deskilling work allowed women to take over tasks previously done by men. 'Patriarchy first' historians dismiss the family wage as a concession to male breadwinners, while others argue that it was a necessary negotiation between men and women in a family setting. Jane Humphries (1991), for example, suggested that the family wage was not 'a sexist device adopted by nineteenth-century working class men'. Rather it was 'a strategy adapted by both men and women against exploitation by the capitalist system' (Roberts, 1995, p. 15).

The intervention of feminist thinking in the process of historical research has thus revealed levels of meaning that would have remained obscure. Much of this new sensitivity to women in the writing and reading of history was driven by a large group of socialists and feminists who in 1970 gathered at a conference in Ruskin College, Oxford, to argue that women be written back into history. Before looking in a little more detail at their intervention, let us consider why the meeting took place in the first instance. What was the nature of their grievances? Why and how had women been obscured in the historical record?

History abounds with examples of determined women who were able to overcome gendered norms and emerge as historical figures, many making original and striking contributions to politics, arts and the social sciences. Boudicca, warrior queen of the Iceni tribe who led a successful revolt against the Romans in c.60 CE, Joan of Arc, a French peasant girl who took arms against the English army in the early fifteenth century, Elizabeth I, the first female queen of England and arguably its greatest monarch and Rani of Jhansi, who, following the death of her husband, led large-scale resistance to British forces during the Indian uprising of 1857 are a few who immediately spring to mind. Women such as Mary Wollstonecraft made significant contributions to political theory, and figures including Marie Curie, Dorothy Hodgkin and Rosalind Franklin remain among the most important scientists of modern times. Female authors were instrumental in laying the foundations for the rise of the modern novel. More generally, thousands of women whose names were never recorded took part in the great revolutionary movements and wars of liberation.

So why is it that the historical records of women's achievements have been systematically understated? This under-recording is in some respects a reflection of a profound historical reality, namely, that most women lived in patriarchal societies, the male members of which imposed suffocating restrictions on what they were allowed to do. But it goes further, for in addition to the subordination of women, their contributions have rarely been fully represented. The historiography, in other words, has also been highly gendered.

Take, for example, the field of intellectual history. From the fifteenth century small but significant numbers of women wrote political treatises of various kinds but they have been largely ignored. For the most part, the history of political thought is the history of writers such as John Locke, Edmund Burke and Thomas Hobbes. Recent attempts have been made, however, successfully to retrieve the writings of women, particularly those who featured in the development of Enlightenment thought. Mary Astell, Anne Laetitia Barbauld and Mary Wollstonecraft are relatively well known, but there were many others including Octavie Belot, Marie-Armande Gacon-Dufour and Catherine Macaulay who used histories, plays, poems, novels and newspapers to engage fully with debates on such burning issues as slavery and the rights of women

(Curtis-Wendlandt et al., 2013; Knott and Taylor, 2005). Much of this was written against and therefore necessarily challenged the taken-for-granted assumptions of their male counterparts.

Although feminist scholarship has done much to recover the presence of such women who had previously been 'hidden from history', this was not necessarily the principal objective. Rather more important was the felt need to challenge those historical perspectives that had systematically omitting women from the historical record. In no area was this more evident than in challenges to class-based analyses of industrialization.

12.2 The Attack on Class

As we have seen, the history of industrialization has been centred on the male experience. Before 1970, labour history and conventional political histories that dealt with, say, high politics or the politics of government tended to tell the story of male power. Unsurprisingly then, some of the more traditional historians were in the feminist firing line but so also were historians such as E. P. Thompson – in fact, E. P. Thompson in particular. His classic *The Making of the English Working Class* (1963) was essentially a study of the formation of a male culture; women were present only at the margins. Thus, his various accounts of radical movements in pre-industrial society argued that a largely homogeneous (and seemingly male) proletariat had gone underground during the state oppression associated with the French wars only to remerge during the 1820s as a major political force in the land.

The essay that really riled feminists, however, was that on wife sales republished in *Cultures in Common* (1991). This explained how a largely male plebeian class had used unofficial forms of divorce to assert their independence from the patrician ruling class and in so doing demonstrated their independence as a class. As a thesis it attracted venom from feminists precisely because it tended to focus on men in the history of class struggle at the expense of women's experiences, suggesting that women had not resisted either capitalist or patriarchal power. Thompson protested that he was simply following evidence presented to him in the archive, but from the 1970s onwards feminist historians would re-read the primary sources and in so doing bring some balance to what they believed to be a skewed historical record in favour, as the joke went at the time, of 'his – story.'

Eric Hobsbawm, to take another example of a noted historian who attracted criticism from feminists, put together a collection of his writings entitled *Labouring Men* (1964). These foregrounded the conditions of the male working class in different industries and their struggles in trades unions for improvement, almost totally neglecting those of women. Thus, Thompson and Hobsbawm on the question of gender, even though part of a radical historical tradition, represented more conventional histories of manual labour and trade union struggles which for the most part had been dominated by men.

It was at this moment that a wave of feminist scholarship began to revisit not only these histories but the male-dominated historiography more generally. The National Women's Liberation Conference of 1970 at Ruskin College was convened by History Workshop and led by feminists including Sheila Rowbotham, Sally Alexander and Anna Davin. It marked the beginning of a new wave of feminist scholarship. Initially, conventional historians viewed these developments with suspicion, even ridicule. Some saw an interest in gender as a passing fashion; others were unwilling to accept that gender was as important a determinant of the human experience as class or race. In the years that followed, however, many of those who attended became prominent feminists and their ideas of gendering history were (almost) totally accepted into the mainstream of historical writing. The feminists of 1970 also made significant breakthroughs in institutional terms, intervening in the upper echelons of the academy, influencing many academic disciplines and creating the subdiscipline of 'Women's Studies', which showcased the experience of women as historical subjects in their own right. From this movement came a host of journals in the 1970s, founded within a few years of each other, such as *Feminist Review* and *History Workshop Journal*, the latter subtitled at its inception as 'a journal for socialist and feminist historians'.

A fresh subjectivity was also introduced into the writing of history evoking women's personal experiences. It was probably the radical American feminist, Carol Hanisch, who coined the phrase in 1969 that 'the personal is political'. Its enduring meaning was that for women their personal problems had become political problems and for them barriers between the private and public spheres had largely broken down. For a number of reasons then, the 1970s proved to be a breakthrough in a consciousness that women and women historians had something important to say.

Although this generation of women influenced the way many historians today read, research and write history, it is important to note that they were not the first. Historians such as Ivy Pinchbeck (1898–1982), Eileen Power (1889–1940) and the great M. Dorothy George (1878–1971) pioneered research into and teaching on the position of women in a man's world, as did Alice Clark, *Working Life of Women in the Seventeenth Century* (1919); Barbara Drake, *Women in Trade Unions* (1920) and Barbara Hutchins, *Women in Modern Industry* (1915). Many of these books continue to have an enduring appeal. Similarly, Mary Ritter Beard's *Woman as a Force in History* (1946) enjoyed an afterlife in the 1960s, perhaps because it argued across a long period (from prehistoric to modern times) and because its polemic against the 'myth' of female subjection in history appealed to the new feminist historians who by now enjoyed a large and popular audience associated with women's liberation.

In order to 'liberate' women or even to celebrate women's role in history, however, women had first to be 'found'. *Hidden from History* was the title of a book by Sheila Rowbotham (1973). Its subtitle, *300 Years of Women's Oppression and the Fight Against It*, said much about the stance of women fighting against sexism and injustice both in the workplace and the home

Figure 12.2 The women's liberation movement in the United States: march in Washington from Farrugut Square to Lafayette Park, August 1970

Contributor: Courtesy of the Library of Congress Prints and Photographs Division, Washington DC, 20540, News and World Report Magazine Photograph Collection, LC-DIG-ppmsca-03425

at this time of radical change. Like Beard, Rowbotham attempted to write women back into national historical narratives over a long timeframe, starting with 'early capitalism' in the seventeenth century and ending around the First World War. It was a product of feminist politics of the 1970s, crystallizing discussions among politically aware women. Published by Virago, the first major publisher dedicated to literature produced by women, it bore witness to an approach that was to transform the writing of history.

By the 1980s, many of the leading feminists had come to realize that because traditional Marxism was gender blind, it offered no usable blueprint in their quest for a new historical paradigm. Bolstered by critiques of previous male-centred histories, they launched attacks on class-based narratives. At that moment, Sally Alexander observed, Marxist ideas about the 'determining social relationship between wage labour and capital, exploiter and exploited, proletarian and capitalist' were unsustainable. Women's history and feminism had together proved that 'subjective identity is also constructed as masculine or feminine, placing the individual as husband or wife, mother or father, son or daughter, and so on' (Alexander, 1984, p. 132). These identities may be conveyed in political language and may occasionally turn into political action but were not necessarily expressed in the form of class interests. Nor could we understand the female historical experience through a simple analysis of their roles, which were largely determined physiologically.

Anne Clark's *The Struggle for the Breeches: Gender and the Making of the British Working Class* (1995) was a conscious attempt to challenge class-based narratives not simply by replacing a history of male labourers with a history of female labourers but instead by integrating considerations of gender into the analysis of class. By comparing the experiences of male artisans with female textile workers, she demonstrated that the story of the Industrial Revolution was not merely about productive relations at work but also featured histories of families and communities, and here women played a vital role. Indeed, the Industrial Revolution could be recast as a struggle over gendered divisions of labour.

That women and men experienced industrialization and working-class culture in very different ways was also explored by Catherine Hall. Her article 'The tale of Samuel and Jemima: gender and working class culture in nineteenth-century England' put yet another nail in the coffin of the triumphal narrative of (largely male) labourers and artisans and revealed women in history where once they had been 'hidden' (Hall, 1990). Taking the account of the radical Samuel Bamford's experiences at the Peterloo Massacre in August 1819, she contrasted it with the story told by his wife Jemima Bamford around the same event. Each account conformed to gender stereotypes: he marched and organized the protesters; she acted as mother and support to the men. These testimonies were not new; they had been available to historians for some time, but Hall, like Clark, showed that accounts of the working class in the workshop or factory where skills fell inevitably to men tell only part of a more complicated story. This new reading of sources did two things: it placed women and gender at the heart of labour narratives but also, as Clark put it, 'ultimately muted the radicalism of the British working class', for within radical culture women were defined principally as wives and mothers (Clark, 1995, p. 271).

One prominent example of the rereading of what had been thought of as the conventional sources of social history was undertaken very effectively by a former student at Ruskin College during these tumultuous times. Sally Alexander was a key figure in these new radical circles fusing, like so many of her contemporaries, the writing of history with political activity. Her long essay on 'Women's work in nineteenth-century London: a study of the years 1820–50' was a passionate example of how women's history could interrogate previously well-worked historical sources to reveal the roles of women in the past. The 1851 Census in the hands of male historians had been curiously silent on women's work, but with a close and creative reading by Alexander, women's roles were revealed not only in the domestic sphere but also in a host of occupations, even if most of them were low status and poorly paid. She thus located a division of labour based on gender, income and skill, thereby demonstrating how patriarchy and capitalism worked hand in glove to ensure 'the economic dependence of women upon their husbands or fathers for a substantial part of their lives' (Alexander, 1976, p. 77).

One of the most eminent of feminist theorists in the United States, Joan Wallach Scott, made a telling intervention in 1986 with an essay entitled 'Gender: a useful category of historical analysis'. Scott had long rejected women's history per se – that is, an historical approach that simply retrieves women from historical oblivion – and was critical of any analysis that involved men and women in relationship to one another because it limited gender histories to histories of power struggles between them. Scott followed this with her important book *Gender and the Politics of History* (1988), in which she retained an interest in power and politics, although not through the lens of class or gender but the production of knowledge about sexual difference or class. The chapters of her book reflected a lifetime seeking to understand gender inequalities and the importance of gender differences in history. For Scott, gender was an historical category that, created through discourse, could be analyzed. Accordingly, she devoted separate essays to the relationship between gender and class, especially in labour histories of the previous thirty years, the influence of feminist history, the role of discursive histories and the uses historians make of representations that construct meanings about class and gender. Following a discussion of Gareth Stedman Jones' analysis of Chartism (see Chapter 21), she summarized well the feminist critique of labour history:

> Class . . . was offered as a universal category even though it depended on a masculine construction. As a result, it was almost inevitable that men represented the working class. Women then had two possible representations. They were either a specific example of the general experience of class and then it was unnecessary to single them out for special treatment; for they were assumed to be included in any discussion of the working class as a whole. Or, women were a troubling exception, asserting particular needs and interests detrimental to class politics, objecting to husbands using household money for union dues, demanding different kinds of strategies in strikes, insisting on continuing religious affiliations in an age of secular socialism. Both representations are evident in the history of labor movements and in the writing of their histories and they help us to locate reasons for the invisibility of women in the making of the working class.
>
> (Scott, 1988, p. 64)

By this time feminist historians had begun to challenge other great themes of scholarly inquiry, and their works were part of most publishers' catalogues. One notable example was Joan Kelly's brilliant study 'Did Women have a Renaissance?' (Kelly, 1984), which argued for the gendered nature of the Renaissance and thereby addressed the nature of the interrelationships among economic, cultural and biological factors in shaping women's lives and identities. Like so many feminist commentators in the 1960s and 1970s, Kelly argued that woman is a cultural being who could never be defined solely by her physicality or body. It followed that gender relations were not biologically given but historically created and thus that 'the relations between the sexes is a social and not a natural one' (Kelly, 1984, p. 1). Within this framework, Kelly's reinterpretation of the Renaissance was important. In particular, she took issue with conventional definitions of the Renaissance as the consolidation of states in Italy from 1350 to 1430, the development of a mercantile and manufacturing economy that could support these states, and a set of social and cultural relations which emerged from these new formations, arguing that such features were shaped unduly by the gendered perspectives adopted by previous historians.

As an alternative, Kelly focused on the Renaissance as a moment of cultural renewal for women and identified four major areas of social and cultural life: the regulation of female sexuality, women's economic and political roles, governing their access to property, politics, power and education, the ability of women to shape their society, and the emergence of a gendered ideology which determined the role of women in production of art, literature and philosophy. Women's roles, Kelly further noted, were performed within the constraints of 'courtly love'; noble and chivalrous love that demanded that women of high social standing marry well and obey the rules of chastity, civility and virtue, which tended to act as a brake on their freedoms. In essence, according to Kelly, personal and public life separated the sexes in Renaissance society. From this a gender division emerged, which Kelly argued marked the origin of modern relations – that is, separate spheres where men exist and thrive in public spaces and women are constrained within the domestic or private sphere.

Also reflecting on the changing state of knowledge about women, Merry Wiesner (1993) was able to sum up the major advances that had taken place in feminist histories of early modern Europe. Feminist history began with studies of 'women worthies' as a means of revealing figures who had previously been hidden. What was the contribution of women as individuals and groups to the great artistic, scientific and intellectual movements of the time? This question had continued to inform research, but it was now augmented by different questions as historians came to appreciate the limitations of analyses that simply attempted to place women on the historical agenda. More interest followed in excavating the distinct female experience in the private and domestic spheres. Here biological experiences around menstruation, pregnancy and motherhood have yielded fine studies, as have friendship networks, devotional practices and patterns of consumption and taste, particularly so given that many of the topics were scantily documented in public archives. Finally, the creation in the early modern period of a gendered division between public and domestic spheres had been subject to scrutiny, and related to this, questions around the emergence of distinct identities of femininity and masculinity were investigated. In certain respects, this trajectory has also been evident in recent feminist histories of other periods and across different parts of the world.

12.3 Gender and Identity

Monks with lactating breasts, boys turning into girls, animals transforming into human beings and vice versa are all medieval and early modern representations where sex, sexuality, identity and gender are very much more ambiguous than images of women and men were to become after the eighteenth century. In Renaissance and medieval paintings, Jesus is depicted with breasts flowing with maternal milk for the soul, or his wound from the Crucifixion is open (it has been argued) like a vagina, symbolic of the largely feminine compassion of God's only begotten son. His heat, moisture and bodily fluids had the power to purify through the sacred juices of his blood, semen and milk – themselves all signs that Christ was independent of sex or gender or else was feminine. God made flesh with female attributes inverted or neutralized ideas of Jesus as a man, making a huge impact on Cistercian and other traditions within the Catholic Church.

Caroline Walker Bynum has explained this gender ambiguity in her books *Jesus as Mother: Studies in the Spirituality of the Middle Ages* (1984) and *Holy Feast and Holy Fast: The Religious Significance of Food to Medieval Women* (1987). Fasting was a means of female self-control, erotic expression and a way of controlling their space in the context of a male-dominated church. In defiance of their husbands and families, religious women, according to the sources, would drink pus from the sick while abstaining from ordinary food. Or else they would give food away to the poor or live for years on the bread of the Eucharist alone until the normal functions of the body such as menstruation or excretion ceased. As Christ was in the Eucharist broken and sacrificed for humanity, hunger through fasting became a sign of female vulnerability and women's inherent understanding of the suffering of Jesus on the cross. When women consumed the blood and body of Christ they became his flesh, thereby fusing their own female identities to the extent that it made it impossible to base those identities purely on their sex.

Bynum's work is an example of how to move women's history on from its initial project of simply writing women back into history in ways that we saw in the last section, to a history that addresses issues around the relations between genders and gender identities. Bynum's approach to medieval aesthetics and food concentrated on the experiences of women themselves but also, critically, on feminine and masculine attributes that she finds in ritual, symbolic practices, cultural artefacts and so on. From Bynum's analysis, therefore, men and women in her medieval world are 'fragile constructs', and the usual way of constructing women around what they do in the family or by the functions of their genitalia underplays what it was to be feminine in medieval culture.

Such new approaches drew in part upon psychoanalytic techniques which have been especially useful to historians concerned with the irrational and with human experiences where *social* anxieties bring out *individual* psychic behaviour – instinct, emotion and bodily drives that were suppressed and, where, by the eighteenth century, both private and public conduct was mannered, restrained and disciplined. Histories using these techniques have been concerned with how these changes in society influenced individual psyches. The problem is to understand subjectivity or, to put it another way, personal responses from women that involved fantasy, memory, sexuality, the unconscious and gender ambiguity (as we saw with the example that opened the section).

So how has the important question of gender identity been approached in recent years? Feminist thinking about identity has drawn problematically upon the work of Freud, in particular his notion that children develop senses of identity through identification with their father, a process that leads to a sense of estrangement for girls. To deal with this problem, feminists such as Julia Kristeva have sought to define a distinct feminine identity by looking at the ways it is constructed not through biology but through language, that is, how images and the written and spoken word in, say, art and literature come to define sexual difference. Such ideas suggest that identity is never fixed or stable but dynamic and subject to change over time brought about by the rhetoric of difference employed in past societies.

No work has had more influence on thinking around femininity than Simone De Beauvoir's *The Second Sex* (1949). The title itself referred to the notion that the terms masculine and feminine are asymmetrical, for the male is considered as the norm in society, against which the female is the other. Using a synthesis of biological, psychological and Marxist theories, De Beauvoir then explored how the creation of this female 'other' can be traced to prehistory. In virtually all past societies, women's relegation to their unique capacity for reproduction underpinned the sexual division of labour and may have led to their subordination. It is not merely or primarily a matter of biology, however, for this ordering is not given as a product of biology but is created:

> One is not born, but rather becomes, a woman. No biological, psychological, or economic fate determines the figure that the human female presents in society; it is civilization as a whole that produces this creature, intermediate between male and eunuch, which is described as feminine. Only the intervention of someone else can establish an individual as an *Other*.
>
> (De Beauvoir, 1997, p. 295)

Feminist historians working within this paradigm have understandably been interested in masculinity as well as femininity. One of the more important studies has been Graham Dawson's *Soldier Heroes: British Adventure, Empire and the Imaginings of Masculinities* (1994), in which he explored how masculinities were fashioned in the national imagination. The soldier hero, he argued, has been a remarkably enduring figure in the Western tradition, in part because it was bound up with the emergence of the modern nation state. Henry V, Drake, Nelson and a host of others were constructed and remain potent symbols of British national identity. Such figures represented the 'true Englishmen', a status which was complemented and completed by visions of domestic femininity at home, vulnerable and requiring protection. Processes of representation and identification have shaped the cultural production and circulation of images of the soldier hero. War adventures, comics, television series, novels, tourist sites and now computer games helped to sustain an intense fascination with the military side of conflict in contemporary society, but the processes have long been evident. In detailed studies of Sir Henry Havelock, 'hero' of the Indian uprising in 1857 and T. E. Lawrence (of Arabia), Dawson showed how the psychic and the social intermeshed in the production of powerful public narratives which furnished idealized forms of masculinity to allay anxieties generated in a world deeply divided by nation and ethnicity, class and gender. In other words, such 'heroes' offered (and continue to offer) psychic reassurance of the eventual triumph of 'good' over the threatening sources.

In a similar fashion, Mrinalini Sinha's *Colonial Masculinity: The 'Manly Englishman' and the 'Effeminate Bengali' in the Late Nineteenth Century* (1995) demonstrated how important notions of masculinity were for the British imperial enterprise. She started from the premise that the identities of colonizer and colonized were never fixed or self-evident but had to be constantly defined and redefined in the context of the imperial social formation. As a result of this, their interrelationship was rearticulated according to the changing imperatives of British rule. As one aspect of this, the figure of the 'manly Englishman' was counterposed to the 'effeminate Bengali' in a descending scale as a means of asserting and maintaining authority. Senior officials within the administrative and military apparatus of rule were constructed as 'manly', while the corpus of politically self-conscious Indian intellectuals (dominated by middle-class Bengalis) who were recruited into the colonial service were seen as 'effeminate'. This representation of Bengalis in colonial discourse as an unnatural or perverted form of masculinity coincided precisely with their rising demands for a share in the economic and political privileges enjoyed by the British. This was not a blatant imposition, but, more subtly and powerfully, this categorization came to be adopted by the Bengalis themselves. This valuable work coincided with other interventions on related themes such as Antoinette Burton, *Burdens of History: British Feminism, Indian Women and Imperial Culture, 1865–1915* (1995); Clare Midgley, *Women Against Slavery: The British Campaigns, 1780–1870* (1992) and overtly on the question of racism from a feminist angle, Vron Ware, *Beyond the Pale: White Women, Racism and History* (1992).

Also notable in this area of national identities are histories that not only talk about the nature and extent of the nation but which also ask questions about the limits of citizenship in the modern period, especially the Second World War. Concerned with the role of class, region, race and empire but also gender in history, the list here might include Sonya Rose, *Which People's War: National Identity and Citizenship in Wartime Britain, 1939–1945* (2003) and Wendy Webster, *Imagining Home: Gender, Race and National Identity, 1945–1964* (1998). Rose is particularly interesting, as an account of the 'home front' and her *What is Gender History* (2010) provided a helicopter view of the genre.

It would be remiss of us to close this chapter without mentioning a topic which has attracted considerable interest among feminist historians. In the West of the sixteenth and seventeenth centuries, between 50,000 and 100,000 people were tried and executed as witches; most of them were women, and most of these were old and poor. Within the vast literature devoted to the topic a variety of social, cultural, economic and psychoanalytical explanations has been offered. Christina Larner (1981), for example, has argued that the Reformation saw an intensification of religious commitment, proof of which was sought by male rulers in fighting religious wars or suppressing heretics within their kingdoms. Social and economic approaches have pointed to the felt need for communities to find explanations for the periodic famines created by bad harvests and the attendant increase in vagrant populations. Such thinking has informed specifically feminist perspectives. Mary Daly (1979), for example, has argued that at this time of profound uncertainty many women were seen to challenge normative views about their position in society, even by confronting male supremacy, and witch hunts occasioned one way of suppressing and eliminating the perceived threat posed by independent women who inhabited spaces beyond conventional social norms. In this context the figure of the witch was literally demonized through association with the Devil and was seen to possess those attributes of aggression, independence and sexuality that set her apart from the acceptable woman of chastity, obedience and domesticity.

Starting with *Oedipus and the Devil* (1994), the work of Lyndal Roper has signalled a more determinedly psychoanalytical approach to an understanding of witchcraft. The work was prompted by unease about the relationship between culture and individual subjectivity, in particular about what she considered to be the excessive emphasis on the cultural and linguistic creation of identity. Witchcraft and the figure of the witch cannot be understood fully without reference also to psychic dimensions, that is, the extent to which fantasy, memory, subliminal desire and the unconscious intervened. The irrational and unconscious were vital dimensions of the witch craze and associated beliefs in such rituals as sex with the Devil, diabolic Sabbaths and cannibalism, and our task is to reveal how they informed the nature of masculinity and femininity, the cultural impact of the Reformation and Counter Reformation and the vital role of witchcraft and magic at the time. Such a perspective has broader implications, for it invites us to reconsider the Reformation not as heralding the birth of the rational, ascetic individual who paves the way for the modern world but as a time of renewed interest in magic and the irrational.

Looking back at the enormous contribution of feminism to the writing of history and in the way that gender studies has continued to produce a cadre of leading scholars in the field, we cannot help but wrap up the chapter by considering the impact of feminist historians (as well as feminist histories) on the academy. In an excellent summary of the journey from women's history to feminist studies to gender history, June Hannam recalled that the innovative approaches to the past with which we have thus far been concerned coincided with the expansion of higher education and the ability of women to (eventually) take top academic jobs to influence what was actually taught at university (www.history.ac.uk/makinghistory/resources/articles/womens_history.html, accessed 20 July 2016). Another product of the ascendency of feminist history and feminist historians was that the women's press, most notably *Virago*, was followed by new journals that included the *Journal of Women's History, Feminist Review, Feminist Studies, Australian Feminist Review, Gender and History* and the *Women's History Review* to which can be added the already discussed *History Workshop Journal*.

Jane Rendall and Keith McClelland recently recalled that Leonore Davidoff (1932–2014) established *Gender and History* in 1987. This journal, perhaps more than any other, 'went far beyond the straightforward recovery of women's lives in the past, and beyond the works bequeathed to us by first-wave feminism in a project to grasp the shifting landscapes of gender history'. (Rendall and McClelland, 2016, p. 283) Determined to bring in classicists and ancient historians and mindful of her own training in sociology and the importance of multi-disciplinary approaches, the first editorial stated a wish 'to examine all historical and social relations from a feminist perspective':

> Gender was to be at the centre of the historical agenda, as a set of lived relations and as a symbolic system. The journal was to encourage interdisciplinary thinking and also to be reflexive about the practice of history itself. And every article was to have something significant to say about gender.
>
> (Rendall and McClelland, 2016, p. 284)

The competition to place an article was fierce. This gives as proof, if proof was needed, that women's history, feminist history and now gendered histories have progressed into the very heart of global historiography. Accounts of the past that fail to take note of gender expose themselves to the charge of being radically incomplete and poorly considered.

12.4 Sexuality and Identity

Sexualities and Identity

When looking for the origins of gay liberation as an expression of sexual identity, the historical imagination is irresistibly transported back to the so-called cultural revolution of the 'Sixties' (see Chapter 22). It is in June 1969 that we find Marsha P. Johnson (1945–1992) as a drag queen and local celebrity in Greenwich Village, throwing the first brick or shot glass, as some have said, against homophobia and in frustration at the denial of sexual freedom. Or that is how it has been recalled in the notable case of Stonewall, a word that evokes the struggle for gay and eventually transexual rights. Stonewall began as a mafia-owned bar (the Stone Wall Inn), one of many gay bars in New York City owned by the mob. That June day developed into a riotous protest provoked by a police raid which itself was allegedly provoked by a bogus missing liquor license. The memory of the rebellion and the reforms that followed it were a guiding star during the darkest days of the AIDS epidemic during the 1980s and 1990s. As Martha led the clientele of Stone Wall against the police in New York City, it appeared to foresee a process that would usher in (at least in the West) political rights, the growing economic strength (in the UK) of the 'pink pound' and now the equal treatment of 'gays in the military' with, further, parity in the state's treatment of formal gay partnerships and, finally, marriage.

Important as this rights-based agenda has proven, it could not provide the historian with a complete picture of the importance and influence of sexuality in the human experience over time. Indeed, any history of gay liberation or histories of sexuality more generally needed to add, for equal consideration, transsexuality and otherwise other non-binary identities (more on this later) whose experiences are, incidentally, replete with a rich vein of unique primary sources. Yet sexuality and identity are such very large topics. Many have only come into historical view very recently and increasingly so since the 1960s. Often this awareness has been shaped by activism during the sixties and in the decades since. And more often still the solidarities that led to the opening of a so-called second phase of feminism meant a self-conscious sense that gender, sexuality and the liberation of sexuality historically could not be contained or controlled. Johnson writing in 1972 expressed this in a fashion which would see its mirror in the historiography of sexuality but which, although in tune with activist demand and opinion, would come to develop a more comprehensive understanding of sexual identity that was not limited to gay men:

> We still feel oppression by other gay brothers. Gay sisters don't think too bad of transvestites. Gay brothers do. I went to a dance at Gay Activists Alliance just last week, and there was

not even one gay brother that came over and said hello. They'd say hello, but then they'd get away very quick. The only transvestites that were very friendly with were that ones that looked freaky in drag, like freak drag, with no tits, no nothing. Well, I can't help but have tits, they're mine. And those men weren't too friendly at all. Once in a while, I get an invitation to Daughters of Bilitis [the first lesbian civil rights organisation in the United States that dated from 1955] and when I go there, they're always warm. All the gay sisters come over and say, 'Hello, we're glad to see you,' and they start long conversations. But the gay brothers. . .

(Marc Stein (ed.), *The Stonewall Riots*, 2019, p. 214)

Johnson herself was vocal on the rights agenda, but as we witness earlier, she abhorred the split in solidarities between homosexuals (both men and women) and transsexuals arguing forcefully that trans people had been left behind in the wake of the Sixties reforms. She was not alone. This was a decade or period which in 1972 was about to fade into a rather less utopian period of neo-liberal economics and Conservative politics. Hence, since then, both activists and historians have been keen not to see sexual identity as either fixed or final but provisional. The historiography of gender could do little else but follow that approach.

Gay Power, then, like 'Flower Power' and anti-war demands for peace, seemingly became a creature of the rights-based demands of that formative decade. As described in a 2017 Netflix documentary, *The Death and Life of Marsha P. Johnson* by David France, on the possible cover up of Johnson's alleged murder, LGBT Co-Founder Acosto Machado summarized Johnson as an 'out' black figure with enormous charisma. But she was also 'like a Holy person', 'wandering the streets in whatever adornment she wanted'. Johnson (also known as Malcolm Michaels Jnr) as the founding spirit of the Gay Liberation Movement was found dead in the Hudson, a victim in 1992 of drowning that was either a result of misadventure or foul play.

Historiography then echoed these changes in activism and protest. The notion of non-binary sexual identity is now largely accepted as a plausible and lucid way to understand sexuality in the past, and with it has come the history of both non-binary sexuality and identity. Together, these histories have at the very least 'rescued for posterity' historical actors that have been hitherto abstracted – made of marble in the Greek or Roman classical world, heretics or sinners in Western Christendom, painted 'Mollys' in the modern world during and after the Enlightenment. Only later did these historical players see the light of day in history books but only then as exotic creatures or objects of derision, deviance and perversion. Take as two examples, the (now) shocking treatment meted out by the British state to the great literary figure Oscar Wilde (1854–1900) in the 1890s or the master mathematician and computing/artificial intelligence pioneer Alan Turing (1912–1954) in the wake of his most extraordinary contribution to the allied war effort. As we write, so-called psychological, pseudo-scientific or religious-based 'conversion therapies' for homosexuals and bisexuals to become heterosexual or their gender identity to shift from transsexuals to cisgender (a gender identity corresponding with the birth sex), remain legal in very many parts of the world, including the UK.

It would be tempting in these most important of areas of historiography to identify a moment of origin in the developing relationship between sexuality and identity. Identity, whether it be gay or straight, bi-sexual, transgender, cis-gender or transitioning, is now widely recognized as a crucial component to understanding both individual and group solidarities behaving in ways that explain the critical building blocks of our understanding of change over time. Agency is equally crucial here and like, say, race or class, sexuality has thrown up movements that the historian would be enormously foolish to ignore.

Before looking at some outstanding examples of how sexuality and identity have been represented by historians in several contrasting ways, let us first acknowledge the important theoretical works that have taken our understanding of sexuality in the past into fresh pastures of historical research. In this context, it would be remiss of us to ignore the work of Michel Foucault (*The History of Sexuality* published in 1977) or Judith Butler (*Gender Trouble*, 1990, 2006) in this process but also to some extent Mary Poovey (*Making a Social Body*, 1995) and *Uneven Developments* (1988). Finally, we should mention Joan Scott's "Gender: A Useful Category of Historical Analysis" that in many ways established the field of gender history (Scott, 1986).

Of these eminent theoreticians, two names stand out. Foucault we shall say more about throughout this section. Butler, on the other hand, deserves the briefest of mentions before we proceed. *Gender Trouble: Feminism and the Subversion of Identity* argued forcefully for the decoupling of *gender* and *sexuality* with women having been mistakenly separated by the feminist movement (it was argued) and attributed common characteristics that are essentially fixed; that is, they were thought of as women by virtue of not being men. This only served to underline for Butler the false nature of binary relationships as a way of understanding or describing sexuality as an essentially human experience. Also influenced by Foucault, this binary approach according to Butler linked sexuality to gender in ways that acknowledged the functioning of power relationships while allowing desire to be 'flexible' and 'free floating'. Enter common usage pronouns located on a spectrum of identity. This individual identity we shall explore as the 'historical self', the attributes of which are not inherent: He/She/They. You are a man or a woman if you *feel* like a man or a woman, but this too is fluid and need not be consistent. Like desire, identity is first felt and then 'performed' accordingly. Butler's work has formed the cornerstone of so-called Queer Theory.

It is within these foundational theoretical contexts, then, that we should consider Frank Mort's *Dangerous Sexualities* (2002), and in so doing we shall inevitably look at how historians have both revealed sexualities (note, plural) as vital to our current understanding the past in respect to sexualities and identity but also how this literature has developed into a search for lost voices and missing origins. We can only note in this context and in passing histories such as Susan Stryker, *Transgender History* (2017), Leah DeVun, *The Shape of Sex. Non-binary Gender from Genesis to the Renaissance* (2021), Matt Cook, Robert Mills, Randolph Trumbach, & H. G. Cocks, *A Gay History of Britain. Love and Sex Between Men Since the Middle Ages* (2007) and Annette F. Timm and Joshua A. Sanborn, *Gender, Sex and the Shaping of Modern Europe. A History from the French Revolution to the Present Day* (2016). So much of the important recent historiography has emerged from the shock of the AIDS crisis and the politics that emerged from the 1960s. Let us explore this notion a little further.

By 1981, the medical establishment had identified early cases of what they first called 'Gay-Related Immune Deficiency' or (GRID). Only later did the pejoratively labelled disease – 'The Gay Plague' become Acquired Immune Deficiency Syndrome (AIDS). With this was 'revealed the competing and unequal ideologies of sexual difference which called into doubt scientific progress [notions of modernity set in train by the Enlightenment] by looking again at the "medio-moral complex of sexuality" in the shadow of the AIDS crisis' (Mort, 2002, p. vi). This 'challenged permissive morality, reasserting the historical links between health and disease and moral and immoral notions of sex' (ibid, p. xiii). Here then is Mort's motivation and the meaning of the subtitle to *Dangerous Sexualities*, 'Medico Moral Politics in England Since 1830'. Many of the histories that followed the emergence of the disease were conceived both in the shadow of the AIDS iceberg (the theme of a doom-laden public announcement in the UK which warned about what was unseen and hidden below) and also against the backdrop of 'Queer Theory'. Queer Theory regarded sexuality as constructed with a rejection of heterosexuality as 'normative', and in turn, as Mort insists, with histories 'forged out of anxieties with conduct perceived to be troublesome or dangerous'(ibid, p. xix). Non-normative sexuality, it was assumed in the older histories, equated to sexual and social disorder.

If Foucault articulated what he called 'the historical present', his commentary on sexuality in history did so in advance of the AIDS crisis. Nonetheless he was keen to ascertain the meaning of sexuality or, more accurately, sexualities within a complex of disciplinary power that included medical authority. Mort took this further by insisting that sexuality as a category of historical and archival enquiry should be considered as part of, not separate to, the 'social forces' that tended to be the everyday concern of historians. Using the usual tools of the historian, there should be any routine historical enquiry, a gendered representation of the self, while there should be an increased production of histories of emotion and fantasy and a sensitivity towards how this might be represented spatially (ibid, pp. xxv–xxvi).

This throws up a variety of fronts for us to explore sexuality and identity and how they relate to a developing historiography. For now, we shall organize these various categories – that have come about since the cultural formations that originated in the 60s and the intervention which Foucault in the 70s – into the useful themes suggested by Mort (ibid, p. xv) All, it could be argued, sit within the context of cultural history (Chapter 11):

- The self in history.
- The representational quality of desire.
- The national and colonial dimensions of sexuality.
- The uses of sexuality and space.

We shall examine each in turn.

The Self in History

There are tensions running through the early studies of gender, not least of these is the exclusive focus on women and the absence of *plural* sexualities. Equally, social movements and individual actors in gendered histories were discursive in form but had the 'historical self' subsumed within structural sources of power such as 'the state' or 'the economy'. Hence Poovey in 1988 has individuals (women) as 'agents of social change' or the 'objects of intersecting social forces' (quoted in Mort, 2002, p. xv); that is, there is a built-in assumption 'that the representation of biological sexuality, the definition of sexual difference, and the social organisation of sexual relations are social, not natural, phenomena' (Poovey, 1988, p. 2). Few would now argue with that, but at the same time, class and the structures of society here are in a narrow sense unproblematically gendered with little sense made of the 'historical self' that lived apart from, say, the state etcetera or of thinking much about how the nature of these 'structures' have changed.

There are obvious similarities here with the approach of Leonora Davidoff and Catherine Hall whose now classic *Family Fortunes: Men and Women of the English Middle Class, 1780–1850* was published just a year before the Poovey tome in 1987. We will not detain the reader too long here, not least because *Family Fortunes* has been already introduced during this chapter, but we must underline the importance of *Family Fortunes* to the understanding of the contribution of women and the family to the framing of 'separate spheres' that in turn has revealed the extent of gendered economic engagement. Excellent and as ground-breaking as this book was, there was no acknowledgment of varied sexualities, masculinities, homosexuality and so on, instead 'They preferred to relate shifts in the gender regime to broader sociocultural forces, aligning particular masculine ideals more simply to social class' (Gleadle, 2007, p. 779). In this narrow sense, the Davidoff and Hall/Poovey approach to gender and structures such as class was very much a creature of its time.

In contrast, R. W. Connell (styled Raewyn Connell since 2006) is a sociologist. *Gender and Power: Society, the Person and Sexual Politics* was published in 1987 while *Masculinities* appeared in 1995. By then she was writing as a 'trans woman', suggesting a theory of 'hegemonic masculinity' that can be applied to the past but is rather more fluid in its historical application. Certainly, in the latter case, hegemonic masculinity is 'not a fixed character type, always and everywhere the same. It is, rather, the masculinity that occupies the hegemonic position in a given pattern of gender relations, a position always contestable' (Connell, 1995, p. 76). This principle could be applicable to consideration of various types of historical evidence and thus speaks to our topic; '[She] He observed that there might be considerable disjuncture between the idealised vision of social norms produced by the "organising intellectuals" – the doctors, clerics, writers and the like – and the actual personalities and performances of men themselves' (Gleadle, 2007, p. 779). While we appear to have an entrenched dominance of a particular form of masculine ideal, we can also discern in the approach by Connell both *social structures* – 'the organising intellectuals' – and the 'personalities and performances' that make up the 'historical self'. These elements interact. This is important if we are to fully understand the historical relationship between sexuality and identity.

John Tosh and Robert Shoemaker likewise followed suit with *A Man's Place: Masculinity and the Middle-Class Home in Victorian England* (1999) and co-edited *Manful Assertions: Masculinities in Britain since 1800* (1991) while R. Shoemaker's *Gender in English Society, 1650–1850: the Emergence of Separate Spheres?* was published in 1998. This was, of course, at the same moment that gay and transsexual activism in the wake of AIDS and the reaction to AIDS had made its influence felt in an emerging historiography. With Foucault and his *History of Sexuality* still present, the influence on historians of both psychology and geography, as we will explain later, would lead Mort to conclude that 'it is the gap between the social and the psychic that some of the most significant historical insights are to be found'. (Mort, 2002, p. xvi)

The Representational Quality of Desire

So it was that histories began to be written 'to map class and gender in the nineteenth century on to each other' (Nead, 2016, p. 179). Lynda Nead, reflecting on her own work in the *History Workshop Journal*, was clear in 2016 that her earliest research depended on that 1977 intervention by Michel Foucault who 'had dislodged the conventional view of Victorian morality; rather than seeing the Victorian age as a period of silence and suppression, he described sexuality in the nineteenth century in terms of a constant process of definition and regulation' (Nead, 2016, p. 179). Certainly it could be said that historians had begun to uncover previously hidden narratives of sexuality. The extraordinary story of Arthur Munby and Hannah Cullwick, told through their respective diaries, was restricted within the Trinity College, Cambridge library until the early 50s. When it was finally opened to the public it revealed a complex sexual relationship between a middle-class man and a working-class woman who had been in service since the age of eight. They married. If this was not transgressive enough, they lived their lives through sexual fantasy:

> After some eighteen years – they never seem to have had sex in its conventional definition, although there were certainly sadomasochist and masochistic tendencies in the relationship – Munby and Cullwick married in 1873. In secret. They visited Europe as man and wife, but back in England they played out their fantasies. In public, she dressed and acted the part of

his maid. He paid her wages for the work she did. In the studio, she posed for his camera as a rural maiden, a serving maid, a ('blacked up') male slave, an angel, a man, and a 'middle class lady', which by marriage she had become. Munby, a barrister, educator, and minor man of letters, did work, but he was mostly subsidized by his family.

(<https://daily.jstor.org/the-bizarre-victorian-diaries-of-cullwick-and-munby/> accessed, 21 April 2022)

Nead's own excellent work explored representations via, say, the historical relationship between art, pornography via the female nude or Victorian 'Babylon'; its' people, streets, and images or 'myths of sexuality', seen through representations of women, took a clear conceptual framework and definition of sexuality from Foucault into the archives. Project forward to 2016, and Nead's questions are as follows. They are pertinent to our own consideration of sexuality and identity in the historical past:

1. What is the relationship between the archive and the conceptual framework and what demands does the archive make on the history of sexuality?
2. What is the nature of resistance beyond the web of power evoked by Foucault? How does the history of sexuality work with and relate to the history of emotions and feeling?
3. What role, if any, does the historical imagination of the researcher play in understanding nineteenth-century sexualities?

'These questions differed from those I had framed in the 1980s, inflected by shifts in historical methodologies that had created a space for concepts such as feeling and imagination, which had been excluded in the earlier Foucauldian work' (*Ibid*, p. 180). The connecting tissue here is the notion of sexuality as representation or performance, which, once again, has its roots in the work of Foucault published, we should note again, in the 1970s, which is argued by some – not least Nead – as a moment of sexual upheaval. But it was to transcend Foucault, taking histories of sexualities and identity in a somewhat different direction.

The National and Colonial Dimensions of Sexuality

If we are to convincingly frame sexualities and identities historically, then it has become increasingly clear that Foucault's theoretical framework has limits and that there are areas in which alternative approaches to sexuality had some purchase. Mort is careful to emphasise that Benedict Anderson's work on nationalism, for example, while all but silent on sexuality, still has nationality and nationalism as a 'cultural construct' a la Foucault and is 'underpinned by recognisably modern institutions of knowledge and power' (Mort, 2002, pp. xx–xxi). The link between national and colonial dimensions of sexuality, we are told, are similarly facilitated by largely metropolitan and bourgeois networks. Before we explore this proposition a little further, let us look at the important work of George Mosse who had touched on the theme of nationalism and sexuality quite early in our chronology of the historiography of sexuality that stretches from the 1960s to the present day.

George L. Mosse (1918–1999) published his *Nationalism and Sexuality: Respectability and Abnormal Sexuality in Modern Europe* in 1985. Again, working with the grain of Foucault and as a homosexual whose German Jewish family had fled the Nazis, Mosse was interested in exploring gender, sexuality and power through so-called 'perverse' sexualities that included homosexuality. Yet, as we have established, Foucault's theories as a guiding star were clearly blinking. For example, Mosse concluded that nineteenth-century sexuality was repressed, while

Foucault disagreed. *Nationalism and Sexuality* argued that a modern set of bourgeois norms was the key to understanding both largely accepted sexual norms and nationalism itself:

> For men these included manliness, stoicism, and the obligation to provide for and protect one's family. To be an upstanding citizen of a particular nation, men had to comply with these behaviors [sic]. Manliness in the form of discipline, restraint, and heterosexual love served as the foundation of the nation. . . . As religion diminished as a cultural force in the nineteenth century, nationalism was increasingly necessary to assure that people behaved in a 'respectable' way. Both men and women were to refuse unconventional sexual expression and instead form nuclear families in which they could raise children. Sex was acceptable only within a marital, heterosexual framework. Men were to remain faithful to their wives. Sexual deviance of any kind – prostitution, homosexuality, masturbation, and lesbianism – were considered evils to be avoided at all costs.
>
> (Mosse, 2020, p. xi)

Now it could be clearly seen that individual erotic impulses could turn into a collective love of nation – 'psychic causality', as it has been labelled. Yet, this was a love that could speak its name. Naked male bodies, for example, became the very ideal of Nazi German youth.

In sum, according to Mosse,

- Contemporaries would strongly disagree with Foucault that they were anything else but repressed because they were 'more often than not frustrated in their fight to wring even a few concessions from society'.
- Deeply buried erotic energies began to bubble up 'closer to the surface' at the *fin de siècle*. Repression, however, still carried the day as freer sexual expression won only a few 'concessions from society'.
- While Foucault historicized Freudian categories as typical of a new science of sex, Mosse was still implementing them uncritically.

(Mosse, 2020, p. xii)

The connections between national and colonial notions of sexualities are important to our understanding of sexuality and identity and probably were understood by contemporaries in the modern era through 'reciprocal networks of empire' and as such, it has been argued, are very much a reflection of the modern era.

Here, briefly, the work of Julie Peakman is interesting. Her *Licentious Worlds. Sex and Exploitation in Global Empires* (2019) is cognizant of a sophisticated theoretical background available to historians of sexuality and imperialism. Foucault is prominent but not excessively so, while we ought not forget a book published contemporaneously, Edward Said's *Orientalism: Western Conceptions of the Orient* (1977), which, as we detail in Chapter 9, has the oriental conceived as 'the other' by Western imperial cultural representations. Studying the fantasies and exploitative sexuality imposed by empires globally and over a long period, Peakman finds four central features that can be applied to very different forms of imperialism and the application of sexual behaviours and cultures usually imposed by men:

1. The importance of religious influences religion affected the creation of laws which in turn affected the marginalised such as women and homosexuals.
2. The significance of relations, heterosexual, or homosexual (religion is seen again as a determinant).

3   The effects of cultural clashes (the imposition of the enlightenment and European-based sense that there was a 'civilising mission' to be imposed by the colonizer on the colonised).
4   The understanding of 'normal' and 'abnormal' sexual behaviour (which sometimes suggests a double standard with the indigenous peoples often seen as licentious and without morality. This could justify sexual exploitation).

(Peakman, 2019, p. 195)

Above all, Peakman emphasises 'that the shifts in sexual behaviour and attitudes in the world over the last four centuries have hinged on a dual combination of the influences of old religions and new developing empires, both steeped in male power and control' (Peakman, 2019, p. 14). Peakman's sources include various erotica alongside the more usual court records, diaries, correspondence and anthropological records but the real departure – not really explored elsewhere in her study – is the survival of religion in sexualized behaviours.

Sexuality and Space

Judith R. Walkowitz, *City of Dreadful Delight: Narratives of Sexual Danger in Late-Victorian London* (1992) used multiple examples to connect the 1880s metropolis with varied discourses of gender and sexuality from accounts of child sex rings by the 'Northern Puritan', W. T. Stead, the short-lived Men and Women's Club that defied heterosexual conventions led by the eugenicist, Karl Pearson and the evocation of 'the darker and erotic elements of the fantastic' via the Whitechapel murderer, Jack the Ripper. Important to our understanding of the historiography of sexualities, therefore, is the construction of moral geographies.

City of Dreadful Delight is a case in point. Typically, the focus is on the metropolis. Mort observed,

> One of the most significant aspects of her analysis was the insight that these socio-sexual relationships were not only embedded in the physical geography of London but were also present in a series of imaginary urban landscapes, which were shaped by the social scripts of melodrama, science, and masculine and feminine versions of cosmopolitan.
>
> (Mort, 2002, p. xxiii)

And so it is that we return to Gay New York but not Stonewall this time. This time, we must consider the work of George Chauncey and his *Gay New York. Gender, Urban Culture and the Making of the Gay Male World, 1890–1940*, published in 1994. It is the city that brings us diverse cultures and diverse sexualities while these sexualities play off the urban environment in which they are situated. Prosaically, this might relate to nineteenth-century Paris as the 'city of love' where wide boulevards facilitate a sexualized gaze or the 'monkey walk' in the back lanes of London's East End when heterosexual youth would parade up and down in an obvious display to the opposite sex. But this is not Chauncey's point; according to Mort, 'Chauncey's analysis points to the extremely porous nature of modern sexual identities which are fluid and contingent partly because of their special proximity to other cultures and ways of life' (Mort, 2002, p. xxiv). These 'ways of life' might (over time) be influenced by disease, or riot, or plain urban zoning leading to gay corners in neighbourhoods that together created differing sexual lives. But also, we would think, they were influenced by the restrictions and marginalization that led to the Stonewall riot.

Not necessarily so, according to Chauncey who argues for the influence of moral geographies in the lives of homosexuals. Gay lives differed across decades with discriminatory laws not always enacted, on the one hand, with the Stonewall riots in 1969 not necessarily acting as a watershed or a high point of homosexual visibility. In all cases place is important. The trend towards the consideration of place continues with Matt Cook, Alison Oram and Justin Bengry (eds.) in *Locating Queer Histories. Places and Traces Across the UK* (2022).

Postscript

Historiography has tended to be a male preserve. Not only have a large majority of studies been undertaken by men, but they have featured men as the movers and shakers of history. History is often said to be written by the victors, that is, historians who have recorded the triumphs of nations and empires. But this can apply also to gender, for men who have dominated the recording of history have chosen to write about the exploits of other men who have dominated nations and empires.

There were notable exceptions. Talented women historians have documented the lives of women, thereby revealing the contribution made by prominent and lowly alike to the functioning of past societies. This may have been a conscious attempt to place women onto the historical agenda, but it had its limitations, for histories that attempt fully to integrate the female experience require more than the inclusion of women in order to fill the gaps – they require a fundamental realignment of historical thinking around the fault lines of past societies. To class divisions we must add those based on gender and race, understood as a dynamic and integrated whole.

These have been the concerns at the centre of the wave of feminist historiography that emerged during the 1970s. Dismissing conventional historical accounts and those inspired by Marxism as sexist, that is, dominated by a tendency to record the male historical experience, feminists set about rewriting history. There were different currents and different political projects, but shared was a desire to integrate more fully the female experience into history. Here the most satisfying attempts were not those that concentrated exclusively upon women but those that considered history as driven by women and men in relation to one another. It was impossible to approach matters of class formation, the Industrial Revolution, family, community, nation state or empire, they argued, with a blindness to gender relations.

In recent years questions of gender subjectivity and identity have attracted attention. We now have a much better understanding of the importance of notions of femininity and masculinity to the organization of society into separate spheres, political and industrial struggles, conflict and the imperial project. Here again, approaches differ depending upon the roles attributed to physiology, culture and language in creating gender identities. Most recently, psychoanalytical approaches have instead argued for the crucial role of the unconscious and fantasy. In no area has this been more important or revealing than with regard to witchcraft.

All historians are under an obligation to remember that approximately half of all societies comprised women, and any account that marginalizes the female experience is impoverished not only because it takes undue account of women but equally because it provides a one-dimensional interpretation of the male experience. So too with the urgent need to acknowledge the work undertaken since the 1960s/1970s on sexuality. Inspired by the Stonewall riots and the terrible ravages of the AIDS epidemic, cultural formations that originated in the 60s and the intervention of Foucault in the 70s have been re-worked in subsequent years, not least by Frank Mort, into themes such as the self in history, the representational quality of desire, the national and colonial dimensions of sexuality and the uses of sexuality and space and the relationship between them.

Further Reading

Sally Alexander (1994) *Becoming a Woman: And Other Essays in 19th and 20th Century Feminist History.*
American Historical Review Forum (2008) 'Revisiting "Gender: A Useful Category of Historical Analysis"', *American Historical Review* 113 (5), pp. 1344–429.
Judith M. Bennett (2006) *History Matters: Patriarchy and the Challenge of Feminism.*
Joan Kelly (1984) *Women, History and Theory: The Essays of Joan Kelly.*
Frank Mort (2002) *Dangerous Sexualities. Medico-Moral Politics in England since 1830.*
Lynda Nead (2016, August) 'Fallen Women and Foundlings: Rethinking Victorian Sexuality', *History Workshop Journal* 82, pp. 177–87.
Sheila Rowbotham (1973) *Hidden from History: 300 Years of Women's Oppression and the Fight Against It.*
Joan W. Scott (1988) *Gender and the Politics of History.*
John Tosh (2005) *Manliness and Masculinities in Nineteenth-Century Britain.*

13 Public History

Introduction

This chapter examines public history and its chief elements: present-mindedness, promiscuity in its choice of what constitutes historical evidence, multi-disciplinarity and anti-intellectualism. It reaches out to historical constituencies such as family historians or popular collectors who are quite untouched by university style history, what is called here the 'academy'. These are not necessarily readers of popular histories that fill the shelves of booksellers but local and community 'historians' who are themselves potentially well placed to tell their own stories without acting as passive participants in histories written by professional historians. However, if these are the claims of its advocates, public and popular forms of history have a soft underbelly. Academic historians sometimes perceive public history at its worst as untheorized and uncritical. History becomes heritage, nostalgic and conservative, packaged in such a way that celebrates the past by dressing it up to encourage social consensus, an antiquarian ruse to make us believe that consent and conformity are natural features of the present. By collecting evidence of past societies, however, public historians have allowed those scholars working in the academy to rewrite histories in ways that would have remained quite impossible. In so doing, the basis of historical knowledge has been challenged.

In order to explore these issues, the first section uses the Battle of Cable Street in 1936 as a way of discussing the range and scope of sources used by the public historian, the definition of public history and how it differs from the publishing phenomenon of popular history and is perceived differently across the world. Section 2 explores differing views about heritage and the 'heritage industry' and the ways that the past is conceptualized and ways too that public history is 'consumed' by the general public. While public history seems to be a different enterprise from university history, it nevertheless produces evidence that professional historians and students can utilize. This is the subject of the third section while the last section explores the tensions created between public history and the academy in what precisely constitutes historical knowledge.

13.1 What Is Public About History?

According to local folklore, in October 1936, Catholics, Jews and Communists fought a pitched battle on the streets of East London against the so-called 'Blackshirts' – or the British Union of Fascists – led by English aristocrat Oswald Mosley (1896–1980). Mistaken in the detail though much of the narrative is, the Battle of Cable Street has passed into mythology, especially among those on the left of British politics who still regard it as the opening salvo in a longer battle for multicultural and multi-ethnic solidarity. Reputedly, priests took up arms alongside rabbis to oppose a brand of fascism largely modelled on Mussolini's fascists in Italy and that along with

German Nazism now choked mainland Europe like a miasma. Waves of protesters dispersed Mosley's Blackshirts with no help from London's police force, who had allowed the march to thread its way through areas heavily populated by Irish and Jewish immigrants. 'They shall not pass' was the rallying cry of the anti-fascists that day, a slogan borrowed from the Spanish Civil War. As a cause célèbre of Popular Front politics from the period, it is immensely important as a moment when otherwise divided and disparate groups came together under a unified banner, while the defeat of the Blackshirts cleared the political air by removing any lingering odour of anti-democratic politics in Britain.

Conventional historical approaches can help one to understand the main facets of this event. Political historians would be keen to tease out the power relations at work that day: the machinations of Communist, trade union and leftist politics; the internal dynamics of Jewish groups (pro- and anti-Zionist, socialist and reformist, religious and secular); the tactics of the London Metropolitan Police; the divisions within fascist ranks and so on. Similarly, social historians may be less interested to divine power relations, feeling themselves better placed to consider gender relations at work on that day, the role of children and young people, religious influences and the like. Methodologically, the social historian may well be more sensitive to oral history approaches (as we will see in Chapter 24), exploring the living testimonies of those that experienced these momentous events, comparing these witness testimonies with newspaper records, contemporary diaries and so on. Cultural historians, perhaps influenced by related subjects such as social or cultural anthropology, psychology, sociology and geography, may be more inclined to look closely at the expressive aspects associated with the day such as posters and banners, language, the role of leadership cults, the socio-economic make-up of the participants, the use made of public space and so forth. Public historians, on the other hand, may well employ a synthesis of these approaches but will focus instead on surviving public nomenclature such as street names and buildings – in particular, how the event resounds in the present.

What precisely then is public history? There is no ready and encompassing definition, but with the words from Robert Kelley, a practitioner of public history, we may have a start:

> In its simplest meaning, Public History refers to the employment of historians and the historical method outside of academia: in government, private corporations, the media, historical societies and museums, even in private practice. Public Historians are at work whenever, in their professional capacity, they are part of the public process. An issue needs to be resolved, a policy must be formed, the use of a resource or the directions of an activity must be more effectively planned and a historian is called upon to bring the dimensions of time: this is Public History.
>
> (Kelley, 1992, p. 111)

He tells us that public history and public historians are anything but creatures of the academy or a trained professional vanguard, but as museum curators, tour guides and genealogists, they take the historical record beyond the fetishized scholarly footnote and cloistered academic seminar into a less rarefied public consciousness.

Shifts in contemporary preoccupations of the historian have changed over time and necessarily alter the subject position of history, revealing new vistas, sources and perspectives; the same might be said of the altering the professional, geographical and social position of the historian. Public history has been particularly adept at meeting these changes, especially given its promiscuous approach to historical evidence. Raphael Samuel (1934–1996), for instance, an enthusiast if not a pioneer of public history approaches, made much of incorporating unofficial sources into the canon of history and giving due regard to scholarship generated outside of professional history and the academy as the product of what is essentially a social form of knowledge. Therefore, the genealogists, canal enthusiasts, railway buffs and amateurs that people his *Theatres of Memory* (1994) enjoy equally the status of historians alongside the professoriate of the old universities as both consumers *and* producers of history. Emma Wilmer, however, sees public history not simply as history practiced outside the university but as the dissemination of history through a broad medium of methods and approaches:

> Public history is history, practically applied. It is based on the understanding that history is not taught solely in the classroom, but is learned in a variety of places, and in a variety of ways. Public historians disseminate historical information to a wide audience through institutions such as archives, historical houses or societies, museums, consulting firms, history libraries, and Web sites. They are providers of primary and secondary source materials, and they often present information to patrons so that the patrons can form their own ideas of history and historical events through exhibits and research. My particular experiences with public history are diverse, and they have helped inform my definition of public history. In providing historical information to visitors, public historians give these visitors a chance to form their own opinions and ideas about history and to create books, essays, dissertations, works of art, and other products that in turn shape other people's ideas about history. Practical and entertaining, applications of history are what set public history apart from classroom history, and both have their place in the overall process of teaching history.
>
> (www.publichistory.org/what_is/definition)

It is historians working outside the academy who have been responsible, it should be emphasized, for actually producing historical evidence, adding to the sum of our historical knowledge, say by collecting political badges generated after the Battle of Cable Street or creating forms of public art (as we shall see later). Moreover, the popular disseminators of history have encouraged the consumption of history by and to a wider public. Public historians have done both these things: produced historical evidence as collectors of evidence that historians working in the academy can readily use, and consumed popular forms of history, sometimes simultaneously.

Figure 13.2 is a photograph of the battle taken on the day that it took place, shop signs hanging from the Jewish-owned shops, burning barricades, paving stones ripped from the pavement. Figure 13.1 is a detail of the massive mural that today takes up a side of a building on Cable Street. The photograph constitutes the primary remains of the battle, perhaps taken by a participant and rescued as historical evidence only later. The mural emerges later as a public memoriam to the event, although as a representation of officially sponsored street art, it has its origins in semi, if not wholly, illegal gable-end graffiti. The historical moment that gave rise to the Battle of Cable Street has passed – as have the making of films about the battle or the historical circumstances that gave rise to the mural and even films about the making of the mural. Yet the event itself – and subsequent public expressions of the event – all have histories that exist in public narratives or stories about the battle. This interface between historical evidence in its primary form influences history in its secondary form and vice versa; whether it is a mural, a school play or even in a more nebulous form, as local legend, they all survive and evolve and eventually transform, taking on lives of their own.

To the public historian, representations of the event enjoy equal resonance with the event itself, building and layering to become part of the received account of what went on during that October day in 1936. Whether via a photograph as primary source or mural as secondary source, these historical echoes exist in a more durable half-life of the battle and its responses, in

224 *Varieties*

Figure 13.1 Mural of The Battle of Cable Street in East London, which depicts the fight against fascism
Contributor: Douglas Lander/Alamy Stock Photo

Figure 13.2 'Battle of Cable Street' in 'Jewish Aldgate', London, 5 October 1936
Contributor: Heritage Image Partnership Ltd/Alamy Stock Photo

public spaces such as the Internet, encouraging discussions about 1930s fascism in Europe more generally as well as informing current debates about multiculturalism, citizenship and national identity. This is how public history operates in the historical present.

Indeed, by using a wide variety of media, collecting oral histories or making a film, we aid accessibility to history as a genre and produce yet more knowledge about the public aspects of an historical event such as this. In addition, the advent of digital cameras means that films made on very small and very sophisticated movie cameras facilitate the production of more narratives about the battle but also determine how stories about it are consumed. Online technologies such as blogs and wikis or moderated online discussions have precisely this dual function as producers and disseminators of yet more knowledge about the battle. The use of technologies that help to develop a more critical understanding of how to analyze history produced and consumed in a public forum has become one of the defining aspects of the public history approach.

Public history, however, is not simply the type of popular history that is now ubiquitous on cable television channels and in the best-selling lists of paperback history, some of them excellent (see Chapter 19). Simon Schama and his BBC *History of Britain* programmes and accompanying volumes and books, Richard Hamblyn's award-winning *The Invention of Clouds* (2001), Dava Sobel's *Longitude* (1998) or Adam Hochschild's *Bury the Chains: Prophets and Rebels in the Fight to Free an Empire's Slaves* (2005) are not, to use a term from the nineteenth century, 'curious histories' but have made a real contribution to historiography. These popularly consumed histories illustrate popular sentiments about what at any one moment is important in history whether or not these histories finally migrate to television or radio. Schama's volumes are constructed wholly from the point of view of a professional historian; with Hamblyn, Sobel and Hochschild, although their perspective originates outside professional history, they too kick over the traces of a given historical phenomenon while attempting to engage with a mass audience.

What then is the extent of public history's concerns? It champions the democratization of the archive and of accessible history, but it is perplexingly difficult to fathom the depths of its interests: treating the public histories of the ancient stones of Avebury at one turn (as a study of history and heritage) and the historical plight of red squirrels at the next (as a study of history and nationalism; Kean et al., 2000). The definition of what public history actually *is*, therefore, must be tempered by what it is *not*, that is, how it differs from political, social or cultural history or from popular histories.

Public history also differs in its practice across the world. It began life in Australia and the United States and accordingly is seen in those places in a somewhat different light than it is in Europe. In Australia, the term has inspired histories based on the indigenous Aboriginal population; in the United States, it serves a more consensual vision of the past, dealing with almost endless lists of individuals and organizations whose interests range from genealogy to the corporate past. Britain, however, hosts a weaker strand of public history. Insofar that it has bothered to be reflective about its own existence, public history British-style imagines itself concerned with bottom-up history, a subgenre of the new social history of the 1960s that, as we shall see in Chapter 22, is couched in class conflict or else is a celebration of heritage. Therefore, a single definition that crosses geographical boundaries is elusive.

If Australian, American and British approaches to public history differ, they are all concerned with widening the public audience for history while employing diverse ways of disseminating history using museums and other forms of popular culture. In this way local and family experiences are brought alive through plays and artwork, community histories or old newspapers, poor law records, diaries and memoirs and travel writing, giving renewed vigour and life to present-day issues such as family breakdown, gender equality, child cruelty, moral sexual dilemmas, 'anti-social' behaviour and developing ideas of masculinity or citizenship. This approach has profound implications for the role of the historian in a modern society in the here and now, but it also asks searching questions about the public function of academic history.

Philip Scarpino, writing in the dedicated journal *The Public Historian*, argued that if public history is concerned with unusual sources and with unusual approaches to sources, with opening the archive to a wider historical public and with addressing a wider historical public, it is only because the academic world continues to confine itself to a relatively limited audience:

> As public history has evolved from a quest for 'alternative careers' to a way of understanding and practicing the craft of history, it has on the campuses run headlong into the sacred trinity of research, teaching, and service – with the greatest of these being research embodied in refereed publications.... Despite the peer review and many other strengths, the present reward system has contributed to an unproductive 'academic vs. public' debate; encouraged a trend towards co-opting public history by defining it as another specialized subfield and obscured the common ground shared by the community of professionals who practice the historian's craft. As historians, we all do research, we all analyze and interpret our findings, and we all communicate the results. The primary difference between public and academic history is in the area of communication – in the audiences that we attempt to reach and in the products that we use to convey our scholarship to those audiences.
>
> (Scarpino, 1993, pp. 55–61)

Professional historians working in universities have begun to argue, however, that we need to take popular forms of knowledge about history as seriously as knowledge generated in the academy. Some of these sentiments may have been encouraged, in Britain at least, by the 'quest for alternative careers' among those academics tenuously employed within the academy. In other words, addressing a wider historical public in the way attempted by public history has become the side effect of changes introduced into higher education. These include an increased student population and an attempt to increase skills levels and to introduce greater cooperation between universities and the private sector, linking funding for research to knowledge transfer initiatives. Because of structural changes within universities, especially the 'new' universities who now work in a wholly different climate from the ancient universities (now operating in a global marketplace) or the Russell Group or the 'red-bricks', there is an increasing division between institutions that predominately teach and institutions that maintain the traditional mix of teaching and research with funding distributed accordingly. Public history, therefore, has a very practical use for a stratum of professional historians who cling on to the profession by their fingertips, as well as others whose business is the past more generally, who do not teach or research history in a university setting but who potentially challenge the status of the professional historian as expert.

Definitions of public history are elastic enough to stretch across geographical borders and to allow the Australian, American and British experiences of public history to mean something different in each context. The focus of public history is the non-expert, and since the sources associated with public history are various, historical knowledge among 'untrained' historians working outside universities tends to be knowledge that is socially constructed. If this distinguishes public history from mainstream, university-based history, then it is because public history engages with forms of history inevitably connected to a wider public. This creates problems. To engage with the public, to really be the public face of what history is and to do this successfully, public history must be accessible and interesting but must also develop as a recognizable genre of history. It is because history in its popular and public forms is so very familiar that it is sometimes difficult to argue that it has the same scholarly weight as conventional history. In effect it is a struggle to ensure that it is taken seriously at all, especially since one of its strengths is that it is indeed accessible and to some degree anti-authoritarian.

Hilda Kean is a pioneer in diverse forms of public history in Britain and she insists this new approach to evidence can be promiscuous in its scope and scale from the archives of the local streets to the souvenirs and trinkets or memories collected informally (Kean, 2000). In doing family history as one important aspect of 'non-expert' led public history, the 'archaeology of lives' as Kean put it, we are as likely to use the 'unofficial' sources of family photographs, diaries and so on as the 'official' sources of the state such as census returns, probate, ecclesiastical records and court case files. According to Kean, public history is not only about the 'historical self' in the historical present or challenging the historian as expert but also about collaboration across fields and a commitment to what she calls 'praxis', that is, history as it affects people and communities:

> Public History acts as an umbrella, under which the historical mind can be brought to bear on areas of research and thought which are too often seen as mutually exclusive. It draws upon the magazine racks of W. H. Smith for source material as much as it draws on academic texts. It looks as much to images and textual conceptions on commercial packaging and television advertising as it does to the art gallery and museum. It seeks oral opinion conveyed through the domestic images recorded by camcorder, constructed images and visual texts on television, and the holistic nature of the idea of knowledge expressed by the Internet. Public History relies on a collective and collaborative effort of people often working in different fields. This very process, of itself, helps to avoid academic navel gazing. In examining the 'historical self' in the concept of our perception of time and sense of place, for instance, then necessity for the enlargement of our terms of reference becomes apparent.
>
> (Kean et al., 2000, pp. 13–14)

There is one very real sense, therefore, in which public history has served to widen our horizons as historians, and if we use family history as but one example of the practice of public history, we will find that millions practice it. History from this perspective has never been more popular.

Public history as a popular form of history acting as an 'umbrella' for different approaches to history has indeed drawn upon a range of both familiar and unfamiliar sources, and this, if nothing else, will be its legacy. Nevertheless, one distinguishing feature of public history is the way it is consumed by a television watching, 'big house' visiting public, which now in many ways seems quite smitten with all things past. This consumption of the past, very much associated with history outside of the academy and the ways in which it connects in a controversial way to the 'heritage industry', is the subject of the next section.

13.2 Consumption of Public History

Sir Edwin Landseer (1802–1873), Victorian court artist par excellence and a great favourite of the Queen, did not exaggerate the ancient splendour of the scene when he painted Victoria and Albert as royals from the fourteenth century, Edward III and Philippa of Hainault. The occasion was a sumptuous and extravagant Plantagenet Ball in May 1842. The young Queen and her Prince wore medieval garb amid a hall decked in medieval decor designed at huge cost (Schama, 2009). The antiquarian James Planche recalled how Victoria and Albert dressed up this way, self-consciously re-enacting the story of a Queen in the Middle Ages who made a successful plea to her 'warrior husband' to spare the burghers of Calais. Schama was keen to emphasize not only the enormous cost of the ball staged at a time of economic distress in the industrial areas but that the proceeds of the ball were donated to the unemployed weavers of Spitalfields.

For Schama, therefore, the acting out of a medieval story of clemency by the appeal of a Queen to her 'King' was no longer simply a fable about the saving of Calais burghers as an example of medieval royal compassion but instead 'is given a modern gloss as a philanthropic melodrama of the nineteenth century' (Schama, p. 127). This worked well enough as a reading of early Victorian class relations at the time. However, our concern is to explain how heritage is employed as an historical narrative and its relation to public history.

The historian Peter Mandler in *The Fall and Rise of the Stately Home* (1997) dedicated the opening chapter of his book to the 'Victorian idea of heritage':

> Whatever the truth of this, it is clearly not necessary to explain the Victorian turn to history – as British historians, less comfortable with cultural nationalism than their French or German counterparts, tend to do – by reference to ruling-class anxieties about the pace of social change and the fear of political upheaval. The use of history is not necessarily prescriptive or conservative, and is often very far from being a device of social control. On the contrary, elite culture's longstanding disregard of national history in favour of classicism and cosmopolitanism gave the past an intrinsically democratic appearance. Long before the early Victorian period of cultural democratization, political radicals had made arguments for constitutional change based on the idea of a lost 'ancient constitution', more popular and national, which had been subverted in the recent past but which could still be reconstructed. It was a natural instinct for advocates (*not* opponents) of change in a highly stable and hierarchical society to seek a pedigree, a tradition for their programme. In much the same way, the Victorian culture industry called into existence an old world to redress the new.
>
> (Mandler, 1997, pp. 28–9)

Here we find the Victorian discovery of the 'olden times', which served to confront anxieties about rapid change or acted as a side-effect of what Mandler calls 'cultural nationalism' – the building of the nation using history. Heritage became a foil to all things modern and this explains the clothes worn by Queen Victoria and the Prince Consort on that May evening in 1842 and again in June 1845 and June 1851 when they became Georgians for the evening or mimicked the style of the Restoration. We need to dig deeper still if we are to understand the power of heritage in the public understanding of history, especially in contrast to the type of history conventionally practiced in university departments today.

Significantly, Mandler was rightly reluctant to dismiss heritage in the nineteenth century or in the present-day as a symptom of ruling-class anxieties about the pace of change and the fear of political upheaval. Before the reforms of the 1830s, the aristocracy quite often looked less to national history as a way of defining the nation, preferring instead to view the past by concentrating on the classical civilizations of Rome and Greece. With the gradual displacement of the aristocracy as a governing class, the past became for the newly enfranchised classes 'intrinsically democratic' and progressive. Heritage became a way of remaking the nation in the image of the new governing classes. After all, as Mandler said, it was radical opinion that lamented the disappearance of the 'ancient constitution', an indigenous and localized constitution displaced by the centralizing tendencies of the so-called Norman Yoke after the invasion of 1066. Radicals looked back (not forward) to what they believed was a perfect Anglo-Saxon constitution that had been swept away by the Norman regime.

Changes in the constitution during the nineteenth century, however, and the inclusion of new classes within the pale of the constitution inspired what Mandler further called the 'culture industry'. This culture industry, probably for the first time, facilitated the consumption of history among the masses, remaking the present through Victorian architecture and the 'improved' built environment, taking the nation back to its medieval foundations. This process of historicizing the nation meant that when Victoria and Albert donned medieval clothes at the Plantagenet Ball of May 1842 and gave the proceeds of this exquisitely grand event to the unemployed, it could be coherently argued by contemporaries that, as Mandler put it, heritage 'called into existence an old world to redress the new' (Mandler, 1997, pp. 28–9). From this vantage point, heritage 'is not necessarily prescriptive or conservative, and is very far from being a device of social control' (ibid.).

This is important to note when we consider the role of heritage in public history; to understand heritage is to understand how a past is created and consumed and to judge to what extent public history is useful within the canon of history as a discipline. Patrick Wright wrote his provocative and wide-ranging *On Living in an Old Country: The National Past in Contemporary Britain* (1998) upon returning from a spell abroad when he found Britain tottering on the brink of a Conservative-led Thatcher government and its population enthralled with what Wright contended was essentially backward-looking tradition. The 'heritage industry', according to Wright, confirmed a cultural conservatism in the country by restructuring a monolithic national identity through an appeal to jingoism and imperial values, and the way that 'heritage' was consumed merely confirmed to Wright a populace stupefied by images and narratives of an apparently consensual past. By trooping around the big houses and castles of rural Britain, people were living the imaginative life of the gentry while being encouraged to forget the vicious class distinctions manifested in life below stairs. Nowhere was this truer than in properties owned by the National Trust, the same organization whose founders, so we have learnt from Stephen Fry at the very opening of this book, were anything but conservative or prescriptive.

The National Trust is not an organization where history is passively consumed but where activity and popular participation are in evidence. The 'One Day in History' event in October 2006, for example, was an event organized by the National Trust precisely to encourage public participation in matters concerned with the past and to produce a level of popular interest that most historians working in the academy could only dream about and one relevant to the lives of many millions of people.

Heritage has been a major concern of public history in Britain where monuments and the packaging of the past – National Trust tea towels and cream teas – have been seen as an object of legitimate study. For Wright this packaging has prevented an historical public from realizing the harsh realities of history. Yet this 2006 event held by the National Trust saw a million badges sold, 10,000 postcards completed, 20,000 declarations of support for the National Trust, 46,000 blogs registered online and 1 million people accessing a virtual heritage site. History from this perspective appears designed less as a trick to manufacture consent and more as a way that a mass audience for history could be galvanized into action; after all, the encouragement of mass participation is an aim of public history. To its detractors, however, the consumption of history succeeded only in 'prettifying' the past, dressing it up in order to support political consensus and suppress political divisions in the present.

On a slightly different trajectory from that of Wright, David Lowenthal has identified nostalgia as a feature of our everyday lives, above all how we deal with the boundaries that he argues separate history from heritage. *The Heritage Crusade and the Spoils of History* (1998) saw heritage and the adherence of a vast public to an uncritical past as essentially situated against progress. Both Wright and Lowenthal, despite their erudite and theoretically sophisticated take

230 *Varieties*

on what after all to the discipline of history is an important question – that of history's relation to the past – saw the consumption of history by a nonprofessional public as regressive. In so doing, it might be argued, they ignored the myriad ways in which amateurs and enthusiasts add to the sum of historical knowledge and how the 'heritage industry' throws up legitimate historical evidence that can be used by historians working in the academy.

Used, that is, by historians like Raphael Samuel who revived the argument, suggested in Section 1 of this chapter, that studying the consumption of the past should be part of what public history does. In precisely this spirit, Samuel undertook research in his local supermarkets. What he found were products literally wrapped in traditional images from the past and he drew conclusions from this evidence about how the past reacts with the present in contemporary culture. To Samuel, history could be done in the supermarket:

> The shelves of the supermarkets are full of newly-minted traditional goods – ploughman's pickles, 'country ales', 'Wiltshire' mustard, 'Norfolk' turkeys, and an astonishing range of technicoloured English Cheeses in which county is distinguished from county by its speckles. Sainsbury's offer 'harvest slims' crispbread and 'all-fruit preserves'. Tesco market their own farmhouse brunch. Heinz have turned from the vivid oranges and browns of their 1960s tins to the yellowy-greenery of their 'ploughman's' pickles.
>
> (Samuel, 1994, pp. 106–7)

Our apparent care for the environment was revealed in 'dolphin-friendly' tuna; county-based 'technicoloured cheeses' which emphasized local belongings and wrappings with bucolic images of England suggested our country longings. Furthermore, 'newly minted traditional goods', a contradiction between the needs of now and a longing for then – products once synthetic and flush full of chemical additives, now revealed our ecological soundness.

Samuel was undoubtedly right about the importance of consumer packaging as a sign of present-day obsessions about the past – his examples reflect the place given to tradition and are true to the time he researched and wrote his book. Now we are more likely to see products wrapped in ways that represent our aspirations for a world village or take into account our concerns for ethical or 'fair trade' products. These preoccupations will undoubtedly change again. Given that we have established that public history is concerned about uses of the past in the present, that it attempts to reach a mass audience, challenge the practices of the professional historian as expert and reconceptualize what constitutes the archive, the public historian ought to monitor the changes in the consumption of heritage. Indeed, the type of evidence suggested by Samuel makes up the very stuff of public history.

Yet a view of public history that concentrates only on heritage and the public consumption of history will fail to take account of public historians as producers of historical knowledge, non-professional historians who by the simple act of collecting artefacts or ephemera of the past have added to history as a social form of knowledge. It is to these producers of public history archives that we now turn.

13.3 Producing Public History

One way of illustrating the importance of such producers is to look at the collections of George Thomason – a seventeenth-century London bookseller and collector of political tracts from St Paul's Churchyard in London – and Robert Opie, who has collected the most astonishing archive of junk leftovers from our own consumer society. It is almost impossible to imagine a reading of the seventeenth century that does not acknowledge the importance and worth of the

Thomason Collection of Tracts held at the British Library. Now bound into about 2,000 volumes, these 22,000 pamphlets, tracts and early newspapers together give a unique account of the political and religious controversies at a moment of fundamental change in England. Thomason acted as an unofficial commentator on the unfolding drama that he himself was a witness to. He collected a remarkably diverse literature that would never have survived if he had not deferred to his own historical sensibilities, possessing the presence of mind to realize that he lived in momentous times. Nor was this collection put together without considerable financial cost to himself and with his own safety on occasions being compromised – he went to prison briefly in 1651. Faced with danger to the collection and himself, he even moved it from location to location to ensure its safety. As he collected the documents of Civil War, the rise of the Commonwealth under Cromwell, the Interregnum and finally the Restoration of the monarchy, he also annotated these printed materials. Here was a public historian providing us with documents, priceless sources that would become the basis of future histories.

In less personal danger but no less heroically, Robert Opie brought together a fantastic collection of packaging and advertising memorabilia, which, but for his determination to record the fleeting imagery of what we might consider to be everyday and mundane, might also have disappeared into the ether. His attention to the flotsam and jetsam of a consumer society and his willingness to repackage the collection as nostalgia is not, it might be argued, comparable to Thomason's efforts in the seventeenth century. Yet, his collection of drink cans, old radios, pedal cars and 'traditional' lawnmowers only hints at his contribution to the documentation of our own age and will one day prove its worth as an astonishing archive. If this collection will be a boon for historians in the future, then we have its conceptual moment articulated by Opie himself when he describes the founding of the collection on a Sunday afternoon in Aberdeen:

> It was impossible to get anything to eat on a Sunday, at least in those days in Scotland. I found a vending machine and purchased a packet of Mackintosh's Munchies and a packet of McVitie's and Price Ginger Nuts. These machines made a good sound in those days – a real 'crunch' when they came down. I got back to my room at the hotel and I was consuming the Munchies, I suddenly looked at the pack and thought, 'If I throw this away I will never, ever, see it again, and yet here is a whole wealth of history!' It was something along those lines. But you see, I was looking at the packet as if it were a stamp, something that I had been saving for thirteen or fourteen years up to this point. So I had had my 'apprenticeship' and I had come to this pivotal moment. I can virtually remember the room I was in. The sudden realization came to me that this was something I should be saving, and I thought what an enormous part of social history I was about to throw away. That packet was going to change and develop into other things. It was no longer going to be priced at seven pence, it would soon be priced at eight pence, or whatever it was. Yet I was about to throw it away, damage it. I knew I should be saving these things. The next packet was the McVitie's one. I still have these things, and they have a date on them. It still says 'wrapped in Sellophane' on them. Spelt with an 'S'! I had my training – as with Matchboxes [an earlier obsession]. I would write the prices in and the date and everything else. When I went up to my friends in Scotland, I was already saying, 'Can I have those packets?' When I got home, my mother was told about the momentous event and from that time in, I have saved every packet that I've consumed the contents of.
>
> (Elsner and Cardinal, 1994, pp. 32–3)

Clearly this is seriously obsessive behaviour, a point illustrated when he talks elsewhere in the interview about the thrill or 'the play' between 'what's useful to save and what's boring to save', emphasizing that the subject matter is not the overriding stimuli but rather the act of collecting itself. These are not the instincts of an historian or even, as we shall find out in Chapter 23, of an archivist. The result, however, is most certainly useful for historians yet to be born who will be able to enjoy a vast archive based on the cultures of twentieth-century consumption. Public history, at least in this guise, provides a useful mode of historical production, concerned as it often is with consumption patterns of the everyday, with contemporary politics and family relations. This affords angles of interpretation of sources not considered as such in the circles of traditional history.

Perhaps the most straightforward way of approaching public history is as a method to reconfigure the archive in ways done by public historians like Thomason and Opie, producing collections useful to scholars. Let us examine this point more fully by considering war games, war gamers and uses made of the past by children's board games made during the Second World War. The work of the public historian is as likely to be found in the magazines of war gamers as in the journals of the military specialist at Sandhurst, for gamers display an impressive ability to engage in complex arguments about the accuracy of the historical record and in present-day historical debate. In an edition of *Miniature Wargames* from 1980, one public historian asked whether Constantine III was 'just another usurper?' This is a question to grace any university examination paper. In another, we find history told as a narrative of flashing swords and booming guns with the rhetorical flourish at the end – 'Bloody, isn't it?' Being both informed about the conventions of an historical approach and able to make history engage and excite is one of the interesting features of public history practiced in this way. It takes precisely the approach no longer taken by school or university history departments, which may, of course, account for its popularity among a large group of people who nevertheless imbibe history in a variety of ways and work tirelessly with the stuff of the past. If nothing else, it appeals to boys:

> Personally, I am drawn to the Pechenegs (800 AD to 1050 AD). Admittedly as a nation they did inspire the proverb 'As stupid as Pecheneg', but on the other hand they did decline the orders of a Byzantine emperor to attack the Turks with the polite response that they did not wish to comply as the Turks were fierce and more numerous, and they sincerely hoped that the Emperor would be tactful enough not to mention the matter again. A glance at the Army List shows, however, that it is possible to upgrade the Pechenegs from the 'cowardly' to the 'pragmatic'.
>
> (Anon., 1989, p. 13)

And:

> If you wish to hijack the mob first both players state exactly where they want the mob to go and what they want to attack. Both then roll a dice and the winner has control of the mob which now must move to its new destination. If the loser has lost by more than 7 he is rendered limb from limb. Bloody, isn't it?
>
> (Webster, 1989, p. v)

These sources give us a strong indication of how at any moment in history the past in a dialectic relationship with the present actually plays out in areas of everyday life that would otherwise go unnoticed. Board games manufactured and played during the years 1939–1945 are sources open to interrogation from several angles. They may even take us back to our opening concern, the public manifestation of attitudes to fascism and anti-fascism in Britain that we saw writ large at the Battle of Cable Street and on the mural created in its memory. Played in the air raid shelters of the Blitz, games like 'Decorate Goering – A Party Game', 'The Allies Dart Game' and 'Chase Your Enemy' showed the German Foreign Minister Ribbentrop with a snake's body and a caveman club or Goering as a victim of a patriotic version of 'Pin the Tail on the Donkey'. Similarly, in the *Dandy* comic, Goering became Hermy in 'Addy and Hermy – The Nasty Nazis', Desperate Dan punches Hitler and anti-Italian racism (that certainly survived into our childhoods) is manifest with Mussolini portrayed as 'Musso the Wop' ('the bigger der flop'). Once again, as in the study of the Battle of Cable Street and the mural that came from the battle, the concern from a public history angle is with the event itself but also with the traces of the event in the present.

These board games work as part of a study of propaganda, of attitudes to warfare as derring-do adventure, as a study of childhood during this critical period or even, if we examine the raw materials from which they are made, an indication of the level of shortages during the conflict when the Norway campaign in 1940 cut off the supply of cardboard. They also demonstrate that the evidence for public history is (a point made by Hilda Kean in Section 2) as likely to be fished out of the attic as dug up in the more conventionally defined archive. The question that Section 4 will seek to answer is whether public history really constitutes a serious alternative to conventional historical approaches.

13.4 Public History as Contested Knowledge

David and Andrew Whelan from Leeds took out their tools for 'doing' history and made their steady way to a field somewhere near Harrogate in England. This father and son metal-detecting team from Yorkshire had already secured permission from a local farmer to scour his land for 'treasure', the sort of 'treasure' that classicists and historians working in universities prefer to call 'evidence'. On their hands and knees, they managed eventually to unearth 617 silver coins, some gold rings and silver bars, all stuffed hard into a silver vessel decorated with depictions of animals and vine-scrolls. Some coins related to Islam and came from areas that stretched from Russia and Afghanistan to Scandinavia, Ireland and the far reaches of Continental Europe. In so doing, these amateur archaeologists (as we might now think of them) added to the sum of expert knowledge, emphasizing the multicultural nature of Britain's ancient history:

> Jonathan Williams, the British Museum's keeper of prehistory and Europe, said that the 'remarkable' find shed new light on a period overshadowed by bloodshed and brutality. 'This was a crucial moment in the country we now live in,' he said. 'The treasure may have been buried for safekeeping by a wealthy Viking during the conquest of the Viking kingdom of Northumbria in AD 927 by the Anglo-Saxon King, Athelstan. He could have been killed – or even forgotten exactly where he buried it.'
>
> (*The Times*, 20 July 2007, p. 25)

From this perspective, history is as much an activity as a profession. It takes its evidence from all around, never privileging the 'official' written document over the 'unofficial knowledge' that decorates our public spaces. Public history, therefore, is practiced in the spaces that we do not recognize as relating to history at all. Could metal detecting, for instance, be credibly seen as the binary opposite of the established methods of archaeology? Could elite biographies as a way of retelling power relations be regarded as less important than family history? Professional historians view family history with scepticism for two chief reasons: first, it lacks a real overarching purpose and a necessary sense of detachment; second, it can collapse quickly into nostalgia, symptomatic of felt absences in the present. 'Top people's' biography is not treated with anything like that routine scepticism. As we know from accounts of the Labour governments in the 1960s, written in diary form or in the form of memoirs by Tony Benn, Barbara Castle and Richard Crossman, while all these people were in the same Cabinet, attending the same meetings, they gave radically different versions of events and, unaccountably, placed themselves centre stage.

We also cannot confidently know what is omitted in elite biography. The former Conservative Prime Minister John Major wrote his voluminous memoirs without ever mentioning his extramarital affair with Edwina Currie. Much of the 'contested knowledge' that Paul Martin – historian, theorist of collecting and part of the new wave in museum studies – describes in Table 13.1 is what he calls 'rarefied' approaches to the past that have been transformed by a 'popular' counterpart. Learned academic journals from a public history angle are less important to the historical public than the potted histories of a holiday destination featured by an in-flight magazine. Similarly, television programmes that invite an audience to bring along their family heirlooms or antiques for scrutiny have, at least in Britain, attracted stunning audience figures while emptying the lofts or attics of the nation. If it is true to say, therefore, that history is now popularly understood through television and film, then in this respect at least, probably the most watched 'historian' in the field today is the actor and director Mel Gibson, with his wildly inaccurate historical dramas that seek to take the lid off Jewish or Anglo-Saxon plots to domicile subject peoples.

Social sciences have been rather quicker off the mark than the arts or humanities regarding questions of cross-disciplinary activity and the use of knowledge gleaned from outside the academy. Sociologists of medicine, religion and environmental politics have all confronted the problems associated with maintaining the status of the expert: the doctor, the cleric, the scientist. Natural scientists are arguably even quicker to break down barriers between the amateur and the professional expert, a legacy, perhaps, of the gentlemen scientists of the eighteenth and nineteenth centuries. In the United States, amateur astronomers complement the academy by identifying comets, variable stars and stellar occultations; field biologists help collect data for bird counts and enumerate flora and fauna and geologists do likewise for the study of rock formations to the extent that together there is now a Society for Amateur Scientists actively engaging with professional science. In Britain, the Zoological Society of London (ZSL) regularly appeals for amateurs to join the search for dolphins, porpoises and seals in the Thames Estuary. Meteorologists rely on public feedback on weather conditions, while archaeologists have long appreciated volunteer diggers and even, as we have seen in the opening example of this section, appreciate amateurs with metal detectors as unpaid scouts for future sites. Indeed metal-detecting works within a raft of legislation and the British Council of Archaeology (Chapter 17) as the professional body of the discipline even runs workshops for enthusiasts while the National

Table 13.1 Contesting knowledge – a table of binary opposites

Rarefied domain	Popular domain
Archaeology	Metal detecting
Elite biography	Family history
Classical music	Popular music
Academic journals	Popular magazines
Classical literature	Pulp fiction
Antique appreciation	Popular collecting

Source: Martin (1999)

Council of Metal Detectors, founded in 1981, represents a host of local clubs – the USA apparently has hundreds (de Groot, 2016, p. 285).

The spin-off to all this is a welcome interest in history more generally, rather in the same way that the brass-rubbing craze of the 1960s and 1970s or metal detecting made the past genuinely popular. Brass-rubbing involved tracing the outside of tombs and monuments in order to gain a likeness, stoking a renewed public interest in heraldry and medievalism more generally. Remarkably, this practice became so popular that, in some churches and cathedrals, facsimiles replaced the originals, raising questions about how we understand the place of the 'original', thus promoting another craze of later decades: conservation and yet another area in which public history works. In the same way, public history has undoubtedly brought a new perspective to conventional historical study. It has questioned the definition of who an historian is and what history does. In this respect, it has enfranchised whole classes of enthusiasts hitherto too often summarily dismissed by professional historians.

Postscript

We have attempted in this chapter to suggest that contemporary historical practices take different forms. Usually thought of as a discipline confined to the rarefied atmosphere and structure of the academy to be pursued by appropriately qualified historians, what is often overlooked is the fact that history features powerfully in the public imagination, and there are many other 'lay' practitioners who undertake research that could be considered to be history. Indeed, before the emergence of history as a profession in the nineteenth century, most historians of repute were amateurs. Today, people who delve into their family history, community activists who attempt to reconstruct aspects of an historical event such as the Cable Street riots, writers of broadcast history programmes, local historians who explore the historical significance of particular lives or buildings and heritage workers who conduct guided tours of buildings or streets all enthusiastically practice and disseminate forms of history despite the fact that many have not been through the rigours of formal historical training.

The existence of this popular, public history has posed many challenges to history as a profession, and this has created real divisions. Some historians have welcomed the emergence of public history. For them, it has served to democratize the practice of history and to change for the better the social production of historical knowledge. There is no obvious reason, they argue, why history should be confined to the academy or for the academy to define what constitutes legitimate historical knowledge. It may be that much history was 'done' in the 'Rhodes must fall' campaigns which began at the University of Cape Town in South Africa in March 2015, spreading to Oriel College, Oxford. With statutes coming down in places like Bristol, the slave owner Edward Colston (1636–1721) was toppled and thrown into a nearby river. Meanwhile, the plinth that supports Sir Winston Churchill in Parliament Square was daubed with the word 'racist'. This was a very public and very accessible path to the past. Too much history is inaccessible since it is written for a small audience of like-minded individuals. In contrast, others argue that public history is not progressive, for it produces knowledge for a popular audience which rarely goes beyond common sense understanding. The heritage industry, for example, manufactures representations of the past for mass consumption, which, in pandering to populist nostalgia, remains conservative and incapable of critically addressing sources of conflict and dissent.

All this suggests that history matters. The huge interest in various forms of history indicates that people are attracted to stories about the past, and these are part of an endeavour to make sense of who and where they are in the present. Perhaps under these circumstances, history is too important to be left to the historians. If that is the case, we as historians have a responsibility to widen and hence democratize the production and dissemination of critical forms of historical knowledge.

Further Reading

Jerome de Groot (2016) *Consuming History: Historians and Heritage in Contemporary Popular Culture*.
John Elsner and Roger Cardinal (1994) *The Cultures of Collecting*.
Ludmilla Jordanova (2006) *History in Practice*.
Hilda Kean et al. (eds.) (2000) *Seeing History: Public History Now in Britain*.
Raphael Samuel (1995) *Theatres of Memory: The Past and Present in Contemporary Culture*.

14 Visual History

Introduction

As a discipline that emerged in the nineteenth century under the guidance of von Ranke and others, history has tended to rely almost exclusively on documentary evidence for its sources. For most historians, written documents remain the most reliable to hand and thus provide the best access to the period under study. Belatedly, however, other sources broadly considered as visual are now treated with seriousness, and so we will investigate how films, television programmes, paintings and photographs are increasingly employed as legitimate means of engaging with history. In certain respects, this is surprising given that they are generally considered as works of the imagination and therefore not 'reliable' sources. And it is true that our techniques for reading them are little developed in comparison with those we bring to bear on documentary evidence, and yet when used skilfully images can enhance the historical imagination and provide at least part of the basis for good history.

In Section 1 we discuss the considerable interest films and television exert on the popular historical imagination. Using specific examples, we investigate how they convey a sense of history and whether they can be considered as historical documents. Denying that, because they are works of imagination, they ought necessarily to be dismissed as evidence, our contention is that in particular ways they can offer valuable interpretations of historical events.

In a similar way, Sections 2 and 3 view the roles played by paintings, prints and photographs. Before the advent of moving images, paintings and prints provided some of the most eloquent representations of contemporary and past societies and as such must be taken seriously as historical evidence. In this respect they are no less reliable or 'true' than documentary evidence. But as with such evidence, we need to understand the conventions and languages used to construct them, and these skills have yet to be fully developed by historians. The final section brings up to date the importance of visual sources by surveying how video games have created fantastic virtual environments and alternative histories that have informed new audiences about the past by lighting up the historical imagination.

14.1 Visual Histories in Film and Television

David Lean's adaptation of the Charles Dickens classic *Oliver Twist*, made in England by a politically conservative director at the height of the Labour Party's power in 1948 when the modern welfare state was coming of age, said something about contemporary attitudes in post-war Britain. 'Please, Sir, I want some more', a plea from Oliver for a second helping of food, had a particular resonance when shown in the austerity of the period. It is a source, therefore, that can only reproduce an almost mythic idea of Victorian England but in so doing may say something more about attitudes to Victorianism in the postwar period.

There can be little doubt that film and television have provided the most popular access to a real or imagined past. Ever since the emergence of cinema in the early years of the twentieth century, historical themes have featured strongly. D. W. Griffith's *The Birth of a Nation* (1915), Sergei Eisenstein's *Battleship Potemkin* (1925), and Lewis Milestone's *All Quiet on the Western Front* (1930) are just three extraordinary examples of how powerful film has been in conveying representations of events from the past. Indeed, Griffith himself believed that film was so powerful that it would eventually displace books as the source of historical knowledge.

During the 1930s and 1940s cinematic depictions of the famous were in vogue as biopics including the *Private Life of Henry Eighth* (1933) and *Ivan the Terrible* (1942) received critical acclaim. In the postwar period, historical films proliferated, many of the more important of which tackled momentous events such as the Holocaust (*Schindler's List*, 1993), Vietnam War (*Apocalypse Now*, 1979), and racial segregation (*Malcolm X*, 1992). As with an iceberg, beneath these peaks lay hidden the bulk of costume dramas, parodies and biopics with little abiding artistic or historic interest.

As television came of age, it too displayed a willingness to take on historical themes with real ambition. The documentary series *The Great War* (1964), *The World at War* (1974) and *The Civil War* (1990) were by any standards milestones in televized historical documentaries. Simultaneously, British producers developed a particular skill in extended historical dramas, at the peak of which stood *The Caesars* (1968), *I, Claudius* (1976) and *The Borgias* (2013), along with many adaptations of historical dramas including *Bleak House* (1985) and more recently *Wolf Hall* (2014).

Visual history has attracted much attention from media theorists and historians. Three broad and related questions have occupied them in recent years: How do historical films and programmes reflect – and thus provide insights into – the periods in which they were made? Do films and programmes ever provide reliable historical evidence which can be taken as seriously as, say, that in documentary sources? How do such historical representations engage with the audience? Take, for example, two films with related concerns. *Little Big Man* (1970), which recounted the story of Jack Crabb – played by Dustin Hoffman – who at well over 100 years old is interviewed by an oral historian about his life among the Indians, his encounters with General George Armstrong Custer and his role as a scout at the battle of the Little Big Horn. *Dances with Wolves*, a feature film directed by and starring Kevin Costner in 1990, is a story about a Union Army Officer, Lieutenant John J. Dunbar, who, injured in a US Civil War battle, finds himself posted to the Western frontier. Here he encounters and befriends his Sioux neighbours. Both films discuss and stress the humanity of a people transformed – annihilated on occasion – by the invasion of another (European) civilization and how this common humanity is unrecognized by the conquering power. *Dances with Wolves* testifies to a post-Vietnam, post-Cold War sensitivity in late-1980s America to the role and place of minorities when faced with the overwhelming power of a 'civilized' nation. In so doing it has something to say about American attitudes towards imperialism and liberal multiculturalism in the postwar period and the folk memories of the West that survived in American society and culture.

Documentaries and news coverage have, on the face of it, fewer layers of interpretation and analysis. Surely, we are simply watching events unfolding, unadulterated and straightforward. Of course, this is rarely the case. Pathé News was a prominent voice in a range of media. After expanding to London in 1902 it continued to appear in cinemas until 1970, accumulating 3,500 hours of filmed history amounting to over 90,000 individual items, all of which is now available online and provides a wonderful resource for analysis of the genre (www.britishpathe.com).

While the newsreel is, of course, invaluable as a primary source, we as historians must decide its purpose, its audience and, in its selection of material, what it wished to convey. Most of all we have to determine, in both documentaries and newsreels, when 'fact' becomes the manipulation of fact – in short, when it becomes propaganda.

Leni Riefenstahl's *Triumph of the Will* is probably the most notorious of propaganda films. It was an account of the Nazi Party congress in 1934, and it clearly sets out to celebrate German power and the role of Hitler as its great leader and saviour. It begins in the clouds as Hitler's plane begins its descent to the ground accompanied by the strains of Wagner. Above all, its use of aerial photography, telephoto lenses and the clever movement of cameras reminds us of the importance of symbols and images. As Riefenstahl intercuts the main players such as Hitler and Hess, the use of angles and close-ups makes it a classic of the genre and above all technically and artistically advanced. We should, therefore, be routinely sceptical about documentary film as an historical source, treating it as we would any other text.

The documentary film has probably been most utilized by historians concerned with the Second World War and has been studied by Anthony Aldgate in *Britain Can Take It* (2007). The title comes from a short propaganda film, *London Can Take It* (1940), which was made under the inspired direction of Humphrey Jennings, a documentary filmmaker and a founder of Mass Observation, a research project that recorded the everyday lives of people between the 1930s and late 1950s (see www.massobs.org.uk/). As historians, what are we to make of the film? It depicts a determined people stoically facing down a merciless enemy. Employing real footage of the Blitz, it is not only a legitimate record of those days but conveys the experience in ways more expressive than the rather limited form of the written word. These images and sounds, however, are interspersed with staged scenes and scripted dialogue which might seem to compromise any sense of authenticity. Furthermore, the film was intended principally for an American audience as a means of persuading them to join the war and therefore had an American narrator as a 'neutral' observer. Ultimately, is the film a reliable record of the response of Londoners to the Blitz? We would argue that in important respects it is, but the narrative of heroic resistance must be considered against sources such as the Mass Observation archive (www.massobs.org.uk/index.htm), which suggests evidence of mass hysteria among the population and the presence of criminality, greed and selfishness – a very different picture from the received idea of wartime Britain as a plucky, united and determined nation.

Film – documentary or feature – can convey a sense of context from which historians might better understand a period or historical moment. This is nicely illustrated by two important films made during the 'sixties', part of the counterculture during this distinctive time of fundamental change (Chapter 22). *Saturday Night and Sunday Morning* was premiered in 1960 and immediately fell afoul of both national and local censors (the English county of Warwickshire banned it because the main character – shockingly – appeared to enjoy the illicit sex portrayed). Directed by a central European Jew – Karel Reisz – and produced by the future producer of the Bond franchise, Harry Saltzman, it centred upon the life and times of a working-class character played by a youthful and then largely unknown but classically trained actor, Albert Finney, who played Arthur Seaton. Its screenplay was by an equally little-known Alan Sillitoe, himself a working-class lad from Nottingham where the film was set. Seaton, a semi-skilled factory hand, looked with disdain at the older men on the production line as defeated and cowered by the depression of the 1930s and was motivated only by hedonism: 'Everything else is propaganda.' *Saturday Night* in that sense was a faithful attempt at social realism (Sillitoe used his mother's house in Nottingham for some of the key scenes) and documented accurately the changing shape of working-class communities as a greater affluence began to take hold in the postwar period.

With a co-starring role for the glamorous Rachel Roberts, *Saturday Night* also proved to be an early source for the period in that its sexuality was both overt and dismissive of conventional family structures. The last scene proved especially provocative, with Seaton and Robert's characters lying on a grass plain on the edge of the city, planning an imminent marriage. With the building of a new housing estate in the background, symbolic perhaps of the coming of a new consumer age, Arthur throws a stone in its direction and off screen we can hear the sound of breaking glass. Finney reflected in an interview in 1972 that this was the first stone thrown in a future protest against consumerism and a materialist society. Reisz, on the other hand, saw it for what it was: surrender to domestication and the last gesture of a defeated rebel. Yet, the film can serve as an historical argument about the character or the meaning of the 'sixties' and as such should be noted as a useful primary source that helps us to understand the 1960s *as* a discrete period.

Dr Strangelove or How I Learned to Stop Worrying and Love the Bomb, released in 1963, is political in another sense and frames much of what historians argue makes up the counterculture of the 'sixties' as an epoch. Directed by Stanley Kubrick, it was described by him as a 'nightmare comedy'. Its anti-war message is conveyed by the multiple roles played by Peter Sellers as the dense RAF officer, as the mad scientist and Nazi refugee and as the hapless President of the United States. Like *Saturday Night*, Kubrick's film has been presented as a leitmotif of the sixties. It resonates with the paranoia of a Communist plot to topple the free world, its Cold War rhetoric, its hope and despair surrounding the life (and then death) of a young president like Kennedy and, most of all perhaps, the realization after the Cuban Missile Crisis that the plot, which ends with country music star Slim Pickens riding a nuclear warhead into oblivion, was not so far-fetched. Historians can treat this as a legitimate source because it reflects the machinations of the Cold War itself, both its advocates and detractors, even if they are portrayed as absurd. Indeed, this very fact will give some sense to future historians how humour became a weapon of mass destruction for political or military figures who would have the general populace believe every last detail of Cold War propaganda.

Such analyses of the extent to which film reflected and represented processes of social and cultural change have in recent years been supplemented with useful questions about the process of filmmaking, the role of the studios, censorship and the state and cinema exhibition. Sue Harper and Vincent Porter's *The Decline of Deference: British Cinema of the 1950s* (2003), for example, examines production and distribution of film, finance, the use of language and reception theory (what the audiences thought about these historical 'texts'). More recently, theorists have carved open exciting new lines of inquiry into the film as history and not simply as a reflection of the broader society. Historical films have rarely been accepted by historians as proving evidence. For the most part they have dismissed the genre as historically inaccurate and unreliable and therefore not to be taken seriously. Such attitudes are beginning to change as we shall see, but in order to develop the arguments further first let us turn our attention to television.

Ken Burns' The Civil War

Over five consecutive evenings in September 1990 a documentary attracted an American audience on a scale unprecedented in the history of public television. An estimated 40 million watched Ken Burns' *The Civil War* as it recounted the story of an American conflict which had redefined the nation in the late nineteenth century and now defined it again for new generations. How did a series lasting eleven hours in total attain such phenomenal success? How does it stand as a work of history? Part of the success lay in its ability to address the concerns of generations troubled by the nation's recent part, but in part also the series clearly worked as a piece of

Figure 14.1 A scene from the decisive second battle of Fredericksburg during the American Civil War, 1863

Contributor: The Print Collector/Alamy Stock Photo

broadcast history. No one could imagine a book on the American Civil War gaining more than a fraction of the audience.

And yet in many respects the documentary was a book, only one which was read to a television audience. The text was fairly conventional as an historical narrative; indeed, an accompanying volume containing the dialogue, many of the images and four essays by historians involved was published simultaneously (Ward et al., 1990). Following a strict chronology, an authoritative narrator recounted the story of the conflict, interspersed with comments from American historians such as Shelby Foote and Barbara Fields who had acted as consultants. Occasionally, the narrative was interrupted by detours into important historical questions, for example, the origins of the conflict and the role of military technology. Although disputes over such detail in the final version erupted, few could deny this was a work of solid history, executed with consummate skill (for a critical assessment, see Toplin, 1997). Unlike a book, however, the narrative was accompanied by an astonishing visual record. Hundreds of photographs from the conflict – the first event of world importance to be captured thus – had been gathered by scouring the nation's archives, and these appeared as a slide show, without further commentary or caption but in a way that was seen to embellish the narrative. Furthermore, comments made by contemporary observers including Lincoln, Frederick Douglass, Jefferson Davis and Walt Whitman were read by well-known actors such as Morgan Freeman and Jason Robards; with the exception of the theme, the background music consisted of melodies from the time and colour images of the sites of battlefields contrasted with the black and white photographs taken 130 years earlier. The critical acclaim of the series from academics and the public alike thus derived from a beautifully presented narrative, reliable even if perhaps comfortingly conventional; its success, measured by the audience, reception and the showering of awards, suggested powerfully that the screen could be used to make history.

This does not tell the whole story, however. Ken Burns, who produced and co-wrote the series, was above all a filmmaker, and it was this background that played the decisive role in shaping the final product. As he recounted in an interview:

> I would have loved more on the congressional sorts of intrigues during the Civil War. I would have loved to do more on women and more on emancipation and more on Robert E. Lee and more on the western battles, but limitations of photographs or just time or rhythm or pacing, or whatever it is, conspired against those things. And they were there, but they were taken out to serve the demands of the ultimate master, which is narrative.
> (Burns interview 1993, cited in Edgerton, 2001, p. 306)

It was the priority given to narrative that gave rise to some of the criticism levelled by historians, especially when narrative displaced what they considered the more important role of the historian, namely, analysis of the historical record. Burns responded:

> I am primarily a filmmaker. That's my job. I'm an amateur historian at best, but more than anything if you wanted to find a hybridization of those two professions, then I find myself an emotional archaeologist. That is to say, there is something in the process of filmmaking that I do in the excavation of these events in the past that provoke a kind of emotion and sympathy that remind us, for example, of which we agree against all odds as a people to cohere.
> (Edgerton, 2001, p. 308)

These, we wish to argue, are the salient issues to be considered in understanding visual history. And they have applicability over the entire range of such histories from documentary to costume drama, from historical epic to biopic. In an influential study, Robert Rosenstone (2006) has persuasively put the case that we have to take visual histories seriously as sources of evidence. While this may run counter to all we have learnt about history since our days at school, visual histories have an increasing influence on our relationship with the past and to dismiss or neglect them is irresponsible. Truth about the past is told not merely by words on a page but also by moving images. If, however, these images cannot perform the same task as words, then the important question is not 'Do they tell the truth?' but 'What kind of truth do they tell'? Filmmakers, he insists, are historians, 'but of necessity *the rules of engagement of their works with the stuff of the past are and must be different from those that govern written history*' (ibid., p. 8, emphasis in original). While conventional historians work with evidential facts to recreate the past, filmmakers invent facts to provide an overall sense of the past and thereby to illuminate it. Much goes on in historical film that we do not yet understand fully. None strives to attain a literal truth about the past as an historian might (as if this were ever possible); rather, the filmmaker works in a 'separate realm of representation and discourse' and with a rich vocabulary of images, symbols and visual metaphors to encourage us to think and understand more about the past than we can from the ingestion of factual material. Furthermore, because the documentary evidence is limited and incomplete, aspects of human experience such as our innermost feelings are retrievable and hence transmittable only through fictionalized forms.

Recent studies have inquired into the ways in which such films operate in what are termed experiential and affective modes of historical engagement as distinct from the analytical and distanced modes found in books (Landsberg, 2015). Our senses are so assailed that we are taken in, thereby abandoning those critical faculties that are necessary for any assessment of the validity of historical representation. And yet affect can be a valuable means of conveying history, and the audience need not necessarily be naïve; if, in other words, the affective mode of engagement can be combined with the analytical, then the acquisition of historical knowledge will be enhanced.

This, surely, is the 'emotional archaeology' of which Ken Burns spoke. Film does not simply provide an image of the past; through a range of devices including image, dialogue, commentary, sound effect and music, it encourages an emotional – often a moral – engagement with that past. Underpinning the whole is a strong sense of narrative which, despite contradiction and tragic turns, offers redemption and therefore optimism about the future of the human condition. This is so of both documentaries and historical films. All too often critics make crude distinctions between the two on familiar grounds that the documentary is truthful while the film is fictionalized, but every documentary, like every history book, deploys invention, and every film can make intelligent and persuasive observations which illuminate historical contexts and events.

Francis Ford Coppola's Apocalypse Now

To illustrate these points let us return to the cinema and consider as a final example Francis Ford Coppola's epic film *Apocalypse Now*. First released in 1979, it used the narrative of Joseph Conrad's *Heart of Darkness* to follow an army captain (Martin Sheen) on a special assignment to 'terminate with extreme prejudice' a renegade Special Forces colonel Kurtz (Marlon Brando) who had set himself up as a god-like leader of a small tribe deep in the Cambodian jungle. By the time the film was released it was widely known that its production had been bedevilled with problems resulting in endless delays and a large overbudget; Coppola himself provided the funds to allow the film to be completed. Even then the release was postponed several times as Coppola struggled with the final editing. Critics were divided. Some such as the *Guardian*'s critic Philip French considered the film a towering achievement; others thought it chaotic, self-indulgent and with nothing say about the experience of Vietnam. With the passage of time allowing perhaps due deliberation, the film is now widely regarded as a masterpiece, not only winning major awards but also featuring strongly in critics lists. In 2009, for example, the London Film Critics' Circle voted it the best film of the last thirty years.

How does *Apocalypse Now* work as history? In some respects, it can be regarded as part of an increasingly critical awareness among filmmakers of the futility of the Vietnam War. *The Deer Hunter*, *Platoon* and *Good Morning Vietnam* among others exposed in their various ways the violence and degradation of the conflict. But while these were concerned above all with the *morality* of America's involvement, *Apocalypse Now* questioned its *reality*. From the opening scene when Captain Willard awakes from a drunken stupor to smash a mirror with his fist, the vision of a descent into hell constructed by the film is nightmarish and hallucinatory. Many of the characters are comic book, smoking dope and with faces painted as grotesque masks, and the aptly named Colonel Kilgore (Robert Duvall) insists on playing *Ride of the Valkyries* over loudspeakers as he leads a helicopter assault on an enemy position and later declares that the smell of napalm in the morning reminds him of victory. And at the very heart of the darkness is the brooding and enigmatic presence of Kurtz. The set scenes are highly stylized and mystical, none more so than the napalm bombing of enemy positions in the jungle or the sudden encounter at night in a clearing of a tacky show staged for the entertainment of the American troops. All this is combined with an extraordinary attention to authentic detail in the weaponry, scenery, costumes and soundscape. Ultimately, however, this does not serve to support the narrative but acts as a juxtaposition to the sense of madness at the heart of the whole experience.

Figure 14.2 Discovery of the heart of darkness in Francis Ford Coppola's *Apocalypse Now*, 1979
Contributor: Pictorial Press Ltd/Alamy Stock Photo

Little of this suggests that *Apocalypse Now* is a reliable record of the Vietnam War. Its vision is not one that could have been built from the archives. What it does is convey brilliantly the unreality, experiential madness, chaos and stupor of the Vietnam War. As Coppola himself said at a press conference following a screening at the Cannes Film Festival, 'My film is not about Vietnam. It is Vietnam'. As historians, we have some way to go before we understand better how films such as *Apocalypse Now* achieve this kind of truth and so render the past meaningful. In the meantime, however, we can speculate along with Rosenstone whether film offers a new form of historical practice. Living in an increasingly visual age, we may find that visual thinking about the past, and the use of metaphor, dream and symbol becomes more relevant than creating logical and coherent arguments from documentary data (Rosenstone, 2006, p. 163). Better still, we might hope that historians of visual history and of written history talk to each other and learn from one another.

14.2 Ways of Seeing: Paintings

The idea of a visual age is based on the premise that images rather than words or sounds dominate our senses. Television and film are a vital component of this world of imagery but of course these creative media are the products of the modern age. In a premodern world static images including paintings, photographs and prints were the visual media of the day, and hence they exerted and arguably continue to exert a profound influence on our perceptions. There is, perhaps, some truth in the adage that an image is worth a thousand words, for images can bring us face-to-face with the past in ways words cannot. This applies to evidence on aspects of everyday life such as clothes, villages, the interior of houses, faces and processes of production that are rarely described in texts, as well as on the belief systems of societies which images have promoted with considerable power, particularly when the majority of the population could neither read nor write.

Clearly, we face a choice about how we deploy visual sources: Are they a 'snapshot' or 'mirror' held up to reality *or* visual evidence in the form of conventions and symbols which the historian can unpick? Too often, it has been argued, historians have been content to settle on the former, to see visual evidence as simply evidence that reflects or illustrates reality. Here visual sources are minimized in importance, appended to the narrative as a way of giving life and colour to the more serious matter of the written text but not used as evidence. More profitably, visual evidence can be read as a series of signs: the portraits of a king or the photograph of an American Civil War battlefield are raked over for tell-tale symbols of everyday life and mores. The dress and deportment of a leader – from the posture of Elizabeth I to Mussolini, the Italian fascist leader, jogging bare-chested – tell us much we need to know, it would seem, about femininity and masculinity in their clothes, posture or deportment at these very different historical moments. Or about class: the aristocracy in photographic portraits tended to steer their gaze away from the camera while the working class or the poor looked straight down the lens. There is then more to visual sources than the opportunity to bolster an historical narrative researched in conventional ways. Historians need to peel away the layers to reveal a story to be told.

The act of 'eyewitnessing' performed by images predates the written word (Burke, 2001). Cave paintings are the earliest and perhaps most obvious example, but there has been since then a continuous use of visual imagery across cultures. It is important to remember, however, that this record has been shaped by revolutionary transitions, for example, when the invention of woodcuts provided artists with the opportunity to produce multiple printed images or when photography provided both reproducibility and a degree of verisimilitude previously unattainable. A vast literature has addressed the question of how images created meanings and opined on their artistic merits; important though some of it is, we are more interested here in whether such images are legitimate sources of historical evidence and, if so, how they may be approached.

As we have already seen, because of the privileged role of the written and printed word in historical work, other potential sources of evidence have been neglected. This has meant that visual images have rarely been taken seriously and in turn that the techniques appropriate for their analysis remain relatively underdeveloped. And yet the questions we need to ask of visual images are precisely the same:

- How, when, why and by whom was the image created?
- How does the image relate to the historical reality it seeks to represent?
- How was the image perceived by contemporary observers?

Images are not neutral or innocent records of the events that they seek to describe. No matter how accurate their creators strive to be, artists, engravers and photographers inhabit mindsets that shape their points of view. Consciously or otherwise, they follow distinctive genres or produce images which through a process of inclusion and exclusion selectively appropriate what they see. It is tempting, for example, to see artistic portraits created during the classic period of European art as reliable representations of their sitters. We think here of the wonderful portraits by masters including Rembrandt, Rubens, William Hogarth and Joshua Reynolds and Thomas Gainsborough. As it developed as a genre, however, portraiture tended to follow distinct conventions that changed little over time. In addition to any desire to present a flattering portrait, the composition of the whole, the staged postures and gestures of the sitters, their costumes and the paraphernalia that often accompanied them were imbibed with symbolic meaning. Monarchs and male aristocrats evoked the symbols of ancient Rome in order to convey a sense of power and statesmanship, while their female equivalents tended towards purity, respectability and virtue, as exemplified by the elaborate iconography displayed by the portraits of Elizabeth I (Figure 14.3).

No matter how realistic such portraits are, therefore, we cannot think of them as reliable records of the past; they are necessarily highly selective and distorted representations of historical reality. Does it follow that they are therefore of little value as historic evidence? On the contrary, such images provide us with access to the mentalities, senses of identity and ideologies of the age. As a means of exploring further ways in which images have been used to shed light on historical episodes, consider Marcus Wood's *Blind Memory* (2000), which detailed the visual representation of slavery in Britain and the United States over 1780–1865 (when the slave trade was finally abolished in America). Wood argued that even though much of the vast historiography of slavery uses images, these are rarely subject to the close critical reading employed on written sources. Maybe, he reasoned, this is because there abides a questionable belief that pictures speak for themselves or that only a tiny proportion of this imagery can be thought of as high art. To overcome this neglect, he embarked on an analysis of oil paintings, rough wood cuts, graphic satire, photographs, book illustrations and advertisements, all of which helped to represent the slave trade, the enslaved and the enslavers. From the outset, however, he faced a dilemma: can art that attempts to describe horrors such as slavery be understood using aesthetic criteria? His answer is yes, but there are limits, for the actual experience of those enslaved stays beyond our comprehension, for ultimately the imagery was created by whites.

Harriet Beecher Stowe's *Uncle Tom's Cabin* is included in the case studies. The book appeared in 1852 and has been regarded as one of the most significant and popular statements on slavery. Wood is interested in how the power of the novel was 'drowned in a visual rhetoric of colossal vulgarity' (p. 143), that is, how the illustrations helped to convey representations of black slaves in ways which were more telling than the written text itself. Indeed, the imagery transformed the book and in so doing provided genuine insight into how English and American audiences wished to remember slavery and how it shifted the language of racism in the mid-nineteenth century.

Figure 14.3 The 'Darnley Portrait' of Elizabeth I by an unknown artist *c.*1575, which was used to promote her mythical status as the virgin goddess Astreia

Contributor: Digital Image Library/Alamy Stock Photo

Paintings (like film and documentary) are therefore cultural texts – imaginative, yes but possessing a language, sense of narrative and symbolism which reflected or challenged broader societal values. The task of the historian is to read paintings as a means of revealing precisely how they operated to create ranges of meaning for the audience. To take another genre, consider the important body of work that was produced at the time of the Industrial Revolution. What kind of records were these paintings? Were they reliable records of the experience, or did they attempt to express either the sense of wonder or horror that greeted the Industrial Revolution? Did, for example, the landscape of industrialization with its fearsome and noisome machinery pumping out black, fetid pollution evoke feelings of awe and terror in the same way that human beings would once have responded to the power and might of nature? And how far can we go in suggesting that the idea of an Industrial Revolution was constructed through its representations? In other words, have we understood the Industrial Revolution not through the data collected by economic historians but through the more evocative images (and text-based reportage for that matter) that accompanied it?

The imagery of industrialization has been explained in magisterial detail by the art historian Francis Klingender (1907–1955), who in his *Art and the Industrial Revolution* (1972) comprehensively recorded expressive aspects of the rise of industry. From John Constable's *Chichester Canal* in 1828 to J. M. W. Turner's *Rain, Steam and Speed* (1844), which terrifyingly portrayed a new-fangled steam train at full throttle (perhaps at 30 miles per hour) or the science-based paintings of a prominent member of the Birmingham-based Lunar Society of scientists and industrialists, Joseph Wright of Derby, to the nightmarish visions of 'Mad' John Martin who sketched industry on a biblical scale as a vision of Hell, it is clear that artists responded in very different ways to the new age of industry and science, and from these responses we can gain insight into some of the hopes and anxieties of the nation as a whole.

Industrial scenes were first painted during the Reformation when aristocratic Catholicism was challenged by popular currents intent on asserting the dignity and self-sufficiency of labour (Klingender, 1975, pp. 57–9). From early in the sixteenth century, workshops, blast furnaces and mines began to feature in European painting. Any hope, however, that these paintings provide reliable guides to the nature of early industrialization is mitigated by the fact that they featured mythological figures such as Venus, Cupid and Vulcan as well as Roman landscapes to render a sense of the momentous changes afoot. The decisive shift occurred with Valesquez. In 1630 he painted *The Forge of Vulcan*, which, while depicting the smiths' bodies and tools with dramatic realism, included the mythic messenger as a surprise visitor. At the height of powers in 1657 he chose in the *Tapestry Weavers* to abandon completely any reference to mythology and thereby create one of the earliest and greatest images of industrial production. When Joseph Wright, arguably the first painter to represent the spirit of the Industrial Revolution, set out, he inherited this tradition. The *Blacksmith's Shop* (1770–1771) draws heavily upon figures and scenes found in paintings of the Italian Renaissance, somewhat incongruously combining classical illusion with realist detail (Figure 14.4). Later, in *The Iron Forge*, Wright also abandoned mythic references, preferring instead to focus on the workers involved in the manufacturing process.

As a counterpoint to such expressions of industrialization, it is worth looking briefly at how rural labourers were depicted. The Industrial Revolution was accompanied by a transformation in the British agricultural economy. The so-called age of improvement witnessed the introduction of new technologies into the countryside, rationalization of productive relationships through 'scientific management', enclosure of land and the displacement of rural labour from farms to the large urban centres. These forces were met with determined resistance by labourers, who sought to defend age-old customary practices and rights which had provided them with a degree of security against the encroachment of a new system that led increasingly to uncertainty

Figure 14.4 Joseph Wright's *The Blacksmith's Shop*, 1771, an early depiction of the process of industrialization
Contributor: Artokoloro/Alamy Stock Photo

and poverty (Thompson, 1963). How, then, were these changes represented by the foremost painters of the rural landscape? The answer is that they simply were not, at least not directly. In the paintings of George Morland, Thomas Gainsborough and John Constable we see for the most part images of a stable, ordered and peaceable society which helped to create a 'mythical unity' (Barrell, 1980). Although working firmly within the tradition of landscape art, these three broke with the convention of depicting rural labour. Previously, the great pastoral artists such as Claude Lorrain (Chapter 14) and Nicolas Poussin had treated human figures simply as sources of colour rather than detailed interest; English artists, on the other hand, strove for a much more acute sense of realism by including recognizable details of tattered clothes and boots, faces and the agricultural implements being used. However, in complete contrast to the commissioned portraits of large landowners, for example, Gainsborough's '*Mr and Mrs Andrews*', in which gentry were larger-than-life figures presiding over the countryside, rural labourers were shown as honest, cheerful and industrious figures, located firmly in the background. What does such imagery reveal to historians about contemporary attitudes and concerns? According to John Barrell (1980), the gradual erasure of rural labour from the landscape, their powerlessness to determine the 'meaning' of the culture of the countryside, is evidence that by the nineteenth century the rural labourer is no longer regarded as the typical English worker. Interest had shifted to the industrial worker upon whose shoulders the progress of the nation depended but whose capacity for resistance threatened that progress (ibid., pp. 32–3). Furthermore, the intimate relationship they have with the natural world expresses a consensual harmony in the class relationships of the countryside which acted to mask the tensions of the eighteenth century and to help create a new rural order without such injurious divisions.

14.3 Ways of Seeing: Prints and Photographs

In marked contrast to paintings, prints were multiply reproduced and therefore tended to reach a much wider audience. Perhaps because of this, prints – either as stand-alone editions or as book illustrations – are generally viewed as lesser works of art. It is true that cheaply produced prints were crude and had no detectable artistic merit, but the best engravings were works of considerable skill and complexity, and in figures such as Thomas Rowlandson, James Gillray, George Cruikshank and William Hogarth resided a brilliant tradition of graphic satire. How are such prints to be read by historians? Were prints ever more than decoration to the weightier texts? If so, how did they contribute to the messages being conveyed?

In a review of recent studies of British print culture, the cultural historian Roy Porter once pleaded 'Would there were schools of "visual history" paralleling "oral history"!' (Porter, 1988a, p. 186). This at a time in the late 1980s when the images seemed at last to be taken seriously. But Porter remained pessimistic, declaring that 'if historians have become more sensitive to juxtaposing what people said against what they read, we still have a long way to go in "seeing" what people saw, and in interpreting the significance of visual signs'. He proceeded to map out an agenda for understanding the historical significance of prints, which is relevant to this day.

It was no accident that literary historians first persuaded us of the importance of the visual; text and image were never alternatives or rivals for the attention of the public. Nor was it ever the case that words were for the literate while prints targeted those who could not read. Generally, illustrated books, chapbooks, broadsheets and ballads strove with varying degrees of success to bring together text and image and as such tended to aim for a popular, literate audience. And since printmaking demanded time and skill, the production and consumption of prints were normally restricted to the metropolis.

What, therefore, is the value of prints to the historian? In certain respects, the issues raised by this question are similar to those related to paintings. No print can be seen as an innocent, direct and authentic record of the historic moment. Representations of, say, the dandy or the pauper, let alone a Frenchman or Irishman, drew upon a stock repertoire of stereotypical images. Furthermore, no less than a painting, a print was deeply embedded in aesthetic, ideological and political currents; indeed, many prints from the genre of graphic satire consciously promoted political agenda. Whether they influenced public opinion or merely preached to the converted will have to remain an open question, but it is worth bearing in mind that many politicians including Charles James Fox and William Pitt in the eighteenth century feared the damage from being lampooned in prints more than that inflicted by disparaging remarks in parliament.

Despite these problems, cultural historians have found ways to tap into the potential offered by prints. Take, for example, Linda Colley, who in her influential study *Britons* (1992) skilfully employed them to reveal the ideological underpinnings of British national identity (Chapter 4). In 1774 John Dixon published a mezzotint in which Father Time gives a magic lantern show in the unlikely setting of a cave to a small, assembled audience comprising allegorical maidens who represent England, Ireland, Scotland and America (Figure 14.5). The image projected by Time is that of a brilliant future in which an angelic host banishes forever the forces of darkness and evil. Britannia smiles at the prospect while Hibernia at her side gestures happily to the victory secured over dissent and discord. Sitting aside from this contented group, however, is an enigmatic figure representing the American colonies. Dressed as a Native American armed with a bow, brown skinned and with her face obscured, she is a troubling, shadowy presence that spatially, culturally and politically remains distant from the reach of the British empire. Just over a year after the print appeared, the first shots were fired by American colonists at Lexington, and the war of independence began in earnest.

Figure 14.5 'John Bull and the Sinking Fund', the brilliant satirist James Gillray's cartoon showing how Britain's wealth was being plundered by a profligate establishment, 1807

Contributor: Heritage Image Partnership Ltd/Alamy Stock Photo

Print culture was also vital in attempts to capture the landscape of the big city at a time of industrialization, and here the pictorial record offers a stark reminder of its limitations as historical evidence. Understandably, London dominated the attention of illustrators from the late eighteenth century, but paradoxically the vivid literary descriptions of the city's modernity were not accompanied by the same impulses to express its human profusion and diversity (Potts, 1988). Reflecting sentiments that defined the age of improvement, influential pictorial surveys such as T. H. Shepherd's *Metropolitan Improvements* (1828) and *London and its Environs* (1830) represented the streets and built environment of London as spectacular, ordered, rational and almost devoid of human bustle. Above all, by focusing on prominent buildings and streets, they offered celebratory accounts of the transformations in the physical landscape which contemporary London was experiencing, presenting a largely mythic picture of splendour and uniformity. It was as if the medium was unable to escape from the traditions of picturesque topography which had dominated prints of the eighteenth century. Completely absent was any sense of the sprawling and ragged areas behind many of the streets featured. Only with the publication over 1841–1844 of Charles Knight's six-volume *London* do literary and pictorial narratives begin to converge, for here there is an attempt to capture working-class districts which remained largely unaffected by the impulse of improvement. It was, however, a vision which failed to draw the moral and political lessons from the extraordinary disparities between rich and poor London; that had to wait until the 1870s when Gustav Doré began to publish shocking prints depicting the gloom and despair of the city's notorious slum areas.

Consider also the tradition of radical satire that sprang to life in the era of the American and French revolutions and gave rise to some of the most memorable prints. During this tumultuous period a large market developed for political prints. Most were expensively produced and hence beyond the means of the poor, but they were often displayed publicly in coffee houses, taverns and shop windows and so reached a wide audience. Their political tone was overwhelmingly in support of the American War of Independence, but when the events of the French Revolution unfolded and fears of a French invasion intensified, political support for the government increased dramatically (Wood, 1994, pp. 58–9). Sympathy for the American cause derived from the belief that Americans were in reality Englishmen struggling to free themselves from a tyrannical government which restricted their freedom. Invective was directed against government ministers who were held responsible, military leaders and eventually the king himself. So vicious were some of the characterizations that, had it chosen, the government could have brought charges of libel, but it was reluctant to bring the prints to court as evidence, so providing them with further publicity.

It was during this campaign that the wayward genius James Gillray developed his unique style, later to create a body of prints unrivalled in their skill and imaginative power before his descent into insanity. Gillray elevated into a fine art the use of distorted caricature, sophisticated narrative, minute detail and brilliant metaphor which was endlessly imitated by his successors (Figure 14.6). As a political satirist, however, Gillray has resisted all attempts by historians to categorize him as radical or loyalist. If his attacks on establishment figures place him in the radical camp, then how is his furious denouncement of French revolutionaries to be explained? It is known that at the time he was in the pay of government and therefore open to the charge of selling his talents to those who offered most. It is certainly the case that print makers made little money and often resorted to other means of raising money, including the publication of bawdy materials which always found a ready market, but it is more likely that Gillray simply stood above political cause, delighting instead in the indictment of indiscriminate violence no matter what its source. Such considerations suggest the intricacy necessary in reading his prints and by extrapolation those of the wider radical tradition.

Figure 14.6 John Dixon's 1774 mezzotint *The Oracle*, suggesting the threat posed by the thirteen colonies to the British Empire

Contributor: Artokoloro/Alamy Stock Photo

In making possible the faithful reproduction of images, print making revolutionized visual culture, particularly in the late eighteenth and early decades of the nineteenth centuries when it was at its height. The evident success of print making, however, led to its ultimate demise, for the technological developments it had pioneered laid the foundations for photography, which from mid-century exerted an increasing influence on the visual arts.

The camera never lies, we are told; after all, photography is a purely physical and chemical process in which the object is imprinted faithfully on a light-sensitive film or plate, then to be printed onto photographic paper. When in the late nineteenth century scientists turned enthusiastically to photography as a means of capturing aspects of the human body, they did so because it was considered capable of representing the truth. The very process of creating a photograph through 'neutral' optical and chemical mechanisms was seen as natural and therefore guaranteed scientific truth. The photograph, unlike the artistic painting, spoke for itself. In certain respects, of course, the photograph had distinct advantages over painting. Those recording industrial scenes of the late nineteenth century, for example, provide us with a more reliable, detailed and comprehensive view of the machinery of cotton manufacture than do paintings of the time. So marked was its ability authentically to reproduce the object that when photography emerged as a cultural form, artists feared that it would consign them to an irrelevance. Happily, this never happened, largely because the historical veracity of photographs came under critical scrutiny. It was recognized that photographers, like painters, worked within distinct genres or deliberately constructed images to engender particular responses from their audience. Family portraits often followed the convention of painting and used fake backgrounds to enhance the effect. Many photographs of pauper children on the streets of Victorian London were staged by charitable organizations as a means of raising money. The 'street Arabs' photographed were ordinary children who were hauled into a photographers' studio, had their faces blacked and were made to dress up in ragged clothes and shoes.

The important point here is that having selected the subject, photographers worked selectively on the image they wished to capture and preserve. The creation of an image, however, does not stop with the flick of the shutter, for with the coming of the digital age, photographers could manipulate captured images in a remarkable number of ways. Note also what powerful associations are transmitted by the colours of the photograph itself. Images printed on sepia paper tended to engender a nostalgia for scenes, events and persons in an irretrievable past, while black and white photographs, widely used in newspapers, convey a sense of a harsh but authentic past in an authoritative way. Colour photographs are somehow 'new' and because of that seem less able to command historical authority.

Photography then is not the simple recording of a factual subject; it is just as open to manipulation as any work of art and its provenance is every bit as significant. It is important here to remember that the rise of photography in the second half of the nineteenth century was intimately connected to the emergence of new practices of observation and record keeping which were integral to institutions designed to regulate and discipline. In this respect, photography was bound up with power. The police, prisons, mental asylums, schools, hospitals and factories all pioneered photography as a means of monitoring and surveillance (Tagg, 1988). The photographs they gathered were generally considered reliable records which, if necessary, could be submitted as evidence in courts of law, the press or respectable criminological, sociological and medical journals. The taking of such photographs, however, was a highly structured process in which criminals, paupers, patients and colonial peoples were required to adopt particular, formal poses rendering them as passive objects of knowledge and devoid of agency.

In one important respect, however, photographs have transformed our ways of seeing. This was one of the arguments taken up by the art critic John Berger in *Ways of Seeing* (1990). Written in the wake of a 1970s television programme of the same name, the book was heralded as a path-breaking response to Kenneth Clark's magisterial but more traditionally minded television series *Civilization: A Personal View*, which was first broadcast in 1969. For Berger, photography had irrevocably changed our perspective. Unlike, say, an artist painting a portrait that stands staring at us and us at it, the camera provided the potential to subvert previous constraints of time and space by constantly changing the angle of vision. There was no longer a static centre to our gaze but a centre that moved. It is true that artistic movements such as Impressionism and Cubism also sought to confront the relative lack of mobility of paintings, but with photography came the ability for subjects to be recorded and looked at in close detail or one part of the subject to be juxtaposed with another or even another image introduced altogether. Furthermore, in arguments which drew upon the work of the cultural critic Walter Benjamin, Berger argued that the camera changed the ways in which paintings were viewed. Before photography a painting was unique, often an integral part of where it was housed, and because of this it possessed auric qualities, that is, the appeal derived from authenticity. This uniqueness is destroyed by photography for now reproductions of the painting enter the public and domestic realms; whereas previously the viewer travelled to the painting, the reproduction travels to the viewer.

What, then, is at stake in using photographs as historical evidence? In approaching them we need to challenge any notion that they possess a naturalness or neutrality. Every photograph – whether a mug shot, a family portrait, an urban scene, or an image of war – is of a particular moment and space and bears the imprint of the conditions of production, the conventions and genre that shaped its composition, lighting and so on and the economic, social and political realities that determined the reasons behind its creation. In this sense, a photograph is less historical evidence than the historical process itself. We cannot use photographs as unproblematic sources of evidence that reveal a 'reality'. Rather we must ask why they were taken, by whom, under what conditions, what choices were taken and for what reason, for whom they were intended and how they might have been read.

Take, for instance, the astonishing photography of the Vietnam War. It has been estimated that around 58,000 Americans and close to 2 million Vietnamese were killed in the conflict. In certain respects, the war was also played out on a domestic front; so far approximately 750 novels, 250 feature films, 100 shorts and nearly 1,500 personal recollections of one sort or another have appeared. The war, at least a popular notion of the war, was thus created and recreated in many senses through its representations, which included photography. Photographers did not simply record the horror of Vietnam, but in many ways they were also combatants. Reporters were given free access to the conflict in a way that is now unthinkable, and in the process many of them lost their lives, including Britain's Larry Barrows and America's Robert Capa. One war photographer who survived and whose extraordinary work remains for the scrutiny of the historian is Don McCullin, whose book *Sleeping With Ghosts* (1996) reveals the power but also the limitations of a history of war using photographs. A review of the book identified well some of the problems faced by McCullin in his attempt to document the conflict:

> McCullin doesn't shoot propaganda photos; in fact, his purpose is to show the horror of the conflict. But the nature of the job determines the side he shoots from. He is there for the duration of the assignment, and then goes onto the next one. He photographs some of the most political moments in history, but the nature of the job requires disconnecting the politics, and the images of them, from the politics which produce them.
>
> (www.dbacon.igc.org/Art/03PolWar.html)

So, here again there are questions to be asked about the role of the photographer. It was not merely that many of the photographs appear to be 'over composed' but also that McCullin got too close to the American soldiers and that his camera was too sympathetic to their plight. Conversely, there might be an argument that as a professional photographer on an assignment, McCullin remained too detached, with war treated merely as a landscape, like his beloved Somerset in England's West Country where he was to retire or the urban landscapes of his impoverished London youth.

We have argued in these sections that visual images can provide valuable historical evidence. The arguments and examples presented suggest strongly that when used with due care, paintings, prints and photographs serve well to enhance the source material of historians. To do so, however, we need to sensitive to the analytical skills required, many of which have heretofore been rather neglected. Peter Burke (2001, pp. 187–8) has usefully summarized some of the issues that we should routinely address:

- Visual images provide evidence of aspects of past human activity including dress, the built environment and work processes and insight into contemporary attitudes towards, for example, the aristocracy, labourers, revolution and national identity.

256 *Varieties*

- Such imagery, however, must be placed firmly in context. Political, cultural and economic influences were all brought to bear on the creation of images, and we should recognize that conventions played a major role in determining modes of artistic expression.
- In order better to capture the complex realities of historical situations, we need to investigate as full a range of contemporary images as possible.
- Historians should be aware of what we might call the unwitting testimony of visual images. In addition to the principal messages conveyed by images, we need to read for clues contained within intimate details, many of which were probably not consciously created by the artists.

Does what is true for visual technologies that have variously been with us for some time remain true for much newer ways of seeing the past and representing history? In order to address this question, we shall now have to disappear into the labyrinth of the modern video game. We shall start at the first level.

14.4 Playing With History: the Rise of the Video Game

The advent of the computer game can probably be dated from 1940 with the Westinghouse display of the 'Nimatron' at the World's Fair held in New York City, an electronic machine capable of playing a human opponent at the ancient game of Nim. The 'father of the video game', however, was Ralph Baer (1922–2014), a German-Jewish émigré to the United States from pre-war Cologne. His Magnavox Odyssey was the first home video games system. Released in 1972, it sold 333,000 units and was the first generation of games console. At the time of writing (2022), we are now in the ninth generation. The technical or commercial details of gaming need not concern us; instead, our intention in this brief overview of video games is to emphasize how such a medium can prove to be an enriching tool when visualizing or reimagining History. We shall organize these games into strands and discuss each in turn. Some of these areas overlap, but no matter.

Historical Saga

The first strand is the historical saga or chronicle that tells a story of characters and themes over a long period; indeed, the idea of the saga is taken originally from the Viking or Icelandic stories. Most of these games are set in the past and contain 'levels' or 'missions' that are based on historical fact despite being created around a fictional character(s). So, for example, the Bay of Pigs or 'Operation 40' sequence in *Call of Duty Black Ops* employed a narrative that is loosely factual. The player is able to take part in the failed assassination attempt of Fidel Castro during the Bay of Pigs invasion despite their character (Alex Mason) being entirely fictional. Another shooter-style franchise, *Sniper Elite*, allows the player to assassinate Hitler; something that, of course, departs from the historical record. Following the chronology of the Second World War itself, Sniper Elite 5 (published in May 2022), takes us to France in 1944: 'As part of a covert US Rangers operation to weaken the Atlantic Wall fortifications along the coast of Brittany'. Here our marksman hero, Karl Fairburne, as American as apple pie (although we learn in the narrative that he is German born but 'has picked a side'), makes contact with the French Resistance. Square jawed, short tempered but as cool as a cucumber, the French allies are also likely to be not entirely bereft of stripey jumpers, berets or even the odd string of onions around their Continental necks. Now the realism is checked. While sites of battle in the American-sponsored coup in 1961 are not real, the hardware that the CIA and others use (weaponry and so forth) is highly accurate and this is also true of *Sniper Elite*. In both examples, the ultimate historian's fantasy is alluring – to almost travel in time – but also the nightmare of changing history in a way that would set off an unknowable chain reaction of events.

Sometimes fictional characters may encounter real historical characters and are charged with real historical missions (Paul Revere's Midnight Ride in *Assassins Creed 3* is a good example). Indeed, the *Assassins Creed* franchise is probably the best example of how historical record can interact with fictional narratives within the game genre of historical saga. As a generational drama played out between liberty and the enemies of liberty (The Assassins versus The Knights Templar), historical periodization is used as an active backdrop over time. Interestingly, this moral designation can lend an alternative perspective of historical figures widely accepted as being 'good' or 'bad'. For example, Alfred the Great, seen through the Viking protagonist's eyes in *Assassins Creed: Valhalla*, is portrayed as understandably less 'great' than his epithet suggests. After all, there is a reason that Alexander III of Macedon was called 'the accursed' rather than 'the great' by his conquered Persian rivals. This notion, of course, is not unique to 'viewing' history through video games; as historians we must be constantly vigilant in assessing the viewpoint from which our sources come. For example, it has often been posited that the Borgia's infamously cruel reputation has been borne from a concerted effort by other wealthy noble families of the time to besmirch their name. By the application of a storyline borrowed from science fiction (the detail here is not important) where the future seeks to observe the past, our heroes and their adversaries in *Assassins Creed* pop up variously in the twelfth-century Levant, Renaissance Italy, the sixteenth-century Ottoman Empire of Suleiman I (1494–1566), the American Wars of Independence (reference the Paul Revere example), the Golden age of Piracy, the French Revolution in Paris, Victorian London, Ptolemaic Egypt, Ancient Greece and most recently (2020) Viking England.

Hence fictionalized characters merge with fictionalized scenarios, although material culture is often represented accurately such as High Renaissance architecture or steam-driven locomotives. This action is also interspersed with well-known historical actors from Machiavelli to Karl Marx. The narrative content, however, can often be seen as lacking in the details of the historical events themselves but, more seriously, storylines can also have gaping holes in the representation of period and place. The historian Alana Harris reminds us, for instance, that the nineteenth-century metropolis as portrayed by *Assassins Creed: Syndicate* seems quite deficient in some elements of the capital which really should have been included in the post Second Reform Act period (after 1867) such as – disturbingly – evidence of prostitution, feminist agitation and evidence of popular politics or radicalism more generally. Instead, child labour is overexposed in a way that reinforces received notions of the period. Yet, as she says, *Assassin's Creed: Syndicate* has a truly arresting visual representation of Victorian London that almost transports the player:

> The amount of detail, the aesthetic, the meticulous attention to the roofscapes and chimney stacks, I think it's beautiful. In many ways there's a lot to it if you have a sufficient grounding to be able to decipher, unpack, augment and supplement what's here, but it works on a fairly superficial level of engagement.
>
> (*The Guardian*, 9 December 2015)

Well, we might respond by saying that it's only a game. We would, however, be wrong to make light of video games that have historical themes such as these – the influence that they can bring to bear on the visualization of history remains extensive and important.

Historical Re-enactment

Some games stay closer to the historical truth. Produced by the French developers Ubisoft (who employ historians as translators of historical documents and as consultants to ensure a degree of historical accuracy), *Brothers in Arms* is the series that follows the progress of the real-life 502nd Parachute Infantry Regiment, part of the 101st Airborne Division, from the D Day invasion of June 1944. Like *Assassins Creed*, the built (or destroyed) environment is breathtakingly detailed in the sense that it can immerse the player. Buildings and landmarks such as churches and town halls become battlegrounds that disintegrate under fire but are topographically accurate. Here the Allies and the German armies clashed in what was the struggle for western Europe. These places are made real because the producers and developers of the game researched contemporary maps to ensure authenticity. In addition,

> Gearbox, the developer, took the time to go to France and record the exact layout and look of the scenery, to trace the steps of the soldiers who fought there. They've interviewed the veterans, shot the actual weapons, hired military advisors, and based the game's levels on period aerial photography. This attention to detail marks it out from other games and sets a historical tone which seeks to take you back in time rather than place you on a film set.
> (Review by Philip Morton, April 2007, www.thunderbolt games.com/review/brothers-in-arms-road-to-hill-30)

There are a host of other war games such as *Battlefield*, *Call of Duty*, and *Medal of Honor*. They have allowed us to travel back to 1942, to Vietnam, and then forward decades to an imaginary war and back again to the more recent past, fighting the Taliban. In comparison, *Brothers in Arms* grips far more emotionally, precisely because it strives towards a greater level of historical truth and social realism (its sound effects alone could bring on virtual shellshock) that makes the others appear positively 'Hollywood' by comparison. Similarly, *Battlefield 1* (2016) by Electronic Arts was launched on the 100th anniversary of the Battle of the Somme, which takes the player into the trenches and tanks but swaps identity at the point of death in the game from one actual combatant (with names and terminal dates) to another. Personal engagement is also foregrounded in *JFK Reloaded* (2004), which invited the player to take the role of Lee Harvey Oswald and then to be scored based on how close the player got to assassinating Kennedy as it was reported to the real-life Warren Commission. It was released to coincide with the anniversary of the death of Kennedy and as such was controversial. Other games that rather uncomfortably recreated historical incidents but with a reconstructed twist include *Super Columbine Massacre RPG!* (2005), which, while initially following the events of the Columbine Massacre in 1999, takes a supernatural turn following the suicides of the perpetrators and their journey through perdition.

Past Regarding

Some games generally ignore historical events but make up for it in social, economic and political authenticity. *Red Dead Redemption* and its prequel *Red Dead Redemption 2* are set between 1899 and 1911 at a moment of historical transformation in America from the 'wild west' to a new modern world. This is captured perfectly in the game when the player wandering in an open world format is permitted to discover what is a (relatively) cosmopolitan city, with motor cars (in the case of *Red Dead Redemption*), trams and First World War weaponry. Other details become apparent such as the presence of early Suffragette movements, proponents of racial eugenics and even a climate scientist warning of the perils that such massive industry will bring to future generations. There is evidence that the silent movie is about to come into vogue.

Another good example of video games that evoke the past is the *Mafia* franchise, which is variously set between 1930s and 1960s America. Although the names used for cars, characters and places are fictional, they are all based on real designs and authentic architecture. For example, the player can shop for a new three-piece suit under the shadow of the Empire Bay Building (Empire State Building) or even drive his ageing mother to the Empire General Hospital (a faithful reconstruction of the LA City Hall). *Mafia 2* has all the ambiance of the 1940s and achieves it by having car radios playing big band, blues and jazz music; these stations adapt as the game progresses through to the 1950s. There is also a demographic element that is visually present between in-game neighbourhoods; Chinatown and Little Italy are visibly populated by the ethnic minorities that gave these areas their names. Perhaps most striking is how the game manages to convey the appalling lack of opportunities for African Americans during this period simply by designing their neighbourhoods as run down and otherwise undesirable. This detail becomes shockingly clear when the character's friend asks him to steal a car from a 'moolie' (an Italian-American racial slur for black person) just before going on a rant espousing stereotypes regarding laziness and drug-use in the black community. Again, an attention to detail is present, with the blues radio station being a clear favourite when visiting shops and bars in such areas. Similar devices are used by *Grand Theft Auto*, a series that includes a 1970s scenario. In the same way that we know *Mafia* is set in the 30s because of the clothes and music we also know that *GTA (Vice City)* is set in the 70s because of the neon lights that adorn buildings, flared trousers, afros and general disco theme.

Historical Simulations

The last type of historical video game involves simulation and tends to take anthropological and geographical approaches to the past. *Civilization* involves role play, strategy and historical scenarios. The strap line invites the player to 'build an empire that stands the test of time'. It begins around 4000 BCE and takes us to modern times, even taking in future technologies. *Europa Universalis* also invites historical thinking around colonial strategies, diplomacy, resource management and so on; however, this series is based specifically between the late Middle Ages through the Early Modern period. *Hearts of Iron* is its World War Two equivalent, made by the same developers. Such games make the aforementioned dream/nightmare of the historian a reality – to play with history and alter its outcome. Thus, if one can suspend their imagination for just a moment, we are left with a device that can answer all our historical counterfactuals or 'what ifs'. For example, what might've happened if Neville Chamberlain declared war on Nazi Germany in response to the 1938 occupation of the Sudetenland? Well according to *Hearts of Iron IV*, if Germany's war support and economy is low enough, Hitler is assassinated, and Himmler takes the reins. This is just one of many bizarre counterfactual historical scenarios that can unfold from a starting point rooted in reality. In fact, with enough tampering, players can find themselves leading a fascist Britain (Oswald Mosely as Prime Minister) into war against a Communist coalition between France and Germany. Thus, the video game evokes a more philosophical debate surrounding historiography – one of contingency and determinism. Is history pre-written, or can anything happen? The author Laurent Binet explores these very questions, imagining a reality where the attempt on Reinhard Heydrich is successful and, in his more recent *Civilisations*, imagining the invasion of Europe by sixteenth-century Inca. *Civilisation*, the game series mentioned earlier, takes these notions a step further. The player may start the game by choosing a real-life leader from history; they may choose government policies very loosely based on real moments in history (for example enacting collectivization or serfdom to boost agricultural output) however, unless specifically playing on an 'earth' map, the geography will be entirely randomized. This leads us to notice the enormous effect that geography (and therefore resources) can have on a civilization; fighting without iron is difficult, feeding a population in a desert is hard and so on and so forth. Again, questions of contingency and determinism are thrown in our faces. Who would Trajan (a Roman Emperor) have been without horses and Cleopatra without a river?

Postscript

For the majority of people, a sense of history is not acquired through books written by trained historians but at school and through various visual media. We make no apology for devoting the most attention in this textbook to such scholarly books, for these are still the staple fare of history students, but it would be remiss of us not to consider at some point the more popular forms of historical production and consumption.

Thus it was that in this chapter we looked in some detail at broadcast history and how it is represented in other visual media. Anyone doubtful of the continued popularity of history need only consider just how pervasive history programmes are on television, either in the form of documentaries or fictionalized reconstructions. Compared with 'serious' books, such programmes are lightweight; indeed, they are often dismissed by historians as trivial and inaccurate on those grounds. We beg to differ. To our minds, many forms of producing history are based on the same depth of historical research and adopt the same broad narrative structures as do history books. Even films, fictionalized historical novels and video games display a profound knowledge of the context. It goes further. Most history books, like broadcast history programmes and novels, attempt to tell a good story; indeed, that is one of the great and seductive attractions of learning about the past. But films and broadcast programmes, it could be argued, are able at the same time to convey affect through sound, vision and word in an even more emotionally engaging way.

We have glanced at paintings, prints, photographs and even video games as sources of historical knowledge. We may live increasingly in a visual culture, but it is not so obvious that such images need to be taken seriously; indeed, our capacity to analyze them does not compare well with our skills in reading printed textual sources, but again, when used appropriately, they are vital sources of evidence. No image is a neutral record of the moment; all images are the product in part of generic convention, and thus they give us real insight into the mentalities and ideologies of the time. Think, for example, how landscape paintings convey a discrete range of feelings or how English prints of the 1790s reveal fissures in politics of the age.

Finally, it is apparent that among younger generations these visual media are increasingly being superseded by digital technologies. If most historians are somewhat nervous at the suggestion that television and film are legitimate sources of historical knowledge, then you might imagine their sense of disbelief that so too are, say, video games. Yet, as we have seen with video games, there is an inbuilt expectation that the player will play with context, chronologies and even facts. Well, even if such games seem remote from the strictures of historical inquiry, for legions of the young they are sources of historical knowledge. The questions are, therefore, what historical knowledge is being conveyed, and what devices are used by the games to produce it? The answers are perhaps unexpected.

Further Reading

John Berger (1973) *Ways of Seeing*.
Peter Burke (2001) *Eyewitnessing: The Uses of Images as Historical Evidence*.

Tristan Donovan (2010) *Replay. The History of Video Games.*
Francis Haskell (1993) *History and its Images: Art and the Interpretation of the Past.*
Stephen L. Kent (2001) *The Ultimate History of Video Games*, Vols. 1 and 2.
Alison Landsberg (2015) *Engaging the Past. Mass Culture and the Production of Historical Knowledge.*
Robert Rosenstone (2006) *History on Film/Film on History.*
Robert Toplin (ed.) (1997) *Ken Burns's The Civil War: Historians Respond.*
Marcus Wood (1994) *Radical Satire and Print Culture, 1790–1822.*

15 Global History

Introduction

This chapter focuses on the genre of global history. Section 1 discusses contemporary interest in globalization and investigates whether processes that operate at a global level are a modern phenomenon or have their lineages in the distant past. Although recent years have experienced an acceleration of globalization, many of the features now considered to be part of this process can be traced back to earlier periods, and it is possible to devise a periodization of global history based on such features. Section 2 develops this theme by looking at the extent to which writers of the premodern period shared a concern with thinking beyond their immediate environments, whether local or national. Here we examine the accounts of some of the great travellers who were responsible more than any others for bringing an awareness of other regions of the world to popular attention and helped to lift Europe out of what might be thought of as the insularity of medieval times. Such accounts were marginalized when history emerged as a discipline during the nineteenth century and turned its interest to nationalist narratives based on notions of the nation state that are associated with the period after the French Revolution. Finally, the chapter considers the promise of fresh approaches to global history that have appeared in the last 30 years, not only in how these accounts reveal a multiplicity of global interconnections but also in challenging views of historical change that have placed the West at centre stage.

15.1 The Challenge of Global History

It is said that on a visit to Europe in the 1960s Chou En Lai, one of the leaders of the Chinese revolution, was asked what he thought about the impact of the French Revolution. 'It is too early to say', he replied. It was a mischievous but astute observation. The revolution was of such momentous significance that its reverberations are still being felt, and these, like ripples on a pond, have extended farther and farther until they have reached every corner of the globe. He appreciated that it was merely part of a crisis which affected and was manifest in popular uprisings in many global theatres. Equally, this crisis gave birth to a host of ideas about human rights, citizenship and democracy which inform the lives of so many of us today and yet are still being contested. Chou En Lai thus revealed a sensitivity to how such events operated on a world stage and to the notion that they can only be understood in global terms.

If history has operated on the global stage ever since human societies had the potential to trade over long distances, it is only in recent years that the historiography of global history has revealed something of its potential for understanding more fully critical moments in the human story. It has done this by demonstrating that such moments were not bounded by distinct regional or national movements but emerged from complex interconnections which reached across land masses and oceans. This, therefore, is the task of global history. If we can make an important distinction, global historians do not attempt a history of the world. This has been the task of those who may be described as world historians (see later). In contrast, global histories tend to focus on a countries, regions or episodes to recognize and takes account of the contacts and connections, linkages and interrelationships that have characterized human activity over centuries and that shape patterns of historical change in all corners of the globe. What we suggest, in this chapter, is that global history is situated somewhere between the 'total' and the 'micro'. In other words, it is almost always much less than a universal history of the world but, at the same time, much more than a narrowly defined and patchwork history of a specific incident or region. Global historians strive to investigate the particular without ever losing sight of the complete whole that it inhabits.

A recent survey of the field has pointedly inquired into the value of global history (Belich et al., 2016). Dismissing those studies that seek to provide a 'history of everything, everywhere, all the time', the editors contend as an alternative that three approaches to global history hold a particular promise:

1 What is often characterized as comparative histories, that is, how different historical problems have been encountered and resolved across time, space and specialism. For example, what were the roots of industrialization, how was it experienced and with what consequences?
2 Pursuit of an understanding of the interconnectedness of historical events. How, for example, the granting of a charter to the East India Company in 1600 for monopoly trading rights in the East set in motion a chain of events – many of which were unanticipated – culminating in a new world imperial order.
3 Attempts to map the process of globalization, that is, the formation of relationships and movements that transcend regional, cultural and political boundaries to embrace at times the entire planet. Human migration is a good example here, not only to show how widespread such movements are but, equally, how far back in time they can be traced.

This chapter then explores the significance of a global imagination to the study and writing of history. Its argument is that overcoming regional boundaries which have defined much of the historiography, global history – or big history, as it is sometimes known – promises fruitful and challenging perspectives on the nature of historical change. A good point to start is Eric Wolf's *Europe and the People without History*, which opens with the following: 'The central assumption of this book is that the world of humankind constitutes a manifold, a totality of interconnected processes, and inquiries that disassemble this totality into bits and then fail to reassemble it falsifies reality' (Wolf, 1997, p. 3). First published in 1982, it is an eloquent statement of what Wolf saw as one of the crucial problems besetting intellectual inquiry, and it serves nicely as an introduction to some of the concerns of this chapter.

From some of the earliest records of human existence it is apparent that people have travelled across land masses, seas and oceans to make contact and enter into economic and cultural exchange with others. These patterns of intercourse refute any suggestion that human societies were enclosed and sealed off but instead encourage us to seek interchange and fusion. The implications of this insight are profound. First, apart from a few isolated communities, societies have existed, indeed have been actively formed, in relation to others. Second, under these circumstances, if historians try to separate societies by considering them as impervious to outside influences, then we run the risk of providing a distorted account of their identities, histories and cultures.

Wolf proceeded with examples of these 'interconnected processes'. Ecologically, New York is hit by the Hong Kong flu; European grapevines are devastated by American plant lice. Economically, when oil wells in the Persian Gulf cease production, generating plants in Ohio are forced to shut down; when the United States suffers an unfavourable balance of payments, American dollars drain into the bank accounts of Frankfurt and Yokahama; Italians manufacture Fiat cars in the Russian Federation. Politically, European wars reverberate around the world; American troops are stationed on the rim of Asia, and Finns guard the border between Israel and Egypt. Wolf chose these examples in the early 1980s; think of what has happened since then, and how the unfolding of world history around such incidents as the destruction of the twin towers in New York on 9/11, 2001, the invasion of Iraq in 2003, the banking crisis of 2007–2008 and Russia's invasion of Ukraine in 2022 has given his message even greater weight.

What may be true of the present is equally true of the past. Diseases brought by the Spanish to South America in the sixteenth century decimated the native populations; from that time, American plants such as the potato, maize and manioc spread through the Old World. Beginning with Portuguese incursion into Africa during the fifteenth century but reaching a peak in the eighteenth, enslaved Africans were forcibly transported to the New World. With the abolition of the British slave trade early in the nineteenth century, indentured labourers from China and India were shipped to Southeast Asia and the Caribbean. As a result of early contact with Asia in the sixteenth century, Europeans learnt from skilled Indians the techniques of producing fine cotton textiles and, from the Chinese, the art of making porcelain. From that time also Arabic numerals were widely adopted, and Europeans entered into a long – and deadly – relationship with Native American tobacco.

Such examples, concludes Wolf, demonstrate 'contact and connections, linkages and interrelationships'. Yet scholars who seek to understand the past choose largely to ignore them. Instead, historians, economists and political scientists take nations, separated by historical and cultural boundaries, as their paradigm. We might then well ask why an anthropologist like Wolf had such a keen sense of the importance of world histories. The argument in this chapter is that all disciplines that seek further understanding of the development of human societies, looking beyond the artificial barriers imposed by national boundaries, need to have an historical imagination, that is, a sense of historical change and how the past continues to live in the present. And it is not merely a question of taking a broader view; there is an imperative to recognize and appreciate the contribution of those who have been written out of the historical record. What does the title of his book reveal about Wolf's approach? Does it seriously suggest that peoples outside Europe have no history? On the contrary, it soon becomes clear that it is precisely the histories of those peoples that have been grievously ignored by writers of European history and now as a matter of urgency need to be placed onto the agenda.

Since the 1980s, there has been a phenomenal growth of interest in globalization. It is difficult these days to switch on the radio or television without hearing an economist, politician, sociologist or even historian talk of globalization as if it was part and parcel of conventional wisdom. More importantly, globalization has emerged as a political issue of some magnitude. When linked to war, hunger, corporate greed or ecological catastrophes, globalization has the ability to mobilize increasing numbers of activists onto the streets to campaign against what they see as the damage caused by global processes to those who live and work at the margins.

Sadly, our understanding of globalization does not quite match our enthusiasm for or against its role in the contemporary world. So what are its defining features and how does it link with the writing and understanding of history? The following have all been proposed by writers in the past 30 years and summarized by the political theorist David Held and his co-authors in *Global Transformations* (Held et al., 1999):

1 An intensification of connections among nation states, leading to a diminution of state policy and a decline in the importance of the nation state.
2 The emergence of political, economic and cultural bureaucracies which operate on a global scale, including multinational firms, banks, the International Monetary Fund and the United Nations.
3 The creation of global cities that act as hubs of global interaction such as London, New York and Tokyo.
4 A dramatic increase in the flows of commodities, peoples, information and cultural products. Millions of people now move around the world in search of better jobs and opportunities or in order to find refuge from persecution. Consumer and perishable goods now reach our shelves in the West from virtually every corner of the globe. The World Wide Web has transformed the speed and passage of information.
5 The worldwide spread of Western-style consumerism. Western brands such as Coca-Cola, McDonald's and Apple, rituals of consumption and shopping malls identical to those found in London or Chicago are to be found from Delhi and Beijing to Abu Dhabi and Rio de Janeiro.

On reflection, there are probably few who would disagree strongly with such a list. Under these circumstances it would be tempting to consider, as many do, that globalization is a process brought about by the ways in which corporations, banks, communications and the movement of people have increasingly transcended national boundaries in the post-Second World War period. The problem is, however, that if we scrutinize the historical record, it is apparent that these processes have been in place for a very long time.

This is where some of the difficult problems arise. For while there may be a degree of consensus on what globalization is, there is little on when it began. Many of the features of globalization can be traced back centuries. The following periodization usefully lays out how global processes have originated and changed over time (Held et al., 1999):

Phase 1 Premodern (before 1500)

- Early imperial systems.
- World religions.
- Nomadic empires and agrarian expansion.
- Plagues and pandemics.
- Long-distance trade.

Phase 2 Early modern (1500–1800)

- Political and military expansion.
- Europe and the new world: demographic, environmental, epidemiological flows.
- Development of European empires.
- New transatlantic exchanges.

Phase 3 Modern (1850–1945)

- European global empires: military, political, economic, cultural flows.
- Global circulation of Western secular discourses and ideologies.

- Transatlantic migrations.
- Asian diasporas.
- Development of a world economy.

Phase 4 Contemporary (1945–present)

- Cold War and post-Cold War global military relationships.
- Systems of global governance and international law.
- Economic globalization: trade, financial markets, multinational production and investment, technology transfer.
- Global environmental threats.
- New patterns of global migration.
- Global spread of media multinationals, Western popular culture and thought.
- New global networks of communication and transport.

We could write many histories of human interaction across many areas and themes but let us take, for example, the case of industrialization. Here is a story familiar to many. Sometime in the late eighteenth century, Britain led the Industrial Revolution. A combination of advantageous natural resources and native genius created a system of factory production which guaranteed for the first time in human history self-sustained economic growth. The revolution was initially based on the manufacture of cotton goods in the large mills of northern England, but later, through the production of iron and steel, reached into every corner of the economy, transforming the working lives and living conditions of the people forever. The problem with this narrative is its insularity. Simply stated, we cannot understand the Industrial Revolution exclusively as a British experience. In a remarkable passage from his massive study of capitalism penned about 150 years ago, Karl Marx provided an alternative interpretation:

> The discovery of gold and silver in America, the extirpation, enslavement, and entombment in the mines of the aboriginal population, the beginning of the conquest and looting of the East Indies, the turning of Africa into a warren for hunting black skins, signalised the rosy dawn of capitalist production. These idyllic proceedings are the chief memento of primitive accumulation. On their heels treads the commercial war of the European nations, with the globe for a theatre.
>
> (Marx, 1974, p. 345)

Marx thus locates the origins of industrial capitalism in the nascent colonial system rather than in the textile factories of England. The flow of plunder from the Spanish colonization of South America and later the British annexation of India, the wealth created by the slave trade and the establishment of a world market enabling manufactured goods to be sold, all helped to create the conditions that underpinned the Industrial Revolution and the ascent of capitalism. The origins of capitalist production, therefore, are not necessarily to be found among English textile weavers alone but have to be sought also among the cotton producers of India, America and Egypt and the sugar workers in the slave plantations of the Caribbean, for here too can we find the skills, technology and forms of labour organization that have come to be seen as typically capitalist (Williams, 1966).

Despite such observations, historians have for the most part been reticent to grasp the potential of global history. After all, the challenge is a formidable one. Historians trained in Western academies tend to be conservative creatures, resistant to new ways of looking at the world.

History is written by the victors, and so they have been taught that the West is a society that has developed independently of other societies and civilizations, according to distinct stages from ancient Greece to Rome, Christendom, the Renaissance and the Enlightenment, ending up with the advanced capitalism of North America, the zenith of human civilization (Wolf, 1997, p. 5). This teleology marks and celebrates the historical unfolding of a self-contained and self-fulfilling prophecy: Why do we need to take account of peoples outside its orbit? Historians are also encouraged to become increasingly specialist, especially in research that is more tightly bounded by period and location. Under such circumstances, it requires something of a bold imaginative leap to think across narrowly defined contours and embrace different historical experiences and to overcome a profound historical amnesia by thinking sympathetically about 'the people without history', that is, those who have rarely featured in conventional historical accounts.

One rather arresting and notorious instance of this historical amnesia is worth recounting. In a series of lectures at Sussex University in 1963, later published in *The Listener*, Professor Trevor-Roper (1914–2003), Regius Professor of History at the University of Oxford, speculated:

> Perhaps, in the future, there will be some African history to teach. But at present there is none, or very little; there is only the history of Europeans in Africa. The rest is largely darkness, like the history of pre-European, pre-Columbian America. And darkness is not a subject for history.
> (www.davidderrick.wordpress.com/2010/06/09/there-is-no-african-history/)

At face value, this may appear uncontentious. In 1963 the historiography of Africa and Mesoamerica *was* little developed within the Western academy, and there were few if any courses offered on these areas. But Trevor-Roper, a traditionally minded historian, implacably opposed to all those with radical leanings, had something rather more troubling in mind. He proceeded:

> I do not deny that men existed even in dark countries and dark centuries, nor that they had political life and culture, interesting to sociologists and anthropologists; but history, I believe, is essentially a form of movement. . . . It is not a mere phantasmagoria of changing shapes and costumes, of battles and conquests, dynasties and usurpations, social forms and social disintegration. If all history is equal . . . then indeed we may neglect our own history and amuse ourselves with the unrewarding gyrations of barbarous tribes in picturesque but irrelevant corners of the globe: tribes whose chief function in history . . . is to show to the present an image of the past from which, by history, it has escaped.
> (Ibid.)

For Trevor-Roper, because Africa had no written records and no historical development that could be discerned, it was not an 'historical continent'. Indeed, it was a continent inhabiting a distant past long abandoned by the West and seemingly incapable of historic development. It is surely fair to add that this view would no longer be accepted in the academy and would be seen as hopelessly Eurocentric – racist even – and empirically naïve. Ironically, however, such views provoked a response that gave rise to postcolonialism and hence a much more comprehensive and nuanced view of how the developing world contributed to the modern.

15.2 Origins of the Global Imagination

Histories in the form of genealogy, myth, biography, dynastic chronicle and military conquest have existed ever since people developed a sense of the passing of time. Most of these were culturally and geographically limited and were meant to establish and help maintain the authority of particular peoples, groups and families. There were also, however, a relatively small number with inquiring minds who were interested in exploring beyond the boundaries of knowledge in which they had been raised, to nurture a sense of world history. They tended to come from the intellectual powerhouses of the time. In China of the first century BCE, for example, Sima Qian, the official historian of the Han Dynasty, gathered and synthesized evidence from early times and from far distant lands to provide a narrative reaching beyond its formal boundaries (Manning, 2003, p. 33). Some were travellers who undertook remarkable journeys across the known world, later to record their observations on the nature of the civilizations and peoples they had encountered.

A few examples must suffice. Marco Polo (1254–1324), the son of a Venetian merchant, set out in 1271 on a journey along the silk route to Xanadu (Shangdu), capital of the Mongol empire, where he was reputed to have stayed for over 20 years. He was not the first European to visit China, but he travelled much more extensively than his predecessors. On returning to Venice in 1295, he published an account of his travels, which was a huge bestseller even though much of the book was regarded as fiction by contemporary readers. Whatever its authenticity, the travelogue opened European eyes to East Asia for the first time and retrospectively established his reputation as one of the great European travellers. Thirty years after Polo's return, the lesser-known but much more widely travelled Moroccan scholar Ibn Battuta (1304–1368/1369) embarked on a 75,000 mile journey traversing the Muslim world from Africa, across the interior of Asia and then on to China. Returning finally to Morocco in 1354, he dictated an account of his travels which was then forgotten, even in the Islamic world, until recently when its rediscovery and translation into English belatedly sealed his reputation as the greatest of medieval travellers and the most reliable chronicler.

This important tradition of writing continued. In the sixteenth century, al-Hasan al-Wazzan (1488–1548), born in Granada, raised in Morocco, also travelled around the Islamic world. As Leo Africanus, he published *The Description of Africa*, which revealed the complex ways in which the histories and cultures of the African, Muslim, Christian and Jewish worlds were interlinked (Zemon Davis, 2007). Take, for example, the vital question at the time of the spread of disease. Syphilis, he claimed, was introduced into North Africa and subsequently spread by Jewish women, many of whom as prostitutes had transmitted the condition to Muslim men:

> Don Fernando, King of Spain, chased the Jews from Spain. Many of the Jews who came to Barbary . . . carried the disease from Spain. Some unhappy Moors mixed with the Jewish women, and so little by little, within ten years, one could not find a family untouched by the disease. At first the disease was judged to be leprosy, and those infected were chased [from their houses] and forced to live with the lepers. Then, as the number of those infected increased every day, it was discovered that many people in Spain had the ailment. So the people who had been chased from their houses returned to them.
> (Cited in Zemon Davis, 2007, p. 137)

Once the disease spread in North Africa, al-Wazzan continued, it inflicted great damage on the cities of Tunisia and Egypt. By contrast, nomadic Arabs and people in the 'Land of the Blacks' (Namibia) were unaffected. It was therefore believed that in order to be cured it was sufficient to breathe the air of the countryside. More recent studies have challenged the account by demonstrating that the syphilis was in fact brought from the Iberian peninsula by both refugee Muslims and refugee Jews; if that is the case then al-Wazzan's interpretation of events was misleading, probably because it was shaped by a number of anxieties about sexual relations

Figure 15.1 The great medieval Muslim traveller Ibn Battuta being shown around the ancient ruins of Pharaonic Egypt. Born in Tangier 1304, he died in Morocco circa 1368 or 1369

Contributor: Classic Image/Alamy Stock Photo

between Muslims and Jews and the 'civilized' values of Arabic cities when compared with nomads and blacks.

Travel accounts like these played a crucial role in helping to lift Europe out of the superstition and religious dogma of the medieval period. By exposing the minds of Europeans to an appreciation of lands and peoples previously seen as fabled, even monstrous, thereby uncovering remarkable sources of knowledge from which Europe had been excluded since ancient times, they helped pave the way for the intellectual revolution of the Renaissance and laid the foundations too for the eighteenth-century Enlightenment. These intellectual transformations in turn provided fertile ground for the planting of novel ideas about world history. The Renaissance witnessed the first flowering, even though its thought remained highly contradictory. The supreme political theorist of the time, Machiavelli, embraced the idea of Western civilization but linked the cultural flowering witnessed in Italy directly and linearly to the Old World, notably the classical era. He therefore had no need to engage with the world outside Europe. Others were more mindful of the existence of other peoples, most especially after the 'discovery' of the Americas at the end of the fifteenth century. For the historian Francesco Guicciardini (1483–1540), the existence of Native Americans raised a host of vital questions about the human condition. How was it, he asked, that such people, many of whom lived in highly organized and successful societies, had been able to progress without knowledge of the Bible or European thought? The opening up of the Americas therefore invited reconsideration of the whole of the past and offered possibilities for future progress.

The Renaissance laid the foundations for the ascent of the West in part by mapping, however patchily, the non-European world. It was not until the Enlightenment, however, that these other cultures were studied seriously and the lessons learnt applied to an analysis of contemporary Western society. Chapter 3 was devoted to the impact of the Enlightenment on the writing of history, and we have no wish to repeat the arguments here, but it would be worth saying a little about how Enlightenment figures furthered the study of global history. Combined with a commitment to rational inquiry based on the laws of natural sciences, many writers were fascinated by societies beyond Europe and determined not only to learn more about their distinct cultures but also to think of ways they could be brought together imaginatively into a grand evolutionary scheme. Thus, one of the leading Enlightenment figures, Denis Diderot (1713–1784), began to compile the *Encyclopédie des Sciences, des Arts et des Métiers* in 1751 with the aim of collecting all the knowledge scattered over the face of the earth. By the time the 28th volume had been published 14 years later, an enthusiastic reading public could learn from the entries of nearly 200 leading writers about, say, the vital contributions made by Islamic intellectuals to the modern world and the important advances in science and philosophy made by ancient Indian and Chinese civilizations.

Simultaneously, many Enlightenment thinkers were busily applying themselves to the task of locating different civilizations in an evolutionary hierarchy, thereby fostering the fledgling interests in world history. Some of the foundations for this reasoning had been laid earlier. Jean Bodin (1530–1596), a French professor of law, wrote *Methodus ad Facilem Historiarum Cognitionem* (1566) in which he reinterpreted the course of world history by identifying three crucial geopolitical regions. The first two millennia had been dominated by the Orientals including Babylonians, Persians and Egyptians because of their knowledge of philosophy and mathematics. They were displaced by Mediterranean peoples (Greeks and Romans), who through politics and practical knowledge controlled the next two millennia. Finally, Northern peoples, that is, Europeans, ascended to power through their skills in warfare and mechanical inventions and their ability to utilize the scientific and philosophical work of ancient Greece and Rome. The English philosopher John Locke (1632–1704), now widely recognized as one of the founding figures of the Enlightenment, published in 1690 *Two Treatises of Government*, which opened the path for what later became known as the 'stages theory of development', which we have already discussed in Chapter 2. Challenging scriptural and ancient accounts which suggested a universal scheme of societal evolution, Locke argued that primitive modes of human subsistence, such as found in hunter-gatherer and early pastoral societies, existed at different times in the development of Asia and Europe, thereby suggesting that their civilizations had progressed at different rates.

How, Enlightenment thinkers asked, were different civilizations to be ranked according to their state of advance? Just as the discovery of 'civilized' Native American societies had posed awkward questions about the status and relevance of Christian knowledge, so astonishing revelations in the *Encyclopédie* about the achievements and longevity of Indian and Chinese civilizations prompted demands to know precisely how these were to be located in the grand order of things: if not at the apex of European civilization or at the level of Africa, which was dismissed as pagan and primitive, then where? In the eighteenth century, particularly with the writings of Adam Smith, Jacques Turgot and Quesnay, the stages theory of development reached maturity. Using overarching and teleological schemes which identified different societies based on their division of labour, commodity exchange and accumulation of capital, they identified various stages through which these societies had passed, from the primitive nomadic ones found in the South Pacific to the advanced commercial nations of Europe. What distinguished these studies was their use of abstraction. None was intended to be a detailed account of historical change, rather the historical record was selectively called upon to support grand, overarching theories about the nature and development of human societies.

Influential writers such as J. G. von Herder and G. W. F. Hegel continued something of this tradition into the nineteenth century, as we witnessed in Chapter 6. Herder's *Ideas for the Philosophy of History of Humanity* (1784–1791) emphasized the unity of humankind but argued that divisions appeared on the basis of ethnicity and it was the 'national genius' possessed by particular ethnic groups that drove historical change. And Hegel's *Lectures on the Philosophy of History* (1837) saw human desire for freedom as the moving force of change towards an ultimate universal spirit. Both drew upon historical examples from around the world, but the focus was on national progress, and the nation was invariably European. Despite his sensitivity to the importance of the world outside Europe, even Karl Marx in his emphasis on the advanced stage of (European) capitalism can be viewed in the same light.

Evident in these writings was the germination of the idea of the nation, and it was this that was to determine the course of historical writing over the next two centuries. It was no accident that the rise of the nation state during the nineteenth century coincided with what has been seen as the coming of age of history as a scientific discipline, for the foundations of historiography were laid by historians who pioneered studies of the nation. We will encounter Leopold von Ranke in Chapter 21 and learn of his approach to evidence, but he can be located also within the changing paradigms of global history. Influenced by Hegel, von Ranke worked within a tradition of philosophical idealism, that is, a system of historical thought based on the application of more abstract rational principles such as the progress of civilizations rather than factual evidence, which he never really abandoned; indeed, he left unfinished at the time of this death an ambitious history of the world. And yet, unlike Herder and Hegel, this idealism was tempered by an attempt to recover the past 'as it really happened' through a meticulous and painstaking examination of documentary sources.

For those fledgling historians seeking to establish themselves, their discipline and their nation, this was an exciting prospect, and so was launched a vast project to record and disseminate the histories of nation states to patriotic audiences. Jules Michelet's *History of the French*

Revolution (1847–1853), Lord Macaulay's *History of England from the Accession of James II* (1849–1861), George Bancroft's *History of the Unites States of America from the Discovery of the Continent* (1873–1874), and a host of other sizable nationalist narratives both illuminated the past and provided lessons for the present. The skills demonstrated in gathering, assessing and interpreting documentary evidence – and the enthusiastic response of a reading public – helped to establish the dominance of national history and the virtually unassailable authority of the professional historian trained in the West (Manning, 2003, p. 28), all at the cost of new initiatives in the writing of global histories.

This paradigm has survived more or less intact to the present day, the difference being that historians have become so specialized in their interests that they tend to talk to one another rather than reaching out to a broad audience. There have been notable exceptions, in particular ambitious studies of world history that inherited Enlightenment thought and engaged with a more popular audience in the aftermath of the horrors of the First and Second World Wars, but somehow they have not successfully entered the canon. A few examples must suffice. In 1918 Oswald Spengler published *Decline of the West*, in which he charted the rise and fall of successive civilizations. It was a profoundly pessimistic vision of a world which he saw as standing on the edge of the abyss. According to Spengler, there was no universal science or spirit of humanity, rather cultures had their own character and way of reasoning, which meant that there was little communication among them. Each, however, went through a predetermined path of development. Starting from a heroic age of war and religion, cultures were then subjected to the influence of industrialization, urbanization and science, which led to commercialization and the domination of the masses. Chaos and a loss of creativity were the inevitable result. H. G. Wells' *The Outline of History*, published in 1920, was a skilful synthesis of the work of world historians stitched together by a single vision. Written in the immediate aftermath of the First World War, the book was meant to answer the need expressed by people for an understanding of the unfolding of the events of world history rather than the narrow national histories they had been taught at school. Wells set about what soon appeared to be an epic task because he was persuaded there were no 'proper' historians who were 'sufficiently wide and sufficiently shallow to cover the vast field of the project'. The story he told was one of progress, of lives of countless people struggling towards consciousness and understanding until we reach the world of today with its tragic confusions and perplexities and yet so full of promise and opportunity.

Arnold Toynbee's twelve-volume *A Study of History* (1933–1961) is the most comprehensive attempt to chart the course the rise and fall of world civilizations while paying due regard to those cultures of Asia, South America and Africa that had been systematically ignored by others. Having said that, *Study* is not a narrative history of the world based on original sources but a comparative and synthetic analysis of all the world's civilizations which relies heavily on the work of previous historians. Thus, like Spengler, he chronicled the changing fortunes of civilizations, using as a template the idea of genesis, growth, breakdown and disintegration, and to an extent he shared his pessimism, but he stressed the critical role of human freedom and posed a universal spiritual renewal as a solution to the world's ills. This suggests that the study of – and respect for – religion was a key to understanding Toynbee's approach, but at the same time he was at pains also to incorporate the impact of Enlightenment reason and rejected any religious dogma that conflicted with reasoned argument and evidence. (We encounter Spengler, Wells and Toynbee in a slightly different context in Chapter 22.)

Finally, Lewis Mumford's trilogy *Technics and Civilization* (1934), *The Culture of Cities* (1938) and *The Condition of Man* (1944) appeared at the same time as Toynbee's magnum opus and also focused on the changing fortunes of world civilizations. He argued that the twentieth century had witnessed the steady disintegration of Western civilization quite unlike those of the Greek, Roman, Chinese or Indian experiences. The loss of faith in progress and the end of expansion can only be reversed by restoring balance in the community and the human personality through drawing upon human energy, knowledge and wealth without being discouraged.

What is interesting about these authors of world histories is that none was a 'proper' historian; indeed, their engagement with history was highly ambiguous. Perhaps this is because no professional historians were sufficiently ambitious or reckless to take on the task, but more importantly they remained deeply suspicious of the sorts of grandiose structures erected by these authors, occasionally seeing their commercial success as a sure sign of an amateur historical scholarship. Spengler had studied philosophy and history as an undergraduate but was equally interested in science and art. He failed his doctoral dissertation in Heraclitus and remained outside the academy, choosing instead to teach in a school. He was deeply critical of the evidence-based approach of historians. Wells' mind was seemingly too eclectic and expansive to be confined to history. He had no academic post, making his name as one of the best-known writers of early science fiction. When confronted with the immensity of the world history he had embarked on, Wells decided that a writer of speculative essays and works of fiction was better qualified than an historian. Toynbee studied archaeology in Athens for a time, and although he did have a chair in Modern Greek and Byzantine Studies for five years, he went on to the Royal Institute of International Affairs and later the Research Department at the Foreign Office. And Mumford did not complete his undergraduate degree, had no academic post and considered himself a writer rather than an historian, urban theorist or literary critic. It is almost as if the discipline of history and the training of historians militated against an imagination of the world required in undertaking such a study.

15.3   Enter 'New World History'

There emerged in the aftermath of the Second World War another current of world history. Less concerned with broad synthesizing narratives covering long historical periods or with the articulation of overarching themes such as progress, spirituality and reason, its protagonists chose rather to focus on more discrete historical problems within a global context, using as evidence conventional documentary sources. The shift was so dramatic that we might well wonder if we are still talking of the same species of world history. Two remarkable studies from seemingly unexpected and unlikely sources led the way. In 1944, Eric Williams, a Trinidadian who had just completed a doctoral dissertation at Oxford, published *Capitalism and Slavery*. Bestriding the continents of America, Africa, Europe and India, Williams confronted much of the orthodoxy that had beset the study of the institution of slavery – in particular the belief that it was an enclosed system of exploitation – and that its eventual eradication owed most to the determined campaigns of enlightened Britons led by William Wilberforce. Like Marx, Williams identified the links between the slave trade and the Industrial Revolution, arguing that profits from slavery provided the necessary finance for the early entrepreneurs. And the whole wretched system was not eventually abolished because of Wilberforce; rather, British capitalists realized that the trade, no longer profitable and increasingly under threat from slave revolts, was a liability. Better by far to do away with it and claim the moral high ground. The book launched a brilliant wave of historical scholarship on world slavery which continues to this day, and although details of Williams' arguments have been subjected to criticism, all historians work with the agenda he first laid down (see Chapter 5 where we investigate this historiography in more detail).

While imprisoned by the Nazis during the Second World War, the French historian Fernand Braudel (1902–1985) began work on an ambitious project. In 1949 his labours saw fruition with the publication of *The Mediterranean and the Mediterranean World in the Era of Philip II*, one of the truly seminal works of the twentieth century. Before the war Braudel had, significantly, spent nearly a decade teaching in the French colony Algeria and later became an important member of the *Annales* group, an influential cohort of historians organized around the journal *Annales d'Histoire Économique et Sociale*, which was committed to a larger and more open approach to history. The book, however, sealed his reputation.

Braudel dedicated it to his fellow historian Lucien Febvre, for good reason. Febvre, along with Marc Bloch, had founded *Annales* in order to promote a new, larger and more human history accessible to audiences beyond the academy. They were highly critical of traditional approaches and were relentless in their attacks on elite political or diplomatic histories. They wished to downgrade the status conferred on individuals and events and instead set out to understand and reveal the deep structures that underpinned human behaviour as a means of writing what they called a 'total history'. In so doing, they borrowed freely from the insights of other disciplines, most notably geography, sociology and anthropology.

Conceiving the Mediterranean during the Renaissance as a part of world history, Braudel's account knew no national or cultural boundaries but embraced the ancient regions of Iraq and Egypt, the Sahara, Europe and Russia. And eschewing the traditional focus of historians on the rich and powerful few and times of rapid change, he broadened his approach to include details of the lives of ordinary people which changed only slowly and over long periods of time. All of this was informed by a deep knowledge and profound historical imagination.

Interestingly, the book started out in 1923 as a routine study of Philip II's Mediterranean policy. Braudel claimed that his teachers strongly approved of it for it conformed well to the pattern of diplomatic history, which was little concerned with the broader economic and social movements that affected the lives of the mass of people. He began to write about the roles played by the Spanish king and his counsellors through changing circumstances, thereby reconstructing a model of Spanish foreign policy of which the Mediterranean was one small part. While thus engaged, Braudel came to recognize that beyond the intervention of Spain, the Mediterranean had a history and destiny of its own, a 'powerful vitality' which suggested that it deserved to be treated better than a 'picturesque background' to the actions of the Spanish court. He therefore embarked on a history of the Mediterranean in its complex totality. Thus, beginning with an account of the relationship between humans and the environment, the passage of which is almost imperceptible, he proceeded to inquire into how economic systems, states, societies and civilizations worked and finally described how these profound underlying currents shaped the lives, decisions and behaviour of individual men (and, yes, it was mostly men).

Critics may at this juncture inquire whether a study of modern slavery or of the Mediterranean, no matter how broadly conceived, can be legitimately considered as a global history. It is a good point but one based on a rather pedantic approach to the topic. Of course, neither Williams nor Braudel set out to write a history of the world; Williams did not even write a world history of slavery, saying nothing about its ancient forms, and Braudel's historical sweep was confined to a few centuries. What Williams showed with great skill was how modern slavery was built not merely upon the Atlantic system that united America with Europe but interconnected also Africa and Asia, and it is this that qualifies it as a world history. And what Braudel did similarly was to show how the destiny of the Mediterranean was intimately linked to all the civilizations that comprised Europe at the time, as well as some in Africa and the Middle East. Global history, you may recall, does not require that every corner of the globe be covered in a grand work of synthesis; rather, what is important is that we reveal Wolf's 'totality of interconnected processes' in ways that transcended conventional national, cultural, and even regional boundaries, so shedding a powerful new light on older historical problems. This explains the enduring influence and appeal of Williams and Braudel.

But if the critics are insistent that world really does mean world, then the foundational text for the new world history was William McNeill's *The Rise of the West* (1963). As the title suggests (note the inversion of Spengler), this was a study of how the West ascended to world dominance, seen not as part of a linear and triumphant trajectory from the ancients or as part of what some have seen as European exceptionalism but as the unfolding of awkward and complex interrelationships with other world powers such as the Ottomans in which knowledge was diffused freely across cultural boundaries. This was history at its grandest and most ambitious, perhaps not surprising since McNeill worked with Toynbee in preparing the last volumes of his monumental series. Unlike Toynbee, however, he avoided the identification of particular patterns in the historical record – which for him derived not from the evidence directly but from the imposition of abstract themes such as secularization – and addressed the evidence directly to create chronologies that offered a range of novel perspectives not only on the West but on world history. Given the focus on the ascent of the West, there was a certain inevitability about the criticism that the book overstated its power and thereby understated the contribution of China, Africa and the Islamic world, but the book did give a considerable boost to the study of interactions and eventually a less skewed picture of the relationship between the West and the rest.

Since these pioneering studies we have seen a great flowering of a new world history. Some of our leading historians have been emboldened to take on afresh the task of writing grand syntheses. Hugh Thomas's *An Unfinished History of the World* (1979), Felipe Fernández-Armesto's *Millennium* (1995), David Abulafia's *The Mediterranean in History* (2003) and Christopher Bayly's *The Birth of the Modern World, 1780–1914* (2004) all demonstrate wide erudition and have opened up new avenues of inquiry into the ascent of the West, the role of industrialization and conflict and the contributions of empires. And many undergraduates have benefited from books such as Wolf's *Europe and the People without History* (1982) and the more recent textbook *Worlds Together, Worlds Apart* (2008) put together by Robert Tignor and his colleagues at Princeton University. Equally, world history has immeasurably enhanced our understanding of topics such as slavery, modern empires, the epidemiology of diseases, diasporic movements, the transfer of technologies, ecological change, commerce and trade and the transmission of culture.

There is a now a considerable body of work to feast upon, the pick of which is as rich and satisfying as any history published in the last hundred years. Take, for example, Marshall Hodgson's *Venture of Islam*. A colleague of McNeill at Chicago before his untimely death in 1968 at the age of 47, Hodgson published posthumously a three-volume magisterial survey of Islamic civilization from before the birth of Muhammad to the mid-twentieth century. *The Venture of Islam* (2011) succeeded spectacularly in countering what Hodgson saw as the Western bias in world histories by locating Islamic civilization within the extraordinary mix of other cultures with which it came into contact.

It is invidious to choose from among the works which make up the brilliant historiography of slavery, but David Brion Davis' *The Problem of Slavery in Western Culture* (1966) is a quite wonderful comparative survey of how slavery was viewed from antiquity to the 1770s, and his *Slavery and Human Progress* (1984) a magisterial account of that extraordinary moment in world history when, after millennia of uncritical acceptance of its existence, the West finally abolished the horrors of slavery (see also Chapter 5). The historiography of empire has also benefited greatly. Sometime before his history of the modern world, Bayly published an account of the reconstitution of the British empire following the loss of the American colonies. Brief and speculative, *Imperial Meridian* (1989) is bursting with ideas about how this episode can only be understood in the context of a world crisis during 1780–1820 and repays careful scrutiny.

What does this new genre offer? One of the most powerful features of world history is the challenge it poses to ways in which the West has been foregrounded in dominant historical narratives. By locating the West in the context of Afro-Eurasia as a whole, we begin to understand more fully its complex trajectory and simultaneously accord space to other world powers and peoples. As we have seen, Wolf's *Europe and a People without History* was a sustained critique of Western centrism, but the most powerful assault was launched by Marshall Hodgson, who had not only published the *Venture of Islam* but pioneered world history. Using examples from cartography and the status of Greenwich Mean Time, he argued that the West has dominated notions of geographical space and time (Hodgson, 1993). How did this come about? Of course, the West did ascend to world dominance, but equally important was the story it told of its own rise to power. According to this narrative, the history of civilizations began in Egypt and Mesopotamia – that is, the East – but then passed successively to ancient Greece and Rome, and Christendom of north-western Europe where medieval and later modern life developed. During this time, the torch of science was temporarily held by Islamic civilization until it was rightfully assumed by Europeans. It is true that China, India and Japan also had important civilizations, but they were on the margins of world history and contributed even less than Islam to the modernizing impulses of Europe. Africa is not even mentioned.

We must locate the history of these civilizations with greater precision. Until 200 years ago most the world's population lived in the Afro-Eurasian landmass. Conventionally this is seen to comprise Europe, the Middle East, India and the Far East, each of which developed autonomously, but in fact they were secondary groupings fused together in a single complex of economic and cultural development promoted principally by trade and diasporic movements. Well into the Middle Ages, Europe, which appeared as little more than a north-westerly outpost to Eurasia, played a peripheral and backward role, evident in the fact that the flow of learning was overwhelmingly from the 'East', something we saw in Chapter 2 when comparing the relatively puny library belonging to Bede in the sixth century with contemporaries from the Islamic world. But Europe was on an upward march, in part by using weapons technology, navigation and ships which had originated in China and the Islamic world. At the cusp of the modern era – roughly the long eighteenth century – power was distributed among these three powers. There was no inevitability to the eventual rise of the West to dominance; it was a process dependent on the common conditions that had underpinned Eurasian culture and that were now beginning to break down.

We must therefore distinguish the history of the West from world history:

> Just as an understanding of the history of Europe cannot be reduced to the history of England because industrialization first developed there, so the history of the world cannot be reduced to the history of the West, because industrialism first spread there.
>
> (Wolf, 1997, p. 268)

The West was one region among others and in premodern ages was distinctly peripheral to the main contours of historical development. Even now it does not define the modern world. Instead of posing the dichotomy of 'East' and 'West', therefore, historians should find ways of thinking about interregional exchanges and mutualities. This is not merely a matter of geography, for such a project also requires that they address anew the question of periodization that has been largely defined by the Western experience. When, in other words, was the medieval, the premodern or even the modern?

These are some of the important questions addressed by Dipesh Chakrabarty in *Provincializing Europe* (2000). His argument is that the so-called European age yielded to other global powers sometime towards the middle of the twentieth century and the idea that the European experience can somehow stand for a universal human history no longer obtains. Important though Europe was to the development of the modern world and concepts such as citizenship, the state and human rights, Europe cannot be seen as a unity or in isolation from the non-European world. We need, therefore, to talk of different Europes with different historical trajectories, each of which had a distinct relationship to the colonized world. The imperial experience was integral to the genesis of the modern world, and therefore it is necessary to trace carefully the genealogies of those ideas that have framed modern societies. This does not mean a rejection of all things European, such as modernity, liberalism, science and reason but rather a recognition of the necessity to 'provincialize Europe'. Without an understanding of its elements and their relationship to regions of the non-European world no longer seen as subordinate, our grasp of the complex totality of world history will remain skewed and unreliable.

What of the future of global history? You will know by now that prediction forms no part of the historian's remit, but it might be worth making one or two tentative suggestions (Christian, 2010). The signs are encouraging. Courses in world history are flourishing in the USA, Britain, Russia and Australia, and the number of studies that come under the umbrella of big history is steadily increasing. Equally important, many of these begin to break down the boundaries between history and the natural sciences by, for example, investigating the long-term trends in biodiversity and consumption of energy (Chapter 16). Part of the reason for this resurgence is, of course, the Internet and the access it provides to historical data on regions previously seen as beyond the reach of most professional historians. If this encourages historians to recognize that their specialist interests are just part of a larger and more complex universal history, then their discipline can only benefit. It may be too optimistic to expect a paradigm shift in what is essentially a rather conservative discipline, but if it means that historians ask new and more exciting questions of their material then for the time being this may be enough.

15.4 Global Pandemics

At the time of writing, the world seems to be recovering slowly from a pandemic popularly known as COVID-19. The numbers of cases and the deaths that follow remain worryingly high in some countries, but overall, there is a sense that the worst is over. Vital in the fight against COVID-19 has been the extraordinarily rapid development and roll out of vaccines which have successfully cut the rates of infection and hospitalization, the foundations of which were laid by the years of painstaking research to advance our understanding of virology and epidemiology. Nonetheless, when COVID-19 struck and the death rates soared, we found that scientific opinion on the nature of the pandemic and its eradication was deeply divided. Furthermore, despite the early successes of the vaccination programme and convincing evidence of the risks involved in failing to have a jab, a significant section of the population continued to defy scientific advice and appeals from the government.

COVID-19 transformed our lives by forcing restrictions on our movements and contacts with others, by impacting drastically on the physical and mental well-being of individuals and the health professionals who cared for them and by economic measures taken in response to the emergency. To date, over 4.5 million people have died of COVID-19; untold millions have suffered in a variety of ways. It is too early to say what the longer-term damage will be or precisely how the pandemic will transform the ways in which we work or conduct ourselves as social individuals or what lessons we can learn, but are there useful questions that historians can ask at this stage? Does the historical record offer us insights into the nature and trajectory of such pandemics?

First, pandemics provide us with a wonderful, if grisly, example of the need to think globally. No pandemic can be understood simply by investigating a single country or even continent. The clue is in the terminology, so we need to be clear. When we refer to a pandemic, we are talking of a health condition which has a global reach; in this respect, it differs from an outbreak or an epidemic where the spread of the disease is regional or national. And it is generally accepted that the term *pandemic* must meet several criteria including wide geographic spread, movement across populations, high attack rates and impact, low immunity among the population and high infectiousness (McMillen, 2016). By their nature, pandemics have historically been much rarer; even so, a recent survey have identified over twenty in the past two millennia, all of which can be classified as plague, cholera, smallpox, influenza, malaria, tuberculosis, HIV/AIDS or a variety of coronavirus and all of which inflicted catastrophic damage on human populations (Piret and Boivin, 2021; McMillen, 2016). Estimates of deaths caused vary widely, in part because of the nature of the impact. Pandemics such as the Black Death acted with a relatively short-lived intensity, while those like cholera, malaria and tuberculosis have been with us for centuries, making it impossible to provide anywhere near reliable data. To give some examples, the Plague of Justinian, 541–543, is reckoned to have killed 50m (more later); the Black Death, 1347–1351, 200m (ditto); smallpox from the sixteenth century onwards, 56m and the so-called Spanish flu of 1918–1919, 50m.

Though they shared many distinguishing features, the cause of infection varied widely from fleas associated with rodents in the plague, to contaminated water in cholera, to birds and pigs in influenza. Historically, what is of particular interest is that of the pandemics, approximately seventy-five per cent occurred after 1800. Does this suggest that there is something about the modern world that actively nurtures the incidences of pandemics? This despite more advanced medical knowledge? Well, the arguments appear persuasive. Since pandemics rely on concentrations of people where pathogens can spread, any move towards the settlement and interaction of populations was likely to increase their vulnerability. Early human populations in the form of nomadic hunter-gatherer groups were likely infected with parasites, worms, lice and ticks but because transmission rates were low, we cannot rightly talk of epidemics or pandemics (Dobson and Carper, 1996; McNeill, 1994). The transition to more sedentary agricultural societies increased infection and transmission, leading to higher infant mortality rates and levels of disease. When humans from groups of neighbouring towns began to communicate, diseases such as smallpox, measles and tuberculosis which had evolved from animal pathogens were seen for the first time. It might be supposed that as towns grew into cities, the chances of epidemics increased but none of the ancient cities of the Egyptian, Greek or Roman empires seemed capable of sustaining common diseases. A certain caution has therefore to be exercised in interpreting sudden outbreaks of disease at this time. Although contemporary accounts referred to them as plagues, there is no evidence to suggest it was bubonic plague which later descended on Europe with devastating results. Perhaps the one contemporary account on which we can rely was that of the father of Greek – and Western – medicine, Hippocrates. Here there was sufficient detail to identify the existence of mumps, malaria, tuberculosis, diphtheria and influenza (McNeil, 1994, pp. 98–9). It was only from the beginning of the Christian era that cities emerged in China, India and the Mediterranean which provided conditions necessary to sustain diseases such as measles, diphtheria and scarlet fever, and then we began to witness pandemics with their unprecedented death tolls, the most catastrophic of which were the Plague of Justinian and the Black Death.

The origins of the Justinian Plague are unknown, but it seems likely that it was transmitted by infected fleas in search of new supplies of blood after the death of their rodent hosts. It broke out in 541 and was first recorded in Egypt before travelling via trade routes across the Mediterranean to Persia (McMillen, 2016, pp. 7–10). By the time it passed two years later as many as 50m people had perished, but it continued to erupt intermittently for two more centuries, reaching the shores of Britain in 664. Contemporary accounts spoke of the annihilation of communities, fields left unploughed, fruit unpicked and animals turned feral. Overall, rural depopulation and the collapse of economies weakened the Mediterranean region and might have contributed to the fall of the Roman empire, although the evidence is inconclusive (McNeill, 1994, p. 123).

The Black Plague of 1347–1351 was of the same bubonic strain but took an even more devastating toll of European lives. Up to half the population succumbed, in total approximately 200m deaths, swelled later by the regular outbreaks in Europe and the Islamic world until 1770. The existing state of medical knowledge had no answers further than forcing infected families to quarantine for forty days; instead people turned to the notion of a wrathful god and sought out scapegoats, most notably Jewish communities, which were obliterated wholesale. The long-term impact of the Black Death on European demography, economics and culture was not quite what we might first have suspected. The reduced population levels led directly to labour shortages creating in turn inflated demand for farm workers. Higher wages and an unprecedented political consciousness among the rural peasantry followed as many found themselves in a position to secure more favourable conditions from their employers and landlords. In Britain, the Peasants' Revolt of 1381, when under Wat Tyler the rebels demanded an end to serfdom, was the apotheosis of such a raised consciousness. Labour shortages also promoted changes in the rural economy and advances in technology as large swathes of land were converted from arable to pastoral, which was less labour intensive, and the tenure of land abandoned feudal ties as it moved to a system based increasingly on market-based relations. Within a century, agricultural output, including wool production – which rose dramatically – and population levels recovered, even surpassed, pre-plague conditions, leading some historians to conclude that the plague was largely beneficial in accelerating the decline of feudal society (McMillen, 2016, p. 16).

Ancient societies therefore witnessed wide fluctuations in health and disease, patterns which we are far from understanding. The dynamics between disease and factors such as diet, densities of human settlement, customs and practices let alone vector hosts, be they insects or water, were extremely complex (McNeill, 1994, p. 31). Nor do we yet understand fully why under certain conditions sustained levels of infection very occasionally led to epidemics and pandemics. One vital factor has been globalization and the momentum it gave to travel, trade and migration (Lindahl and Grace, 2015). Such movements accelerated the transmission of pathogens to new areas so that large-scale migration and mixing of populations has often been accompanied by the spread of pathogens followed by significant outbreaks of disease. At times of war and colonization, the effects have been particularly acute. So too has been the impact on ecosystems. The massive changes wrought by interventions such as deforestation, irrigation, intensification of farming and destruction of natural habitats may have boosted production of foodstuffs and natural materials, but they also promoted the growth of vector habitats and hence vector and parasitic diseases.

How pandemics are linked inexorably to a range of environmental and societal factors and have in their impact reconfigured human societies are complex issues which in some instances serve to challenge conventional wisdom. This complexity has been explored with great skill and erudition by Geoffey Parker in his monumental study of the global crisis of the seventeenth century, a book to which we return in the next chapter (Parker, 2013). The organizing theme is at first sight uncomplicated: a prolonged and intense period of global cooling 'coincided with an unparalleled spate of revolutions and state breakdowns around the world . . . while other states came close to revolution' (ibid, pp. xix–xx). Furthermore, war was adopted by Europe and the Ottoman, Chinese and Mughal empires as the accepted means of resolving domestic and international problems. This 'coincidence', however, becomes something stronger in the course of the book as the relationship between the 'Little Ice Age' and social turmoil assumes that of correlation, that is, climate is linked causally to revolt. At this point the complexities arise, for there were a multitude of ways in which climate change provoked social and political unrest. Disease was one of the principal suspects (ibid, pp. 82–7). Smallpox was one of the great killers of the seventeenth century. Even though its impact was felt in almost every corner of the world, across the century it became more widespread and more deadly. Plague was the only other disease to kill as many. Pandemics were intermittent but the plague struck with speed and intensity – as Naples, Seville, Moscow, Amsterdam, London and other great cities were soon to discover. Now the courses of both smallpox and the plague closely followed harvest yields, and so the virulence of the outbreak to some extent was conditional on the food supply that differentially affected people's diets. By impoverishing the diets of most of the population, the famines of the Little Ice Age necessarily aggravated the severity of smallpox and the plague.

The years of climatic misfortune, coupled with poor harvests, were those of the major revolts. Poor harvests had been a regular occurrence in the premodern period, and yet historically few of these had led to pandemics or provoked unrest, but perhaps it was the case that the privations of the seventeenth century were so extreme that revolt was seen by rural labourers to be the means of last resort. In this case, it seems likely that hunger, not disease, provoked unrest. Communities under ever-present threat from an unknown killer which had already taken a massive toll on its members were fearful, not rebellious. The Peasants' Revolt of 1381 took place approximately fifty years after the outbreak of the plague in England. When revolts occurred, the demands were for a return to a previous order free from want, conflict and repression. If this meant the overthrow of political regimes, so be it. And most revolts were led not by peasants but by intellectual, political or religious elites, as was the case of the English Revolution.

We wish to finish by considering the COVID pandemic in the light of these deliberations. The first point worth making is how much the experience of COVID shares with earlier pandemics:

1 There is great uncertainty over data on the number of fatalities. In the past, record keeping of life experiences was poor, and beyond the major urban centres it was impossible to keep reliable information on, say, the numbers who succumbed daily. The current figure of 4.5m COVID deaths is certainly a gross underestimate, not because we do not have the means of more accurate data but because death tolls have become a political issue. Governments across the world, most notably those of the United States, Great Britain, India, Russia and Brazil, have found it in their political interests to understate the death tolls because actual totals may raise too many questions about their competence in handling the pandemic.

2 In seeking to explain COVID when medical opinion is far from consensual, many have turned to bizarre conspiracy theories little different to those of the past. COVID was deliberately started, many have argued, as a means of subjecting the population to close surveillance by the state. And these theorists point to the great success of this strategy. In most countries, much of the population have complied with government orders to stay at home, wear face masks and maintain social distancing, often at great social and emotional cost to individuals. Evangelicals, as ever, invoke the notion of God's will as a punishment for the sins of society while other religious traditions offer other explanations.

3 More worrying have been attempts to identify members of society supposedly responsible for the spread of COVID. These attempts have sprung from and in turn feed into brands of nationalism in which poor and migrant sections are viewed with distrust, even alarm. Mercifully, we have not witnessed the wholesale annihilation of particular communities or demographics, but in the United States, Great Britain, China and India, amongst others, xenophobic sentiments and punitive sanctions against vulnerable sections of the population are on the increase.

It is too early to say with any confidence what the longer-term effect of COVID will be on human society. Development of vaccines has dramatically cut incidences of the virus and the numbers of those infected who subsequently need hospitalization. There are gross inequalities, however, in its availability. The proportion of the population fully vaccinated is very much lower in countries of the developing world than in the west; as in previous pandemics, the spread of the disease has cruelly exposed the fault lines of class and race. Given that the eradication of COVID is predicated on the successful vaccination of a large majority of the world's peoples, this seems unlikely to occur in the near future. In the meantime, COVID in its variants will revisit us on a regular basis.

Is there any evidence that COVID has permanently altered either the machinery of Western capitalism or in China, which appears to have produced a sub-standard vaccine, that brutally locked down its' population and appears to be in pursuit of a 'zero-COVID policy leading to social dislocation, that may not yet have played itself out? As seems always to have been the case when faced with a financial crisis or war, the power and scope of state action has increased. In Britain, the Tory government, operating well outside its comfort zone, felt compelled through the furlough scheme to pay workers who were not working, provide grants and loans to firms faced with closure and prevent landlords evicting tenants who were unable to pay their rents. Faced with extraordinary levels of popular support for the National Health Service during the pandemic, plans for privatization by stealth have temporarily been put on hold. To help pay for the damage wreaked by COVID, the government is to raise national insurance and taxes in defiance of pledges made in the Tory manifesto. Similar programmes are on the agenda of Western economies, broadly with the tacit approval of the International Monetary Fund (IMF). Does all this point to a shift in balance away from the corporate power and untrammelled capitalist enterprise to (big) domestic states working more for the common good? Well, we shall see. In the meantime, we, like millions of others, are adopting what is generally referred to as the new normal, but that is another part of the story for another time.

Postscript

Whatever sort of global history is being written, the task is not a simple one or one for the faint hearted. Traditionally, an historian is trained to be a specialist or soon becomes one as a means of carving out a niche in what is a competitive market. Global or world history confronts this tradition in a direct way, for it requires the historian to transcend such limitations by thinking on a much wider canvas. It is possible to write a history of Britain, for example, without venturing beyond its shores. But this would be an insular and impoverished history. 'What do they know of Britain', inquired Rudyard Kipling, 'who only Britain know?' Given that the rise of Britain to world power happened because it was able to dominate other countries and at the same time defeat its imperial rivals, any self-respecting history needs to take account of those relationships, and that in turn requires detailed study of the histories of other countries.

Quite apart from the sheer scale of such a venture, certain problems arise which can only be alluded to briefly here. To write an account of the relationship to another culture, it is necessary to understand how the culture works not from the perspective of an outsider but from the inside. This in turn requires some knowledge of other languages, thus providing access to archival sources. To illustrate the point, consider Britain's colonization of India. It would be possible to write a top-down history of how Britain imposed its rule, but it would be highly skewed. Britain was never able to exercise complete authority; it had therefore to enter into dialogue with individuals and sections of Indian society. How that dialogue worked depended in part upon how Indians themselves viewed the occupation of their country by a foreign power, how they viewed attempts to interfere with their own ancient customs, rituals and beliefs. Some of these responses may have appeared in English, but even here without an appreciation of the codes, philosophies and histories that shaped them, our understanding is impoverished.

There can be few areas that better illustrate the importance of thinking globally than that of disease. Pandemics are rightly thought of as global because it has been evident from their long history that their transmission and impact on human and animal populations knew not national or physical boundaries. The recent outbreak of COVID-19 has reminded all with an historical consciousness that such pandemics are nothing new but have since the beginnings of recorded history inflicted untold pain, misery and death on societies. Not only that, but pandemics have also demonstrated remarkable similarities in their development, transmission and impact, and if we are to manage with any degree of success future pandemics (which there will certainly be) then we would be well advised to seek guidance from the past.

The promise of world history is considerable; if we are prepared to put in the work and fire our imagination, then the discipline of history may at last be able to shed the legacies of its founding impulses. Indeed, with the unfolding of recent events there is a strong argument that we need global history more than ever before (Adelman, 2017). As the popularity of global histories soared, with the works of such as Jared Diamond (1997) and Sven Beckert (2014) appearing on every best-seller list, the political tide seemed to turn against globalization. In the past five years we have heard Donald Trump, Vladimir Putin, Marine Le Pen and Xi Jinping speak enthusiastically about the rise of nationalism as an antidote to globalism and the welcome insularity of national interests. In Britain, the successful Brexit campaign has signalled a retreat into a 'Little Englandism'. Furthermore, in the academy the engagement with global histories has not necessarily led to a proliferation of historical interest in the non-Western world. Under these circumstances, global historians have to become even more serious about an integrated, interconnected and interdependent world in which the voices of all of its peoples are heard.

Further Reading

Marshall G. S. Hodgson (1993) *Rethinking World History: Essays on Europe, Islam and World History.*
Georg G. Iggers and Q. Edward Wang (2008) *A Global History of Modern Historiography.*
Patrick Manning (2003) *Navigating World History: Historians Create a Global Past.*
Robert Tignor et al. (2008) *Worlds Together, Worlds Apart.*
Michel-Rolph Trouillot (1995) *Silencing the Past: Power and the Production of History.*
Eric Wolf (1982) *Europe and the People without History.*

16 Environmental History

Introduction

At first glance the scope of environmental history is immense. Given that it conventionally includes the dynamic and reciprocal relationship between human behaviour and natural world and the ways in which the latter has been viewed by peoples over time, there are large areas of the sciences and arts which could legitimately be encompassed by its remit. Section 1 considers these issues before moving on to discuss how the environment has been understood in the past. Given the utter dependency of early societies on the environment, it comes as no surprise that from the beginnings of recorded history peoples have thought about the natural world and the climate. They lacked knowledge derived from modern science, but their understanding of the relationship between humans and their environment was sophisticated. Later, historians of the ancient Greek and Roman world demonstrated an awareness, albeit limited, of the natural world and its impact on societal change, before medieval historians and travellers began to paint much larger pictures of the globe. Later, in the long-running General Global Crisis debate, historians argued whether evidence exists to find a causal connection between the very real extremes in climate that is a feature of the seventeenth century and the no less real anomalies of conflict, rebellion, revolution and war which were also such a distinct feature of the period until the eighteenth century ushered in a relative stability.

As was so often the case, however, the age of European imperial expansion witnessed the most rapid advances. In India, for example, the need of colonial authorities to understand and hence control the environment promoted major research projects (Section 2). What emerged was an increased sensitivity both to the vulnerability of the natural world in the face of human depredation and the reciprocal impact that such change had on people, as evidenced, for example, in devastating famines that swept through large areas of India.

It is something of a paradox that, despite the long recognition of such problems, academics were not attracted to environmental science and history until the postwar years (Section 3). Paralleling the rise of concern about the impact of human behaviour on the environment, university courses were offered that attracted large numbers of students, and there appeared several pioneering studies that for the first time foregrounded the environment in the history of the modern world. Arguably, more than any other area of inquiry associated with history, environmental history remains truly interdisciplinary.

16.1 The Scope of Environmental History and Historical Precedents

It is no easy task to define environmental history, pinpoint when it began as a discipline in its own right or identify its lineages. We do know that a consciousness of the environment began in the earliest times when humans were forced to confront the natural world and develop strategies for survival against hostile elements. It was hardly accidental, therefore, that such an awareness was evident in the first figurative representations and written recordings of human existence. And there is abundant evidence that ancient and medieval philosophers speculated on the nature of the environment, often with regard to the human condition. It was not until the age of European colonial expansion when data on the natural world were first systematically and accurately recorded that historical changes in topography, climate, flora and fauna were analyzed. Much of this work encouraged an interest in the interrelationships between the human and natural worlds, but it arguably it was not until the postwar years that environmental history as a species of historical inquiry emerged, arguably as part of the dramatic growth in anxiety about the damage inflicted on the planet by human intervention and the human costs of deforestation, desiccation and extreme weather.

In this chapter we seek to explore these themes. Because the topic is potentially vast – literally the entire history of human interaction with the environment – it is necessary at the outset to define limits. J. Donald Hughes (2006, p. 3) has usefully identified three broad questions that together have mapped the boundaries of environmental history:

1. What influence has the environment exerted on human history?
2. How has human intervention altered the environment?
3. How have humans thought about the environment?

These themes rarely work in isolation and so have tended to run into one another. For example, studies on environmental influences or human intervention have considered also how the environment was regarded, and those on human intervention have considered how changes in the environment rebounded to affect the course of human affairs. Perhaps environmental history is therefore simply (!) a quest to understand how humans over time have interrelated with and thought about the rest of nature.

Even if the borders can be drawn in this way, more detailed scrutiny of the individual themes suggests just how wide their terrain remains. In considering the influence of the environment on human history, scholars have considered the topography, soil types and mineral resources of the land; the crucial juxtaposition of land with rivers, lakes and seas; changes in the atmosphere, weather and climate and the living world of nature, in particular plants and animals that have a direct influence on humans. The theme of human intervention, which has tended to dominate the agenda of environmental history, has focused attention on our need to provide sustenance through such means as agriculture, fishing and hunting; the extraction of essential materials by mining, forestry and the management of water and the damaging impact of waste production evident in the pollution of the atmosphere, land and the living world. Finally, the study of human thought on the natural world has explored the ways in which the religions, philosophies and political ideologies of different cultures have perceived and thereby acted upon the environment.

Such an agenda has attracted the attention of scholars from an extraordinarily wide range of disciplines. Anthropologists, philosophers, geographers, biologists, meteorologists, economists as well as historians are among those who have made important contributions to the debates. In this respect, it could well be argued that environmental history has developed as one of the truly interdisciplinary areas of inquiry. Part of the reason for this is that from the beginnings of time humans have reflected on the natural world, and many of the questions of contemporary relevance have historic lineages traceable to ancient cultures and philosophies.

In the tradition of Western thought, for example, ancient Greek and Roman scholars considered the environment entirely fit for human habitation (Glacken, 1967, p. 147). There existed a harmony between nature and humans which was ordered, perhaps even the product of a grand design. All the natural and human world, therefore, conformed to and confirmed the existence of a plan in which everything had its place. Furthermore, because the ancients were sufficiently knowledgeable about the earth's diversity, it was possible to point to other areas where the design had been able to adapt to different climates and conditions and thereby to suggest the ability of the environment to influence human life and culture. Simultaneously, and somewhat contradictorily, humans as the highest form of creation could improve nature through invention. Farming, irrigation and drainage schemes and the clearance of forests and waste lands were seen to improve nature by making it more productive and thus better fitted to human needs. At its extreme, this line of thought led to an unqualified hubris about human mastery over nature and the idea that nature existed only to serve the interests of humans.

Unsurprisingly, the two greatest historians of the ancient world were conscious of these matters (Chapter 1). Herodotus' account is replete with detailed descriptions of the topography of Europe, the Mediterranean world and Egypt. These are frequently linked to the cultures of its peoples. Take, for example, his description of the Scythians:

Having neither cities nor forts, and carrying their dwellings with them wherever they go; accustomed, moreover, one and all of them, to shoot from horseback; and living not by husbandry but on their cattle, their wagons the only houses they possess, how can they fail of being unconquerable, and unassailable even? The nature of their country, and the rivers by which it is intersected, greatly favour this mode of resisting attacks. For the land is level, well-watered, and abounding in pasture; while the rivers which traverse it are almost equal in number to the canals of Egypt.

(Herodotus, 2003, p. 321)

It was Thucydides, however, who in detailing the influence of topography and climate on human populations developed a more rigorous approach to the problem. In a complete break with Herodotus, Thucydides refused to acknowledge the influence of gods, oracles or omens; what we have is a history in which humans control their own destiny but only under conditions they inhabit. Important here was geography, which from the very outset Thucydides signals was a critical influence on the historical development of the Greek empire:

the country now called Hellas had no settled population in ancient times; instead there was a series of migrations, as the various tribes, being under constant pressure of invaders who were stronger than they were, were always prepared to abandon their own territory. There was no commerce, and no safe communication either by land or sea; the use they made of their land was limited to the production of necessities; they had no surplus left over for capital, and no regular system of agriculture since they lacked the protection of fortifications. . . . Where the soil was most fertile there were the most frequent changes in population . . . for in these fertile districts it was easier for individuals to secure greater powers than their neighbours: this led to disunity, which often caused the collapse of these states, which in any case were more likely to attract the attention of foreign invaders. It is interesting to observe that Attica, which, because of the poverty of her soil, was remarkably free from political disunity, has always been inhabited by the same race of people.

(Thucydides, 1972, pp. 35–6)

An environmental consciousness in early times was by no means a concern exclusively of the West; indeed, as is becoming increasingly apparent, most established communities came to perceive interrelationships between human and natural worlds. During the period of Indian history around the time of the Romans, ancient texts such as the *Arthasastra*, a handbook of public administration, revealed the presence of a rich and powerful Mauryan state based in the agricultural lands and village communities to the north and the centre which organized ambitious schemes to protect forests and indigenous fauna, most notably the elephants. Furthermore, the handbook displays a rudimentary sense of environmental determinism. It recounts, for example, that in seeking to extend its influence by clearing new lands for cultivation, the kingdom under its legendary leader Ashoka (c.268–232 BCE) encountered tribal societies of nomadic herding peoples and forest dwellers who were seen as savage because they inhabited alien landscapes previously beyond the civilizing influence of the agrarian economy (Parasher-Sen, 2011). This trope proved remarkably enduring, for by the eleventh century CE Sanskrit literary sources commonly referred to the contrast between the untamed forest and settled village communities (Chakravarti, 2011), and it was to underscore many of the anxieties expressed by the British over the troublesome presence of tribal communities at the outer limits of its empire.

The period from 500 to 1300 witnessed the expansion of Indian agriculture. As a concomitant, there emerged a finely tuned sensibility to the geographical distribution of different land types within agrarian settlements. Charters granting land in the Deccan region from the eighth century CE, for example, define the boundaries of marsh land, pasture and cattle-grazing lands, orchards and even a village area with timber, grass and straw (Lal, 2011). This was combined with an awareness of the critical importance of climate and natural and artificial hydraulic systems. Eleventh-century charters from Bengal and Bihar include frequent references to rivers and embankments and from the arid topography of Rajasthan to the beneficial effects of irrigation technologies on the cultivation of a diverse range of crops including cotton, indigo and sugar cane.

The Middle Ages in the West seemed to offer few advances in understanding of the environment. Compared with theological disputations, astrology and alchemy, the earthly world outside the human attracted little interest (Glacken, 1967, p. 286). There was one endeavour, however, which did lift medieval scholars out of the prosaic. Travellers and the popular accounts they wrote of their voyages not only opened up new and unknown vistas to European minds but helped to promote the extraordinary intellectual transformation that culminated in the age of science and reason. Tales of Christian pilgrimages, especially to Palestine, may not have been concerned with environmental causation but they did provide detailed mappings of the topographies of holy sites mentioned in Biblical narratives (Elsner and Rubiés, 1999). These accounts – part travelogue, part spiritual achievement of divine grace – would become a paradigm for travel writings in the West until the modern era. Geographically, however, they, like the accounts of crusaders that followed, were for the most part focused on the Holy Land, and so had nothing to say about the world beyond Europe and the Middle East. Toward the late Middle Ages, a crisis in the feudal order attendant on a certain loss of confidence in faith promoted alternative travelogues. Allegorical tales were displaced by ones offering not only narrative truths based on first-hand empirical observation but also a much greater sense of ethnographical diversity. The hugely popular accounts of Marco Polo and John Mandeville from the thirteenth and fourteenth centuries may have relied heavily on myth, but there was sufficient material of seeming authority effectively to introduce large parts of the world to a European audience.

At the same time, a tradition of travel within the Muslim world was gathering momentum, largely through the exploits of Ibn Khaldun and Ibn Battuta. Of the fourteenth century, of Berber descent and of wide scholarly background, they are both now regarded as among the most remarkable figures of the age. In his best-known work, *Muqaddimah*, Ibn Khaldun attempts a history of world civilizations based in part upon his own travels around the Islamic empire. It identifies the various climatic regions and how these had shaped the lives of their inhabitants;

unsurprisingly, most attention was devoted to the desert lives of Bedouin tribes. Although Ibn Battuta was a judge and scholar, he is best remembered for his extensive travels over thirty years throughout the Islamic world, Africa, China and South Asia. His subsequent account, commonly referred to as the *Rihla* or Journey, was composed largely from memory and in parts from other accounts, but it displayed an extraordinary knowledge of the environments and cultures of lands previously beyond the Islamic and European worlds. The impact of the *Muqaddimah* and *Rihla* outside the Arab world, however, was limited. Extracts from the *Muqaddimah* were first translated into French early in the nineteenth century, while an abridged manuscript version of the *Rihla* was first translated into English in 1829. Since then, both have come to be recognized as pioneering works of history, economics and geography, ranking alongside the greatest of the ancient world.

It is often claimed that while the medieval world tended to contemplate human subordination to and dependence upon the environment, modern sensibilities were rather more inclined to celebrate man's (and it was man's) mastery over nature (Glacken, 196, p. 349). The case is overstated for it is evident that the Middle Ages witnessed human intervention on an unprecedented scale, but even that was dwarfed by the changes wrought since, say, the sixteenth century. This is where European imperial endeavour entered the stage and began a new phase in environmental history, not only in the transformation that took place but also in the development of environmental history as a discipline in its own right.

16.2 European Colonialism and the Environment

In the *Wealth of Nations* Adam Smith famously declared: 'The discovery of America, and that of a passage to the East Indies by the Cape of Good Hope, are the two greatest and most important events recorded in the history of mankind' (Smith, 1997, p. 622). He made this claim in 1776, that is, on the cusp of the new age and at a time before he could realistically assess the consequences for humankind, but arguably, and despite the tumultuous change that modernization has brought about, Smith's vision still holds. Smith was interested in political economy, specifically how the nations of the world could best secure the futures of their peoples through industry and commerce. In so doing he demonstrated an awareness of historic developments of agrarian and industrial economies, sea-born and land-based trade and how they were shaped by the environment. Take, for example, the following discussion of the origins of civilization:

> The nations that . . . appear to have been first civilized, were those that dwelt round the coast of the Mediterranean Sea. That sea, by far the greatest inlet that is known in the world, having no tides, nor consequently any waves, except such as are caused by the wind only, was, by the smoothness of the surface, as well as by the multitude of its islands, and the proximity of its neighbouring shores, extremely favourable to the infant navigation of the world; when, from their ignorance of the compass, men were afraid to quite the view of the coast, and from the imperfection of the art of ship-building, to abandon themselves to the boisterous waves of the ocean.
>
> (Smith, 1997, p. 24)

These insights aside, it would be difficult to think of the *Wealth of Nations* as a ground-breaking work of environmental history. Smith's discussion of the two 'greatest events', for example, hardly touches on the environment. And yet, as we shall see, in the long term the opening up of the Americas and India to Europe transformed the political economy of the world *and* had as profound an influence on the natural world as any before or since. We will come later to consider the opening of the Americas but first wish to explore the vital impact of European imperial endeavour and the body of work it has attracted. There is no better starting point than Richard Grove's *Green Imperialism*, a ground-breaking book which has done much to define the agenda for studies that were to follow (Grove, 1995). Grove argues that, far from being a fashionable concern of the twentieth century, distinctly modern ways of thinking about the environment were born out of the experience of colonial rule in the tropics. In particular, an awareness of the vulnerability of the environment to human depredation emerged from and was shaped by the complex thinking of European colonizers – a thinking which stood in many ways in sharp contrast to the material and mental exploitation that occurred. Not that this enhanced awareness was a construction of an exclusively European natural philosophy; to the contrary, the diffusion of indigenous knowledges of the environment not only preceded European incursions but exerted a critical influence on the development of modern epistemologies.

The first flowering of this sprang from anxieties about the damaging effects of plantation agriculture on island sites including Madeira, Mauritius and the Caribbean. From the sixteenth century, urgent demands were expressed to mitigate deforestation, soil erosion and desiccation, which resulted from colonial intervention. In so doing scientists such as Richard Norwood and William Sayle in Bermuda, Thomas Tryon in Barbados and Edmond Halley in St Helena sowed the seeds of a sustained critique of environmental degradation (Grove and Damodaran, 2012). This age of exploration and colonial expansion also seemed to provide the bodies and theories of botany, medicine and science more generally as a means of recording and understanding the damage and in some cases devise appropriate strategies of conservation. The many botanical gardens established in virtually all the colonies were part of this project. Powerful merchant trading companies, in particular the East India Company in Britain, employed trained scientists and doctors to investigate the putative interrelationships among irrigation, deforestation and climate and the incidence of famine and disease. Their findings alarmed the Company and provided the necessary impetus for the pioneering forest-conservation programmes that followed (ibid., p. 11).

Important among early scientists was William Roxburgh who in the latter decades of the eighteenth century supplemented his work as a Company surgeon by analyzing what he saw as the intimate relationship between climate and ecological change. He pioneered the meticulous recording of meteorological data, which he harnessed in a sustained critique of the damage brought by colonial intervention (Grove, 1995 pp. 399–408). He happened to be in India during a particularly powerful phase of El Niño activity when devastating famines struck Bengal and Madras, leading him to speculate on the periodical incidence of drought and the abject failure of the Company to respond adequately to the high levels of mortality that ensued.

The ready exchange of ideas among scientists working in different locations laid the foundations during the eighteenth and nineteenth centuries for the first global environmentalism. Although this was funded and driven by Western concerns, indigenous systems of thought were integral to the development of modern thinking. In India, for example, concepts of nature, many of which had ancient lineages in Hinduism, Islam and Zoroastrianism, fed into and hence shaped environmental concern. When this was combined with an appreciation of customary methods of irrigation, water conservation and forest management, it is difficult to avoid the conclusion that the overall influence of indigenous thought on colonial environmental policy in India was weightier than any ideologies imported from outside (ibid., p. 382).

The influence of pre-modern thought was evident also in some of the foundational work of a global environmentalism. The environmental philosophy of the German explorer

Alexander von Humboldt, the influence of which was felt around nineteenth-century Europe, was rooted in the universalism of Johann von Herder, whose *Outlines of a Philosophy of the History of Man* (1800) had sought a 'comprehensive view of the geography and history of man, in order to complete for all of nature . . . the picture of which we have but a few, though clear, outlines' (cited in Grove, 1995, p. 368). Herder viewed human life as intimately related to the natural world. The physical universe provided a matrix within which humans emerged and developed over time. Differences in the environment, however, created distinct hierarchies. Because of its geographical and climatic conditions, Europe alone provided the centre for a human life that was 'genuinely historical'. By comparison, in China, India and pre-Columbian America there was no historical progress, merely static civilizations with little experience of steady cumulative development. In this quest von Herder had drawn heavily upon Hindu teachings on the relations between man and nature which had been widely disseminated by German and French orientalists and which espoused the vital notion of the unity and interdependence of all things. Few historians nowadays would accept Herder's somewhat dismissive and racialized depiction of the non-European world, but without him, the environmental holism that came to define much of Humboldt's work would have been poorly developed.

We must caution against any notion, however, that colonizers and indigenous peoples worked in harmony to improve the landscape or at the very least mitigate the damage inflicted by imperial reform. There were often considerable discrepancies between professed ideals and the practical realities of environmental policies. When hydraulic engineers, many from a military background, set about improving the irrigation of nineteenth-century India in order to boost agricultural productivity and eradicate famines, they came into conflict with indigenous practices. Over millennia, Indians had developed a sophisticated network of canals, dams and reservoir tanks to provide sufficient water in times of drought. Occasionally, these were admired by government engineers, but in general they were considered primitive, inferior and inefficient schemes when compared with those based on the scientific and mathematical knowledge imported from the West. In the event, however, this knowledge and many of the schemes upon which they were built led to disastrous increases in malarial disease and a decline in agricultural productivity (Beinhart and Hughes, 2007, Chapter 6).

The wholesale destruction of Indian forests was just one part of the story of environmental degradation brought by European colonizers wherever they chose to venture. Massive schemes to clear land for agriculture or to provide timber first for company ships and then for sleepers in the construction of the fast-expanding railway system during the second half of the nineteenth century destroyed large swathes of India's forests. It was an act, like water management, which blindly ignored practices of conservation and regeneration followed by indigenous populations over centuries (Gadgil and Guha, 1993). Some officials, however, sensing an irreversible environmental crisis, added their voices to the critique of environmental degradation, making major contributions to debates on the untold damage caused by human intervention. Hugh Cleghorn, Conservator of Forests in Madras and now widely regarded as the founder of Indian forestry, first drew attention to the alarming state of India's forests in 1851 when, in a report commissioned by the British Association for the Advancement of Science, he revealed the disastrous effects of colonial policies. The administration had failed to manage forests with due care; the real potential offered by them had never been realized, instead they had been remorselessly exploited by the demands of the state. This critique later reached maturity in *The Forests and Gardens of South India*, a compilation of earlier reports from the various regions, which brought to public attention the extent of wholesale plunder and wastage. In sentiments

290 *Varieties*

Figure 16.1 Alexander von Humboldt, scientist, traveller and environmentalist, on an expedition to South America, *c.*1800

Contributor: Chronicle/Alamy Stock Photo

prefiguring many of the contemporary concerns about the disappearance of rain forests in South America, Cleghorn wrote:

> It is only in late years that attention has been drawn to the importance of preserving tropical forests. . . . The question when viewed simply in its physical relations, and the propriety of clearing forest lands in order to enlarge the area of food-producing soil, pointed perhaps as much to extensive clearance as vigilant conservancy. The matter of complaint was, that

throughout the Indian empire large and valuable forest tracks were exposed to the careless rapacity of the native population, and especially unscrupulous contractors and traders, who cut and cleared them without reference to ultimate results, and who did so, moreover, without being in any way under the control or regulation of authority.

(Cleghorn, 1861, pp. vi–vii)

And the plunder was staggering. Cleghorn estimated that the construction of railways would require an annual supply of timber (mostly teak) for 250,000 sleepers or some 35,000 trees. Even though England, Ceylon and Australia would help to meet this demand, the Madras Presidency would continue to suffer from a massive drain on its forest resources (ibid., p. 33). But even this grossly underestimated the scale of tree felling, for routinely only ten per cent of the timber cut was found to be suitable. But action followed in 1865 and 1878 when two Indian Forest Acts were introduced that offered a degree of protection against the rampant commercial exploitation of previous decades.

Cleghorn's work must be seen as part of an extraordinary flowering of global environmental consciousness in the second half of the nineteenth century. Paul Strzelecki, *Physical Description of New South Wales* (1845); Ferdinand von Mueller, *Australian Vegetation, Considered especially in its Bearing on the Occupation of Territory* (1867); Berthold von Ribbentrop, *Forestry in the British Empire* (1899) and John Croumbie Brown, *The Hydrology of South Africa* (1875) were a few of the important studies written by scientists working in the colonial peripheries, which meticulously mapped the damaging consequences of environmental change (Grove and Damodaran, 2012, p. 570). This work, however, was not confined exclusively to the (British) empire. George Marsh, for example, who served as the US ambassador to Italy, developed a keen interest in how human action affected the physical condition of the landscape, most notably that of the Mediterranean and North America. His *Man and Nature* (1864) declared that, unless we learnt the lessons from the past about the damage inflicted by human ignorance, the fate that befell earlier civilizations would revisit those of the present.

16.3 Modern Environmentalism

By placing firmly on the agenda the notion that the human and natural histories were intimately linked, this body of work laid the foundation for the environmental histories of the twentieth century. Early on, theories of global desiccation began to command renewed interest among geographers and climatologists. Since the late eighteenth century when data on climatic conditions and agriculture were first gathered systematically, there had been speculation on their mutual influences, but the cataclysmic Indian famine of 1877–1879 and the opening up of Africa to scientific exploration promoted a surge of interest in historic patterns of extreme weather, most notably drought and monsoon rainfall, coupled with heightened concerns about the extinction of indigenous peoples and large animals (Davis, 2001; Grove, 1998). John Croumbie Brown, *The Hydrology of South Africa* (1875); David and Charles Livingstone, *Narrative of an Expedition to the Zambesi and its Tributaries* (1866); J. D. Falconer, *On Horseback through Nigeria* (1911) and J. Tilho, *Documents Scientifiques de la Mission Tilho* (1910–1911) provided compelling evidence that great lakes had existed in central areas, glaciers from Mount Kenya and Kilimanjaro had extended much further, and large expanses of the Sahara had once been fertile, in other words, that the climate of Africa had been much cooler in the past (Grove and Damodaran, 2012, pp. 570–1).

Simultaneously, small groups of geographers operating mainly from the metropolitan centre began to construct a more global environmental history by synthesizing the writings of colonial scientists. Much of this work was framed by the experience of the British empire and bore its indelible stamp, but it had the merit of transcending regional boundaries. Halford Mackinder, *Britain and the British Seas* (1902); H. B. George, *The Historical Geography of the British Empire* (1901) and J. L. Myre, *The Dawn of History* (1911) were typical of a body of writing that was both innovative and popular. In the interwar years, no doubt reflecting heightened anxieties about the threats to the empire posed by nationalist movements, publications appeared warning of the dangers of environmental degradation. Using examples from empires in the past C. E. P. Brooks, *The Evolution of Climate* (1922) and *Climate Through the Ages* (1926) and the American Ellsworth Huntington, *Climatic Changes* (1922) described the potentially catastrophic consequences of climate change even for mighty empires. This rather doom-laden scenario was evident also in works which tackled the potential for human destruction either by direct intervention or through the failure to take appropriate action to mitigate climatic change. The relationship between desiccation and human activity was amply if alarmingly investigated by William Macdonald, *Conquest of the Desert* (1913); E. H. L. Schwartz, *The Kalahari; or Thirstland Redemption* (1923) and J. C. Smuts, *Holism and Evolution* (1926). Much of this set the scene for sensationalist and journalistic books such as Graham Jacks and R. O. White's *The Rape of the Earth: A World Survey of Soil Erosion* (1939), which did more to spread panic about environmental degradation, particularly against a backdrop of the appearance of dust bowls in the vast plains of North America.

Heretofore, approaches to the environment had been pioneered by geographers, including some with a distinct historical bent. During the interwar period, largely independent of this work, scholars from other disciplines began to make what were arguably the first significant contributions to our understanding of the relationship between geography and societal evolution. No more so than in France, where the *Annales* school was particularly creative. Lucien Febvre, *La Terre et L'evolution Humaine* (1924), unimaginatively entitled *A Geographical Introduction to History* when published in English translation the following year, proclaimed the vital role of geography in explaining historical change, not as a determinant but rather as a factor that shapes or sets boundaries to human action. In this respect, Febvre may well have set the agenda for the study of environmental history in its own right. Having paid due regard in the introduction to the earlier work of luminaries such as von Humboldt, Jules Michelet and Comte de Buffon, Febvre then insists – and with some justification – that 'we know in reality little or nothing as yet of the influence of the geographical environment on human societies'. We need to develop, therefore, a 'geographical spirit' in order to understand 'what conditions are imposed on history . . . by the habitable earth'. Such a venture requires us to 'free ourselves from any pre-determined historical or topographical order, and from any systematic or pre-conceived design of forcing certain general data to fit in with reality, or of making certain abstract characteristics true for all history and all countries' (Febvre, 2003, p. 124). This insistence on acknowledging the historical specificity of different geographical regions was never fully realized in Febvre, but the cause was taken up some twenty years later by his colleague Fernand Braudel. In *The Mediterranean and the Mediterranean World in the Age of Philip II* (1946), long regarded as a classic, Braudel devotes almost all the first half to a detailed study of the environment and the economy before going on to consider the 'history' of the region. Even then, he ignored national boundaries and eschewed the conventional narrative description of events that had characterized most historical writing in order to understand the broad and enduring structures inhabited by human societies.

Elsewhere, this approach to world history began to attract the attention of scholars from a range of disciplines. The Australian archaeologist V. Gordon Childe (1892–1957) published a number of studies which gained wide popular and scholarly appeal (see also Chapter 17). *The Oriental Prelude to European History* (1934), *Man Makes Himself* (1936) and *What Happened in History* (1942) employed rich archaeological evidence to map the course of human evolution prior to the Industrial Revolution. And the British anthropologist Daryll Forde (1902–1973), based at the University of California, published to great acclaim *Habitat, Economy and Society* (1934), a collection of writings on the environmental impact on the economy and customs of various communities from Siberia to the Kalahari.

In the postwar years the centre of gravity for the study of environmental history shifted decisively to North America. Fuelled by increasing concerns over threats to the environment and popular protest against the Vietnam War, the writings of W. L. Thomas, *Man's Role in Changing the Face of the Earth* (1956), Clarence Glacken, *Traces on the Rhodian Shore* (1965), Clifford Geertz, *Agricultural Involution; the Processes of Ecological Change in Indonesia* (1963), Carl Sauer, *The Early Spanish Main* (1966) and Roderick Nash, *Wilderness and the American Dream* (1967) skilfully captured the mood and led to soaring demands for university courses on environmental history. Then in 1972 Alfred Crosby published *The Columbian Exchange: Biological and Cultural Consequences of 1492*, followed fourteen years later by *Ecological Imperialism: The Biological Expansion of Europe, 900–1900*, at which point environmental history came of age.

Columbian Exchange followed the movement of plants, animals, diseases and material cultures criss-crossing the Atlantic in the aftermath of the opening up of the Americas in 1492. Its wide appeal resided in the way Crosby overcame disciplinary and geographical boundaries and a certain American insularity to provide a compelling account of the rise of Europe – a rise, he emphasized, which owed as much to the biology of micro-organisms as to a superiority of manpower, technology and weaponry. The extraordinary, long-term impact of the event was later expanded in the lively and accessible study *1493* by Charles Mann (2011). He argues that the bringing together of two previously separate worlds set in motion a chain of events which touched every corner of the globe, the consequences of which we still live with. It is a story that involved the cultivation and consumption of tobacco and the humble potato, the conveyance of micro-organisms carrying malaria and yellow fever, the mining and transhipment of vast quantities of silver, huge demographic shifts caused by the enslavement of Africans and revolutions in agricultural and industrial production.

Ecological Imperialism opens with a challenge: 'European emigrants and their descendants are all over the place, which requires explanation' (Crosby, 1986, p. 2). Striking is the observation that those parts of the world that most closely resemble Europe in terms of culture and demography are far away across major oceans. They have climates and terrains, however, which are similarly hospitable, enabling European flora and fauna to thrive, especially where the competition is mild. In an age of European imperial expansion over a millennium, that dominance was won against indigenous populations, not merely or principally by force of arms but by ecological factors including the skilful exploitation of winds and currents; cultivation of crops, grasses and even weeds which overwhelmed native species and spread rapidly; use of domesticated animals for motive power, transport and a source of protein and the exportation of deadly infectious diseases such as smallpox, which took a terrible toll on indigenous peoples.

Such approaches to an understanding of the experience of European imperial endeavour reveal what environmental history can bring to the table. More than is the case in conventional histories, an appreciation of ecological factors provides a forceful explanation of why vast territories in the Americas and Oceania were conquered by so few European settlers. And it points to powerful associations across time and space. Looking at imperialism through the lens of environmentalism reveals processes of changes to the relationship between the natural and human which had commenced long before but were then intensified and accelerated. It follows that imperialism must be inserted into longer narratives of development and natural change rather than conferring on it an autonomy around which periodizations such as pre-colonial, colonial and post-colonial or premodern, modern and postmodern are constructed (Pomeranz, 2009, p. 16).

The appearance of these studies coincided with sharp increases in concerns over putative ecological crises created by human intervention. Especially in the States, this period gave rise to a surge of imaginative studies which sought to provide broad narratives of global environmental change, and were attractive to both academic and public audiences. Among the more important was the trilogy of William McNeill (1978, 1982, 1990) who has done more than anyone to further the study of global history with due regard to environmental factors. Eric Wolf (1997) opens his fine exploration of old and new worlds since 1400 with the bold assertion that 'To understand the world of 1400, we must begin with geography' and proceeds to reveal the manifold economic, ecological, political and cultural interconnections that shaped the humankind as it entered the modern era (Chapter 15). J. Donald Hughes (2001) was among the first historians to write a global environmental history, while the ecologist Jared Diamond (1997) attempted a socio-ecological world history which although criticized as derivative and somewhat deterministic has succeeded in attracting a huge readership.

The seventeenth century has hosted a theory that has helped greatly to enhance the worth of environmental history. The theory of General Global Crisis had seemed terminally out of fashion until the military historian Geoffrey Parker wrote *Global Crisis: War, Climate Change & Catastrophe in the Seventeenth Century* (2013). This was a book long in the planning. An earlier book *The General Crisis of the Seventeenth Century* had appeared in 1975, been republished in 1997, and in February 1998 Parker had written an email to his publishers, the contents of which, in their sheer scope and ambition, most of us could only dream about:

> I always thought that the idea of my next book would come to me quite unexpectedly. Last night I awoke at 4AM and realized that I wanted to write a book about the General Crisis of the seventeenth century – not a collection of essays (been there, done that) but an integrated narrative and analytical account of the first global crisis for which we possess adequate documentation for Asia, Africa, the Americas, and Europe. My account would adopt a Braudelian structure, examining long-term factors (climate above all), medium-run changes (economic fluctuations and so on) and 'events' (from the English Civil War and the crisis in the French and Spanish Monarchies, through the murder of two Ottoman sultans, the civil wars in India and sub-Saharan Africa to the collapse of Ming China and the wars around the Great Lakes of America). Besides examining each of the upheavals of the mid-century, the book would offer explanations of why such synchronic developments occur with so little warning and why they end. Although not the first 'general crisis' known to historians, it is the first one for which adequate data exists worldwide. Since it addresses issues of concern today – the impact of global climate change and sharp economic recession on government and society – it should not lack interested readers.
>
> (Parker, 2013, p. 705)

And this is almost precisely what he delivered, all 700–800 pages of it. Historians had looked at the idea of a seventeenth-century crisis before. Eric Hobsbawm had suggested in 1954 that the transition between the feudal and capitalist economies (the precise location and nature of transition was a common debate in Marxist circles at the time) meant that the rise of nascent capitalistic mercantile and commercial interests had led to popular uprisings as feudal elites attempted to hold onto their power. At root (because it was a Marxist argument) this was a crisis stoked by economic interests that were ultimately contradictory. A few years later, in 1959, the more traditionalist historian Hugh Trevor-Roper (Chapters 21 and 22) saw the crisis, not in economic terms but in terms of politics and fiscal policy with courts and governments rubbing up against provincial and local powers with dramatic results. This debate culminated in an edited collection by T. S. Aston called *Crisis in Europe, 1560–1660* (1965).

But by then interest in the theory of a General Global Crisis had begun to lose pace. A review of Parker's book by early modernist Derek Parrott examined why:

> Trevor-Roper's political crisis suffered a slower disintegration, through a revisionism which steadily sapped the life out of binary models that pitted a radical centre against a backward periphery, or new bureaucratic functionaries against reactionary nobles. In the end, both interpretations were of course thoroughly Eurocentric. How useful was the concept of the transition from feudalism to capitalism when examining political upheavals in mid-17th-century China? Did it make any sense to discuss the crisis of the Ottoman Empire in terms of a struggle between a centralising monarchy and reactionary provincial nobility?
>
> (Parrott, 2015)

The General Crisis of the 17th Century was seen as a sequel to Ashton's *Crisis in Europe*, but this time climate change was very clearly the main explanation for increasing conflict not only in mid-seventeenth century Europe but elsewhere:

> This pattern of world-wide upheaval suggests that beneath the more obvious local precipitants lurked very basic global causes. The most plausible candidate is climatic change: a world-wide deterioration in prevailing weather patterns, leading to relative over-population and related food shortages, to mass migrations (perhaps armed) from poorer to richer lands, to swift spreading pandemics, and to frequent wars and rebellions. However, for a climatic explanation to be valid, evidence of crisis must be apparent in many parts of the globe – at least over large parts of the northern hemisphere (where the bulk of the population then lived) – and not merely in a small region such as Europe. The mid-seventeenth century seems to meet this criterion.
>
> (Parker and Smith, 1997, p. 6)

Perhaps with the onset of a greater sensitivity about the need to take a global view of historical phenomena (Chapter 15), Jack Goldstone's *Revolution and Rebellion in the Early Modern World* (1991) examined multi continent cycles of population expansion and decline. However, Goldstone saw a crisis of the state as prime cause that explained social and political disarray. Here Goldstone drew a rather straighter line from commentators such as Barrington Moore and Skocpol that we looked at in Chapter 8.

Parker differed in identifying climate as a principal cause of massive social, economic and political disruption, as evident in the cycles of war, famine and disease. In a later work by which time new sources of evidence had become available, he listed the major revolts and revolutions of the seventeenth century suggesting the global reach of the revolutionary turmoil.

Contemporaries were aware of this general crisis and tended to blame God and the Devil in equal measure, while natural philosophers searched in vain for a rational explanation. Some, such as the English philosopher Francis Bacon, hinted at the importance of climate to good government, but it was not until new archives became available in the postwar years that historians began to elaborate on the dynamic relationship between climate and human affairs. Parker was among them and sought carefully to identify areas of natural variation in climate that were causally related to the major revolts and revolutions of the seventeenth century.

The climax of these upheavals occurred in the 1640s. Here was a time of peculiarly low solar activity when temperatures plummeted to record levels. Historians and climatologists talk of a Little Ice Age in which prolonged droughts were experienced in some regions, disastrous floods in others, leading to sharp increases in the cost of essential foodstuffs including rice and corn. Faced with unprecedented highs in the cost of food, popular revolts broke out in Portugal, Japan, Spain, Italy, Russia, Scotland, China, indeed around the globe (Parker, 2013, pp. 1073–5). More global wars took place than at any time until the 1940s, more than one occurred every three years, and over 1611–1669 Europe was constantly at war.

Parker insisted that the new archives that radically altered our ability to identify correlations between climate and social upheaval were human and natural:

Human Archive

- *Narrative* information contained in written texts (chronicles and histories, letters and diaries, judicial and government records, newspapers and broadsheets) and oral traditions
- *Numerical* information compiled from documentary proxy data (such as the changing date on which the harvesting of certain crops began each year, or the annual volume harvested) or, occasionally, from narrative reports ('Rain fell for the first time in 42 days')
- *Pictorial* information contained in dated visual representations of natural phenomena (paintings that show the position of a glacier's tongue in a given year or that depict ice floes in a harbor [sic] during a winter of unusual severity
- *Epigraphic* or *archaeological* information, such as inscriptions on structures that date flood levels, or excavations of settlements abandoned because of climate change

Natural Archive

Ice cores: the annual deposits on ice caps and glaciers around the world, captured in deep boreholes, provide evidence of changing levels of volcanic emissions, precipitation, air temperature, and atmospheric composition

Glaciology: the altering advance and retreat of glaciers, together with and analysis of the debris left behind, sheds light on both precipitation and ablation

Palynology: changes in pollen and spores deposited in lakes, bogs, and estuaries reflect the natural vegetation at the time of pollen deposit

Dendrochronology: the varying size of growth rings laid down by trees during each growing season reflects local conditions in spring and summer. A thick ring corresponds with a year favourable to growth, while a narrow ring indicates a year of adversity

(ibid, pp. 1065–6)

This serves as a useful example of the intimate relationship between evidence and theory, but Parker concludes in sombre tone. Despite the advances made in the study of climatic change, historians in the North American academy seem to resist the notion that climate has exercised a decisive influence on human affairs in the past.

We wish to close with two collections. The first by Donald Worster, *The Wealth of Nature: Environmental History and the Ecological Imagination* (1993), written by one of the most respected environmental historians, sets out an intellectual and political manifesto for the study of environmental history that has probably not been bettered:

I want to draw attention back to the material reality of the natural world as it impinges on human society, now shaping, now being shaped, by that society. My dissatisfaction with non-environmental history is that it commonly ignores that material reality, an ignorance that extends far beyond the cloisters of history into contemporary popular attitudes. . . . Whatever terrain the environmental historian chooses to investigate, he has to address the age-old predicament of how humankind can feed itself without degrading the primal source of life. Today, as ever, that problem is the fundamental challenge in human ecology, and meeting it will require knowing the earth well – knowing its history and knowing its limits.

(Worster, 1993, pp. ix, 63)

In the edited collection *Environment and World History* (2009), two eminent historians, Edmund Burke III and Kenneth Pomeranz, take up the task. New forms of global history which have emerged over the past thirty years, they claim, have challenged us to rethink the modern world less as a history of the West, more as a shared history of the peoples of Asia, Europe, America and Africa. Environmental history possesses a similar intellectual agenda but by comparison has been slow to develop or make its influence felt. Most world histories have simply ignored the environment or relegated it to the margins, C. A. Bayly's *The Birth of the Modern World* (2004) and W. Roger Louis (ed.), *Oxford History of the British Empire* (1995–1999) being cases in point. The task, therefore, is to persuade global historians that in its attention to global, regional and local ecologies, environmental history offers global history the chance to break free from boundaries defined largely by nation or civilization. 'Putting the environment into world history', they conclude, 'is therefore an urgent intellectual project' (Burke and Pomeranz, 2009, pp. xi–xiii).

As an example of this project, let us look briefly at one of the contributions to the collection. In 'The Big Story', Burke explores what he terms the deep history of humanity through the lens of energy (Burke, 2009). By mapping the dynamics and storage of planetary bioenergy, he claims, we challenge the historical narratives underlying conventional accounts of human development since Palaeolithic times. The use of fire ensured the survival of the species and humans gradually peopled the world. Over ensuing millennia changes in the relationship between the human and natural worlds culminated in the Neolithic revolution when hunter-gatherers discovered in farming a means of sustaining a reliable supply of food. This revolution in energy gave rise to civilizations and unprecedented concentrations of population and a transformation in the use of domestic animals as a source of power. During the age of empire, the calculus of energy remained the same, but as wood and charcoal were abandoned and the potential of fossil fuel at last realized, the Industrial Revolution took off, leading to vast increases in human populations and to dramatic environmental degradation. In describing industrialization, Burke contends, historians have tended to focus on the scientific and technological, but if as an alternative we foreground transformations in bioenergetic systems then it becomes one of several that have taken place in the *trés longue durée*. Today, as the use of fossil fuels is increasingly questioned, are we on the eve of another?

Such attempts to bring together environmental and global history into a constructive dialogue are, however, in their infancy. In the meantime, despite the longevity of an environmental consciousness, the emergence of a powerful body of writing in the postwar years and a crescendo of doom-laden prognoses of ecological catastrophes, environmental history has not been able to penetrate mainstream historiography. Part of the reason lies in the innate conservatism of the discipline, part in the very infancy of environmental history as a subdiscipline with its own priorities. Any productive coalescence in the future will depend upon social, economic and cultural historians coming to acknowledge the importance of environmental influences and upon a willingness among environmental historians to combine broad, overarching narratives with an acute sensitivity to the more specific and particular trajectories of different regions and localities.

298 *Varieties*

A sensitivity to environmental factors in human history cannot be our whole concern. In some respects, environmental history is too important to be left to the historians. As Parker acutely observed, studying the impact of the environment on the seventeenth-century crisis will not

> prevent the onset of further climatic catastrophes in the twenty-first century; but if historians can identify the structural, political, economic, and ideological characteristics in each afflicted society around the world that prevented (or facilitated) an appropriate response during the General Crisis, and consider how the outcomes could have been different, we may learn some valuable lessons for dealing with the climate challenges that undoubtedly await us and our children.
>
> (Parker, 2013, p. 1079)

Postscript

In addressing environment history, we face something of a paradox. If for the sake of argument, we consider that the field seeks to understand the dynamic and reciprocal relationship between the environment and human activity, then how can we explain why it has only recently appeared in university programmes, and why it has failed to intervene in mainstream historical research? The paradox is even more striking when we realize that the environment has attracted the interest of scholars, administrators, rulers and indigenous communities from early times. Ancient Greek and Roman philosophers, for example, were aware of the influence of topography and climate on human populations. And in medieval India indigenous communities developed a sophisticated – but largely unwritten – sense of how humans best manage different land types. Historians have also been debating the possibility that changes in the natural environment such as rapid climate change might even been causally linked to historical events.

As was the case in so many other fields including anthropology and medicine, the colonial experience was instrumental in placing environmental history on a more secure and scientific basis. Through empirical studies on fields, forests, famines, and irrigation systems, in particular, colonial administrators began to understand something of the vulnerability of the environment to the destructive influence of human depredation. And it was largely from such studies that historians began to consider how the global environment shaped the course of societal evolution at a global level.

If environmental history reached maturity in the postwar years with the publication of groundbreaking studies such as Alfred Crosby's *Ecological Imperialism*, it was as an adolescent. A growing awareness of human destruction of the planet provided much of the impetus for this resurgence of interest, but this level of concern has not been matched by the same determination to write the environment into historical accounts. Until this happens, there is always the chance that the environment will – like many other historical fashions – gradually fade from the scene. For our understanding of the planet, this will be unfortunate to say the least; for the discipline of history, it will be deeply damaging because it threatens to stifle not only the development of global history but also the one area of truly interdisciplinary study.

Further Reading

Fernand Braudel (1972) [1946] *The Mediterranean and the Mediterranean World in the Age of Philip II*.
Edmund Burke III and Kenneth Pomeranz (eds.) (2009) *Environment and World History*.
Alfred Crosby (1972) *The Columbian Exchange: Biological and Cultural Consequences of 1492*.
Mike Davis (2001) *Late Victorian Holocausts: El Niño Famines and the Making of the Third World*.

Clarence J. Glacken (1967) *Traces on the Rhodian Shore: Nature and Culture in Western Thought from Ancient Times to the End of the Eighteenth Century.*
Richard Grove (1995) *Green Imperialism: Colonial Expansion, Tropical Island Edens and the Origins of Environmentalism, 1600–1860.*
Donald J. Hughes (2006) *What Is Environmental History?*
Charles Mann (2011) *1493: How Europe's Discovery of the Americas Revolutionized Trade, Ecology and Life on Earth.*
Geoffrey Parker (2013) *Global Crisis: War, Climate Change & Catastrophe in the Seventeenth Century.*

Part 3
Interdisciplinarities

17 Archaeology

Introduction

For many there seems to be no significant difference between archaeology and history. Both are devoted to uncovering the past (although literally in the case of archaeology), both recognize the importance of historical chronology and in broad terms there are strong parallels in how the two disciplines have developed. Are archaeologists, therefore, nothing more than historians with dirty hands?

If we dig beneath the surface (to continue the metaphor) then certain significant differences can be detected. As we have seen in Chapter 2, the writing of history has an ancient lineage in Greece and Rome, while archaeology has developed only in recent times (Section 1). True, for millennia people have unearthed the remains of previous civilizations, but this was in the search for precious artefacts. Indeed, this motive impelled much of the work of unearthing the past until the modern era. At this point, underpinned by the intellectual transformations of the nineteenth century, archaeology emerged as a discipline and embarked on a quest to understand more about the ancient past through the collection and classification of material artefacts.

In the early decades, despite the tentative identification of stages of societal development, the emphasis was on empirically based description. In the mid twentieth century, archaeology came under the spell of theory as Gordon Childe urged his contemporaries seriously to address the matter of explanation (Section 2). In other words, it was no longer sufficient to collect and organize artefacts; they were there to help us provide explanations of how societies changed. This move unleashed in the post-=war years an extraordinarily diverse and fragmented body of work, from which emerged one strand that attempted to bring together archaeology and history. So-called historical archaeology has to our minds offered considerable potential in overcoming artificial barriers between the disciplines, as evidenced, for example, in the recent work on early imperial formations (Section 3).

17.1 The Lure of Archaeology

Archaeology retains a considerable hold on the popular imagination. Quite apart from the fictional exploits of Indiana Jones in the films made by Stephen Spielberg, enthusiastic audiences are guaranteed for the documentary programmes that appear frequently on television. The variety on offer is extraordinary. Arguably the most popular ancient site is ancient Egypt, fascination for which shows no signs of trailing off, followed by programmes on the enduring legacy of the Greek and Roman empires, but even practical demonstrations of British archaeology featured in the regular *Time Team* series that ran in Britain for many years. The discovery of the wreck of the Tudor warship *Mary Rose* under the waters of the Solent in 1971 and the excavation and identification of the remains of Richard III under a Leicester car park in 2015 captured the nation's imagination. More widely, Howard Carter's discovery of the tomb of Tutankhamun in 1922 and the accidental uncovering of the Terracotta Army of Shaanxi province by local farmers in 1974 were among the defining moments of the twentieth century. More recently – and tragically – the destruction of the Bamiyan Buddhas in Afghanistan and of the ancient city and world heritage site of Palmyra, Syria by Islamic extremists has provoked international outrage. Finally, as a practical pursuit, archaeology is now more popular than ever. Degree courses are offered by a significant minority of American and British universities, including most of the top-ranked ones, and amateur archaeological societies can be found in many regions.

Despite its appeal, archaeology has posed some challenging political and moral issues, not least in the various attempts to highjack excavations in pursuit of pernicious ideologies. In 1931, for example, Gertrude Caton-Thompson (1888–1985) reported from her careful excavation of Great Zimbabwe in Rhodesia that the monument was entirely consistent with medieval Bantu culture. Most white Rhodesians, indeed, archaeologists at the time, refused to accept that Africans ever possessed the necessary skills and that it must therefore have been built by Phoenician or even early Portuguese traders. Only with independence were African origins acknowledged, and the new country took its name from the monument (Renfrew and Bahn, 2012, pp. 466–7). And in 1930s Germany archaeologists provided tools to help promote plans of the Nazi regime to annex territory. With the enthusiastic support of the SS leader Heinrich Himmler, archaeologists and scholars from the humanities and social sciences undertook work on the remains of the lost Viking village of Haithabu in Scandinavia as a means of affirming a narrative that, since Germanic peoples had in the prehistoric past migrated into and subjected these lands, the German nation had prior claim to them (Hare, 2014).

But what precisely is archaeology, and what is its relationship to history? Let us begin with Gordon Childe, a pioneering archaeologist who did much to establish the ground rules of the scholarly discipline in the twentieth century (see later). To the question 'What is archaeology about?' he answered:

Archaeology studies all changes in the material world that are due to human action – naturally in so far as they survive. The archaeological record is constituted by the fossilized results of human behaviour, and it is the archaeologist's business to reconstitute the behaviour as far as he can and so to recapture the thoughts that behaviour expressed. In so far as he can do that, he becomes an historian.

(Childe, 1956, p. 1)

This quotation raises a host of important questions that we need to consider in a little more depth. Few would contest the notion that at the heart of archaeological endeavour is the material world. Childe proceeds to argue that archaeologists' attempts to recover artefacts can conveniently be divided into relics and monuments. Relics include tools, weapons and a host of personal items that can be removed to be studied in a laboratory, while monuments include houses, temples and earthworks, which need to be studied in situ. Thus, archaeologists strive to recover the material remains of human activity, and the picture we have of enthusiastic groups excavating ancient sites is a familiar, even stereotypical one. However, it does pose two rather important questions, namely, what periods of human history are the concern of archaeologists, and how are the discovered remains best to be used to shed light on the past?

What Historical Periods?

Most would think that archaeologists deal with the ancient past, that is, with those peoples that inhabited a material rather than a written culture. In some respects, this may be a convenient division of labour between archaeology and history: simply stated, archaeologists use artefacts as evidence, historians use written sources. Given that the origins of human culture can be traced back three million years and that writing did not appear until, say, 3,000 BCE, this may appear an uneven division for archaeologists could legitimately claim as their territory ninety-nine per cent of the human record. But note that the division has become increasingly blurred as archaeologists increasingly contribute to an understanding of periods using documents and inscriptions, just as historians have extended their interests to material artefacts. Furthermore, advances in technology have played a vital role in the development of areas such as underwater, industrial and battlefield archaeology, all of which have made significant contributions to our understanding of the modern age.

What Use Are the Artefacts?

A large majority of archaeologists would accept that the collection and studying of artefacts cannot be an end in itself. As Childe argued, they are of value only in what they reveal about the nature of human cultures. This process, however, is neither simple nor self-evident, for to allow the material remains to speak and hence reveal their secrets they have to be identified, classified, ordered and dated, then interpreted. This, above all, requires the appropriate application of theory, and it is this fractious issue that has essentially determined the emergence of archaeology as a scholarly discipline and been responsible for struggles over its soul.

We wish to return to these issues later but first we need to take a detour into the history of archaeology better to understand its changing role. Since ancient times artefacts from previous civilizations have been sought for their material or historical value, but it was not until the Enlightenment that their excavating and collection became a serious matter. 'Cabinets of curiosities' were built around a large variety of ancient natural and artificial specimens to be displayed to the edification of invited audiences (Renfrew and Bahn, 2012, p. 22). Reflecting a revival of interest in classical learning, much of the material centred on objects and monuments from the Greek and Roman empires, but these were supplemented by local finds. Simultaneously, ancient monuments began to draw the interests of early archaeologists, all of whom were amateur and would not have recognized they were members of a fledgling profession. Early in the eighteenth century, the Anglican clergyman William Stukeley (1687–1765) undertook detailed surveys of English monumental sites, including Avebury and Stonehenge, producing plans which are still of value. About the same time the sites of Herculaneum and then Pompeii were discovered. At first, they were plundered by the King and Queen of Naples seeking objects with which to adorn their palace, but the excavations soon revealed the sites had immense historical importance, and so the work became more careful and systematic.

Sometime before helping to write the Declaration of Independence, Thomas Jefferson (1743–1826) was known largely through the study of burial mounds, thousands of which were scattered over the American landscape. Containing stratified burials of humans, many of which were adorned with beautifully crafted items, they were widely thought at the time to have been built not by native Amerindians – who at the time were in a depressed state – but by a mythical and long-vanished race that had migrated from South America or even Scandinavia. During excavation of a mound near to his home at Monticello in the late eighteenth century, however, Jefferson speculated on links to Native American culture (Jefferson, 1954). He recalled,

Figure 17.1 Excavation by Dr Montroville Dickeson of an Amerindian burial mound in Mississippi, *c.*1850. Scene from the Mississippi Panorama, a large-scale painting on linen by John Egan and Dr Dickeson

Contributor: GRANGER – Historical Picture Archive/Alamy Stock Phot

for example, an early incident when a party of Indians passing through the country proceeded straight to a barrow (as he called the mound) set in a wood, paused for a time to mourn and then returned to the main road approximately six miles away.

And credit should certainly be accorded to Jefferson for the scientific way in which he proceeded, making a perpendicular cut in the mound, not to retrieve the objects but in order to observe their arrangement in stratified layers, all of which was subsequently recorded systematically. However, Jefferson's reputation as the father of American archaeology has recently been challenged (Hatzenbuehler, 2011). 'Scientific' his methods might have been – arguably a century before their time – but his desire to distance himself from any notion that he was simply collecting artefacts led him to some highly questionable theories on Native American culture. While defending the view that the burial mounds were part of that culture and therefore to study them was to understand better its origins, Jefferson's archaeological work was integral to a wider project to assimilate Native Americans into modern American society and hence reach the levels of development enjoyed by Europeans.

Despite the work of such pioneering archaeologists, the beginnings of modern archaeology can be traced back to the nineteenth century, during which antiquarian and somewhat amateur investigators were superseded by professionals with a keener sense of what the discipline had to offer. Whereas previously most excavations were driven by a desire to amass artefacts, now archaeologists directed their energies to reveal what these artefacts, properly excavated, recorded and classified, said about the historic cultures that created them. Pithily stated, this was a move from a search for finds to a search to find out.

Such a transformation cannot be seen as purely internal to the discipline, for it was largely predicated on the massive intellectual shifts that occurred at the time (Renfrew and Bahn, 2012, p. 26). In the first place, Charles Lyell (1797–1875), a child of the Scottish enlightenment, published in 1833 *Principles of Geology*, which demonstrated the gradual geological evolution of the earth, so challenging the widely held belief, stated in the Bible, that in a great labour of six days God created the world. Lyell also suggested that the world had a much greater antiquity than was popularly thought. Based on ingenious calculations of historical lineages, enterprising individuals had estimated that the earth was created at approximately 4,000 BCE, but after Lyell such fanciful ideas were no longer tenable. With the opening of this door, people began to argue for the existence of prehistoric peoples, especially after the publication of John Lubbock's *Prehistoric Times* (1865), which introduced the term into the English language.

Although Lyell never fully accepted the evolutionary theory of Charles Darwin (1809–1892), his role in preparing the ground cannot be disputed, for while Lyell spoke of the gradual evolution of the earth's geology, Darwin's concern was with the evolution of the biological world. The idea of the evolution of living things had been around for some time, but with the publication of *On the Origin of Species* (1859), hastened by the dramatic appearance of Alfred Russell Wallace (1823–1913) who independently had arrived at the same conclusions, Darwin showed for the first time precisely how the evolutionary mechanism operated. Any such notion that humans had evolved over time from other species directly challenged prevalent Christian belief in the creation of man in the image of God; indeed, this irreconcilability was a source of much anguish for Darwin who originally had intended to enter the church.

Out of this same intellectual environment emerged another theory that was to have a lasting impact on archaeology. Early in the nineteenth century the English antiquarian Richard Colt Hoare (1758–1838) – another of independent means – carried out a detailed series of excavations in his native Wiltshire, including the sites of Salisbury Plain and Stonehenge, recognizing among the artefacts of stone, brass and iron a temporal sequence, on the basis of which stages in societal evolution could be identified. But it was with the work of the Danish archaeologist C. J. Thomsen (1788–1865) that the stages theory gained rigour and consistency. Scandinavia proved an exceptionally rich environment for prehistoric tools and tombs, large collections of which were displayed in the National Museum of Northern Antiquities in Copenhagen. In organizing the exhibits, Thomsen, who had been appointed curator in 1816, decided to group them together according to their putative age (Childe, 1956, p. 23). Since the artefacts were all preliterate, there were no written records to help, and so he turned to an older idea that people had originally used stone tools and weapons, then bronze and finally iron. This formed the basis of the three-age typology, which proved remarkably versatile for it found useful application over the whole of Europe. Thus, the Stone, Bronze and Iron Ages entered into the intellectual realm of archaeology as a principle with which to organize cultures chronologically.

Now the conditions were in place, and work of some of the great archaeologists began. It is worth mentioning a few of them. Like so many archaeologists of the time, General Augustus Pitt-Rivers (1827–1900) was a military man. While serving abroad he developed an interest in archaeology to which he brought his considerable skills in surveying and organization. Over seventeen years he excavated prehistoric, Saxon and Roman sites in England, pioneering the methodical collection and recording of even the most mundane artefacts – what he called typical objects, which revealed much about the life of ordinary people – as a result of which he is widely held to be the founder of modern archaeology. Simultaneously, he amassed a considerable collection of ethnographic objects from around the world, not from personal travels but from connections he fostered with London dealers. In 1884 part of the collection formed the basis of the Pitts Rivers Museum in Oxford where, in an inspired move, he displayed similar objects in distinct groups in order to reveal a sense of their development over time.

Since Napoleon's military incursion into Egypt in 1798–1800, Europeans had been captivated by the splendours of its lost civilization. Napoleon himself had been well prepared, ensuring that the expedition was equipped with an adequate supply of archaeologists to record any finds. When in 1822 Jean-François Champillion (1790–1832) deciphered the Rosetta Stone to reveal the secrets of Egyptian hieroglyphs, the stage was set for an extraordinary phase of archaeological endeavour which has continued to the present. William Flinders Petrie (1853–1942) was among the most important, not only in what he was able to reveal about pharaonic Egypt but also in advancing the field techniques of archaeology. As a young man, Petrie began work on various sites near his home (in God's own country) at Charlton, South London but was to devote most of his considerable energies and tenacity to ancient Egypt and Palestine. Here he discovered a number of significant sites, including the stela (stone tablet) of Merneptah, which bore the first ever mention of Israel in an Egyptian inscription. His methods advanced the cause of archaeology. His attention to the smallest detail and the systematic way in which he went about his work provided a lasting legacy, but arguably his most important contribution was in the use of pottery and ceramics to date sites with an unprecedented accuracy. As a firm believer in eugenics and the inferiority of African and Latinate peoples, however, it could be argued that Petrie hindered rather than advanced the interpretation of the culture of ancient Egypt.

In North America, nineteenth-century archaeology was driven by questions arising from its own historical experiences of settlement in an occupied land (for good surveys of the development of American archaeology, see Fitting, 1973, and Willey and Sabloff, 1993). While something was known of the background of European settlers, widespread ignorance existed on the indigenous peoples they encountered. How did they make their way to the American mainland? Where did they come from? How in their physiologies, languages and cultures did they compare with Europeans? These were questions that for the most part sprang from anthropological concerns, and they do help to explain the affinity in the United States between archaeology and anthropology, while in European archaeology the touchstone has always been history.

The American Philosophical Society, founded in 1743, provided a forum for luminaries including Thomas Jefferson, Benjamin Rush and Benjamin Smith Barton, who from the late eighteenth century defined an agenda which continued well into the nineteenth (Fowler and Wilcox, 2010, p. xiii). The call was for systematic compilations of ethnographic, archaeological and historical data on Amerindian peoples. As European Americans moved west, so they discovered ever more mounds to excavate in the elusive quest for the race of mound builders. As in Europe, much of the work was carried out by amateurs such as Caleb Altwater (1778–1867), a local postmaster, who excavated burial mounds in Ohio and Ephraim Squier (1821–1888), a journalist, who surveyed over 200 mounds in the Mississippi Valley (Renfrew and Bahn, 2012, p. 30). This work collectively began to challenge the mound builder myth. In 1839, Dr Samuel Morton examined nearly a thousand skulls from the tombs, concluding that there were no significant differences between those of the mound builders and contemporary Amerindians (Brose, 1973, p. 85). In 1845, Squier was commissioned by the American Ethnological Society to report on the mounds in Ohio. With Dr Edwin Davis, he published *Ancient Monuments of the Mississippi Valley* (1848), which, although largely descriptive in intent, demonstrated the existence of different types of mounds related to distinct aboriginal cultures. It was not until Cyrus Thomas (1825–1910) published the *Annual Report of the Bureau of American Ethnology* (1894) that the fanciful idea of a race of mound builders was finally laid to rest. Following a detailed review of previous work, he concluded that mounds had been built by ancestors of the Indians and that their diversity reflected the cultural practices of different tribes or nations (Stoltman, 1973, p. 126).

In the belief that linguistic connections could reveal the origins of ancient cultures, Jefferson and Barton also embarked on a detailed classification of Amerindian languages. By mid-century, following the lead of European archaeology, Americans turned their attention to other sites, including middens (rubbish deposits) scattered along rivers and seashores. Here important figures including Clarence Moore (1852–1936) and William Holmes (1846–1933) proved that the shell middens were of human origin and that, through the systematic collection and analysis of ceramic remains, diverse regional cultures could be identified and dated. By the end of the century, the professionalization of archaeology had gathered pace, and there were clearly enough large collections of materials to justify the opening of museums such as the Field Columbian in Chicago and University Museum in Pennsylvania; indeed, most of the important archaeological and natural history museums were established in this period (Fowler and Wilcox, 2010, p. xvii).

As with anthropology (Chapter 18) and the environmental sciences (Chapter 20), much progress in archaeology occurred in an imperial context and so was necessarily shaped by prevailing attitudes on the relationships between colonizer and colonized. Let us take as an example the role of the British in India. From the eighteenth century, so-called orientalists such as the great linguist William Jones (1746–1794) began for the first time to recognize the longevity and worth of Indian civilization. Under the aegis of the newly established Asiatic Society of Bengal, they embarked on a detailed study of India's ancient Sanskrit texts and drew up a comprehensive balance sheet of its monumental remains, best represented by Thomas Maurice's seven-volume *Indian Antiquities or Dissertations on Hindoostan* (1812–1814), which described Indian temples as magnificent as any found in Greece or Egypt. This project, however, was largely abandoned in the early nineteenth century as British colonial authorities increasingly viewed it in negative terms. They surmised that, while Indian culture had an extraordinarily rich past, it had subsequently declined and degenerated into idolatry and superstition.

Faced with this, from mid-century they embarked on an archaeological survey of India in order to identify what best represented the ancient culture and was therefore fit to be recorded and preserved. In an historical survey of British archaeology in nineteenth-century India, K. Paddayya has argued that despite the affinity between this work and the imperial formation, colonial archaeologists did much to develop the discipline and hence an understanding of India's past (Paddayya, 1995). The foundations were laid by outstanding figures such as Colonel Meadows Taylor (1808–1876), Robert Foote (1834–1912) and Alexander Cunningham (1814–1893) none of whom was an archaeologist, but they combined an interest in India's past with their work as engineers, scientists and military men.

Taylor, who lacked a formal education, studied archaeology along with science, engineering, art and history. While serving as the political agent in Karnataka, he came across megalithic tombs which, he surmised, were broadly like sites in Western Europe and therefore must have been built by Druids who had migrated to India in ancient times. Such suspect reasoning, however, needs to be seen against genuine advances made by Taylor in the preparation of site maps, the use of the principle of stratification and the careful drawing of artefacts and skeletal remains, which were years ahead of their time, later influencing the work of Pitt-Rivers and Mortimer Wheeler.

As a military engineer in India, Cunningham developed a lasting interest in archaeology, and on his retirement he berated the wholesale neglect of the monuments, many of which were now threatened with ruin. He approached the governor-general Lord Canning, who in 1861 agreed to set up the Archaeological Survey of India with Cunningham as its directory. Its brief was to provide an accurate description of the 'remains as most deserve notice'. Cunningham travelled the whole of northern India preparing detailed site maps and recording evidence of artefacts including coins and inscriptions, so providing the framework for the continued work of the Survey, which to this day remains the leading authority of India's archaeological heritage. His contribution was duly acknowledged by future directors, including Mortimer Wheeler.

Although archaeology is often viewed as the preserve of the rugged, patriarchal male, there have been outstanding female pioneers. Because of highly gendered attitudes towards female employment, many were able to play only a marginal role, but those with the determination could make their name. After graduating in the classics, Harriet Hawes (1871–1945) left her comfortable life in America to search for prehistoric sites in Crete, eventually being the first to discover a Minoan town. Professionalization, however, had to await the twentieth century with figures such as Dorothy Garrod (1892–1968) who through her excavations in Iraq and Palestine revealed the prehistory of the Middle East. In 1937 she was appointed as the first woman professor at Cambridge (Renfrew and Bahn, 2012, p. 34). And there was also Gertrude Caton-Thompson (1888–1985), the excavator of Great Zimbabwe. She also worked notably in Malta and South Arabia, introducing new techniques to the discipline while holding senior positions in the Prehistoric Society and the Royal Anthropological Institute.

17.2 The Theoretical Turn: Collingwood and Childe

In important respects paralleling the discipline of history, the founding and early development of archaeology was driven by a desire to excavate, record and classify ancient remains. Over time, a sense of cultural development through evolution intervened to help shape these classifications, but rigorous theory was worn lightly. Even though Darwinian theory was generally accepted within the academic community by the end of the nineteenth century, evolutionary schemes could not be applied to material artefacts. Sadly, where evolutionary thought was taken seriously, it was in order to define the racial inferiority of peoples whose cultures were being explored. During the early decades of the twentieth century, increasingly sophisticated chronological sequences were devised. Equally importantly, in a move away from the determination of broad universal patterns of human development, archaeologists were drawn to what historians described as regional studies, and thus foundations were laid for the archaeology of Mayan, Peruvian, Egyptian, Amerindian, Mesopotamian and Minoan civilizations.

Enter R. G. Collingwood (1889–1943) and V. Gordon Childe (1892–1957). Few could have been further removed from the boisterous figures of nineteenth-century archaeology. Collingwood (whom we have met on several occasions) was educated at home by his father until the age of thirteen, principally in the classics, history and philosophy (typically, attempting to read – but not fully understand – Kant's ethics when he was eight; Boucher, 1995). He gained a scholarship to Oxford and for three years devoted himself to studying to the extent that he became a recluse, graduating first in Classical Moderations and later in Literae Humaniores, after which he was elected as a fellow at Pembroke College, Oxford. From there, until his untimely death from pneumonia following years of chronic ill health, he wrote and taught on the philosophy of history. There was another Collingwood, however, who despite his fragility travelled around the country in pursuit of a passion in archaeology, which he inherited from his father at an early age. He recounted a story of being taken to his father's dig at a Roman fort in a carpenter's bag when three weeks old and later accompanying him to many other sites (Collingwood, 1939, p. 80).

Since we have already spoken of Collingwood's contribution to historical thought, here we wish to discuss briefly the legacy of his work in archaeology for which he is less well known.

In *The Archaeology of Roman Britain* (1930), *Roman Britain* (1932) and *Roman Britain and the English Settlements* (1936), Collingwood summed up his thoughts on and work in archaeology. At the time these studies were reviewed positively and have subsequently been considered authoritative, but arguably of more importance has been his influence on archaeological theory. Collingwood challenged what he considered as the artificial separation between material artefacts and written documents which had erected barriers between archaeology and history. Largely because archaeology was empirically driven, the sorts of questions that historians were beginning to ask about written sources rarely applied to artefacts. In *The Idea of History*, he cited with approval the words of the Italian historian Benedetto Croce:

> Do you wish to understand the true history of a neolithic Ligurian or Sicilian? Try, if you can, to become a neolithic Ligurian or Sicilian in your mind. If you cannot do that, or do not care to, content yourself with describing and arranging in series the skulls, implements, and drawings which have been found belonging to these neolithic peoples.
> (Croce, 1921, pp. 134–5, cited in Collingwood, 1961, p. 199)

This advice, Collingwood proceeded, was good. Neolithic man was an historical reality. If he made a flint axe it was with a particular purpose in mind. In that sense the artefact expresses something of his spirit. To write the history of neolithic man, therefore, you need to be able to enter his mind and 'make his thoughts your own'. If you fail to do this, then all that is left is to arrange his relics in some sort of order: the result is not history but ethnology or archaeology.

Collingwood contended that this had to change and to this end laid down three guiding principles not only for any aspiring archaeologist but also for any kind of historian:

> I have been preaching to my archaeological friends the duty of never digging either a five-thousand-pound site or a five-shilling trench without being certain that you can satisfy an enquirer who asks you What are you doing this piece of work for?
>
> Since history proper is the history of thought, there are no mere 'events' in history: what is miscalled an 'event' is really an action, and expresses some thought (intention, purpose) of its agent; the historian's business is therefore to identify this thought.
>
> No historical problem should be studied without studying what I called its second-order history, that is, the history of historical thought about it.
> (Collingwood, 1939, pp. 126–7, 132)

Early archaeologists had dug blindly with purpose from the collection of artefacts, and although things have changed in recent times, inadequate attention was still being paid to this important question. For Collingwood archaeologists should not undertake excavations simply to find artefacts any more than historians should diligently trawl the written archives to accumulate data. And funds should no longer be made available to excavate sites to the point where they were dug out before moving onto another.

The second principle suggests that archaeologists need to identify the purpose behind all objects and 'events' on the basis of sound historical evidence. Why did it happen? What was it for? Was its purpose successfully accomplished? In other words, rather than viewing events from the outside, it was necessary to understand them from within by identifying the human values and intentions that determined particular courses of action. Competing interpretations may well arise from this, but this encourages debate and the search for answers. This feeds into the third principle. Debates over interpretation should necessarily be informed by the work of others, for we need to understand the strengths and weaknesses of previous theories.

These may all appear sound common sense; indeed, the first and third principles are now widely followed by archaeologists, for few would embark on an excavation in the blind hope that something would turn up (Leach, 2009, p. 17). For some, however, the stress Collingwood places on human motivation brings us too close to individual psychology. But he, in ways similar to Fernand Braudel, recognized that such intents had to be located within broader structural histories of collective endeavour, which in turn were underpinned by the deep, long-term currents of historical change.

We do not know if Collingwood ever met his contemporary V. Gordon Childe (1892–1957) or even how well they knew each other's work, but they shared a common purpose in bringing about a radical overhaul of archaeology. Childe was born in Australia, and after graduating from Sydney University he made his way to Oxford where, under the influence of Arthur Evans and John Myres, he was drawn increasingly to prehistoric archaeology (see Trigger, 1978 and Orser and Patterson, 2004 for good reviews of his life and intellectual development). A period of political activity and unemployment ended when he was appointed as librarian at the Royal Anthropological Institute in 1925, which he used as a platform to travel to archaeological collections around Europe. Several large works of synthesis followed with astonishing speed – *The Dawn of European Civilization* (1925), *The Aryans: A Study of Indo-European Origins* (1926), *The Most Ancient East: The Oriental Prelude to European Prehistory* (1928) and *The Danube in Prehistory* (1929). These works not only established Childe's reputation but arguably revolutionized archaeological thought, and he was soon offered the chair in archaeology at Edinburgh University and in 1946 at London University's Institute of Archaeology, which he held until his retirement in 1956. In the following year while trekking in the Blue Mountain near Sydney, he fell to his death; it was apparently an act of suicide.

It is difficult to summarize in a few words the prolific output of Childe or assess his immense – and contested – contribution to archaeological thought. At the core of his work, in complete contrast to his predecessors, was a commitment to historical explanation. If he was also interested in formulating general laws of human behaviour, as were those archaeologists in the United States who had been nurtured on anthropology, then this was secondary, a means only of advancing explanation. Childe's affinities were with historians, but here also he broke with conventional wisdom, particularly in challenging the approaches of Leopold von Ranke, which formed the basis of traditional historical practice (see Chapter 21). Far from considering factual evidence as the foundation, Childe emphasized the role of interpretation and hence theory. He agreed with Collingwood that archaeologists do not excavate innocently to collect materials but should do so in order to test hypotheses and that historical processes do not operate according to universal laws but through human consciousness; actions, not events, must be our guide. At times, he may have found that Collingwood's *The Idea of History* overstressed the role of thought, but as a guide to the nature of the relationship between human agency and material processes it was sound.

But if the collection and classification of artefacts revealed little about historical change, which body of theory could? Childe was politically and intellectually a Marxist, and although he never reconciled fully his archaeological work with Marx's historical materialism, it provided him with a model of historical change which remained an important influence throughout his life. Toward the end, at a time when contemporaries were still concerned with mapping the cultural chronologies of regions, he adapted historical materialism to address some of the big questions, including the origin of human civilization. Childe thus contended that a Neolithic Revolution in the Near East had given rise to farming and later the development of large urban settlements.

17.3 Historical Archaeology

At about the time of Childe's death and as a result of his and others' dissatisfaction with the state of archaeology, the so-called new archaeology was born. During what has been labelled the explanatory period, archaeologists struggled to forge innovative approaches to the collection and interpretation of evidence that made explicit the framework of their arguments (Willey and Sabloff, 1993). The most influential strand to emerge was processual archaeology, which distanced itself from previous traditions through a series of dualisms:

Explanation vs Description. Through the explicit use of theory, archaeologists need to explain the past not simply attempt to reconstruct it through the collection of materials

Cultural Process vs Cultural History. Instead of focusing on particular, geographically-bound historical experiences, it was necessary to think of generalized cultural processes such as the emergence of farming

Deductive vs Inductive Logic. Archaeology should not resemble a jigsaw where the pieces are assembled and put together to reveal a picture. We need initially to formulate hypotheses, construct models with which to test the evidence.

(Renfrew and Bahn, 2012, p. 41)

The zeal with which new archaeologists set about their mission led many to call upon diverse and often arcane bodies of theory. It was not a happy time. Somewhat paralleling developments in historiography, archaeologists doggedly sought niche positions which they defended aggressively against critics. Many stopped speaking to others in the field.

There is little point here in elucidating the structural, evolutionary, functionalist, cognitive, ecological, symbolic, Marxist, post-processual, post-structural and other archaeologies which emerged in this period, so helping to fragment the discipline, often in harmful ways. Much more useful as a means of illustrating different approaches and of summarizing the main intellectual shifts during the twentieth century is a comparison among the explanations offered for the existence of megalith monuments on the mainland of western Europe (here we are indebted to ibid., pp. 47–8). Since the nineteenth century, migrationist and diffusionist explanations have seen the megaliths as the creation of a single people who migrated in the prehistoric period. Early in the twentieth century the emphasis shifted to the diffusion of ideas from the higher civilizations of the east Mediterranean such as Crete and Greece via Italy and Spain. However, radiocarbon dating proved that the megaliths of Western Europe were earlier than those of Crete, so processual explanations attempted to explain them as territorial markers of egalitarian, dispersed groups or of ancestral rights to the land. Marxist explanations of the 1980s saw the monuments both as expressions of power in an inegalitarian society and as a means of naturalizing that power. Finally, post-processual interpretations insisted that the historical contexts need to be understood. Megaliths did not serve economic or demographic ends but were above all symbolic significations of social relationships associated with houses, including gender roles. As is so often the case, these contrasting approaches that at first sight seem mutually exclusive in practice could well be complementary. Much of the fractiousness has now dissipated, and the intellectual fashions have passed by, but they have left the same fundamental questions unanswered.

We wish to finish this section by returning to the matter of the distinction between archaeology and history. As we have seen, archaeology has broadly been considered as the study of the material culture from the (ancient) past. This has served to distinguish it from history, which has tended to rely on the written records of later societies. If this is the core distinction, then others necessarily follow, which can be expressed as a series of dualisms (Johnson, 1999, p. 24):

Archaeology	History
Artefact	Document
Physical	Symbolic
Objective	Subjective
Vernacular	Elite
Colonized	Colonizer
Long term	Event/Action

These dualisms are overstated – there is little to suggest, for example, that archaeology is any more objective than history – but they do help us to think about the distinctions between the disciplines. Such distinctions, however, have in recent years come under scrutiny (Funari et al., 1999). It is not only that many archaeologists have long studied literate artefacts such as inscriptions and have developed an interest in historic as well as prehistoric societies – but that the ready distinction between preliterate and literate societies has been criticized as unhelpful, even ideologically flawed. Some have referred to the tyranny of history simply because the focus on literate societies has tended to validate them while denigrating preliterate societies. And necessarily this has privileged the rise of the West, its role as a colonial power and, of course, those elite sections of society that were part of its literate culture. It is as if the rise of the West has simultaneously constituted the history (or lack of it) of the non-Western world – an idea captured acutely by Eric Wolf's classic *Europe and the People without History* (1997).

An encouraging response to these concerns is the recent rise of what is termed *historical archaeology*. The implication here is not that archaeology should now be seen as historical but rather that it should occupy a critical position in all forms of documentary history. There is potentially much of benefit in the unification of history and archaeology, for it will break down artificial oppositions between non-literate and literate societies, and the refusal to privilege documentary over material evidence challenges any notion posing the innate superiority of literate civilizations. This is not to deny the transformation brought about by writing but to set it in historical context. Documentation was integral to the centralization of power and therefore the rise of early states and empires. It also played a critical role in constructing the past in ways that broadly reinforced those in power.

Historical archaeology also attempts to break down the opposition between material artefact and written text. Martin Johnson explains some the questions that arise if the two are brought together in dialogue:

> If material culture is text, text is also material culture. How, physically, were documents generated? What, for example, do different scripts tell us about the bodily discipline of writing? What of the physical production of printed books? How does the conceptual ordering of a feudal text like the Domesday Book or Boldon Book correspond (or fail to correspond) to the material ordering of the planned feudal landscapes found across much of Europe?
>
> (Johnson, 1999, pp. 31–2)

To illustrate these concerns let us have a look at how some archaeologists have approached the study of empires. Most of the previous work on empires has relied on written sources or occasionally transcriptions, but what is to be done when a written record does not exist or is poor? The Wari empire of Peru, which lasted from approximately 750 CE to 1000 CE, presents particularly interesting problems for it was aliterate, that is, it produced neither written documents nor eyewitness accounts handed down through the generations (Schreiber, 2001). Its history is thus more likely to be the province of archaeologists, not historians, but even here there are major obstacles to be overcome. Because the archaeological remains are fragmented and scanty, it has been impossible to reconstruct in detail the course of imperial expansion and decline. What remains, however, are the residues of its military infrastructure, and from these it has been possible to map some of the broad contours of the development of the Wari Empire. Garrisons, roads, and urban centres have proven of particular value here. Although it is not easy directly to date them, the network of roads provides valuable insights. Those used for military purposes are identified by virtue of the fact that they connected garrisons, which can be dated more precisely, thus building up a picture of the limits and chronology of imperial expansion. Meanwhile, urban centres are located through the survival of the distinct Wari architecture of the temples and the large houses of the ruling elite. This imperial built environment and infrastructure provided evidence of the extent to which the ruling elite were prepared to invest resources in order to maintain sovereignty over the region and of changes in the military, economic and political organization at a local level through which this control operated. Hence we know the chronology, speed and direction of the expansion of the Wari empire but as yet have no explanation for its sudden collapse after a period of two or three hundred years.

Studies on the Satavahana dynasty of the Deccan of central and southern India (c.100 BCE –200 CE) provide another fascinating example of historical archaeology (Sinopoli, 2001). While predated by the better-known Mauryan empire of northern India (c.300–180 BCE), which reached its zenith under the legendary king Asoka, Satavahana was arguably more extensive and longer lasting. Much of what we know comes from textual and material sources including sacred writings, inscriptions, coins, monuments, monastic sites and Roman and Greek histories. Coins have been especially significant. Thousands of lead, copper and alloyed coins have been excavated, together with smaller numbers of silver and gold. Most featured the names of contemporary rulers and had highly restricted geographical distributions thus helping to untangle what were complex and dynamic political systems and shed light on the partially monetized economy. And, as with the Wari Empire, numerous monumental sites exist, which, despite problems in dating them and disjunctions between rates of material and political change in the period, do offer insights into the regional patterns of imperial expansion. Where chronologies are contradictory and therefore difficult to construct, inscriptions of the histories of royal families have helped to address the problem. What emerges is a picture of settlement patterns suggesting the growth of numerous small-scale regional polities and identities with porous boundaries. These regional systems were then incorporated into a larger imperial formation which imposed formal administrative structures and novel regimes of revenue collection. After the chaos that followed the death of Asoka, the Satavahanas thus brought a large measure of peace and order to the Deccan.

Such studies demonstrate that valuable evidence derives from diverse sources which cannot usefully be divided into texts and material artefacts. Indeed, it is from a constructive dialogue among them – and between archaeologists, anthropologists and historians – that real progress can be made in advancing our understanding of the pasts of these ancient empires.

17.4 Jerusalem and Its Layers

If I forget thee, O Jerusalem, let my right hand forget her cunning.
Let my tongue cleave to the roof of my mouth, if I remember thee not; if I set not Jerusalem above my chiefest joy.

So says Psalm 27, and so say religious Jews in their daily prayers. The sentiments here convey the profound sense in which Jerusalem has entered Jewish mythology. But it is a mythology that has been and remains highly contested among the historical narratives that are believed and defended by all of the various groups that live cheek by jowl in Jerusalem or even 'know' Jerusalem as a distant dream. Written by the singer and songwriter Naomi Shemer on the eve of the Six Day War in 1967, the words of *Jerusalem of the Gold* became an unofficial hymn for many Israelis as they faced what they earnestly believed would be (wrongly as it turned out) another Holocaust at the hands of the surrounding Arab countries (Segev, 2007). It began as a lament for something lost, even, we might say, an ancestral longing. The first line tells (allegedly) of how the 'market place is empty', the second on how 'no-one' goes to the Temple Mount while the last line is a promise that Jews will one day be able to go to the Dead Sea via Jericho, impossible at the time because East Jerusalem was controlled by Jordan – a prophecy that, controversially, came to pass after the Six Day War. This modern psalm of return became so iconic for both Israeli and diaspora Jews that it was ripped out of its 1960s context in the film *Schindler's List* by Steven Spielberg and became the powerful backdrop to the scene where 'Schindlers Jews' walk over the brow of the hill after the war is over in 1945 seemingly walking to liberation and to Jerusalem itself.

Where once Jews dreamt of a return to *Jerusalem of the Gold* (the Old City and the Temple was largely out of bounds to Jews until 1967, controlled as it was by Jordan), so do Palestinians mourn the *Nakba* or disaster that saw a Jewish state established in 1948 and the beginning of the Palestinian diaspora. The marketplace was not empty, and someone did frequent the Temple Mount. Simon Goldhill captured something of Jerusalem's complex and contested legacy:

> For it is how these different inheritances are interwoven with one another, or set in conflict, or layered on top of each other, that makes Jerusalem so perplexing and complex. . . . This is the place where Abraham prepared to sacrifice his son, where David danced before the Lord, where Jesus walked, spoke to his disciples, and was crucified, where Mohammed's night journey took him to heaven to learn the rules of proper Muslim behaviour.
>
> (Goldhill, 2008, p. 5)

Rudimentary efforts then to establish a simple timeline or chronology or find agreement about the story or stories of Jerusalem are fraught with controversy, although most recently, in 2022, *Nine Quarters of Jerusalem: A New Biography of the Old City* by Matthew Teller has made an attempt. Just look at the diversity that is suggested in the 'quarters' of the Old City: The Armenian Quarter; Christian Quarter; Jewish Quarter; Muslim Quarter and, above all, the Temple Mount (or *Haram esh-Sharif*, as the Muslims call it). Teller sees this sort of division as a leftover and would add 'different denominations of Christians, African and Sufi Muslims, Gypsies (known as Rom) and Israeli Jews (largely Orthodox)' (*Observer*, 6 March 2022). Each group has its own narrative and even common landmarks are named differently. A cursory glance at pro-Palestinian and Zionist websites reveals comments from each of these two groups that reveal how the buried layers of Jerusalem history allow each to vie for legitimacy, evidence from the long covered past which might make the case for the politics of the present or threaten it:

Some facts:

There has not been a country that is called Israel.
Jews had been screwed in Europe, because they are dirty, lier [sic], greedy

Europe wanted to get rid of Jews.
Palestinians hosted Jews in Palestine.
Jews came to Palestine as refugees.
Thereafter, Jews have been murdering Palestine since 1945
In 1945 Jews took Palestine over
Since 1945 Jews have been trying to find one evidence that proves there was a country that is called Israel, and yet nothing has been found.
It has been called Palestine since, Ancient Egyptians, Canaanites, Ancient Israelites, Assyrians, Babylonians, Persians, Ancient Greeks, Romans, Byzantines, the Muslims, the Crusaders, Ayyubids [sic], Mameluks [sic], Ottomans, the British, The Hashemite Kingdom of Jordan.
Jews a group of people who are not Muslims or Christians.
Jews are relating to Judaism.
Jews can be found in Africa, USA, Europe, Asia, Arab Countries and everywhere.
Jews are not a nation as such.

(www.palestinefacts.org/pf_early_palestine_name_origin.php)

For their part, Israeli Jews claim legitimacy by claiming antiquity – here by telling a joke about a representative rising during a session of the United Nations:

Before beginning my talk I want to tell you something about Moses. When he struck the rock and it brought forth water, he thought, 'What a good opportunity to have a bath!' He removed his clothes, put them aside on the rock and entered the water. When he got out and wanted to dress, his clothes had vanished. A Palestinian had stolen them. The Palestinian representative jumped up furiously and shouted, 'What are you talking about? The Palestinians weren't there then.' The Israeli representative smiled and said 'And now that I have made that clear, I will begin my speech'.

Now these narratives need not be true in order to become stuck in the tramlines of popular beliefs and understandings about history that may or may not have much validity. This is where archaeology can help and why it is so important politically. Was there a place called Israel? Are there traces of a Temple in Jerusalem? Where do the scriptures stand in the face of archaeological evidence? This contested past has been heightened, no doubt, with the American recognition of Jerusalem as the sovereign capital of modern Israel (along with Honduras, Guatemala and Kosovo).

Tearing ourselves away from the endless strife over Jerusalem for a moment we can see examples where the results of archaeological digs elsewhere have led to a deepening or repositioning of pre-existing historical narratives. It was revealed in June 2016, for instance, that archaeologists in London had been working covertly during the previous two years translating from Latin the sunken wooden manuscripts found during a dig in the financial City. It was revealed that a 57-CE financial document had been found, while the variety of the characters in the texts told the story of London's cosmopolitanism: from 'Tertius the brewer, Proculus the haulier, Tibullus the freed slave, Optatus the food merchant, Crispus the innkeeper, Classicus the lieutenant colonel, Junius the barrel maker, Rusticus (one of the governor's bodyguards) and, last but not least, Florentinus the slave' (*The Independent*, 1 June 2016). This was no threat to the dominant consensus of London as a gloriously diverse world city and financial hub. Instead, it was a welcome meeting with 'early Londoners' that reinforced the consensus. Or take the example from a Viking find in Canada where the discovery of a possible settlement may mean an earlier European presence on the North American continent than had been thought previously (*The Independent*, 3 April 2016). Like our example from London, the result may be interesting in its own terms but (in this case) it only unsettles existing understandings of the chronology of European colonization 500 years before Columbus.

More controversial is the recent archaeological excavations in the Somme, the site of the First World War battle that witnessed an unimaginable loss of life. As the largest group of trees on the battleground, Mametz Wood was to be cleared of the Germans by the 38th (Welsh) Division in just a few hours (or so the generals thought). In the event, face-to-face fighting raged between 7 and 14 July 1916 with 4,000 causalities among the allies and 600 dead. While the Welsh won eventually, they faced a torrent of abuse from critics at home and there were even accusations of cowardice. Archaeologists can now tell us what really happened. We knew that the enemy were experienced and well dug in but what was not apparent from the contemporary British maps or reconnaissance reports was the extent of the defensive strongholds. Using aerial mapping techniques, archaeologists have found power cables and a telephone network that gave the Germans a massive advantage (*Sunday Times*, 3 July 2016). The archaeologists on this dig were from the British Ministry of Defence and so the subsequent vindication of the men fighting in what became known as Death Valley was no longer politically charged. As with our London and Canadian examples, the altering of the historical record found little traction in contemporary disputes beyond, perhaps, very small numbers of Welsh nationalists.

Jerusalem is different. The Israel Antiquities Authority (IAA) took over statutory responsibility for archaeological works from the British in 1948, and the rich record of archaeological remains in the Holy Land discovered during the nineteenth century. While there is little doubt about the academic integrity of the body archaeology more generally became the battleground on which each side – Israeli and Palestinian – affirmed their historical legitimacy in the city and region. Doron Ben-Ami, an archaeologist with the IAA, for example, searched in an area near the Temple Mount/*Haram esh-Sharif* for evidence of a Greek citadel that had once overshadowed the Temple:

> His team dug through successive layers, from an early Islamic market, through a Byzantine orchard and a hoard of 264 coins from the seventh century, under an elaborate Roman villa, and then beyond a first-century place for ritual Jewish bathing. Under buildings that pottery and coins demonstrated to be from the early centuries B.C., the archaeologists found layers of what looked like random rubble.
>
> (www.news.nationalgeographic.com/2016/04/160422-israel-jerusalem-hellenistic-archaeology-passover-hanukkah/)

That 'random rubble' was in 164 BCE a focus point for Jewish rebels led by Judah Maccabee. The Greeks were seen as colonizers bent on imposing idolatry on the Jewish people. When Simon Maccabee finally overwhelmed this imposing building in 141 BCE and expelled Hellenistic culture from Jerusalem, he effectively introduced one of two post-biblical festivals into the Judaic calendar: the mid-winter festival of *Hanukkah*. Not only were the layers uncovered controversial, so too was the site – it sat between the Temple Mount/*Haram esh-Sharif* and a Palestinian village to the south. 'This excavation is not searching for history', said Jawad Siam, director of the Madaa Community Center based in Silwan, 'it's designed to serve a settlement project.' The response to this observation was equally instructive: 'When Jerusalem calls, you never say no', said Ben-Ami. 'My expertise is in archaeology, not politics' (*National Geographic* online, April 2016).

Let us look further at the stormcentre of the archaeological dispute between Israelis and Palestinians: the Temple Mount. When the Arab historian, Aref el Aref, wrote *A Brief Guide to the Haram al-Sharif* (1929), the acknowledgment that there was once a Jewish Temple in Jerusalem seemed uncontroversial. Not so now. In recent years, the site has become a focus for bitter dispute. In 2010, it seems that a report was published by the Palestinian Authority that argued that the Western Wall (the 'wailing wall' has it has been called traditionally or *Kotel* in Hebrew) was merely part of the Al-Aqsa Mosque and not a remnant of the Temple:

> This wall was never part of the so-called Temple Mount, but Muslim tolerance allowed the Jews to stand in front of it and weep over its destruction, . . . No Muslim or Arab or Palestinian had the right to give up one stone of Al-Buraq Wall or other religious sites.
> (*Jerusalem Post*, 22 November 2010)

Although Jerusalem has been controlled by the Israelis since 1967, against international law it should be said, the site itself is managed by the *Waqf*, an Islamic religious trust that remained under the control of Jordan but which was first installed after the Muslim invasion of Jerusalem in 1187. It is they that have responsibility for the religious sites and archaeological matters in the immediate vicinity. In 1996 an archaeological war broke out. In a compound across from the Al-Aqsa Mosque, an underground and vaulted area called Solomon's Stables, the *Waqf* decided to turn the area into a place to pray and renamed it El-Marwani Mosque. Electric light illuminated proceedings; floor tiles lent some aesthetic qualities. With a nod from the Israeli government, an exit was planned by excavating a vaulted area where worshippers could egress in the event of an emergency.

Excavate anything in Jerusalem and an archaeologist will get twitchy. Bring in a bulldozer and dig a pit that is 131 feet long and 40 feet deep (it has been said) and then take hundreds of tons of dirt and debris (archaeological treasures?) to the local dump and you will need to answer some questions. Were Israeli archaeologists going too far when they accused the *Waqf* of attempting to (re) bury Jewish history, or perhaps was this just a very large oversight? 'That earth was saturated with the history of Jerusalem', said Eyal Meiron, an historian at the Ben-Zvi Institute for the Study of Eretz Israel. 'A toothbrush would be too large for brushing that soil, and they did it with bulldozers.' Yusuf Natsheh, as the *Waqf's* archaeologist, was absent when the deed was done but said in forthright terms nonetheless: 'The Israelis were "exaggerating" the value of the found artefacts. Every stone is a Muslim development. . . . If anything was destroyed, it was Muslim heritage' (www.smithsonianmag.com/history/what-is-beneath-the-temple-mount-920764/#hBDr4jfVPrQQOGtG.99).

Archaeology, then, has become a weapon in Jerusalem. It is a silent weapon, perhaps, but one that has sought quite deliberately (at least in some instances such as the one related earlier) to kill those already dead by denying they ever existed. Each side forgets that the Old City may be a large archaeological dig, but it is also a 'hive of new construction'. Everything changes and everything has changed:

> Many of the most iconic images of Jerusalem – the golden roof of the Dome of the Rock, the mass of worshippers in front of the Western Wall – looked quite different even a hundred years ago, when the dome was a dull lead, and the Western Wall approached only by a few sad mourners down a dank alleyway. The famous walls of the walled city are from the

sixteenth century only, the walkway around the ramparts, so beloved of current tourists, a product of the 1920s. This is a city that fabricates, forgets, and forges its past – in both senses of 'forge' – through misrepresentations and politically motivated fictions.

(Goldhill, 2008, p. 5)

Happily, archaeology is usually a good deal more routine and objective. It may involve piecing together the history of human communities by a reading of parchment, papyrus or paper-based documents. It may be about understanding the consumption of meat and different types of meat in the waste material of past societies, helping to unravel the wealth and belief systems of ancient communities. It may be about the analysis of bones and the types of cooking implements used in Israel, for instance, that suggest that the ancient peoples of Palestine and, before it was Judea, probably avoided eating pig earlier than any religious injunction turned pork into a forbidden food. Archaeology can offer that unique type of evidence to the historian. It is not always so politically charged.

Postscript

The similarities between archaeology and history are obvious enough. Both disciplines seek to reveal the past through the recovery and interpretation of what remains from the period in question. Both have lineages that can be traced back to antiquity and have similar trajectories in their emergence as scholarly disciplines, especially during the nineteenth century when they came under the thrall of professionalization. There are, however, important differences. Conventionally, archaeologists have been concerned with preliterate cultures and because of this have relied principally on material artefacts as sources of evidence, while historians have been concerned overwhelmingly with literate cultures and therefore have focused on written, documentary sources.

Types of evidence have tended to influence the respective approaches of the disciplines. Initially, the archaeologist set out to discover finds, which later were classified according to increasingly elaborate schemes which had the immense merit of providing reasonably reliable guides to dating. Only in the twentieth century, largely under the influence of Collingwood and Childe, did archaeology acquire theoretical predispositions, which led to unseemly splits into warring factions. Historians have not been spared from such developments. Thus, while the discipline has remained conservative – tied to Rankean notions of historical practice – it too has been punctured in recent years by attacks from the likes of postmodernism.

Now we see evidence of a certain convergence as archaeologists move into periods and cultures that have previously been the concern of historians, and historians accept with greater enthusiasm material artefacts as forms of evidence. Maybe this rapprochement means that the only real distinction is the state of their hands.

Whatever the case might be, it is evident that both archaeology and history have lost something of their innocence in recent times. Whether we are talking of the excavation of burial mounds in eighteenth-century America or interpretation of the rise of European civilization, it is likely that no work was simply a quest for the truth. But lately, as we have seen in the case of Jerusalem, such work has become highly politicized, probably to the detriment of all concerned.

Further Reading

Susan Alcock, Terence D'Altroy, Kathleen Morrison and Carla Sinopoli (eds.) (2001) *Empires: Perspectives from Archaeology and History*.

Pedro Funari, Martin Hall and Siân Jones (eds.) (1999) *Historical Archaeology: Back from the Edge*.
Katharina Galor and Hanswulf Bloedhorn (2013) *The Archaeology of Jerusalem*.
Simon Goldhill (2008) *Jerusalem: City of Longing*.
Jerome Murphy-O'Connor (2008) *The Holy Land: An Oxford Archaeological Guide (Oxford Archaeological Guides): An Oxford Archaeological Guide from Earliest Times to 1700*.
Colin Renfrew and Paul Bahn (2012) *Archaeology: Theories, Methods and Practice*.
Bruce Trigger (2006) *A History of Archaeological Thought*.
Peter Ucko (ed.) (1995) *Theory in Archaeology*.
Gordon Willey and Jeremy Sabloff (1993) *A History of American Archaeology*.

18 Anthropology

Introduction

This chapter begins by outlining the differences between anthropology and history before going on to explore the considerable areas of common ground between the two disciplines. The use of ritual in historical studies influenced a whole generation of historiography, especially apparent since the 1960s. In the course of the discussion in Section 2 we look at how theories like functionalism and structuralism, so influential in anthropology, were understood by major historians such as Alan Macfarlane, Keith Thomas and Natalie Zemon Davis. The third section will examine the rich and fascinating universe of history and mythology within the framework of anthropology. The case study used here is the so-called blood libel, which across centuries and different cultures has maintained a myth that Jews require blood for their religious rituals. Anthropological approaches used by historians have gone some way in obtaining more sophisticated historical explanations for why this myth has enjoyed such extraordinary longevity. The common ground between anthropology and history includes the use of historical methods by anthropologists interested in ethnography that in turn has had a significant impact on how historians approach social and cultural history – a relationship that we find entwined in Section 4. Without sensitivity towards pre-literate societies such as those encountered in the anthropological writings about Captain Cook we would never have understood the full circumstances of his death. Finally, we will look at how microhistories, influenced by approaches associated with social anthropology seek 'to detect the large in the small'. Here the work of Carlo Ginzburg is recognized as especially significant.

18.1 Pens and Pith Helmets: the Influence of Anthropology on History

Emma Crewe's *Lords of Parliament: Manners, Rituals and Politics* (2005) studied the cultural practices of peers in the British House of Lords:

> Most were mystified by why I was there, and some seemed displeased that I had done research in East Africa and South Asia, as though ceremonial robes of ermine (the winter coat of the stoat) [worn by peers on ceremonial occasions] should not be considered in the same light as those of fish skins, or feathers, or cowry shells and they were puzzled when I lingered on aspects that appeared to them to have little to do with politics.
>
> (Crewe, 2005, p. ix)

In the same way that anthropologists have understood their own societies by using insights gathered while investigating the lives, rituals and narratives of societies very different from their

DOI: 10.4324/9781003156086-21

own, historians have applied the methods of anthropology in order to study another 'foreign country' – the past.

What is anthropology? With Greek roots – *anthropos* (human) and *logos* (science) – anthropology is concerned with 'the study of man', and yet there are a few branches. In the United States, for example, it includes biological anthropology, archaeology (see Chapter 17), anthropological linguistics and cultural anthropology. In this chapter we deal with the largest of these subdisciplines, namely, cultural anthropology, which at its simplest is the study of the cultural diversity found in both 'primitive' and 'complex' societies. (Quotation marks are used here because the terms 'complex' and 'primitive' are value-laden – 'complex' being somehow better than 'primitive'). The value-laden term *primitive* may mean 'exotic' or can be used as a byword for pre-industrial societies, while *complex* may mean the study of behaviours or mythologies of a distinct group within industrial or 'advanced' societies. Occasionally we find anthropologists seeking to understand more about complex societies by applying methods usually associated with the study of primitive societies.

While there is no succinct definition of what anthropology *is*, it does have methodologies that serve to distinguish it from related disciplines such as sociology and history. The methodologies of anthropology are diverse but usually involve participation and observation. By going among those peoples to be researched, the anthropologist hopes to read their language, images, gestures, sounds and objects and a system of signs that are to be found in spoken, written and visual documents.

What then is special about anthropology and how might historians learn from its approaches? Anthropology as a discipline developed both intellectually and institutionally through the eighteenth and nineteenth centuries. It had its origins in the experience of European imperial expansion. Explorers, colonial officials, traders or missionaries of church or chapel would be dispatched to locate, govern, plunder and convert unfamiliar non-European societies; the success of this venture depended in part upon learning about the nature of the peoples they encountered. Yet this process does not begin to explain the changing institutional or theoretical framework in which anthropology as a discipline developed, operated and continues to operate.

Early anthropological endeavour crystallized into a more familiar modern shape with the creation of the Royal Anthropological Institute of Great Britain and Ireland (RAI) in 1871. The RAI was an amalgamation of the Ethnological Society of London founded in 1843 and the Anthropological Society of London, which had emerged in the 1860s. Unlike its amateur forbears (the word 'anthropology' first appeared in the *Edinburgh Review* in the early 1800s) or the Paris-based *Société des Obervateurs de l'Homme*, founded as early as 1799, the RAI was a learned institution which expressed its professional aspirations through discussion and debate, meetings and conferences, the promotion and dissemination of research findings, the maintenance of standards and employment opportunities and the provision of bibliographic services.

By the late-nineteenth century when anthropology had pushed its way into the halls of the universities, it was an institution that was already seen as halfway respectable. The American Anthropological Association was founded in 1902 and, most recently, these professional institutions have been joined by the Association of Social Anthropologists of the Commonwealth (1946), the European Association of Social Anthropologists (1989) and the World Council of Anthropological Associations, founded in Brazil in 2004.

The establishment of the RAI in the nineteenth century announced a breakthrough in ideas and approaches to anthropology, which was to have a profound effect on the usefulness of anthropology for historians and the attraction of history to anthropologists. Between the 1840s and the 1870s a theoretical storm in the discipline was brewing, and we can date the rather awkward relationship between social or cultural anthropology and history from this moment.

Anthropology as a discipline was quite often couched in Darwinist or evolutionist terms and at first anthropology regarded itself as a behavioural science – using scientific method to study the behaviour of living creatures. A recognition that the past could bring context to studies of 'primitive' societies and peoples led to accusations that history as a discipline was less rigorous than anthropology. By the 1920s, anthropologists working in the field had dismissed any attempt to construct a history of the tribe as simply 'guesswork'. Historians were themselves regarded as theoretically primitive or backward while history as a discipline was thought to be conservative and traditional in outlook, producing research that often failed to consider 'exotic' societies. Fixated on documentary or written archives, correspondence, diaries and so on, blind to non-literary societies, history was thought ill-equipped to investigate anyone besides those that had produced the archive – the colonizers, not the colonized. There seemed, then, to be little alternative to imperial histories which recounted the experiences of explorers, traders, colonial officials, missionaries – all set within a perspective of imperial expansion, free-trade and evangelical Christianity.

In the twentieth century, the relationship between history and anthropology fluctuated and was dependent on developments in each discipline. The pioneering anthropologist E. E. Evans-Pritchard (1902–1973), for example, trained as an historian before turning to anthropology as a postgraduate. He saw history as central to the approach that anthropology should take in its encounters with people from other cultures. His book on witchcraft, oracles and magic among the Sudanese Azande (a people located in Central Africa between the Nile and the Congo) was significantly entitled *The Azande: History and Political Institutions* (1971). Evans-Pritchard compares very well with the image of the pith-helmeted anthropologist-explorer but he remained firmly wedded to historical method and was emphatic about understanding the history, culture and social system of his subjects. This was a point made in a pamphlet which had a colossal influence on a young generation of historians starting to engage with a new kind of social history (Evans-Pritchard, 1971).

In 1970, Alan Macfarlanes' *The Family Life of Ralph Josselin; A Seventeenth-Century Clergyman: An Essay in Historical Anthropology* and his later studies of witchcraft in Tudor and Stuart Essex pioneered work produced within functionalist anthropology in an historical context. This started a trend that would help to redirect the way in which whole areas of historical research and writing were undertaken. Historians like Keith Thomas, soon to be famous for his magisterial *Religion and the Decline of Magic* (1971) but then working in the relatively untrodden field of women's history, acknowledged this debt.

By the 1970s, therefore, 'context' was reintroduced to anthropological study. With both disciplines in a reforming mood, the result was a rapprochement between anthropology and history. On the one hand, anthropologists rediscovered older bodies of ethnographical writing and so developed a renewed interest in the provenance and progeny of their discipline. On the other hand, approaches used by historians were finding currency among anthropologists. By the 1960s, both Victor Turner (1920–1982) and Clifford Geertz (1926–2006) were making imaginative use of available historical evidence, developing an anthropological and historical interest in culture, ritual, performance and symbolism. Turner argued that anthropologists should turn their attention to medieval religious politics as a well-documented period open to the methods of anthropology. The emphasis on ritual was to have a profound influence on historical research and writing in this period.

Bernard Cohn (1928–2003), whose interest in the Indian caste system was already well known, wrote an article entitled 'History and anthropology: the state of play' (Cohn, 1980; see also Cohn, 1987). The central idea was that 'history can become more historical in becoming more anthropological' and that 'anthropology can become more anthropological in becoming more historical'. In recommending a growing conjunction between anthropology and history, Cohn set in train a coming together of the two disciplines. Culture and how culture is constituted and represented, particularly in the historic 'otherness' of non-Western peoples, formed the basis of this new hybrid of historical anthropology.

Others took up the cause. John Adams recommended that historians adopt anthropology's interest in the everyday, the meanings of the mundane and commonplace and also be more self-aware of historical method and theory than they had heretofore been inclined to be. Historians, he contended, had become too preoccupied with what they took to be anthropology's fascination with the exotic, and cultural history was setting off hurriedly in pursuit of the unusual rather than the typical. From the historians' camp, Natalie Zemon Davis argued something similar. Anthropology, she suggested, could help historians to free themselves from the need to order events in terms of relative importance and so constructing narratives that hide the detailed fabric of life behind the great tapestry of the story. Anthropology can lend itself in practical ways by leading the eye of the historian towards 'the living processes of social interaction', providing ways of 'interpreting symbolic behaviour' (behaviour in history, such as faith, that can be seen as a symbol or sign of some historical phenomenon or experience) and understanding 'material cultures' or the non-literary cultures that had previously been beyond the realm of historical research (Adams, 1981, pp. 253–65).

Peter Burke, an historian who has made a very specific engagement with historical anthropology, has summed up the influence and utility of anthropological approaches to history by emphasizing a number of areas of impact:

1 There is an emphasis on qualitative over quantitative evidence. Historical anthropology tends to emphasize the use of imagery, symbolic meanings, social and cultural processes and so on over the statistical and the numerical. In fairness, the quantitative approach (related to the measurable quantity of something) has always had a place in the discipline of history, but the relative emphasis most definitely falls on the qualitative (the quality of observation or evidence and its utility for historians).
2 The use of microhistory as highly intensive local studies of the type written by Emmanuel Le Roy Ladurie and Carlo Ginzburg are entirely characteristic of social anthropology and now of history. Understanding societies by examining communities at smaller levels of social aggregation is analogous with the practices of social anthropology.
3 The third area where historical anthropology helps to augment the work of the historian borrows specifically from the anthropologist Clifford Geertz who is concerned primarily with the interpretation of culture (Geertz, 1973). Culture for Geertz, following the German social theorist Max Weber (1864–1920), is a 'web of significance' of our own making, and the job of the anthropologist (and the historian) is to find its meanings. Historians often analyze events and processes in the past in terms that would not have been intelligible to the contemporaries who acted out those events and processes. Geertz, on the other hand, used the term 'thick description' in his famous account of the 'deep play' of the Balinese cock fight, which provided a layering of detailed description of the event and built a picture and an explanation that would be intelligible to the people of that time and place. The cock fights in Bali, therefore, were seen as symbolic enactments of local status conflicts.
4 Historical anthropology imports into history a concern with the role of symbolism in everyday life and this applies to cultural life in the form of art, work, clothes, food, gesture (such as the wink that can be either flirtatious or conspiratorial) and so forth. The desire to unpack symbols is nicely described in Robert Darnton's *The Great Cat Massacre: And Other Episodes of French Cultural History* (1984), which asked why the ritual slaughter of cats was

found funny by Parisian journeyman printers in 1730. Briefly, the torture of cats was something important in the 'rough music' of the religious-based charivaris in parts of early-modern France and in rituals associated with witchcraft. It was deemed hilarious by the workers to subvert these rituals by killing the cats of their masters' wives and in so doing they turned tradition against the bourgeoisie. This, according to Darnton, anticipated the revolutionary events of the 1780s and 1790s.

Anthropologists who study communities traditionally concentrate their energies on the study of peoples living in parts of the world remote in space and in culture from the Western industrial societies to which they themselves belong. This makes the appearance of difference an inescapable, even blinding fact. More often, especially for functionalist or structuralist anthropologists, whom we shall define and examine in closer detail in the next section, they focus on the identification of recurrent patterns contained within people's ritual and symbolic practices. Now anthropologists are just as likely to study rural communities or discrete urban groups within modern industrial societies, and they are often acutely sensitive to particularities and difference within what historians might too easily see as homogenized mass culture.

Many historians have learned another habit of mind from anthropology, one that many more historians could do with learning, that is, to read against the grain of generalization: to work against our instincts and to hunt down the particular, the peculiar and the odd and understand what it meant to people in the past. Approaching historical subjects from the point of view of an anthropologist, seeing them 'as a race apart', makes for better historians who have fully absorbed lessons learnt from the 'pens and pith helmets' of the pioneering historians and anthropologists that we will review in this chapter. Above all, it is the ability to 'decode' behaviours and cultures, a skill borrowed from anthropology, which retains ultimate value for historians. It is to the theories that underline these approaches that we shall now turn.

18.2 Functionalism and Structuralism: Understanding the Lord Mayor's Show

The Lord Mayor's Show celebrated a local office that dated back a thousand years and recounted the national story in an imperial age. Sometimes peaceful, sometimes not, before the mid-nineteenth century the show travelled by water up the Thames from London Bridge to Westminster and was held each year on the 'Glorious Ninth' of November. Later it progressed through the streets of the City of London and by the 1870s it had become 'a holiday show' with the Committee of the Stock Exchange authorizing a day off for its members since little business was done in the City anyway. In 1880, the *Daily Telegraph* spoke of the City as the 'finest site in Europe' and its show as being 'alive with holiday makers'. By then the show had reallocated to the first Saturday in November when thousands turned up, not just from the London suburbs and the Home Counties but from across England. This was a ritual known and revered across the empire.

One of the features of the show by the 1880s was an overwhelming concentration on historical images, great men and glorious events, drawing on symbols well known to a wider historical culture. Yet, the late-Victorian City of London was truly modern; but then to be truly modern was also to be in touch with antiquity and tradition. What are we to make of the changing contours of this ritual that had been played out annually on the streets of the City of London for centuries? Clearly ritual of any kind depends somewhat on context and meaning and that meaning can be often masked or layered. Anthropologically, then, there are perhaps several questions that can be asked about a ritual such as the Lord Mayor's Show. Any explanation of the place of the pre-modern office of Lord Mayor operating in the modern world must successfully explain the relationship that the City had as a modern centre of finance with tradition or historical memory.

It must also answer other questions thrown up by the anthropological method. What was the function of the Show, did it support existing social structures by simply representing them, did it legitimize social authority by concealing that authority in 'harmless' ritual and how much can this ritual tell us about City society – about dissent and rebellion, as well as change? To what extent was the Show malleable, not so much a receptacle for uncontested narratives about the national past – of tradition and continuities – but open to different groups and contested views of that past?

Answers to the evident paradox of the show, which apparently represented simultaneously the modern and the archaic, is found in anthropological explanations from both functionalist and structuralist viewpoints. Functionalism developed during a period when anthropologists little valued history. During the 1920s and 1930s the pioneering Polish anthropologist Bronislaw Malinowski (1884–1942), for example, took no account of the history of people and societies that he described in *Sexual Life of Savages* (1929). His interest was in societies regarded as static and 'backward', evidenced by their primitive reproductive practices, their apparent ignorance about the process of procreation and their indiscretion in publicly describing their own sexual lives:

> An interesting personal account was given to me by Monakewo. . . . It was hardly discreet of him to speak of his mistress by name; but the ethnographer's love for the concrete instance may excuse my not emending it.
>
> 'When I sleep with Dabugera I embrace her, I hug her with my whole body, I rub noses with her. We suck each other's lower lip, so that we are stirred to passion. We suck each other's tongues, we bite each other's noses, we bite each other's chins, we bite cheeks and caress the armpit and the groin. The she will say 'O my lover, it itches very much . . . push on again, my whole body melts with pleasure . . . do it vigorously, be quick, so that the fluids may discharge . . . tread on again, my body feels so pleasant'.

(Malinowski, 1929, pp. 286–7)

Malinowski was concerned with understanding the varying needs of the human organism and how those needs related to the social system to which the individual belonged. Central to his view is the idea that society is a system in which social processes like courtship and marriage and artefacts such as shrines and other objects of religious veneration are to be understood through the *function* that they fulfil within that system. The object of studying a society, therefore, is to appreciate how it works as a system at any given time rather than how it had historically developed.

Malinowski is known as the founder of functionalist anthropology because of this emphasis on understanding objects, rituals, symbols and practices through their social functions. In this he inherited much from the French sociologist Emile Durkheim (1858–1917), who stands at the head of this tradition of sociology and anthropology. The legacy of Malinowski is clearest in the work of English anthropologist A. R. Radcliffe-Brown (1881–1955) who argued that the function of cultural phenomena like social ceremonies and the structures of kinship was social maintenance or the conservation of society in its current arrangements.

We introduced the anthropologist Alan Macfarlane in the last section. Like Evans-Pritchard, Macfarlane trained as an historian and went on to produce works of historical erudition and value within both disciplines. In a review of the developing relationship between history and anthropology, published in the *Times Literary Supplement* in January 1973, Macfarlane explained the benefits that a functionalist anthropology can bring to the study of history:

> [A]nthropology is based on a timeless but satisfying explanatory system which has been termed 'functionalism'. Rather than seeing the roots of actions and thoughts in random past events, it was argued that both actions and ideas could be explained by their present 'functions'. This was especially important since it helped to de-mystify much of what had earlier been dismissed as 'irrational' or 'superstitious'. For example, witchcraft beliefs serve a 'function' in many societies, both to explain misfortune and as a form of social control. . . . Functionally a witch doctor is only a psychiatrist writ large.
>
> (Macfarlane, 1973, p. xx)

In 1981, Macfarlane, who by then was aware of the limits of functionalism, reflected on the ground-breaking qualities of Keith Thomas' *Religion and the Decline of Magic*. It had introduced fresh ways of looking at previously obscure sources such as the records of the ecclesiastical courts or astrologers' notebooks, making respectable research on fairy beliefs, popular prophecies, village healers and popular religion. Thomas was well aware of how functionalism, derived from anthropology, could be applied to an historical subject. Take, for example, the disputes that emerged in the guise of accusations of witchcraft practice, which were apparent only because of structural weaknesses in that system caused by 'the position of the poor and dependent members of the community':

> Witch-beliefs are therefore of interest to the social historian for the light they throw upon the weak points in the social structure of the time. Essentially the witch and her victim were two persons who ought to have been friendly towards each other, but were not. They existed in a state of concealed hostility for which society provided no legitimate outlet. They could not take each other to law; neither could they have recourse to open violence. In Africa accusations of witchcraft frequently spring from conflicts within the family, for example, between the co-wives of a polygamous husband. But in England the witch and her accuser were very seldom related. The tensions which such accusations usually reflected arose from the position of the poor and dependent members of the community. The charges of witchcraft were a means of expressing deep-felt animosities in acceptable guise.
>
> (Thomas, 1971, p. 669)

Using the tools of anthropology, then, historians can know why witches were found on the boundaries of the village and on the margins of society. Interestingly, again according to Macfarlane, it was a book researched and written precisely at a moment when functionalism was subject to a devastating attack by an alternative theoretical tradition, that is, structuralism.

Claude Lévi-Strauss (1909–2009) is generally regarded as the most influential anthropologist of the second half of the twentieth century and is considered as the modern founder of structuralism (see Chapter 11). Simultaneous to the development of structuralism and perhaps of greater moment to the historian was the birth of semiotics, which Lévi-Strauss regarded as a limb of anthropology. Semiotics, put at its crudest, is the study of signs. For Ferdinand de Saussure (1857–1913), Swiss linguist and originator of structural linguistics, it was 'the study of the role of signs as part of social life'. Applied to the archive, especially to visual sources, semiotics has attractions for the historian; it seeks to get beneath the 'surface features' of phenomena and reveal how the organization of signs and systems as a form of language create meaning. In this way, the definition of 'language' may be widened to include 'images', 'gestures', 'sounds' and 'objects', all of which have systems of signs and symbols.

One example of the usefulness to historians of 'reading the signs' can be examined through something common to us all: death. Rituals of death are culturally constructed and change over time. In most societies and in most times, after death we find a ritual or process of mourning and a sign of mourning is that we might wear clothes that are different from our everyday clothes. In the West the symbol of mourning has been traditionally black; in India it has been white. Only particular knowledge of the context can allow us to know what a particular sign or symbol means and what it means in any one historical period or place.

Reading the signs can also be of value in revealing the nature of the myths, which to an extent we all inhabit in various ways. Generally considered to be 'false' belief systems, endemic to primitive societies that do not have the capacity to know better, myths are complex ideologies created in most societies as a means of helping people interpret and hence confront often worrying aspects of their lives. In the next section, we wish to explore one particular pernicious myth, that of the blood libel.

18.3 Myths and History: Jewish Conspiracies and the 'Blood Libel'

Anthropologists are also deeply interested in myth and mythology; in many respects the interpretation of myth as a cultural artefact is fundamentally what anthropology is about. History, on the other hand, has always had a more troubled relationship with the mythic and mythological. We shall examine these relationships by looking more closely at a myth that survived across centuries and across cultures and many different types of societies and still exists despite being verifiably untrue. This is the myth that Jews require blood for their religious rituals and practices.

Martin Luther (1483–1546), who was a priest in a critical moment of Christian reform, was once a friend to the Jews, calling them the 'blood-relations of our Lord'. He even announced to the Catholic Church that 'if you become tired of abusing me as a heretic, that you begin to revile me as a Jew'. It was the bit about blood that stuck, however, especially after 1543 when he wrote his now infamous *The Jews and Their Lies*. No longer did he defend the Jews as kith and kin ('as blood-relations' to Jesus the Jew), now he stirred mythologies about Jews and Judaism that only confirmed Christian prejudices of a people who had, they thought, conspired to kill Christ by initiating and prolonging the 'Passion' or crucifixion.

From early medieval times, the Jews had stood accused of consuming blood for the ritual purposes of making *matzah* (the unleavened bread Jews eat at Passover). This blood was said to have been extracted from Christian children. 'William' in Norwich in 1144 and 'Hugh' in Lincoln in 1255 were both said in various ways to have been crucified by Jews and drained of blood for these ritual purposes. There were similar reports of incidents in England after this period that were transported in subsequent centuries to mainland Europe, to Germany and France in particular, with truly terrifying consequences. It was blood that Jews needed to dab on the eyes of their young, as everyone knew in medieval Europe that Jews were born blind and needed the blood of a Christian child in order to see. They needed Christian blood in order to heal their circumcision – a stubborn reminder of their adherence to the old covenant and denial of the new. Everyone knew too that Jewish men menstruated. The mythology then of Jewish culpability in the death of Jesus and Jews as a 'cursed people', the 'children of the Devil', laid the groundwork for what has become known as the 'blood libel'.

How this mythology has transliterated across cultures and religious traditions, retaining a remarkable coherence, keeping its basic shape, is a deep-seated historical problem that is not confined to Europe. Indeed, the most infamous incident of the myth of Jewish cannibalism emerged dramatically in Syria in 1840 with the so-called Damascus Affair (Green, 2010, pp. 133–41). An arresting example of the myth travelling over time, distance and culture, however, comes from the United States. The conversation related below happened in the immediate aftermath of the disappearance of a four-year-old girl in September 1928 from a small town in upstate New York. The child was found safe – she had apparently fallen asleep in the woods – but crowds continued to congregate near the local synagogue with accusations that Jews had been responsible for her kidnap. The 'foreigner' in question was a recent immigrant from Salonika in Greece who provided the direct link back to European mythologies about Jews:

Mickey McCann   'Can you give any information as to whether your people in the Old Country offer human sacrifices?'
Rabbi Brennglass (indignant) 'I am surprised that an officer of the United States, which is the most enlightened country in the world, should dare to ask such a foolish and ridiculous question'.
McCann   'Was there ever a time when the Jewish people used human blood?'
Rabbi Brennglass 'No never, that is a slander against the entire Jewish people'.
McCann   'Please don't think that the idea originated with me; somebody else, a foreigner, impressed me with it'.

(Perry and Schweitzer, 2002, pp. 43–4)

All societies have myths. They provide a sense of who we are, where we come from and why we are here but they do not necessarily relate to real or even plausible accounts of the past. While we have comprehensibly established that there are myths that existed and exist about Jews, we might have chosen to focus on myths that Jews may have about themselves or about others. We could have raised the more general question of conspiracy and myth in history or focused on other groups that have historically featured in myth-making over the years.

In one view, myths are a fanciful collection of stories created for important reasons but they do not amount to accurate descriptions of the past as it is understood by historians. The functions of myths are acknowledged but they are the proper concern of other disciplines such as folklore or anthropology. This does not mean that the historian is not interested in myth; as we have seen, it is simply too important to be ignored. Even if we think that the myths of the ancient Greeks, for example, do not describe accurately the development of Athens or Sparta, the history (including politics, sociology, culture and economy) of those societies cannot be understood without appreciating the great importance of their myths to *them*, for the thoughts and deeds of people in the past are guided by what they believe to be true as much or more than by any objective reality that can be dug up in the archives.

Historians have adopted several different positions regarding the relationship between myth and history. Some, like Eric Hobsbawm, have seen myth and history locked in a competitive struggle to explain reality. *The Invention of Tradition*, edited with the anthropologist Terence Ranger, caused quite a stir when it was published in 1983. According to the contributors, myth acts as a sort of illegitimate history, explaining past events in a way entirely subservient to the prevailing interests of dominant groups within society. The Aryan myth, the myth that some North European peoples share a common and racially pure origin, so central to Nazi ideology, is one example. Another might be what the historian Angus Calder has called the *Myth of the Blitz* (1991), which finds a population under German attack in London during the Second World War but who are themselves locked in a competitive struggle for survival, not unified on a common front but 'all in it together', a myth that has been handed down to Britons as victors of the war.

Such myths are seen by Hobsbawm and others as being essentially untrue, harmful and as such must be combatted. The main means of fighting against pernicious myth is history. History, as a discipline, with its methods, formal procedures and insistence on the use of evidence, is said to provide an alternative account of the past that challenges the political manipulation of myth. Thus, one job of the historian is to debunk myth, whether it is the myth of the grasping, manipulative, conspiratorial and blood-thirsty Jew or the Western myth, according to Edward Said's *Orientalism* (1979), of the so-called destructiveness of the Arab mind. It is all the better then, when refuting these migrating, transforming, durable mythologies, that we have the tools of anthropology at our disposal, for what they can provide is a deeper understanding of the processes of thought and the symbolic worlds constructed by us in our search for solutions.

18.4 The 'Dying God': Captain Cook and Ethnohistory

In popular perceptions of their roles, anthropologists and historians cut very different figures. The anthropologist wears a bush hat or pith helmet and tirelessly trudges up mountains or hacks through jungle in search of lost tribes and ancient, unchanging, folklore. He or she is a cross between Indiana Jones and a colonial official associated with the imperial literature or poetry of Rudyard Kipling (1865–1936). The historian heads resolutely in the opposite direction, plunging ever deeper into the mysterious and dusty world of the archive, meticulously piecing together our collective past. A dishevelled figure that stands guardian as a remembrancer of how we became who we think we are. Despite their comic pastiches, the traditional images of the adventurous anthropologist and the book-bound historian do nonetheless reflect persistent differences in subject matter and approach. Anthropologists do sometimes study people who live in remote places and historians do spend a lot of their time in archives. However, neither of these images will do for the present day. Anthropology is now a highly theoretical discipline and is as much a creature of the library as of the field trip. Historians have long woken up to the fact that they have a claim on the whole of human experience and are no longer confined to the archives alone.

Ethnohistory looks at the variety of human existence from an historical point of view but quite often using evidence gleaned from indigenous sources. Now absorbed within cultural anthropology in keeping with its American roots, it is one area where history and anthropology more generally have come closest to shading one into the other. Ethnohistory began in the United States in the early and mid-twentieth century as an attempt to understand the culture and history of Native American peoples from the inside. Edward S. Curtis (1868–1952), for instance, between 1907 and 1930, captured the popular culture of the native Indian by photographing 'the old time Indian, his dress, his ceremonies, his life and manners', which has provided an archive for both the anthropologist and historian alike (Library of Congress, 2009).

From the anthropologists concerned with the history of societies that were pre-literate and often small in scale, ethnohistory became open to linguistics and archaeology while vocabulary and the structure of language became the primary materials of historical inquiry. This type of cultural anthropology tries to free itself from the historian's traditional dependence on documents, focusing instead on oral traditions, storytelling or the artefacts of material culture such as pottery, earthenware and similar objects, visual images and artwork. The emphasis on orality, objects and the visual allows histories of non-literate societies to be written. There are then moments when not only does anthropology throw light on an historical question but that history has complemented the work of anthropologists.

By looking closely at the murder of Captain Cook, it can be seen how successful ethnohistory or cultural anthropology has been in suggesting plausible explanations. The more standard account of Cook's life and death has become a part of the narrative of the expansion of Europe into the non-European world: of heroic discovery and sacrifice, of a civilizing force and noblesse oblige, of a Christian mission to savage peoples and to bring further glory and riches to the mother country. The job of the historian is to interrogate this narrative, not simply to debunk it but to understand it in the context of the history of the British empire. This is critical

332 *Interdisciplinarities*

for any consideration of Marshall Sahlins' important approach to cultural anthropology and to the rituals of the Hawaiians themselves. For, more than anyone else, Sahlins has led the way in interpreting the mutual discovery of James Cook and the Hawaiians in a way that makes sense in relation to Hawaiian culture as well as British imperial history.

In his book *Islands of History* (1987), as well in longer treatments of the subject in academic journals and elsewhere, Sahlins' starting point was to ask what the Hawaiians themselves understood to be happening when Cook anchored off their shores and to insist that societies such as these have their own histories and cultures, although they have been influenced by Europe and the West. Princeton anthropologist Gananath Obeyesekere takes up this theme in his book *The Apotheosis of Captain Cook: European Mythmaking in the Pacific* (1997), arguing that the deification of Cook was a European invention which presented the 'natives' as dupes, a representation of 'primitive' peoples that lives on in Western popular imagination.

On 17 January 1779, the ships *Resolution* and *Discovery* sat at anchor in Kealakekua Bay on the black-sanded shore of the island of Hawaii. The British seamen, confined for month

Figure 18.1 Captain Cook, Western explorer and 'hero'
Contributor: GL Archive/Alamy Stock Photo

after month on the long sea journey across the Atlantic, through the treacherous waters off Cape Horn and the endless watery wastes of the Pacific, thought they had landed in paradise. In the memories of generations of British schoolchildren, their commander Captain James Cook (1728–1779) has been credited with discovering the island. Hawaii was of course already known to its own native inhabitants, even if they had a very different understanding of how their home related to the rest of the universe from that of their putative discoverers. Cook and his crew remained among the Hawaiians enjoying lavish hospitality, the sexual favours of the women and the sumptuous bounty of the verdant green island. As is famous from the crews' own accounts as well as that of historians after the event, they were treated as if they were gods in a land of natural splendour and plenty.

Cook's discovery, the way he arrived, and the timing of his presence led to his deification by the islanders – he was thought to be *Lono*, the god of natural growth and reproduction. This god lived among them for a time. When Cook returned to his ship, the islanders thought they had been abandoned by their god, and their child-like generosity turned suddenly to fury as their savagery won out over their natural nobility – or so it appeared from a European perspective. When, on 14 February, Cook returned from the ship with some marines to take the Hawaiian king, Kaniopu'u, as a hostage against goods stolen the previous evening from the *Discovery*, the islanders brutally murdered their fallen idol. The encounter, once peaceful and friendly, had turned to bloody confrontation: 'The structural crisis, when all the social relations began to change their signs' (Sahlins, 1987, p. 107).

Sahlins' explanation involved seeing the incident from the point of view of the Hawaiians, taking note of the local ritual cycles of the year. Cook's appearances and reappearances happened to coincide with the expectations of local lore and custom in relation to the movements of *Lono*, of sexual overtures made by the Hawaiian women who in keeping with their own knowledge of the rituals and narratives of their role in this performative cycle were 'looking for a lord' among their visitors whose very presence, in turn, was part of the prophecy of local religious belief. In this sense, quite apart from the conduct of Cook and his men or the 'savagery' of the 'child-like' indigenous peoples, the encounter between 'native' and 'European' ended in the way (for the islanders) it was expected and deigned to have ended: a face-off between king (Kaniopu'u) and god (Cook) in which the king was destined to prevail. Cook, as the 'dying god' *Lono*, unwittingly played out the death rituals of local religious custom and, therefore, that of his own death.

Sahlins here posed a challenge to structuralism. According to Sahlins, Cook's death was certainly the result of a 'structural crisis' but that it was predicated on a remarkable set of 'ritual coincidences'. These could only be explained through an understanding of the indigenous culture of Hawaii. While not entirely rejecting Lévi-Strauss's linguistic frame of reference, his was a synthesis of a structuralist approach but with a heavy emphasis both on history and the importance of local custom or culture. This approach yields a plausible account of what went on that St Valentine's Day in 1779 in ways that we might never have considered possible. Only by recognizing the structures of this society – its symbols and signs – and using the tools of anthropology could historians challenge existing explanations of the circumstances of Cook's death.

This interest in the impact of the West and particularly the impact of states expanding outside of their territorial boundaries amounts to common interests for the anthropologist and historian. The recent contribution of Sahlins is particularly suggestive here. Assumptions are often made about the impact that contacts with developed Western societies have had on the others that they encountered in the course of their economic and political expansion. Key to these assumptions is the idea that the local, the culturally particular, the distinctive folkways and ways of life of native peoples were disrupted fundamentally by imperial contacts.

More recently, the globalization of the world economy and the expansion of Western-based multinationals such as McDonald's and Coca-Cola have had a homogenizing effect on local cultures – making all cultures look the same, simplifying them into the workings of a basic machine, as the anthropologist Edmund Leach (1910–1989) argued. When we arrive at our 'exotic' holiday destination it also has already been 'spoiled', reduced to a bland similarity in the face of a dominant Western culture as regional and local cultural forms are obliterated. Sahlins makes a strong case for recognizing the resistance of these cultures. Not that they remain unaffected either by imperialism or modern capitalism but that they can engage with and absorb cultural influence on their terms as well as on the terms of the greater economic powers. They exist as genuine hybrids of the general and the local and this may mean that local cultures are more resilient than we give them credit for.

The problem is that historians remained for a very long time well equipped to research and write the history of the British venturers and imperialists from the manifold sources available but less able to research the history of the Hawaiians. Not so anthropologists. They are, after all, expert in the interpretation of non-literate cultures and cultures at the point of first contact with Europeans. If we do not understand the part that Hawaiian history played in these events and the part that these events and subsequent relations with Europeans played in later Hawaiian history, we will never fully understand the imperial past and the events that take place after the 'age of empire'. In the case of the death of Cook this might have always meant a search for explanations from one (European) side of the equation, but by considering the local and the discrete we now know better. It is to the local and the discrete or the 'micro' that we now turn.

18.5 Microhistories: Cheese, Worms, Night Battles and Ecstasies

Foregrounding aspects of the cultural life of two communities in the remote Friuli region of north-east Italy, the intellectual development and ideas of a poor sixteenth-century miller known as Mennochio can be traced through their many intricacies. Although Friuli had surprisingly high levels of popular literacy, Mennochio was strikingly literate for someone from such lowly origins. From his reading of learned texts, from the folk-culture of his region and from the fertility of his own imagination, Mennochio conjured up his own cosmology. Creation, he argued to his neighbours, consisted of ripe cheese and life was made up of maggots and worms living upon its substance.

This view of the universe, that it had anarchic beginnings, clearly questioned the Christian understanding of God's design. Mennochio even questioned the divinity of Jesus. Unsurprisingly, his querulous and incautiously talkative nature soon attracted the attention of religious and civil authorities. Interrogation, prosecution and ultimately conviction followed and, although found guilty of being a *heresyarch*, someone who not only repeated heresies but created them, Mennochio was sentenced only to prison. His confinement lasted until the authorities were persuaded that he was truly repentant, whereupon he was released but warned under the direst penalties never to lapse into his old heretical ways. For a number of years, he was silent but gradually his need to express his views and propound his own theology fought its way to the surface; he began once more to harangue his neighbours. This time the courts acted with swift severity and, on being found guilty for a second time, Mennochio was executed.

The tale is taken from Carlo Ginzburg's *The Cheese and The Worms: The Cosmos of a Sixteenth Century Miller* (1982), which remains a fine example of a microhistory, a small-scale and highly localized attempt to reconstruct cultural processes and social relations in great detail. Heavily influenced by historical anthropology, his approach made the local and the particular its starting point. By the 1980s, following the pioneering lead of historians like Keith Thomas during the 1960s and 1970s and the impact of 'history from below', historians have developed new areas of the history of culture: turning their gaze not to the world of the high culture of social elites but, like the historical anthropologist who studied the lowly tribesman, to the world of the common people: the peasant, the villager and the urban poor.

Ginzburg scouted out historical detail in symbols and signs, squeezing these signs from the smallest and the most insignificant historical trifle and then describing and connecting that evidence on macro social structures. We will look now at two of his major works in order to fathom how he managed to tease out the larger trends and concerns of history in the tiny and seemingly insignificant. His particular skill was in reading signs and in those signs detecting a rich context for the more important structures to be found in society. In doing this, in concentrating on the discrete, he drew upon an approach of Italian (and to some extent, French) historiography that had, as its starting point, the local.

In the second of his noted works, *The Night Battles* (1983), Ginzburg analyzed what appeared to be the incidence of a secret cult known to themselves as the Benandanti, again in a remote Friulian community. Extensive records created by Dominican inquisitors sent by the Catholic Church to investigate them suggest that these people believed that nocturnal dream world battles were fought out between the Benandanti and forces of darkness trying to invade their world while they slept. The Inquisitors wanted to know if these stories of 'night battles' were related to witchcraft and, in particular, if they contained any evidence of demonic activity: Did the devil have a hand in these dream world events of the night?

In different ways through the intensive description of the life of Mennochio and the nocturnal world of the Benandanti, Ginzburg is interested to retrieve aspects of popular culture at the humblest levels of society and in its more remote geographical reaches: a long way from the concerns of high politics and court society. In this he represented, like Sahlins, a venture into the field of historical anthropology. As Ginzburg himself would acknowledge, however, there were issues of methodology to be attended to here. Popular culture could not really be understood outside of its interactions with elite, literate culture. For Mennochio, it was his literacy, his reading of learned texts, that was one source of his own private cosmology that finally led to his destruction. In the case of the Benandanti, what we know of their beliefs we recover from records produced by their inquisitors who not only recorded what they were told of the views of the poor villagers but also framed and wrote the questions they were asked. We also must recognize that the inquisitors conducted their inquiries over such a long period that the responses of the Benandanti might well have come to take on the meanings and shapes implicit in the kinds of questions they were being asked. The poor peasants may have been providing the answers they thought were expected of them; popular culture may have learned to mould itself around the preconceptions of the inquisitors themselves.

In his third and by far most ambitious work, Ginzburg's new edition of *Ecstasies: Deciphering the Witches' Sabbath* (2004) investigated why ideas of a conspiracy against Christianity spread in the early part of the fourteenth century, why accusations of conspiracy were first aimed at discrete social and ethnic groups – lepers, Jews, Muslims or conspiring combinations of these groups – and then ended up with witches as the arch-conspirators, their numbers drawn from the general population. It was only then that Christian society could imagine that it faced a single external enemy: the devil. And it was this idea of a conspiracy of the devil that came to dominate Europe over the next two centuries:

> From a relatively restricted social group (the lepers) one passes to a larger, but ethnically and religiously delimited group (the Jews), finally reaching a potentially boundless sect (male and female witches). Like the lepers and Jews, male and female witches are located at the

margins of the community; their conspiracy is once again inspired by an external enemy – the enemy par excellence, the devil.

(Ginzburg, 1992, p. 72)

Ginzburg wanted to establish where this phenomenon began and his use here of historical anthropology is unmistakable. His starting point is the internment of lepers and the prohibition on their having children and then the mass murder of French Jews in the spring of 1321. Burning at the stake, the confiscation of property and the exclusion from trades and commerce were followed by accusations that Jews were behind the Black Death, more burnings and eventually expulsion from France under royal edict. He worked back to these events by investigating the provenance of the Witches' Sabbath, which comprised homage to the devil, rejection of Christ and the Christian faith, magical ointment, sacrifice of children, animal metamorphoses, magical flying, nocturnal gatherings, feasting and sexual orgies. In doing this, focusing on a particular time and place (fourteenth- and fifteenth-century France) he had hoped to chart how conspiracy – or the idea of conspiracy – worked and from whence it came. Moreover, he also wished to determine how the microhistory of a small community, a discrete group, a lone individual, could impact on the mighty structures of church and state.

For all Ginzburg's erudition, he did what all good historians should do: he connected evidence; he drew conclusions from the particular and applied those conclusions to the general. Above all, he treated chronology with tremendous respect: poring over evidence year by year, day by day and hour by hour. His influences were anthropological, and he had an astonishing ability to read signs and tear symbolic fragments of evidence from one context and apply them imaginatively to what was previously thought to be an entirely unconnected context. His inspiration, however, was surely that of an historian seeking to understand human change.

Postscript

At first sight there appears to be little in common between history and anthropology. History, after all, is concerned with the study of past societies, while anthropology explores societies in the present. The work of the founding anthropologists in the early nineteenth century was very much part of an imperial project, for it arose from a need to understand more about the societies that the imperial powers – most particularly the British in India and Polynesia – encountered. Thus, the aim was to understand as a means of better controlling the ways in which these 'primitive' societies operated, and although there may have been passing reference to the histories of these societies, the overriding concern was to reveal the significance of their ritual beliefs and activities and the role of myth and custom.

During the twentieth century, the relationship between history and anthropology altered. Anthropologists increasingly recognized the importance of providing historical context, but more important was the acceptance among historians of the value of anthropological approaches. Their interests remained in past societies, but many began to appreciate that the ways in which anthropologists had approached an understanding of, say, ritual and symbolism, could be applied to the past. In the postwar period, we have witnessed the creation of a body of work about past societies by scholars who to great effect have straddled the worlds of history and anthropology. To take one outstanding example, Keith Thomas' *Religion and the Decline of Magic* was a path-breaking attempt to understand an important moment in European history, and he did so by viewing with the eyes of an anthropologist how and why societies at the time responded to the rise of religion and the impact it had upon ancient folk beliefs and rituals.

Anthropology has also encouraged a certain theoretical awareness among historians. Although functionalism and structuralism were not the exclusive preserve of anthropology but were developed also in disciplines such as sociology and literary studies, historians learnt most about their practical application from anthropologists. For historians, functionalism provided a means of explanation of the 'whole way of life' of a society through an understanding of what particular functions were served by customs, rituals or particular patterns of behaviour more generally. An emphasis on the maintenance of social coherence, however, has over time led to a loss of confidence in functionalism. Rather more important has been the influence of structuralism. Here a preoccupation with revealing the hidden structures of social mores, read more or less as a giant language, has led to an influential body of historical inquiry, deeply critical of more traditional approaches.

Finally, anthropology has opened an interest within history with the whole question of myth. It is no exaggeration to say that we live through myths as taken-for-granted systems of beliefs, and anthropology has played a vital role not only in explaining to historians the importance of myth but also in providing them with the tools to untangle their inner workings and social consequences.

Further Reading

Alan Barnard (2000) *History and Theory in Anthropology*.
Alan Barnard and Jonathan Spencer (eds.) (2002) *Encyclopaedia of Social and Cultural Anthropology*.
Clifford Geertz (1973) *The Interpretation of Cultures*.
Carlo Ginzburg (1980) *Cheese and the Worms: The Cosmos of a Sixteenth Century Miller*.
Carlo Ginzburg (2004) *Ecstasies: Deciphering the Witches' Sabbath*.
Emmanuelle Le Roy Ladurie (1978) *Montaillou*.
Marvin Perry and Frederick M. Schweitzer (2002) *Antisemitism: Myth and Hate from Antiquity to the Present*.
Marshall Sahlins (1987) *Islands of History*.
Marshall Sahlins (1995) *How 'Natives' Think: About Captain Cook, for Example*.
Marshall Sahlins (2004) *Apologies to Thucydides: Understanding History and Culture and Vice-Versa*.

19 Literature

Introduction

Literary cultures provide sources of historical evidence that greatly enrich understandings of the past. In the opening section we discuss how literary scholars have historicized their examination of the novel in ways that blur the boundaries between historical and fictional narrative and provide both challenges and opportunities for the historian. New Historicism is discussed in the second section. This approach favours an informed interaction between 'imaginary' texts and the 'real' evidence that has resulted in an interdisciplinarity between literary scholars and historians. The third section takes as its focus the graphic novel and how it too can hold up a mirror to both individuals *and* society and as such may be worthy of examination, telling us something about our contemporary preoccupations with the past. The final section uses the literary and historical writing of the metropolis in order to illustrate how literature and history can enjoy a fruitful and productive relationship.

19.1 Literature as History

When Sherlock Holmes and Dr Watson inadvertently meet in a City of London opium den called the Bar of Gold in Upper Swadham Lane, 'a vile alley lurking behind the high wharves which line the north side of the river to the east of London Bridge', we not only travel with them into London's back streets ('Between a slop-shop and a gin-shop') but journey downwards into its darkest and most dangerous places. But what as historians are we to make of Sir Arthur Conan Doyle's story, *The Man with the Twisted Lip*, serialized in *The Strand Magazine* from July to December 1891? One reading would take note of this submerged layer of the City of London's economic life. We know that many figures in the City straddled many types of existences and moved freely across the cityscape from the West to the East Ends, and so this fictional story could tell us something about notions of identity in the period and how poverty was spatially organized.

Holmes and Watson are searching for a respectable City man, Neville St Clair, who has disappeared near this unsavoury house run by a 'rascally lascar', a 'man of the vilest antecedents'. St Clair lives in Lee, Kent as a gentleman who 'appeared to have plenty of money'. He bought a large villa and eventually married the daughter of a local brewer. And as a 'gentleman' he had no occupation. However, St Clair was said to be 'interested in several companies' and travelled into the City by train in the morning and returned by the 5:14 from Cannon Street every night. A man, it would seem, without problems, not, that is, until his wife made an unplanned trip to the City on an errand and to do a little shopping. This was risqué behaviour unaccompanied by a man as she found herself in a lesser-known part of the City.

DOI: 10.4324/9781003156086-22

Glancing up at a window (of an opium den as it turns out) she glimpsed her husband, who quickly slides out of view.

The police were called and so eventually is Holmes, the one man who can make sense of the confusion and dangers of modern London. Save for clothing and a trickle of spilt blood leading down steps towards the perilous tides of the Thames there is no sign of St Clair. However, following the investigation we learn that St Clair has taken 'employment' in the lucrative business of professional beggary. In order to avoid the police regulations, he pretended to a small trade in wax vestas (matches). Here, after he changed clothes at his den in Great Swadham Street, he proceeded to the heart of the financial City, Threadneedle Street:

> upon the left-hand side, there is, as you may have remarked, a small angle in the wall. Here it is that this creature takes his daily seat, cross-legged with his tiny stock of matches on his lap, and as he is a piteous spectacle a small rain of charity descends into the greasy leather cap which lies upon the pavement beside him.
>
> (Doyle, 1891, pp. 107–8)

That the fictional St Clair 'could every morning emerge as a squalid beggar and in the evenings transform [himself] into a well-dressed man about town' stretches our imagination but by reading a fictional account about the 1890s that was written at the time, we may identify a real, not fictional, anxiety about the nature of identity in this decade and the troubling presence of the poor located adjacent to the financial centre of the nation, indeed the empire. His 'greasy leather cap' served as a trope to identify the repellent dirtiness of the poor and gives a textual clue while reference to 'vile' antecedents comes straight from gothic assumptions about the inherited nature of corruption.

Conan Doyle never intended the story to be true in any conventional sense. As we have suggested, the main character strains credibility, and even when Doyle attempted to capture in striking realism and detail the topography of London's streets he was in error (Glinert, 2003, pp. 172–3). It is a useful example, however, for us as historians to pose questions about the boundary between history and literature.

This boundary is not rigid or well defined. Indeed, until the emergence of what we would consider historical writing in the nineteenth century, it was difficult to detect at all. From earliest times, historical accounts have been suffused with mythical tales and incorporated fictional elements such as speeches and conversations which were clearly the invention of the authors or had been passed down through the centuries. It was only with the emergence of a sense of time based on the calendar and the dating of historical sources that boundaries began to be drawn between the rather more fixed genres of historical writing and literature.

Let us elaborate a little further these important suggestions. In ancient Greece and Rome, both history and literature were recognized to be exercises in rhetoric, but already history was thought to record real events and actors, while literature dealt overwhelmingly with imaginary happenings. Aristotle made the classic distinction:

> the distinction between the historian and the poet is not whether they give their accounts in verse or prose (for it would be possible for Herodotus' work to be put into verses and it would be no less a kind of history with verse than it is without verses). [No] the difference is this: that the one tells what happened, the other the sorts of things that *can* happen. That's why in fact poetry is a more speculative and more 'serious' business than history: for poetry deals more with universals, history with particulars.
>
> (Aristotle, 1997, p. 81)

This distinction between the historian, who observes and records – and the poet, who philosophizes and constructs was to prove remarkably enduring, although not always enforceable as a universal and consistent rule of thumb. While it may be said that in general historians have used literary sources as a means of illuminating context – something that the historian E. P. Thompson described, pejoratively, as adding frivolous 'colour' – literary scholars have used historical context as a means of illuminating literary forms. Some have clearly felt comfortable in both camps. Indeed, fine studies such as Michael McKeon's *The Origins of the English Novel* (1987) and James Chandler's *England in 1819: The Politics of Literary Culture and the Case of Romantic Historicism* (1999) show the extent to which the two forms continued to overlap well into the modern period.

With the consolidation of the discipline of historiography and the rise of the novel, however, historians devoted themselves to recording things 'as they actually happened' while literature was seen increasingly as the province of authors exploring human fantasies and emotions. Using appropriate methodologies and sources, historians were concerned with events in the past that could be observed and 'proven', in contrast to novelists, playwrights and poets who conveyed a world of the imagination. Given this distinction, historians rarely considered fiction as a source of historical truth. Rather, when historians and historically minded literary theorists approached the novel, it was as a means of understanding the historical context of its production and reception. Thus, the literary text is seen primarily as a

> mirror image or at least a symptom of some sociohistorical or perhaps transhistorical process or structure such as capitalism, colonialism, the rise of the individual, the emergence of a distinctive if not unique form of experience or subjectivity. . . . The text thus becomes a document of the times or perhaps of transhistorical forces.
>
> (LaCapra, 2013, p. 13)

Such studies have tended to dominate the field. Seemingly endless doctorate dissertations, articles and books have appeared which attempt to uncover how particular novels inscribe their historical contexts through the formal procedures of the genre, its style, form and structure. (As an exercise, you might wish to see just how many studies have appeared of such favourites as Joseph Conrad's *Heart of Darkness*, Emily Brontës *Wuthering Heights* or Charles Dickens' *Bleak House*.)

We opened this section with a brief exploration of how a Conan Doyle short story can be read to reveal something of its historical context and engagement with contemporary concerns. Morag Shiach's *Modernism, Labour and Selfhood in British Literature and Culture, 1890–1930* (2004) extends the discussion. Shiach's background is in literature rather than history, but she draws upon both to show how modern forms of labour were experienced and represented. The years 1890–1930 were chosen deliberately, for the period was coterminous with the moment of modernism when distinct forms of labour and notions of the self emerged. These issues may seem to be the provenance of the historian, and yet Schiach skilfully charts the shifts that occurred by using primarily literary sources. What particular technologies, she asked, reshaped our understanding of labour and the self? How did writers and artists seek to capture and at the same time create such understanding? With these questions in mind, Shiach explored the writings of D. H. Lawrence, Sylvia Pankhurst and others to show that work came to define human individuality at a time when more efficient work routines, new technologies and intense divisions of labour, most notable among women employed in the sweated trades, reduced the number of hours worked.

It is important to remember that fiction and poetry come in a bewildering variety of forms, as does their engagement with historical 'truth'. Chaucer's tales were largely fictional but at the same time drew directly from his experience of real events and places to reveal something of the nature of medieval England. Shakespeare also drew heavily upon such historical references but to tell us about the time of Richard III or late Tudor England. And what forms of historical engagement are evident in more modern works like T. S. Eliot's *The Waste Land*, Margaret Mitchell's *Gone with the Wind*, James Jones' *From Here to Eternity*, Salman Rushdie's *Midnight's Children* or Hilary Mantel's *Wolf Hall*?

Few historians would deny the importance of masterpieces such as *The Waste Land* and James Joyce's *Ulysses* in illuminating the human condition during the early years of the twentieth century. By comparison, popular works of historical fiction are generally held in low regard as being fanciful, trivial and historically unreliable. But it is necessary for a moment to eschew such prejudices and try better to understand how these novels operate.

Let us take as an example Hilary Mantel's *Wolf Hall*, first published in 2009 to wide critical acclaim and recently adapted for television by the BBC. It is clear from the outset that Mantel has read the full range of primary and secondary sources dealing with the Tudor court under Henry VIII. And she is unhappy with some of the standard accounts, especially those that portray the Chancellor Thomas Cromwell in an unfavourable light. The image of him as an evil and scheming megalomaniac who rose to prominence from lowly origins is largely a product of Victorian times, taken up and recycled by modern historians such as G. E. R. Elton and David Starkey. For Mantel, there is another Cromwell whose personal and family life paints a rather different picture. Through letters and the observations of those who knew him it is possible to gain access to this Cromwell, a man who was not without feeling but one who in the heat of the Tudor court had to exercise iron self-control. Mantel admits there are many gaps which the novelist fills through, say, fictionalized conversations, but if the research has been done thoroughly, and you can manage to know the characters and allow them to speak, then the guesswork is plausible.

Ultimately, she claims, with any such book it is hard to please both the literary critic and the historian. The critic wonders why the history cannot be slicker and more dramatic; the historian asks why some of the detail has been omitted. Mantel does not profess to be an historian for she lives inside the consciousness of Cromwell and his associates and tries to capture much of the uncertainty and risk that governed their lives. In this endeavour, however, she is happy for historians to pass judgement on whether her interpretation of the events makes sense (Mantel, 2010).

It is important to stress that historical novelists like Mantel now make a point of researching the period as thoroughly as any historian. It is routine for a novelist to discuss their 'sources' and to base a storyline around known or contested historical facts in which they immerse their reader while taking artistic licence with the facts, often by inventing characters, conversations and situations. William Boyd is a prime example of a novelist who extends this technique by using footnoting or even providing an index. His themes are historical, and he purports to use historical sources (that are actually fictional) to place his fictional characters into the maelstrom of real historical events. An early novel *An Ice Cream War* (1982) used letters as a prop to tell a story about conflict in East Africa during the First World War while *Sweet Caress* (2015) used photographs that purport to have been taken by the main character in the novel but which had been randomly collected (or in one instance found randomly in a bus station) and spread generously across the narrative as if they provided a factual support to the story. Boyd went as far in his *Nat Tate: An American Artist: 1928–1960* (2011) as to write a biography of an artist that never actually existed. The book launched on the eve of April Fool's Day with David Bowie providing readings to an audience of critics in New York, apparently oblivious that Nat and Tate were an amalgam of the National and Tate art galleries in London.

These examples provide yet more evidence of how fact and fiction are often the playthings of the historical novelist but for historians can provide thought-provoking, interesting and provocative results. Perhaps the greatest strength of the historical novel, though, is an ability to set alight the imagination, to prompt an independent search for more information about a specific event, personage or detail that especially captures an interest.

Similar arguments can be made about studies that are consciously historical but at the same time variously use devices which are normally considered within the realm of literature. Orlando Figes' *A People's Tragedy: the Russian Revolution, 1891–1924*, for example, is based on a sound factual knowledge of what events surrounded this momentous moment and consequently has what Michael Bentley called a 'persuasive authenticity' (Bentley, 2005, p. 160). At the same time, however, it tells a 'good story' using a full range of literary characteristics. At the heart of Figes' project was a desire to write a history of the revolution as a personal tragedy. Hoping to challenge those histories that celebrated the achievements of the Bolshevik leadership, he determined instead to reveal the immense human costs, in part by 'listening to the voices of individual people whose lives became caught up in the storm'. Here he recounts the thoughts of the Empress Alexander soon after a grand event staged in St Petersburg early in 1913 to mark the three-hundredth anniversary of Romanov rule:

> Now you can see for yourself what cowards these state ministers are,' the Empress Alexandra told a lady-in-waiting shortly after the jubilee. 'They are constantly frightening the Emperor with threats of revolution and here – you see it for yourself – we need merely to show ourselves and at once their hearts are outs.' If the rituals of the jubilee were intended to create an illusion of a mighty and stable dynasty, then they had convinced few people except the court itself. The Romanovs became victims of their own propaganda. Nicholas, in particular, returned from his tour of the provinces confirmed in the self-delusion that 'My people love me'. It aroused a fresh desire to travel in the Russian interior. He talked of a boat trip down the Volga, a visit to Caucasus and Siberia. Emboldened by the belief in his own popularity, he began to look for ways of moving one step closer towards the system of personal rule which he so admired in ancient Muscovy.
>
> (Figes, 1997, p. 12)

Arguably, this passage owes more to literature than history. Since the conversations are not referenced, it is difficult to verify them. Without this, we cannot decide whether the words were actually spoken or simply invented by Figes – like an historical novelist – to convey feelings and emotions of the protagonists in an engaging way. These problems are compounded when he comes to discuss the Russian peasantry. Here was a population that left no written records, and so the historian looks in vain for recorded conversations. Under these circumstances, Figes turns to the contemporary writings of the great Russian novelists for insights into the peasant world; but Leo Tolstoy, Maxim Gorky and Anton Chekhov are hardly conventional sources of historic evidence.

We can reveal more about the complex relationship between fiction and historical truth through a discussion of Simon Schama's *Dead Certainties* (1991). Schama approaches important historical questions in a highly unorthodox way and simultaneously reflects on the role of narrative in both forms of writing. Let us first establish the 'plot' or rather the historical narratives as presented by Schama. He adopted two main storylines. One narrative is organized around the fate of General James Wolfe, killed in 1759 by the French at the Battle of Quebec. His death was remarkably low key. Wolfe was shot at the foot of a cliff close to a small bush; it went unnoticed and unreported until his body – already showing signs of decay – was discovered by a lowly foot soldier. Schama presents us with various narratives which offer alternative interpretations of his demise, what Schama called 'the many deaths of General Wolfe'. Most notable, perhaps, is the one recounted by a soldier using fictionalized dialogue. The second main narrative is an account of the murder offered by Wolfe's biographer, Francis Parkman, whose book *Montcalm and Wolfe* (1884) ensued that Wolfe would be remembered as a national hero. Schama explained his approach:

> Both the stories offered here play with the teasing gap separating a lived event and its subsequent narration. Although both follow the documented record with some closeness, they are works of the imagination, not scholarship. Both dissolve the certainties of events into the multiple possibilities of alternative narrations. . . . These are stories then, of broken bodies, uncertain ends, indeterminate consequences. And in keeping with the self-disrupting nature of the narratives, I have deliberately dislocated the conventions by which histories establish coherence and persuasiveness. Avoiding the framing of time sequences supplied by historical chronologies, the stories begin with abrupt interventions – like windows opening suddenly – and end with many things unconcluded.
>
> (Schama, 1991, pp. 320–1)

A third narrative, embedded in the famous painting of 1771 by the Anglo-American Benjamin West, complicates further the historical recovery of Wolfe's death. Determined that Wolfe 'must not die like a common soldier under a bush', he created an image in which the sorry ordinariness of Wolfe's death was displaced by a grandly theatrical and symbolically loaded staging, guaranteed to evoke in the minds of the audience the highest ideas of noble sacrifice (and to secure West's reputation and livelihood).

These stories serve to explore a 'border country' between fiction (what is made up) and history (what is constructed from evidence) as a means of showing that the distinctions between the two are not as hard and fast as conventionally thought. This is a vital issue which we wish to examine a little further by considering evidence, narrative and causality.

Historians are in general poorly served by the evidence when attempting to recreate the past. Documentary evidence, upon which most historians rely disproportionately, is fragmented, incomplete and contains loud silences on the topic being researched. What exists has by accident or design survived from the past while the vast bulk has been lost forever. The records of the English Poor Law, for example, are essentially those written by officials in the course of their duty, and even when they exist as a fairly complete series, they say next to nothing about the attitudes of those subject to its harsh rules or its impact on the lives of poor families. And, of course, evidence is never pristine, raw data: it exists because it has already been processed to fulfil particular functions or meet specific demands. Sadly, we can only test its veracity against other evidence, never against the events themselves, and so it follows that events described are not 'real' but only possible objects of perception.

By inventing evidence of events, characters and conversations, fiction may appear yet further removed from the past, but much historical fiction is not merely invention or imaginary – it too relies upon the same body of hard factual evidence to forge a creative synthesis between the real and imaginary. Importantly also, fiction enables the writer to enter areas of the human condition normally out of bounds to the historian simply because no hard evidential data exist. Human fears, hopes and aspirations are often better explored through fiction, as are areas such as the lives of the poor and enslaved. Fiction, in other words, is not necessarily escapism but can offer new ways of speaking and thinking about experiences beyond the grasp of the historian. Without recognition of this point, we would find it difficult to account for the work of, say, Dickens, Joyce or Eliot.

19.2 Historicism: Text and Context

We should perhaps pause a moment to consider the respective roles of the scholar of literature and that of the historian, between those who at first sight deal with 'the real' against those who play with the imaginary. There was a time when the literary critic would treat a text as autonomous, and therefore judge it on any independent merits as if a 'pudding' or 'machine'. The only consideration (as in the intrinsic merits of the poem, novel or short story) was whether it was good or whether it worked. With the development of what has been termed the 'New Historicism', texts were brought into juxtaposition with contexts, thereby creating fresh and productive relationships between literature and history. This shift is mapped out by the essays in Harold Veeser's *The New Historicism* (1980). They claim that since words are an intrinsic part of a culture, not free floating or devoid of context, any literary work, any text, should be considered a creation of the time in which it was produced and consumed. Thus contextualization, the lifeblood of the historian, became important to literary analysis, and this was to change literary studies and more importantly (for our purposes) the research and writing of history.

The New Historicists facilitated a renewed understanding of how 'history and culture define each other'. The understanding and interpretation of texts was subject to the ever-altering preoccupations of the here and now. It was recognized, moreover, that as texts and historical actors comingled and together produced cultural texts, these texts could not be studied outside culture. Hence literary specialists needed to understand, say, *Oliver Twist* within the context of mid-Victorian responses to poverty and urbanization, while historians now needed to pay more attention to the form, content and structure of language itself.

Renaissance scholars such as Stephen Greenblatt took the scepticism about the existence of the autonomous text and equally autonomous historical self – implicit in the 'New Historicism' and argued that both texts and the self are defined by relationships shaped in the culture. It was in this way that Greenblatt (and other scholars, especially in Renaissance and Victorian studies) have eschewed 'standard' history and instead 'fashioned . . . criticism from anecdotes, unusual events, and incidental objects to animate old texts' (Williams, p. 47).

Perhaps the most advanced and accomplished example of this approach can be found in the work of Alison Light. Her histories of servants and more recently her use of genealogy illustrate the past lives of the working poor. She moves from an informed narrative that we might associate with a 'straightforward' social history of the Industrial Revolution to a literary style that occasionally leaves 'hard' evidence or 'strict' chronology behind. The tense used is that of the continuous present, which has the effect of almost turning history writing into a prose more usually associated with literature:

> When shall we say it was? And where? Sometime in the 1800s, and two brothers are walking a track which runs, pitted and rutted, across the smooth slopes of the chalk downland. It is a raw morning, the mists lifting. This is Wiltshire, a large county to the west of England, 200 miles from London, and they are high on Salisbury Plain, heading south-east to the coast fifty miles on. A carter will take them part of the way, but they have no money to squander and will walk if they have to. The chalk is their country but they have seldom been further than Salisbury, a stretch of fifteen miles. Sheep shuffle off as the strangers approach, their wool glistening with damp. Across the Plain there are hundreds of sheep, closely cropping the grass; corn will be planted where the flock has been folded, making the most of the manure. To the north, though, the soil turns dark and clayey, good for cattle and dairy. Wiltshire is two different countries: chalk and cheese.
>
> (Light, 2015, p. 67)

When compared with the organization of evidence, which is thought to be the proper role of the historian, narration such as this (beautifully crafted) is generally regarded as the realm of the novelist attempting to 'tell a good story'. The distinction between pure literary scholarship and history writing, however, does not stand scrutiny in this excerpt from Light. Such interdisciplinarity has been instrumental in the realization that history cannot work through the simple amassing and presentation of evidential data. Rather, evidence must be linked in order to transform data into a dynamic sequence with due regard to time and hence to convey a coherent picture of the past. The historian is thus necessarily involved in acts of narration which correspond and overlap with those of the novelist. It is recognition of the virtually indistinguishable narrative strategies of history and literature that underpins the influential work of Hayden White. White has importantly argued that, in communicating a realistic representation of the past, history and literature employ the same archetypal narrative forms that operate at a deep structural level (White, 1978). These modes he describes as comic, romantic, tragic and ironic, and they refer not to the world as it is but as it is represented by historians and novelists; an appreciation of how such narrative works is the first step in its transcendence and hence a certain liberation from constraints that have affected their writings.

Deliberation on these matters has led some modern philosophers of history to striking conclusions. R. G. Collingwood, whom we have already met on several occasions, pointed to the striking similarities between historians and novelists:

Each of them makes it his business to construct a picture which is partly a narrative of events, partly a description of situations, exhibition of motives, analysis of characters. Each aims at making his picture a coherent whole, where every character and every situation is so bound up with the rest that this character in this situation cannot but act in this way, and we cannot imagine him as acting otherwise. The novel and the history must both of them make sense; nothing is admissible in either except what is necessary, and the judge of this necessity is in both cases the imagination. Both the novel and the history are self-explanatory, self-justifying, the product of an autonomous or self-authorizing activity; and in both cases this activity is the *a priori* imagination.

(Collingwood, 1961, pp. 245–6)

More recently, Alun Munslow, although schooled in postmodern theory, has reached the same conclusions. He argues cogently that history is primarily a form of literature. Historians do not resurrect the empirical reality of the past but rather gather and present evidential facts in order to endow them with coherence and meaning. While some might devote themselves to discovering the facts as a means of revealing the 'truth' about the past, what they do in effect is aim to tell a story that plausibly explains what the evidence means:

the content of history, like that of literature, derives its meaning as much by the representation of that content, as by research into the sources, tracing the causes and effects of events as well as the hidden but discoverable structure(s) of historical change. This approach maintains that history, rather than discovering the most likely meaning to the past either by virtue of the evidence and/or its theoretical underpinnings can, rather, only offer a representation of pastness.

(Munslow, 2003, p. 6)

This does not deny the importance of the evidence but challenges the notion cherished by most historians that contemporary sources provide the foundation for historical inquiry.

We have already considered the extent to which history and literature share thinking on causation (Chapter 21). Stephen Kern stresses the point that causal theories are ubiquitous because they have universal application. Although he is concerned principally with the homologies between literature and natural sciences such as genetics and physiology, his arguments can readily be applied to history. The emergence of a more complex and circumspect perspective on causation has encouraged many historians to abandon monocausal explanations. This is evident, for example, in the move from linear narratives to a more fluid handling of time and an appreciation of the difficulties in adjudicating between different interpretations of the past.

We wish to bring these issues together by looking briefly at a modern American masterpiece. Toni Morrison's *Beloved* (1987) is an innovative attempt to capture aspects of the history of American slavery. At first sight, there was nothing necessarily new in this venture; after all, the historiography of slavery is considerable; the best of it is brilliant. Morrison was familiar with this body of work, including slave autobiographies and the extensive narratives of ex-slaves recorded in the interwar period, and she recognized its worth in recording slavery as an institution, but on the other hand she found large and worrying silences on the experiences of the enslaved themselves, for these narratives stopped when confronted with experiences too terrible to relate. This omission, she argued, was responsible for a 'national amnesia', in response to which Morrison determined to retrieve aspects of that past, not as a means of overcoming the amnesia but rather of burying its horrors once and for all, hence enabling 'us' to move on.

The novel is steeped in the actual past. At the centre of a complex, fragmented narrative is the story of Sethe, who slits the throat of her two-year old daughter rather than allowing her to become a slave. The child subsequently returns as a spiteful ghost to take possession of the house in which her mother now lives as an emancipated woman. Beloved is not merely another character, however; rather she embodies a past which has to be remembered and confronted before it can be forgotten. Such elements of magical realism, which are so embedded in American folklore, may at first sight seem to compromise the work of an author committed to retrieving the 'truth' about the past, but throughout the book there are constant references to 'real' places and events. The infanticide, for example, was based on a real-life incident in 1856 when a slave Margaret Garner killed her daughter, although in circumstances which now are not entirely clear. Morrison's endeavour, however, is not that of the conventional historian, simply because the historian has no evidence or means of gaining access to – and recovering the conditions and feelings of – the anonymous enslaved. It is consciously an act of remembering, a desire to find and reveal a truth about a 'people without history', so giving a voice to the 'disremembered', unrecorded and unaccounted for. If this involves disclosing the horrors of slavery – of thinking the unthinkable – then so be it.

A sense of history weighs heavily. At the end of the novel, Sethe's husband, Paul D, turns and says 'Sethe, me and you, we got more yesterday than anybody. We need some kind of tomorrow' (Morrison, 1993, p. 273). In order to accomplish this, Sethe had found it necessary to confront and thereby come to terms with the past. Beloved embodied this past, and hence a vital part of the struggle to keep the past at bay was not to forget her but to lay her memory to rest. This act of disavowal, however, was difficult, for nothing ever dies, as Sethe tries to explain to her daughter, Denver:

> I was talking about time. It's so hard for me to believe in it. Some things go. Pass on. Some things just stay. I used to think it was my rememory. You know. Some things you forget. Other things you never do. But it's not. Places, places are still there. If a house burns down, it's gone, but the place – the picture of it – stays, and not just in my rememory, but out there, in the world. What I remember is a picture floating around there outside my head. I mean,

even if I don't think it, even if I die, the picture of what I did, or knew, or saw is still out there. Right in the place it happened.

(Ibid., pp. 35–6)

This desire to expose the truth about the interior lives of people who had no means of recording them themselves (Light has surely attempted something similar in her *Common People*) cannot be achieved through conventional historical methods. Access to the memories within is possible only through an act of imagination which takes responsibility for the creation of characters, events and even the language. This may seem the province of the novelist, but again any consistent distinction between fiction and history (as we have sought to argue) is difficult to uphold. Morrison describes her strategy as literary archaeology, that is, an imaginative retrieval and reconstruction of the past in which fiction is historicized and history is fictionalized. All this is rather redolent of what Collingwood was writing some seventy years ago.

Beloved was received with critical acclaim and helped secure its author the Nobel Prize for Literature. If, at the same time, the book has partly filled a cavernous gap in the American imagination of its past in ways that could never have been achieved by history alone, then there is no greater testament to the power of the symbiosis between literature and history.

19.3 Nostalgia and the Graphic Novel

There are occasions when physical sites – places, spaces or buildings – can act as a confluence for thoughts about the past and preoccupations with the present, when streams of time, in a sense, come back on themselves allowing a conduit for the past to become redolent in the present. The built environment, the material culture of 'artefacts', even smells can succeed in connecting present and past through an affinity of the mind, spirit or temperament. The Twin Towers were an iconic symbol of America and global free trade and one such site of memory. In the aftermath of the horrors of 9/11 the comic book (the genre had morphed into the graphic novel by the 1980s) vividly historicized this seminal event while earlier acts of violence were simultaneously re-remembered. The mutuality of text, context and image that work together to illustrate the power and importance of the past make the comic and the graphic novel a distinct genre running between the two disciplines. As such, the visual and the written texts that characterize this form of narration are very much part of the nexus between literature and history.

For Art Spiegelman, 9/11 threw up dark recollections about the Holocaust. *In the Shadow of No Towers* was published in 2004 and, in a sense, was a rejoinder to his *Maus: A Survivor's Tale*, which was serialized through the 1980s and which adopted or borrowed the memories of his father, Vladek, a former inmate of Auschwitz who experienced the horrors of attempted genocide. David Haydu writing in the *New York Sunday Review* (September 2004) noted how father and son confronted mass murder and what he called 'arrogant' and 'power-hungry regimes' while each made sense of these historical events (the Holocaust and 9/11) by focusing on family and what it meant to be a Jew in both these historical moments.

For Spiegelman, the events of 9/11 had a direct personal relevance. Living in Manhattan and watching on television what was perhaps (as the critical theorist Jurgen Habermas suggested) the first truly globalized event witnessed universally, he ran to rescue his daughter at a school near what was about to become Ground Zero. This Swedish-born veteran of the underground comic or comix book genre was seized by panic. He had the natural fears of a father but as he ran from the smoke and fire of the falling second tower with his daughter in his arms, he was gripped with an apocalyptic feeling that the sky was falling and the US government had somehow colluded in this tragedy or at least had failed to protect its citizens; in short, history was revisiting calamity on his own family in an eerily familiar way. Those charged with protecting its citizens had somehow turned into their persecutors. His early illustrations after 9/11 reveal the author threatened by both sides – terrorist and his own government (see www.sequart.org/magazine/2693/on-in-the-shadow-of-no-towers/from-in-the-shadow-of-no-towers). In the days and months that followed, Spiegelman found an extraordinary creativity in his obvious pain and in the dislocation in time that 9/11 had prompted in his imagination.

Finding himself at the very centre of an historical watershed on 9/11, Spiegelman wrote and drew in order to understand the self – himself – but in the context of global history. In *Maus* his family were represented as mice and so he now transformed himself back into a mouse on the comic pages of *In the Shadow of No Towers*. He was very clear on how the self in the present was juxtaposed with the past, '[O]utrunning the toxic cloud'. His own experiences on that day recalled for Spiegelman how his father had tried (and failed) to describe the stench of a death camp, for Spiegelman now needed to find a way to depict the foul smell of New York ablaze in an effort to establish an historical record through a form of literature. He went on:

> the 'faultline' between World History and Personal History suddenly emerged after the north tower of the World Trade Center [WTC] collapsed, but that the collapse itself unveiled the ever-presence of such a Janus-faced locus. Like Walter Benjamin's 'angel of history' at whose feet, the past collects as a 'single catastrophe'.
> (www.americanpopularculture.com/archive/venues/spiegelman)

The reference here to the literary critic and writer Walter Benjamin, whose suicide in 1940, is telling. For Benjamin, history did not necessarily point in the direction of progress but 'flashes up in a moment of danger' such as Nazism in the 1930s or the attack on the US by Al-Qaeda in 2001. In a short essay called *Illuminations*, Benjamin described the angel of history (an image that he took from a 1920s painting by Paul Klee) where history is not a 'chain of events' but a tempest where all history (as it were) can be gathered into the cataclysm of a single moment: 'His [the angel of history] face is turned toward the past. Where we perceive a chain of events, he sees one single catastrophe which keeps piling wreckage upon wreckage and hurls it in front of his feet' (Benjamin, 1968, p. 257). The angel would stay to make whole what has been smashed, but it propelled towards a future which he can neither resist nor adequately represent. Thus, in Spiegelman's short graphic novel that followed the horrific tragedy of that September morning, he and other writers and artists of graphic novels reflected the global event back on the personal, the 'single catastrophe' where all history is assembled. While historians could not possibly work exclusively within this personal context and we would not collapse (as Spiegelman does) the Holocaust and 9/11, it does work well as an attempt at historical reconstruction from an intensely personal viewpoint but also from the perspective of an historical event that has a context. For Spiegelman that main context is a politics that was about to turn into 'The War on Terror' and his art became nothing less than an attempt at self-therapy with history informing a reflective commentary on 'the' event itself and the fear of events yet to come. Other writers and artists approached events differently. 'Before' and 'After' served as a literary device for establishing 9/11 as an event which existed in linear time, a story to be told within a narrower context and which did not attempt to compare an earlier historical event or speculate either about the future. In effect and perhaps even as an intention, this was the record of 9/11 organized as a graphic memoir called 'Tuesday' by cartoonist Henrik Rehr who, like Spiegelman, lived very close to Ground Zero. What strikes the historian here is the attempt to frame an historical event in the ordinary and mundane. On return to the apartment after the attack, the commentator notes a layer of dust everywhere but with toys still on the floor, a newspaper still open on the same page and a coffee mug 'waiting for me on the kitchen counter.' This could not be further from the depiction of 9/11 by Spiegelman, which was smothered by history; instead, time appeared to have come to a gentle halt.

The form, structure and organization of these works are important. Again (as in the *Beloved* example that we gave in the last section) we might examine the non-linear way that the story unfolds. With Spiegelman's approach to time, the narrative is as impacted as the event itself; 'the jumps between panels, between strips and within the page layout, recreates the chaos of a complex and hurting situation' while 'At first sight, each page is a shapeless mass of frames which is closer to a collage than to a comic. Paces multiply and there are no clear directions to read it' (Claudio, 2011). This takes us some distance from historical narratives that tend towards sequence and the unfolding of a story but it is, nonetheless, storytelling. It certainly combines storytelling and pictures with time flowing through the comic artwork just as it flows through an historical narrative. It would seem that whereas time becomes disrupted (so to speak) by 9/11 so too did the sequential organization of the comic genre.

The visual style and format used by Spiegelman to represent the 'single catastrophe' of 9/11 departed from *Maus*, it has been argued, by a loss of 'rawness'. It was replaced by a 'formulaic slickness of mainstream comics' (www.americanpopularculture.com/archive/venues/spiegelman). His underground and edgy art was (it was argued) supplanted by 'digital design' and 'packaging' that was printed on thick cardboard paper and even sold on a separate shelf from other graphic novels. It was also expensive. It looked and felt, it was further argued, like an elite product. Certainly, Spiegelman was content to design the memorable cover page of the late September edition of the *New Yorker*, that bastion of metropolitan elitism, with the Twin Towers barely visible as a black backdrop – the black of mourning – that was indistinguishable from the grey that dominated the foreground of the cover.

Purists may have objected to the distance Spiegelman had travelled from the crude productions of the underground comix, but more notable from a historiographical perspective than his so-called repudiation of comix was his artwork. This was seen as 'simultaneously contemporary and antique':

> appropriations of long-forgotten newspaper comic-strip characters. Five or six story segments or graphic elements in different styles – one running vertically, one in a large circle, one broken up into images laid out like snapshots on the floor. . . . At the same time, the book's main pages are intended as a homage to the first American newspaper comics from the turn of the 20th century – principally in having been designed originally for serial publication . . . reproducing seven vintage Sunday newspaper strips that dealt, a century ago, with war, patriotism, Arabs, Lower Manhattan and buildings threatening to fall.
> (www.americanpopularculture.com/archive/venues/spiegelman.htm)

We shall have cause to return to Spiegelman's motivation for the use of the early comics as he worked out the shock of a visit from the 'angel of history' on 9/11. Before that, we should first establish the origins of the comic book in order to understand fully why Spiegelman revived some of their more familiar tropes in his depiction of 9/11.

While North American comics have become iconic in the English-speaking world (Marvel and DC Comics, for example), comix and then graphic novels have evolved to become a global phenomenon with France and Japan very important contributors to the genre. Attempts to understand their impact have tended to focus on the visual as either a system of signs or a branch of contemporary art rather than for a genre primarily concerned with historical narratives. Thierry Groensteen in *The System of Comics* (2007) and *Comics and Narration* (2013) has provided the most instructive guide to this form of storytelling. There are notable cartoonists who are associated with the graphic novel. Robert Crumb (b. 1943) is one who takes the past as a central concern (chiefly the 1920s) while Will Eisner (1917–2005) probably did more than anyone to popularize graphic art. His *Comics and Sequential Art*, published in 1985, categorized the graphic novel as a form of narration as much as an art form. More recently the historiographical significance of the graphic novel has been emphasized. Here the name of Alan Moore must be reckoned with. While Eisner often returned to historical themes with his *Contract with God* (1978) that turned the Bible into a graphic novel and probably signalled the beginning of the modern form, it was Moore's *Watchman* (1987; the artist was Eddie Campbell) who lent both a deeper psychology to his characters and an imaginative approach to historical counterfactuals. In *Watchman*, the 'superhuman' named Manhattan 'ensures that America wins the Vietnam conflict, that the US has the edge over the Soviet Union in the Cold War and that Nixon is able to change the Constitution and stay on for a fourth term' (Tony Venezia, 2009, p. 23).

Yet a Benjamin-like scepticism about linear time or any sense that time stretched forward with a singular and determined end or purpose is a constant. In a sense, the graphic novel as a form of historical narrative is against determinism or a sense that history inevitably will travel in a single direction. Even a conventional narrative that focused on the story of Jack the Ripper and the late nineteenth century Whitechapel murders in Moore's *From Hell* (serialized between 1989 and 1996) was an exploration of how time and perception in the human mind interacted. This was not a conventional narrative. It involved a rich and varied historical depiction of the Victorian age and a comprehensive understanding of the era that becomes in Moore and Campbell's hands a prerequisite to identifying Jack.

From Hell is a plausible account of the rise of the modern world when Victorian London is the epicentre of urban living with its pressures of inequality and overcrowding, ethnic and religious strife, new art forms, sexual transgressions, the replacement of laissez faire economic assumptions with fresh ideas about collectivism, plus new criminal phenomena such as the serial murderer. If historical accuracy is not a concern (and the plot line is decidedly implausible) there is a need presented to understand society and mythology holistically in order to understand the 'whodunnit' but also to demonstrate how the graphic novel as a form of literature has historiographical significance.

We have sought to establish the variety of motivations that have informed the graphic novel as a form of narration, but how might the genre be distinguished from other forms? Some graphic novels concern themselves with telling historically based stories. Yet not all graphic novels are concerned with the past. Some use the format to discuss a single historical event. Unlike Spiegelman who collapsed the Holocaust and 9/11 into closely related events, others have taken the First World War (like Ground Zero) as a site of memory, a site of mourning but also a locus for a steely patriotism. These disparate writers and artists are brought together by a strong sense of nostalgia:

> Like many people involved in comics, Spiegelman is a nostalgist. Even underground artists, for all the radicalism in their depiction of sex and drugs and rock 'n' roll, drew inspiration from the 'big foot' characters of early Disney animation, funny-animal cartoons of the 1930's and the EC Comics horror stories of the 50's. Spiegelman, in reaching back farther to the turn of the 20th century . . . struggled to come to terms with the losses of Sept. 11, he lost himself in nostalgia for an irretrievable era in his art – the Old World of comics – much as his aging father longed for the Europe that had existed before the war.
> (www.americanpopularculture.com/archive/venues/spiegelman)

Theorists are inclined to link nostalgia to a longing for an irretrievable age made distant by an accelerated passing of time. The forces of globalization have displaced familiar landscapes, a once-settled community, ways of life that may prompt 'nationalism, heritage policies, vintage consumerism, the tourism industry, and religious and ecological movements' (Ange, 2015, p. 2). It may even prompt a longing to return to a lost world of Communism. Put this way, anything in the culture that is 'retro' can act as a solace in rapidly changing times with nostalgia as an escape from modernity and mass consumerism.

According to Jan Baetens and Hugo Frey in *The Graphic Novel: An Introduction* (2015), Spiegelman is more sophisticated and nuanced in his use of history, and it goes beyond mere escapism:

> Thus the material that he includes from the 1900s in *In the Shadow of No Towers* is open to being read as marking out themes that are haunting him rather than reassuring him after 9/11. The comics are restored as problematic ephemera that are all apiece with Spiegelman's questioning and critique of 9/11 and the 'war on terror'. The historical comics are not silent museum pieces but rather open images that pose questions about American culture. Spiegelman knows they are reassuring, but he also selects them because they are disturbing and nightmarish too.
>
> (Baetens et al., 2015, p. 240)

Nostalgia is nonetheless a useful way of thinking about author motivation and suggests one reason why an historian may wish to explore a subjective past and why too that enterprise should be approached with caution. It may mean, for example, that a graphic novel might express a longing for the golden age of the metropolis with Batman and Gotham City representing the moral certainty of a bygone age, especially in the more uncomfortable context of the here and now. This might also be said of the disappeared world of Sephardi Jews in the Maghreb, which found an expression for a lost world in the bittersweet, sad and funny story of the *Rabbi's Cat* by Joann Sfar set in 1930s Algeria, largely by exploring faith, tradition and secularism. By 1963 the vast bulk of the Jewish community had left Algeria (about 130,000 in total) while most others who had remained departed hastily after terrorist threats in the early 1990s. With all the synagogues converted into mosques, many looked back with nostalgia to a shared existence where Jews and Muslims lived in relative harmony until the influence of Nazi Germany prompted a pogrom in 1934 and support for Vichy France during the Second World War brought harassment and threats to property and later in the 1950s and 1960s the independence movement in Algeria pitted Muslims and Jews on opposite sides.

This example (and there are others like it) illustrate what Ed S. Tan has restyled 'graphic narration' (Baetens, 2001, p. 45) The comic may not have a closer proximity to history than fiction, but it certainly does poke a creative stick at the old certainties and provides yet another example of how the gap between literature and history is usefully filled by a mixture of words and pictures.

19.4 Writing the Metropolis

In this section we return to a theme implicitly raised at the beginning of the chapter, namely, how have writers represented the metropolis? How, in other words, have they attempted to capture the manifold complexities of London, and have these writings provided reliable representations which are of value to historians investigating its past?

Literary expressions of the metropolis can usefully be traced back to the late sixteenth century when the city emerged as a great commercial and cultural centre (Marriott, 2000). Guide books appeared which provided a new urban elite with factual information on its theatres, mansions, churches, historic buildings and places of public edification such as museums. For the most part these were reliable accounts of the city's built environment, but they remained highly selective, for none included details of sites frequented or inhabited by the poorer sections of the population. There was, however, an alternative literature, popular and countercultural, which expressed the political and social tensions created by an ascendant merchant class. In cheaply produced pamphlets and lexicons, writers such as Thomas Dekker and Thomas Nashe explored areas of metropolitan life previously beyond public gaze, in particular, the dissolute lives of those inhabiting a criminal underworld, and in so doing they exposed also the fraudulent nature of all those operating in the market place.

By the eighteenth century this subversive literature had been displaced by the writings of Daniel Defoe, Jonathan Swift and Alexander Pope and the images of William Hogarth and Thomas Rowlandson, which in depicting the diverse cultural geography of London retained subversive elements but overall tended to consolidate the moral vision of an ascendant bourgeoisie. London low life was also represented in popular fictional travelogues which claimed to expose taxonomies of criminal behaviour by describing how the naïve visitor is assailed on the streets by varieties of tricksters and fraudsters intent on depriving him of any money about his person.

By the end of the eighteenth century, this body of literature had become stale and unimaginative. The picture it provided was of London as a great imperial city, ordered but apart from rogue elements almost entirely devoid of people. This was all to change in the first decades of the next century when, in an unprecedented move, a small group of writers and publishers working at the margins of society attempted to capture the lives of those inhabiting the metropolitan underworld and so laid the foundation for the urban novels of Charles Dickens and the great surveys of Henry Mayhew. In important respects, this literature was a response to increasing anxieties about the troublesome presence of the poor on the streets and in the dockside areas who were seen to present a threat not only to individual pedestrians but the commerce and moral fabric of the city, made even worse by the fact that respectable society knew nothing about them. When Pierce Egan, George Smeeton, George Cruikshank, James Grant and others set about their work, it was in large measure to reveal to the public who, where and what the poor were. Two hundred years later, however, the pertinent question for us is: Was their literary depiction of the metropolitan poor historically reliable?

To explore this, we wish initially to have a look at the founding and most remarkable text of this new literature, namely, Pierce Egan's *Life in London*. Egan was an Irish journalist who moved into the world of Grub Street or hack publishing in London. He had previously published town guides and books on sport, including *Boxiana*, which remains one of the finest studies of the sport, but *Life in London* provided his memorial. After appearing in serial form, it was published as a book in 1821 and took London by storm. Arguably, no other book had such an impact on the cultural life of the nineteenth-century metropolis, for it was endlessly adapted and plagiarized. The extraordinary popularity of the book derived from its depiction of the complex totality of London life, most notably the haunts and characters of the impoverished underworld that had never before appeared in print. For Egan, London was a 'complex cyclopaedia' wherein extremes of life happily co-exist. And in order to understand it, Egan claimed, first-hand was vital:

> An accurate knowledge of the manners, habits and feelings of a brave and free people is not to be acquired in the CLOSET, nor is it to be derived from the formal precepts of tutors.

It is only by means of a free and unrestrained intercourse with society . . . that an intimate acquaintance is to be obtained with Englishmen: for this purpose it is necessary to view their pastimes, to hear their remarks, and, from such sources, to be enabled to study their character.
(Egan, 1821, p. vi)

Such an approach may in retrospect be closer to that of an anthropologist involved in field work (even though anthropology was yet to emerge as a discipline in its own right) than to an historian who tends to spend a lot of time in one closet or another, but it did yield some telling results. Employing the narrative form of a tricks-of-the-town travelogue, the book charts the adventures of Corinthian Tom and Jerry Hawthorn (the original Tom & Jerry) who, accompanied by their friend Bob Logic, travel around the metropolis. Despite the fictional nature of this narrative, the locations and many of the characters encountered by the three heroes were real enough and undoubtedly known to Egan.

One evening, for example, they visit a riverside tavern known as All Max in the East – reputedly based on one at Limehouse – which Egan describes in some detail, often as a counterpoint to Almack's, a gentleman's club in the West End. No card of admission was required; everyone was welcome, 'colour and country considered no obstacle'. Among the clientele were 'lascars, blacks, jack tars, coal-heavers, dustmen, women of colour . . . and a sprinkling of the remnants of once fine girls', all jigging together so long as the fiddler remained sober enough to play. Bob Logic, who is shown in an etching by George Cruikshank of the proceedings with a black woman on his lap, declares to Tom it is only the lower orders which seem able to enjoy themselves. Can this image be considered historically accurate? Quite apart from the fact that it is the only description of an early nineteenth-century riverside tavern we have, there is little to suggest from what we know of the maritime community in which it was located that it is fanciful or contrived. Similar arguments apply to Egan's descriptions of many of the other locations visited including Vauxhall Gardens, Drury Lane Theatre, the condemned yard at Newgate Prison and the Masquerade Supper at the English Opera House.

Many of the characters identified were real historical figures. At one point Tom has boxing lessons at the self-defence academy run by the champion pugilist John Jackson, and at Westminster Pit the trio witness a fight between a dog and Jacco Maccacco, a monkey which had famously killed all-comers. And there are frequent references to the great figures of the age including Mozart, Gibbon, Wellington and Reynolds.

Finally, historical realism and hence any claim to authenticity are enhanced by Egan's determination to reproduce something of the popular language of the time. The account is littered with words which were part of a metropolitan jargon – or cant. What, for example, would the reader have made of:

Washing the *ivory* with a prime *screw* under the *spikes* in Saint George's Fields, or in tossing off, on the sly, some *tape* with a *pal* undergoing a *three-month's preparation* to come out as a new member of society, is a scene that develops a great deal of the human heart.
(Egan, 1821, p. 32)

Helpfully, Egan provides the meanings of such cant in numerous footnotes, so we can surmise that he refers in this passage to the progress in the human mind brought about by education, even in the unprepossessing environment of a prison (*ivory* is head, *screw* is prison guard, and so on).

Being a comic literary tale, Egan spares the reader from the more unedifying details of metropolitan life – we learn nothing, for example, of the routine hardships of the destitute, nor do we follow the condemned to the place of execution. This is ultimately an anecdotal picture of metropolitan life which can be enjoyed at a distance and in the safety of your own home. But at the same time, it does offer an historically reliable account of many features of the time; indeed, *Life in London* remains the first – and for a while, the only – attempt to capture the full complexity of the city. From the book, we would argue, it is possible to reconstruct the sites, nature and characters which defined the cultural life of the early nineteenth-century metropolis.

Other accounts inspired by Egan soon followed, the most notable of which was George Smeeton's *Doings in London* (Smeeton, 1828). Smeeton sought to provide an alternative vision of London to Egan, which he dismissed as a fanciful product of an 'inventive genius'; instead, claimed Smeeton, 'It has been *my* aim to show vice and deception in all their *real* deformity; and not, by painting in glowing colours the fascinating allurements, the mischievous frolics, and vicious habits of the profligate, the heedless, and the debauched' (ibid., p. iii). And yet the debt to Egan is obvious in the title, many of the places visited and real-life characters encountered by the two urban travellers Peregrine Wilson and his guide Mentor and the illustrations based on work by Robert Cruikshank. Ultimately, however, does Smeeton succeed in his endeavour to reveal the true state of London? The itinerary provides a flimsy narrative for an extraordinary miscellany of information on topics including begging, fashion, gin and card games compiled from an equally striking variety of sources such as police records, novels, newspapers, parliamentary records and treatises which are thrown together in a seemingly haphazard manner. At the heart of the book was thus a tension between empirical veracity and a seemingly chaotic structure which led nowhere in particular.

What was the legacy of this tradition of urban literature and the work of Egan in particular? Out of this literary subculture, representing as it did a struggle to grasp the complex totality of London and now largely forgotten, sprang Charles Dickens and Henry Mayhew, whose writings came to define what the nineteenth-century metropolis was. Dickens displayed strong links with Egan's celebration of the exuberance of metropolitan life. Best evidenced in the early novels *Sketches of Boz* and *Pickwick Papers*, Dickens brought to life and made familiar the sorts of characters met by chance encounter in Egan. But his sympathetic vision remained rather detached from the members of the poor or the working class who tend to be viewed as minor and shadowy figures unrepresentative of the wider culture. Although Dickens occasionally conveyed a sense of London's poverty, it is there as a backdrop to the main plot, and we actually learn little about the lot of the poor.

The images of characters with which we are so familiar were created less by Dickens' prose than by the remarkable illustrators whose etchings accompanied the text. Most notable among them was the same George Cruikshank who had provided the plates for *Life in London*. The unforgettable image of the rogue Fagin from *Oliver Twist*, for example, which has since entered the popular imagination is his, not Dickens'. Likewise, those of Mr Pickwick, David Copperfield, Mr Micawber and others were created by the graphic illustrator Hablot Browne.

Nonetheless, the historical veracity of Dickens is evident in his representation of London's topography. Like Egan, Dickens loved to walk around its streets and so gained an intimate knowledge of their character. His novels are replete with detailed descriptions of the urban atmosphere, sometimes to the extent that the sense of place assumes centre stage of the narrative. Take, for example, the justly celebrated opening to *Bleak House* in which mud and fog become a metaphor for the bureaucracy and creeping stagnation of the High Court of Chancery. Sadly, brief extracts will have to suffice:

> London. Michaelmas Term lately over, and the Lord Chancellor sitting in Lincoln's Inn Hall. Implacable November weather. As much mud on the streets, as if the waters had but newly retired from the face of the earth, and it would not be wonderful to meet a Megalosaurus,

forty feet long or so, waddling like an elephantine lizard up Holborn Hill. Smoke lowering down from chimney-pots, making a soft black drizzle, with flakes of soot in it as big as full-grown snowflakes – gone into mourning, one might imagine, for the dearth of the sun. . . . Fog everywhere. Fog up the river, where it flows among green aits and meadows; fog down the river, where it rolls defiled among the tiers of shipping, and the waterside pollutions of a great (and dirty) city. Fog in the Essex marshes, fog on the Kentish heights. . . . The raw afternoon is rawest, and the dense fog is densest, and the muddy streets are muddiest, near that leaden-headed old obstruction, appropriate ornament for the threshold of a leaden-headed old corporation: Temple Bar. And hard by Temple Bar, in Lincoln's Inn Hall, at the very heart of the fog, sits the Lord High Chancellor in his High Court of Chancery.

(Dickens, 2012, pp. 8–9)

A sense of realism in Dickens is also conveyed by his use of conversational language. Again, like Egan, he attempts to reproduce working-class idioms as a means of providing a measure of seeming authenticity. Here from *Pickwick Papers* is the archetypal cockney Sam Weller intervening to prevent his master, Mr Pickwick, from entering a fracas at a lawyer's office in Cornhill:

You just come avay. Battledore and shuttlecock's a wery good game, vhen you an't the shuttlecock and two lawyers the battledores, in which case it gets too excitin' to be pleasant. Come avay, Sir. If you want to ease your mind by blowing up somebody, come out into the court and blow up me; but it's rather too expensive work to be carried on here.

(Dickens, 2003, p. 343)

It is difficult to gauge the authenticity of this representation of the cockney language any more than that offered by Egan, but it does point to particular features that survived into the late nineteenth century when, say, music hall popularized working-class jargon.

It is instructive to compare Dickens' fiction with his journalism in which he did strive to reveal in more detail the working and living experiences of the metropolitan poor. In articles contributed to the periodicals *Household Words* and *All the Year Round*, both of which were edited by him, Dickens vividly exposed the inhumanities of a system that condemned the poor to a life of drudgery and toil. Among the best were 'A walk in the workhouse', 'A December vision', and 'On duty with Inspector Field', which were based on first-hand observation and offered accurate portrayals to the reading public and to later historians (Slater, 1994–98).

Links between Egan and the great urban explorer Henry Mayhew are evident. Mayhew inhabited the same literary subculture and worked around periodicals and theatrical productions which would have been familiar to Egan. They were both close personal friends of and collaborators with George Cruikshank. And there can be little doubt that in embarking upon his monumental study of the London poor Mayhew was influenced by the low-life characters identified by Egan. But Mayhew took Egan in a different direction. What in Egan is the comical frenzy of an underground culture becomes for Mayhew the object of detailed observation as a means of revealing the disastrous economic and social consequences of wholesale neglect.

Arguably, more than anyone then or since Mayhew recorded and gave voice to the lives of the metropolitan poor when originally in the *Morning Chronicle* during the 1840s and later in the four volumes of *London Labour and the London Poor* (1851–61) he published the results of his work. His original project was to map metropolitan poverty in its entirety, but it soon became clear that this was far too ambitious, and in the event he focused on street sellers, performers and labourers who made up a relatively small proportion of the poor as a whole. His sources were direct observation, a large variety of reports and social surveys and the personal testimony of a variety of people including flower sellers, costermongers and dock workers, from which he wrote about the experiences, cultures and economies of poverty and the feelings of those forced to live within its clutches. Typical was the testimony of an eight-year old girl selling watercress at Farringdon Market:

> I go about the streets with water-creases, crying, 'Four bunches a penny, water-creases.' I am just eight year old – that's all, and I've a big sister, and a brother and a sister younger than I am. On and off, I've been very near twelvemonth in the streets. Before that, I had to take care of a baby for my aunt. No, it wasn't heavy – it was only two months old; but I minded over it for ever such a time – till it could walk. . . . The creases is so bad now, that I haven't been out with 'em for three days. They're so cold, people won't buy them; for when I goes up to them, they say, 'They'll freeze our bellies.
>
> (Quoted in Allen, 1998, p. 128)

Almost certainly Mayhew shaped the testimony in order to provide it with coherence and perhaps dramatic effect, but what remains is a striking and historically reliable record of the experience of a young girl which must have resembled that of hundreds if not thousands of others at the time. Little wonder that contemporary readers saw in Mayhew the extremes and pities of human experience rarely found in fictional accounts.

Ultimately, however, Mayhew strove unsuccessfully to organize and hence make sense of the scale and diversity of the material he gathered, as if it overwhelmed him. Drawing on contemporary anthropology, he attempted to provide a theoretical framework with which he classified the poor into different sections, but these ideas were never applied rigorously, and in the end, we are left with the impression that Mayhew was simply overwhelmed by the evidence.

In their different ways, Egan, Dickens and Mayhew imaginatively mapped the metropolitan poor. All had an intimate knowledge of London and drew directly upon first-hand observation to portray its streets and characters. To a greater or lesser extent, fiction featured as part of their imagination. So how do they stand in the eyes of an historian? Are their accounts too inclined to the anecdotal and fictional to be taken seriously, or do they provide genuine insight into London low-life? Given previous arguments about the impossibility of distinguishing rigidly between historical fiction and 'proper' history, we are inclined to the view that the three provide different forms of evidence on the poor, as legitimate and reliable as any other nineteenth-century sources including police records and the biographical accounts of evangelicals working in their midst. Because of Mayhew's methodology and focus, he has tended to attract the most attention from historians investigating urban poverty; perhaps it is now time that due regard is paid also to Egan and Dickens.

We wish to finish by considering briefly a body of fiction, the lineages of which can be traced back to Mayhew and Dickens but which provided a distinctly modern perspective on the darker aspects of metropolitan life. The various authors of what came to be known collectively as slum literature looked with a penetrating and often knowledgeable gaze upon the mean streets of London in ways that both exposed the myth of outcast London and perpetuated its underlying features (Whitehead and White, 2013). Much of their popularity derived from sensationalized images that touched directly on the readers' shared anxieties about the threat posed by the persistence of poverty on the streets of the capital.

The tone was set by George Gissing's *The Nether World* (1889). A Yorkshireman by birth, Gissing had migrated to London and there found inspiration for his creative energy by living among the poor he wrote about. Radically inclined, he was deeply angered by the conditions of working-class areas in the capital and set out to expose not only the effects of poverty on human lives but the futility of remedies that had been tried to mitigate them. *The Nether World* presents an unrelentingly depressing picture of slum life in Clerkenwell, an area to the north of the City. As with Dante's picture of hell – an association which was often made – the slum is inhabited by filthy, crazed and physically deformed characters who have lost all sense of hope. Various attempts are made to eradicate the worst excesses by well-meaning, even honourable political radicals, philanthropists and planners intent on clearing the slums, but they have all come to nothing. Ultimately, we are left with the prospect that the slum offers no escape for its denizens.

Arthur Morrison, who had been born and brought up in Poplar but then devoted his life to moving away from the East End, wrote his realist and melancholy tale *Child of the Jago* (1896) about the notorious slum area of the Old Nichol in Shoreditch. In describing scenes of savage violence, diseased and malnourished infants, sexual depravity including hints of incest, he drew upon the full range of tropes which had been used to depict the residuum. And while he laid much of the blame for the festering conditions in which the poor are forced to live on the neglect and abuse of the respectable middle classes, he saw the poor as a degenerate and self-destructive race incapable of lifting itself out of the pit of moral and social degradation. Gissing was scathing of the novel because of its sensationalism and lack of sympathy for the poor, but *Child of the Jago* has remained an iconic text within the genre of slum literature.

Around this time, a more distinctive voice was emerging. For many years, Israel Zangwill had chronicled Jewish life in the East End through articles and essays, plays, short stories and poems which appeared in the columns of popular magazines, but then in 1892 he gained international fame with the publication of *Children of the Ghetto: A Study of a Peculiar People*. Based on his own childhood memories, the novel offered a sympathetic and humorous picture of an immigrant community even more removed from the gaze of middle-class observers than the slums of Old Nichol or Clerkenwell. Zangwill makes no attempt to mask the squalid conditions in which many lived, but shining through this deprivation is a powerful sense of the dreams, romances and fantasies of Jewish life enriched by detailed descriptions of its customs and rituals. Above all, he captures the depth of Yiddishkeit inherited by this resourceful immigrant community, now under threat from demographic change and an inevitable assimilation into the host culture. Let us finish with a brief description of the main protagonist Moses Ansell and his family, which conveys with wit and a degree of realism, something of this life:

> [The family] was tossed about on the battledores of philanthropy, often reverting to their starting point, to the disgust of the charitable committees. Yet Moses always made loyal efforts to find work. His versatility was marvellous. There was nothing he could not do badly. He had been a glazier, synagogue beadle, picture-frame manufacturer, cantor, peddler, shoemaker in all branches, coat-seller, official executioner of fowls and cattle, Hebrew teacher, fruiterer, circumciser, professional corpse watcher, and now he was tailor out of work. . . . It was as a hawker be believed himself most gifted, and he never lost the conviction that if he could get a fair start, he had in him the makings of a millionaire.
>
> (Zangwill, 1998, pp. 121–2)

Postscript

We all know that history is different from fiction. Historians rely above all on the collection of evidence, on the basis of which they provide reliable accounts of what happened in the past, while novelists spin tales which are largely the product of their fertile imaginations – except that many historians and literary theorists increasingly recognize that these distinctions really do not bear scrutiny.

For a start, the distinction between the two is largely modern, forged when history sought to establish its own identity over the nineteenth century. Prior to that it was never clear where the boundaries between history and literature were to be drawn. But while the attempt to define history as distinct may have promoted certain procedural rules such as the primacy accorded to (written) evidence, in practice history could not be sectioned off entirely from literature. The similarities were too powerful. Both history and literature tell stories using a range of shared narrative devices (how often have we been told that history is stranger or more interesting than fiction?). Indeed, we have seen that some of the most innovative work of recent years has identified distinct narrative strategies in history writing that have clearly derived from literature.

Furthermore, the whole matter of evidence, far from dividing history and literature, tends to bring them together. Historical novels such as *Beloved* and *Wolf Hall* are built on a comprehensive and detailed knowledge of primary and secondary sources. Where gaps exist – as they inevitably do – writers imaginatively fill them with conversations and events which, while fictionalized, are entirely consist with the historical interpretation being constructed. This process is little different from that followed by historians. Historical evidence is scant; rarely is it sufficient to put together a complete account. Instead, historians too fill the gaps in the evidential record in order to build up a persuasive and coherent narrative conveying their interpretation of events. Both history and literature are therefore ultimately only representations of the past built on a poor and incomplete evidential record.

One final point. The historical novel is extraordinarily popular and remains along with broadcast media one of the most powerful means of producing history for a popular audience. Such novels sell in their tens of thousands, 'serious' history books in their hundreds. This needs to be explained, perhaps in part by invoking the notion of affect. Do such novels work because they are able to engage directly with our emotions rather than simply our intellects? Is there something about the act of storytelling, particularly if it is able to enter the minds of historical actors, which we find compelling and attractive? We will leave you to ponder on that.

Further Reading

Dominick LaCapra (2013) *History, Literature, Critical Theory*.
Alison Light (2015) *Common People: The History of an English Family*.
Hilary Mantel (2010) *Wolf Hall*.
Toni Morrison (1987) *Beloved*.
Alun Munslow (2007) *Narrative and History*.
Simon Schama (1991) *Dead Certainties*.
Art Spiegelman (2004) *In the Shadow of No Towers*.
Harold Veeser (1989) *The New Historicism*.

20 Geography

Introduction

Geography and its methods have been especially useful to historians in recent years, particularly for those historians working on urban topics and on empire. The first section acknowledges the way place and space have been understood in both urban and imperial studies and charts the development of historical geography as a subdiscipline. We concentrate on the contribution of historical geography and its importance to the historical method in the study of space or place, using examples that illustrate how geographical approaches to history have become of interest to historians. The second section investigates geographies of empire: geographies closely aligned with postcolonial criticisms of imperialism, postcolonial discourses and the problem of how power was wielded in imperial spaces. The final section concentrates on urban spaces and the mapping used by Charles Booth, the late-nineteenth-century statistician, philanthropist and social investigator. Maps have been a constant if changing focus for historical geography and are useful as a way of illustrating the extent to which geography has moved away from the social sciences and towards the arts or humanities, facilitating the use of maps as historical sources.

20.1 History, Space and Place

Space and place orientate historians, allowing us to analyze historical context in a dimension other than time. Historical or cultural geography helps us to understand how spaces or places shape historical processes. At its simplest, historical geography charts change in a single place, looking out for altering power relations in that place or examining cultural, social, political relations in comparison with other places. Historical geographers are interested in places – what they represent over time – and often proceed using the conceptual tools of historians and sociologists, so breaking with the more traditional concerns such as the movement of tectonic plates, river courses, volcanoes or climate fluctuations.

A brief focus on a place can reveal much. Bank is a junction at the heart of London's City, which both iconically and in reality was the financial and imperial powerhouse of British imperialism, providing much of the money in the form of loans and insurance for expansion and a site for the transaction of a good deal of global business. As a confluence of roads abutting the Bank of England, this space has unsurprisingly attracted a good deal of attention from historians. Niels Moeller Lund (1863–1916), a painter born in Denmark, focused on this place in his *The Heart of the Empire*. Looking down at Bank Junction and the Mansion House from the roofscape of the Bank of England, while gazing further afield to older spaces in the City, here is an image of national identity that is uniquely organized around the business zone of an important urban place, the very epicentre of Britain's imperial might (Figure 20.1).

Figure 20.1 Niels Moeller Lund, *The Heart of the Empire*, painted in 1904
Contributor: Heritage Image Partnership Ltd/Alamy Stock Photo

Taking this painting as a single source, we may be forgiven for thinking that it defined the City as exclusively modern, bereft of a residential population, even if other (written) sources identify a flourishing associational life. In fact, Lund's portrayal of city space picks out St Paul's Cathedral, churches, the halls of the Livery Companies and the Lord Mayor's Mansion House, symbolizing the City Corporation as the ancient local government of the square mile, all nestling between the cracks of the otherwise dominant financial palaces. In the painting, places celebrated for their grandeur and modernity sit cheek by jowl with historic sites and buildings. To put it another way, the image depicts a space containing the fragments of the past as well as the essence of the present.

One way of challenging the received view of the City as exclusively the centre of business and power is to turn to other sources. By fixing our gaze on the level of the street, we find the many workers who serviced its business. The City of London becomes more than the sum of its economic interests. Rather it is a place that contains pockets of overcrowding, working-class housing and poverty and is alive with social dangers such as criminality and violence. Contenting ourselves with visual sources for the moment, a painting entitled *The Heart of Empire* by Frederic Marlett Bell-Smith (1846–1923), an émigré to Canada in 1867, in many ways stands in contrast to that of Lund. Bell-Smith was influenced partially by Lund, but unlike Lund he gave a strong sense of how City spaces were about much more than big business. Painted in 1909, *The Heart of Empire* emphasizes the workforce of a City that was miles away from the impression of the City as almost unpopulated, jam-packed with imperious buildings. Featured instead in the foreground are working-class Londoners. We find a newspaper boy, costermongers, soldiers and sailors, drivers and a motley collection of pedestrians going about their daily business against a backdrop created by the imposing architecture of financial power.

The City of power, modernity and business may be one way (it might be concluded) to understand the City in history, but it can be seen that these spaces were populated by the poor and powerless. Thinking about this place as essentially contested is, therefore, an example of how geographical approaches can be useful to historians. While historians have been keen to map the City's boundaries and write copiously about its function within modern capitalism, it is only by using geographical approaches to place that we can begin to see the City's history as existing in social and economic layers: from the stockbroker and the clerk to the newspaper boy, carriage driver, chestnut seller and sailor. By looking closely at the City's diverse spaces through the lens of historical geography, we gain an alternative view of the City that is not dependent upon a simple nexus between modernity (what it means to be modern), business and empire.

From this example, we should have some idea of what historical geographers do and some sense of the range or limits of their concerns. Yet we should pause to recognize that the work of historical geographers is premised on the notion that historians cannot take place as given – a mere backdrop where events are played out. Places, such as the City of business or the City of the casual poor, are cultural places that affect the thoughts and behaviour of those who inhabit that place.

What is historical geography and what of value does it offer to historians? Historical geography is the study of spaces in the past, how they have been represented and how they have influenced the behaviour and thinking of those who inhabited and passed through them. The relationship between geography and history has been explored by the historical geographer David N. Livingstone. His *The Geographical Tradition: Episodes in the History of a Contested Enterprise* (1992) hit on the idea of geography as a developing discipline, its preoccupations and approaches changing with society. Once, according to Livingstone, the geographer was concerned with the scientific problem of navigation. One thinks immediately of the Royal Geographical Society in this respect. Later involved in Enlightenment-driven science, geography became 'an instrument of imperialism', manipulated to serve the interests of racial theory. At another moment geography has helped find geographical patterns of diversity, adapting models of evolutionary theory and the importance of regions and 'zones' that have all fed into urban sociology (see Chapter 12). It has been concerned with environment and resources, sometimes embracing quantitative methods, sometimes emphasizing culture and imagination (such as the City example earlier).

As we found with anthropology (Chapter 18), it is sometimes easier to determine what historical geographers do than to pin down what historical geography is. Let us therefore take as an example of the actual use of geography in history, the *Annales* school in France. Part of the cross-disciplinary work of *Annales* (also discussed in Chapter 15) spans the twentieth century and has had a considerable impact on the use of geography by historians. A prominent member, Fernand Braudel, wrote a magisterial work of history that attempted to understand how the course of events in the Mediterranean was influenced enormously by geographies of the region. Thus, *The Mediterranean World in the Age of Philip II*, which was first published in the late 1940s, concentrates on climate, terrain, agriculture, cities and trade, transport and demography – all the raw materials of geography – as a means of accounting for the histories of its peoples.

Among the more important topics addressed by historical geographers is the urban form, and perhaps the most interesting geographer and urban activist to take us forward in understanding the urban from a cultural history point of view was Jane Jacobs (1916–2006). Cities, to Jacob, were the historical powerhouses of advanced civilization and the economic roots of any complex culture. Her extraordinary body of work, evidenced by *The Death and Life of Great American Cities* (1961), *The Economy of Cities* (1969), *Cities and the Wealth of Nations: Principles of Economic Life* (1984), *Systems of Survival: A Dialogue on the Moral Foundations of Commerce and Politics* (1994) and *The Nature of Economies* (2000) posit the city as an organic system with all the moral life of an advanced life form. In a sense, it might be argued that her optimism about the power of cities to both represent all of humanity and simultaneously to hold up the potential to transform it was the antithesis of Lewis Mumford's work on the city – Mumford, who in *The Culture of City* (1934) and *City in History* (1961) was, for all his humanity, largely pessimistic about modernity and the accompanying mechanization of urban life (see also Chapters 9 and 19). Not until the end of her life did Jacobs reveal her own pessimism about the weakening of social responsibility, the cheapening of culture in North America and the general amnesia about history – something that her *Dark Age Ahead* (2004) both articulated and predicted in areas as diverse as education, the family and the effects of technology. In so doing she evoked a diverse range of historical examples, examples that she felt could allow lessons to be learnt and a remedy to be put in place even at this late hour.

Historical geography has moved now towards postmodernism. This, in brief, has led to a concern with how place has been represented in what might be called cultural texts. Edward Said and his *Orientalism* (1978) have been enormously influential in the area of postcolonial theory (see Chapter 9). Said described how knowledge and culture can work together in the application of power. Through representations of its culture, the 'Orient' was viewed by the West as backward and exotic, while the West could be seen by comparison as modern and rational. Through European involvement in Egypt from the time of Napoleon's invasion, the Middle East and eastern cultures were constructed in Western texts – mostly paintings and literature gathered through journeying to the East – in this way, thereby consolidating rule over its place and peoples.

Take another example from British rule of India, well described by David Ludden (1999). The British recognized that for millennia India had been seen as an agrarian space, and yet they had no ready means of understanding that space as a prelude to taking effective control. It was not only that they lacked access to the history and culture of India, but also any attempt to appropriate the space was likely to be fiercely contested by indigenous farmers. In order to secure control over the administration of land and land revenue in the eighteenth and nineteenth centuries, the British thus represented the rural world of India – the fields, peasants, villages and landlords – as ancient, backward, inefficient and unchanging, desperately in need of the modernizing impulses that they could bring:

> Agrarian sites now appear as standardized objects of administration, policy debate, and political struggle. Idiosyncratic local histories and old agrarian territories were in effect buried by imperial modernity under mountains of homogeneous, official data, as villages, towns, districts, and provinces became standard units for conventional studies of politics, economics, culture, and society. The non-modern quality of the agrarian past became quaint stuff for gazetteers and folklore, irrelevant for history except as a reflection of archaic peasant memory and tradition – marginalia – cut off from the modern historical mainstream. . . . [British] voices expressed a distinctive middle-class middleness by translating (vernacular) village tradition into the (English) language of modernity. They made the problems of the country into a critique of colonial policy so as to make agrarian South Asia a colonial problem, calling out for national attention.
>
> (Ludden, 1999, pp. 7–8, 10)

As in the example given by Said, to have knowledge of a place is to have power over it. Maps and mapping, therefore, have become as instrumental to the study, for instance, of imperialism as they were once vital to imperialism itself. This relationship between maps and space, including maps of empire, as will be seen in the following sections, has become equally invaluable to historical geography.

20.2 Geographies of Empire

The Victorian author Charles Dickens wrote a book in 1838 which brought to life one of the most reviled characters created in the English language. Dickens notoriously portrayed Fagin as a Jew who manipulated the children of London's slums into learning the dark arts of robbery and picking pockets. In a famous scene from *Oliver Twist*, Fagin traversed the highways and hidden spaces of the city, criss-crossing through back alleys and underpasses, apparently knowing the city in ways considered wondrous yet sinister by contemporaries. A contrast, perhaps, is Joseph Conrad's *Heart of Darkness*, a novella serialized in 1899 before it was published as a book in 1902, in which the hero, Marlowe, a seaman and wanderer, did not penetrate the heart of the city like Fagin but went in the opposite direction, taking a psychological journey to the edges of the imperial imagination – going to the borders of what reasonably could be known.

These examples from literature illustrate how important geographies – the understanding of place – are to our efforts as historians to tease out how place influences history. The metaphor of centre and periphery is especially significant to our historical understanding of both urban spaces and empire spaces. That is to say, the urban metropolis is imagined at the centre of our understanding of place and the empire at the periphery, by definition on the borders or edge, and occasionally in the way it is described it can, as in *Heart of Darkness*, tip over into the mythical or menacing. We touched on this metaphor in the first section when discussing Lund's painting that focused on the roofscape of the mighty imperial City (in the centre) but then adjusted its gaze out towards the colonies (on the periphery). Geographies of the urban and geographies of empire both in a sense rely on knowledge of, as historical geographer Felix Driver put it, 'cultures of exploration' that existed in both Dickens' London and Conrad's Africa. This section will therefore concentrate on how geographies of empire and geographies of the urban interacted and how historical geographers have treated this interaction.

Driver's chapter on social investigation in the 1890s metropolis in his *Geography Militant: Geography, Exploration and Empire* and Alan Lester's work on *Imperial Networks: Creating Identities in Nineteenth-Century South Africa and Britain*, both published in 2001, connect urban with imperial geographies. Driver noted the influence of domestic accounts of London such as that of the Salvationist William Booth and his much read *In Darkest England* (1890). (William Booth is not to be confused with his namesake Charles who will be discussed later.) This book is in many ways graphic and hard-hitting. Typical for an evangelical tract of the period, it was both keen to save souls and dire in its warnings for those who choose the wrong path in life. The Salvation Army under Booth became a feature of the industrial metropolitan landscape, and with tambourine and military-style uniform, Booth and his followers explored London while rescuing its miserable and downtrodden people. It was also a book that in turn was influenced by the publication in the same year of the explorer and journalist Henry Moreton Stanley's *In Darkest Africa*. As Driver put it in his *Geography Militant*, 'The language and politics of exploration abroad were recycled in the context of debates over social policy at home as the frontiers of geographical knowledge were mapped onto the heart of empire' (Driver, 2001, p. 23). There was then a relationship between exploring the 'unknown' city of the poor and destitute and exploring the unknown paths and tributaries of empire.

In some respects, the centre/periphery metaphor is considered somewhat dated. Yet, both Driver and Lester demonstrated a mutual interest in knowing how the exploration of foreign lands abroad linked with a growing knowledge and exploration of the unknown city. The metaphor is still useful then as a way of explaining the extent of historical geography's interests and preoccupations. Lester recounted how each settler colony was a hub for communication between 'certain social and political groups that concerned themselves, even if only periodically and half-heartedly, with events at the margins of empire' (Lester, 2001, p. ix). Exploring London and exploring empire forged both the identities of people that occupied these spaces and informed discourses about these spaces. Historians sensitive to the methods and approaches of historical geography have been keen to stress how describing unknown metropolitan and imperial spaces helped map those places onto the contemporary imagination. John Marriott, for instance, argued in *The Other Empire: Metropolis, India and Progress in the Colonial Imagination* (2003) that imperial centre and colonial periphery, to some extent, constructed each other through what he called a 'unitary field of analysis'. Issues of poverty and race pressed on the 'explorers' of both London and Delhi and are described in London-published evangelical tracts and Indian travelogues in very similar ways. This notion that influences between centre and periphery are interlocked and are reciprocated has proven to be tremendously useful to historical geographers, urban historians and historians of imperialism.

It is the emphasis on power and uses of power in the colonial and postcolonial interest, that is, how imperial powers took over space and used it for their own purposes, that has excited the most interest among historical geographers. The expression of this power can be found in the mapping of empire geographies and its importance to the work of historians.

According to Eric Wolf in his enormously influential *Europe and the People Without History* (1982), to understand the world of 1400 we must begin with geography and space – how the world was spatially ordered and how that ordering was transformed by the opening up of the Americas at the end of the fifteenth century. Wolf, first discussed in Chapter 10, was trained initially as an anthropologist and then turned to geography. His emphasis was on topography, the climate, and the extent to which these factors influenced the development of trade routes and the interconnections between people within the overall context of the rise and fall of empires. Many travel accounts, for example, that may have helped understand how space was organized globally remained little known or never saw the light of day; whether these accounts were published and distributed depended upon varieties of social, economic and political factors. Although it is possible that some of these travel accounts were written with a degree of objectivity and that others contained a substantial amount of imaginative writing, such distinctions would have meant little to the medieval reader. Places like India and China were so beyond the mental horizons of people in the 'known world' that they simply had no way of assessing the validity of travellers' accounts.

This is why maps became a more direct and accessible way of conveying a sense of the spatial ordering of the world and why they remain such invaluable sources for historians. We cannot think of maps as inert records of landscapes or passive reflections of objects – these are above all socially constructed images. They cannot be judged in terms of their veracity or falsehood but have to be viewed as ways of representing, conceiving, articulating and structuring the human world – and as such they are influenced profoundly by the social relations from which they were created. This was true at the very beginning of mapping. Their production was subject to all the factors relating to literature; indeed, many of the early maps were drawn from literary accounts, including biblical accounts, such as a map of the Garden of Eden, which before the advent of accurate techniques of surveying are to our eyes so fantastic.

So what was the state of cartography in 1400 and how from maps can we get a sense of how people *at the time* saw the world? How too does the development of cartography connect to imperial geographies? Maps have been around for many centuries. The earliest-known example is from 5 BCE. Perhaps not surprisingly, it was the Romans who put cartography on the map. There is an important historical lesson here which links to what has already been said in this section. Maps have always been associated powerfully with empire in that they were used actively in the pursuit of colonial objectives. Lands were claimed on paper before they were effectively occupied and so in a way anticipated and facilitated empire. Surveyors marched alongside soldiers, initially mapping for reconnaissance, then for general information and eventually as a tool of pacification, civilization and exploitation of the colonies. Maps were used to legitimize the reality of conquest and empire.

Strabo (64 BCE–20 CE) was the first great Roman geographer. Ptolemy (90–168 CE), who with some justification can be described as the father of modern geography, followed him. He did not really extend the spatial knowledge of Strabo but ordered it in a more systematic way. It was Ptolemy who established the convention that places north at the top of a map, using a grid of latitude and longitude, who perceived the earth as a sphere divided into 360 degrees and who devised a means of projecting the spherical earth onto a flat map. He gave his name to this and so maps today are consequently labelled Ptolemaic (Figure 20.2).

Europe lost its supremacy over cartography in the Middle Ages. Roman Catholic orthodoxy dictated that the special ordering of the world be determined by Christian principles. So emerged what came to be known as 'T O' maps, in which a 'T' in an 'O' or circle represented everything that was known of the world: Europe, Asia and Africa (beyond Asia was Paradise). The 'T' represented the large oceans: to the left the Black and Aegean Seas, to the right the Nile and Red Seas and through the middle the Mediterranean. Jerusalem was at the centre (Figure 20.3).

Such maps must be among the most expressive and ideological of all cultural objects. They describe not only the perceived world spaces of the Christian period from the Middle Ages to the great age of discovery but reveal the minds and values of their creators. Their portrayal of space is replete with Christian ethnocentrism and the marginalization of alien, that is, non-Christian peoples. For on these maps, the peoples of Africa and Asia are divided off from those of Europe.

Indeed, the whole map divides the world into Noah's post-flood allotment of the world to his sons: Asia to Japhet, Europe to Shem and Africa to Ham; the first son, being the eldest, receives the largest land mass. Occasionally, a fourth area is depicted, boldly separated from the others. Here resided the people that were most unlike Westerners – an antipodal region somehow beyond description.

Cartography was transformed by the so-called age of exploration, attendant upon the ascent of the West. This began in the Renaissance in the fifteenth century. Scholars rediscovered the works of ancient geographers such as Strabo and Ptolemy at the same time as they embarked on an unprecedented wave of discovery (see Chapter 1). Portuguese and Spanish explorers and navigators were the most determined and ambitious. The Portuguese made their way down the coast of West Africa and eventually around the Cape of Good Hope in search of a sea route to India, completing the return journey in 1498. At the same time Columbus set off westwards across the Atlantic in the hope of reaching the rich empires of China and Japan. When he reached the Caribbean, he thought he had found Indians, laying the foundation for the distinction between East and West Indies. Soon after, Pedro Álvares Cabral, Portuguese navigator and explorer, sailed from Lisbon and accidentally discovered Brazil on his way to India.

These discoveries opened up the world to Europe, so transforming its sense of space and its geographical imagination. The entire project of discovery was in one decisive sense a direct

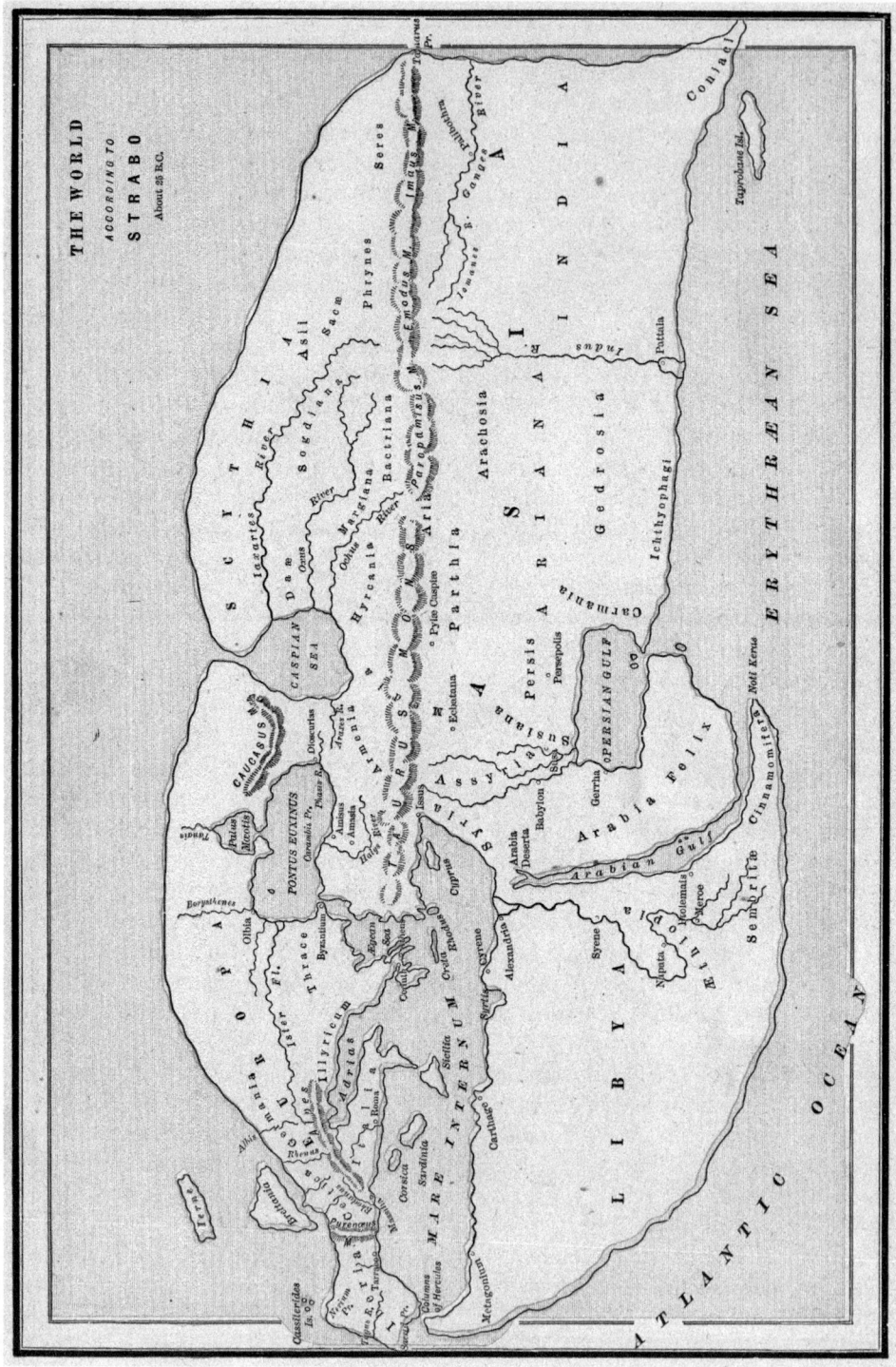

Figure 20.2 Strabo (c.25 BCE), *Map of the World*, printed c.1888

Contributor: Old Paper Studios/Alamy Stock Photo

Figure 20.3 'TO' Map after Isidore of Seville, c.630 CE, which later appeared as the first ever printed map in 1472

Contributor: INTERFOTO/Alamy Stock Photo

refutation of Christian cartography; in another, it altered the use of maps – no longer were they seen as visual commentaries of divine purpose and as repositories of legends, monsters and marvels but as instruments to use practically. Cartography became a matter of transcribing and measuring the visible world, rather than a means of speculating on its nature, form and structure as the ancients once thought. Thus, the discovery of the Americas was not merely a matter of finding some new land mass but also of rethinking a world that could contain it. To do this it was necessary to reinvent the world. In the geography of the fifteenth century, there were no continents and no oceans. The world was seen as an island – something essentially insular, self-enclosed, surrounded by the dark, inhuman and unknowable void of the deep waters. It was not that the ocean was as yet empirically unknown but rather that it was, in principle, unknowable. The ocean had been a nothingness or void that marked the boundaries of the world – now it was necessary to think of the world as discontinuous, divided by an ocean that became no more significant than a river or a mountain range that divides two land masses.

This process of learning and development focused on space and the imagination of space had a tremendous effect on the modernizing process, part of which was the perceived need to understand and map urban centres.

20.3 'How to Lie With Maps': Maps, Methodology and the Metropolis

Shetland is not located in a drawn box, just off the coast of mainland Britain. Yet it is shown that way, and as if it is nearer to Scotland than it is to Norway, and every evening this falsehood is represented on BBC weather maps and across countless news organizations. London Underground lines do not move in straight lines (like the schematic map designed by Harry Beck in 1931) but in reality, travel in crooked and circular motions; topographically (the features on the ground such as a railway) are correct but geographically incorrect. Maps are the stuff of historical geography and maps lie. One commentator, Mark Monmonier, in his book *How to Lie with Maps* (1996) argued that maps in general are a 'selective, incomplete view of reality' that they, 'like speeches or paintings, are authored collections of information subject to distortions arising from ignorance, greed, ideological blindness, or malice' (Monmonier, 1996, p. 2). Not all maps, of course and not always. As the last section witnessed, the way we see maps has changed radically over time. From the perspective of historian Jeremy Black in both his books on this subject, *Maps and History: Constructing Images of the Past* (2000) and *Maps and Politics* (1997), maps are selective in what they show and convey a sense of art or artifice; that is, they are constructed or, to a limited extent at least, made up. The argument of this section, therefore, is that cartography is not a science: objective, precise, technically mathematical; it is now a branch of the arts. Cartographers can now make maps with pinpoint precision, but the choice of what to map, what to include and exclude in a map, what colour legend to use, are all subjective judgements.

Two views of maps as mathematically accurate and faithful to an objective truth (like a photograph) and maps as an interpretation or representation of reality (like a painting) are played out in the methodological problems that historians face in the interpretation of maps and their use in the past. Perhaps one way of illustrating this tension is to look closely at Charles Booth, the nineteenth-century philanthropist and social investigator (see Chapter 19). Booth was an innovator in urban cartography, but before discussing his contribution in this area, more needs to be known about the man and his methods.

Charles Booth (1840–1916) was concerned with social statistics and social reform. He was also concerned with morality and with moral character – facets that every individual ought to have as part of a civic ideal. This stance was not uncommon among his Victorian contemporaries. A lack of civic virtue was judged against the notion of 'fitness', recalling, perhaps, the social reformer John Bright's appeal for constitutional rights in 1867 to be extended to the 'fit', that is, those that had the rationality and property to grasp the rights and obligations of the franchise and thereby of full citizenship. A lack of the wherewithal to be fit and independent would suggest a failure of moral will and was a sign of defective citizenship, although for Booth this might be explained by defects in the social environment. The Left, therefore, has tended to dismiss Booth, with historians E. P. Thompson and Eileen Yeo (most notably) regarding him as a middle-class moralist with inferior informants and little direct contact with the working class.

Booth's ability to be detached is important for our consideration of him as urban map-maker because it would inevitably say something about the nature of his maps. The point about Booth in this respect is that his own perceived sense of what constituted a 'fact' was but a short conceptual hop from what we now can see clearly as the fiction of late-Victorian novelists, artists and journalists. Booth and the fiction, art and reports filed by sensationalist journalists to the mass-circulation journals and newspapers of the time drew on official reports for their ideas, although there is no guarantee that either parliamentarians or those that sat on Royal Commissions and the like could declare themselves entirely free from assumptions about the London poor which social reportage expressed in such vivid and vulgar colours. If social reportage is the sum of literature, art and journalism, perhaps its most detailed and lurid exponent was Henry Mayhew, a journalist and social investigator in the 1840s and 1850s (see Chapter 14). His sensational descriptions of poverty and criminality were part and parcel of social reportage, an influence that if anything intensified between 1889 and 1902 when Booth wrote the bulk of his reports about London poverty, industry and religious influences. Not only did the language used by Charles Booth place grave doubt on his claim of scientific objectivity, but these descriptions, which seem to chime so perfectly with what science thought it knew about human evolution (and degeneration), are reflected in the way Booth constructed his maps.

Like Booth in his *Life and Labour of the People in London* (1889–1902), historians want to map the unknown, to explore but also to find the 'underlying' truth of places like London as a 'myriad of subcultures'. Booth's ground-breaking attempt to use statistical material in order to provide a social classification for all London's streets, displayed in the colour coding of his *Descriptive Map of London Poverty* in 1889, was startlingly innovative and given expression in the form of a map.

Bearing in mind Booth's use of contextual evidence in the construction of his maps, we might want to ask: did Booth's maps describe poverty as he intended or were they a distortion of reality, more a reflection of Victorian moral values? The following table shows the method Booth used to classify classes: black represents 'the lowest grade', while yellow is the lightest and most transparent of the primary colours and is ascribed to the wealthy.

The use Booth made of colour should make historians wary, and an analysis of this may go some way to answering the central question about the accuracy of Booth's maps and the imposition of Victorian moral values on what Booth would have claimed to be the objective claims of science. We need, therefore, to interrogate his mapping as we would any other source. Any historian worth his or her salt should ask questions, although answers to these questions now are not our chief concern. Were Booth's choices influenced by the technical limitations of printing at the time? Was he influenced too by contemporary innovations in art such as Pre-Raphaelite art and his friendship with the Pre-Raphaelite artist, Holman Hunt, thus explaining his own innovative use of colour coding? Might his own cultural presuppositions and perceptions of social hierarchy have found expression in darkness as a byword for vice and depravity while light colours suggested civility and virtue? To what extent was Booth open to contemporary assumptions and theories regarding the degenerate nature of the poor (Englander, 1995)?

The language of the reports and notebooks (as the historian Geoffrey Crossick and others have argued), like his maps, was shaped by contemporary concerns that the respectable working class would be infected by an underclass. We know that Booth supported the exclusion of the 'residuum' or those thought by biological predisposition to sully the gene pool of an imperial race and who by necessity had to be banished to labour colonies. In this, Booth only succeeded in holding up a mirror to late-Victorian respectability and social theory. Whether Booth and others presented a true representation of their subject – or rather more simply mapped moral prejudices – have implications for Booth's methodology and for his claims of value-free investigation. It also tells us something about our use of maps as historical sources – whether, indeed, they might be considered to be more like photographs or more like paintings.

Table 20.1 Booth's street classification

Colour code	Social character	Class groups
Black	The lowest grade	A
Dark blue	Very poor	B
Light blue	Standard poverty	C, D
Purple	Mixed with poverty	C, D + E, F
Pink	Working-class comfort	E, F
Red	Well-to-do	
Yellow	Wealthy	

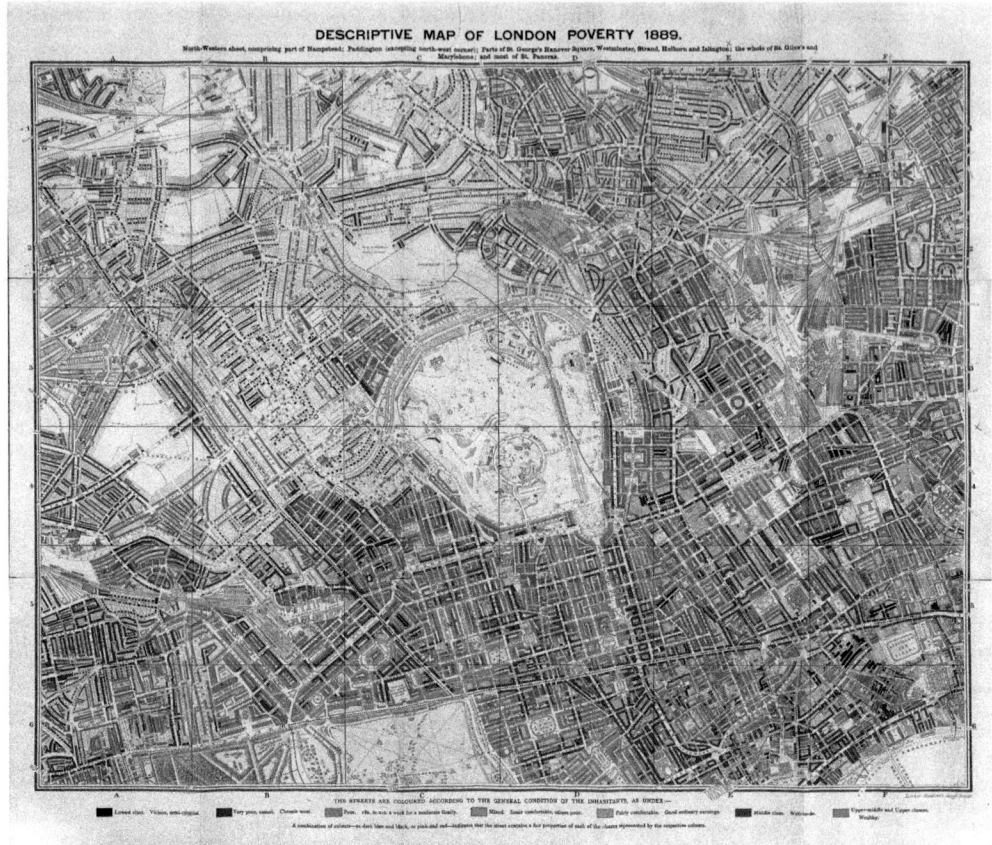

Figure 20.4 Charles Booth, *Descriptive Map of London Poverty*, 1889. Descriptive map of London poverty, 1889 (north-western sheet). A poverty map is a map that provides a detailed description of the spatial distribution of poverty and inequality within a country

Contributor: Science History Images/Alamy Stock Photo

Booth, like contemporary sensationalist journalists, writers and social-realist artists, wanted to map the unknown. He also claimed that he wanted to get beneath the more lurid accounts of the urban poor. That is perhaps one reason why the emphasis placed on cartography by Booth was very innovative – he wanted to present his findings as unimpeachable science and with a certain grandeur. When he displayed his map of London at Toynbee Hall and the Oxford House settlement at Bethnal Green in London's East End it measured an enormous sixteen feet by thirteen feet. Its scale was twenty-five inches to the mile, and he had it specially hand coloured by his staff (Figure 20.4).

David Reeder (1995) has discussed this innovation in social cartography. The subjectivity of Booth's maps drawn from his poverty survey, suggested Reeder, derived from Booth's initial feeling that the metropolis was essentially so large and so diverse that it was unknowable. Booth was keen to provide a context to data which could not be strictly quantifiable and which reflected the fluidity and almost mystery of London life, but he went much further in portraying more data on his maps than was strictly necessary. This suggested, perhaps, a continuing need to understand not simply what he *thought* about London but how he *felt* about London in all its disturbing complexity. This subjectivity was compounded, it could be argued from a reading of Reeder, by the very methodology of the survey itself – its use of School Board Visitors, schoolteachers, policemen, clergymen, social workers and local administrators to collect data which, no matter how widely gathered, could never be free from the inherent bias of those who collected the information. That Booth thought that this bias could be eliminated by the sheer weight of the collected data suggests a naivety about the nature of social investigation as a credible science. It owes something to Booth's mistaken assumption, moreover, that information (and by extension the representation of information on his maps) could ever be an unsullied truth.

But what does Booth reveal about contemporary attitudes to how space and place affected shifting poverty patterns and the movement of people? It is evident that Booth's study was informed, for example, by standard assumptions about Jews and the Irish and some dogmatic views about areas that seem somehow inherently of the 'lowest grade'. One way to consider to what extent Booth may have simply mapped his subjective moral values is to place two of Booth's maps side by side. The left side of one map is a representation of an area in East London called the Old Nichol, what Arthur Morrison called in his fiction the Jago, an area explored forensically by Sarah Wise in *The Blackest Streets: The Life and Death of a Victorian Slum* (2008). High Street Shoreditch and Hackney Road bound it to the north with Spitalfields to the south. On the right of the same map is the area portrayed after the newly created London County Council (LCC) had built the model Boundary Street Estate by clearing 15 acres of slums, displacing 6,000 slum-dwellers and providing new, modern housing for 5,500 people. The Jago (or Old Nichol) was characterized by dirt, decay and degeneracy. A local clergyman, the pugnacious Reverend Osbourne Jay, had been resident in the area at Holy Trinity Shoreditch since 1886 and recorded his shocking experiences in his evocative *Life in Darkest London* (1891). Five years later, Morrison's *The Child of the Jago* cast Jay as Father Stuart and Toynbee Hall as the 'East End Elevation Mission' and arrived at similar, pessimistic conclusions about the area. But while the Old Nichol, imagined by social and literary observers as intemperate, violent, crowded and dark, the development promised temperance, order, space and light. Put simply, as seen by contemporaries, it was an exercise in social cleansing.

The two maps, as described earlier, give some sense of the scale and scope of the demographic shift that occurred and provide a dramatic example of how historical geography and maps can record change over time. Both these representations (before and after) should be treated with care for their combined effect on those in Booth's team charged with representing social reality in his maps. Maps used in isolation rarely give a wholly convincing account; indeed, there are three alternative sets of evidence that contradict the generalized negative descriptions of the area represented by Booth on the left-hand map. The ramshackle street on the left is contrasted with the 'post-development' map on the right, underlining a perceived improvement in the area: namely the replacement of the original inhabitants by artisans and clerks. Yet the map on the right is a blueprint or prospectus, an account of a space in the throes of becoming a different kind of space. In it we are invited to *imagine* that the factory provides steady work, not casual work, for residents who live nearby. As the School Board building is represented on the map, indeed a plethora of School Board buildings, they fulfil the promise, not the actuality, of public education. The reader of this map is invited to muse, to daydream that, when the day is done, the citizen, maybe the very citizen looking at the map, might stroll to a place of recreation: the centrepiece of the development, the garden or bandstand as it eventually became. Again, students of historical geography and students of the metropolis must ask, considering its topographical accuracy, whether these features were exaggerated in number or size. This is most certainly the case with the bandstand, which in fact is a lot smaller. Does this map really represent space that is scientifically constructed and objective? We would suggest not. Booth was reported in an obituary to have protested otherwise:

> East London lay hidden behind a curtain on which were painted terrible pictures: starving children, suffering women, overworked men; the horrors of drunkenness and vice; monsters and demons of inhumanity; giants of disease and despair. . . . Did these pictures truly represent what lay behind, or did they bear to the facts a relation similar to that which the pictures outside a booth at some country fair bear to the performance or show within? This curtain we have tried to lift.
>
> (Quoted in Abbott, 1917, pp. 195–200)

Either way, it should be reiterated that Booth's maps were constructed like any other artefact: subjective in their representation of what might be or be regarded as one view – but only one view of social reality – a reality or knowledge that can be at least partly unlocked using the tools of historical geography.

Maps can thus present a facet of history that is colourful and evocative. In the nineteenth century, maps were seen in mathematical terms: a form of knowledge final in its conclusions, built on the Enlightenment notion that the information contained therein was transparent, objective, neutral and 'scientific', both verifiable and falsifiable. Since then, historical geographers have shifted perceptions of what it is that we think maps can do. What emerges from a brief study of the geography of the Victorian metropolis and the use of social cartography – or social mapping – is that maps can be used to investigate, communicate and inform, but as a primary source they must be read with immense caution. Maps are not simply mathematical; they evoke the 'remembered, the imagined, the contemplated' (Cosgrove, 1999, p. 2). Maps depict neither the material nor the actual, but instead they convey the immaterial or the desired. From this perspective, the map is just another cultural 'sign' that is selective, that omits, that is essentially opaque and we also look now as much for its silences as its obvious pronouncements.

What has prompted this shift in our understanding of maps? One factor is our use of information technology. When maps are used online, for example, the spatiality is altered and the data synthesized; spatial coordinates are juxtaposed and manipulated. This is surely a decisive move away from Booth's flap-top table mentioned earlier – no matter how impressive in size, no matter how vivid its colours, no matter how plural its audience.

Postscript

It is something of an aphorism that historians are interested in time, while space is the concern of geographers. Thus, history is built around notions of the passing of time considered for the most part as a process of linear progress within a space which is never questioned. In this scenario, space is a given, a constant, a background against which historical events unfold. Now it has been apparent since the work of Einstein that time and space are not constants, but since these distortions are only apparent under extreme conditions at the subatomic level, they hardly have relevance for historical processes. It is therefore only in recent years, largely under the influence of geographers and sociologists, that space has come to be recognized as a dynamic dimension of historical change. Far from being an inert backdrop, physical space and the ways in which it has been represented have contributed massively to the ways in which historical actors have behaved. The work of influential writers including Fernand Braudel and Eric Wolf have shown that geography matters because the physical landscape defined and set limits to the movements of people, and these limits have had a profound bearing upon what was possible.

Equally importantly, we are defined and define others in part by the ways in which space is represented and experienced. This process is ultimately political because there have been constant struggles to define the nature of spaces. It is no exaggeration to say that those who have been able to define, order and represent space have tended to be the ones who have prevailed in struggles, either at the micro level of, say, individual households or at the macro level of the global. It is for this reason that European imperial endeavour was built not only upon the appropriation of space but also its representation in particular ways. To define a space as wild, untamed or a wasteland was often a vital prelude to its subsequent annexation by colonizing forces. And we have seen from Chapter 12 that the isolation of domestic space in early modern Europe was crucial to the history and politics of gender relations.

No sphere of activity in this regard was more important than cartography. The making of maps was never an attempt to capture physical space in a neutral and accurate way. Maps were very much part of an endeavour to define and hence ultimately control space, and it was no accident that all the major advances in cartography occurred at times of imperial expansion. Maps also played a vital role in ordering space at a more local level. The metropolitan poverty maps created by Charles Booth, for example, represented in distinctive ways the spatial distribution of the poor but were also deeply inflected by ideological assumptions about who and what the poor were.

We need therefore to keep constantly in mind the spatial dynamics of historical processes. From mountain ranges and oceans to cities and even streets and houses, space has played an import role in determining how people moved and defined themselves and others.

Further Reading

Jeremy Black (1997) *Maps in History: Constructing Images of the Past.*
Felix Driver (2001) *Geography Militant: Geography, Exploration and Empire.*
David N. Livingstone (1992) *The Geographical Tradition.*
David Ludden (1999) *The New Cambridge History of India, Vol. IV, No. 4, An Agrarian History of South Asia.*
Eric Wolf (1982) *Europe and the People Without History.*

Part 4
Methods

21 Proof and the Problem of Objectivity

Introduction

This chapter introduces history both as a discipline and as an approach to historical knowledge. While it cannot be comprehensive, we aim nevertheless to explore some of the fundamental problems faced by historians as they seek to understand past societies. How they do this is determined by many factors. At its simplest, however, it largely depends upon whether history is regarded as a science which has the historian as objective fact finder and analyst, or alternatively as an art in which the historian presents an interpretation of the past that is a result of either personal experience or the social and cultural milieu in which the historian is located. The first section introduces these issues by looking afresh at the argument first raised in the 1960s between historians E. H. Carr and Geoffrey Elton but in the newer context of postmodernism. It sets out the varying ways in which these prominent historians approached the discipline and dealt with historical evidence in all its varied forms. Section 2 uses historical writing concerned with the events of 1857, the Indian 'Mutiny', to discuss whether history is a dependable basis of knowledge that can provide a comprehensive and reliable explanation of how past societies change. The third section focuses on another dispute between historians, that of Chartism. Chartism was a mid-nineteenth-century radical political and social movement in Great Britain that demanded far-reaching reform. We shall see how historical facts are generated and also how historians select evidence and then use innovative techniques to inform our historical understanding. This section will explain how historical explanations for a single historical event or period can radically change over time, either by the discovery of new evidence or, more likely, by shifts in the ways historians approach the evidence. Finally, we investigate the problem of causation in history. Since the Enlightenment, which we encountered in Chapter 3, historians and social scientists have attempted to identify precisely what caused historical episodes to take place, but have these efforts been successful? Can we ever know for certain what the causal factors were, or is this ultimately a futile quest?

21.1 History: a Science or an Art?

Why bother? Why study history? Why does history matter? For professionals who teach and research history it provides, let it be said, a source of income and occasionally a very pleasing one at that. But it is much more than that. Most historians are deeply engaged in trying to uncover the past, not only because there are fascinating stories to be told but also because the telling of the past has enormous contemporary importance. Our understanding of the present relies in large part upon how we view the past, and this vital issue is of concern to us all, whether or not we are trained historians. This recognition lies at the very heart of what we would describe as historical imagination – an imagination possessed by all those who look to the past as a means of understanding their place in the contemporary world.

Although this raises a series of important points about the nature of history, it does not address the question of precisely *what* history is. Here we encounter the first difficulty, for as you make your way through this chapter, you will realize that this seemingly simple matter masks some complex issues. Note, for example, that there is a profound ambiguity in the term 'history'. When we talk of 'history', do we mean what happened in the past? Or do we mean what is written and taught about the past, that is, historiography? It is usually clear from the context which meaning we are using, but the very fact that we have the same term to describe both meanings suggests something rather important. Studying history at a more advanced level should make us a little more circumspect about the nature of the relationship between the past and what is written and taught about the past. Fry uses the term *history* as writing about the past; that too will be the approach of this chapter. We shall examine the extent to which history as a discipline can be seen, crudely put, as either a science or an art and the consequences of taking one view over the other.

The former Regius Professor of Modern History at the University of Cambridge, Sir Geoffrey Elton (1921–1994), put it succinctly: history is at once interesting and exciting, amusing and instructive, but above all it encompasses a quest for the past. Yet Elton opposed the idea that historians should have an empathy for the past, for such an emotional engagement displaces what should be the object of the historian, namely, rational enquiry into past events. As a traditional historian, he believed very much in the possibilities of history as an exercise in empirical or fact-based truth and the ability of the historian to analyze objectively the results of research with a high degree of precision.

These ideas were expressed in Elton's *The Practice of History* (1967), which remains a useful elaboration of how history is conventionally viewed. It is a book, however, which was written consciously as a rejoinder to E. H. Carr (1892–1982) and his *What is History?* (1961), which had argued for a rather more sensitive approach to historical evidence. For Carr, history is subjective because historians are recognized as part of the process of doing history, unable to separate prejudices and presuppositions from conclusions drawn solely from evidence. It is this factor above all others that has secured his reputation as a radical historian, while Elton is seen as a defender of the conservative approach to history. If both views are caricatures – arch conservative and radical – each historian has left us with a legacy upon which we can build.

This spat between Elton and Carr on the status of historical knowledge is by common consent the defining debate about how the study of the past should be approached. While Elton was unquestionably suspicious of history's ability to predict the future, he nonetheless understood the role of the historian and saw history as 'scientific', that is, a method based upon rational inquiry. By approaching evidence critically, he argued, historical truth can be revealed. 'Hard work' and 'clear thinking' would promote a healthy scepticism as the historian investigates the primary sources or considers the views of other historians.

According to Elton, the successful resolution of all historical problems depends upon the appropriate use of evidence. To this end three main stages of reading evidence are required: a review of the available evidence (what sources exist?), the informed criticism of that evidence (what does it testify to?), and from that process the framing of answers (what happened in the past?). Historical research must therefore 'arise from the evidence not from the mind of the enquirer', thereby avoiding the 'preconceived notions' of the historian. By following these guidelines, the historian 'well trained in the principles of scholarship' can reveal the truth or 'as near to the truth of the past as he has any hope of getting' (Elton, 2002, pp. 46, 80). In his *Return to Essentials: Some Reflections on the Present State of Historical Study* (1991), Elton develops these arguments by rejecting theory, 'theory mongers' and the abstraction of history because theory imposes ideas upon the evidence in ways which compromise its objectivity or distort its use. Elton was adamant that the involvement of the historian as a subjective individual, the 'infiltration of historiographical methods' and the 'problem of historical reconstruction' should be 'reduced to a minimum'. The historian must act only as a conduit through which the experiences of the past travel; indeed, a relationship with the dead provides the thrill and challenge of history. If nothing else, for the 'honest historian', as Elton put it, just doing history allows 'the enormous enlargement of one's acquaintances', a list that is renewed and refreshed with every visit to the archive (Elton, 2002, pp. 79, 83, 142).

Yet historians are social and cultural animals, prompting the suggestion that history is less a science and more an art: it is constructed through the imagination of a particular moment rather than discovered through experiment or objective methodology. The past can reveal truths that are part of our personal and collective lives. If, for example, we consider a landscape beautiful, it is because we have absorbed historical assumptions that influence how we understand that landscape. Mountains were seen only as obstacles to easy travel before the eighteenth century and then subsequently regarded as glorious monuments to nature; these changing views were not based on objective approaches to the evidence but on sensibilities that emerged from the Enlightenment; that is, notions of the sublime majesty of nature that quite simply changed dramatically with the influence of Romanticism that emerged from or against the Enlightenment (see Chapter 3). In this context, for example, we may have an idea of the English village that is bucolic, charming and seemingly unchanging, the very epitome of Englishness. It may consist of a church, a duck pond, a war memorial, a cricket pitch or a village green and a public house or 'pub', a sense of England as a pastoral idyll symbolized by the thatched roofed house or, perhaps, the 'babbling brook' or haystack, even if this particular feature of the countryside actually disappeared from English fields more than half a century ago (Samuel, 1994, p. 107). It is an image that contrasts with landscapes of smoking chimneys or rows of terraced houses that make up the 'pit' village of the former mining communities, the 'dark satanic mills' demonized by writers such as William Blake, Charles Dickens and Arnold Bennett. These images and narratives of industrialization were evoked when Victorian artists and writers described industrialization or the 'condition of England'.

Outside a European sensibility, this aesthetic may never be known, and instead the thatched roof in an English village could be seen as a sign of poverty. People of earlier periods might have read the picture differently not because they lacked humanity, sensibilities or taste or because they should somehow be considered inferior to those who lived in Western cultures but because the historical milieux in which they lived were simply different. William Cobbett (1763–1835), pamphleteer and social commentator, recalled in his *Rural Rides*, sometime in the 1820s, travelling through the rolling hills of the Cotswolds in England, not far from the city of Oxford. He hated the picturesque scenery: to Cobbett the livestock that populated its gentle hills and slopes would feed the 'Great Wen' or large drain – the teeming multitudes of London. Before Cobbett, certainly in the century before he was born, the argument that the Cotswolds was a storehouse for the industrial masses could not have been made or would have been made in a quite different way.

It could be argued then that whatever period or era of history we live in is steeped with sensibilities and aesthetics that colour our lives and shade how we learn or write history, thereby challenging our efforts to be dispassionate in the way we read evidence. This may give us pause to consider whether our consciousness of eras and epochs can ever be identified in an objective manner. Did the middle classes feel themselves to be continually 'rising' or could the ancients have known that they were ancient any more than we can know precisely that we are somehow 'postmodern'? Johan Huizinga's highly speculative but extremely stimulating *The Waning of the Middle Ages* (2001), first published in 1924, looked at the culture of fourteenth- and fifteenth-century France and the Low Countries and concluded that artists, as well as theologians, poets, chroniclers, princes and statesmen should be treated 'not as the harbingers of a coming culture, but as perfecting and concluding the old' (Huizinga, 2001, p. x). Chivalry, hierarchy, gothic forms and symbolism that were so important to medieval architecture, art and life were not the rotten remains of a stagnant, 'dark' or 'middle' age in history whose only real purpose was to stand in contrast to the bright, humanist 'Renaissance period' that was about to be born. If we were alive then, unknowingly on the cusp of the medieval and early modern eras, we would surely have been subject to a maelstrom of influences that dictated our attitudes to what might be uniquely considered *at that moment* to be pleasing in appearance.

If the contemporary observer can therefore differentiate between the beauty and ugliness of the rolling hills of the Cotswolds and make historical judgements about what a landscape represents or how it has changed, it is because our experiences in the present are altogether more encompassing than attempts to recapture the past through the acquisition of analytical skills or training for historians proposed by Elton. Examples from the history of landscape, aesthetics or the competing ideas of the English village serve to illustrate the message at the heart of this section: that history does indeed matter in a way that would find agreement between both Carr and Elton, yet in differing ways.

'The past is a foreign country' is the opening line to the novel by L. P. Hartley called *The Go-Between*, and it is a place where 'they do things differently'. This articulates how from the perspective of Elton and others, the present is indeed separated from the past: 'They' are separated from 'us'. And yet as David Lowenthal noted in his 1985 book *The Past Is a Foreign Country*:

> During most of history men scarcely differentiated past from present, referring even to remote events, if at all, as though they were then occurring. Up to the nineteenth century those that gave any thought to the historical past supposed it much like the present. To be sure, the drama of history recorded major changes of life and landscape, but human nature supposedly remained constant, events always actuated by the same passions and prejudices. Even when ennobled by nostalgia or depreciated by partisans of progress, the past seemed not a foreign country but a part of their own. And chroniclers portrayed bygone times with an immediacy and intimacy that reflected the supposed likeness.
>
> (Lowenthal, 1985, p. xvi)

Only with the rise of scientific-type methodology when importance came to be placed on ways of gathering evidence objectively could distinctions in time be made between 'then' and 'now'. This is a theme that we shall return to in the next chapter. Some commentators interested in questions that arise from the quest for historical objectivity and coherent narratives, such as the historian Gertrude Himmelfarb, have articulated an overwhelming need to revive histories that promote synthesized or unified themes concerned with class, nation, ideas and so forth. However universal or 'whole' narratives such as the story of nation or class have been, efforts to foster and promote a single, coherent and integrated history have become increasingly difficult, precisely because of renewed efforts to write histories of gender, race and so on that speak to our lives in the here and now.

Like Elton, Himmelfarb has argued that a downplaying of political history over several years has encouraged historical knowledge to be treated in isolation, with each topic treated like a piece of a jigsaw but where seldom a complete picture comes into view. The real distinction that Himmelfarb makes, however, is between an 'old' history that attempts to understand contemporaries in their own terms and the 'new' history, which, while laudable in taking notice of, say, the historical role of women or black people, tends to interpret the past solely through the optic of the present (Himmelfarb, 2004). This fragmentation of historical narratives into stories about 'identities' has happened under the influence of literary theory, which, she argues, deconstructs the language used in historical sources to the point where the voice of the author is given no authority and the meaning of which can never be truly known. The text and the language of the text, from this perspective, have no context besides the preoccupations and concerns of the historian in the present day (see Chapter 7).

We are presented then with a serious choice about how history as a discipline works, what it can reasonably do and how it is approached. Taking our cue from historians such as Elton or Himmelfarb, is objectivity something we should strive for? Or is the subjectivity and (to an extent) present-mindedness of Carr and others more convincing? What are the pressures and influences bearing down on us as we 'do' history, and can we resist these pressures to the extent that we can really know things about the past? To address these questions – and to introduce others – we shall need to take a trip to India and the British Raj.

21.2 History and the Status of Historical Knowledge

The Indian Mutiny began in the summer of 1857 and was finally crushed nearly a year later. It has entered our popular imagination, but just note how. The use of the term 'mutiny', rather than, say, revolt, suggests that this was a traitorous act perpetrated by subjects of the British crown. This was how it was seen at the time, and it helps to explain why the retribution of the British was so brutal. A memorial in Delhi remembers the mutiny. Built by the British in 1863, it takes the form of an octagonal shaped tower and ornamental facade in the gothic style. It is dedicated to the memory of those soldiers and loyal Indians of the Delhi Field Force who were killed or died of disease during what now might be considered as the initial war for Indian independence. In 1972 a new plaque was added, correcting any impression given by the original memorial that the 'enemy' were anything else but, as it is inscribed, 'freedom fighters and martyrs of India'. And so, this was how the history of the Mutiny was first built and then reconstructed.

The mutiny was ostensibly sparked by the replacement of standard issue Minie rifles with Pattern Enfield's rifle-muskets. Both Hindu and Muslim soldiers were now required to bite off the end of the cartridge, which was widely rumoured to be caked with cow or pig fat, thus in one stroke causing offence to each religious group that made up the Indian ranks of the East India Company's Bengal Army. The origins of the revolt, however, were complicated, and drew variously upon a range of grievances over the ways in which the British had intruded in the economic and cultural life of Indian peoples. Many of our generation learnt nothing about the Indian Mutiny of 1857–1858 at school. Parents, no doubt as part of the general reassessment of the empire that took place in the midst of postwar decolonization, may have told stories about the cruelty of the British as they took revenge on the hacking to death of 260 women and children in the massacre of Kanpur in July 1857 or by lashing the mutineers to the mouths of cannons and blasting them to oblivion – a form of execution that the British reasoned was quick, yet spectacular, so giving fair warning to would-be protesters who harboured any lingering doubts about the wisdom and might of British rule. Above all, these were acts of calculated cruelty since – as the British knew full well – Hindus believed that the body needed to be intact for it to be reincarnated.

As far as the historiography of the revolt is concerned, let us look at an account by a noted, if traditional, historian of India and ask what it reveals about his approach to an understanding of the repercussions of the mutiny. Percival Spear's *A History of India*, first published in 1965, contains the following passage:

> In the summer of 1858 northern India lay inert and lacerated. The wisdom of Canning and strength of men like Sir John Lawrence restrained and soon ended the punitive measures and clamours for vengeance which followed the wake of the armies. But much remained to be done. Most of the rebel leaders were killed in battle like the Rani of Jhansi, or disappeared like the Nana and Bakht Khan of Delhi, or were executed like Tantia Topi. The Emperor Bahadur Shah had been promised his life. After a trial of doubtful legality he was exiled to Rangoon where he died in 1862 at the age of eighty-seven. The Mughal family lost its royal status. Delhi and Lucknow slowly returned to normal life, but Delhi with its territory lost its semi-independent position and was attached to the Punjab. A number of implicated princelings lost their states and their lives. In Oudh Canning's confiscatory proclamation was not withdrawn, but its application was left to the discretion of the new Chief Commissioner Montgomery, and its rigour mitigated by a system of regrants.
>
> These were the immediate and local results; there followed a number of measures of great importance. The East India Company ended its long career as the ruling power in India; a new attitude was adopted toward the princes; the army was reorganised; a new beginning was made in associating Indians with the supreme of their country. The new age was ushered in and its intended spirit defined in the Queen's proclamation of 1 November 1858. If good

Figure 21.1 Summary executions by the British of Indian rebels in 1857, depicted by the Russian artist Vasily Vereshagin in 1884

Contributor: Pictorial Press Ltd/Alamy Stock Photo

can come out of the evil the mutiny can claim the credit for most of these measures. There remained the psychological gulf between the peoples of India and Britain. This gulf was not created by the Mutiny as we have seen. The forces of separation had outstripped that of cooperation and the hope of self-government. This spirit was reinforced by that of fear on the British side and the resentment which it aroused was deepened by the memory of defeat and vengeance on the Indian. In this sense the Mutiny was a calamity whose effects only time could heal. Happily the progressive forces of reform and cooperation were not consumed but only consumed by the smoke of passion. They had received a severe set-back, but the next fifty years showed that it was a check rather than a halt.

(Spear, 1990, pp. 227–8)

Given that Spear, as a traditional historian, stressed the value of factual evidence, what facts did he use in this passage? We noted the following:

1 The Indian Mutiny ended in the summer of 1858.
2 Most of the rebel leaders were killed, executed or had disappeared.
3 Clamour for vengeance against the Indians was tempered by the Viceroy Lord Canning and the Governor of the Punjab, Sir John Lawrence.
4 Delhi lost its independence and was absorbed into the Punjab.
5 The East India Company lost its colonial authority, the Indian army was reorganized and Indians began to be incorporated into the apparatus of government.
6 Queen Victoria issued a proclamation in November 1858 which outlined new policies towards India.

To save time, these 'facts' are listed in a rough chronological order. They are all evidential facts that cannot seriously be disputed, at least not without some difficulty. But in themselves – even when arranged in the order that they happened – they say nothing about the nature of the British response to the revolt. Alone these facts do not constitute history; that is, they are part of the past but beyond their mere selection they are not yet part of historiography. They are like a catalogue of information and so only become history when they are linked one to another as part of a narrative framework. Spear has done precisely this. Let us, however, look in a little more detail at what is going on in the passage. What he does here is use the chronicle of events as building blocks of a particular story with a beginning (the end of the revolt) and an end (the subsequent fifty years of British rule). A few important points follow from this:

1 The story is put together by linking the various chronological elements in causal relationships. The Indian Mutiny resulted in the death or disappearance of many of the rebel leaders. In the immediate aftermath there were demands for vengeance, but these were silenced by the British authorities. Lessons were learnt from the mutiny. Measures were introduced to heal the wounds. The separation between Briton and Indian that had caused the mutiny were mitigated by the Queen's proclamation, the end of the reign of the East India Company and the introduction of Indians in colonial administration.
2 The story thus unfolds as a secondary narrative of British colonial authority in India. Britain ruled with humanity and harmony until events forced a separation, resulting in the mutiny, the defeat of which left India devastated and humiliated. But although the mutiny was a tragedy, in the longer term it promoted progressive forces of cooperation and hope which once again led to a happy and benign colonial relationship. Just consider how the language in the

passage reinforces this narrative. India was 'inert' and 'lacerated'; the 'wisdom' of Canning, the 'strength' of Lawrence muting the cries for vengeance; 'good came out of the evil of the mutiny'.

This narrative is part of a larger narrative that Spear inhabits in which colonial rule is exercised by the British as progressive and benign and operates for the benefit of both colonizers and colonized. The story, however, is only one of many that can be constructed using this chronicle. Another, from the perspective of an Indian rebel, could certainly be imagined or even retrieved from *exactly* the same evidence, but it is one absent in Spear. As an alternative history we could interpret the evidence as follows:

- After years of suppression large sections of the Indian population decided to take matters in their own hands and drive the British out of India.
- The revolt was nearly successful, but because of the military superiority of the British and their access to technology such as the telegraph, the nationalist struggle was defeated.
- The British press cried out for vengeance against those who had been responsible for the atrocities. Many of the rebels were executed but not on the scale that some had wished for.
- The British government now recognized that their rule could no longer be based on military power alone and therefore decided to take due account of India's religion and customs in order not to cause offence and assimilate influential sections into the British ruling elite as a means of diverting them from future nationalist struggle.

What this example illustrates is that seemingly objective accounts based on hard factual evidence are riven by ideological influences, such as the historians' feelings about the nature of British rule in India. Here there is a critical difference between historical and evidential truth. There are certain truths in history, but these tend to be evidential. Interpretations can never be self-evident truths because they are always open to challenge. All we can hope for is that through a dialogue between theory and evidence we can approach historical truth even though we never truly arrive there.

The received 'story' about the British Raj and others like it – the attacks by white settlers on American 'red' Indians in countless Westerns ('Got him', we shouted as they were shot from their horses) and ruthless Nazis in comics, forever exclaiming *Achtung* – take us directly to questions about the nature of history, our understanding of the past and the role of the historian. Bearing in mind that many of us don't come to these subjects without prejudice, how can we gain access to the past with enough understanding and complexity that we neither accept unquestioningly an impressionistic historical narrative nor reject one that is broadly convincing to an intelligent reader? In short, how might we determine the status of historical knowledge?

In order to consider this question, we must return to the historian Geoffrey Elton. The rather comfortable view held by Elton that the past is there and all we must do is record it in a logical and coherent way is one that formed the cornerstone of the discipline of history when it emerged in the nineteenth century, largely with the life and work of the German historian Leopold von Ranke (1795–1886). Von Ranke, whom we met in Chapter 6, lived by his famous maxim that the job of the historian was to show the past as it really happened. Since then, many important historians, with Elton-inspired rationalism, have attempted to do precisely this. From the perspective of Carr-like subjectivists, however, the whole edifice of that maxim is built on the mistaken premise that the past is out there just waiting to be discovered and then recovered by professionals trained in all the appropriate skills of gathering evidence and putting the fragments together again to form a whole picture true to its original likeness.

According to Elton 'the reality – yes, the truth – of the past exists in materials of various kinds, produced by the past at the time that it occurred and left behind by it as testimony' (Elton, 1998, p. 52). What Elton is claiming here is that evidence is the basis of proper History with a capital 'H'. Historians are firmly bound by its authority and must not use fiction to fill in the gaps that inevitably exist. It is in the sources – the evidential facts – that Elton's 'truth' can be found. But it is, of course, only the skilled, the professionally trained historian, who can do the proper work with such sources – only he or she who with an objective and open mind will select, evaluate and arrange them into a meaningful account of the past. These then are questions that take us to the heart of what it means to be objective in our approach to history, that is, how we can be free of bias or prejudice caused by personal feelings, excessive imagination or memories, and who it is that we can regard as a bone fide historian.

Now there are elements of this argument with which no historian, professional or otherwise, could quarrel. Elton recognizes that history is not the study of the past (we have no time machine to allow us to travel back in time) but the study of what remains of the past in the present. Clearly, we must take evidence seriously – approach it with honesty and integrity, even it if we find it does not accord with an argument we are trying to make. Historical facts found in the evidence cannot under any circumstances be squeezed into preconceived notions of what it is that we wish to argue and made to fit a pre-existing theory. Similarly, evidence ought not to be disregarded if we find it does not accord with our argument, no matter how beautifully designed that argument may be. We certainly should not make up evidence, making doubtful causal links between persons and events that may strengthen that argument but that would make that argument false. Even with these basic provisos, there remain real problems in relying purely on evidence as the necessary basis of an historical account.

Underlying Elton's approach to history is the premise that somehow the process of research and writing can be undertaken in an objective way by the historian. In a sense, Percival Spear's book on India contained that assumption. Others argue that subjectivity is unavoidable, that we are all creatures profoundly influenced by both the past and by history. Perhaps what Elton fails to recognize is the sheer impossibility of tackling evidence with neutrality. Not that all historians have a particular axe to grind – most are not engaged in propaganda work which blatantly sets out to assassinate historical characters or causes. Nor are we especially motivated by emotions such as anger, love or contempt. Rather, we all inhabit particular social and political environments which will inevitably influence how we construct our histories. For the new social historians of the 1960s and 1970s, subjectivity became a virtue when certain historians were encouraged to use their own experiences in the present to shape their reading of historical evidence (Chapter 10). This was true of socialist and feminist historians who encouraged a dialogue between workers and historians.

It is the increasing recognition of the importance of historical truth that has given rise to something of a transformation in historical thought over the last twenty years. Such has been this transformation that there are now currents in the philosophy of history which almost completely invert the relationship between evidence and interpretation. As we have seen, for Elton evidence is the origin and basis of all historical knowledge, whereas more recent interventions point to the critical importance of the interpretation of evidence and indeed the status of evidence. We introduced the term *postmodern* in the opening section and in Chapter 7, but for now it is enough to say that postmodern historiography denies that historical truth is possible. The past is not out there simply to be grasped but is actively created by historians working with particular values, ideologies and interpretations. The task, then, is not only to scrutinize the evidence but also to reveal the processes through which that evidence is used to create interpretations of past events. This in many ways can be seen as a healthy development, not least in revealing the hidden ideologies in historical accounts. Unfortunately, as in all such movements when established orthodoxies are being challenged, an awful lot of heat is wasted in vituperative debate, insult and misrepresentation.

Both these positions are unfair and untenable. We cannot dismiss the whole corpus of previous historiography as theoretically naive simply because emphasis is given to this evidence rather than to the problem of interpretation. Many historians working within this tradition have provided us with rich, sophisticated accounts of historical events and change. If we subsequently wish to read them with due recognition of the moment they were produced and the framework they inhabited, then they must retain their value. Yet, equally, we cannot dismiss postmodern history as a mere figment of their imaginations. To our knowledge, no historian working within this tradition would dismiss evidence as inconsequential – that, for example, the Holocaust had no material reality; all take it seriously. Postmodern historians, however, argue that, for it to be understood, that materiality must be appropriated by ideas and theories about the nature of historical change, of the rituals of human behaviour and the very status or form of writing itself. Historians, needless to say, are not neatly divided between 'empiricists' and 'postmodernists'. When we say 'empiricists' we mean (in brief) historians that rely on fact-gathering and the narrow use of our senses to interpret those facts. All historians, however, are cognizant of the need to explore the limits of historical knowledge and the place of the historian in the creation and transformation of knowledge as they encounter the fragments of the past in the present. To do this well, something must be known about choosing and interpreting evidence – the very issues confronted in the next section with a survey of the historiography of Chartism.

21.3 Choosing Evidence, Challenging Interpretations

Monday was a traditional day of riot and protest in Britain and was derived from a traditional holiday called St Maundy. Probably for this reason, on Monday, 25 September 1838, the Manchester Political Union organized a rally at Kersal Moor, Salford in the north of England, where an estimated 300,000 people gathered and marched from the Manchester factories to the moors accompanied by bands and carrying banners rescued from the 'massacre' at Peterloo in 1819. 'More pigs less parsons' or 'For children and wife, we war to the knife' exclaimed the banners as they were carried that day by the so-called Chartists who demanded the 'six points' of political reform, namely, universal male suffrage, annual parliaments, vote by secret ballot, abolition of the property qualification for members of parliament, payment of MPs and equal electoral constituencies.

Chartist activity, intense though it was, had all but ceased by the final National Convention in 1858. Nonetheless, in its aftermath, all Chartism's demands were subsequently granted except, mercifully, annual parliaments. Since then, the rise and fall of Chartism has attracted much attention from historians: was it economic, social or political in nature? Was it a national or a regional movement? Was it well or badly led? Was it revolutionary? Did it succeed or fail? The purpose of this section then is to use Chartism as a case study to demonstrate how historians build knowledge through innovative approaches to research and the deployment of evidence and in so doing transform our historical understanding.

Some historians have located Chartism in the long history of radicalism beginning with the seventeenth-century agitation by the Levellers and their 'People's Agreement', which included demands for popular sovereignty and the extension of suffrage – or the dissenting, agrarian communism of the Diggers. Alternatively, the election of the radical John Wilkes in the Middlesex elections of the 1760s and 1770s (mentioned briefly in the opening section and discussed again in Chapter 8) is sometimes regarded as the beginning of the democratic impulse in Britain (see Chapter 6). Whatever its origins, radicalism in Britain received a boost from the American and French Revolutions and the radical pamphleteering of such activists as Obadiah Hulme, James Burgh and Major John Cartwright in the 1770s, which acted as counterweights to popular loyalism and led to the state suppression of radical agitation in the mid-1790s. Radicalism revived at the end of the French wars or else went underground, while political radicalism such as that of the Tory William Cobbett (he from the first section who despised the Cotswolds because it fed the industrial masses in London) prospered, taking us down to Peterloo in 1819 and beyond. Next, the rise of philosophical radicalism and economic reform gave rise to influential figures such as the utilitarian Jeremy Bentham and promoted a heightened interest in parliamentary reform. A quiescent state in the mid-1820s, during a period of relative prosperity, was followed by revival of activity over religious disabilities in 1828–1829 which informed middle class agitation down to the First Reform Act of 1832, the repeal of the Corn Laws in 1846 and emergence of working-class agitation that fed Chartism until (and beyond) the European revolutions of 1848.

This largely working-class agitation demanded land nationalization and legislative change to free workers from 'industrial slavery'. Reforms to the poor law, support for the unemployed and calls for the disestablishment of the Church of England as administrators of relief to the poor and for a system of free education (including the establishment of industrial schools) anticipated the rise of the welfare state of the early twentieth century. Likewise, the reforms to the state

Figure 21.2 Chartist meeting at Kennington Common, London, April 1848. Although large, the gathering signalled the demise of the movement

Contributor: Chronicle/Alamy Stock Photo

anticipated an inclusive pluralism that brought nonconformists (non-Anglican Protestants), Catholics, Jews and atheists into the 'pale of the constitution' in advance of the introduction of universal suffrage and the rise of mass politics.

Given this narrative, how has Chartism been treated by historians? How have they chosen which evidence to highlight and how have they interpreted that evidence? What, more generally, has characterized the changing approaches to these questions? Early histories of radicalism made an explicit link between the political and social motivations for Chartism – 'the knife and fork question'. Both Fabian (the intellectual arm of the British labour movement that argued for the evolutionary transformation of capitalism) and Marxist histories regarded Chartism as the forerunners of the modern Labour movement. A key figure in the movement and in its subsequent historiography was Francis Place (1771–1836). A follower of the radical William Godwin (1756–1836) and a member of the London Corresponding Society, which boasted of its unlimited membership sympathetic to the egalitarian aims of the French Revolution, Place had made his name as part of the Westminster elections with Francis Burdett. He also, in 1838, with the London Working Men's Association, helped to draft the People's Charter, only thereafter becoming disillusioned with Chartism and its rainbow coalition of currency reformers, socialist and cooperative followers of Robert Owen, and local heroes with their almost infinite variety of colourful views. After opposing factory reform and supporting the Anti-Corn Law League, he retired to write the voluminous account of his times, which Robert Gammage's *History of the Chartist Movement* (1894), Graham Wallas' *Life of Francis Place* (1898) and countless scholars have drawn upon since.

The Place collection held in the British Library has been known and used by historians since at least the 1890s. Evidence of the Chartist experience, however, was not yet fully known until the 1940s, and the interpretation of Chartism had advanced little. Marxist histories highlighted 'physical force' Chartism as part of a heritage of revolutionary politics and this too was of a piece with contemporary Communist politics. Likewise, both Theodore Rothstein's *From Chartism to Labourism* (1929) and Reg Groves' *But We Shall Rise Again* (1938) emphasized the evolutionary and revolutionary strands within Chartism but did so with a Popular Front agenda in mind (the touchstone of radical politics and historiography in the 1930s that argued for a united force on the left to counter right-wing and reactionary politics). Fabian historiography (in which for these purposes we can count G. D. H. Cole's *Chartist Portraits* (1941), continuing the biographical tradition begun by Gammage) tended towards framing the 'moral force' element of Chartism as part of a constitutional and gradualist politics that he largely supported in his own day. Cole and then the historian George Kitson Clark (1900–1975), in a 1953 book, were keen to emphasize how 'rational Chartism' or 'hungry Chartism' was a movement broken by working class divisions of the sort that wrecked the 1950s Labour Party – then out of power – and that served as a warning to internal dissidents of the danger of division. The concern was with contemporary working class unity as much as it was with the objective truths thrown up by historical research.

That Chartism served as a cautionary tale for those on the Left facing a formidable foe was emphasized less by the Liberal historians J. L. (1872–1949) and Barbara (1873–1961) Hammond who in their very popular *The Age of the Chartists, 1832–1852* (1930) did something to address the ambivalence Liberals had hitherto felt towards Chartism. Likewise, Asa Briggs (1921–2016) wrote *Chartist Studies* (1959) and introduced a commentary from a social democratic perspective. Questions were posed about the effect of the trade cycle on the ebb and flow of Chartist militancy, seen very much as a local and regional phenomenon. As a celebrant of the radical tradition, Francis Williams, journalist and Labour Party activist, wrote *Fifty Years' March: The Rise of the Labour Party* (1949) and *The Magnificent Journey: The Rise of the*

Trade Unions (1954) but did so in a way that presented the history of radicalism as the history of class, which by then had become a shared determinant among historians of various political traditions.

Enter Dorothy Thompson (1923–2011) who was perhaps the most influential historian of Chartism. Her students and followers – James Epstein, Neville Kirk, John Saville and Geoff Eley – together transformed Chartist studies, emphasizing the national characteristics of Chartism as the culmination of a 'literate and sophisticated' working-class radicalism which simultaneously renewed Chartism as a political rather than an economic movement. In the intervention launched by *The Chartists: Popular Politics in the Industrial Revolution* (1984), Thompson:

- Saw a need for a general survey of what we thought we knew about Chartism.
- Rejected local studies that suggested that Chartism was simply a series of protest movements.
- Introduced a longer timeline for Chartism (back to 1832).
- Placed less emphasis on the heterogeneity of Chartist support, rethinking the occupations of Chartists.
- Detected a common language based on what she argued to be a coherent political and social programme.

Chartism is thus an example of an historical question that has been through several phases of historiography, its parameters set firm by both the evidence and the conceptual boundaries of the discipline. Biographical accounts focused on leadership, placing emphasis on 'moral force' or 'physical force' Chartism, the political or social aspects of their demands, Chartism as a series of local protests versus Chartism as a systematic national movement – all at one time or another came to prominence. The archive, such as the Place papers, had been all but exhausted but still historians have found ways of reading evidence in new and interesting ways; this leads us to an important recent intervention in our understanding of Chartism by Gareth Stedman Jones.

Stedman Jones, in an essay called 'Rethinking Chartism', republished in *Languages of Class* (1983), transformed our knowledge of Chartism and simultaneously the methodology of modern historical studies. Stedman Jones adopted the notion that language – how we describe the world – is prior to our experience of it. In short, for Stedman Jones social being was not reflected simply in consciousness to be revealed through empirical procedures of Marxism; it was organized by language. By studying the language used by Chartists, he insisted that the movement was not a perfect contemporary reflection of a revolutionary class-consciousness in the 1840s but instead employed language that was situated as a challenge to the 'Old Corruption' of land, church and aristocracy that belonged to the period before 1832. This language was of the eighteenth century, not the 1840s, the decade in which Chartism ostensibly thrived. It was language used by Wilkes in the 1760s and 1770s and by other radicals in the 1790s following the French Revolution, not a language that could possibly be used to critique a new industrial order. Thus, the banners carried onto Kersal Moor in 1838 with which we began the section – 'More pigs less parsons' – was indeed a political language but one aimed at the church, not the poverty induced by industrialization. Nor could Chartism be a mirror held up to Peel's 1841–1846 government measures.

As suggested by Miles Taylor (1996), an historian of nineteenth-century popular politics, Thompson and Stedman Jones had much in common:

- Both were sceptical about Chartism as a local phenomenon.
- Both said Chartism was not simply a protest movement but had greater coherence.
- Both wanted to emphasize the political elements of Chartism.

- Both recognized the rational nature of Chartist arguments.
- Both located Chartism within a longer chronology of radicalism.

They disagreed profoundly, however, about why Chartism collapsed, and they did so not because new evidence had become known but because new interpretations were now available. For Thompson it was because the working class had lost the collective belief that they could reform politics in the conditions thrown up by mid-century capitalism; for Stedman Jones it was the collapse of the Chartist critique of the state, a critique inherited from a pre-reform politics (see Chapter 8). This disagreement was as much a disagreement of approach to the relevant facts: for Stedman Jones, Chartism could not respond to the limited nature of factory reform – new policing legislation, reform of local government and the New Poor Law; for Thompson, the state restricted newspapers and trade unions and crushed class consciousness, which in turn led to the collapse of Chartism.

The result of this debate about what we consider to be evidence and how we approach it has led to fresh strands of enquiry: especially the systematic study of language and symbols, what the early historian of Chartism Robert Gammage once called the 'gaudy trappings' of Chartism – poetry, ballads, hymns, banners and flags. Thompson was always inclined to seek out the expressive aspects of the movement, but this and revisions based on the languages of what the historian Edward Royle called 'Chartist culture' have seen some rich work undertaken in popular politics more generally. Patrick Joyce in his *Democratic Subjects* (1994) attacked class as a universal category and looked instead for 'other discourses of "the People" that were not confined to Chartist agitation'. Margot Finn (1993) took Chartism beyond its usual periodization, connecting it to European nationalism and socialism of the 1860s, while Eugenio Biagini and Alistair Reid took up Chartism, like Stedman Jones, as one part of a radical tradition that stretches forward to influence both Gladstonian Liberalism and a nascent Labour movement.

The most recent contributions to Chartist scholarship have not successfully challenged the approach of Stedman Jones, although Ariane Schnepf's *Our Original Rights as a People* (2006) has attempted just that. Instead, there are studies which take the reader across the whole narrative of Chartism, such as Malcolm Chase's *Chartism: A New History* (2007) and W. Hamish Fraser's *Chartism in Scotland* (2010). There is even a turn back to biography that had originally characterized historical writing about the Chartists from the 1850s with Stephen Roberts looking at the career histories of Chartist figures Thomas Cooper and Arthur O'Neill in his *The Chartist Prisoners* (2008). Yet none of these worthwhile additions to the genre was content to make do with accepted 'facts'; instead, they did what historians ought to do – they concentrated equally on both the choice and selection of evidence and balanced theory and evidence.

By focusing on this one area of historiography we should be now able to pull together some of the themes of the chapter. Whether the historian is objective or subjective about the Chartist phenomenon is not important if it is believed that historical evidence remains unsullied by the unreasonable prejudice of the historian or even influenced by the time in which the history is researched and written. Nor should an approach that regards the historian as objective, treating the past as quite unconnected to the present, necessarily be a right-wing or conservative idea. The radical historian E. P. Thompson (1924–1993), for example, saw wife sales (like his essays on 'rough music' in 1972 or the 'moral economy' in 1971) as an instance of a 'rebellious traditional culture' among the masses against a background of industrialization, an illustration of 'the disassociation between patrician and plebeian cultures'. This suggested a concern for radical and class-based experiences, but these historical experiences were, Thompson maintained, first revealed to him through primary sources.

Thompson as a Marxist did not collapse into a subjective empathy – an historical imagination applied to the past may well have been far too soft focused and woolly for Thompson. He used the archive to glimpse social relations among a stratum of society previously treated with condescension: an attempt by the mainly rural poor to claim rights in the face of a rapidly changing economy and a plebeian culture that was separate from its patrician counterpart. In using that archive he applied method just as surely as Elton. Indeed, in an argument with Raphael Samuel in the pages of the *History Workshop Journal* in the 1990s, Thompson railed against the 'modish subjectivism now so current' and argued that the evidence of the archive was not 'silent and inert to be manipulated into any form the questioner proposed. Nor can the choice of context or setting be decided by the flip of a coin'. When Samuel suggested that the idea of wife sales as an unofficial form of divorce was 'like any piece of historical reasoning and research, it was a child or creature of its time', Thompson insisted instead and not without irritation that his argument had derived 'from the instances which kept popping up in the newspapers when I was researching' (Thompson, 1992). From this debate alone we can see that advances in our knowledge of the past depends upon – indeed thrives on – the judgements of historians and continued debates among them. History is about argument and so solid advice for any student would be to 'go argue'.

21.4 Causes in History

We wish to end this chapter by focusing on the most important – and intractable – question faced by historians today, namely, can historians ever *explain* what happened in the past? The question may seem an obvious one, but it is perhaps surprising how little attention it has commanded among historians in the long term. As we saw in Chapter 3 when reviewing how the discipline developed, the question of interpretation was not taken seriously until the Enlightenment. Previous historians had tended to work to chronicle events as a means of celebrating past achievements or of bolstering the claims of particular rulers. In this respect, history rarely rose above the level of propaganda. Furthermore, if ever they articulated a sense of historical process by describing, say, how a particular society progressed, this was almost invariably seen as the result of divine providence or accident.

The other barrier which modern historians needed to overcome was that of positivism, a system of thought that had dominated historical inquiry since the nineteenth century. We have already touched on this in the earlier discussion of Geoffrey Elton, a twentieth-century historian who continued to adhere to this philosophy, but now it is necessary to flesh out the arguments a little. Positivism was a philosophy of knowledge that had its roots in and came to define the methodology of the natural sciences in the early modern period. It held that priority be given to the compilation and organization of facts based on which general (scientific) laws could then be induced. Historians were seduced by this approach and so set about gathering all the facts they could lay their hands on. Not only that, but they also recognized that the facts – or historical evidence as they preferred to call this material – needed to be as reliable and authentic as possible. Much time was therefore devoted to a critical examination of the gathered evidence before it could be given their seal of approval. The result was a vast increase in the store of evidence, almost all of which derived from documentary sources such as commentaries, state papers, court records and correspondence. (It was to be many years before other sources including archaeological, literary and photographic were taken seriously.)

The transition from facts to general laws, however, which seemed to be accomplished with great success in the natural sciences, worked less well in history. The main problem was in the evidence itself. Scientific evidence tended to be much more secure, reliable and controllable.

Facts were gathered by scientists under strictly monitored conditions. They derived from firsthand observation which, if necessary, could be repeated time and again. No historian enjoyed such privileges. The inevitable outcome was that history remained rooted in the compilation of facts that came to be seen as its sole raison d'être. Thus it was that nineteenth-century historians such as von Ranke could claim that the task of the historian was to report things as they actually happened.

Alternative currents of thought emerged in the course of the century which challenged this comforting orthodoxy. Sociological thinking gained momentum. Led by Auguste Comte (1798–1857), sociologists began to argue that historical evidence offered something more important and interesting than the mere recording of events (Collingwood, 1961, pp. 128–31). If historians could not follow the example of natural scientists, then he proposed a new social science of sociology, which would use historical and contemporary evidence as the platform to launch into an investigation of the causal connections among the facts, on the basis of which sociologists could explain patterns of human behaviour and derive laws of societal change. According to Comte, the sociologist was a super-historian because he or she elevated history to the rank of a science and historians to scientists instead of mere collectors and recorders of evidence.

The second impulse for change came from the work of Charles Darwin. The idea of a static natural world had long been discarded before *The Origin of Species* first appeared in 1859, but that of evolution through natural selection was truly original and seismic in its impact. Despite its many detractors, evolution conquered science *and* began increasingly to appeal to historians. Evolution, after all, was predicated on the notion of progress over time, and so it came to be viewed as a theory that could be applied as much to historical as natural change. Grand theories about the steady progress of civilization – particularly in the modern era when the Enlightenment had banished the age of bigotry, darkness and superstition – and industrialization and liberalization provided great hope, for the future of a free and prosperous human race owed much to this current of thought.

This exciting opening of historical inquiry, however, presented a whole new range of philosophical and methodological questions with which historians still grapple. Many historians employed narrative as a vehicle to identify causal links. Story telling was an integral part of positivist approaches to the past, especially in biographical accounts where the motives of individual actors could readily be unearthed, and so it was a matter of framing their narratives with a greater rigour. Diplomatic and political histories have been and continue to be prone to approaches relying on the stated intent and tactics of the main players (Tosh, 2021, pp. 142–50). Individual motive, however, has proven an uncertain and unreliable guide to historical causation. There is often a real discrepancy between what historical actors say about their motives, understandings and policies and how they actually choose to act in particular situations. The stated aims of the Court of Directors of the East India Company, for example, are poor guides to measures taken by company officials on the ground in eighteenth-century India. Equally importantly, individuals rarely display an awareness of structural changes such as modernization, demography or popular sensibilities within which they worked and which necessarily underpinned the historical changes they witnessed.

Ultimately, because human behaviour is extraordinarily complex, as are its causes, one-dimensional explanations are unreliable and inaccurate. Stephen Kern has recently highlighted some of these issues by exploring the changing interpretations of murder in Western culture and the bodies of knowledge upon which they have drawn (Kern, 2006). His emphasis is chiefly on literary forms but the same motifs operate in works of history. Concomitant with the rise of sociology in the early decades of the nineteenth century, Kern argues, Western thinkers transformed understanding of human behaviour and its causes. Advances in disciplines including genetics, economics, biology, criminology and philosophy provided the impetus, but they were most popularly evident in the novel, which came to act as a filter for 'scientific' explanations. Crime fiction is a particularly good example. Early novels of this genre strongly displayed determinist causal factors such as monomania in *Moby Dick* and poverty in *Oliver Twist*, but as the century wore on these factors became increasing layered and multifaceted. With this, the search for unambiguous causality found in many Victorian novels was abandoned as writers more willingly accepted open-ended plots with no definite closure (ibid., p. 12).

The pleasing irony here is that this move to complexity and uncertainty reflected broader structural changes in society, notably the increasing interdependence and remoteness of social and economic relationships which resulted from the expansion of industrial capitalism and urbanization. History, in other words, caused shifts in the ways in which causality itself was viewed. And these changes were manifest in the broad causal themes identified by Kern, namely, ancestry, childhood, language, sexuality, emotion, mind, society and ideas, all of which featured strongly both in scientific research and crime fiction. A few examples from Kern must suffice. In *Dracula* (1897), Bram Stoker skilfully combines ancestry and criminality. The count is heir to predatory impulses passed down through the bloodline from one generation to another. But Stoker also drew freely upon the work of the influential Italian criminologist Cesare Lombroso who had done much to popularize the notion that 'criminal types' had clearly recognizable features. Thus, the count was identified as a criminal type with an imperfectly formed mind, evidence of which could be detected in his aquiline nose, bushy eyebrows and pointed ears. Aldous Huxley's *Brave New World* (1932) depicts the use of hormones to activate and quell aggressive impulses. In his dystopian vision, female embryos are injected with male sex hormones, the urges of adult females are placated with mammary gland extracts, and adults chew sex-hormone gum. When necessary to discharge aggression, hormones are even used to simulate murder. And when in John Steinbeck's *The Grapes of Wrath* (1939) the house of a poor farmer is about to be bulldozed, his murderous intent is defused by the driver's assertion that there is no one to blame and therefore no one to be shot. Anonymous, remote corporate greed is ultimately responsible for the farmer's desperate plight.

These are solitary fictional characters whose experiences may not translate that readily into history, except that there are abundant examples from biographies of real historical actors that employ the same strategies and narrative devices in identifying causal relationships. The all-too-numerous studies of Hitler, for example, include the full range of sociological, psychological, economic and sexual motives in attempting to explain his monstrous behaviour. Rudolph Binion's psycho-history *Hitler among the Germans* (1976) is typical. Binion proposes that traumas from Hitler's early life were largely responsible for his subsequent genocide of the Jews. Before his birth, Hitler's mother lost three children to diphtheria, in response to which she became over-protective of Adolf, breast feeding him well into teething but simultaneously conveying feelings of guilt and inadequacy. Later she was diagnosed with breast cancer and had a double mastectomy, largely on the recommendation of a Jewish doctor. But the cancer returned, and Hitler insisted the doctor – against his better advice – apply daily a pungent drug Iodoform to the suppurating scars, but to no avail for the mother died, probably from ingesting the drug. Using notions of oral trauma and Freudian oedipal theory, Binion uses these events to explain Hitler's hatred of Jews and the constant references he makes to the removal of the poison and cancer within German society (Kern, 2006, pp. 79–85).

Most historians, however, justifiably remain sceptical of such approaches. The elevation of largely accidental events to principal causal status in explaining momentous historical happenings is misleading, even foolhardy. Quite apart from Binion's reliance on uncertain psychoanalytical theory, there remains the whole question of whether historical change can be explained by reference to a single factor. Arguably, Hitler's hatred of the Jews had just as much to do with Germany's crisis following defeat in the First World War, the ancient lineages of antisemitism and an aggressive nationalism.

In order to develop the critique of monocausal explanations let us consider examples of somewhat limited historical thinking about other momentous events. It is widely believed that the United States was eventually compelled to enter the Second World War by the bombing of Pearl Harbor in December 1941, but as John Gaddis shows with admirable clarity, the reality was rather different:

> It would make no sense . . . to begin an account of the Japanese attack on Pearl Harbour with the launching of the planes from their carriers: you'd want to know how the carriers came to be within range of Hawaii, which requires explaining why the government in Tokyo chose to risk war with the United States. But you can't do that without discussing the American oil embargo against Japan, which in turn was a response to the Japanese takeover of French Indochina. Which of course resulted from the opportunity provided by France's defeat at the hands of Nazi Germany, together with frustrations Japan had encountered in trying to conquer China. Accounting for all this, however, would require some attention to the rise of authoritarianism and militarism during the 1930s, which in turn had something to do with the Great Depression as well as the perceived iniquities of the post-World War I settlement, and so on.
>
> (Gaddis, 2002, p. 95, cited in Hewitson, 2014, p. 105)

The oft-quoted claim – to take another example – that the First World War was caused by the assassination of Archduke Ferdinand is likewise suspect, for it ignores the deeper structural shifts brought by imperial and industrial rivalries, the struggles over resources, inept diplomatic manoeuvrings and even the destructive impulses of modernization. And so it is simply not true (as we have found in this very chapter) that the Indian Mutiny was caused by forcing sepoys to bite rifle cartridges smeared with pig fat or that the abolition of slavery was driven solely by humanitarian desires to free enslaved Africans and their descendants.

So where does all this leave the question of historical causation? If we reject the idea of a single causal factor or of the determining influence of individual actors, then are we necessarily forced to accept the view that historical causation is multivalent and multi-layered? Yes, we think we are, and yet does this get us any further? It may well be that the sheer plurality of causation prevents us from achieving a totally satisfactory – and satisfying – explanation of any historical event. Perhaps the philosopher of science K. Codell Carter was right when he insisted 'how totally pointless, hopeless, and downright silly it is to think one can ever state *precisely* what it is for one thing to cause another' (Carter, 2003, p. 199 cited in Kern, 2006, p. 26).

Inspired by the call of Comte and others, many historians applied themselves to the task of uncovering general laws that could explain the course of historical change. One of the most influential was, of course, Karl Marx (see Chapter 6). All history is the history of class struggle, he declared, and it was this that acted as a motor force to drive historical transformation from primitive communism through distinct stages to capitalism and eventually communism. Such approaches proved extremely resilient and versatile as they gave rise to most of the subsequent schools of interpretative history striving for a narrative of universal application. Marxism, the *Annales* school, modernization theory and the histories of imperialism were all built on nineteenth-century precursors. In the past thirty years, however, these have come under increasing attack. Few historians would now accept Marxist narratives. Not only do they rely too heavily upon determinist conceptions of the relationship between the economic base and societal infrastructure, but they are also wedded to a teleology of historical change, which when compared with the detailed record is unreliable. It goes further, for now, as part of the postmodern critique of historical practice, all such grand narratives have largely been abandoned (Chapter 7).

What, then, is left to the hapless historian in pursuit of the holy grail of causation? If we are still interested (as we should be) in explaining human behaviour, then it remains the case that this must be seen in the appropriate historical context in all of its manifestations. This is easier said than done. The paucity and fragility of much historical evidence, the distinction of relationships which are causal rather than merely linked and the ordering of causal hierarchies according to their relevance continue to present significant challenges, and if we find monocausal approaches unattractive or are overwhelmed by causal plurality, then perhaps we might make progress by thinking in terms of limits or boundaries. Recourse to an understanding of broad, underlying structural processes may provide the key also to an understanding of human actors, not in the sense of determining their behaviour but rather of setting limits to or defining the boundaries of the options that are available to them. Joan Wallace Scott has nicely stated the case:

> [S]ubjects do have agency. They are not unified, autonomous individuals exercising free will, but rather subjects whose agency is created through situations and statuses conferred on them. Being a subject means being 'subject to definite conditions of existence, conditions of endowment of agents and conditions of exercise. These conditions enable choices, although they are not unlimited'.
>
> (Scott, 2007, p. 793)

Precisely what a subject is or what conditions we are interested in takes us into debates that cannot be pursued here. Such complex debates on causation continue to exercise the more philosophically minded historians, and the obscure detail need not trouble us unduly. But it is vital to retain a critical perspective on historical writing by constantly asking what notions of causality obtain and with what results?

Postscript

Many of us were encouraged to believe at school that since history books recorded events as they happened, they were reliable and truthful statements about the past. Hopefully, anyone who has continued an interest in history – whether an established researcher or someone reading a history book or watching a television documentary as a source of relaxation and entertainment – has had the resourcefulness to develop a more critical awareness of such accounts and therefore should be sufficiently aware of the need to ask probing questions about the nature of the evidence presented and how it has been used by the writers.

What is clear from the consideration in this chapter of how historians have approached the past is that there is no consensus; indeed, the topic has remained a contentious one. Over the nineteenth century when history emerged as a discipline in its own right, the task of the historian was seen to be that of recording things as they actually happened. This seemed obvious enough. Under appropriate circumstances, any historian trained in the techniques of working with evidence could produce a solid picture of the past. This vision of the role of the historian has proven to be remarkably enduring; indeed, many historians today would accept in large measure that this is what they strive for.

Recent scholarship, however, has begun to unsettle this rather too convenient approach. Until we have a time machine, it is argued, historians cannot work in the past but examine in the present what evidence has survived from the past. Even historians are creatures of their time and so are in some ways influenced by the spirit of the age no matter how much they may wish to rise above such mundane considerations. The debate between Geoffrey Elton, in the blue corner, representing the traditional historian and E. H. Carr, in the red corner (no necessary significance here in the colour coding), representing a more critical approach to evidence, directly addresses these sorts of concerns. Unlike Elton, Carr contends that since we are all unable to divorce ourselves from contemporary political and social concerns, our approach to historical evidence can never be objective or dispassionate. This challenges the idea of the potential neutrality of the historian as recorder and questions whether we can ever gain access to historical truth.

In certain respects, we can. We know beyond reasonable doubt, for example, that Earl Cornwallis surrendered to the combined forces of North America and France on 19 October 1781, that a Bosnian nationalist assassinated Archduke Franz Ferdinand on 28 June 1914 and that Jawaharlal Nehru declared Indian independence from British rule at midnight, 17 August 1947. Yet historical debates still rage on the historical significances of these events and whether (another preoccupation of this chapter) historical cause can be established by the historian.

The topic of historical causality is neglected at our peril; that one agent, structure or event is the 'cause' of an historical trend is difficult to defend. Although we have access to what might be described as evidential truth, that same evidence can be used in very different ways by historians to construct a narrative and hence interpret the historical significance of the episode. When Percival Spear wrote of the aftermath of the Indian Mutiny, he used limited evidential truths to forge a distinct account that in many respects is open to challenge by historians who have less sympathy for British rule. Theories on nationalist struggles, the role of the individual in historical processes, the nature of imperial power and so on will thus shape how historians view evidence.

Carr concluded that evidence and theory must be in continual dialogue, that is, theories must be tested against evidence and evidence viewed through the lens of theory. The theory in question can be that suggested by Gareth Stedman Jones to historians of Chartism. Without digging up a single new fact, Stedman Jones has suggested an approach to existing evidence that has utterly transformed the way modern historians think about both Chartism as a movement and popular politics more generally.

These, then, are the sorts of questions we should bear in mind when approaching the past. The past is gone – we can never gain access to it except through the evidence that has survived to the present. What we do with that evidence determines the sort of accounts that are written.

Further Reading

E. H. Carr (2001) [1961] *What is History?*
Codell Carter (2003) *The Rise of Causal Concepts of Disease: Case Histories.*
R. G. Collingwood (1961) *The Idea of History.*
Geoffrey Elton (2002) [1967] *The Practice of History.*
John Gaddis (2002) *The Landscape of History: How Historians Map the Past.*
Mark Hewitson (2014) *History and Causality.*
Stephen Kern (2004) *A Cultural History of Causality. Science, Murder Novels, and Systems of Thought.*
Joan W. Scott (2007) *The Politics of the Veil.*
Gareth Stedman Jones (1983) 'Rethinking Chartism', in *The Languages of Class.*
Miles Taylor (1996) 'Rethinking the Chartists: Searching for Synthesis in the Historiography of Chartism'.
Dorothy Thompson (1984) *Chartism: Popular Politics in the Industrial Revolution.*
www.history.ac.uk/ihr/Focus/Whatishistory/carr1.html.

22 Ordering of Time

Introduction

This chapter explores the connection between history and time. The very idea of time, its relationship to human history and our understanding of it as either circular, coming back on itself, linear where it moves inextricably forward or as existing in isolated pockets of experience, differs within *and* across cultures. Notions of time then relate to the nature of society, for example, whether the society under review is pre-literate, agrarian or advanced industrial. Time is also a site of struggle; the modern world is the outcome of a reordering of time driven by capitalist rationalization.

Historians tend to order past time by slicing it up into epochs and periods, but there are incongruities in so doing. The decade that we call the 1960s is not necessarily congruent with the 'sixties' as an historical period. The 1960s is measurable as a block of time, not so the cultural phenomena that we associate with the 'sixties'. And as a distinct period that, for example, was detectable in the United States, France, Britain and Italy, it may have passed almost without trace in, say, South America or the Soviet Union.

Questions follow from this. What are the elements that might be associated with historical periods? To be a Victorian, for example, is to be associated with a particular time but also with an historical style. Think Victorian and, more likely than not, we can conjure up a world of extreme richness and extreme poverty – shoeless children working in chimneys and gentlemen in top hats making their way through the London fog carrying silver-topped canes. Sex and hypocrisy sleep together. When do historical periods begin and end? Is the decade we call the 'sixties' actually a discrete period with its own associations of free love and countercultural protest, quite unlike the period that came before it, the 'age of austerity' characterized by war, food shortages and drabness? Answers to questions such as these and to others like it must always be given in the knowledge that historians impose 'periods', 'eras', 'epochs' and 'ages' on time. In a recent controversy at the University of Oxford about a demand for the removal of a statue of Cecil Rhodes with unpleasant imperialist associations, the Chancellor of the university was not alone in saying that 'you can't rewrite history'. This is, of course, precisely what historians do, and our conception and reconception of a period is a great aid in this endeavour.

22.1 Time, History, Modernity

To live in any modern Western society is to be a narrative junkie. We crave stories (in whatever medium) that have a beginning, middle and end. These narratives relate primarily to an understanding of time that we think we know best – our own lives. Time is projected towards an end-point, moving forward in stages, which Shakespeare in *As You Like It* identified succinctly as infant, schoolchild, lover, soldier, wise man or woman ('justice') and old age ('pantaloon'). Finally, there is second childhood – 'sans teeth, sans eyes, sans taste, sans everything' – and then death. Time in our own personal 'life cycle' is circular. From the writer of the book of *Ecclesiastes*, however, we learn there is a 'season set for everything, a time for every experience under heaven'. Yet:

> Only that will happen
> Which has happened,
> Only that occurs
> Which has occurred;
> There is nothing new
> Beneath the sun!

Time in an advanced, industrial society is conceived – not as cyclical – but progressive; it runs in a forward direction. It is linear. It has a beginning, middle and end with the next age seemingly improving on the last. Although personal cyclical time and public linear time cannot be reconciled, important questions arise: where does this sense of time as progressive and linear come from, and why is it important for historians?

Understandings of the passing of time are dependent upon social factors such as age and gender as well as culture. Educationalists and psychologists have suggested, for example, that children understand the passing of time in wholly different ways from adults. They soon learn that the day is broken down, seemingly for the convenience of grown-ups. There is a time to get up, a time to work and a time to play and, most certainly, a time to go to bed. With the onset of industrialization came differing understandings of time in the experiences of women, men and children depending upon the work that they did and the roles that they performed. In this respect, some feminist historians have regarded time as socially constructed through the domestic or private sphere in which the experience of so-called 'maternal' or 'family' time prevails. For men there was the experience of work and decision-making in the public sphere, influenced by other factors such as social class.

Social historian Tamara Hareven (1937–2002) examined 'family time' and compared it to 'historical time' in a New England industrial community, emphasizing how perceptions of time vary in different places and cultures:

> Historical time is generally defined as a linear chronological movement of changes in a society over decades or centuries, while individual lifetime is measured according to age. But age and chronology both need social contexts to be meaningful. Social age is different from chronological age: in certain societies, a twelve-year-old is an adolescent; in others, he is old. How were typical lives 'timed' in the past, and how did these life-course patterns fit into their economic, institutional, and demographical setting?
>
> (Hareven, 1983, p. 59)

Time works differently for adults and children and, critically, within different contexts. As the male experience of time has been dominant over female experiences of time in modern or industrial societies, it is the 'chronological' and linear understanding of time that dominates history as both a process and as a discipline. To answer fully the question of why this should be so, however, we must move beyond understanding time through personal experience and the narratives of our own existences. While individual lifetimes are measured according to the particular social context of age and gender, industrial or 'historical time' (as Hareven put it) is the linear movement of change in the public sphere and is measured conventionally over years, decades and centuries.

Divisions between pre-industrial and industrial approaches to time and history are profound. Pre-industrial societies or pre-literate societies had no idea of time running either forwards or backwards. As there was no established or agreed chronology, there could be no established or agreed calendar. It was impossible to conceive history as either linear or progressive. The chronology of past events could not, therefore, be determined by objective criteria. In pre-industrial societies there could be no assumption that any event had any universal significance, not least because of the absence in these societies of a recognized dating system. Nor could it be assessed for its significance or be seen objectively as part of an historical pattern or trend.

Sociologists and anthropologists have revealed something of the comprehension of time in different parts of the world. When the anthropologist Pierre Bourdieu (1930–2002) studied Algerian peasants in the late 1950s and early 1960s, painstakingly retrieving the social and economic world of the indigenous Kabyle Berbers, he observed that time in this society was understood as 'so many experiences' that existed in 'self-enclosed units', usually with some social, political or religious significance but not at any rate as industrial society assumed time as part of a continuous line leading to an endpoint in history:

> [E]vents in the past are located by reference to memorable occurrences: one speaks of 'the year in which there was misery', 'the year in which there was a plague', 'in which there was snow for many years', or, in Algiers, 'the year when the ship burned in the harbour'. Temporal points of reference are just so many experiences. One must avoid seeing here points of division, which would presuppose the notion of regular measured intervals, that is to say, a special conception of the temporal. The islands of time which are defined by these landmarks are not apprehended as segments of a continuous line, but rather so many self-enclosed units.
> (Bourdieu, 1963, p. 59)

Subjectively, members of such societies could measure the *relative* ages of say the elder, the novice or, indeed, the *relative* importance of an event compared to another event: one year becomes the year of the drought, another the year of the exploding volcano. Without an agreed method of measuring and keeping time, however, they could not conceive of 'eras', 'ages' or 'periods' any more than they would measure in objective terms the age of an individual within a group.

In contrast, attitudes towards time in the West are tied to the industrial process of the last couple of hundred years or so. In the phenomenon of industrialization and all that accompanied it, we find a critical divide over time and between cultures. According to Peter Laslett's *The World We Have Lost* (1965), time before industrialization was located in the rhythm – not of the machine – but of the natural seasons and with it the organization of pre-industrial family life. Rural time had a different shape from what was to become 'urban time'; time measured not by clock but by season. Weather, the movements of the moon and sun, sowing and harvesting, dictated the cycles of rural life, while feast days, fast days and days dedicated to the saints maintained religion at the centre of rural life. As the first industrial nation, Britain was at the apogee of much that was to develop elsewhere. 'Time-discipline' imposed on workers newly arrived from the countryside, according to the historian E. P. Thompson in his path-breaking *Time, Work, Discipline and Industrial Capitalism* (1967), ensnared the industrial proletariat and chained them to the incessant and remorseless rhythm of the machine. To give one illustration from Flora Tristan, French writer and radical activist, in 1840, we can glimpse just how violently human conceptions of the world were changed by industrialization and how, too, perceptions of time were transformed by the context of what it must have been like to abruptly become (as Thomas Carlyle put it) 'mechanical in head and heart':

> I have seen a steam engine with the strength of 500 horses! Nothing is more formidable than the sight of the motion imparted to these iron masses whose colossal proportions frighten the imagination and seem to surpass the power of man! This motor of hyperbolic power is located in a vast building where it runs a considerable number of machines which work iron and wood. Its enormous polished iron bars go up and down forty or fifty times a minute and impart a backward and forward motion to the tongue of the monster which seems to suck in everything in order to swallow it up, the awesome groans it utters, the rapid turning of the enormous wheel which emerges from the abyss to plunge immediately back again, never revealing more than half of its circumference to the eye, fills one's soul with terror. In the presence of the monster one sees nothing else, one hears nothing but its breathing.
>
> (Tristan, 1840, p. 71)

Like labour itself, time now had a value and a price. Time was money. Taking a place on a production line of a factory or workshop, 'clocking out' eventually became the lot of the industrial working class. Only the pursuits of popular culture, football and the like provided a respite, although with commercialization even the football match came to have a regular kick-off time and was governed by a measurable length of season. It too, therefore, relied on a secular, civil calendar.

With industrialization came urbanization, then the railway and the usurpation of local time by national time. To have a national railway timetable, each major town and city conformed to a nationally agreed time where once localities had kept their own, and railway journeys from, say, London to Bristol took longer according to these clocks than journeys from Bristol to London. Industrialization generally heralded the introduction of both national and international time – Greenwich Mean Time (GMT) – and the notion of linear progression in time. This notion had profound consequences for the understanding and writing of history – whether or not 'progress' or 'decline' could be determined in the present by knowing what happened to civilizations in the past. For Victorians, history worked in the knowledge of the fate that once befell Greece and imperial Rome. As empires rose (such as the British Empire) so too could they fall. In other words, history could run backwards as well as forwards. Herbert Spencer, philosopher, sociologist and social Darwinist, announced in 1851, the same year as the erection of that beacon of Victorian optimism, the Crystal Palace, that progress was evolutionary but that evolution could also run backwards. Like so many others, Spencer was devastated when he learnt that the second law of thermodynamics meant that the world had from its very creation begun to grow cold and become more chaotic: it was degenerating (Spencer, 1862). This is what natural scientists now call entropy. It is this that provided late-Victorian Britain with its most pervasive dialectic, that of progress and degeneration. If 1851 marked the high point of the 'age of equipoise' or the 'age of improvement', by the 1890s notions of degeneration overtook or challenged these ideas of progress. Even Charles Darwin, while optimistic in his *On the Origin of Species* (1859), could offer no guarantee of human progress by the time of the publication of his *Descent of Man* in 1871.

With the context of industrialization (at least in the West) came both a different understanding of the mechanics of time, a changing idea of progress and with it changing ideas of how both society and history worked. The sociologist Emile Durkheim noted how time was divided technically between seconds, minutes, days, months and years but could also be understood through public events such as feasts, rites and public ceremonies which were particular and peculiar to different cultures. Durkheim had in mind, however, the processes of modernity and the differences apparent between mechanical societies (by mechanical he confusingly meant pre-industrial) and organic societies and how in these advanced, industrial societies, time was just another form of globalized commercial property to be bought, sold, bartered or negotiated (Durkheim, 2015, p. 10).

Thus far we have examined the cultural and ideological dimensions of time, but in many respects 'political time' has been the most important in world history. In general, political authority has been exercised in part through an ability to control time. Consider, for example, the fascinating story of how Western global hegemony in the modern period was secured by the imposition of a world system of time. In 1714 the British parliament instituted a prize of £20,000 in order urgently to locate longitude at sea. For centuries, sailors had employed various celestial methods as a means of mapping the vertical lines that circle the globe. The need to measure longitude accurately was urgent for several reasons. Latitude – or the horizontal lines on the globe – was well-known, so well-known in fact that the sea lanes were dangerously crowded with ships sticking to these narrow routes, including pirate ships. Without longitude, the ability to trade across unknown seas, to discover, to conquer would be quite impossible or would remain (like the discovery of America by Columbus) a matter of luck.

Astronomers, from the German Johannes Werner in 1514 to the genius of the Italian Galileo in 1610 – and before them some of the greatest figures from the classical world – had attempted to find the position of a ship by variations of a single method. This method in some way involved mapping the skies, sun, planets and stars and then, in a hideously complex process, measuring the relation of the moon to a point fixed in time and space. Galileo, more simply, even hit on the idea of fixing longitude by measuring the ellipses of the moons of Jupiter. All of this could work, except it was extremely time consuming, not particularly accurate and impossible when skies were cloudy.

The problem of finding longitude, however, was solved finally by a clockmaker who was neither an astronomer nor a gentleman but happened to be a genius. Between 1737 and 1760, John Harrison built four clocks for use on board the British fleet, each an improvement on the last. The fourth was able to overcome the problems of the destabilizing conditions found on board ship to keep time with astonishing accuracy and hence allow navigators to calculate the longitude of the vessel at any time of the day or night, whatever the weather. Harrison was eventually awarded the prize, but it caused more than a ripple of disquiet on otherwise calm naval waters. Although resistant to his method and the very fact of his being a mere maker of mechanical devices, not a 'scientist' steeped in the mysteries of astronomy, the authorities abandoned celestial approaches – that is, those approaches that looked to the sky for a fixed longitudinal point – but decided to retain the convention of using the Observatory at Greenwich as 'Mean Time'. Greenwich, at '0' degrees latitude and longitude, thus became the centre of the world and ships could traverse the seas quicker than ever before. Now Britain controlled both time and space and because of this, Britannia ruled the waves. This invention was unbelievably difficult in conception, long in gestation and painfully drawn out in its delivery, but it had momentous repercussions in the understanding of time in relation to history. Above all, it was to have long-term consequences for Western hegemony, for it can be argued that to control time and space is to control history and the writing of histories.

David Harvey in his book *The Condition of Postmodernity* (1990) argued that money, power and capital combine to ensure that the conquest and control of time and space were never independent of social relations any more than history, and history writing, it might be argued, could be anything else but part of the society from which it emanated. As the enclosure movements transformed the landscape of eighteenth- and nineteenth-century Britain, for instance, so imperialism empowered a new mercantile class. Turnpikes, canals and trains changed special relations (bringing hitherto remote areas 'nearer' to London) and in so doing led to a redistribution of wealth and power. This 'pulverisation of space', Harvey tells us, meant that capital could move faster along lines of communication than ever before, via say the network established by the Rothschild family that spread over Europe in the early part of the nineteenth century. Specifically, during the changes evoked by industrialization, time and space compressed as technological changes increased speeds of travel and communication, transforming relations of distance.

Stephen Kern in his *The Culture of Time and Space 1880–1918* (2003) investigated the apogee of this process at the fin de siècle through the fields of physics, philosophy, psychiatry, sociology, art and literature. He labelled Harvey's description of this process of 'space-time compression' as 'one-sided', arguing that new transportation and communication technologies expanded as well as compressed space-time. Taking the newly invented telephone as an example, he suggested that telephones 'compressed space in that they reduced lived distances' but also expanded space 'by extending the special reach of an individual from one place to another' (p. xii). This 'space-time' relationship was experienced in a variety of ways, according to Kern: in cultural forms such as art, distance, direction and speed. This is especially highlighted between 1880 and 1918 through changing modes of production (Taylorian time management systems in Ford factories, for instance); diplomacy and perceived abilities to communicate quickly across geographical boundaries; cinema and the phonograph, which modified perceptions of the past; luxury liners such as the Titanic and military endeavours like the Schlieffen Plan, which relied on speed. Or take the synchronized wristwatches that were distributed from headquarters and passed along the trenches at the Somme. At precisely 7:30 a.m. on the morning of 1 July 1916, the whistles blew and the greatest loss of life in a single day ever experienced by the British army began. Without the concept of standard time and without the technical means of measuring time, events could not have happened as they did. In any case, war had made time homogeneous once again, experienced not as James Joyce had described it in *Ulysses* (1922) as flowing or broken consciousness or as Marcel Proust in his *Remembrance of Things Past* (1913–1927) had conceived it through memory and private reflection: vague, arbitrary and inexact. Capitalism had rationalized time in areas that would affect the writing and popular understanding of the past. A need to understand the past and to locate the present, however, was not exclusively a product of modernity.

Any reckoning of the relationship between history and an understanding of time must take in, therefore, religious contexts. Rabbi Lord Jonathan Sacks (1948–2020) suggested, for instance, that

> Jewish time is not linear but something more profound. I call it covenantal time. This is time, not as continuous advance, but as a narrative with a beginning and a distant end, in whose midst we are and whose twists and turns continue to surprise us.
>
> (Sacks, 2003, p. 80)

'There is no guarantee of progress', he quickly adds. The Jewish God (as it were) is encountered via the narratives of creation and prophets as a space where humans meet, confront and wrestle with the divine. A God of history is unusual, perhaps unique, among religions and civilizations, for most religions associate God with timelessness, not as a figure to bargain with. As the philosopher Isaiah Berlin recalled, the Jews had 'a great deal of history but all too little geography. Much time, but little space' (ibid).

Figure 22.1 The third of John Harrison's four marine chronometers, now held at the Royal Observatory, Greenwich, London. Started in 1740, it took him nineteen years to build but was then abandoned as too unreliable in his quest to determine longitude at sea

Contributor: Ian Dagnall Commercial Collection/Alamy Stock Photo

Similarly, Islam is a tradition where an idea of linear history or history as progressive is quite absent. There is, however, a definite chronology at work, a need to measure time for profound reasons attached to religious law but where there appears to be a real difference between Western and Eastern conceptions of time or at least between Islam and Judeo-Christianity:

> The Qur'anic vision of history rests upon a certain conception of time and space and a certain style to express that conception. Islam and history are coeval: 'It was God who called you Muslims from days of old' (22:78). A community or *umma*, of God has from time immemorial been the 'witnesses of God on earth, aligning to virtue and forbidding evil'. It is a 'community of the centre' which came into being with Adam. Thereafter, the Qur'an pans over a landscape where time is less a chronology than a continuum, where Abraham, Moses, Jesus and Mohammed are all described in a grammatical tense which one is tempted to call the eternal present. The whole of history is present at once to God. Within this design, events are arranged in clusters repetitive in form. This means that a Qur'anic *quissa* or tale, is closer in function and meaning to a 'case in point', an 'affair' or even a 'parable' than it is to a story or narrative.
>
> (Khaldi, 1994, p. 8)

Instead of the industrial model of time first conceived in the West, history is a 'continuum' or an 'eternal present'. In the concept of Islamic time and its expression through Arabic, there is no sense at all of past, present or future or yet of a 'continuum', but rather time is 'complete or incomplete' depending on whether or not an action willed by Allah has been fulfilled:

> The link of causality that appears to rule the world and human life becomes subordinate to Allah, and natural causes give way to divine will. As a rule, God does not interrupt the continuity of events . . . though He is able to intervene at any moment by what is commonly termed a miracle but simply means an interruption of His customary activity. Atomism was not only most congenial to a vision of God acting instantaneously in the world as the sole true cause, it also proved most closely akin to Arabic grammar, which lacks genuine verbs for 'to be' and 'to become'. Neither does Arabic employ the tenses of past, present and future. Instead, it uses verbal aspects of complete and incomplete, marking the degree to which an action has been realized or is yet to be realized without distinguishing precisely between present and future.
>
> (Bowering, 1997, p. 60)

Other, if different, understandings of time can be also taken from Buddhism or even Aboriginal Dreamtime. In all these traditions, our understanding of time and history should be deeply contextualized.

22.2 Newton and the 'Time Reckoner'

A Scottish grandmother named Helen Duncan was arrested under the 1735 Witchcraft Act, along with a seventy-two-year-old Londoner, Jane Yorke. The year was 1944. By consulting a linear timeline or chronology, it can surely be deduced very quickly that these arrests were not prompted by a society that believed these women were actually witches and there was not a general belief in witchcraft. Thus, without knowing much about their cases but because of an agreed chronology of events, it can be said emphatically that the witch craze belongs to an earlier period and that these women could not represent a continuity from fifteenth- and sixteenth-century Europe, seventeenth-century America or even parts of present-day Africa, although comparisons between modern Africa and pre-modern Europe are fraught with dangers. It turns out, instead, that both women were seen as security risks in wartime Britain. Séances held by each of the women, at the bequest of the apparently grieving relatives of serving seamen, had inadvertently revealed the names of torpedoed ships whose fate had not yet been announced by the British authorities. As survivors of these vessels had fed details to the women contrary to the best interests of the war effort, the Witchcraft Act became the most convenient way to bring these apparent fraudsters to trial and to shut them up. The Act was not abolished until 1951.

The mere existence of an agreed and rational chronology could look critically at seemingly unimportant historical events such as the incarceration of two apparently harmless old ladies. The stakes (no pun intended) were higher, but it was equally essential for Christendom in the Middle Ages to record with accuracy the birth and death of Christ, to know precisely when Christmas should be marked in relation to the solar and lunar calendars. The overall purpose was to use astronomy and mathematics to confirm that biblical sources could support an agreed chronology and to allow Christians to celebrate Easter (and other moveable feasts) together and at the same time. Theologically speaking this was vital. Without the precise ability to build a Christian chronology that could pinpoint the Creation and the Incarnation, it would be impossible to calculate the End of Days.

One such 'time reckoner' was the historian we know as the Venerable Bede (672–735 CE) (of whom we speak more in Chapter 2). He argued for the concept of a Leap Year as a way of catching up on a calendar which was losing days in relation to the really quite advanced calculations about the motion of the Sun around the Earth and the measurements of equinoxes. In doing this, he used a specially designed sundial and observed the tides around Northumbria in northern England. By the time he had finished, the word 'calculator' had entered the language, although to what extent Bede was a prime mover in this enterprise is contested. Certainly, the Muslim world (and the Jews of Iberia) had stolen a march on Christianity, with calendars of much greater accuracy and complexity, while Bede himself tends to be placed into the context of contemporary and near contemporary writers on time and the calendar, especially Irish commentators. More recently the Bishop of Lincoln, Bishop Grosseteste (c.1170–1253), has been especially noted for his ground-breaking work on the medieval calendar and his influence on those that came subsequently (Flood et al., 2013).

Bede, however, took much of his chronology from Dionysius Exiguus (d. c.544), agreeing with his dating of the birth of Christ and designating this year as 'year one'. He also shared with Dionysius a concern properly to date Easter. As an abbot (some say monk), Dionysius was summoned to Rome to catalogue the pontifical archives and by 525, at the bequest of Pope St John I, he created a chronology that is to some extent in use still today, introducing the term Christian Era to our lexicon.

The origin of the 'Christian Era' was argued to be the Incarnation. What had previously been known as the 'Era of Martyrs' became known in Italy and Spain (in the eighth and ninth centuries) and in England (in the tenth century) as 'Era of Incarnation' (Stiglmayr, 1909). There had been earlier attempts to date the Creation of the world. In the third century Julius Africanus (c.160–c.240 CE) established a Christian chronology that was to prove a huge hostage to fortune as it predicted the Second Coming of Christ (it would be around 500 CE). What were known as Pauline divisions of time (named after Paul the Apostle) charted a journey between Creation and Apocalypse: the age before Mosaic Law (the state of nature), the Mosaic Law (erroneously, it was thought, still accepted by the Jews) and the age of grace under Christ. This age would conclude with the Second Coming. Where precisely the present was located in the Christian chronology, however, was something that Calabrian Abbot Joachim of Fiore (1135–1202 CE) elucidated with his proposal for history and time to be understood through a trinity of ages: Father (before Christ), Son (the time of Christ) and the age of the Holy Ghost (the future). His was an apocalyptic vision that assumed that eschatology – the study of church doctrine – would reveal a divine plan that could chart all human experience to the End of Days, or at least this is how it looks to the eyes of most modern historians.

Bernard McGinn's *The Calabrian Abbot: Joachim of Fiore in the History of Western Thought* (1985) argued that Joachim's 'theology of history' was similar in range and method to the better known St Augustine of Hippo (354–430 CE). Works by Augustine such as *De Civitate Dei* – or the City of God – posited ages starting with Adam and Noah, which finished with Christ and the present. Before the Christian era, however, historians such as Herodotus (*c.*490 BCE) had said little about chronology, with dating deduced by using the reigns of Emperors and Kings. Indeed, much of classical scholarship, as we saw in Chapter 1, was concerned with locating golden ages and to a limited extent at least, as in the examples from Shakespeare and *Ecclesiastes* with which we started the chapter, recurrent cycles of ages.

A quest for mathematical exactitude united attempts by medieval scholars such as Bede and the natural philosopher and mathematician Sir Isaac Newton (1642–1727) to establish a Christian chronology. The imperative to establish both religious and civil calendars coincided in the seventeenth century. It became vital to know where humanity was on the journey to judgement and redemption and to have a chronology that would allow 'epochs' and 'eras' to be identified and examined for the purpose of charting the rational progress of time. Time, the measurement of time and the theological need to agree a calendar, therefore, simultaneously emerged out of the Enlightenment, predated perhaps by the work of scholars such as Bishop Grosseteste (*c.*1175–1253) whose command of Jewish, Islamic and early Christian interpretations of time and apparent understanding of natural phenomena anticipated some of the scientific assumptions of the European Enlightenment (Flood et al., 2013). In any case, this is critically important for historians because we, uniquely perhaps, work with time and chronologies in order to make sense of the world.

Newton's chronology provided a new basis for measuring time, conforming to laws of motion that he argued governed the entire universe. The *Chronology of Ancient Kingdoms Amended*, published a year after his death in 1728, included a preface of 'the first memory of things in Europe', in other words, a chronology of what he regarded as significant historical events that demonstrated how history moves forward. Yet it was one also deeply influenced by Christianity. Taking his dating system from the French Jesuit scholar Dionysius Petavius (1583–1652), who had first set out the BC/AD categories in 1627 and who wrote *The History of the World or, an Account of Time*, which was published posthumously in 1659, Newton devised a system of time that was absolute in the sense that it removed anomalies associated with cultural and religious differences. Newton was, however, standing on the shoulders of previous giants in the field, something that Grosseteste also acknowledged tacitly.

Newton's assumptions remained those of the Christian narrative of creation (birth of Jesus), death (Crucifixion) and resurrection (second coming). The story of Jesus in the New Testament is an account of man and God, an account of the ages of man and the fate and redemption of humanity. After all, this was a religious man who dedicated much of his time trying to turn base metals into gold, proving the existence of fairies or determining the best theological course for rebuilding the second Jewish Temple destroyed in 70 CE. The time Newton spent, however, on cosmology or what we might construe as modern physics, also turned out to be significant for the writing of history. As the historian William Gallois argued, time from the perspective of the Enlightenment is 'neutral and progressive':

History is therefore utterly dependent upon a new means of picturing time which emerges in western Europe at a distinct moment. It conceives of itself as neutral and progressive because it is self-evidently different from earlier conceptions of time, and because it is part of a complex of ideas about space and time which enabled huge advances in productivity, in making histories as much as in making paintings or machines. As a human creation, this idea of historical time is just as subject to critique and innovation as any other invention.

(Gallois, 2007, p. 46)

While Newtonian ideas of time were born from Christianity and nurtured in western European society as a continuation of a specifically Christian attempt to understand time, historians continue to owe Newton a debt for another important reason. Simply measuring time was once *the* basic task of the historian – to chronicle all that has been and to use prophecy to reveal all that might yet be. With Enlightenment science and rationality came an attempt to construct a narrative of progress. The establishment of a chronology was essential in order that historians could lay the foundations from objective historical reasoning. Future historians could identify specific eras, periods or epochs or 'timeframes' within which events could be organized, analyzed and understood. No longer could the 'year in which there was a plague', as Pierre Bourdieu's Algerian peasants might have put it, be understood in isolation or the origins of history dated arbitrarily from the Creation or the Incarnation.

Newton's 'general laws' of the universe applied to the writing of history, an 'absolute' chronology that was true in all times and all places – and as such it was constant. As the time of an historical event could be known precisely, it could also be compared to an event on another part of the timeline. An explosion of European writings and works of art in the fourteenth, fifteenth and sixteenth centuries, for instance, suggested, when taken together, a new sense of individualism – a Renaissance.

Because of Enlightenment-inspired approaches to chronology, historians can make comparisons over time and analyze the meaning of events. As Wilcox put it, following this Western innovation in history writing and historical knowledge, 'judgement follows measurement' and not the other way around:

The dating systems in use before Newton were not absolute and did not contain the implications about absolute time that characterize the BC/AD system. Pre-Newtonian time had no conceptual grid to give universal applicability to numbers. Dates in that time were tied to specific themes, events and moral lessons, and they gave a meaning and shape of their own to the events they dated. Without the conceptual grid the fundamental sequence/measurement and judgement was radically different from our own. Whatever our attitude towards the function of history and the possibility of objectivity, we assume that an historian answers the question of when an event occurred before determining its meaning; judgement follows measurement. . . . Historians writing before Newton reversed this order. Events created their own time frames. Before locating an event in time, the histories had to make judgements about its meaning and its thematic relation to other events. New insights, synthesis, or major events, such as the rise of Rome, the coming of Christianity, the development of modern nations, or the revival of culture in the Renaissance all created their own time frames . . . the time frame did not include a group of events; a group of events contained the time frame.

(Wilcox, 1987, p. 9)

Post-Newtonian historians could now judge and measure events against an agreed and 'rational' timeline, determining both the existence and importance of distinct historical periods:

the 'antique' period, the 'Middle Ages', the Reformation and counter Reformation, Renaissance, Enlightenment and so on. Although this timeline has become difficult to defend from a postmodernist perspective (Chapter 7), with history seemingly unfolding in a progressive direction that relentlessly moves forward, a judgement about the importance of an historic event within a chronology was easier to agree when the whole of Europe went over to the Gregorian calendar. It is worth recounting this story briefly because it was to have consequences for Western historical practice.

The Gregorian reforms in western Europe introduced an arithmetical system that counted days in a similar way as the previous Julian calendar, a product of Pagan Rome. It allowed for the drift caused by previously incorrect calculations of the year's length in relation to the vernal equinox. As the Gregorian dropped ten days to correct this error and brought the calendar back into line with the seasons, historians could agree a chronology of events from mainland Catholic Europe to its Protestant fringes, which in turn required general agreement based on simple, verifiable and agreed historical facts. How, for instance, could two people die on the same date but not on the same day? The explanation could be that one died in Spain, which had been one of the first countries to adopt the Gregorian calendar, while the other person died in Protestant England, which was among the last. (Scotland had made the change in 1600.) Understanding the precise occurrence of battles, enthronements, peace treaties and plagues, dating for tombstones, all recorded by contemporaries either according to the Julian or to the Gregorian calendars, still today creates enormous difficulties for historians. Even the relatively straightforward business of dating a birth is contentious: certificates often append both the Old Style (OS) and New Style (NS), expressed as (for example) 1752/53. The first date denotes OS, the second NS. Both are correct.

Such difficulties were overshadowed in the early twentieth century with the revolutionary transformation in the measurement and concept of time brought about by the work of Albert Einstein. Contrary to Newton, Einstein established that time was subjective, not absolute. This theory suggested that there could no longer be a single 'objective' clock but many clocks spread across the universe, 'each telling a different correct time'. Einstein used his now famous metaphor of the moving train to argue that while space was a fixed and absolute concept, time was relative. Placing a clock at either end of a moving train, Einstein imagined a flash of light that illuminated each clock face. Sitting in the middle of the moving train, the clocks told the same time. When a stationary person observed the moving train from a platform, however, the flash lit up the clocks at what appeared to be very slightly different times. The work of Einstein has had little direct impact on historians, not least because the changes in time he talked of occur only under exceptional circumstances. However, the principles that arose from this work suggested two things. The first was that time is not absolute and unchanging but relative. The second is important for historians because it suggests that the observation of time changes time itself. That is, time is not a Newtonian constant only to be measured objectively from the outside but is something that can be experienced subjectively.

22.3 Time, History and the Shape of Things to Come

Futurology is no longer a respectable form of history. It aimed to predict the future by understanding historical trends in the present. Very often the suggestion that history had predictive qualities is to be found among previous generations of historians but also with non-academic commentaries on the past and particularly, perhaps, in science fiction. Tales such as *The Time Machine* (1895) and *The War in the Air* (1908) that came from the pen of H. G. Wells (1866–1946) often saw the positive benefits of science to human development. Yet by the time of his death Wells, autodidact, author and socialist, was pessimistic about the direction of history. His *Outline of History*, published in twenty-four fortnightly parts from November 1919 until November the following year, sold two million copies and was translated into many languages. Running to 780 pages, this was no sketch and neither could we describe it as an outline. Nor, indeed, was his *Short History* – published in 1922 and revised constantly until 1945 – actually short. Its range, however, was simply breath-taking. The opening chapter began with 'The world in space', where Wells described the Earth as 'a spheroid, a sphere slightly compressed, orange fashion'. By locating the origins of time in space, not with Creation, the birth of Jesus or the Council of Nicaea (where in 325 the Christian calendar became largely independent from the Jewish calendar), he immediately took issue with the Christian account of human origins and traditional Christian chronology.

As we have seen, changes in understandings of time that led to ideas of history as linear and forward-looking were histories heavily influenced by both Christianity and the Enlightenment. In the shadow of the two world wars of the twentieth century, however, popular histories such as those by Oswald Spengler, Arnold Toynbee and H. G. Wells did not necessarily or inevitably point forward. Indeed, in his fictional *Shape of Things to Come* (1933), Wells made sneering reference to the 'Chronological Institute', a band of enthusiastic amateurs who from at least the mid-1850s produced transactions of their deliberations and who underwent a review of 'the cardinal dates in our social evolution':

> Until the Chronological Institute has completed its present labours of revision and defined the cardinal dates in our social evolution, it is best to refer our account of the development of man's mind and will throughout this hectic period of human experience to the clumsy and irrelevant computation by centuries before and after the Christian Era, that is still current. As we have explained more fully in a previous book . . . we inherit this system of historical pigeonholes from Christendom; that arbitrary chequerwork of hundred-year blocks was imposed upon the entire Mediterranean and Atlantic literatures for two thousand years, and it still distorts the views of history of all but the alertest minds. The young student needs to be constantly on his guard against its false divisions . . . we talk of the 'eighteenth century', and we think of fashions and customs and attitudes that are characteristic of a period extending from the Treaty of Westphalia in C.E. 1642 [which was actually 1648] to the Napoleonic collapse in C.E. 1815; we talk of the 'nineteenth century', and the pictures and images evoked are those of the gas-lighting and steam-transport era, from after the distressful years of post-Napoleonic recovery to the immense shock of the World War in C.E. 1914. The phase 'twentieth century', again, calls forth images of the aeroplane, the electrification of the world and so forth; but an aeroplane was an extremely rare object in the air until 1914 (the first got up in 1905), and the replacement of the last steam railway train and the last steamship was not completed until the nineteen-forties. It is a tiresome waste of energy to oblige each generation of young minds to learn first of all in any unmeaning pattern of centuries and then to correct that first crude arrangement, so that this long-needed revision of our chronology is one that will be very welcome to every teacher. Then from the very outset he or she will be able to block out the story of our race in significant masses.
>
> (Wells, 2005, pp. 25–6)

This section dwells on the problems posed by notions of 'progress' and its relation to the non-linear development of history to the writing of history itself. To be able to identify histories that are implicitly either linear or non-linear in their methodological prejudices is an essential skill for the historian. Difficulties remain of defining periods or even the problems involved in establishing the appropriate timeframe to be studied, from geological time, which moves at a glacial pace and begins before human beings occupied the planet, to spans of time that cover mere decades or even a single year, as, for example, does William Fishman's *East End 1888: Life in a London Borough Among the Labouring Poor* (1988).

In the world in which Wells wrote and worked, it was quite natural for historians to ascribe periods with certain characteristics and attribute to them moral values. It was also quite normal, increasingly so between the First and Second World Wars, to be pessimistic about the forward trajectory of history. Both popular and professional histories, however, are now built on time-lines that break time down into stages of development with 'civilization' as the most advanced stage of history. Among eminent writers of the past who identified stages of development were Adam Smith (1723–1790) with his unfolding economic-based model (the Age of Hunters, the Age of Shepherds, the Age of Agriculture, the Age of Commerce), Auguste Comte who attempted to theorize social progress through a philosophy of science and came up with three stages (Theological, Metaphysical, Positive) and Karl Marx who also had used historical stages as a way of explaining historical movement (see Chapter 6) that could be scientifically observed and predicted. Astonishingly, as late as the 1980s, archaeological survey courses at reputable universities in the United Kingdom maintained the three-stages model of time – 'Civilization', 'Barbarism' and 'Savagery' – that had been established by the anthropologist and social evolutionist Lewis Henry Morgan (1815–1881) in his *Ancient Society* (1877). By presenting history in stages and attributing to them certain properties and characteristics, historians of very early societies could make value judgements, which, if applied to the contemporary world, would label, say, the Aboriginals of Australia as barbaric or savage.

Equally, historians, while influenced by science and scientists (Newton and Einstein are obvious examples) remain ignorant of the methods and approaches with which scientists would measure change and locate the origins of life. Here time is measured as geological time or as 'deep time' where physical factors such as destruction of rock formations or the onset of an ice age act as 'turning points' or 'watersheds' in history but remain evolutionary. Modern historians envisage time differently, but they sometimes connect time with stage theories. Jacques Le Goff, including in his book on *The Birth of Europe* (2005), on the one hand, identifies 'antique', 'medieval' and 'modern' as the dominant divisions in Western historiography, while R. G. Collingwood (1889–1943), on the other, wondered what determined an age as 'modern' especially when contemporaries would never have recognized it as such, and the boundaries between these artificial periods might be decided. These are legitimate questions for historians. How then do we understand the relationship between history and time after Newton and Einstein and after the discredited futurology of Wells and others? After all, Greeks and Romans would not consider themselves to be ancient, and if we think of ourselves as historical beings, we may think of ourselves as 'modern', perhaps – but only in comparison with them.

The historian Penelope J. Corfield in her *Time and the Shape of History* (2007) has called for a return to 'big histories' and an end to histories that are so narrow and particular that they have the tendency to disconnect one 'period' from another. The trend for historians to research, write and teach according to these confined periods prevents consideration of *longue durée* narratives of the type now routinely written, for example, by geologists. Corfield's is an important work in the philosophy of history and in some senses takes us back to histories pioneered by Wells and those popular historians of that period who underlined the big picture and the long term, stressing continuity over change in history writing. It also recalls the *Annales* approach to history, which we outlined in Chapter 10.

Corfield was a prominent figure in 1970s historiography, part of a generation that, unwittingly perhaps, became ever more specialized and narrower in their concerns but which has now emerged from the wreckage of 1960s feminist and Marxist historiography. She sought histories that confronted 'diachronic change', that is, change which looks over the long term, even the deep geological past of millennia – historical change which is not simply determined by considerations of gender or class. From this perspective, micro change prompted by changes to the environment, shifts in religious or secular movements or natural environmental disasters like the Lisbon earthquake of 1755, produced 'turning points' as important as the more conventional watersheds such as political revolution, invasion or war. This diachronic approach is, she tells us, in sharp contrast to the 'synchronic immersion' of specialized periods and histories focusing on a fairly specific moment in time that in recent decades has seen the kind of narrow history inevitably produced by professional historians addressing narrow subject communities (Corfield, 2007, pp. 14–15).

Whichever way historians (professional or otherwise) define historical periods, great and momentous events are made important by the writing of history. These watersheds can define a generation or even a century. Yet, these watersheds do not always survive as seminal events. The attacks on Washington and New York in September 2001 – or the so-called Arab Spring of 2011 – seem destined to define our own age, and the surprise attack on Pearl Harbor in December 1941 is clearly of enormous importance to the development of the twentieth century. But who now remembers an event such as the Papal Aggression of 1850? This attempt to reintroduce a Catholic hierarchy of bishops into Britain for the first time since the Reformation was a moment when anti-Catholicism in England bubbled violently to the surface, only to submerge just as quickly. Look through the records of the period, almost any record, and we find priests attacked in the street, churches burnt to the ground, and editorials of the *Times* which were equally inflammatory in tone as intention. This so-called watershed in British religious and political life, the entry of the post-Reformation Catholic Church into mainstream British social and ecclesiastical life, iconically every bit as large and important as an aircraft hitting the Twin Towers of the World Trade Centre, in the end produced relatively minor aftershocks and has all but disappeared from view.

These watersheds or 'turning points' are constructed by historians, but historians can also suggest counterfactual histories that work along different timelines. What would have happened, for instance, if the British had prevailed at the battle of Saratoga in 1777 and the American colonists failed to raise a coalition of major European powers against the colonial power? Not only would this momentous event have failed to constitute part of the American War of Independence – known universally as the American Revolution – but also the course of modern history would have been radically different. Such counterfactual history is useful as a questioning device and allows history to be imagined along different imaginative tramways. Niall Ferguson in his *Virtual History: Alternatives and Counterfactuals* (1997) described these 'what if' histories as an exercise in 'imaginary time'. In any case these scenarios are sparingly used among historians and probably rightly so. Ferguson's target was the Christian determinism that so troubled Wells and the seemingly inevitable progress of history (Creation, the Fall, the election of Israel, the Age of Prophets, exile and the rise of Rome, the Incarnation, the Crucifixion, the Resurrection and promise of return). He was offended too by the determinism of other grand theories but most particularly Marxism (the stages of primitive Communism, Feudalism, Capitalism and back to Communism) and their apparent sense of progressive history as inevitable. To this extent, he had a serious point to make.

Yet the need for narratives remains. Although these narratives differ radically from East to West with the 'shape of things to come' imagined in spectacularly different terms across societies and at different moments in history, to tell or listen to a story is one very powerful way of being human. It also true that periods are still attributed characteristics. To be a Victorian, as we shall see in the next section of this chapter, is to be associated with a particular time but also with an historical style. The question is why we associate characteristics to a particular period. Likewise, how do we determine when a period begins and ends? When, for example, did the 1960s or the 'sixties' happen? Dating, chronology and periodization present profound theoretical problems for history as a discipline. How do we decide on periods as worthy of research and study? By looking at very definite and readily identifiable periods, we shall now attempt to answer that question but also examine how we establish the terminal dates of any given period.

22.4 Events, People and Periods: What Is 'Victorian'? When Were the 'Sixties'?

It is New Year's Eve, 1959. As the chimes of midnight sound, party revellers throw off their stiff suits and wool skirts, changing into Afghan coats and the horribly bright hippie gear that is to become a motif of the 'sixties'. Hairstyles become a remarkable sight. 'Teenagers' suddenly look less like their parents: a subspecies has evolved; although there had been earlier sightings with Teddy Boys, Rockers and Beatniks. Someone changes the vinyl record from jitterbug, skittle or plain 'rock n roll' to Eastern-influenced music that tears conventional orchestration to shreds (Marwick, 2005). Dancing stops and, sitting cross-legged on the floor, partygoers actually listen to the 'composition' as if it were a work of art: not a conventional work of art but one that is innovative and experimental. Out goes the canon of accepted art, in comes the psychedelic. Men can dress like women; women like 'chicks'. They all fervently hope they die before they get old. Guilty sex becomes open sex and even public sex. With the introduction of the contraceptive pill, love becomes 'free' while abortion is available on demand. There is no church next Sunday, just a drug-fuelled spiritualism heralding a sudden and catastrophic secularization (Brown, 2009). Rigid social hierarchies, repressive sexuality, respect for all forms of authority – from the park keeper to the family doctor – dissolve. Racism slowly becomes unacceptable and a plethora of opposition to conventional politics through civil disobedience is born with the Civil Rights Movement and violent opposition to the American war in Vietnam. Countercultural movements seemingly transform every area of life and every institution, including the university, much to the disgust and puzzlement of establishment figures such as the respected and vastly influential Cold War diplomat, the American George F. Kennan (1904–2005). Kennan is instructive because he represented an older generation who were marked by the rise of Communism (to which he became an implacable foe) and fascism (to which he became briefly attached) and the duty or disciple of war and public service. Kennan represents everything that the 'sixties' did not:

> And one would like to warn these young people that in distancing themselves so recklessly not only from the wisdom but from the feelings of parents, they are hacking at their own underpinnings – and even those of people as yet unborn. There can be no greater illusion than the belief that one can treat one's parents unfeelingly and with contempt and yet expect that their own children will some day treat one otherwise; for such people break the golden chain of affection that binds the generations and gives continuity and meaning to life.
>
> (Kennan, 1968, p. 14)

What a party. 'Turn on, tune in, drop out.' Then in 1979 with the election of Margaret Thatcher in Britain and in 1980 with Ronald Reagan in the United States, the final nail is driven in the coffin. The hangover begins.

Thus the 'sixties' is a period labelled as such by historians – not simply a decade measured on a timeline. Whatever constitutes this period had, in fact, started well before New Year's Eve

1959 and ended just a few years before the election of Thatcher and Reagan. But then historians select aspects of history such as these as worthy of particular attention. They construct chronologies *through* their narratives, in the stories they tell, breaking down time into comprehensible chunks that they define as 'periods', 'ages' or 'eras'. Their descriptions of a period eventually become illustrative of that period. Of course, historical periods rarely, if ever, fit the exact contours of a decade or century. Arthur Marwick (1936–2006) in his comprehensive if overlong work on the 'sixties', *Cultural Revolution in Britain, France, Italy and the United States* (1998), saw the period as beginning in 1957–1958 with various cultural changes and ending in 1974 with the results of a massive oil price rise in 1973, brought on by the Yom Kippur war and a crisis in the Middle East that is with us still. From this came mass unemployment and a more conservative politics. Marwick also made clear the difference between a period and a decade, between history and time:

> Is it legitimate to make contrasts and comparisons between the 'fifties', the 'sixties', the 'seventies'? We readily think in decades, but that is only because we count the years as we would our fingers or our toes. In historical study we do need a concept of periods, or eras, or ages, though such periods do not automatically coincide with decades or with centuries, nor do they have any imminent or natural existence, independent of the analytical needs of historians. Periodization, the chopping up of the past into chunks or periods, is essential because the past in its entirety is so extensive and complex; but different historians will identify different chunks, depending upon their interests and the countries they are dealing with – a periodization which suits the study of Western Europe will not suit the study of Africa or Japan. The implication of periodization is that particular chunks of time contain a certain unity, in that events, attitudes, values, social hierarchies within the chosen 'period' seem to be closely integrated with each other, to share common features, and in that there are identifiable points of change when a 'period' defined in this way gives way to a new period.
>
> (Marwick, 1998, p. 5)

In the same way that the 1960s is a decade that is identified with the 'sixties' as a singular period, the Victorian period is also discernible by the way that the nineteenth century is understood by historians. The project of 'inventing the Victorians', for example, can be traced back to an immensely influential single source. Lytton Strachey published *Eminent Victorians* in 1918. By demolishing great Victorian figures such as Cardinal Manning, Florence Nightingale, General Gordon of Khartoum and Thomas Arnold, Strachey condemned a whole age as excessively religious, sexually repressed, jingoistic and moralistic. He and the Bloomsbury set – that is, the group of notable and enlightened artists and writers of which he was a prominent member – almost alone hastened the modern age. At least, so they believed. It has taken the concerted effort and scholarship of subsequent historians to give greater balance to this rather skewed picture.

If the 1960s added up to the revolutionary ideals of discernible and clearly identified countercultural movements, quite opposed to the world of the previous generation, then the Victorian period ended – not with a great event or the end of a reign – but with a conversation. Uttering the word 'semen' hastened another age, a period when 'the word bugger was never far from our lips', heralding what Frank Mort has called 'a new modernist chronology of sex'. Modernity, according to Virginia Woolf began at this very moment in 1910:

> [One] scene has always lived in my memory. . . . It was a spring evening. Vanessa and I were sitting in the drawing room. . . . Suddenly the door opened and the long sinister figure of Mr

> Lytton Strachey stood on the threshold. He pointed his finger at a stain on Vanessa's white dress.
>
> 'Semen?' he said.
>
> Can one really say it? I thought and we burst out laughing. With that one word all barriers of reticence and reserve went down. A flood of the sacred fluid seemed to overwhelm us. Sex permeated our conversation. The word bugger was never far from our lips. We discussed copulation with the same excitement and openness that we had discussed the nature of good. It is strange to think how reticent, how reserved we had been and for how long. It was, I think, a great advance in civilization. When all intellectual questions had been debated so freely, sex was ignored. Now a flood of light poured in upon that department too. We had known everything but had never talked. Now we talked nothing else.
>
> (Woolf, 1985, pp. 195–6)

While it is clearly ludicrous to say that an historical epoch could begin or end with a conversation, equally it would be folly to suggest that there is no such thing as a Victorian period at all. Even at its most basic, the Victorian period must begin with the ascent to the throne of a monarch and end with the death of a long-reigning Queen. It could also be argued that the 1960s as a decade (as opposed to the 'sixties' as a period) cannot be detached from the context of a century. Eric Hobsbawm (1917–2012) did just that by identifying a short twentieth century that stretched from the end of the First World War to the destruction of the Berlin Wall and the end of Communism in 1989. Within this 'age of extremes', to use the title of his 1994 book, Hobsbawm situates a 'golden age' of prosperity, with terminal dates at 1945 and 1973. The 'sixties' from this angle is not a separate period but a time of profound social, cultural, political and economic change that begins, not in 1957–1958 as Marwick suggested but with the reforming governments established after the Second World War in 1945. Unlike Marwick, there is also an assumption by Hobsbawm that the 'sixties' was the result of freedoms won after the experience of global conflict. This is as may be. The point that needs to be understood is that history and historians impose a narrative on time; that the Renaissance is a period identified by historians, as is the 'short eighteenth century' (1789–1832), the 'long nineteenth century' (1815–1914) and the 'short twentieth century' (1914–1991). Each period or date has significance, chosen precisely because it is deemed to constitute a fundamental watershed. Periods can only be successfully identified if the relationship between time and history and the ways in which historians construct chronologies and analyze historical periods is given due consideration.

The chapter began with a bold statement: that we are all narrative junkies. In 1979, the journal *Past and Present* began a series of articles that reflected on the theory and practice of history. Lawrence Stone (1919–1999) fired a controversial opening salvo by suggesting that historians were in the throes of moving away from a preoccupation with science-derived method and the study of impersonal forces which had sought to question 'why' as opposed to the 'how' and 'when' questions presented by the discipline. From the 1930s to the 1960s/1970s, non-personal structural forces had been the focus of very many historians. Now, he argued, there was a return to a more personalized narrative, that is, historical evidence placed in chronological sequential order which would form a coherent story, with a narrative arc and replete with plots and subplots. This suggested a trend towards histories less likely to be analytical and more likely to be descriptive with (as Stone put it) a 'central focus [which] is on man not circumstances'. He was indeed prescient in his description of a changing historiographical landscape:

> Historians are therefore now dividing into four groups: the old narrative historians, primarily political historians and biographers; the cliometricians who continue to act like statistical

junkies; the hard-nosed social historians still busy analysing impersonal structures; and the historians of mentalité, now chasing ideals, values, mind-sets, and patterns of intimate personal behaviour the more intimate the better.

(Stone, 1979, p. 21)

These are areas that we shall unpick in future chapters. It is enough to underline here that Stone personified a shift in historical fashions that was real: moving from the narrowly analytical to the more descriptive, highlighting the particular and the peculiar over the collective aggregate of the statistician, revelling in the challenges of using archives with imagination and just telling a good story well. That there was such a shift is undeniable. To understand it in its complexity, however, we need first to comprehend how historians have approached the ordering of time. This chapter has sought to aid that understanding and to stress the importance of narrative and period in the reading and writing of history.

Postscript

If geographers are interested primarily in space, then it could well be argued that time is the province of the historian. The study of history is, after all, concerned with change over time – how episodes took place, how we passed from one age to another – and in order to provide a semblance of order to the record of human activity, historians have found it convenient to divide it up into periods of manageable duration. These periods have become the great building blocks of the past. Although there are squabbles over the precise dates, we have an almost taken-for-granted understanding of when and what was, say, the medieval and Victorian eras, the ages of discovery and imperial expansion, the seventeenth century, even the 1960s.

In constructing these blocks or slicing up the past in this way, time is taken as a given, a constant that somehow is just there as a backdrop. The notion of time we tend to work with is that inherited from Newton, and it is one that pervades the Western world. This has set a precedent with very real and damaging consequences, not least in asserting the dominance of the West. When historians talk of the age of empire or the feudal era, for example, it is the Western experience that is being referred to. For one thing, it masks the extent to which time is not only uneven and changing but is subject to contestation. Our sense of time and how it impacts on our lives is constantly changing. Thus, although most in the West, including historians, see history changing linearly and progressively, in other parts of the world change is thought to be cyclical or even regressive. It is on the basis of such conceptions of time that particular teleological narratives are constructed. If, for example, time is linked to progress, as it is in Whig interpretations, then historical change is thought to be the gradual unfolding of events towards a better (more liberal, more democratic, more equal) world. History is replete, however, with struggles over time. The introduction of more precise measurements of time in the early phases of industrial capitalism was part of an attempt, it could be argued, to control the working lives of people in ways which led to longer and more intense forms of labour. At a broader level, the general acceptance of GMT as the absolute standard with which to divide up the world into time zones was a triumph of Western hegemony. Such episodes are of fundamental importance not only in themselves but also because they signal radical shifts in the way that the world is organized.

David Harvey has persuasively argued that all significant historical change is accompanied and characterized by a reordering of time and space. Arguably, we are now in the middle of such a change. The development of the Internet has transformed the transmission of messages, which can now be performed almost instantaneously. As we write, there is a war in Europe, while the results of climate change are all too clear. It is perhaps too early to assess the nature of these phenomena or their longer-term impacts, but historians of the future will look back on these years as decisive in redefining our sense of time and hence the course of history and its interpretation.

Further Reading

Penelope J. Corfield (2007) *Time and the Shape of History*.
Niall Ferguson (ed.) (1997) *Virtual History: Alternatives and Counterfactuals*.
R. Flood, J. Ginther and J. Goering (eds.) (2013) *Robert Grosseteste and His Intellectual Milieu*.
William Gallois (2007) *Time, Religion and History*.
Stephen Kern (2003) *The Culture of Time and Space 1880–1918*.
Jonathan Sacks (2003) *The Chief Rabbi's Haggadah*.
D. J. Wilcox (1987) *The Measure of Times Past: Pre-Newtonian Chronologies and the Rhetoric of Relative Time*.

23 Archives in a Digital World

Introduction

The idea of the archive is an ancient one and the archive itself is often a locus of power. Archives can take the form of a stone inscription, a clay tablet or perhaps even a recorded memory and need not simply comprise parchment and paper. The first section moves beyond definitions and interpretations of the archive by examining how an archive is built and developed, the sheer variety of sources that can make up an archive and how the archive can increase or recede in importance depending on the preoccupations and fashions of the day. This explored, the second section examines the preservation of an extensive archive of East European shtetl or small-town Jewry through the YIVO, an institute for Jewish research. The mere existence of the YIVO archive allows, in a sense, a way of life to survive, even to live on, making it possible for historians to map the road to evil and back. This case study shows the possible extent of the archive but also the political nature and dimensions of archives more generally. By discussing The National Archives at Kew and the concept of community archives in the third section, we ask once again not only what an archive is but also whom it should serve. In this way, we move away from an examination of the 'official' or national archives governed by agreed professional standards to the 'democratization of the archive' and proposals for archives to be generated not by the state but by local associations and communities. Finally, the digital revolution has had a massive impact on the archiving of historical materials. In Section 4, we discuss the nature of this effect and think about what it means for historians.

23.1 What Is an Archive?

The Ark of the Covenant contained the Decalogue or the tablets on which was written the Ten Commandments. For the Israelites, it was part of their founding text. Made of acacia wood, lined inside and out with solid gold, richly decorated with gold cherubim, the Ark has been estimated by modern biblical scholars (assuming its actual existence) to have weighed close to ten tons. No wonder it needed oxen and cart to transport its contents from place to place.

Around 1000 BCE David was crowned second king of the whole house of Israel, routing the Philistines in a series of battles, although his importance, if not his existence, is disputed by scholars. The Ark was the organizing symbol of nationhood at the time of a new king and therefore went ahead of a triumphant 30,000-strong army, dancing, according to biblical accounts, to the sounds of 'cypress wood instruments, with lyres, harps, timbrels, sistrums and cymbals'. When the oxen faltered and the Ark began to slip, a man who had been walking alongside the cart when it toppled stretched out an arm to steady it and God struck him dead for his trouble. The music fell silent. Recognizing and fearing its power, King David removed the 'archive',

DOI: 10.4324/9781003156086-27

although eventually the Ark entered David's City to joy and more dancing before becoming the centrepiece in the 'holy of holies', disappearing from history around the time of the destruction of the First Temple in 586 BCE.

The symbiotic relationship between power and the stewardship of an archive is explored throughout this chapter; this includes the power of the archive to influence society: determining the present by its governorship of the past. But there is also the power of archives to 'recover moments of inception: to find and possess all sorts of beginnings' as the historian Carolyn Steedman stated in her book *Dust* (2001, p. 5). First, however, to definition. Dictionary definitions of an archive will only get us so far. There is no need to go back into the mists of an Old Testament past, however, to locate the origins of the word *archive*, but we instead look to the Greek meaning, which associates archive with a 'magisterial residence', 'a public office' and 'that which is old'. As John Burrow (1935–2009) has noted, the archive has been important to historians since Greek times, although Herodotus (see Chapter 1) as the 'father of history' tended to interrogate the keepers of the archive, not the archive itself. Indeed, the 'archive' in both the Egyptian and Greek civilizations is in origin a record (like the tablets of the Ten Commandments) 'inscribed on stones and clay tablets and, for most of the greatest matters, on the walls of temples, tombs and palaces' (ibid., p. 2). As such it was not casually put together as a set of dusty documents, instead it was chiselled in stone and built to last.

Patrick Joyce is an historian known for his innovative histories and the use of sources that are anything but typical. He sees the built environment as a text and asserts that buildings and urban space can be read like any book or manuscript (Joyce, 1999). Joyce is concerned with finding the 'liberal city', its municipal libraries and official repositories of historical meaning that resonate in his own life, providing some order and sense to the changing shape of these things in his own memory. The archive in his vision, therefore, need not be gathered and locked away by the state in a gilded official building. According to Joyce, the archive is all around us – even the building itself should be considered part of the archive. Memory is part of the archive too; something that is stored away, consulted much later and then reinterpreted in the light of present-day concerns or fashions. Buildings and landscapes are part of what might be described, more particularly, as an *unofficial* archive.

The archive and the places where the archive might be kept can then be very eclectic and haphazard indeed. Whether historians recognize that the 'medieval tapestry' or the 'African body tattoo' is historical evidence or regard the 'Victorian house museum' as an archival repository really depends upon the individual historian (Burton, 2005). As a collection of documents or as inscriptions set in stone, an archive is synonymous with 'a place in which public records are kept', housed in a dedicated place and within the bureaucratic context of the modern state. The church had the responsibility and power of maintaining records up until the twelfth century or so. Whether the archive is kept by church or state, the keeping and maintenance of an archive become both controversial and contested, inevitably the object of dispute (Brown and Davis-Brown, 1998). What might be contained in the archive? What ought to be omitted? What are the criteria for the selection of material? Who runs the repository in which it is kept and how? When an *official* archive is collected, catalogued and conserved according to the strict guidelines of the profession, it is done with due reference to agreed norms. The archive is not, moreover, as it is persuasively argued by Burton, 'innocent':

> For archives do not simply arrive or emerge fully formed; nor are they innocent of struggles for power in either their creation or their interpretative application. Though their own origins are often occluded and the exclusions in which they are promised often dimly understood, all archives came into being as used in history as a result of specific political, cultural, and

socioeconomic pressures – pressures which leave traces and which render archives themselves artefacts of history.

(Burton, 2005, p. 6)

The curators, archivists, librarians or directors of the grand institutions who maintain our past in trust on behalf of the public wield significant power, not least in acting as gatekeepers. The Browns argued that knowledge, power and discourse are interrelated, an idea first popularized by the French philosopher, Michel Foucault (1926–1984), who said that power resides in language, surveillance and examination. Put simply, whoever controls language controls the production and reception of knowledge, and therefore the 'discourse of the archive' describes the world. What may seem simply to be a pile of dusty documents, neutral, subject to open and objective scrutiny, is from this perspective part of a struggle for the power to describe and control the past and (therefore) the present. This is why the mobile archive of the biblical Ark has power and this is why it too is contested.

The Browns, like Patrick Joyce, question the relationship between the users and keepers of the unofficial archive, such as the community historians and archivists who are introduced later. These unofficial keepers of our memories are compared with the professional administration of the archive 'with its own pyramid of titles, powers, rights and duties' (Brown, 1998, p. 21). The hierarchies of the official archive, therefore, turn on controlling the ways in which the archive is both understood and described.

Also, this process does not cease when the cataloguing of the archive is complete – meanings for Foucault are never static, they are always unstable and liable to change in accordance with present-day occupations. The archive, therefore, is anything but passive and harmless; indeed, it can be dangerous. According to Foucault, the archives are 'documents of exclusion' and 'monuments to particular configurations of power'. Or, as Antoinette Burton put it, 'they all have dynamic relationships, not just to the past and present, but to the fate of regimes, the physical relationship, the serendipity of bureaucrats, and the care and neglect of archivists as well' (Burton, 2005, p. 6).

The archive should be read in ways that recognize it exists within levels of meaning. The meaning that scholars may place on the archive, however, is largely dependent upon the process of creating and maintaining an archive. Elizabeth Bramm Dunn (2007) has outlined the limits of archival practice. By the time historians have consulted the archive, it has been collected in a way highly susceptible to chance or accident. Documents that survive from the outside world are, as it were, 'weeded', that is, the archivist chooses to keep some material and exclude others. This highly subjective process depend upon arbitrary factors such as the collections policy of the repository in question, economic and staff factors, available storage space, personal interest of the archivist and so forth. Once the item is catalogued it is then stored on a closed shelf. Only at this point can the scholars take an educated guess as to the use of that document in relation to the research question they had posed.

The arbitrary nature of the archiving process provides historians with one of the most enduring pleasures of historical research: the fantasy of finding a document or collection that is undiscovered. The frisson of having in one's hands a book whose pages are uncut gives the delightful and evocative sense of discovering hidden treasure, as yet apparently unseen, with its survival a matter of chance that makes the experience all the more remarkable. All this before historians 'read' levels of meaning into the document itself, tease out the tone and semantics of the language and second guess the intentions of the author using contextual knowledge.

Archives, just by existing, create meanings that historians must unravel in response to the changing preoccupations of the present. There is a sense in which the archive is conceived differently over time – that the archive is not collated or read in a neutral way and, like the Ark and its contents discussed at the opening of this section, it is invested with both meaning and power. This will become clearer when we examine in the next section an archive that grew and moved with its subject matter.

23.2 'When We Return as Human Beings Again': Archives and the Ashes

Ashkenazi Jews once occupied the so-called Pale of Settlement, a huge strip of land that ran across the western borders of Russia and Central Europe. This land was put aside for Jewish occupation until the First World War and the Russian Revolution in 1917 threatened its borders. These communities had a distinctive way of life which remained more or less intact until the decimation wrought by the Nazi Holocaust. An archive of this vivid culture grew from the 1920s to the present day and contains the social memories and artefacts of European Jewry. It stands, perhaps, as an exemplar of a modern archive for its sheer diversity and exists as a remnant of a world now physically destroyed – or at least no longer existing in the form illuminated by the archive. The aim of this section is to chart why an archive such as this was begun, its changing content and the strategies used by its founding spirits to preserve it at all costs and then using this to draw out how it is that archives more generally can preserve the 'figurative remains' of an entire way of life.

With the changing of national boundaries after the First World War (1914–1918) and the trauma of the Bolshevik Revolution in 1917, Wilno in Poland became Vilnius in Lithuania, and so Polish Jews became Lithuanian Jews. They maintained their identities as Jews through religious practice, language, literature and culture. But as the modern world advanced with its opportunities and horrors, the shtetlekh (towns with a large Jewish population) lost their distinctiveness and coherence. This was part of the process later popularly dramatized by *Fiddler on the Roof*, a book by Joseph Stein set in Tsarist Russia during the pogroms of 1905 and based on a Yiddish story by Sholem Aleichem published as *Tevye and his Daughters* in 1894. That other great chronicler of the lost world of the shtetl, the painter Marc Chagall, inspired the metaphor of the survival of tradition amid danger, the fiddler balancing precariously on a roof.

The general recognition that this way of life faced rapid decline resulted in 1925 with the founding in Vilna of the YIVO Institute for Jewish Research, dedicated to the study and preservation of Yiddish and East European culture. Because the rabbinate and secular Jews (for different reasons, perhaps) believed that this rich culture was under threat, they cooperated in making sound recordings of the ancient prayers or collected archives connected to a disappearing art and literature. A network of volunteers (*Zamlers*) collected printed matter of all types. Young people were encouraged to write autobiographies and courses in Yiddish were organized for aspirant Jewish students. But the archive was also partly a response to an expression of national consciousness instilled by the great European powers at the Paris Conference in 1919, which, along with the gradually more persuasive arguments made by Zionists for a Jewish homeland, promoted the idea of the Jewish people as a unitary nation or people. The archive in this context had never been so important.

In 1940 the archive came under threat from Soviet occupation and between 1940 and August 1943 from Nazi domination. With occupation, YIVO headquarters became a Nazi depot for looted collections destined for destruction or, if there was some intrinsic value, for transport to the Fatherland. Under guard, Jews from the Vilna ghetto arrived at this depot each day to, as one witness put it, 'dig the graves for our souls'. Instead of doing the bidding of the Nazi destroyers, those volunteers, once so instrumental in creating the archive, transformed themselves into what became known in subsequent legend as the 'paper brigade'. These brave women and men smuggled out the precious contents of the archive page by page, secreting the fragments of a Jewish past in places where they hoped the Nazis would not look or entrusting the archive to gentile Lithuanians. One diarist central to the rescue of the archive recorded:

> Our work is reaching its conclusion. Thousands of books are being dumped as trash and the Jewish books will be liquidated. Whatever part we can rescue, will be saved with God's help. We will find it when we return as human beings.
>
> (Rose, 2008, p. 72)

More of the dispersed archive came to light after the war: in Vilna itself, in Frankfurt-am-Main in Germany, in a village near Marseilles in France and in the recently opened archives of the former Soviet Union. Now based in New York, the YIVO library contains more than 350,000 books in twelve languages and the archive amounts to over twenty-two million pages.

Only by going through the extensive YIVO archive do we get a sense of its true diversity, for it contains:

- visual records (photographs, paintings, maps, film)
- sound (interviews, music)
- material culture (objects such as postcards and greetings cards)
- manuscripts (private and public, individual and of organizations)
- electronic data (available on CD-ROM or online via the Web)

www.yivo.org/archives-library

The visual material includes photographs from the Yiddish theatre and papers by prominent writers and artists. There are photographs of personalities and places and art produced by those in concentration camps during the Nazi era, especially art produced by children. This aspect is by no means exclusive to the YIVO archive, yet the YIVO archive is nonetheless comprehensive. Films came to the archive from the ghettos in Europe and from as far afield as China. Sound recordings are varied: Yiddish and Hebrew music, both popular and liturgical; Holocaust era songs, choral and Hasidic song, children's songs and Klezmer (Ashkenazi Jewish music); radio programmes from the American Jewish radio stations; oral testimonies from the trade union movement and other leftist groups; orchestrations of all kinds. Private manuscript collections include those donated by prominent Zionists and communal leaders. Organizational records range from the American Jewish Committee (1918–1970s) and the United Hebrew Trades (1899–1979) to the Workmen's Circle (1893–1972). Official records include those of Nazi Governmental Bodies and Institutions and the Union Générale des Israelites de France.

Archivists add constantly to their collections, partly as opportunities present themselves but also in the light of present-day concerns. YIVO is no exception, and so in 1992 it acquired the collection of the *Bund* or the Jewish Socialist Society founded in Geneva; their archive was transferred to Berlin in 1919, smuggled to France in 1933 and, after a period of confiscation by the Germans, to New York in 1951. Somewhat akin to finding a branch of the Chartists in contemporary London, the *Bund* is listed still in the New York telephone directory.

The YIVO collection is especially interesting for several reasons. It gives an account of how an archive builds layer upon layer, how parts of the archive become important in one historical moment, 'flashing up at a moment of danger' and then receding again to relative obscurity. The Holocaust remained relatively obscure, while its survivors maintained a silence in the years immediately following 1945, only coming into focus again in recent years with the breaking of this silence. The example of YIVO gives us a sense in which the archive can act as a compound to heal psychological wounds, to act almost as a surrogate for a culture and way of life now quite vanished.

But the archive has its limits. At its most basic, the archive is a work of the mind or, as time slips, of social memory – that is, memory becomes as important as a pile of dusty documents. The shtetl way of life can be romanticized, of course, or framed in such a way that it seems almost impossible to reveal a picture that historians could regard as credible. The archive can assist in piecing together a lost civilization or way of life, assisting in its romanticization or, looking in retrospect, at the sheer poverty and discrimination suffered by Jews. The Jewish author Theo Richmond repopulated his parents' Polish shtetl by collecting testimonies from those who once lived and worked in Konin. Visiting Konin himself, the realization dawned on Richmond that it only really existed through the oral history he had created or in the local archives, but it was most vivid in his own imagination:

> Every trace of Jewish life had been expunged, and only in the mind could that life be resurrected, perhaps more easily at a distance from this dismal place, which only seemed to deny its past. This was not the market square so many Koriners had described to me, crowded with people buying and selling and haggling, the fishmonger Bim-Bom scooping a wriggling carp from his barrel, shopkeepers leaning in doorways, porters and wheelbarrows, Aryeh-Leib going by with his milk churn, country women with eggs and home-made cheeses, *buba* [grandmother] Mindl selling vegetables fresh from Glinka, Zalman Ryczhe's gramophone horn booming from his tailor's workshop, Jews arguing over Judaism, Zionism, socialism, others hurrying to prayer, Simcha Sarna on his way to the Chevre Shas, the Lame Ryczke limping back to his *cheder*, peasants and pedlars, pots and pans, noise and chatter, and everywhere the lively, singsong cadences of Yiddish. . . . Only memory can keep that world alive.
> (Richmond, 1995, p. 426)

Without the YIVO archive, we would know much less about the Jewish experience in eastern Europe and, perhaps, its aftershocks in the politics of Israel and the United States. In contrast, Sephardi Jews (that is, Jews who were originally expelled from Spain and Portugal and who largely resettled in the Netherlands or the Arab countries of the Mediterranean rim) lived an equally vibrant cultural and religious life in Muslim lands but were mostly expelled after the creation of the Jewish state. While there is now some effort by scholars and others to retrieve these experiences, for example by collecting popular songs and ballads that date back to life in medieval Spain, this lost world of Sephardi Jews will in all likelihood never achieve the vividness of accounts of European shtetl life. The YIVO archive was supplemented by a project led by Professors Jeffrey Veidlinger and Dov-Ber Kerler called 'Archives of Historical and Ethnographic Yiddish Memories, or AHEYM (homewards in Yiddish)' in which historians and linguists went from town to town in Poland and elsewhere, interviewing the very last Jews who live there in isolation from a Jewish population that is now either dead or has made a new life in America, Israel or elsewhere.

23.3 'Speaking for Ourselves': State and Community Archives

A reader at the National Archives of England and Wales at Kew might expect to consult any number of manuscripts and documents from a huge collection of state papers that stretch back over a thousand years: King Henry VIII's signature, perhaps or the 1939 declaration of war on Germany. The Domesday Book dating from the 1080s resides in a glass case, set back in a humidified space of its own, with a highly sophisticated alarm system and doors designed to trap any would-be thief inside the room – testimony to both the antiquity of the document but also to its status as a founding text of the English nation. Only the Magna Carta of 1215 would come close to rivalling this symbol of national pride, similar perhaps to the American Constitution and the Bill of Rights, which are widely accepted by the people of the United States as the foundations of the state and a way of life.

Beer mats are part of this varied collection, originally submitted to the patent office and accordingly kept for posterity. E136\24\3\ is the classmark for a mummified rat that can be found on the miles of shelving (which increases at a rate of approximately one mile every year). Taking the mummified rat as a symbol of the neglect of the national archives in past years and the Domesday Book together for a moment allows a comparison between the national records as they were once kept and the extraordinary lengths to which archivists and conservationists will now go in order to protect the national past.

The public educationalist and one-time reformer at what was then called the Public Record Office, Henry Cole (1808–1882), or at least this is how the story is told, was so distressed in the 1830s about the condition of the national archive that he presented a rat to a Royal Commission called specifically to investigate the decay of the nation's records. He protested that rats had breached the state papers and as this particular rat had eaten so much of the archive, it too should now be part of state records. And so, the rat was kept.

That the public archive was both neglected and widely distributed across the capital is supported by reports received in the seventeenth and eighteenth centuries – something graphically illustrated here:

> [I]n 1709 the records of the Court of Wards were found to be in a house adjoining that of the royal fishmonger . . . near to Westminster Hall. The royal fishmonger, we are told, did as he pleased with the records, which were perishing rapidly. The records of the King's Bench were not far off, but equally under threat. They were stored above a place which had formally been a worsted shop, but was by 1709 partly a wash house and partly a stable 'which is a very Improper situation for records of such consequence'. By 1711 some attempts had been made to rescue both sets of records and the fishmonger's house has been organized as a record repository.
>
> (Hallam, 1990, p. 33)

At a conference in 1988 to commemorate 150 years of the modern existence of the Public Record Office, former Lord Chancellor, Lord Mackay of Clashfern, rightly spoke about the importance of maintaining historical documents in the context of foreign invasion and the relative absence of internal strife. Starting his story in the early medieval period, he highlighted the 'rudimentary' archival 'principles and practices' that once existed, comparing them with the gradual development of modern archival practices.

There was no mention, however, here of records kept with a less-than-diligent fishmonger or of the rather more chequered history of the way in which records were kept in the Middle Ages. Any such attempt then to overstate the continuity and consistency of care given by the state to the records of the state must be treated with caution.

Conservation has not always been the priority of those charged with the maintenance of archives. Initially archives were in the hands of the church and local clerical offices. From approximately the ninth or tenth centuries, charters that pertained to monastic houses in Britain and elsewhere in Europe gave way to the creation of cartularies. These cartularies are essentially transcribed copies of charters in the form of a codex or transcribed manuscript in a book or, more rarely, in the form of a roll. By the eleventh and twelfth centuries the transcriptions largely took place in Benedictine monasteries and other ecclesiastical institutions, increasing in both number and importance.

Patrick Geary (1994) persuasively argued that, because of this process, the archive was transformed between the ninth and eleventh centuries. This transformation, he goes on, had a profound influence on the survival of historical evidence to the present day. Before 920, Britain had the largest collection of original charters in Europe – some 839 were extant in the monastery of St Gall alone. By the twelfth century, however, these archival riches had disappeared, the result of 'neglect', 'selection', 'transformation' and 'suppression', destroyed as a side-effect of the construction of the cartularies and the systematic and deliberate disposal of the original documents from which they had been copied. It appears that Western churchmen 'used this raw material with great freedom, destroying, revising, recopying, and especially reorganizing. The result was a winnowing and restructuring process that provided the parameters within which subsequent generations could hope to understand the past' (Geary, 1994, p. 114). This process, it seems, was somewhat in advance of a properly organized royal chancery archive but appears to have coincided with the rise of a literate state.

Elizabeth Hallam (1990) took up the story in her essay 'Nine centuries of keeping public records' by outlining the emergence in 1100 (or thereabouts) of the so-called pipe record and with it a bureaucracy of state clerks. Later in the reign of Henry II the state archive was kept at Winchester but moved around in (taking us back to the very beginning of the chapter) 'arks' or 'hutches'. By 1200, the archive (now comprised of Royal Charters, Letters of Patent, Close Rolls, Fine Rolls, Inquisition Post Mortems and so on) saw an increase in bureaucratic support. Yet there was still no central repository and parts of the archive were in the hands and under the responsibility of an array of local officials, while the end of the century saw the compilation of lists of the contents of the archive, which then and now are called 'Calendars'. Edward II, especially after the Templars were dissolved in 1312 (they apparently had been the main record keepers of the Exchequer), undertook a preliminary sorting of Exchequer records. This did not represent radical change, however, and the crisis of conservation witnessed at the fishmongers in the early 1700s, and rather glossed over by Clashfern began from about 1500 when government or state departments each kept their own records without bothering to transfer them to the so-called Treasury of Receipt.

This trend had been apparent for some while and surprisingly it seems that the method of keeping government archives or records was widely known among the general populace. So it was, in 1381, when disturbances began at the start of what is now known as the Peasants' Revolt, that the rebels knew enough about state records to identify state documents (especially documents that related to taxation) by the colour of their sealing wax:

> In both counties the Sheriff was captured on Monday 10 June . . . Sir John Sewale of Essex in his house in Great Coggeshall, Sir William Septvans of Kent when Canterbury Castle was successfully stormed. We learn that Sewale was abused, his clothing torn and his house pillaged, and that the rebels then removed 'all writs and sums of the lord King of the green wax or divers writs of the lord King and rolls of the same' and carried them to Chelmsford the next day where they were publicly burnt. Septvans was taken from Canterbury by Wat Tyler, John Hales of Malling, Ael (Ker) of Erith and many others to his Manor some two miles to the south of the city at Milton, where he was forced to hand over 'fifty rolls of the pleas of the county and the Crown', together with whatever royal writs were in his custody; these were taken back to Canterbury and burned there that same day. The desire to destroy documents sealed with green wax, for which we have evidence in Kent and Essex, reflects the fact that this was the colour used for documents issued from the Exchequer. For largely illiterate

insurgents 'green wax' was an easy way of identifying documents that might concern taxation. It is clear that these simultaneous attacks on the Sheriffs of Essex and Kent represent a deliberate attempt to destroy the current records of the fiscal and judicial administration of the two Shires. They imply both careful planning and accurate knowledge of the Sheriffs' whereabouts and likely movements.

(Brooks, 1985, p. 260)

It was not until the passing of successive parliamentary acts in the nineteenth century that centrally funded and professional state record keeping began to emerge. Legislation in 1838 established a need for an acquisitions policy and a central place of storage, while in 1879 problems caused by the accumulation of obsolete departmental records began to be addressed in systematic fashion. It was the explosion in paper records created by the First World War, however, that really gave momentum to the ongoing process of the late-Victorian professionalization at the Public Record Office (PRO). The paper predicament grew until 1952–1953 when the Grigg Committee tackled this problem, but it coincided with a growing popularity in public records from the end of the First World War (Martin, 1990, p. 21).

Calendars and lists based on improving 'objective' standards would provide ever-greater access to the archive, while the 1910 Royal Commission on the Public Records led to the Deputy Keeper Reports, which henceforth provided annually a comprehensive survey of archival practice. At the same time the by now formidable pyramid of postholders within the Public Record Office produced an increasing stream of publishing about the archive. This was not exactly new either: 'careful and critical' publications of archival documents appeared in the seventeenth century and in 1704 *Foedera* was one of the first official (or semi-official) publications of select documents, lists and indexes. By the twentieth century, however, these documents were still 'selected', with all the problems of subjectivity that this entails. By this time there were major figures working on the state archives. For example, James Gardiner at the PRO spent well over half a century working on a single publication or Henry Maxwell Lyte, who from 1886 organized calendars that attempted a listing or cataloguing of documents in chronological order. He also was a long-standing servant of the PRO. Now the trend is towards placing documents online and a purpose-built repository stands on the edge of the Thames at Kew, while the PRO has been rebranded as The National Archives.

The professionalization of The National Archives is not without significance for historians, even if the years of the decayed rat have lasted just as long as the years of what Lord Clashfern liked to imagine as the glorious continuity of conservation and preservation of archives. To this extent then, a professional, state-run institution serving the citizenry is open to question, particularly as it should be apparent from previous sections that archives and the administration of archives cannot be neutral and free of bias.

The National Archives are reputed to be at the service of the citizenry but remain in the ownership and control of government. Permissive legislation in recent years has given the citizenry increased powers of access, of 'freedom of information', yet rules of privacy and secrecy continue to protect both private individuals and public bodies from embarrassment, with the release of documents in certain circumstances delayed by 30 years, 50 years or even 100 years in some instances. As effectively the storehouse for government records, the government itself has a proportionate say in what is kept and what is thrown away (typically ninety-eight per cent of the total documentation produced every year by the state is destroyed). Government on a department-by-department basis can also call back documentation to the department for consultation. Yet we know from some examples of how states behave that they are not necessarily to be trusted in these areas:

Historians and other scholars are increasingly concerned to understand how knowledge is produced and, more specifically, how knowledge of the past is produced. Where previously historians 'mined' the archive for 'nuggets of fact' in a manner conscious of problems of bias in the record, today scholars pay greater attention to the particular processes by which the record was produced and subsequently shaped, both before its entry into the archive, and increasingly as part of the archival record. This approach draws attention to the way in which the record is altered over time, as well as the gaps and omissions in, and excisions from, the record. In South Africa historians have been cautious about relying exclusively on public and more specifically government records, because of their colonial and later apartheid biases. That the record is biased is widely recognized by researchers, but a great deal of work remains to develop our understanding of the circumstances of the creation of the archival record in general, and of specific collections in particular.

(Hamilton et al., 2002, p. 9)

In some contrast, perhaps, to its sharply hierarchical management structures, The National Archives now seeks a role in the community beyond that of keepers of state records. In recent years there have been efforts, variously successful and variously supported within the institution, to reach out to localities and to local cultures which often reconstruct the past via a distinct 'sense of place'. Projects have focused for the most part on oral histories, cultural heritage and social memory, with the aim of enabling communities to respond to the challenges of change brought about by physical and economic regeneration. These community histories have generated community archives that not only consider the legacy of the past but also assess the impact of regeneration in the places from which they come. Archives more generally, it has been argued in several reports commissioned by the government, are the mainstay of traditional scholarship, a vital resource of historical investigation. There is also a deep, popular interest in heritage, which was outlined in some detail in Chapter 13 on public history. This has encouraged increasing numbers of the public not only to use traditional archives but also to create their own, so expanding the sum of the nation's archival heritage. The overall aim of community archives is to improve the accessibility of archives for more diverse users and collections.

The Community Access to Archives Project (CAAP) in November 2003 was carried out in a partnership between The National Archives and a number of national and regional archive bodies. The idea was to encourage social inclusion and enable archives to reach new audiences. It endeavoured to connect archive users in the wider community to work with professionals, identifying sources required in order to develop educational and outreach opportunities and to help foster a template for community involvement. Some regard this trend in professional/amateur collaboration and the new technologies of the 'information revolution' as a challenge to the whole notion of what an archive is and the assumption of recent decades that it should be generated and kept centrally. The archives of the nation may well move from public institutions financed by the state to the archive accessed by and even controlled by local communities.

Events of recent years have transformed the ways in which the archive is conceived, created, managed and used. Conventionally thought of as a repository of written, printed and visual records, the archive has tended to be financed, maintained and controlled by public institutions somewhat remote from the concerns of the public in general, cultural minorities in particular. The information revolution and the continued escalation of interest in various forms of public history, however, have provided conditions for a major reassessment of the ways in which archives relate to the communities they are supposed to serve. It is now possible to transmit archival information with a speed and on a scale not previously possible. This is leading to a democratization of the archive; not only are archives more accessible, but equally communities can actively contribute to them, even create their own.

Arguably, for the first time we thus have an opportunity through use of the archive to enhance community life. Imaginative archival work with local communities can help record hidden lives, excavate and preserve collective memories and provide rich sources for its members to help make sense of their histories and hence their contemporary situations. Local history, family history and community history all stand to gain from this.

In its broadest sense, a community archive can celebrate and rebuild the sense of community in our lives today. Because of the new technologies available to us, an archive, not unlike the Ark of the Covenant, need not be tied to a particular location, and it does not have to conform to a particular format. Its creation, however, does have to involve communities, whether independently or in collaboration with a public archive service. In this respect, the notion of the archive has been transformed from its description in the first section as firmly tied to relationships of state power, to an identification with a particular community as we saw in the second section and to a definition of the archive apparently separate from the tussles of power which emerge from communities themselves. This does not suggest for a moment that 'community archives' can replace 'national archives', but it might challenge archivists to reveal some of the 'mysteries' of their profession in order to create the kind of community-based archive that quite simply we have not seen before.

23.4 Archives and the Digital Turn

In this section we intend to investigate what is generally termed digital history, that is, approaches to the preservation and study of the past that employ advances in information technology. At first sight, this is a broad remit, for software systems are widely used as tools to produce and disseminate knowledge, for example by making sense of large historical data sets, but we wish to focus specifically on historical sources that are being digitized and hence made available online as an alternative to print. Because of the excitement this topic now generates, it is tempting to view the use of digital technologies in historical study as distinctly new. In fact, the history of digital humanities originated in the early 1960s when computing began to be used quantitatively to store and analyze historical data. In 1971 the influential – and significantly titled – Project Gutenberg was launched with an aim to digitize and freely distribute books (www.gutenberg.org). Originally the target was 10,000 titles, but by 2015 it had reached 50,000. The computer-aided study of the putative economic benefits of African-American slavery published by Robert Fogel and Stanley Engerman in 1974 was a good – albeit highly controversial – example of what could be done at the time (Fogel and Engerman, 1974). But most historians remained unconvinced of the benefits offered by a technology that was considered expensive and unfathomable, and so it is only in the past ten years or more that something of a revolution has occurred, particularly in accessing historical sources and the publication of born digital works, namely, books and articles that appear only in digital form. Little wonder that some historians now talk of the printed monograph as an endangered species.

While historians continued in a state of denial about the potential advantages of digital technology for the profession, the shock troops who largely took responsibility for driving this revolution were – and continue to be – archivists and librarians. What they have been able to achieve is simply staggering. The British Library has been in the forefront of such initiatives. Led by Dame Lynne Brindley, its *Digitization Strategy 2008–2011* announced an intent over the ensuing three years to open up access to the library's collection by digitizing 20 million pages of nineteenth-century literature (approximately 80,000 books), 1 million pages of historic newspapers in addition to the 3 million already digitized, 4,000 hours of sound recordings and 100,000 pages of Greek manuscripts. Because of the complexity of the programme, there are no reliable indications on whether or not these targets have been met. Instead, the most recent aggregate data show that 12 million still images were digitized in 2012–2013, 36 million in 2013–2014 and 22 million in 2014–2015. Progress is also being made in the digitization of databases and '900 Greek manuscripts and some of the most important papyri, ranging in date from the first to the eighteenth centuries, are now included in the Digitised Manuscripts site' (www.bl.uk/manuscripts/). Access, normally through subscription or in the library's reading rooms, is now possible for a range of online archives including British Records of the Atlantic World, American Civil War: Letters and Diaries and African Blue Books, 1821–1953 (for a complete list see www.bl.uk/eresources/main.shtml).

This considerable achievement is, however, dwarfed by that of the Internet Archive (www.archive.org). Founded in 1996 as a non-profit digital library with a mission to provide 'universal access to all knowledge' and operating with a modest annual budget of approximately $10 million, the IA had within six years managed to store 100 terabytes of data (10^{14} bytes) – roughly equivalent to 10 billion pages or five times all the books held by the Library of Congress. Astonishingly, by 2014, this had increased to 10 petabytes (10^{16} bytes), representing 400 billion pages.

Many such examples, albeit on a smaller scale, can be cited from around the world (for an overview of the European experience, see Enumerate, 2013). As a result, historians now have online access to a large number of digital libraries which together provide a remarkable resource few could have imagined even ten years ago. Most of these collections comprise printed materials, photographic images, maps and audio files. By comparison, the digitization of older archival materials has not kept pace and overall is underrepresented. For these, we need to look to the rapidly growing number of websites devoted to specialist subject areas which provide access to relevant archives. A few examples must suffice. With funding of $50 million from a combination of private and public donors, the Library of Congress has since 1994 embarked on an ambitious project to digitize written and spoken words, images, prints, maps and music, culminating in the American Memory website (www.memory.loc.gov/ammem). This provides free and open access to over nine million items and stands as an extraordinary collection of personal narratives and detailed background information offering a quite exceptional database for anyone interested in the history of North America. It should be required reading for every American citizen and must be the envy of all modern historians.

In Britain, an important and well-known example is *Proceedings of the Old Bailey, 1674–1913* (www.oldbaileyonline.org), which contains transcribed records of nearly 200,000 criminal trials held at London's most prominent criminal court. Helpfully, the website provides a contextual backdrop to the records, including headings such as gender, community histories of London's minorities, geographies of London and an architectural account of the Old Bailey courthouse. These sources unwittingly provide a collective biography of the thousands of men and women who went to trial at the Old Bailey, and the whole is fully searchable so that anyone can trace their criminal ancestors or determine, say, the numbers of people convicted of rioting between 1750 and 1800 or the numbers transported or executed at Tyburn for petty theft. Such tools also have the potential to reveal previously hidden movements in the history of crime and punishment which would otherwise have been difficult to detect, in this case, the rapid rise in plea bargaining and the increasing tendency within the legal system to treat marriages as partnerships of love rather than convenience.

Slavery has rightly attracted the attention of online projects on both sides of the Atlantic, such as *Voyages*, a project that began in the late 1960s when scholars working independently of one another started to collect records on slave-trading voyages. It subsequently received funding from numerous sources including Emory and Hull universities and the W. E. B. Du Bois Institute, with which the Trans-Atlantic Slave Trade Database was created (www.slavevoyages.org). Here are recorded details of some 35,000 voyages, estimates of the extent of the trade, and the names of all the slaves noted at the time. The *Legacies of British Slave-ownership* project at University College, London, on the other hand, used the extraordinary set of records held in The National Archives at Kew to provide details of all those slave owners who were compensated for the emancipation of slaves in 1833, as well as much contextual information (www.ucl.ac.uk/lbs/). The data show that approximately half of the £20 million paid in compensation was unashamedly claimed by absentee planters, bankers, financiers, clergymen, widows and others living in Britain and used as a vital source of capital to promote early industrial and commercial growth.

Specialist databases are not confined to the modern period. Projects such as PASE (a prosopography of Anglo-Saxon England) run by King's College, London and Cambridge University have attracted major funding. It is built around a database which aims to cover

> the recorded inhabitants of England from the late sixth to the end of the eleventh century. It is based on a systematic examination of the available written sources for the period, including chronicles, saints' *Lives*, charters, *libri vitae*, inscriptions, and coins.
>
> (www.pase.ac.uk)

Similarly, the Clergy of England Database, involving King's London, Kent and Reading universities documents the careers of every Church of England clergyman between 1540 and 1835 (www.theclergydatabase.org.uk). Many other such databases, including some interesting prosopographies of local individuals and groups in 'Survey of Scottish witchcraft, 1563–1736' or 'Mathematical women in the British Isles, 1878–1940', can be located at the *History Data Service* maintained by the University of Essex (www.hds.essex.ac.uk/history/data/prosopography.asp).

Finally, it is worth mentioning an example of the many online initiatives developed by enthusiastic amateurs. Although very much part of the industry that has arisen from the rather morbid interest in the Whitechapel or Jack the Ripper murders, www.casebook.org contains a comprehensive collection of contemporary newspaper coverage, a photo archive and detailed factual information which is invaluable to anyone wishing to investigate the topic.

An increasingly vital source of evidence is the digitized versions of historic newspapers, historical images and video clips. A large number of national and international newspapers including the *Wall Street Journal*, the *New York Times* and the *Times* are now available online, as are those which catered to specific communities, for example, the *Jewish Chronicle*. A comprehensive and up-to-date list of British and Irish newspapers is contained in Richard Heaton's Index (www.freepages.genealogy.rootsweb.ancestry.com). Many of the sites are provided by the newspapers themselves. In the States, historic collections (but not recent issues) of the *Washington Post*, *Chicago Defender* and *Pittsburg Courier* and others are freely available online, while in the UK historic issues of most of the important nationals including *The Scotsman*, *The Times*, *Observer*, and the *Manchester Guardian* are supplemented with weeklies such as *The Spectator*, *Economist* and *Illustrated London News*. Abroad, *Isvestiia*, *Pravda*, *Times of India* have been digitized, as have East Asian titles including the *Japan Times* and *North China Herald*, and an important recent initiative launched by Europeana has begun to digitize an impressive range of newspapers from across Europe (www.europeana.eu). The British Library has the most complete catalogue of what is available (www.explore.bl.uk) and also provides to Reader Pass Holders access to a range of international newspapers (www.bl.uk/eresources/remote/about).

As we have seen, many digital libraries contain images, music and sound recordings, but in addition more specialist archives exist. One example is the so-called DIAMM project run by the Music Faculty at Oxford University and the Bodleian Library, which since 1998 has been concerned with obtaining and digitizing images of medieval polyphonic music, that is, to archive music taken from original music sheets. To date, 14,000 images have been stored (www.diamm.ac.uk). Another is the collection *Extending the Suffrage*, which details the banners used by this late nineteenth- and twentieth-century political movement in the marches and protests of both Suffragettes and Suffragists (www.ahds.ac.uk/creating/case-studies/suffrage). Architecture and the built environment now feature strongly. Run by Sheffield University, *The Cistercians in Yorkshire*, for example, focuses on Cistercian life in the great abbeys of the county and uses multimedia facilities to great effect (www.cistercians.shef.ac.uk).

While these online libraries and archives, funded largely through public, private and philanthropic initiatives, provide free and open access, it is important to remember that online archives have become commercial propositions in recent years. With the cooperation of libraries, a number of companies now supply extensive archival resources on particular themes for those wishing to subscribe. A few examples must suffice. Gale offers major collections including *Sources in US History Online*, which contains extensive materials on the Civil War, Slavery, the American Revolution and struggles for voting rights for women (www.gale.cengage.com). And Adam Matthew Digital includes in recent digitized archives *The First World War: Personal narratives, Foreign Office: India, Pakistan and Afghanistan, 1947–80* and *Jewish Life in America, c.1654–1954* (www.amdigital.co.uk). Although most of such collections are extensive, they do tend to draw selectively upon archives, and so while they might be wonderful resources for teaching and undergraduate work, more advanced research will require access to other sources. In addition, none of these collections is cheap, and so they are beyond the means of most individuals. Institutional subscriptions are normally the only means of gaining access to them, but even here there are limitations. A significant online resource typically costs well in excess of £10,000, putting many beyond the reach of most national libraries.

Limited access sites also include those containing valuable collections of journals. For example, JSTOR has digitized the contents of over a thousand journals, approximately 250 of which are classified as history, so providing a valuable service to those who do not have ready access to comprehensive collections (www.jstor.org). In most cases, however, issues of the past three years are not included. Many journals are available online through subscription to individual publishers.

As a result of such endeavour, historians now have access to source material on an unprecedented scale, and it seems likely that most printed sources from the seventeenth to nineteenth centuries as well as back issues of journals are now accessed online. Many historians have found it possible to complete articles – even books – without leaving the comfort of their own studies. So, are we close now to realizing Internet Archive's mission of providing, if not all knowledge, at least a substantial chunk of it? Do we, in other words, hold in our hands what has been termed the infinite archive? Well, no. We contend that a degree of caution has yet to be exercised by historians in using digital forms and in the remainder of this section hope to explain why this is the case. There are four areas of concern.

First, vast though online resources are for the historian, they give access to merely a small portion of the material available. The physical holdings of the British Library, namely books, journals, newspapers, maps, manuscripts, photographs and so on, are more than 150 million; only a fraction of these – roughly five per cent – have been digitized. Each month these holdings increase by 0.8 kilometres of shelf space, equivalent to 6.8 terabytes of digital content, and so even the British Library must struggle to maintain, let alone increase, this fraction. Such aggregate data disguise significant variations in the digitization of different types of holdings. Some indication of the coverage of books, for example, comes from the partnership between Microsoft and the British Library to digitize predominantly nineteenth-century titles. In 2007–2008, 68,000 volumes were digitized, representing 0.5 per cent of the total. The National Archives is the treasure house of British public records including government papers, census surveys and records of the armed services, crime and immigration. It too, as we established in the previous section, has embarked in recent years on ambitious digitization projects; so far five per cent of the material is now available online (www.nationalarchives.gov.uk/records/our-online-records.htm). A similar picture obtains with newspapers. If current targets are met, then 40 million pages of newspapers will have been digitized by 2020, equivalent to five per cent of the BL's collection. This may appear low, but across Europe it was estimated in 2015 that only 130 million pages of newspaper have been digitized by various libraries out of a total of 1.5 billion, that is, 0.87 per cent (www.europeana-newspapers.eu).

This picture suggests that, despite the extent of digitization, historians engaged in research will still find it necessary to get out of the house and take a trip (almost certainly to be repeated) to where the relevant archives are stored, there to consult the original primary sources. To take one example, anyone interested in the fate of the East India Company will find much valuable printed material including biographies, parliamentary inquiries, reports, charters and histories online. Much relevant material, in particular, selections of correspondence between India House in London and the Governor General in Council at Calcutta and of the minutes of various committees have appeared in print. But the vast bulk of the Company archive comprising handwritten reports and correspondence is stored at the British Library and is available only to the visitor. In areas such as revenue administration, even this archive is not complete, and so the determined researcher may find it necessary to travel to the West Bengal State Archive in Calcutta where much of the original material generated by the Company remains.

Second, an awareness of the limited extent of digitization begs the question: who decides what is to be digitized and for what reasons? Academic libraries are notoriously reticent to give answers to such questions, but it is clear that some vague notion of the public interest is the main driver, in other words, choices are made – largely by librarians and archivists, rather than by historians – on the basis of what is likely to be of most interest and value to the public. This explains why books and newspapers figure so prominently. Needless, to say, what is deemed in the public interest is determined by a complex range of social, cultural, legal and political forces, and it is a matter of regret that historians' opinions on these matters are not more actively sought.

Digitization is, however, expensive, and we find that public libraries are often prepared to enter into partnerships with commercial and other organizations with their own particular agendas. The British Library is currently engaged in large projects with the Qatar Foundation to provide a bilingual, online portal to materials relating to the history of the Gulf and Arabic science (www.bl.uk/qatar/), with the Google Books Partnership to digitize over 250,000 British and European books published prior to 1870 and with publishers including Find My Past, Gale Cengage and Adam Matthew Digital to digitize archives and printed collections, which will be made available only to subscribers. These public-private partnerships with publishers have proven popular but are determined largely by commercial considerations; among the most important are sites such as www.findmypast.co.uk and www.ancestry.com, which have fed successfully on – and in turn have generated – the huge popular interest in genealogy.

Many of the most useful sites, however, have resulted from the determined efforts of historians who with the aid of research funding have not only made available vital, specialist databases but provided a range of valuable contextual materials. In addition to those already described, we might mention notable examples such as the University of Wisconsin's *Foreign Relations of the United States* (www.uwdc.library.wisc.edu/collections/FRUS) and the University of Sussex's *Mass Observation Online* (www.massobs.org.uk).

Digital archives of historical materials are so numerous and fast growing that there is no definitive, up-to-date guide. Too often, tracking down relevant digital sources – as with more conventional ones – is a matter of chance. Furthermore, they tend to operate independently of one another; it is rarely possible to work across different sites. A recent initiative entitled *Connected Histories*, however, has revealed the potential of thinking beyond such boundaries and perhaps points to the direction of future work. The site pulls together a range of digital sources covering British history from 1500–1900, thereby allowing full-text searches for names, dates and places (www.connectedhistories.org).

Third, the worrying problem of preservation haunts all digital archives. If the body of historical evidence has not served historians well, the same cannot be said of the medium, for vellum, paper and good old-fashioned Indian ink have proved remarkably enduring. And it is comforting to know that if properly conserved and protected against unforeseen damage, they will continue to do so. Digital archives present us with an entirely different – and more troubling – dilemma, for the medium here is much less resilient to the ravages of time. In America, the Committee on the Records of Government warned as early as 1985 that the United States was in 'danger of losing its memory' (Rosenzweig, 2011, p. 8). Increasingly since then, archivists and librarians have spoken of the threatened loss of digital records, often in similarly apocalyptic terms. Some may have been prone to exaggerate, but the problem is real enough. Magnetic tapes used to store digital data have a short life span, probably between ten and thirty years. Not only that, but such storage is vulnerable to the slightest damage. While paper records may tear, they remain legible; if, on the other hand, a digital record is infected by a damaged bit, the entire file fails. The problem is compounded by the changes in technology. Older records are now often stored on disks or tape drives or organized in software formats and languages which are obsolete, rendering them unreadable. This reduces even further the effective life time of digital databases, and we now face the frightening prospect of having to renew them every five years or so. Part of the solution is in data migration, that is, transferring records from older to the latest formats, as did the National Archives in rescuing the tapes from the 1960 US Census, but this is an expensive and time-consuming process. It is worth noting also that services are now in place to provide continued access to online content even if a company ceases to exist (www.lockss.org).

Fourth, with the growth of digital texts has come the realization that it is not enough simply to make the original texts available online. This is particularly so of older manuscripts. Few people have the necessary skills to read handwriting from the seventeenth century and earlier, and so many digital archives have introduced Optical Character Recognition (OCR), which allows readers to search through full texts of the archive rather than simply, say, titles of individual items. This has proven to be an invaluable research tool. Google, for example, has used it to scan a large percentage of the holding of the Bodleian Library at Oxford University (www.books.google.com). But transcription can be very labour intensive, and the promise is not often realized, particularly with handwritten manuscripts and those with complicated page layouts. It is worth noting that searches based on OCR encounter significant problems in dealing with older printed archives where the typography is typically uneven and fonts obsolete, while they cannot be used at all to access hand-written records. Some providers have attempted to overcome this problem. In Early English Books Online (www.eebo.chadwyck.com), for example, ProQuest have built a complex thesaurus to support searches of texts written in older forms of English, but this is an expensive process and does not eliminate the difficulties entirely.

Apart from federated sites such as *Connected Histories*, which allow researchers to search across databases, each database must be approached painstakingly. This in turn presents difficulties. A detailed study of some of the main full-text databases of nineteenth-century British history revealed wide variations in the numbers of hits (Upchurch, 2012). Charles Upchurch at Florida State University conducted a comparative analysis of how efficient different search tools were in identifying reports in the press of sex between men. He found that the best results from a search of the *Times* came from *Palmer's Index to the Times*, which existed on CD ROM. This was because all the information in the index was keyed in manually and was thus not affected by misidentifications inherent in OCR.

Part of the problem was in identifying appropriate search terms used at the time to refer to the sex act. 'Indecent assault' was the most important indexing term in *Palmer's Index*, producing over 700 hits between 1800 and 1870; by comparison, it produced only 103 hits using *The Nineteenth-Century Index* and approximately 60 using the *Times Digital Archive*, where 'abominable' and 'assault with intent' were much more in evidence. The *British Library Newspapers 1800–1900 Full Text* came up with nearly 3,000 hits, but many of these derived from provincial newspapers where reports were too brief to be of real value. Upchurch concludes by advising caution in the use of even the most recent search tools and recommends that they be backed up by hits from older indexes and databases.

We wish to finish by considering briefly one or two more theoretical questions raised by the digital turn about the nature and status of historical evidence and its relationship with the historian. There can be little doubt that the access to evidence facilitated by digitization has made historical research and teaching more convenient. It is now possible to consult relevant primary and secondary sources without leaving your desk. And digitization has opened new avenues of research through, for example, data mining and textual analysis. Has this led, however, to *better* research and teaching? Not necessarily. Most historians these days are under pressure to publish and so have little time for critical reflection. Within such a climate, the temptation is to rely as much as possible on such ready sources, because of which the same bodies of knowledge tend to be recycled. This has attracted criticism in some circles that digital archives tempt historians to word search large bodies of material in a highly selective fashion rather than master them using due care and attention. We can now determine in a matter of seconds, for example, how frequently Jefferson used the term 'democracy', but this says nothing about the contexts or the particular nature of the problems he was addressing. Linked to this is the suggestion that research is now being driven increasingly by which databases and word searches are available. And for some of the old fashioned among us, convenient though a computer is, it can never really substitute for the exhilaration of burrowing down into dusty archives and actually handling manuscripts and miscellaneous pieces of paper created by the heroes and villains of ages past.

For students, the great temptation is to rely overly on the 5 million articles written in English which can currently be found on Wikipedia. It is not just that as a ready source of information on an extraordinary range of topics, Wikipedia is simply unchallengeable. With thousands of anonymous authors working on a voluntary basis, the majority of whom are not trained historians, providing open and free access to their materials, this is a venture which represents an unprecedented democratization of information. It is, however, no more than that. Articles vary greatly in their authority and coverage, and although they have been shown to be as accurate as material in *Encyclopaedia Britannica* they are ultimately limited. Vast areas of history are ignored. Furthermore, while academics are invited to contribute, they enjoy no privileges and are barred from writing about original research findings. Overall, therefore, the historical information is dated, lacks analytical perspective and is confined to areas of interest to white males who tend to dominate the Wikipedia community. Any student of the past needs to be aware that

434 *Methods*

just because information on a topic cannot be found in Wikipedia does not mean that it does not exist and that you cannot rely exclusively or even principally on Wikipedia without running the risk of plagiarism or at best of a reliance on recycled materials. Wikipedia is no substitute for an excavation of the relevant primary and secondary materials found in scholarly libraries and archives.

In considering the impact of digitization on the status of historical evidence, Mark Poster has pointedly asked 'What is at stake in the alteration of material structure of cultural objects from the paper forms of manuscript and print to the digital form of computer files?' (Poster, 2003, p. 17). His answer to this important question is that the digitization of sources such as texts, images and sounds presents several problems in defining the nature of historical truth. First, given that much of the information is put together by a variety of historians and amateur enthusiasts, it is not always clear how much reliability can be placed on the individual sites. There is also the worry of the increasing concentration of archival material controlled by media companies which can restrict access. Second, digital sources are rather more prone than archival materials to alteration by their users. Texts can be rewritten, and links made which potentially transform the original, so again throwing into doubt the authenticity of the materials. However, Poster noted that the excitement of working in a real as opposed to a virtual archive can seduce historians into the belief that the 'truth' is to be found only here. Digitization debunks any such notions. Without the same intense emotional engagement, virtual archives can encourage more critical reflection on questions of authorship, reliability and authenticity.

Consciously or otherwise, these arguments rehearse a celebrated essay written in 1936 by the influential German cultural theorist Walter Benjamin. Entitled 'The Work of Art in the Age of Mechanical Reproduction', it reflects on the ways in which modern techniques of artistic reproduction, most notably photography and film, have shaped the aesthetic experience of the audience. Modern technology has divested works of art of their 'aura'; in other words, because they are reproduced in multiple identical forms which are made available to mass audiences, these works have lost the power that derived from their authenticity and the magical, transcendent beauty they possessed. This process is essentially democratizing since it encourages the audience to become critical observers and commentators rather than solitary, passive consumers. Perhaps it is now time for historians to consider more earnestly 'The Work of Archives in the Age of Digital Reproduction' and thereby reflect on whether the same loss of authenticity necessarily accompanies the digitization of archival material and leads to the democratization of our attempts to retrieve the past and precisely how it has altered our engagement with historical evidence.

One graphic way of thinking about this encounter is to ask whether we approach the past as tourist or explorer (Sandle, 2013). Traditionally, students have been tourists, that is, they have followed largely passive and predictable encounters with the past, directed by expert tour guides. In the digital age, is the student an explorer, that is, more autonomous and less guided, more prepared for the unknown and unpredictable and therefore more willing to venture into unexplored regions? We would like to think so, but as with all forms of exploration, forget the lessons learnt from previous encounters at your peril.

23.5 Social Media

'Heinrich Kramer (*c.* 1430–1505), also known under the Latinized name Henricus Institor, was a German churchman and inquisitor. With his widely distributed book *Malleus Maleficarum* (1487), which describes witchcraft and endorses detailed processes for the extermination of witches, he was instrumental in establishing the period of witch trials in the early modern period' (https://en.wikipedia.org/wiki/Heinrich_Kramer#cite_note-1). So begins the *Wikipedia* page of a dissident and remote figure in history that otherwise might have remained under other circumstances obscure, a crank whose wacky theories about women and sorcery morphed into charges of conspiracy that proved to be murderous. His musings and wayward writings caught on like a fire in the driest of Europe's forests, and as a result countless women were tortured and killed to confront a perceived danger which never remotely existed. That this small and otherwise insignificant tinderbox of a book – a work of pure fiction popularly styled 'The Hammer of Witches' – lit pyres across the Continent was due, it might be argued, to a new way of spreading information: the printing press.

It was with Kramer that the journalist Gabriel Gatehouse began his absorbing podcast, *The Coming Storm* (BBC Radio 4, 2022). Here the focus was on the events of 6 January 2021 in Washington DC as Hilary Clinton's 'basket of deplorables' stormed the Capitol convinced by the lone voice of *QAnon* that the American 'deep state' was in cahoots with cannibalistic paedophiles to frustrate the fair re-election of the 45th President of the United States. *QAnon* was a rogue insider sitting, it was thought, erroneously, in the inner chambers of government. Like 'deep throat' during the Watergate affair in the 1970s, this shadowy figure was pointing the way to truth and justice. Millions of 'followers' came to believe that a satanic cabal of elite, liberal child traffickers had stolen the 2020 American Presidential election from the sitting President, Donald Trump. These claims, as false as those made by Kramer in the late fifteenth century, galvanized a deluded and (by their lights, at least) discarded and marginalized group of mainly white men and women. It relied on the pulsating ability of a new medium to spread darkness and lies as quickly and efficiently as it can transmit light and truth.

Gatehouse took his listeners back to the Bill Clinton White House of the 1990s to find the origin of the attempted insurrection that led to the passage of House Resolution 24, a second Article of Impeachment for President Donald Trump by the US House of Representatives and an investigation by Congress that continues as we write. Back then, the Clinton administration was accused of bringing the alleged corruption of Arkansas to Washington DC, with charges that included financial impropriety and rape and even an accusation that Clinton's childhood friend Vince Foster, who shot himself in Fort Marcy Park in Northern Virginia in July 1993, had been murdered on the order of the President himself.

It was recalled by Gatehouse that the earliest manifestation of the Internet was apparent during the Clinton years but played a negligible role in these accusations, coming from the right and all but ignored by the mainstream 'liberal' media. The capacity for the Internet before the World Wide Web existed then in a closed form that amounted to a community of experts exchanging specialist knowledge. But this capacity was changing precisely when Clinton came to power. The earliest platform to take hold was Talkomatic, which developed out of a computer-based education programme called PLATO at the University of Illinois in 1973. Then, in 1980, we find CompuServe, which took on a chat function and only then the so-called golden age that coincided with the Clinton presidency and saw the launch of AOL (*c.*1992), Prodigy (1992) and Yahoo (1997) among others. MSN bought Compuserve in 1998, which marked a massive shift to 'dial in' services and subscriptions by the hour or month, plus a surge in participation by the American public. The massification of Internet use and global hegemony was to come a little later.

Clinton's team, nothing if not moderns in 1993, got their man to host a town hall chat with a screen name 'Clinton Pz.'. The trend was now clear: 'By 1997, the year AOL launched Instant Messenger as a stand-alone chat product, the company boasted an estimated 19,000 chatrooms. Users spent more than a million hours chatting each day' (*Washington Post*, 30 October 2014).

While the early platforms were designed for education and only incidentally for personal exchange, it was noticed that roleplay, anonymity and consequently intimacy between users grew significantly over time. There was no hint in the 90s, however, of the sort of web forums such as *Discord* or *Voat* (which hosted dissidents from the social news and discussion website, *Reddit*) that would induce 'Millions of Americans [who] now believe the US government is being controlled by a cannibalistic child sex-trafficking ring . . . [with] some [others] . . . prepared to pick up machine guns for their cause' (*New Statesman*, 19 January 2022). Nor could Clinton's 'tech specialists' in the 90s be any match for Donald Trump's command of Twitter as a mode of communication. Social media was no longer acting as a remote 'town hall'. Instead, with Trump's use of his thumb, social media became a way to call supporters to arms, as the events of January 2021 were to demonstrate. Social media may well prove to have been the first and most important weapon in the Second American Civil War.

And this history is now being told in real time. Not only an example of a genre that may well sit between journalism and a form of contemporary history, podcasts have become both a 'first draft of history' but also a digital reflection on contemporary events that can also serve to change reactions to the event itself. Podcasts, blogs, tweets and the like challenge the historian to judge to what extent social media is both a platform to debunk myth and conspiracy theories but also a creator of myth and conspiracy theories. Social media might then be seen as the newfangled printing press had been seen in the early modern period: it had the capacity to spread knowledge in the most democratic of ways but also to spread falsehoods in the most democratic of ways. This extraordinary impact was, Gatehouse invited us to recall, predicted by a book by James Dale Davidson and Lord William Rees Mogg (1928–2012), which picked up on both the far-right obsession with the Clintons but also offered a prophecy about the dire (though not necessarily unwelcome to the authors) consequences of the new information age. In *The Sovereign Individual: Mastering the Transition to the Information Age* (Davidson, 2019), there was to be a 'global realignment' and a 'fourth stage in human society'. This, it was contended, would reposition the individual and rebalance the power of the citizen against the power of government. Social media was to have a critical role in this millennial shift in power relationships and so mark the transition from the industrial age to the information age. It is for the historian to understand and explain who it is that will be put to the sword this time around.

The historian then will need to consider all the cultural productions of each manifestation and type of social media: its dangers and distortions, its advantages in networking and knowledge exchange, its possibilities for public outreach and opportunities to preserve the past in myriad ways and, finally, the way that social media has 'scaled up' historical events themselves. When Dr Martin Luther King Jr was jailed in Atlanta in October 1960, just fifty-five souls showed up to bear witness. When Travon Martin in 2013, Michael Browne in 2014 and then, most famously, George Floyd in 2020 were killed in acts of police brutality, with Floyd filmed dying under the boot of a Minneapolis police officer, 218,000 retweeted the bystander video on 23 May. By 28 May, 8 million had retweeted the #BlackLivesMatter hashtag while these extraordinary numbers remained well over 2.2 million per day until 7 June. Black Lives Matters (BLM) had been founded after the Zimmerman/Trayvon Martin case in July 2013 and had grown expeditiously, but the brutal killing of Floyd was now a global event (see also Chapter 5). Clearly, social media as a medium had arrived and arrived too as a tool for historians that must be taken very seriously indeed (Accessed 30 January from www.pewresearch.org/fact-tank/2020/06/10/blacklivesmatter-surges-on-twitter-after-george-floyds-death/>).

The influence of social media was a global phenomenon seen in, for example, the Tahrir Square protests in Egypt, the Occupy Wall Street/City of London protests or the street occupations of Extinction Rebellion. Here social media had the ability to 'scale up' social movements such as BLM with the 'mobilizing of new members, boosting protest turnout or supporting fundraising campaigns' (Mundt et al., 2018, p. 2). It also played a key role in 'coalition building' around common focal points, the most important of which was police brutality but included:

- A rejection of hierarchy and centralized leadership.
- The adoption of a horizontal, not vertical, organizational structure
- An 'intersectional' approach that might, for example, 'lift up' 'queer women of color' (ibid, p. 3)
- The rejection of conventional forms of media in order to 'control their own narrative' (ibid, p. 9).

It would not be lost on historians of civil rights that 'repost' and 'share' options now available via Twitter would appear to break with conventional leadership structures whether personified by Dr King or by Malcolm X. Social media would allow, it was been further argued, 'youth of color [to] challenge dominant ideologies of race' (Carney, 2016, p. 13). It raised 'structural racism' as problem, so presenting a profound challenge to the 'dangerous liberalism' that said that 'all people are the same'. Racism was not a thing of the past, a view that had provided a 'false sense of comfort' and a belief that a 'post racial ideology' could afford an even-handedness across race (ibid, p. 17).

All roads, as with the discussion earlier on networking at the dawn of the Internet, the origins of discontent from the right (via Trump) culminating in the storming of the Capitol and from the left (via BLM), appear to lead back to the 90s. Some aspects of the 'third way' politics of Clinton seem to have stuck with BLM, however, as the Black Lives Matter slogan unaccountably became the darling of a corporate world such as is the NFL (in the US) and Premier League (in England) with the near universal 'taking of the knee' as both a protest against racism and an apparent fresh embrace by business of diversity and inclusion.

Clearly, the very processes of history itself that once hung on a mode of information invented by Johannes Gutenberg in fifteenth-century Germany and introduced to England by William Caxton (c.1422–c.1491) now rest with social media at least in ways that are equal to the printed word. There are advantages to and opportunities for social media and the new information age but dangers also – just as surely as in the case of the printing press that Kramer misused in his search for scapegoats and phantom demons – that might yet thwart the birth of the new or threaten the established order of the new millennium. It is difficult to disagree with the view that social media has fundamentally changed 'the dynamics of academic networking', going way beyond the early days of 'H Net' (www.h-net.org/. (<accessed 30 January 2022) and www.readex.com/readex-report/issues/volume-7-issue-1/academic-networking-20-historians-and-social-media>). Few of us need reminding that social media platforms were of inestimable value during the recent lockdown when seminars and conferences were impossible. Through such platforms historians from across the world were able to meet and exchange ideas, albeit virtually. Such has been their success in eliminating the need for travel and accommodation, these events are likely to continue well after all COVID restrictions have been lifted. And where once someone senior and respected in a field might be 'caught' at a conference, now they can more readily be 'friended' or 'followed' on platforms such as Facebook. Blogs have become popular in the profession such as the group blog 'Religion in American History' (https://usreligion.blogspot.com/), while academics have themselves opened to the possibilities of new forms of knowledge exchange. An historian of dress, Kate Strasdin, for example, author of *Inside the Royal Wardrobe: A Dress History of Queen Alexandra* (2017), worked in a relatively remote rural geography while speaking of the virtues of Instagram and Twitter as a valuable way of airing object-based approaches to research:

> The image rich content on Instagram comprises a slightly different audience. It is broad in its diversity – I have virtual friendships now with decorative arts and textile curators, costume designers, fashion designers, writers, broadcasters, makers and thinkers from across the world, not to mention other historians sharing their work visually. For me it has been a supportive and enriching space and it really can inform new research.
> (<accessed 30 January 2022 https://blog.royalhistsoc.org/2019/07/23/insta-research-kate-strasdin/>)

There are other virtues that historians can readily pin on social media: its potential, for instance, to galvanize public history projects (see Chapter 13). There are, however, potentially negative aspects to the use of social media. Catherine Fletcher, author of *The Beauty and the Terror: An Alternative History of the Italian Renaissance* (2020), has articulated well this concern:

> [S]ocial media favours the quirky, the visual, the gruesome, salacious or conspiratorial. There's a certain tabloid headline quality to it all and, while that can be fun, it has real problems. In a Twitter thread last June, curator Sara Huws wrote of her concern that the histories she tweeted from a Welsh museum account got more attention if she implied they'd been suppressed. The public wanted to believe in a conspiracy to hide the historical truth, even when there was no evidence of such a thing. Huws stopped using the tactic. Yet under pressure to promote an exciting piece of research, it can be all too easy for historians – even those with the best of motivations – to buy into social media's more worrying tendencies.

(<accessed 30 January www.historytoday.com/archive/head-head/social-media-good-history>)

Back then to where we began with *QAnon* and the march on the Capitol, with 'President Twitter' using social media as a new medium articulating old myths, conspiracies and fears. Whether good or ill, the truth, as ever, probably lies somewhere in between and is best articulated by Kevin Kruse who sees real advantages in the use of social media but challenges misunderstandings and untruths generated by the non-expert. In this, Kruse is taking a traditional stance of historian as professional expert, remembrancer, myth-buster and conspiracy denier. Interestingly, he does it reactively by using social media and uses language and imagery that can be understood in public forums (<accessed 30 January 2022 www.youtube.com/watch?v=RnQFCA6Fe40). We cannot help but believe that the professional historian remains a credible expert whatever the medium.

Postscript

Clearly, there is natural overlap here between social media and much that we have said about the digital archive. An archive is generally thought of as a repository for materials of historic interest or social significance. Since the beginning of the nineteenth century when history emerged as a discipline, much intellectual, emotional and financial weight has been invested in the archive, as a result of which it now stands as a store of pristine knowledge, sacred and inviolable. Such perspectives, however, must be tempered by recognition that the archive does not create itself but is shaped by the people who put it together and allow historians or the general public access to the materials. We therefore have to ask of any archive: Who are the collectors? What criteria do they use in collecting material? How is the archive controlled and maintained? Who act as the gatekeepers?

Archives are often put together through chance or accident. Documents that survive are those that an archivist has chosen to keep. That decision is a highly selective process determined by arbitrary factors such as the collections policy, personal interest of the archivist, storage facilities and so on. And what is made available is strongly influenced by secrecy (against the national interest), privacy, preservation and decency.

Archives do not simply arrive or emerge fully formed. Nor are they immune to struggles for power in either their creation or use. Furthermore, their origins may not be that well known and the gaps in knowledge only dimly understood. What is clear is that all archives came into being as a result of specific political, cultural and socio-economic processes, and these leave traces, rendering the archives themselves artefacts of history. And archives are never able to maintain their status as a pristine record of the past; as they are reshaped though cataloguing, classification and conservation, so they continue to create new meanings.

More recent thinking has opened up the boundaries of the archive. It is no longer thought to be exclusively a collection of printed and visual materials from the past. Take, for example, the city. From the early part of the nineteenth century when new forms of observation emerged, it seems that the street and the built environment generally became an archive, a repository of material that can be used a source of evidence.

One recent interesting development attendant on the extraordinary opportunities opened by digital technologies has done much to challenge the orthodoxy of the archive in many ways. The notion of the community archive has attracted recent attention, and we believe it has some potential in democratizing the archive. Thus, while the traditional archive is thought of as a repository of textual records, financed and controlled by public institutions somewhat remote from the concerns of the public in general, cultural minorities in particular, the community archive – digital or otherwise – is created and maintained by communities themselves. There is a democratization of the archives since they are more accessible, but equally communities create or contribute to archives on their own terms. Through the archive local communities can record hidden lives, excavate and preserve collective memories and provide rich sources for its members to make sense of their own historical experiences.

Social media, we found, is a brand-new medium that has grown very, very quickly. It comes in several forms and has been a positive boon for some historians but an obvious bind for others. Dependent on that exact form, it will inevitably act on the course of the historical process itself while generating (it goes without saying) a massive archive. The example of the exponential production of tweets and re-tweets connected with the Black Lives Matter movement between 2013–2020 pays testimony to this potential archive.

Digitization has made available unprecedented levels of archival material to the historical researcher. Such data, however, have not only extended the reach of researchers and reduced the amount of time spent in dusty archives but arguably have begun to change forever the nature of the relationship between the historian and the evidence, in turn transforming the very act of research and writing.

Further Reading

Walter Benjamin (1968) [1936] 'The Work of Art in the Age of Mechanical Reproduction'.
Antoinette Burton (ed.) (2005) *Archive Stories, Fictions and the Writing of History*.
Nikita Carney (2016, April) 'All Lives Matter, But So Does Race: Black Lives Matter and the Evolving Role of Social Media', *Humanity & Society*, pp. 1–20.
Enumerate Thematic Network (2013) *Report on the Thematic Surveys on Digital Collections in European Cultural Heritage Institutions* [www.enumerate.eu].

Carolyn Hamilton et al. (eds.) (2002) *Refiguring the Archive*.
G. H. Martin and Peter Spufford (eds.) (1990) *The Records of the Nation*.
Marcia Mundt, Karen Ross and Charla M. Burnett (2018, October–December) 'Scaling Social Movements Through Social Media: The Case of Black Lives Matter', *Social Media + Society*, pp. 1–14.
Roy Rosenzweig (2011) *Clio Wired: the Future of the Past in the Digital Age*.
Toni Weller (ed.) (2013) *History in the Digital Age*.

24 Oral History

Introduction

This chapter discusses the opportunities offered to the historian by oral history and the conceptual and methodological issues that it raises. In the first instance, this involves looking at the use made of oral history, not just in colleges and universities but also in the wider community where it has found a home. Much of the ideological and political importance of oral history can be understood by examining how it rose to its current popularity. To do this involves describing how it grew out of a background in the social history and 'history from below' movements of the 1960s and 1970s. However, collecting and interpreting oral evidence has a much longer lineage. Sociologists began using interviews and participant observation in urban settings as early as the 1920s, and historians who later adopted such techniques were well aware of this.

Oral history has also been moved by an urgent sense of recovering a world of memory, largely through the reflections of older people which were about to be lost as they slipped over the lip of memory into forgotten obscurity. At a wider level, this informed the fear that whole cultures and subcultures might disappear. This thought alone led to another trajectory for oral history. While anthropologists and ethnographers had long used such techniques in their fieldwork in Africa, Asia and South America, the work of, for example, Jan Vansina in Africa has had a somewhat different purpose. Taking both anthropology and history as his starting point, Vansina aimed not to recover the memories of those who had participated in an historical event but to make use of African oral traditions that passed down stories from the past but which were then manifested as homilies or metaphors for current political or power relationships.

24.1 'Anthropologists of Ourselves': Urban, Rural, Foreign

It is early in the morning. The date is 11 September 2001. Firefighters Alan Wallace and Mark Skipper wait on the heliport at the Pentagon for the arrival later that day of President George W. Bush. While waiting, they prepare fire truck 161. This is what happens next:

> They had just pulled the foam truck out of the firehouse and were standing there when they looked up and saw the plane coming over the Navy Annex building.
> They turned and ran, and at the point of impact were partially shielded by their fire truck from the flying debris of shrapnel and flames. They were knocked to the ground by the concussion, were able to get up, go over to the fire truck, and initially they were able to get it started to call for help at Fort Myer. And then they had to put out parts of their uniform – their bunker gear was actually on fire, so the first thing they had to do was put out their own fire

DOI: 10.4324/9781003156086-28

truck and their fire equipment and they tried to start the truck and move it, but they discovered that it wouldn't move.

They got out and looked, and the whole back of the fire truck had melted. So they turned their attention to trying to rescue people from the building and went over and helped people escape from the building.

(www.americanhistory.si.edu/september11)

The highly dramatic terrorist attack on the United States in September 2001 was an occasion when an event of huge historic importance was recorded and where the spoken testimonies of witnesses instantly became primary sources. As with all such projects, the evidence was then synthesized by oral historians into historical explanations of change and continuity over time, but at no time has it occurred on such a scale.

This oral history project immediately raised a number of issues relating to intriguing problems of method and opened up a universe of exciting possibilities amidst the debris of an extraordinary tragedy. As to the interview: Which respondents to select? Which questions to ask? Which questions to leave out? How should a relaxed, non-threatening, environment for the interview be created? After the interviews are complete, there are problems and opportunities related to using and interpreting the material collected: how to transcribe the spoken word and turn it into text? How should the use of dialect terms be communicated and interpreted, and how should we use and determine the importance of regional accents? What about non-verbal forms of communication like gesture? These are the standard questions associated with oral history. With the attacks on the Twin Towers in New York and the Pentagon in Washington, however, there was no time to consider such methodological niceties. Helena Wright, a Curator at the Smithsonian Institution at Washington responsible for collecting artefacts of national life, including oral testimonies, expressed the practically unique situation that a range of like organizations faced after that fateful day:

> As historians we normally have a period of reflection when we evaluate what's happening. We're not really involved in current events – it's rather contradictory to what historians do. Usually some time elapses before we can evaluate and determine what's to be brought into a collection. So in that sense the immediacy of this situation [9/11] is quite unusual. It does feel different. There is a kind of rush to make sure that we actually do capture and acquire what we need to before it's either destroyed or disappears.
>
> (www.americanhistory.si.edu/september11)

Within the limits necessarily set by living memory, oral history has allowed access to social groups and communities too often inadequately or even completely unrepresented by traditional archival sources. The financially impoverished, immigrant communities, benefit claimants and even children all have their faceless existences reflected in government statistics, but these types of sources tell us little about the lived experience of such people. Thus oral history does not just have a sense of immediacy; it connects with neglected and underrepresented groups and, by focusing on actually lived lives, illuminates them in completely new ways. It does not just discuss these individuals and groups as historical artefacts but gives expression to their own words and idioms, their dialects and folkways. Oral history, in very complex and problematic ways, gives them a historical voice.

Perhaps the most straightforward way of conveying something of the potential value of oral history is to look briefly at the work currently done by three recent projects. This might give greater insight into how historians and community activists have used this method but also allow us to understand their motivations, their presuppositions and their ideological or political orientation. The projects discussed in this section are:

- King's Cross Voices: King's Cross Oral History Project
- East Midlands Oral History Archive: oral history of the village of Newton Burgoland
- South African History [Oral History] Online

Drawing on very different contexts, they typify a much wider range of projects undertaken in a huge variety of communities, languages and countries. The projects also illustrate the diversity of contexts in which the contribution of oral history can be invaluable.

King's Cross Voices

Inner-city regeneration may improve the urban infrastructure but often it is accompanied by the disruption, even dismantling, of the local community. The area of North London behind the great railway terminals of King's Cross, St Pancras and Euston known as Somers Town is one that has undergone several transformations, and the present moment is no exception. The demolition and clearing of redundant industrial sites, railway infrastructure and giant gasholders and the development of wasteland have all taken place, but they have given rise to anxieties among residents that the formerly settled working-class community of the area might itself be transformed. This has reinforced a more general anxiety that, as older members of the community die, a world of memory, a record of lived human experience is about to slip from sight into an unrecorded past. The King's Cross Oral History Project – a project run by community volunteers – addresses itself to that anxiety by attempting to record the voices of people who have lived in that area over a long period and in so doing provide a record of that history from a perspective that would otherwise be lost to us.

The stated aims of the King's Cross project are articulated on their website at www.kingscross.co.uk/kings-cross-voices:

- To create an accessible archive housing the recorded voices and transcripts of the people of King's Cross.
- To provide an educational resource for schools and the wider community.
- To develop publications, exhibitions and sound trails.

The aim to create an archive of the voices of people who were long-term residents of the area is clear. Stories are recorded of people who were born in that part of London or who migrated to it. Likewise, the archive is a resource that is meant to feed back into the community by reinforcing and validating its own sense of self. At a wider level of historical interpretation, the project finally sets itself the task of interpreting and presenting this source material in publications and exhibitions to a wider public – to become, in effect, part of the greater world of published history.

Using the actual material from this project, we can gain a sense of how social change in this area has impacted on the lives of ordinary individuals. From the testimony of Barbara Hughes, for example, we learn how she had been moved into social housing provided by the East End Dwelling Company and how this expressed a form of social solidarity but without being sentimental about traditional working-class community life. Rather, the force of her testimony illustrated the degree of regulation imposed upon tenants in this kind of accommodation:

Where we were was the East End Dwelling Company, it was meant to be for the working classes. You lived according to your block, to your station. We moved to Number 1 Midhope Buildings in 1954. That corner had been bombed, so it was then a very modern block, one of the better blocks. In Tonbridge and Hastings where lots of police officers lived, they didn't encourage people with children. There were sets of rules. I can remember moving in, and on my floor which overlooked what was then the café in Cromer Street and the Church, a very nice view, but it was the top floor, and me with two babies. I'd settled in for 2 or 3 days and there was a knock on the door. It was a very elderly neighbour who handed me a pummel stone and she expected me to clean – to do the stairs up, and the stairs down, and the loo, once a week. If someone couldn't do it for some reason, you'd do it for them. All very responsible. We also had those washing lines that went right across from one side to the other on pulleys.

(Barbara Hughes, King's Cross Voices, 2004, at www.kingscross.co.uk/kings-cross-voices)

In a rather different vein, Reg Hopkins, who was born in the area, recalled the excitement of growing up near a major railway terminus in its heyday, communicating very directly its urgency, noise and colour:

It reminded me of a Turner painting. It was smoke and steam everywhere, great whooshes of steam would shoot forth. The station was so busy then as compared with now. Today it is all commuters. I don't say that it isn't busy today but then it was entirely different you know. If you went over to Platform 1 side, where the cab ranks is, there would be boxes of pigeons there. They were racing pigeons. . . . It probably was the East End of London where there was this tradition of pigeon racing so they would be taken to King's Cross, loaded on the trains, off loaded at York, at Darlington, and fly back. And also the mail. It was very busy. Huge sacks of mail right the way along the platform. Trains would bring the mail in, the lorries would pick it up, the lorries would return with more sacks and load the trains and off they would go. It was an extremely busy station. It was the hustle and the bustle that made it very exciting wasn't it. You felt a sense of living there.

(Reg Hopkins, King's Cross Voices, 2004, at www.kingscross.co.uk/kings-cross-voices)

Finally, perhaps most poignantly, Norma Steel described hearing of the proposed redevelopment of the area in terms that almost turn the coming excavations into a metaphor for the destruction of the community she had spent years defending:

They [were] going to put the biggest hole Europe had ever seen in smack dab the middle of King's Cross. I just couldn't believe it! It was uncanny. It was absolutely devastating. After all the years of fighting for the community. It took a long time for the enormity of the project to sink in. Everything changed then. Everything changed.

(Norma Steel, King's Cross Voices, 2004, at www.kingscross.co.uk/kings-cross-voices)

Oral History of Newton Burgoland

Oral history has very strong roots in studies of rural society. Many British villages, having experienced long periods of seeming changelessness, confronted the disruptive tendencies of modern industrialization and urbanization, which transformed settled agricultural communities to places dependent on regional commerce and industry. Villages suffered from population decline or became little more than residential dormitories for nearby towns that provide the main opportunities in employment, shopping, social life and so forth.

A project carried out by the East Midlands Oral History Archive on 'Growing up in a Leicestershire Village', which focused on Newton Burgoland, captured aspects of rural life by interviewing respondents who grew up in the village in the 1920s and 1930s. It offered a valuable insight into the character of village life in terms of social attitudes, infrastructure and amenities among many other things. The interviewees imparted a colourful sense of the role of religion in village life, education and schooling and at the same time revealed a deeper substratum of meaning to their lives. Take, for example, the following brief extracts.

Interviewee: We had a Congregational Chapel and a Methodist. Eventually the Methodist was sold and the Congregational bought it for the village, for a hall.
EMOHA: Could you tell me something about the differences between the two places of worship?
Interviewee: Well, I think the Congregational were more, what should I say, free and easy really. The Methodists seemed very strict, it was really strict Methodist, and they didn't have any entertainment at all, where we had a marvellous choir mistress and organist who really had the children entertained the whole time, and we had wonderful concerts and outings and everything, and Sunday School anniversaries, of that was a very big day.
(www.le.ac.uk/emoha/community/resources/county/newton/growingup.html)

Even this brief example on religious life provided insight into the diversity of religious experience of the village in the 1920s and 1930s – how, in particular, the very different social attitudes of Congregationalism and Methodism, as strands of nonconformity, shaped village life. This already suggests a great deal more than might have been surmised without oral history techniques to help provoke further questions about how divisions in the village, as well as patterns of social solidarity, worked in this rural community. Taking another example from the experience of rural labour adds to the picture and emphasizes the point:

Interviewee: At harvest time we used to, Mum used to make this beer in what we called a *pancheon*, stand it in the dairy, and at lunch we used to take it down to the fields to the men. We'd take it in bottles or in milk cans, anything like that, and then when we'd take our own lunch with us and we'd sit under the hedge on the sacks and have our lunch with the men down there. That was our life as children really, doin' that sort of thing.
(www.le.ac.uk/emoha/community/resources/county/newton/growingup.html)

There is a great deal about the nature of labour in the village to be gleaned at a time of national economic downturn. The importance of harvest work is emphasized for one thing and the role that children played in taking food to the men while they were at work: men's work and children's work. Here is where the skills of reading documents and interviews overlap; much more can be wrung from this extract. The interviewee talked about making beer and feeding the working men but also revealed that making the beer was their mother's work, that the children spent time with male family members while eating with them. The sexual division of labour, the involvement of the whole family in the work process and the obligations of children were all evoked with a real immediacy in part because of the nature of the medium of oral history.

In another extract, an interviewee talked of school life and, after accounting for the structure of the school by age group, the authority of the headmaster, the heating of the school and the use of the school as a sort of community centre, there was a fascinating and revealing description of the toilet facilities:

EMOHA: What sort of toilet facilities did they have at school?
Interviewee: They were in the school yard. There was a row of them. There was one kept locked for the staff. There was the girls' side and then there was a high wall and then there was the boys' side, and of course, they had the men come and empty the pans once a week.
EMOHA: When you say 'empty the pans' . . .
Interviewee: Never conscious of it being done but it was always done.
EMOHA: What sort of pans were these?
Interviewee: Well, they had metal pans into wooden seats, you see.
EMOHA: So, each toilet . . .
Interviewee: Had a wooden seat and metal pan.
EMOHA: Can you . . .
Interviewee: No chains or anything.
EMOHA: Can you remember what these were like to use?
Interviewee: Horrible. Well, I thought they were.
EMOHA: Was that very different from what you had at home? What sort of toilet did you have at home?
Interviewee: Oh no, we had the same thing at home! Oh yes. Lovely white seat because my sister and I used to scrub it.
EMOHA: What happened to the pan at home?
Interviewee: My father emptied that. That went down the fields.
EMOHA: Did it?
Interviewee: Buried. So we never had an accumulation, it was always kept very nice.
EMOHA: So, the school ones weren't, you said they weren't, you didn't like using them?
Interviewee: I didn't like it but then I was a bit finicky anyway.
(www.le.ac.uk/emoha/community/resources/county/newton/growingup.html)

The structure of society and its relations with children are now known from the organization of the school toilets. One was kept locked for the exclusive use of the staff while the boys and girls toilets were segregated. This is not very surprising and largely still pertains to this day. We also learnt that this village in the heart of England did not have flushing toilets either in the school or in the home of this respondent and that someone in the community had the job of emptying the facilities in the school. Beneath this something deeper can be glimpsed. The clear contrast between sanitation in the home and that in the school says much about how cleanliness and respectability might have been related. There is not much to go on here but there is a hint that might be pursued by further questioning. The interviewee did not just recall details about the school facilities but also made a statement about home and home life.

South African History Online

Oral history can retrieve histories of both urban and rural communities and give voice to people whose views and lives might otherwise go unrecorded. There is undoubtedly an ideological component to this act of retrieval but very often it lives in the background as an unstated assumption. This is not necessarily always the case. In South Africa, where the political turmoil and change of recent decades has operated alongside the legacy of the long-term exclusion of black people from all the major political processes of national life, oral history has a particular immediacy. This context is not only inescapably political but it also makes clear how interviewees and oral history methods live alongside and complement other kinds of sources and techniques.

The South African History Online website, established in June 2000, has as its stated aim to 'break the silence on the historic and cultural achievements of the country's black communities'. To achieve this aim, whether it is an appropriate aim for the historian or not, requires more than just interviewing the urban and rural poor about the nature of their domestic and social lives. Reconstructing the history of the apartheid period in the light of the post-apartheid world in a way that gives a due account of the entire population is going to require every resource, method and conceptual framework that the historian can mobilize. But oral history is certainly part of that process.

At one level, the voice of the voiceless, the ordinary activist caught up in the sweep of extraordinary events can be heard. Here two women, Magdelene Matashdi Tsoane (MT) and Rahaba Mahlakedi Moedetsi (RM), were interviewed about their participation in an early great march against the apartheid regime in 1956:

Q: How did you feel as you were mixed according to race?
RM: I can say I was very happy to work with different people but the people I have enjoyed most were the Indians. I have many friends in India. People like Amina Cachalia were there.
MT: We also worked very closely with people like Lilian Ngoyi and many more. During the march we were together with Ma-Moeketsi and others. I was always with Ma-Moeketsi.
Q: Can you tell us a little bit about the South African Federation of Women?
RM: I am the one who was the member of that organization. I was working with many white women in this organization. We use to attend meetings in Johannesburg.
Q: Were you not afraid for your children during the 1956 March?
RM: No, we had our children on our backs during the March. Many women had their children with them during the March. Some were carrying the white children with them, those who were working for whites.
Q: Tell us about the songs you sung.
MT: We were singing the song, which says 'Verwoerd, the black people will kill you and we do not want Bantu Education'. And the song was saying: 'If you strike a woman, you strike a rock'.

(www.sahistory.org.za/archive/womens-march-interviews)

We learn here about the importance of women in the history of the struggle against apartheid and about the use of children (including white children) in marches and demonstrations that would culminate in the horrors of the Sharpeville massacre on 21 July 1960 when ten children were among the sixty-nine people killed by the police. Song was clearly an important aspect of protest and, above all, the fact that the campaign was 'mixed according to race' – a fact that might be surprising to some. However, this image of inter-racial cooperation should not lull us into thinking that this campaign did not display the usual elements of factionalism and infighting.

448 *Methods*

This next voice was not that of an ordinary protester but that of Johnny Issel, a leader of the United Democratic Front in the Western Cape:

Q: Were there political factions in Cape Town at the time?
JI: Yes indeed. . . . A number of political tendencies seemed to surface during 1980 when we saw an upsurge in mass action. The people were ready for direct political action against the state. A protracted bus boycott ensued. Communities were coming out in support of various worker struggles. Civic protests proliferated, like the one in Mitchells Plain against electricity penalties. With this surfaced a number of political groupings – all very eager to hoist their separate flags. There were three major groups on the left. One such group positioned itself at the leadership of the emerging independent trade union movement and held a critical position towards the ANC. Then there were the remnants of the old Unity Movement. Their base was within the non-racial sports movement, a few civic organizations and the municipal workers union. The largest, by far, were those who pledged allegiance to the Congress Movement. They were quite amorphous at the beginning but found greater cohesiveness. . . . Whilst there was co-operation amongst these left groups on a number of campaigns, bitter tensions surfaced at the time of the UDF launch. [1983]
(www.sahistory.org.za/archive/interview-johnny-issel-key-udf-western-cape-leader-2003)

Recalling events that took place nearly three decades after the marches of 1956, Johnny Issels' voice was that of a campaign-hardened activist, operating at time when the prospect of success of the anti-apartheid movement must have seemed as distant as ever. In this context the tensions between different political interests within the broader campaign were all the more important and recalled by him in a level-headed manner that illustrated this salutary fact without talking it up or, in any obvious way, speaking for his own faction in these debates.

The opening sections of this chapter have suggested a range of contexts within which oral history has made a valuable contribution to historical research. This is true in terms of its contribution to historical knowledge but also in terms of widening the range and nature of historical inquiry itself. Ranging from inner-city London to rural Leicestershire and the political struggles of the South African anti-apartheid movement, oral history techniques can unearth what would remain unrecorded but can also allow space for the reflections of historical actors who have left a significant mark on the written record.

In all of this, however, oral history also has its limitations. In relation to the cases discussed earlier, for example, plans for the 'regeneration' of King's Cross local authority and property developers should also be consulted, as should digests of social statistics like the government publication *Social Trends* to find out at what point running water and flushing toilets became commonplace in the villages of the English midlands. Most urgently, no historian would dream of building a history of modern South Africa on oral history sources alone. Oral history must be seen, therefore, in relation to its balance sheet of advantages offset against disadvantages. How to make such a calculation will be tackled in the next section.

24.2 Oral Historiography

It is difficult to say with any certainty when oral historiography began. We know from ancient times that some of the earliest historians relied upon the memories of people with whom they conversed (as seen in Chapter 1). In the modern era, folklorists, musicians and writers have a long history of interviewing ordinary people about their lives and cultures. Much of this was done in a haphazard fashion and little was recorded systematically. Arguably, therefore, the first work which we would recognize as oral history was conducted in the United States during the interwar years. Financed by the federal government to relieve the effects of the depression, the Federal Writers Project embarked on an extraordinarily ambitious scheme to interview and record the experiences of thousands of ordinary working people. Most notable here were the interviews carried out with over 2,000 former slaves, which provided a unique insight into their lives (now available online as *Slave Narratives from the Federal Writers' Project, 1936–38*, www.memory.loc.gov). In some contrast, the first major academic research for the study of oral history, with recognition then as a subdiscipline, was established at Columbia University in 1948. The moving spirit was Allan Nevins (1890–1971) and the project focused on producing an oral history of white male elites.

An early practitioner of a more popular oral history in Britain was George Ewart Evans (1909–1988), who used interviews amongst other methods to recover the language and lore of ploughmen and agricultural labourers in East Anglia in the 1950s and 1960s and had a keen antiquarian's eye for a world that was rapidly disappearing (see later). Another example of this approach was contained in *Akenfield* (1969), an account of class and status by the writer Ronald Blythe (1922–2023), which was set in a real-life, if tiny, English village in Suffolk and drew upon interviews conducted in late 1967. In a testimony from the local blacksmith, who was born in 1923 and recalled the financial hardship of the 1930s, there was a single paragraph that can be read as evidence of the way memory works. It shows how memories may sometimes be borrowed (he mentioned his grandfather), and the tendency for the brain to airbrush out the worst memories may be in evidence when he insisted that 'people were content', but it also suggested that the village worked on a strict hierarchy of patronage, with power and influence flowing downwards from the 'Big House':

> This was the year [1930] my grandfather had to shut down the forge. He never went back to it. I used to walk by it, eying it and thinking. But nothing was rosy wherever you looked. Nearly everybody went out of business. Nothing was sold. People who had left school began to think about the Big House. You realized that it was there, with all the gardeners, grooms and maids and food. You have to face it, the Big House was then an asset to the village. It paid us to raise our hats, which is why we did it. I hear people run the gentry down now but they were better than the farmers in a crisis. Theirs was the only hand which fed us that we could see. So we bowed a bit; it cost nothing, even if it wasn't all courtesy. Nobody left, nobody went away. People were content. However hard up they were, they stayed content. The boys had the arse out of their trousers, no socks and the toes out of their boots. My brothers and myself were like this, yet so happy. I think other families were the same. The village kept close.
>
> (Gregory Gladwel, aged 44, blacksmith, in Blyth, 1969, p. 126)

The gardener at the 'Big House' in the second of the direct quotations was only thirty-nine when interviewed by Blyth and provides more information on class relationships within the community:

> I went to his Lordship's when I was fourteen and stayed for fourteen years. There were seven gardeners and goodness knows how many servants in the house. It was a frightening experience for a boy. Lord and Ladyship were very, very Victorian and very domineering. It was 'swing your arms' every time they saw us. Ladyship would appear suddenly from nowhere when one of us boys were walking off to fetch something. 'Swing your arms!' she would

shout. We wore green baize aprons and collars and ties, no matter how hot it was, and whatever we had to do had to be done on the dot. Nobody was allowed to smoke. A gardener was immediately sacked if he was caught smoking, no matter how long he worked there.

We must never be seen from the house; it was forbidden. And if people were sitting on the terrace or on the lawn, and you had a great barrow-load of weeds, you might have to push it as much as a mile to keep out of view.

If you were seen you were always told about it and warned, and as you walked away Ladyship would call after you, 'Swing your arms!' It was terrible. You felt like someone with a disease.

(Christopher Falconer, aged 39, gardener, in Blyth, 1969, p. 116)

Early examples of social history also explored the lives of agricultural labourers, both male and female, industrial workers, car workers and political activists of very different persuasions through the techniques of oral history. They did so in a way that simultaneously mobilized social historians, sociologists, folklorists and emerging departments of cultural studies to create an awareness of the value of oral history. In *Fenwomen: A Portrait of Women in an English Village* (1975), for example, Mary Chamberlain retrieved the lives of East Anglian women and their world of work. Later, in *Poor Labouring Men* (1985), Alun Howkins provided a similar account of male agricultural labourers. On the margins of the city of Oxford, the political lives of recently settled and sometimes turbulent quarry workers are recorded in the essay 'Quarry roughs' edited by Raphael Samuel in his *Village Life and Labour* (1975). In a large study that involved collaboration between British and Italian university departments, Paul Thompson and Luisa Passerini headed a project that excavated the lives of car workers in Coventry and Turin. Here, by its efforts to engage with histories across national boundaries, oral history admirably transcended any parochial boundaries it may have been inclined to impose on itself. Newer projects have often focused on the mobility of migrant groups rather than change in settled communities. In Cardiff, Wales, migration into the area now known simply as 'The Bay' and formerly as Butetown or, more notoriously, as Tiger Bay was typical of the use of oral history to trace the history of migrating communities or peoples (see Butetown History and Arts Centre, www.bhac.org).

Oral history developed in a similar fashion in a number of countries and at the same time began to take on a new and more concrete institutional existence. The Oral History Association in the United States was founded in 1966 and the *Oral History Journal* began life in 1971. Courses about oral history or using oral history as a component method began to spring up in university departments across Britain and several other countries. In the United States, Eliot Wigginton's *Foxfire Project* was inspirational not just in its uses of oral historical methods but the place that it found in progressive education. Wigginton created a model of educational practice that was quite unlike any standard classroom approach, motivating students to interview members of the community in northern Georgia. Recipes, local folk remedies, traditions in music and dance illuminated the unique and hitherto hidden culture of these Appalachian Mountain people. In the wake of these developments, a few reflexive studies emerged that discussed the methodology, techniques and historiography of oral history. The most notable of these was Paul Thompson's *The Voice of the Past: Oral History* (1978), which simultaneously argued the case for history written from oral testimony rather than from the more familiar document-based sources and for the potential of oral history methods to democratize history itself.

This all-too-brief survey should nevertheless complete a clear grasp of the chronology and character of this literature, allowing a return now to the political and ideological make-up of oral history. While it would be a mistake to see all writers in this field as belonging to one political camp, it is reasonable to suggest that oral historians were broadly socialist and feminist in this period and driven by a strong imperative to recover the experience of people neglected by the traditional historical canon and under-represented in printed archives. These people were largely poor and working class. The historians avoided sentimentalizing their subject matter despite an obvious empathy but in so doing reminded us that oral history can fall prey to a sentimental over-identification with its subjects, both individually and as social groups. In fact, the noted Italian oral historian Luisa Passerini rightly suggested that oral history can easily move from this identification with the idea of representing the unrepresented into a vulgar populism that is itself a form of historical misrepresentation. As a left-wing historian, she recognized that oral history was not necessarily radical and warned historians not to fall into 'facile democratization' and 'complacent populism', falsely romanticizing the working class and presenting oral history as an unproblematic instrument of democratic scholarship (Passerini, 1987).

Indeed, oral histories need not be anymore 'democratic' than the subjects of oral history. Speech and behaviour are constructed through culture and so oral history from this perspective is like storytelling and is simply another way of representing the self. The evidence provided by oral history methods requires the same critical attention and evaluation as any other source material or history. Democratic intent does not of itself make good history: careful and critical historical practice can.

Even the most enthusiastic advocate of oral history would allow that it comes with a range of conceptual and methodological problems. Oral history concerns itself by definition with living memory, which itself places inescapable temporal limits on its area of inquiry: at this time, it would be difficult imagine a project centred on anything earlier than the 1920s or 1930s. Veracity and accuracy is another criticism often levelled at oral history. Memory is inherently selective, faulty, deluded and fraught with all sorts of problems as well as being revealing and potentially informative. Psychologists, for example, now tell us that our autobiographical memories are used to construct our identities in the present but are played out in scenarios to test what our future reactions should be in similar circumstances. These are problems that are to some extent a product of the way that oral history developed in the later twentieth century.

The directness of the engagement between the historian/interviewer and the historical subject/interviewee means that the problem of interpreting evidence that can be seen in any historical engagement is especially urgent in the case of oral history. When an historical document is read, we are no more a blank sheet than the document itself. We bring our own knowledge, presuppositions and cultural belonging to the table (Chapter 21). Likewise, oral historians play an active part in the interviewing process, not just framing the questions but also playing a vital part in determining the nature of the moment.

Much of the practice of oral history is related to the techniques and complexities of interviewing people, in particular the forensic skills of constructing a table of questions that meet the needs of the research project and also allow the respondent the freedom to express themselves, introducing material of which the interviewer is otherwise unaware. Decisions must be made regarding the technicalities of the material and equipment: is the recorder vital, or might the notebook be less intrusive and so more appropriate? How are the interviews to be transcribed in a way that allows a fuller understanding to emerge? These are technical problems that require a specific kind of training that is beyond our concerns. We wish, rather, to focus more specifically on the historiographical and conceptual issues associated with oral history.

24.3 Interviewing Techniques and the Limits of Memory: Arthur Harding and the East End Underworld

A pioneer in its techniques, Raphael Samuel developed oral history as a way of giving voice to the powerless but also as a device to retrieve historical detail that would otherwise stay beyond the reach of the historian. His interviews in the 1970s with Arthur Harding (or Treserden to give him his real name) are no exception. Born in 1886 and brought up in the notorious neighbourhood of the Old Nichol in Bethnal Green, Harding appeared to offer a direct bridge back to the East End of the late nineteenth and early twentieth centuries.

He presented Samuel with a chance to talk to perhaps the last known survivor of a world we thought quite lost, as well as providing, as Samuel put it, a 'capital document' for future historians. (The archive is now held by the Bishopsgate Institute.) Harding had first recorded his memories on paper, which later arrived with Samuel via a mutual contact, Stan Newens (Newens, 2007). This 400-page typescript focused mainly on Harding's life as a 'terror' in the East End, his stretches in jail (including a 5-year term in Dartmoor), and his evidence to the Royal Commission on the Metropolitan Police in 1908 described him as 'the most slippery customer in Brick Lane' (Samuel, 1981). Fascinating as much of this material obviously was, Samuel believed that, because it focused on Harding's criminal activities, the manuscript did not yield enough of Harding's life as a whole. More particularly, it said next to nothing about Harding's childhood in the Nichol. Samuel wished to develop the everyday aspects of Harding's life: his period as a cabinet maker, domestic life, child–parent relations, the informal networks of the underworld, the relationships among the English, Irish, Jews and what Harding called 'Half-Jews', and gambling, racing and street-trading. In contrast, Harding presented his autobiography as a life of crime but only in the important context of his fifty or so years of going straight.

The relationship between Harding and Samuel was always likely to be difficult. Politically, Harding was a Conservative voter – except in 1945 – and from a family of 'poor but loyal' Conservatives. He had spent a lifetime living on his wits and his physical courage. He even joined Mosley's Blackshirts 'for the excitement', as he put it. Samuel, on the other hand, was a secular Jew brought up in the Communist party and intellectually steeped in its traditions. He gained a First Class degree at the University of Oxford and, although later politically active with the New Left, lived to some extent a life of the mind. They had the East End in common (both saw it as their natural habitat) but generational chasms loomed large. Harding was born in 1886 and Samuel in 1934. By the time Harding was interviewed by Samuel he was old enough (and presumably harmless enough) to be known by the Mosleyites (see Chapter 13) with affection and perhaps with a patronizing touch as 'Uncle Arthur'.

Besides the wish to explain and vindicate his life, Harding wanted to expose what he regarded as the venal corruption of the Metropolitan Police. One in particular, Divisional Detective Inspector Wensley ('the Weasel'), presented as a villain in all but profession, pursued Harding through the back lanes and law courts of London. Harding's role was prominent. At one moment, he was at the heart of gangland London, fighting the Darby Sarbini gang or the Titanic Mob; in the next, he was championing the vulnerable (he was morally offended, for instance, by pimping and the women that suffered from it), a friend and respecter of the immigrant Jew and those physically weak or disabled. His appearances in the dock were always unfortunate accidents or deliberate efforts to put him away but were testimony to Harding's verbal elegance, as well as a genuine autodidactic attitude towards learning the law. He claimed never to have lied to the courts: a truthfulness that contrasted with Wensley's deliberate efforts to send him down.

Samuel's instinct as an oral historian was to let the subject speak for himself, running a danger that Harding's childhood and other areas of interest to the reading public would be neglected. Apparently, Harding even refused at first to focus on the criminal and sub-criminal characters of the East End: Long Hymie, Dodger Mullins, Darky the Coon and others, let alone the more mundane stuff of social history. Instead, he lightened on extraneous events such as the Whitechapel murders and the Dockers' Strike, both of which date back to the 1880s. His evidence, given with no particular respect for structure or chronology, threatened to lead the reader into an unpromising labyrinth of characters and places. This apparent impasse called for a compromise. If the material was to be published and Harding's autobiography not to collapse into a biography authored by Samuel, something had to be done. A 'battle of wills', as Samuel was later to describe it, ensued:

> We settled for a *de facto* compromise, in which each of us pursued our particular hobby-horse – the Jago in my case, Inspector Wensley in Arthur's – while the other waited patiently to return to the main point.
>
> (Raphael Samuel Archive, Bishopsgate Institute)

To an extent then, both witness and inquisitor had tapered perspectives of the nature of the East End and drew upon the copious literature associated with the area, for Harding much of it sensational. For his part, Samuel self-consciously traced a journey from the slums described in the art and literature of the period, of social investigation and other social reportage, to the postwar slum clearances described in the sociology of that time. The result was Samuel's *East End Underworld – Chapters in the Life of Arthur Harding* (1981).

Both interviewer and interviewee tended to draw upon popular constructions of the East End. Harding looked for vindication and (in the style of the melodramas he watched at the Britannia theatre in Hoxton) for revenge. Samuel's first point of reference, on the other hand, was the slum literature of Arthur Morrison and others such as his *Child of the Jago*. Samuel was a pioneer in this hitherto little-known Booth archive at the London School of Economics. No doubt because of his own personal involvement, his knowledge of the tribal closeness of the East End described by the sociology of Young and Willmott (1957), Samuel complained that Harding was unable to separate narrative from analysis, unable, it seemed, to recall events without conceptualizing and interpreting them, hypothesizing or forever speculating on the motives of his enemies. Nor could Harding divorce his own memories from received views of the area. He continuously explained his experiences in clichés, drawing rather more on the 'darkest East End' representation made famous by late-Victorian social reportage than that of the 'golden age' literature of East End writing that celebrates community solidarities. Biography is 'replete', Samuel observed, 'with cultural borrowings, drawing its categories from religious, political ideas and literary imaginings' (www.bishopsgate.org.uk/content/1008/Samuel-Raphael).

The real problem, however, was to agree on the boundaries of oral history: to know whether these were the partially expunged memories and views of Harding or evidence crafted, shaped and even manipulated by a professional historian. Whether too, as there is such a confusion of images and messages about the East End, it was even possible to grasp a truthful, unsullied account by simply using oral history methods. Samuel recognized this tension in how the East End was characterized but also the tension between Harding and himself, both creatures of their time and each the instrument of their own memories where evidence derived by oral history methods is likely to say as much about the historian as the history.

Oral history has added a whole new dynamic to historical research and publication in relation to both method and subject matter but also comes packaged with problems peculiar to itself. The experience of *East End Underworld* revealed, in effect, a balance sheet of advantages and disadvantages. The rewards seem to far outweigh the methodological difficulties, but there may

454 *Methods*

be another perspective from which to view what we do with oral history, and it is these we examine next.

24.4 The Wider Conceptual Problems

When one oral historian wanted to understand the circumstances of the Giriama revolt against the British in Kenya in 1914, he questioned members of the Mijikenda. Despite all historical or documentary evidence to the contrary, they insisted that the conflict was prompted by a rape. Structurally, there is an explanation for this. It seems that in the tradition of this culture, 'the idea of rape was a convenient abstraction denoting a serious social transgression which, when involving outsiders, was a legitimate cause for war' (Spear, 1981, p. 141). This explanation could be applied to all wars: as rape was the cause of one war it became the stock explanation for all wars.

This is an example of a strand of oral history that relies less on autobiographical memory and more on oral traditions that percolate down through the generations of preliterate societies. It is an approach that can be traced back to the early fieldwork of anthropologists and sociologists. Jan Vansina's *Oral Tradition as History* (1985) addressed the shortcomings of his own pioneering 1961 book and made a plea for the reconstruction of history using oral methods. It promoted a considerable debate about the merits of oral history and was couched in anthropological discourses (see Chapter 18). Within anthropology, functionalists were sceptical of oral history, believing that it could do little else but confirm present-day institutions, reflecting the social relations therein. Structuralists, on the other hand, argued that many preliterate societies constructed historical narratives that were transmitted in oral traditions in ways that allowed structural anthropologists to study societies and (we might surmise) for historians to identify change. These oral traditions, which were 'largely composed of collages of universal symbols artfully constructed according to set patterns of thought to express essential human values', were therefore a vital element of the societies they studied (Spear, 1981, p. 134).

Vansina later wrote *Living in Africa* (1994) with a developed knowledge that oral evidence was infused with structural conventions about the past that are accepted by members of the group, layered with mythology and laced with hearsay. The oral transmission of these 'unwritten documents', mediated through collective memory, was later re-explored by Vansina and others in *Oral Tradition: A Study in Historical Methodology* (2009). The purpose of his approach was to reconstruct knowledge by tapping into narratives that existed a priori in society and which were shared by members of a society regardless, for instance, of whether an event like the 1914 rebellion in Kenya was remembered by this or that individual giving testimony at any one time. Ethnographers, whether their subject area is the native cultures of modern Africa or the lives, narratives and rituals of Western societies, use oral-based approaches in societies they study in order to gain insights into whole cultures, social lives and political practices. While Vansina and others do it by identifying the structural assumptions built into pre-literate society, European folk memory has been captured primarily by retrieving individual memories as a way of piecing together what psychologists call 'flashbulb memory', that is, memories that are stirred by momentous social events such as the death of Princess Diana or the attacks on the United States in September 2001. It is to oral history as it has been applied to European narratives that we now turn.

Oral traditions speak to a deeper and more enduring human need that has been consistently present in Western society since at least the transformations associated with large-scale industrialization (and later de-industrialization), urbanization and migration. Most of us, at some point in our lives or in our relationship with older relatives, friends or neighbours have encountered the sensation of something passing from the world and felt that their existence will pass from living memory and become a story told rather than a scene witnessed. In due course, even the story will be forgotten. This loss is apparent in individual lives but also in relation to change in the village, change in inner-city neighbourhoods, changing work-practices and relations, and in religious observance. This fear of loss can act as a powerful imperative to do something to preserve the past and has two consequences for how oral history might be thought about. The first relates to the wider history that provides the context for oral testimony; the second is connected to the idea that people will 'do' oral history with or without the participation of the academy.

These are important sources of inspiration for all strands of oral history. It is interesting that for Ewart Evans, whom we encountered in Section 2, the passing of folkways and traditional language acted as the mainspring that drove his research. He recognized a vocabulary used by East Anglian ploughmen who started work in the 1880s and 1890s that he had earlier found in medieval poetry. This, he knew, would not last. Once this was recognized, he became less insistent on finding academic antecedents, recognizing instead another much older lineage behind the drive to record and recover a world that was about to disappear.

Ewart Evans was not the first to feel this and to act upon it. One point of origin for the study of oral history lies far outside of the formal field of historical inquiry and is deeply embedded in the history of literature and music as well as the scholarly practice of history. Collecting oral tradition and reproducing it in print for a wider audience became a particular enthusiasm in the German-speaking lands. Here it provided one of the many connections between the spirit of inquiry native to the European Enlightenment of the eighteenth century and the growing cultural nationalism of the later eighteenth and nineteenth centuries often associated with romantic literature like that of Walter Scott in Scotland (see Chapter 3). Gotthold Ephraim Lessing (1729–1781), for example, was a poet, philosopher and critic whose collection of stories entitled *Dschinnistan* (1786–1789) used such folk tales alongside original stories. While there was an uncharacteristic emphasis on the triumph of reason over mysticism in these stories, they did help to legitimate the use of such folk tales in literature culture and the Western art tradition. One of Lessing's tales concerns a magic zither that is considered one of several possible sources for Mozart's *Magic Flute* (1791).

Yet, it was the brothers Jakob Grimm (1785–1863) and Wilhelm Grimm (1786–1859) who did most to develop the art of collecting and whose names are best known beyond their native Germany. As leading academics, their first interest was in linguistics and philology (the relationship of languages and their histories), out of which their passion for collecting grew. Despite their popularity and the enduring place of 'Snow White and the Seven Dwarfs' and 'The Frog King' in our popular culture, their collecting was very much a function of their studies of language. They began collecting folk tales and legends in 1807 and rode the wave of enthusiasm for German folklore, publishing their *Children's and Household Tales* (1810) followed by another volume of seventy tales in 1814. They came with the scholarly apparatus and footnotes associated with serious folklore but also remained in more popular circulation. It is their method that is of primary interest to us. Their intention was to offer faithful renditions of folklore rather than adaptations intended for the print market. As with the Dane Hans Christian Anderson, the Grimm brothers expressed through their stories base national sentiments, and these stories represented a significant step towards modern folklore studies and ultimately towards the practice of oral history.

They were not alone in their endeavours. Klemens Brentano (1778–1842), also a novelist and poet, worked with his brother-in-law Ludwig Achim von Arnim (1781–1831) on a collection of folksongs, *Des Knaben Wunderhorn* (1805–1808). Like the Grimms, they were rigorous in their approach and the collecting of folk song and music became another dimension to the systematic retrieval of the non-print worlds of the past. In Britain, a number of collectors started collecting folk song and dance. This was led by Cecil Sharp (1859–1924) who, upon returning from an attempt to develop a teaching and music career in Australia, encountered English folk music anew and particularly the almost-extinct practice of Morris dancing. He used the music he discovered in his own compositions and retrieved and notated music and dance that would otherwise have been lost. The fact that Sharp frequently bowdlerized the lyrics of folksongs before publishing them or using them in teaching also raised an awareness of methodological problems associated with transcription as well as interpretation. In 1911 he founded the English Folk Dance Society, which went on in 1932 to merge with the Folk Song Society. Between 1916 and 1918 he travelled in the United States, contributing to the ongoing work of collecting and recording folk songs in the Appalachian Mountains.

Tracking the development of English and Scottish folk songs and the way in which they evolved over time as they migrated, along with the folk themselves, to North America was very much the concern of Francis James Child (1825–1896). Child made the return journey from his native United States to study not only the folk song of his own land but their countries of origin. In this respect he pioneered the area developed by Sharp. Paralleling work going on in Denmark, he amassed a huge collection of songs (both tunes and words) and their historical lineage, which can be found in his ten-volume *The English and Scottish Popular Ballad* (1882–1898).

By the end of the early part of the twentieth century, folk songs were being widely collected. At one level this was an act of retrieval, undertaken for its own sake, but on another it was also being adapted in contemporary compositions. Lucy Broadwood (1858–1929), who followed her father John into collecting folk songs, was a founding member and moving spirit of the Folk Song Society in England. In 1904, the English composer Ralph Vaughan Williams (1872–1958) was moved by the fear that the tradition of the English folk song would soon disappear and, worse still, disappear without a trace. His method was simply to tramp the countryside talking to people, listening to them sing and transcribing and thus preserving what he heard. This was later incorporated into his music but the act of retrieval was done nonetheless, and Vaughan Williams consciously saw it as contributing to the work of collectors like Broadwood.

The Hungarian composers Zotland Kodaly (1882–1967) and Bela Bartok (1881–1945) had a similar approach to their music. Here, in a way, is a return to the academic origins of the Grimm brothers because Kodaly's interest in folk tales and songs grew out of research for his doctorate on Hungarian folk song. Throughout 1905 he travelled through the Hungarian countryside recording songs and stories on phonograph cylinders. Out of his 1906 thesis came a hugely productive collaboration that made a major contribution to the rise of ethnomusicology. Kodaly met Bela Bartok in 1908 with Kodaly initially acting as mentor to the older Bartok. Their own compositions were profoundly shaped by this research, original and valuable in revealing the origins of Magyar folk music and its relationship with the gypsy music of the region.

Ethnomusicology and oral history are not the same. The early collectors of folk tales and songs did not always, if ever, use the kind of methodological discipline that we would expect of a modern historian. However, from the Grimms through to Child and then Kodaly and Bartok there was a growing awareness of the need to establish critical procedures and methods in the recording of the material collected. More than this though, through the rise of the practice of collecting folkways, including those who helped to popularize it even where they had no awareness of sound methods, there is still common ground with the inspirations behind oral history.

All this leaves us with two dimensions to consider. First, worlds are constantly being lost as cultures change and as the memory of each generation passes from human recall. For Walter Scott it was the taming of the Scottish borders by the spread of modern commerce. For Vaughan Williams in England, it was the loss of an oral tradition that had been overwhelmed by the tide of growing literacy. The anxiety was clear. If this is not recorded now, the world apparent to us now will be gone forever. The second area of common ground is that oral history tends to focus on the spoken, hence its name. This can lead to amnesia: to forget that which could as easily be called aural history. It is about hearing as well as speaking, and hearing is by no means restricted to hearing the spoken word alone.

With the sense of losing a part of the world as individual and social memories fade comes an important motive for doing history by oral methods that in turn answers a deep human need. Either self-consciously in the manner of Scott in Scotland or through the Grimms as part of a rich lineage of folklore in Germany or through unselfconscious storytelling and ballad making, people have always done oral history. Now, in the age of the electronic recording, mass print culture and the Internet and in the knowledge that academic historians, amateur historians and community groups have now practiced oral history with great sophistication, people will carry on doing it using these more modern means. Putting the proverbial genie back in the bottle is not an option. It seems likely that a wide range of people will carry on interviewing and recording the memory of their villages and streets in the face of inexorable change or recording the memories of 'the old country' before the tales of migration are lost. They will do this whether academic historians are paying attention or not. It would be better if attention were paid.

Postscript

Oral history is a strand of historical inquiry that has grown in status in recent years and although still regarded by more conventional historians with a degree of suspicion has also been responsible for innovative studies. Part of its appeal derives from its democratic impulses. Oral history has presented opportunities for thousands of amateur historians in community groups and even schools to undertake research into aspects of the past. At its most basic level, you do not need to be a trained historian to pick up a tape recorder and interview elderly people about their past experiences. And oral history provides ordinary people who are largely absent from the historical record with the opportunity to speak for themselves. Without the work of oral historians, therefore, we would know much less about the lives and working conditions of the men and women who through their toil created the world as we know it.

There have been strands within what might loosely be described as oral history which have not directly addressed the experiences of the elderly trawled from their memories but rather have striven to understand the role of storytelling, particularly in preliterate cultures. Folk tales and music constitute part of vital oral traditions. Their meanings may have been lost over time, but the stories have been resurrected and reconstructed by anthropologists and cultural historians to reveal the attitudes of the inhabitants of ancient societies to vital questions about life, death and change.

Not that oral history is without its difficulties, as conventional historians are quick to point out. For the most part, as a methodology it relies upon the memories of witnesses, and we know only too well how fickle, unreliable and selective these can be. In answer to this, we can say that oral historians are interested not only in the ability of people to recall information reliably but also in how they interpreted the events that shaped their lives. It is clear also that recall of the past is shaped profoundly by the present. People interpret their lives through the prism of the here and now and often attempt to reconstruct personal narratives as a means of making sense of or celebrating them. The process of gathering information is also prone to influence from the presence of the interviewer. All memories are therefore recalled with a particular audience in mind and responses to questions shaped by beliefs in what is required or expected of them. These sorts of criticisms do not necessarily compromise the promise of oral history, however, not least because they can also be levelled at other, more conventional sources. All documentary sources are written with a particular audience in mind and, equally importantly, also depend upon the memories of their authors.

Oral history thus continues to offer much in its ability to access the lives of ordinary people; over time, as it confronts and overcomes its most pressing theoretical and methodological problems, it may even become accepted as part of mainstream historiography.

Further Reading

Robert Perks and Alistair Thompson (eds.) (2006) *The Oral History Reader*.
Raphael Samuel (1981) *East End Underworld: Chapters in the Life of Arthur Harding*.
Anthony Selden and Joanna Pappworth (1983) *By Word of Mouth: Elite Oral History*.
Elizabeth Tonkin (1992) *Narrating Our Pasts: The Social Construction of Oral History*.
Jan Vansina (1985) *Oral Tradition as History*.

Bibliography

The place of publication is London unless otherwise stated.

Abbott, Andrew (1991) 'The Lost Synthesis', *Social Science History* 15 (2), pp. 201–38.
Abbott, Edith (1917) 'Charles Booth 1840–1916', *Journal of Political Economy* 25 (2), pp. 195–200.
Abrams, Philip (1982) *Historical Sociology*, Ithaca: Cornell University Press.
Achinstein, Peter (ed.) (2004) *Science Rules: A Historical Introduction to Scientific Methods*, Baltimore: The Johns Hopkins University Press.
Adams, John W. (1981) 'Consensus, Community, and Exoticism', *The Journal of Interdisciplinary History* 12 (2), pp. 253–65.
Adelman, Jeremy (2017) 'What is Global History Now?', *Aeon Essays*, 2 March.
A'Hearn, Brian, Franco Peracchi and Giovanni Vecchi (2009) 'Height and the Normal Distribution: Evidence from Italian Military Data', *Demography* 46 (1), pp. 1–25.
Alcock, Susan, Terence D'Altroy, Kathleen Morrison and Carla Sinopoli (eds.) (2001) *Empires. Perspectives from Archaeology and History*, Cambridge: Cambridge University Press.
Aldgate, Anthony (2007) *Britain Can Take It*, I. B. Tauris.
Alexander, Sally (1976) 'Women's Work in Nineteenth-Century London', in A. Oakley and T. Mitchell (eds.), *The Rights and Wrongs of Women*, Harmondsworth: Penguin.
Alexander, Sally (1984) 'Women, Class and Sexual Differences in the 1830s and 1840s: Some Reflections on the Writing of a Feminist History', *History Workshop Journal* 17 (1), pp. 125–49.
Alexander, Sally (1994) *Becoming a Woman: And Other Essays in 19th and 20th Century Feminist History*, Virago.
Allen, Rick (1998) *The Moving Pageant: A Literary Sourcebook on London Streetlife, 1700–1914*, Routledge.
Althusser, Louis (1962) *For Marx*, Allen Lane.
Amt, Emilie (ed.) (1993) *Women's Lives in Medieval Europe. A Sourcebook*, Routledge.
Anderson, Benedict (2006) [1983] *Imagined Communities: Reflections on the Origins and Spread of Nationalism*, Virago.
Anderson, Michael (1980) *Approaches to the History of the Western Family, 1500–1914*, Basingstoke: Macmillan.
Anderson, Perry (1964) 'Origins of the Present Crisis', *New Left Review* 23, pp. 26–53.
Anderson, Perry (1974) *Passages from Antiquity to Feudalism*, New Left Books.
Ange, Olivia and David Berliner (2015) *The Anthropology of Nostalgia*, New York: Berghahn.
Ankersmit, Frank (2001a) 'Edmund Burke, Historism, and History', in W. M. Verhoeven (ed.), *Revolutionary Histories. Transatlantic Cultural Nationalism, 1775–1815*, Basingstoke: Palgrave.
Ankersmit, Frank (2001b) *Historical Representation*, Stanford: Stanford University Press.
Anonymous (1989) 'The Runes of Loki. A Mischievous Look at Wargamers', *Miniature Wargames* 71.
Arendt, Hannah (2004) [1968] *The Origins of Totalitarianism*, New York: Schocken Books.
Aristotle (1997) *Aristotle's Poetics*, trans. George Whalley, Montreal: McGill-Queen's University Press.
Arnold, David and David Hardiman (eds.) (1993) *Subaltern Studies*, VII, Delhi: Oxford University Press.

Ashworth, Tony (2000) [1980] *Trench Warfare 1914–1918: The Live and Let Live System*, Pan Books.
Aston, T. H. (1967) *Crisis in Europe, 1560–1660*, New York: Anchor.
Avis, Paul (2002) *Christian Church: Theological Resources in Historical Perspective*, Edinburgh: T&T Clarke.
Ayers, Edward L. (1996) *All Over the Map: Rethinking American Regions*, Baltimore: The Johns Hopkins University Press.
Azzam, Reem (1999) *Modern Historical Methodology vs. Hadeeth Methodology* [www.islamreligion.com/articles/851/viewall/modern-historical-methodology-vs-hadeeth-methodology/].
Bacon, D. (2006) *Depoliticizing War* [http://dbacon.igc.org/Art/03PolWar.html].
Baetens, Jan (ed.) (2001) *The Graphic Novel*, Leuven: Leuven University Press.
Baetens, Jan and Hugo Frey (2015) *The Graphic Novel. An Introduction*, Cambridge: Cambridge University Press.
Bagley, J. J. (1972) *Historical Interpretations: Sources of Medieval History, 1066–1540*, Devon: David & Charles.
Bailyn, Bernard (1992) *The Ideological Origins of the American Revolution*, Cambridge, MA: Harvard University Press.
Bakhtin, Mikhail (1984) [1965] *Rabelais and His World*, Bloomington: Indiana University Press.
Ballantyne, Tony (2010) 'The Changing Shape of the Modern British Empire and its Historiography', *Historical Journal* 53 (2), pp. 429–52.
Bancroft, George (1857) *History of the United States*, Boston: Little, Brown.
Barbauld, Anna Laetitia (1825) 'On Monastic Institutions', in *The Works*, 2 vols, Longman.
Barclay, Katie (2021) 'State of the Field: The History of Emotions', *History* 106 (371), pp. 456–66.
Barnard, Alan (2000) *History and Theory in Anthropology*, Cambridge: Cambridge University Press.
Barnard, Alan and Jonathan Spencer (eds.) (2002) *Encyclopaedia of Social and Cultural Anthropology*, Routledge.
Barnett, Correlli (1986) *The Audit of War: The Illusion and Reality of Britain as a Great Nation*, Faber and Faber.
Barratt Brown, Michael (1988) 'Away with All the Great Arches: Anderson's History of British Capitalism', *New Left Review* 167, pp. 22–55.
Barrell, John (1980) *The Dark Side of the Landscape. The Rural Poor in English Paintings, 1730–1840*, Cambridge: Cambridge University Press.
Barrow, J. W. (1981) *A Liberal Descent: Victorian Historians and the English Past*, Cambridge: Cambridge University Press.
Battuta, Ibn (2005) [1929] *Travels in Asia and Africa 1325–1354*, Routledge Curzon.
Bayly, C. A. (1989) *Imperial Meridian*, Longman.
Bayly, C. A. (1997) *Empire and Information. Intelligence Gathering and Social Communication in India, 1780–1870*, Cambridge: Cambridge University Press.
Bayly, C. A. (2004) *The Birth of the Modern World, 1780–1914*, Oxford: Blackwell.
Beard, Mary (1987) [1946] *Woman as a Force in History: A Study in Traditions and Realities*, New York: Persia Books.
Beckert, Sven (2014) *Empire of Cotton. A New History of Global Capitalism*, Harmondsworth: Penguin.
Bédarida, François (1991) [1979] *Social History of Britain, 1851–1975*, Routledge.
Beinhart, William and Lotte Hughes (2007) *Environment and Empire*, Oxford: Oxford University Press.
Belich, James, John Darwin, Margret Frenz and Chris Wickham (eds.) (2016) *The Prospect of Global History*, Oxford: Oxford University Press.
Bender, Thomas (2002) 'Strategies of Narrative Synthesis', *American Historical Review* 107 (1), pp. 129–53.
Ben-Israel, Hedva (1968) *English Historians on the French Revolution*, Cambridge: Cambridge University Press.
Benjamin, Walter (1968) [1936] 'The Work of Art in the Age of Mechanical Reproduction', in Hannah Arendt (ed.), *Illuminations: Essays and Reflections*, New York: Schocken Books.
Bennett, Judith M. (2006) *History Matters: Patriarchy and the Challenge of Feminism*, Philadelphia: University of Pennsylvania Press.

Bennett, Judith M. (2008) 'Forgetting the Past', *Gender & History* 20, pp. 669–77.
Bentley, Amy (1995) 'Book Review Essay', *Digest*, pp. 20–4.
Bentley, Michael (2005) *Modernizing England's Past: English Historiography in the Age of Modernism, 1870–1970*, Cambridge: Cambridge University Press.
Berg, Maxine (1994) *The Age of Manufactures: Industry, Innovation and Work in Britain*, Routledge.
Berg, Maxine (2005) *Luxury and Pleasure in Eighteenth Century Britain*, Oxford: Oxford University Press.
Berg, Maxine and Pat Hudson (1992) 'Rehabilitating the Industrial Revolution', *Economic History Review* XLV (1), pp. 24–50.
Berger, John (1990) [1973] *Ways of Seeing*, Harmondsworth: Penguin.
Berlin, Isaiah (1976) *Vico and Herder: Two Studies in The History of Ideas*, Chatto & Windus.
Berman, Marshall (1983) *All that Is Solid Melts into Air: The Experience of Modernity*, Verso.
Bernstein, Barton (ed.) (1968) *Towards a New Past: Dissenting Essays in American History*, New York: Chatto & Windus.
Bhabha, Homi (1994) *The Location of Culture*, Routledge.
Biagini, Eugenio F. and Alistair Reid (1991) *Currents of Radicalism: Popular Radicalism, Organised Labour and Popular Politics 1850–1914*, Cambridge: Cambridge University Press.
Binion, Rudolph (1976) *Hitler Among the Germans*, New York: Elsevier.
Bischoff, Bernhard (1990) [1979] *Latin Palaeography: Antiquity and the Middle Ages*, Cambridge: Cambridge University Press.
Blaas, P. B. M. (1978) *Continuity and Anachronism: Parliamentary and Constitutional Development in Whig Historiography and the Anti-Whig Reaction*, Germany: Springer.
Black, Jeremy (1997) *Maps and Politics*, Chicago: University of Chicago Press.
Black, Jeremy (2000) *Maps in History: Constructing Images of the Past*, New Haven: Yale University Press.
Blanning, T. C. W. and Peter Wende (eds.) (1999) *Reform in Great Britain and Germany, 1750–1850*, Oxford: Oxford University Press.
Blythe, Ronald (1969) *Akenfield: Portrait of an English Village*, Harmondsworth: Penguin.
Boddice, Rob (2014) 'The Affective Turn: Historicizing the Emotions', in Tileaga and Byford (eds.), *Psychology and History*.
Boddice, Rob (2018) *The History of Emotions*, Manchester University Press.
Bogdanor, Vernon (2003) *The British Constitution in the Twentieth Century*, Oxford: Oxford University Press.
Bondanella, Peter E. (1973) *Machiavelli and the Art of Renaissance History*, Detroit: Wayne State University Press.
Booth, Charles (1889) *Life and Labour of the People in London*, Macmillan.
Boucher, David (1995) 'The Life, Times and Legacy of R. G. Collingwood', in D. Boucher, J. Connelly and T. Modood (eds.), *Philosophy, History and Civilization*, pp. 1–31, Cardiff: University of Wales Press.
Boucher, David, James Connelly and Tariq Modood (eds.) (1995) *Philosophy, History and Civilization. Interdisciplinary Perspectives on R. G. Collingwood*, Cardiff: University of Wales Press.
Bourdieu, Pierre (1963) 'The Attitude of the Algerian Peasant Towards Time', in J. Pitt-Rivers (ed.), *Mediterranean Countrymen: Essays in the Social Anthropology of the Mediterranean*, pp. 55–72, The Hague: Mouton.
Bourke, Joanna (2003) 'Fear and Anxiety: Writing about Emotion in Modern History', *History Workshop Journal* 55, pp. 111–33.
Bowering, G. (1997) 'The Concept of Time in Islam', *Proceedings of the American Philosophical Society* 141 (1), pp. 55–66.
Boyns, Trevor (2007) 'Accounting, Information, and Communication Systems', in G. G. Jones and J. Zeitlin (eds.), *The Oxford Handbook of Business History*, pp. 447–69, Oxford: Oxford University Press.
Braudel, Fernand (1992) *The Mediterranean and the Mediterranean World in the Age of Philip II*, Harper Collins.
Brewer, John (1976) [1989] *Party Ideology and Popular Politics at the Accession of George III*, Cambridge: Cambridge University Press.

Briggs, Asa (1962) [1959] *Chartist Studies*, New York: St Martin's Press.
Broadberry, Steve (1997) *The Productivity Race: British Manufacturing Performance in International Perspective 1850–1990*, Cambridge: Cambridge University Press.
Bromwich, David (2014) *The Intellectual Life of Edmund Burke: From the Sublime and Beautiful to American Independence*, Cambridge, MA: Harvard University Press.
Brooks, Nicholas (1985) 'The Organisation and Achievements of the Peasants of Kent and Essex in 1381', in H. Hayr-Harting and R. I. Moore (eds.), *Studies in Medieval History*, Hambledon.
Brose, David (1973) 'The Northeastern United States', in J. Fitting (ed.), *Development of North American Archaeology*, pp. 84–96, University Park: Penn State University Press.
Brown, Callum G. (2009) *The Death of Christian Britain: Understanding Secularisation 1800–2000*, Routledge.
Brown, Jonathan (1998) *Painting in Spain 1500–1700*, New Haven: Yale University Press.
Brown, Richard and Beth Davis-Brown (1998) 'The Making of Memory: The Politics of Archives, Libraries and Museums in the Construction of National Consciousness', *History of the Human Sciences* 11 (4), pp. 17–32.
Brown, Stuart et al. (1980) *Adam Smith's Wealth of Nations*, Open University Press.
Brownley, Martine Watson (1985) *Clarendon and the Rhetoric of Historical Form*, Philadelphia: University of Pennsylvania Press.
Bruce, Steve (1992) *Religion and Modernization: Sociologists and Historians Debate the Secularization Thesis*, Oxford: Oxford University Press.
Burckhardt, Jacob (2004) *Civilization of the Renaissance in Italy*, New York: Modern House.
Burke, Edmund (2003) [1790] *Reflections on the Revolution in France*, ed. Frank Turner, New Haven: Yale University Press.
Burke, Edmund (2009) 'The Big Story. Human History, Energy Regimes, and the Environment', in E. Burke and K. Pomerantz (eds.), *The Environment and World History*, pp. 33–53, Berkeley: University of California Press.
Burke, Edmund and Kenneth Pomerantz (eds.) (2009) *The Environment and World History*, Berkeley: University of California Press.
Burke, Peter (1985) *Vico*, Oxford: Oxford University Press.
Burke, Peter (1997) *Varieties of Cultural History*, Cambridge: Cambridge University Press.
Burke, Peter (1998) *European Renaissance*, Oxford: Blackwell.
Burke, Peter (2005) [1992] *History and Social Theory*, Cornell: Cornell University Press.
Burke, Peter (2007) [2001] *Eyewitnessing: The Uses of Images as Historical Evidence*, Ithaca: Cornell University Press.
Burke, Peter (2008) *What is Cultural History?* Cambridge: Cambridge University Press.
Burke, Peter (2009) [1978] *Popular Culture in Early Modern Europe*, Farnham: Ashgate.
Burton, Antoinette (1995) *Burdens of History: British Feminism, Indian Women and Imperial Culture, 1865–1915*, Chapel Hill: University of North Carolina Press.
Burton, Antoinette (ed.) (2005) *Archive Stories: Fact, Fiction, and the Writing of History*, Durham: Duke University Press.
Butler, Judith (2006) *Gender Trouble: Feminism and the Subversion of Identity*, Routledge.
Butterfield, Herbert (1970) [1944] *The Englishman and His History*, New Haven: Archon Books.
Butterfield, Herbert (2005) [1931] *The Whig Interpretation of History*, Continuum.
Bynum, Caroline Walker (1984) *Jesus as Mother: Studies in the Spirituality of the Middle Ages*, Berkeley: University of California Press.
Bynum, Caroline Walker (1987) *Holy Feast and Holy Fast: The Religious Significance of Food to Medieval Women*, Berkeley: University of California Press.
Cain, P. J. and A. G. Hopkins (1986) 'Gentlemanly Capitalism and British Expansion Overseas, I. The Old Colonial System, 1688–1850', *Economic History Review* XXXIX p. 506.
Cain, P. J. and A. G. Hopkins (1987) 'Gentlemanly Capitalism and British Expansion Overseas, II. New Imperialism, 1850–1945', *Economic History Review* XL, pp. 1–26.
Cain, P. J. and A. G. Hopkins (2001) *British Imperialism, 1688–2000*, Harlow: Longman.

Calder, Angus (1991) *Myth of the Blitz*, Pimlico.
Carlyle, Thomas (2010) [1837] *Carlyle's French Revolution*, ed. Ruth Scurr, Continuum.
Carney, Nikita (April 2016) 'All Lives Matter, But So Does Race: Black Lives Matter and the Evolving Role of Social Media', *Humanity & Society* 40 (2), pp. 1–20.
Carr, E. H. (2001) [1961] *What Is History?*, Basingstoke: Palgrave.
Carter, K. Codell (2003) *The Rise of Causal Concepts of Disease: Case Histories*, Basingstoke: Palgrave.
Chadwick, Owen (1975) *The Secularization of the European Mind in the Nineteenth Century*, Cambridge: Cambridge University Press.
Chakrabarty, Dipesh (1989) *Rethinking Working-Class History. Bengal, 1890–1940*, Princeton: Princeton University Press.
Chakrabarty, Dipesh (2000) *Provincializing Europe: Postcolonial Thought and Historical Difference*, Princeton: Princeton University Press.
Chakravarti, Ranabir (2011) 'Natural Resources and Human Settlements. Perceiving the Environment in India', in N. S. Kapur (ed.), *Environmental History of Early India*, pp. 55–62.
Chamberlain, Mary (1975) *Fenwomen: A Portrait of Women in an English Village*, Virago.
Chandler, Alfred (1990) [1962] *Strategy and Structure: Chapters in the History of the American Industrial Enterprise*, Cambridge, MA: MIT Press.
Chandler, James (1999) *England in 1819: The Politics of Literary Culture and the Case of Romantic Historicism*, Chicago: University of Chicago Press.
Chase, Malcolm (2007) *Chartism: A New History*, Manchester: Manchester University Press.
Chaturvedi, Vinayak (ed.) (2000) *Mapping Subaltern Studies and the Postcolonial*, Verso.
Chauncey, George (1994), *Gay New York. Gender, Urban Culture and the Making of the Gay Male World, 1890–1940*, Flamingo.
Cheney, C. R. (2000) *A Handbook of Dates for British Students*, Cambridge: Cambridge University Press.
Cheng, Eileen (2008) *The Plain and Noble Garb of Truth. Nationalism and Impartiality in American Historical Writing, 1784–1860*, Athens: University of Georgia Press.
Childe, V. Gordon (1956) *Piecing Together the Past. The Interpretation of Archaeological Data*, Routledge & Kegan Paul.
Childs, Peter and Patrick Williams (1997) *An Introduction to Post-Colonial Theory*, Upper Saddle River, NJ: Prentice Hall.
Cho, Jennifer (2007) '(Re)Remembering the Apocalyptic Specter: Art Spiegelman's', *In the Shadow of No Towers* [www.americanpopularculture.com/archive/venues/spiegelman.htm].
Christian, David (2010) 'The Return of Universal History', *History and Theory* 49 (4), pp. 6–27.
Clanchy, M. T. (1993) *From Memory to Written Record: England 1066–1307*, Oxford: Blackwell.
Clapham, John (1949) [1926] *Economic History of Britain*, Cambridge: Cambridge University Press.
Clark, Anna (1995) *The Struggle for the Breeches: Gender and the Making of the British Working Class*, Berkeley: University of California Press.
Clark, Kenneth (1969) *Civilization: A Personal View*, BBC.
Clarke, Peter (2007) [1971] *Lancashire and the New Liberalism*, Cambridge: Cambridge University Press.
Claudio, Ester (2001) *Ergodic texts: In the Shadow of No Towers* [http://blog.comicsgrid.com/2011/02/ergodic-texts-in-the-shadow-of-no-towers/].
Cleghorn, Hugh (1861) *The Forests and Gardens of South India*, W. H. Allen.
Cobb, Richard C. (1974) *Modern French History in Britain*, Oxford: Oxford University Press.
Cobbett, William (2001) *Rural Rides*, Harmondsworth: Penguin.
Cohn, B. (1980) 'History and Anthropology: The State of Play', *Comparative Studies in Society and History* 22 (2), pp. 198–222.
Cohn, B. (1990) [1987] *Anthropologist Among the Historians and Other Essays*, Oxford: Oxford University Press.
Cohn, Norman (2005) [1967] *Warrant for Genocide: The Myth of the Jewish World Conspiracy and the Protocols of the Elders of Zion*, Serif.
Cole, G. D. H. (1989) [1941] *Chartist Portraits*, Cassell.
Cole, G. D. H. and Raymond Postgate (1938) *The Common People 1746–1938*, Methuen.

Coleman, D. C. (1992) *Myth, History and the Industrial Revolution*, Hambledon.
Colish, Marcia L. (1997) *Medieval Foundations of the Western Intellectual Tradition, 400–1400*, New Haven: Yale University Press.
Colley, Linda (2003) *Captives: Britain, Empire and the World 1600–1850*, Pimlico.
Colley, Linda (2005) *Britons: Forging the Nation 1707–1837*, New Haven: Yale University Press.
Collingwood, R. G. (1939) *An Autobiography*, Oxford: Oxford University Press.
Collingwood, R. G. (1961) [1946] *The Idea of History*, Oxford: Oxford University Press.
Collini, Stefan (1999) *English Pasts: Essays in History and Culture*, Oxford: Oxford University Press.
Connell, R. W. (1987) *Gender and Power: Society, the Person and Sexual Politics*, Cambridge: Polity Press.
Connell, R. W. (1995) *Masculinities*, Cambridge: Polity Press.
Cook, Matt, Robert Mills, Randolph Trumbach and H. G. Cocks (2007) *A Gay History of Britain. Love and Sex Between Men Since the Middle Ages*, Oxford: Greenwood World Publishing.
Cook, Matt, Alison Oram and Justin Bengry (eds.) (2022) *Locating Queer Histories. Places and Traces Across the UK*, Bloomsbury Academic.
Corfield, Penelope J. (2007) *Time and the Shape of History*, New Haven: Yale University Press.
Cosgrove, Denis E. (1999) *Mappings*, Reaktion.
Cosslett, Tess (ed.) (1984) *Science and Religion in the Nineteenth Century*, Cambridge: Cambridge University Press.
Cowling, Maurice (1971) *Impact of Labour 1920–1924: The Beginning of Modern British Politics*, Cambridge: Cambridge University Press.
Crafts, N. F. R. and C. K. Harley (1985) 'English Workers' Real Wages During the Industrial Revolution: Some Remaining Problems', *Journal of Economic History* 45, pp. 139–44.
Crafts, N. F. R. and C. K. Harley (1992) 'Output Growth and the British Industrial Revolution: A Restatement of the Crafts-Harley View', *Economic History Review* 45, pp. 703–30.
Craig, David (2010) '"High Politics" and the "New Political History"', *Historical Journal* 53, pp. 453–75.
Crewe, Emma (2005) *Lords of Parliament: Manners, Rituals and Politics*, Manchester: Manchester University Press.
Croce, Benedetto (1921) *Theory and History of Historiography*, Harrap.
Crosby, Alfred (1972) *The Columbian Exchange. Biological and Cultural Consequences of 1492*, Westport, CT: Greenwood Press.
Crosby, Alfred (1986) *Ecological Imperialism. The Biological Expansion of Europe, 900–1900*, Cambridge: Cambridge University Press.
Curtin, Philip (1969) *Atlantic Slave Trade*, Madison: University of Wisconsin Press.
Curtis-Wendlandt, Lisa, Paul Gibbard and Karen Green (eds.) (2013) *Political Ideas of Enlightenment Women: Virtue and Citizenship*, Farnham: Ashgate.
Daly, Mary (1979) *Gyn/Ecology*, The Women's Press.
Dangerfield, George (1997) [1935] *The Strange Death of Liberal England*, Stanford: Stanford University Press.
Darnton, Robert (2001) [1984] *The Great Cat Massacre: And Other Episodes of French Cultural History*, Harmondsworth: Penguin.
Daunton, Martin J. (1989) 'Gentlemanly Capitalism and British Industry 1820–1914', *Past and Present* 122 (1), pp. 119–58.
Davidoff, Leonore and Catherine Hall (1987) *Family Fortunes: Men and Women of the English Middle Class 1780–1850*, Routledge.
Davidson, James Dale (2019) *The Sovereign Individual: Mastering the Transition to the Information Age*, New York: Touchstone.
Davis, David Brion (1988) [1966] *The Problem of Slavery in Western Culture*, Oxford: Oxford University Press.
Davis, David Brion (2000) 'Looking at Slavery from Broader Perspectives', *American Historical Review* 105 (2), pp. 452–66.
Davis, David Brion (2014) *The Problem of Slavery in the Age of Emancipation*, New York: Vintage Books.

Davis, Jack (2002) 'Review of Books: Beyond Atlanta: The Struggle for Racial Equality in Georgia, 1940–1980, Stephen Tuck', *American Historical Review* 107 (5), pp. 1595–6.

Davis, Mike (2001) *Late Victorian Holocausts: El Niño Famines and the Making of the Third World*, New York: Verso.

Dawson, Graham (1994) *Soldier Heroes: British Adventure, Empire and the Imaginings of Masculinities*, Routledge.

Deal, Douglas (1993) *Race and Class in Colonial Virginia*, Revision of Author's Thesis.

De Beauvoir, Simone (1997) *The Second Sex*, Vintage.

Degler, Carl (1959) 'Slavery and the Genesis of American Race Prejudice', *Comparative Studies in Social History* II, pp. 49–66.

De Groot, Jerome (2016) *Consuming History: Historians and Heritage in Contemporary Popular Culture*, Abingdon: Routledge.

Deliege, Robert (2004) *Lévi-Strauss Today*, Oxford: Oxford University Press.

Delmas, Candice (2018) *A Duty to Resist: When Disobedience Should be Uncivil*, New York: Oxford University Press.

Delmas, Candice (2020) 'Uncivil Disobedience', in Schwartzberg, *Protest and Dissent*, pp. 9–44.

Delogu, Paolo (2002) *An Introduction to Medieval History*, Duckworth.

Denikin, Anton (1975) *The Career of a Tsarist Officer: Memoirs, 1872–1916*, Minnesota: University of Minnesota Press.

Dennis, Richard (1991) 'History, Geography, and Historical Geography', *Social Science History* 15 (2), pp. 265–88.

DeVun, Leah (2021) *The Shape of Sex. Non-binary Gender from Genesis to the Renaissance*, New York: Columbia University Press.

Diamond, Jared (1997) *Guns, Germs and Steel: The Fates of Human Societies*, New York: Vintage.

Dickens, Charles (2003) *Pickwick Papers*, Harmondsworth: Penguin.

Dickens, Charles (2012) *Bleak House*, Harmondsworth: Penguin.

Dirks, Nicolas (ed.) (1992) *Colonialism and Culture*, Ann Arbor: University of Michigan Press.

Dobson, Andrew and Robin Carper (1996) 'Infectious Diseases and Human Population History', *BioScience* 46 (2), pp. 115–26.

Donovan, Tristan (2010) *Replay. The History of Video Games*, East Sussex: Yellow Ant.

Doyle, Arthur Conan (1891) 'The Man with the Twisted Lip', *The Strand Magazine* 2 (12).

De Genova, Nicholas (2018) 'The "Migrant Crisis" as Racial Crisis: Do *Black Lives Matter* in Europe?', *Ethnic and Racial Studies* 41 (10), pp. 1765–82. http://doi.org/10.1080/0149870.2017.1361543.

Driver, Felix (2001) *Geography Militant: Geography, Exploration and Empire*, Oxford: Oxford University Press.

Du Bois, W. E. B. (1992) [1935] *Black Reconstruction: An Essay Toward a History of the Part Which Black Folk Played in the Attempt to Reconstruct Democracy in America, 1860–1880*, New York: Harcourt, Brace.

Duffy, Eamon (2005) [1992] *The Stripping of the Altars: Traditional Religion in England c.1400 – c.1580*, New Haven: Yale University Press.

Dunn, Elizabeth Bramm (2007) 'Preserving or Distorting History? Scholars Reflect on Archival Repositories', *Historical Methods* 40 (4).

Durkheim, Emile (2015) [1915] *The Elementary Forms of Religious Life*, trans. Joseph Ward Swain, George Allen & Unwin.

Dyer, Christopher (2002) *Making a Living in the Middle Ages: The People of Britain 850–1520*, New Haven: Yale University Press.

Edgerton, David (2006) *Warfare State: Britain, 1920–1970*, Cambridge: Cambridge University Press.

Edgerton, Gary (2001) 'Ken Burns's Rebirth of a Nation: Television, Narrative, and Popular History', in Landy, *The Historical Film*.

Egan, Pierce (1821) *Life in London*, London: Sherwood, Neely and Jones, reproduced facsimile in John Marriott (ed.), *Unknown London*, vol. 2.

Eisner, Will (1978) *Contract with God*, New York: Norton.

Eley, Geoff (2005) *A Crooked Line: From Cultural History to the History of Society*, Ann Arbor: University of Michigan Press.
Eley, Geoff and David Blackburn (1985) *The Peculiarities of German History: Bourgeois Society and Politics in Nineteenth-Century Germany*, Oxford: Oxford University Press.
Elsner, John and Roger Cardinal (1994) *The Cultures of Collecting*, Reaktion Books.
Elsner, John and Joan-Pau Rubiés (1999) 'Introduction', in idem (eds) *Voyages and Visions. Toward a Cultural History of Travel*, Reaktion Books.
Eltis, David (1987) *Economic Growth and the End of the Transatlantic Slave Trade*, New York: Oxford University Press.
Elton, G. E. R. (1998) *Return to Essentials: Some Reflection on the Present State of Historical Study*, Cambridge: Cambridge University Press.
Elton, G. E. R. (2002) [1967] *The Practice of History*, Oxford: Blackwell.
Englander, David and Rosemary O'Day (1983) *Mr Charles Booth's Inquiry: Life and Labour of the People in London Reconsidered*, Hambledon.
Englander, David and Rosemary O'Day (eds.) (1995) *Retrieved Riches: Social Investigation in Britain 1840–1914*, Farnham: Ashgate.
Enumerate Thematic Network (2013) *Report on the Thematic Surveys on Digital Collections in European Cultural Heritage Institutions* [www.enumerate.eu].
Evans-Pritchard, E. E. (1971) *The Azande: History and Political Institutions*, Oxford: Clarendon Press.
Fairclough, Adam (1983) 'Was Martin Luther King a Marxist?', *History Workshop Journal* 15, pp. 117–25.
Febvre, Lucien (2009) [1924] *A Geographical Introduction to History*, New York: Knopf.
Feldman, David and Jon Lawrence (2011) 'Introduction: Structures and Transformations in British Historiography', in idem (eds.), *Structures and Transformations in Modern British History*, Cambridge: Cambridge University Press.
Ferguson, Frances (2004) 'Burke and the Response to the Enlightenment', in Martin Fitzpatrick, Peter Jones, Christa Knellwolf and Iain McCalman (eds.), *The Enlightenment World*, London and New York: Routledge.
Ferguson, Frances (2004) 'Burke and the Response to the Enlightenment', in Martin Peter Jones Fitzpatrick, Christa Knellwolf and Ian McCalman (eds.), *The Enlightenment World*.
Ferguson, Niall (2011) *Civilization: The West and the Rest*, Allen Lane.
Ferguson, Niall (ed.) (2011) [1997] *Virtual History: Alternatives and Counterfactuals*, Harmondsworth: Penguin.
Ferguson, Wallace K. (1956) *The Renaissance*, New York: Holt.
Ferguson, Wallace K. (1981) [1948] *The Renaissance in Historical Thought: Five Centuries of Interpretation*, New York: AMS Press.
Fernández-Armesto, Felipe (1995) *Millennium*, Black Swan.
Figes, Orlando (1997) *A People's Tragedy: The Russian Revolution 1891–1924*, Pimlico.
Finkelman, Paul (2014) [1996] *Slavery and the Founders: Race and Liberty in the Age of Jefferson*, New York: Routledge.
Finn, Margot (1993) *After Chartism: Class and Nation in English Radical Politics, 1848–1874*, Cambridge: Cambridge University Press.
Fishman, William J. (1988) *East End 1888: Life in a London Borough Among the Labouring Poor*, Duckworth.
Fitting, James (ed.) (1973) *The Development of North American Archaeology. Essays in the History of Regional Traditions*, University Park: The Pennsylvania State University Press.
Fletcher, Caroline (2020) *The Beauty and the Terror: An Alternative History of the Italian Renaissance*, Vintage.
Flood, Robert, James Ginther and Joseph Goering (eds.) (2013) *Robert Grosseteste and His Intellectual Milieu*, Toronto: Pontifical Institute of Medieval Studies.
Floud, Roderick, Kenneth Wachter and Annabel Gregory (1990) *Height, Health and History: Nutritional Status in the United Kingdom, 1750–1980*, Cambridge: Cambridge University Press.
Flower, Michael A. and John Marincola (eds.) (2002) *Herodotus, The Histories*, Cambridge: Cambridge University Press.

Fogel, Robert and Stanley Engerman (1974) *Time on the Cross: The Economics of Negro Slavery*, Boston: Little, Brown.
Foner, Eric (1984) 'Why Is There No Socialism in the United States?', *History Workshop Journal* 17 (Spring), pp. 234–49.
Foster, John (1974) *Class Struggle and the Industrial Revolution*, Weidenfeld and Nicolson.
Foucault, Michel (1995) [1977] *Discipline and Punish: Birth of the Prison*, New York: Vintage Books.
Foucault, Michel (2001) [1965] *Madness and Civilization: A History of Insanity in the Age of Reason*, Routledge.
Foucault, Michel (2002) [1972] *The Archaeology of Knowledge*, Routledge.
Foucault, Michel (2003) [1973] *The Birth of the Clinic: An Archaeology of Medical Perception*, Routledge.
Fowler, Don and David Wilcox (eds.) (2010) *Philadelphia and the Development of Americanist Archaeology*, Tuscaloosa: University of Alabama Press.
Fredenson, Patrick (2009) 'Business History and History', in G. Jones and J. Zeitlin (eds.), *Oxford Handbook of Business History*, Oxford: Oxford University Press.
Fukuyama, Francis (1992) *The End of History and the Last Man*, New York: Free Press.
Fulbrook, Mary (ed.) (1997) *German History Since 1800*, Arnold.
Funari, Pedro, Martin Hall and Siân Jones (eds.) (1999) *Historical Archaeology. Back from the Edge*, Routledge.
Furet, François (1998) 'The French Revolution Revisited', in Gary Kates (ed.), *The French Revolution. Recent Debates and New Controversies*, Routledge.
Fussner, Frank Smith (2010) [1962] *The Historical Revolution: English Historical Writing and Thought, 1580–1640*, Westport, CT: Greenwood Press.
Gaddis, John (2002) *The Landscape of History: How Historians Map the Past*, Oxford: Oxford University Press.
Gadgil, Madhav and Ramachandra Guha (1993) *This Fissured Land. An Ecological History of India*, Berkeley: University of California Press.
Gallois, William (2007) *Time, Religion and History*, Harlow: Pearson Longman.
Galor, Katharina and Hanswulf Bloedhorn (2013) *The Archaeology of Jerusalem*, New Haven: Yale University Press.
Gamble, Andrew (2014) *Crisis Without End: The Unravelling of Western Prosperity*, Basingstoke: Palgrave.
Gammage, Robert (1894) *History of the Chartist Movement, 1837–54*, Newcastle: Browne and Browne.
Gardiner, Samuel Rawson (1894) [1863] *History of England from the Accession of James I to the Outbreak of the Civil War 1603–1642*, Longmans Green & Co.
Garnett, Jane, H. C. G. Matthew and John Walsh (1993) *Revival and Religion Since 1700: Essays for John Walsh*, Hambledon Press.
Gay, Peter (1986) *The Tender Passion. The Bourgeois Experience: Victoria to Freud*, New York: Norton.
Geary, Patrick J. (1994) *Phantoms of Remembrance: Memory and Oblivion at the First Millennium*, Princeton: Princeton University Press.
Geertz, Clifford (1973) *The Interpretation of Cultures: Selected Essays*, New York: Basic Books.
Ghosh, Peter (1999) 'Whig Interpretation of History', in K. Boyd (ed.), *Encyclopaedia of Historians and History Writing*, Fitzroy Dearborn.
Gibbon, Edward (1998) [1776] *The History of the Decline and Fall of the Roman Empire*, ed. D. Lentin and B. Norman, Ware: Wordsworth.
Giddens, Anthony (1996) [1971] *Capitalism and Modern Social Theory: An Analysis of the Writings of Marx, Durkheim and Max Weber*, Cambridge: Cambridge University Press.
Ginzburg, Carlo (1983) *The Night Battles: Witchcraft and Agrarian Cults in the Sixteenth and Seventeenth Centuries*, Routledge & Kegan Paul.
Ginzburg, Carlo (1990) *Myths, Emblems, Clues*, Hutchinson Radius.
Ginzburg, Carlo (1992) [1980] *The Cheese and the Worms: The Cosmos of a Sixteenth-Century Miller*, Baltimore: Johns Hopkins University Press.

Ginzburg, Carlo (2004) [1989] *Ecstasies: Deciphering the Witches' Sabbath*, Chicago: University of Chicago Press.
Girouard, Mark (1999) *Alfred Waterhouse and the Natural History Museum*, The Natural History Museum.
Gissing, George (1999) [1889] *The Nether World*, Oxford: Oxford University Press.
Given-Wilson, Christopher (2007) [2004] *Chronicles: The Writing of History in Medieval Britain*, Hambledon Continuum.
Glacken, Clarence (1967) *Traces on the Rhodian Shore. Nature and Culture in Western Thought from Ancient Times to the End of the Eighteenth Century*, Berkeley: University of California Press.
Gleadle, Kathryn (2007) 'Revisiting Family Fortunes: reflections on the twentieth anniversary of the publication of L. Davidoff & C. Hall (1987) Family Fortunes: men and women of the English middle class, 1780–1850', *Women's History Review* 16 (5), pp. 773–782.
Glinert, Edward (2000) *A Literary Guide to London*, Harmondsworth: Penguin Books.
Glinert, Edward (2003) *The London Compendium: A Street by Street Exploration of the London Metropolis*, Allen & Lane.
Goldhill, Simon (2008) *Jerusalem: City of Longing*, Cambridge, MA: Harvard University Press.
Goldman, Eric F. (1952) 'The Origins of Beard's Economic Interpretation of the Constitution', *Journal of the History of Ideas* 13 (2), pp. 234–49.
Goldstone, Jack (1991) *Revolution and Rebellion in the Early Modern World*, Berkeley: University of California Press.
Goldthorpe, John H. (1991) 'The Uses of History in Sociology: Reflections on Some Recent Tendencies', *British Journal of Sociology* 42 (2), pp. 211–30.
Goldthorpe, John H. (1994) 'The Uses of History in Sociology: A Reply', *British Journal of Sociology* 45 (1), pp. 55–77.
Gomery, Douglas and Robert Clyde Allen (1993) [1985] *Film History: Theory and Practice*, Boston: McGraw-Hill.
Gooder, Eileen (1979) [1961] *Latin for Local History: An Introduction*, Longman.
Goody, Jack (1983) *The Development of the Family and Marriage in Europe*, Cambridge: Cambridge University Press.
Goody, Jack, Joan Thirsk and E. P. Thompson (eds.) (1976) *Family and Inheritance. Rural Society in Western Europe, 1200–1800*, Cambridge: Cambridge University Press.
Gospel, Howard (forthcoming) *Skill Formation for British Industry: A Historical and Comparative Perspective*.
Gourvish, Terence Richard and N. Blake (1986) *British Railways 1948–73: A Business History*, Cambridge: Cambridge University Press.
Gourvish, Terence Richard and Mike Anson (2006) *The Official History of Britain and the Channel Tunnel*, Routledge.
Gras, Norman (1939) *Business and Capitalism: An Introduction to Business History*, New York: F. S. Crofts.
Graves, Robert and Barry Unsworth (2006) *I, Claudius: From the Autobiography of Tiberius Claudius, Emperor of the Romans, Born 10 BC, Murdered and Deified AD54*, Harmondsworth: Penguin Classics.
Gray, Robbie (1976) *The Labour Aristocracy in Victorian Edinburgh*, Oxford: Oxford University Press.
Green, Abigail (2010) *Moses Montiefiore: Jewish Liberator, Imperial Hero*, Cambridge, MA: Harvard University Press.
Green, Eric M. (ed.) (1997) *An Age of Transition: British Politics, 1880–1914*, Edinburgh: Edinburgh University Press.
Green, John Richard (1992) [1892–1894] *A Short History of the English People*, Folio Society.
Green, Simon J. D. (1996) *Religion in the Age of Decline: Organisation and Experience in Industrial Yorkshire 1870–1920*, Cambridge: Cambridge University Press.
Green, Simon J. D. (2010) *The Passing of Protestant England: Secularisation and Social Change, c.1920–1960*, Cambridge: Cambridge University Press.
Groensteen, Thierry, Bart Beaty and Nick Nguyen (2007) *The System of Comics*, Oxford: University of Mississippi Press.
Groensteen, Thierry and Ann Miller (2013) *Comics and Narration*, Oxford: University of Mississippi Press.

Grove, Richard (1995) *Green Imperalism. Colonial Expansion, Tropical Island Edens and the Origins of Environmentalism, 1600–1860*, Cambridge: Cambridge University Press.
Grove, Richard (1998) 'The East India Company, the Raj and the El Niño: The Critical Role Played by Colonial Scientists in Establishing the Mechanisms of Global Climate Teleconnections, 1770–1930', in R. Grove, V. Damodoran and S. Sangwan, *Nature and the Orient*, pp. 301–23.
Grove, Richard and Vinita Damodaran (2012) 'Environment', in Philippa Levine and John Marriott (eds.), *The Ashgate Research Companion to Modern Imperial Histories*, Farnham: Ashgate.
Grove, Richard, Vinita Damodaran and Satpal Sangwan (eds.) (1998) *Nature and the Orient*, Delhi: Oxford University Press.
Groves, Reginald (1938) *But We Shall Rise Again: A Narrative History of Chartism*, Secker and Warburg.
Guha, Ranajit (ed.) (1982–1989) *Subaltern Studies, Writings on South Asian History and Society*, Vols. I–VI, Delhi: Oxford University Press.
Gunaway, Bryan (2003) 'Review of Carolyn Steedman, Dust: The Archive and Cultural History', *H. Net Reviews in the Humanities & Social Sciences*.
Gunn, Simon (2006) *History and Cultural Theory*, Harlow: Pearson Longman.
Habermas, Jurgen (1987) [1972] *Knowledge and Human Interests*, Cambridge: Polity.
Hadju, David (2004) Review 'In the Shadow of No Towers', *New York Times* [www.nytimes.com/2004/09/12/books/review/in-the-shadow-of-no-towers-homeland-insecurity.html?_r=2].
Hale, John (1967) *The Evolution of British Historiography from Bacon to Namier*, Macmillan.
Hall, Catherine (1990) 'The Tale of Samuel and Jemima: Gender and Working Class Culture in Nineteenth Century England', in idem (ed.), *White, Male and Middle-Class: Explorations in Feminism and History*, Cambridge: Polity.
Hall, Catherine (ed.) (2000) *Cultures of Empire. A Reader*, Manchester: Manchester University Press.
Hallam, Elizabeth M. (1990) 'Nine Centuries of Keeping Public Records', in Geoffrey Martin and Peter Spufford (eds.), *The Records of the Nation: The Public Record Office, 1838–1988: The British Record Society, 1888–1988*, Woodbridge: Boydell.
Hallam, Henry (1908) [1827] *Constitutional History of England from the Accession of Henry VII to the Death of George II*, 12 vols., John Murray.
Hamblyn, Richard (2002) *The Invention of Clouds: How an Amateur Meteorologist Forged the Language of the Skies*, Picador.
Hamilton, Carolyn, V. Harris, M. Pickover, G. Reid, R. Saleh and J. Taylor (eds.) (2002) *Refiguring the Archive*, Dordrecht: Kluwer Academic.
Hamish Fraser, W. (2010) *Chartism in Scotland*, Pontypool: Merlin Press.
Hammond, Barbara and John Hammond (1947) [1934] *The Bleak Age*, West Drayton: Penguin.
Hammond, Barbara and John Hammond (1962) [1930] *The Age of the Chartists, 1832–1852: A Study of Discontent*, Hamden, CT: Archon Books.
Hancock, David (1995) *Citizens of the World. London Merchants and the Integration of the British Atlantic Community, 1735–1785*, Cambridge: Cambridge University Press.
Handlin, Oscar and Mary Handlin (1950) 'Origins of the Southern Labor System', *William and Mary Quarterly* VII, pp. 199–222.
Hannah, Leslie and Margaret Ackrill (2001) *Barclays: The Business of Banking 1690–1996*, Cambridge: Cambridge University Press.
Hare, J. Laurence (2014) 'Nazi Archaeology Abroad: German Prehistorians and the International Dynamics of Collaboration', *Patterns of Prejudice* 48 (1), pp. 1–24.
Hareven, Tamara K. (1983) *Family Time and Historical Time: The Relationship between Family and Work in a New England Industrial Community*, Cambridge: Cambridge University Press.
Harper, Sue and Vincent Porter (2003) *The Decline of Deference: British Cinema of the 1950s*, Oxford: Oxford University Press.
Harris, Jose (1994) *Private Lives, Public Spirit: A Social History of Britain 1870–1914*, Harmondsworth: Penguin.
Harrison, Brian (1996) *The Transformation of British Politics, 1860–1995*, Oxford: Oxford University Press.
Hartwell, Max (1972) [1965] *The Industrial Revolution in England*, Historical Association.

Hartz, Loius (1991) [1955] *The Liberal Tradition in America: An Interpretation of American Political Thought Since the Revolution*, New York: Harcourt, Brace.
Harvey, David (1989) *The Condition of Postmodernity: An Enquiry into the Origins of Cultural Change*, Oxford: Blackwell.
Haskell, Francis (1993) *History and Its Images: Art and the Interpretation of the Past*, New Haven: Yale University Press.
Hatzenbuehler, Ronald (2011) 'Questioning Whether Thomas Jefferson Was the "Father" of American Archaeology', *History and Anthropology* 22 (1), pp. 121–9.
Hauser, Arnold (1999) [1951] *Social History of Art, 1892–1978*, Routledge.
Held, David, Anthony Mcgrew, David Goldblatt and Jonathan Perraton (1999) *Global Transformations: Politics, Economics and Culture*, Cambridge: Polity.
Helmstadter, Richard J. (1985) *Victorian Faith in Crisis*, Lanham, MD: University Press of America.
Helmstadter, Richard J. (1988) 'The Nonconformist Conscience', in Gerald Parsons, James Moore and Jonathan Wolffe (eds.), *Religion in Victorian Britain*, Vols. I–IV, Manchester: Manchester University Press.
Herodotus (2002) *The Histories*, ed. John Marincola.
Herodotus (2003) *The Histories*, Harmondsworth: Penguin.
Hewitson, Mark (2014) *History and Causality*, Basingstoke: Palgrave.
Higham, John (1989) 'Changing Paradigms: The Collapse of Consensus History', *The Journal of American History* 76 (2), pp. 460–6.
Hill, Christopher (1991) [1972] *The World Turned Upside Down: Radical Ideas during the English Revolution*, Harmondsworth: Penguin.
Himmelfarb, Gertrude (2004) *The New History and the Old: Critical Essays and Reappraisals*, Cambridge, MA: Harvard University Press.
Hinde, Andrew (2003) *England's Population: A History since the Domesday Survey*, Hodder Headline.
History and Sociology (1976) *British Journal of Sociology* 27 (3), pp. 295–412.
Hobsbawm, Eric (1964) *Labouring Men*, Weidenfeld and Nicolson.
Hobsbawm, Eric (1969) *Bandits*, Weidenfeld and Nicolson.
Hobsbawm, Eric (1971) 'From Social History to History of Society', *Daedalus* 100 (1), pp. 20–45.
Hobsbawm, Eric and Terence Ranger (1992) [1983] *The Invention of Tradition*, Cambridge: Cambridge University Press.
Hochschild, Adam (2005) *Bury the Chains: Prophets and Rebels in the Fight to Free an Empire's Slaves*, Basingstoke: Macmillan.
Hodgson, Marshall G. S. (2011) [1974] *Venture of Islam: Conscience and History in a World Civilization*, Chicago: University of Chicago Press.
Hodgson, Marshall G. S. and Edmund Burke (1993) *Rethinking World History: Essays on Europe, Islam and World History*, Cambridge: Cambridge University Press.
Hoffman, John and Paul Graham (2006) *Introduction to Political Concepts*, Harlow: Pearson Education.
Hofstadter, Richard (1950) 'Beard and the Constitution: The History of an Idea', *American Quarterly* 2 (3), pp. 195–213.
Hofstadter, Richard (1989) [1948] *The American Political Tradition and the Men Who Made It*, New York: Knopf.
Hofstadter, Richard (2012) [1968] *The Progressive Historians*, Chicago: The University of Chicago Press.
Hooker, Juliet (2016) 'Black Lives Matter and the Paradoxes of U.S. Black Politics: From Democratic Sacrifice to Democratic Repair', *Political Theory* 44 (4), pp. 448–69.
Hooker, Juliet (2020) 'Disobedience *in Black*. On Race and Dissent', in Schwartzberg, *Protest and Dissent*, pp. 45–63.
Hoover, Dwight W. (1965) 'Comments on Recent United States Historiography', *American Quarterly* 17 (2) Supplement, pp. 299–318.
Hopkins, F. Michael (2007) 'Continuing Debate and New Approaches in Cold War History', *The Historical Journal* 50 (4), pp. 913–34.

Hornblower, Simon (ed.) (1994) *Greek Historiography*, Oxford: Clarendon Press.
Howkins, Alun (1985) *Poor Labouring Men: Rural Radicalism in Norfolk, 1872–1923*, Routledge & Kegan Paul.
Hughes, J. Donald (2001) *An Environmental History of the World: Humankind's Changing Role in the Community of Life*, Routledge.
Hughes, J. Donald (2006) *What is Environmental History?*, Cambridge: Polity.
Huizinga, John (2001) [1919] *The Waning of the Middle Ages*, Harmondsworth: Penguin.
Humphries, Jane (1977) 'Class Struggle and the Persistence of the Working Class Family', *Cambridge Journal of Economics* 47 (1).
Humphries, Jane (1991) '"Lurking in the Wings": Women in the Historiography of the Industrial Revolution', *Business and Economic History* 20, pp. 32–44.
Hunt, Edwin S. and James M. Murray (1999) *A History of Business in Medieval Europe 1200–1550*, Cambridge: Cambridge University Press.
Hunt, Lynn (ed.) (1989) *The New Cultural History*, Berkeley: University of California Press.
Iggers, Georg G., Edward Q. Wang and Supriya Mukherjee (2008) *A Global History of Modern Historiography*, Harlow: Pearson Longman.
Ignatieff, Michael (1994) [1984] *The Needs of Strangers*, Vintage.
Jacob, Margaret and James Jacob (eds.) (1991) *The Origins of Anglo-American Radicalism*, Amherst, NY: Humanities.
Jacobs, Jane (1970) [1969] *The Economy of Cities*, New York: Vintage Books.
Jacobs, Jane (1985) [1984] *Cities and the Wealth of Nations: Principles of Economic Life*, New York: Vintage Books.
Jacobs, Jane (1994) [1993] *Systems of Survival: A Dialogue on the Moral Foundations of Commerce and Politics*, Hodder & Stoughton.
Jacobs, Jane (2000a) [1961] *The Death and Life of Great American Cities*, Pimlico.
Jacobs, Jane (2000b) *The Nature of Economies*, New York: Vintage Books.
Jacobs, Jane (2004) *Dark Age Ahead*, New York: Random House.
Janiak, Andrew (ed.) (2014) [1713] *Isaac Newton. Philosophical Writings*, Cambridge: Cambridge University Press.
Jefferson, Thomas (1954) [1787] *Notes on the State of Virginia*, New York: Norton.
Jenkins, Keith (1991) *Rethinking History*, Routledge.
Jenkins, Keith (1997) *The Postmodern History Reader*, Routledge.
Johnson, Martin (1999) 'Rethinking Historical Archaeology', in Funari, Jones and Hall, *Historical Archaeology*, pp. 23–36.
Jones, Geoffrey G. and Jonathan Zeitlin (eds.) (2008) *The Oxford Handbook of Business History*, Oxford: Oxford University Press.
Jones, Peter (2004) 'Introduction', in Fitzpatrick et al., *The Enlightenment World*.
Jordan, Winthrop (2012) [1968] *White Over Black: American Attitudes Toward the Negro, 1550–1812*, New York: Oxford University Press.
Jordanova, Ludmilla (2006) [2000] *History in Practice*, Hodder Arnold.
Josephus, F. (1981) *The Jewish War*, Harmondsworth: Penguin.
Joyce, Patrick (1994) *Democratic Subjects: The Self and the Social in Nineteenth-Century England*, Cambridge: Cambridge University Press.
Joyce, Patrick (ed.) (1995) *Class*, Oxford: Oxford University Press.
Joyce, Patrick (1999) 'The Politics of the Liberal Archive', *History of the Human Sciences* 12 (2), pp. 35–49.
Kapur, Nandini Sinha (ed.) (2011) *Environmental History of Early India*, New Delhi: Oxford University Press.
Kassow, Samuel D. (2009) [2007] *Who Will Write Our History? Rediscovering a Hidden Archive from the Warsaw Ghetto*, Harmondsworth: Penguin.
Kaye, Harvey J. (1995) [1984] *The British Marxist Historians: An Introductory Analysis*, Basingstoke: Macmillan.

Kean, Hilda, Paul Martin and Sally Morgan (eds.) (2000) *Seeing History: Public History Now in Britain*, Francis Boutle.
Kekewich, Lucille (ed.) (2000) *The Impact of Humanism: A Cultural Enquiry*, New Haven: Yale University Press.
Kelley, Robert (1992) 'Public History: Its Origins, Nature and Prospects', in Phyllis K. Leffler and Joseph Brent (eds.), *Public History Readings*, Malabar, FL: Krieger Publishing.
Kelly, Joan (1984) *Women, History and Theory: The Essays of Joan Kelly*, Chicago: University of Chicago Press.
Kennan, George F. (1968) *Democracy and the Student Left*, Hutchinson.
Kent, Stephen L. (2001) *The Ultimate History of Video Games*, Vols 1 and 2, New York: Columbia University Press.
Kern, Stephen (2003) [1983] *The Culture of Time and Space, 1880–1918*, Cambridge, MA: Harvard University Press.
Kern, Stephen (2006) *A Cultural History of Causality. Science, Murder Novels, and Systems of Thought*, Princeton: Princeton University Press.
Khaldi, Tarif (1994) *Arabic Historical Thought in the Classical Period*, New York: Cambridge University Press.
Kirby, Peter (1997) 'The Standard of Living Debate and the Industrial Revolution', *Refresh* 25.
Klein, Herbert (1999) *The Atlantic Slave Trade*, Cambridge: Cambridge University Press.
Klingender, Francis and Arthur Elton (1975) [1968] *Art and the Industrial Revolution*, St Albans: Paladin.
Kloppenberg, James T. (2001) 'In Retrospect: Louis Hartz's *The Liberal Tradition in America*', *Reviews in American History* 29, pp. 460–78.
Knott, Sarah and Barbara Taylor (eds.) (2005) *Women, Gender and Enlightenment*, Basingstoke: Macmillan.
Kochan, Lionel (1977) *The Jew and His History*, Basingstoke: Macmillan.
Kocka, Jurgen (1997) 'New Trends in Labour Movement Historiography: A German Perspective', *International Review of Social History* 42 (1), pp. 67–78.
Kolchin, Peter (2003) *American Slavery, 1619–1877*, New York: Hill and Wang.
LaCapra, Dominick (2013) *History, Literature, Critical Theory*, Ithaca: Cornell University Press.
Ladurie, Emmanuelle Le Roy (1990) [1975] *Montaillou: Cathars and Catholics in a French Village, 1294–1324*, Harmondsworth: Penguin.
Ladurie, Emmanuelle Le Roy (2003) [1980] *Carnival in Romans: Mayhem and Massacre in a French City*, Phoenix Press.
Lal, Shyam Narayan (2011) 'An Aspect of Rural Landscape in the Rashtrakuta Kingdom', in Kapur, *Environmental History of Early India*, pp. 43–52.
Lambert, W. R. (1988) 'Some Working-Class Attitudes Towards Organised Religion in Nineteenth Century Wales', in Gerald Parsons, James Moore and Jonathan Wolffe (eds.), *Religion in Victorian Britain*, Vols. I–IV, Manchester: Manchester University Press.
Lamoreaux, Naomi R., Daniel M. G. Raff and Peter Temin (2008) 'Economic Theory and Business History', in *Oxford Handbook of Business History*, http://doi.org/10.1093/oxfordhb/9780199263684.003.0003.
Landes, David (1999) [1998] *The Wealth and Poverty of Nations: Why Some Are So Rich and Some So Poor*, Abacus.
Landsberg, Alison (2015) *Engaging the Past. Mass Culture and the Production of Historical Knowledge*, New York: Columbia University Press.
Landy, Marcia (ed.) (2001) *The Historical Film. History and Memory in Media*, New Brunswick, NJ: Rutgers University Press.
Larner, Christina (1983) [1981] *Enemies of God: The Witch Hunt in Scotland*, Oxford: Blackwell.
Laslett, Peter (1971) [1965] *The World We Have Lost*, Methuen.
Laslett, Peter (1977) *Family Life and Illicit Love in Earlier Generations*, Cambridge: Cambridge University Press.
Laslett, Peter (ed.) with assistance from Wall, Richard (1972) *Household and Family in Past Time: Comparative Studies in the Size and Structure of the Domestic Group Over the Last Three Centuries in*

England, France, Serbia, Japan and Colonial North America, with Further Materials from Western Europe, Cambridge: Cambridge University Press.

Lawrence, Jon (1998) *Speaking for the People: Party, Language and Popular Politics in England, 1867–1914*, Cambridge: Cambridge University Press.

Lawrence, Jon (2013) 'Back to Work. The Making and Unmaking of the English Working Class', *Juncture* 20 (1), pp. 80–4.

Lawrence, Jon and Miles Taylor (eds.) (1997) *Party, State and Society: Electoral Behaviour in Britain since 1820*, Aldershot: Scolar Press.

Leach, Stephen (2009) 'An Appreciation of R. G. Collingwood as an Archaeologist', *Bulletin of the History of Archaeology* 19 (1), pp. 14–20.

Lebron, Christopher (2019) *The Making of Black Lives Matter: A Brief History of an Idea*, New York: Oxford University Press.

Le Goff, Jacques (1980) *Time, Work and Culture in the Middle Ages*, Chicago: University of Chicago Press.

Le Goff, Jacques (2007) [2005] *The Birth of Europe*, Oxford: Blackwell.

Lentin, Anthony and Brian Norman (1979) *Gibbon's the Decline and Fall of the Roman Empire*, Milton Keynes: Open University Press.

Lentin, Anthony and Brian Norman (eds.) (1998) *Edmund Gibbon, The History of the Decline and Fall of the Roman Empire*, Ware: Wordsworth.

Lester, Alan (2001) *Imperial Networks: Creating Identities in Nineteenth-Century South Africa and Britain*, Routledge.

Levine, Joseph (1991) *Battle of the Books: History and Literature in the Augustan Age*, Ithaca: Cornell University Press.

Levine, L. W. (1977) *Black Culture and Consciousness: Afro-American Folk Thought from Slavery to Freedom*, New York and Oxford: Oxford University Press.

Levine, Philippa and John Marriott (eds.) (2012) *The Ashgate Research Companion to Modern Imperial Histories*, Farnham: Ashgate.

Lévi-Strauss, Claude (1993–1994) [1958] *Structural Anthropology*, Harmondsworth: Penguin.

Levy, Fred Jacob (2004) [1967] *Tudor Historical Thought*, Toronto: University of Toronto Press.

Light, Alison (2015) *Common People: The History of an English Family*, Harmondsworth: Penguin.

Lindahl, J. F. and D. Grace (2015) 'Consequences of Human Actions on Risks for Infectious Diseases', *Infection Ecology and Epidemiology* 5, pp. 1–11.

Lindert, Peter H. and Jeffrey Williamson (1985) 'English Workers' Real Wages: Reply to Crafts', *The Journal of Economic History* 45 (1), pp. 145–53.

Linebaugh, Peter and Marcus Rediker (2000) *The Many-Headed Hydra. The Hidden History of the Revolutionary Atlantic*, Verso.

Lisle-Williams, M. (1984) 'Merchant Banking Dynasties in the English Class Structure, Ownership, Solidarity and Kinship in the City of London, 1850–1960', *British Journal of Sociology* XXXV, pp. 333–62.

Livingstone, David N. (1992) *The Geographical Tradition: Episodes in the History of a Contested Enterprise*, Oxford: Blackwell.

Louis, W. Roger (ed.) (1995–1999) *The Oxford History of the British Empire*, 5 vols., Oxford: Oxford University Press.

Lowenthal, David (1985) *The Past is a Foreign Country*, Cambridge: Cambridge University Press.

Lowenthal, David (1998) [1996] *The Heritage Crusade and the Spoils of History*, Cambridge: Cambridge University Press.

Lowery, Wesley (2017) *They Can't Kill us All: The Story of Black Lives Matter*, Harmondsworth: Penguin.

Ludden, David (1999) *An Agrarian History of South Asia, The New Cambridge History of India*, IV *(4)*, Cambridge: Cambridge University Press.

MacCalman, Iain (1988) *Radical Underworld: Prophets, Revolutionaries and Pornographers in London, 1795–1840*, Oxford: Clarendon.

MacFarlane, Alan (1970) *The Family Life of Ralph Josselin: A Seventeenth-Century Clergyman. An Essay in Historical Anthropology*, New York: Norton.

MacFarlane, Alan (1973) 'Imaginative Leaps', *Times Literary Supplement*, January.
MacLeod, Duncan (1974) *Slavery, Race and the American Revolution*, Cambridge: Cambridge University Press.
Malinowski, Bronislav (1929) *Sexual Life of Savages in North West Melanesia*, Routledge and Kegan Paul.
Mandler, Peter (1997) *The Fall and Rise of the Stately Home*, New Haven: Yale University Press.
Mandler, Peter (2002) *History and National Life*, Profile Books.
Mandler, Peter (2006) *The English National Character*, New Haven: Yale University Press.
Mann, Charles C. (2011) [1493] *How Europe's Discovery of the Americas Revolutionized Trade, Ecology and Life on Earth*, Granta.
Mann, Michael (1986–2012) *The Sources of Social Power*, New York: Cambridge University Press.
Manning, Patrick (2003) *Navigating World History: Historians Create a Global Past*, Basingstoke: Palgrave.
Mantel, Hilary (2010) *Wolf Hall*, Fourth Estate.
Marchand, L. A. (1957) *Byron: A Biography*, 3 vols., John Murray.
Marcus, Jacob R. (1999) [1938] *The Jew in the Medieval World: A Sourcebook*, Cincinnati: Hebrew Union College Press.
Marriott, John (2000) 'Introduction', in idem (ed.), *Unknown London. Early Modernist Visions of the Metropolis, 1815–45*, 6 vols., Pickering & Chatto.
Marriott, John (2003) *The Other Empire: Metropolis, India and Progress in the Colonial Imagination*, Manchester: Manchester University Press.
Martin, Bernice (1976) 'Review of *Passages from Antiquity to Feudalism and Lineages of the Absolutist State* by Perry Anderson', *The British Journal of Sociology* 27 (2), pp. 267–71.
Martin, C. T. (1976) [1910] *The Record Interpreter*, Dorking: Kohler and Coombes.
Martin, G. H. (1990) 'The Public Records in 1988', in Martin and Spufford, *The Records of the Nation*.
Martin, G. H. and Peter Spufford (eds.) (1990) *The Records of the Nation: The Public Record Office, 1838–1988*, Woodbridge: Boydell.
Martin, Paul (1999) 'Look, See, Hear: A Remembrance with Approaches to Contemporary Public History at Ruskin', in Geof Andrews, Hilda Kean and Jane Thompson (eds.), *Ruskin College, Contesting Knowledge, Dissenting Politics*, Lawrence & Wishart.
Marwick, Arthur (2001) *The New Nature of History: Knowledge, Evidence, Language*, Basingstoke: Palgrave.
Marwick, Arthur (2005) [1998] *The Sixties: Cultural Revolution in Britain, France, Italy and the United States*, Oxford: Oxford University Press.
Marx, Karl (1974) [1886] *Capital: A Critical Analysis of Capital Production*, Chicago: Encyclopædia Britannica.
Marx, Karl and Frie+drich Engels (2002) [1844] *The Communist Manifesto*, Harmondsworth: Penguin.
Mayer, Arno J. (1981) *The Persistence of the Old Regime: Europe to the Great War*, Croom Helm.
McCullin, Don (1996) *Sleeping with Ghosts*, Cape.
McDonald, Forest (1997) 'Colliding with the Past', *American History* 25 (1), pp. 13–18.
McGinn, Bernard (1985) *The Calabrian Abbot: Joachim of Fiore in the History of Western Thought*, New York: Macmillan.
McKeon, Michael (1987) *The Origins of the English Novel, 1600–1740*, Baltimore: The Johns Hopkins University Press.
McKibbin, Ross (1998) *Classes and Cultures: England, 1918–1951*, Oxford: Oxford University Press.
McMillen, Christian (2016) *Pandemics: A Very Short Introduction*, Oxford: Oxford University Press.
McNeill, William (1963) *The Rise of the West*, Chicago: Chicago University Press.
McNeill, William (1982) *The Pursuit of Power: Technology, Armed Force and Society since AD 1000*, Chicago: University of Chicago Press.
McNeill, William (1990) *The Age of Gunpowder Empires*, Chicago: University of Chicago Press.
McNeill, William (1994) [1976] *Plagues and Peoples*, Harmondsworth: Penguin.
Mellor, Ronald (1999) *The Roman Historians*, Routledge.
Mellor, Ronald (ed.) (2004) *The Historians of Ancient Rome*, Routledge.
Merridale, Catherine (2001) *Night of Stone: Death and Memory in Russia*, New York: Viking.

Michie, Ranald (1992) *The City of London: Continuity and Change, 1850–1990*, Basingstoke: Macmillan.
Midgley, Clare (1992) *Women Against Slavery: The British Campaigns, 1780–1870*, Routledge.
Mighall, Robert (1999) *A Geography of Victorian Gothic Fiction: Mapping History's Nightmares*, Oxford: Oxford University Press.
Miller, Cecilia (1993) *Giambattista Vico: Imagination and Historical Knowledge*, Basingstoke: Macmillan.
Miller, Joseph (2012) *Problem of Slavery as History: A Global Approach*, New Haven: Yale University Press.
Mokyr, Joel (2002) *The Gifts of Athena: Historical Origins of the Knowledge Economy*, Princeton: Princeton University Press.
Mokyr, Joel (2009) *The Enlightened Economy: An Economic History of Britain, 1700–1850*, New Haven: Yale University Press.
Momigliano, Arnaldo (1990) *Classical Foundations of Modern Historiography*, Berkeley: California University Press.
Monmonier, Mark (1996) *How to Lie with Maps*, Chicago: University of Chicago Press.
Moore, Barrington (1966) *Social Origins of Dictatorship and Democracy: Lord and Peasant in the Making of the Modern World*, Boston: Beacon Press.
Morrison, Arthur (1982) [1896] *The Child of the Jago*, Chicago: Academy Publications.
Morrison, Toni (1993) *Beloved*, Vintage.
Mort, Frank (2002) *Dangerous Sexualities: Medico-Moral Politics in England Since 1830*, Routledge.
Mosse, George (1985) *Nationalism and Sexuality: Respectability and Abnormal Sexuality in Modern Europe*, New York: Howard Fertig.
Mosse, George L. (2020) *Nationalism and Sexuality: Middle-Class Morality and Sexual Norms in Modern Europe*, University of Wisconsin Press.
Mumford, Lewis (1934) *Technics and Civilization*, Routledge.
Mumford, Lewis (1938) *The Culture of Cities*, Secker & Warburg.
Mumford, Lewis (1944) *The Condition of Man*, Secker & Warburg.
Mumford, Lewis (1961) *City in History*, Secker & Warburg.
Mundt, Marcia, Karen Ross and Charla M. Burnett (2018) 'Scaling Social Movements Through Social Media: The Case of Black Lives Matter', *Social Media and Society*, October–December, pp. 1–14.
Munslow, Alun (2003) *The New History*, Harlow: Pearson.
Munslow, Alun (2007) *Narrative and History*, Basingstoke: Palgrave.
Murphy-O'Connor, Jerome (2008) *The Holy Land: An Oxford Archaeological Guide: An Oxford Archaeological Guide from Earliest Times to 1700*, Oxford: Oxford University Press.
Muthu, Sankar (2003) *Enlightenment Against Empire*, Princeton: Princeton University Press.
Namier, Lewis (1957) *The Structure of Politics at the Accession of George III*, Macmillan.
Narayana Rao, V., D. Shulman and S. Subrahmanyam (2001) *Textures of Time; Writing History in South India, 1600–1800*, Delhi: Permanent Black.
Nead, Lynda (2016, August) 'Fallen Women and Foundlings: Rethinking Victorian Sexuality', *History Workshop Journal* 82, pp. 177–87.
Nead, Lynda (2000) *Victorian Babylon: People, Streets and Images in Nineteenth Century London*, New Haven: Yale University Press.
Newens, Stan (2007) 'The Genesis of East End Underworld: Chapters in the Life of Arthur Harding', *History Workshop Journal* 64, pp. 347–53.
Newton, Isaac (1999) [1713] *The Principia: Mathematical Principles of Natural Philosophy*, trans. Bernard Cohen and Anne Whitman, Berkeley: University of California Press.
Nigam, Aditya (2020) *Decolonizing Theory: Thinking Across Traditions*, Bloomsbury.
Novick, Peter (1988) *That Noble Dream. The 'Objectivity Question' and the American Historical Profession*, Cambridge: Cambridge University Press.
Obeyesekere, Gananath (1997) *The Apotheosis of Captain Cook: European Mythmaking in the Pacific*, Princeton: Princeton University Press.
TheObserver (2006, July 9).
Offer, Avner (1989) *The First World War: An Agrarian Interpretation*, Oxford: Oxford University Press.
Oliver, W. H. (1979) *Prophets and Millennialists: The Uses of Biblical Prophecy in England from the 1790s to the 1840s*, Oxford: Oxford University Press.

Orr, Linda (1990) *Headless History. Nineteenth-Century French Historiography of the Revolution*, Ithaca: Cornell University Press.
Orser, Charles and Thomas Patterson (2004) 'Introduction: V. Gordon Childe and the Foundations of Social Archaeology', in Patterson and Orser, *Foundations of Social Archaeology*, pp. 1–23.
Paddayya, K. (1995) 'Theoretical Perspectives in Indian Archaeology', in Ucko, *Theory in Archaeology*, pp. 110–49.
Paine, Thomas (2004) [1794] *Age of Reason*, Dover Publications.
Pandey, Gyan and Partha Chatterjee (eds.) (1992) *Subaltern Studies*, Vol. VII, Delhi: Oxford University Press.
Parasher-Sen, Aloka (2011) 'Of Tribes, Hunters and Barbarians. Forest Dwellers in the Mauryan Period', in Kapur, *Environmental History of Early India*, pp. 3–22.
Parker, Geoffrey (2013) *Global Crisis. War, Climate Change & Catastrophe in the Seventeenth Century*, New Haven: Yale University Press.
Parker, Geoffrey and Lesley Smith (eds.) (1997) *The General Crisis of the Seventeenth Century*, Routledge.
TheParliament Rolls of Medieval England, 1275–1504 (2005) 16 vols., Woodbridge: Boydell Press.
Parrott, David (2015) '*Global Crisis: War, Climate Change and Catastrophe in the 17th Century* by Geoffrey Parker', *London Review of Books* 37 (5).
Parsons, Gerald (1993) *The Growth of Religious Diversity*, Routledge.
Parsons, Gerald, James Moore and John Wolffe (eds.) (1988) *Religion in Victorian Britain*, Vols. 1–1V, Manchester: Manchester University Press.
Parsons, Talcott (1951) *The Social System*, Routledge and Kegan Paul.
Passerini, Luisa (1987) *Fascism in Popular Memory: The Cultural Experience of the Turin Working Class*, Cambridge: Cambridge University Press.
Patterson, Thomas and Charles Orser (eds.) (2004) *Foundations of Social Archaeology. Selected Writings of V. Gordon Childe*, Walnut Creek, CA: AltaMira Press.
Peakman, Julie (2019) *Licentious Worlds. Sex and Exploitation in Global Empires*, NA: Reaktion Books.
Pederson, Susan (2002) 'What is Political History Now?', in David Cannadine (ed.), *What Is History Now?*, Basingstoke: Palgrave.
Perkin, Harold (1981) *The Structured Crowd*, Brighton: Harvester Press.
Perkin, Harold (1989) *The Rise of Professional Society*, Routledge.
Perks, Robert and Alistair Thompson (eds.) (2006) *The Oral History Reader*, Routledge.
Perry, Marvin and Frederick M. Schweitzer (2002) *Antisemitism: Myth and Hate from Antiquity to the Present*, Basingstoke: Palgrave.
Pietrzak-Franger, Monika (2009) 'Envisioning the Ripper's Visions: Adapting Myth', in Alan Moore and Eddie Campbell (eds.), *From Hell: Neo-Victorian Studies*, pp. 157–85.
Pike, E. Royston (1966) *Human Documents of the Industrial Revolution in Britain*, Allen & Unwin.
Piret, Jocelyne and Guy Boivin (2021) 'Pandemics Throughout History', *Frontiers in Microbiology* 11, pp. 1–16.
Plumb, J. H. (1988) *The Making of an Historian. The Collected Essays of J. H. Plumb*, 3 vols., Brighton: Harvester Wheatsheaf.
Plumb, J. H. (2003) [1969] *The Death of the Past*, Basingstoke: Palgrave.
Pocock, J. G. A. (1985) *Virtue, Commerce and History*, Cambridge: Cambridge University Press.
Pomeranz, Kenneth (2009) 'Introduction', in Burke and Pomeranz, *Environment and World History*.
Poovey, Mary (1995) *Making a Social Body: British Cultural Formation, 1830–1864*, Chicago: University of Chicago Press.
Poovey, Mary (1988) *Uneven Developments: The Ideological Work of Gender in mid-Victorian England*, Chicago: University of Chicago Press.
Portelli, Alessandro (1991) *The Death of Luigi Trastulli and Other Stories*, Albany: State University of New York Press.
Porter, Bernard (2004) *The Absent-Minded Imperialists. Empire, Society and Culture in Britain*, Oxford: Oxford University Press.
Porter, Roy (1988a) 'Seeing the Past,' *Past and Present* 118, pp. 186–205.

Porter, Roy (1988b) *Edward Gibbon: Making Histories*, Weidenfeld and Nicolson.
Porter, Roy (1995) *Enlightenment: Britain and the Creation of the Modern World*, Allen Lane.
Poster, Mark (2003) 'History in the Digital Domain', *Historian* 4, pp. 17–32.
Potter, M. David (1954a) 'Democracy and Abundance', *Challenge* 3 (2), pp. 37–41.
Potter, M. David (1954b) *People of Plenty: Economic Abundance and the American Character*, Chicago: University of Chicago Press.
Potts, Alex (1988) 'Picturing the Modern Metropolis: Images of London in the Nineteenth Century', *History Workshop Journal* 26 (1), pp. 28–56.
Pounds, N. J. G. (1994) [1974] *Economic History of Medieval Europe*, Longman.
Press, G. A. (1982) *The Development of the Idea of History in Antiquity*, Kingston, ON: McGill-Queen's University Press.
Price, Richard (1789) *A Discourse on the Love of Our Country*.
Price, Richard (2006) 'One Big Thing: Britain, its Empire, and their Imperial Culture', *Journal of British Studies* 45 (3), pp. 602–27.
Pryde, E. B. and D. E. Greenway (eds.) (1986) [1941] *Handbook of British Chronology*, Cambridge: Cambridge University Press.
Rabelais, François (1653) *Gargantua and his Son Pantagruel*, trans. Sir Thomas Urquhart, Baddely, Harmondsworth: Penguin for Modern Version, 2006.
Readman, Paul (2009) 'The State of Twentieth-Century British Political History', *Journal of Public Policy* 21 (3).
Reddy, William (1997) 'Against Constructionism: The Historical Ethnography of Emotions', *Current Anthropology* 38 (1), pp. 327–51.
Reddy, William (2001) *The Navigation of Feeling: A Framework for the History of Emotions*, Cambridge: Cambridge University Press.
Reeder, David (1995) 'Representations of Metropolis: Descriptions of the Social Environment in Life and Labour', in Englander and O'Day, *Retrieved Riches*.
Rendall, Jane and Keith McClelland (2016) 'Leonore Davidoff and the Founding of *Gender & History*', *Gender and History* 48 (2), pp. 283–7.
Renfrew, Colin and Paul Bahn (2012) *Archaeology: Theories, Methods and Practice*, Thames & Hudson.
Richmond, Theo (1995) *Konin: A Quest*, Cape.
Roberts, Elizabeth (1995) *Women: Work 1840–1940*, Cambridge: Cambridge University.
Roberts, Elizabeth (1996) [1984] *A Woman's Place: An Oral History of Working Class Women*, Oxford: Blackwell.
Roberts, Stephen (2008) *The Chartist Prisoners*, Oxford: Peter Lang.
Robertson, E. W. (1872) *Historical Essays in Connexion with the Land and Church etc.*, Edinburgh: Edmonston and Doublas.
Robinson, Chase F. (2003) *Islamic Historiography*, Cambridge: Cambridge University Press.
Rohrbacher, David (2002) *The Historians of Late Antiquity*, Routledge.
Roper, Lyndal (1994) *Oedipus and the Devil: Witchcraft, Sexuality and Religion in Early Modern Europe*, Routledge.
Rose, Gillian and Miles Ogborn (1988) 'Feminism and Historical Geography', *Journal of Historical Geography* 14 (4), pp. 405–9.
Rose, Jonathan (ed.) (2008) *The Holocaust and the Book: Destruction and Preservation*, Amherst: University of Massachusetts Press.
Rose, Sonya (2003) *Which People's War: National Identity and Citizenship in Wartime Britain, 1939–45*, Oxford: Oxford University Press.
Rose, Sonya (2010) *What Is Gender History?* Cambridge: Polity Press.
Rosenstone, Robert (2006) *History on Film/Film on History*, Harlow: Pearson Longman.
Rosenthal, Franz (1990), *Science and Medicine in Islam: A Collection of Essays*, Aldershot: Variorum.
Rosenwein, Barbara (2002) 'Worrying about Emotions in History', *American Historical Review* 107 (3), pp. 821–45.
Rosenzweig, Roy (2011) *Clio Wired: The Future of the Past in the Digital Age*, New York: Columbia University Press.

Rothstein, Theodore (1984) [1929] *From Chartism to Labourism*, Garland.
Rowbotham, Sheila (1973) *Hidden from History: 300 Years of Women's Oppression and the Fight Against It*, Pluto Press.
Royle, Edward (1996) [1980] *Chartism*, Longman.
Rubinstein, W. D. (1977) 'The End of "Old Corruption" in Britain, 1780–1860', *Past and Present* 76, pp. 55–86.
Rudé, George F. E. (2005) [1964] *The Crowd in History: A Study of Popular Disturbances in France and England, 1730–1848*, Wiley.
Ryrie, Alex (2009) '*The Canon: The Stripping of the Altars: Traditional Religion in England, 1400–1580* by Eamon Duffy', *Times Higher Education Supplement*, 7 May.
Sacks, Jonathan (2003) *The Chief Rabbi's Haggadah: Hebrew and English Text with New Essays and Commentary*, Harper Collins.
Sahlins, Marshall (1981) *Historical Metaphors and Mythical Realities: Structure in the Early History of the Sandwich Islands*, Ann Arbor: University of Michigan Press.
Sahlins, Marshall (1987) *Islands of History*, Chicago: University of Chicago Press.
Sahlins, Marshall (1995) *How 'Natives' Think: About Captain Cook, For Example*, Chicago: University of Chicago Press.
Sahlins, Marshall (2004) *Apologies to Thucydides: Understanding History and Culture and Vice-Versa*, Chicago: University of Chicago Press.
Said, Edward (1991) [1978] *Orientalism: Western Conceptions of the Orient*, Harmondsworth: Penguin.
Said, Edward (1993) *Culture and Imperialism*, Chatto and Windus.
Samuel, Raphael (1975) 'Quarry Roughs', in idem (ed.), *Village Life and Labour*, Routledge and Kegan Paul.
Samuel, Raphael (1981) *East End Underworld: Chapters in the Life of Arthur Harding*, Routledge.
Samuel, Raphael (1992) 'On the Methods of History Workshop: A Reply', *History Workshop Journal* 9, pp. 162–75.
Samuel, Raphael (1993) 'The Discovery of Puritanism, 1820–1914: A Preliminary Sketch', in Garnett, Matthews and Walsh, *Revival and Religion Since 1700*.
Samuel, Raphael (1994) *Theatres of Memory*, Verso.
Sandle, Mark (2013) 'Studying the Past in the Digital Age: From Tourist to Explorer', in Weller, *History in the Digital Age*, pp. 129–48.
Sarkar, Sumit (1997) *Writing Social History*, Delhi: Oxford University Press.
Satia, Priya (2020) *Time's Monster: History, Conscience and Britain's Empire*, Harmondsworth: Penguin.
Saunders, Peter (1981) *Social Theory and the Urban Question*, Hutchinson.
Savage, Mike and Andrew Miles (1994) *The Remaking of the British Working Class, 1840–1940*, Routledge.
Scarpino, Philip V. (1993) 'Some Thoughts on Defining, Evaluating, and Rewarding Public Scholarship', *Public Historian* 15 (2), pp. 55–61.
Schama, Simon (1987) *The Embarrassment of Riches: An Interpretation of Dutch Culture in the Golden Age*, New York: Knopf.
Schama, Simon (1989) *Citizens: A Chronicle of the French Revolution*, Viking.
Schama, Simon (1991) *Dead Certainties*, Granta.
Schama, Simon (1995) *Landscape and Memory*, Harper Collins.
Schama, Simon (1999) *Rembrandt's Eyes*, Allen Lane.
Schama, Simon (2002) *A History of Britain*, Vol. 3, BBC.
Schama, Simon (2009) *The Power of Art*, The Bodley Head.
Schlesinger, Arthur (1943) 'Presidential Address Prepared for the Columbus Meeting But Delivered on the Evening of the Annual Business Meeting in Washington, December 30, 1942', *American Historical Review* 48 (2), pp. 225–44.
Schnepf, Ariane (2006) *Our Original Rights as a People*, Oxford: Peter Lang.
Schreiber, Katharina (2001) 'The Wari Empire of Middle Horizon Peru: The Epistemological Challenge of Documenting an Empire without Documentary Evidence', in Alcock, D'Altroy, Morrison and Sinopoli, *Empires*, pp. 70–92.
Schwartzberg, Melissa (ed.) (2020) *Protest and Dissent*, New York: Oxford University Press.

Scott, Joan W. (1986) 'Gender: A Useful Category of Historical Analysis', *American Historical Review* 91 (5), pp. 1053–75.
Scott, Joan W. (1988) *Gender and the Politics of History*, New York: Columbia University Press.
Scott, Joan W. (2007) *The Politics of the Veil*, Princeton: Princeton University Press.
Scott, Joan W. (2010) 'Gender: Still a Useful Category of Anaysis?', *Diogenes* (English ed.) 57 (1), pp. 7–14.
Scott, Sir Walter (1834) [1816] *The Antiquary*, Edinburgh: Robert Cadell.
Seeskin, Kenneth (2004a) 'Maimonides Sense of History', *Jewish History* 18, pp. 125–8.
Seeskin, Kenneth (2004b) *Maimonides on the Origin of the World*, Cambridge: Cambridge University Press.
Segev, Tom (2007) *Israel, the War, and the Year that Transformed the Middle East*, New York: Metropolitan Books.
Selden, Anthony and Joanna Pappworth (1983) *By Word of Mouth: Elite Oral History*, Methuen.
Sellar, A. M. (ed.) (1907) *Bede's Ecclesiastical History of England. A Revised Translation with Introduction, Life, and Notes*, George Bell & Sons.
Sellar, W. C. and R. J. Yeatman (1930) *1066 and All That*, Methuen.
Semmel, Bernard (1960) *Imperialism and Social Reform. English Social and Imperial Thought 1895–1914*, Boston: Allen & Unwin.
Semmel, Bernard (1986) *Liberalism and Naval Strategy. Ideology, Interest, and Sea Power during the Pax Britannica*, Boston: Allen & Unwin.
Semmel, Bernard (1993) *The Liberal Ideal and the Demons of Empire. Theories of Imperialism from Adam Smith to Lenin*, Baltimore: The Johns Hopkins University Press.
Sexton, Jay (2005, Spring) 'The Transnational Turn in American Historical Writing', *Historical Journal*.
Shiach, Morag (2004) *Modernism, Labour and Selfhood in British Literature and Culture, 1890–1930*, Cambridge: Cambridge University Press.
Shorter, Edward (1975) *The Making of the Modern Family*, Collins.
Singh, Jyotsna (1996) *Colonial Narratives/Cultural Dialogues. Discoveries of India in the Language of Colonialism*, Routledge.
Sinha, Mrinalini (1995) *Colonial Masculinity: The 'Manly Englishman' and the 'Effeminate Bengali' in the Late Nineteenth Century*, Manchester: Manchester University Press.
Sinopoli, Carla (2001) 'On the Edge of Empire: Form and Substance in the Satavahana Dynasty', in Alcock, D'Altroy, Morrison and Sinopoli, *Empires*, pp. 155–78.
Skinner, Quentin (1981) *Machiavelli*, Oxford: Oxford University Press.
Skowronek, Stephen (1982) *Building a New American State: The Expansion of National Administrative Capacities, 1877–1920*, Cambridge: Cambridge University Press.
Skowronek, Stephen (2004) *The Search for American Political Development*, Cambridge: Cambridge University Press.
Slack, Paul (1985) *The Impact of Plague in Tudor and Stuart England*, Routledge and Kegan Paul.
Slater, Michael (ed.) (1994–1998) *The Dent Uniform Edition of Dickens' Journalism*, 3 vols., Dent.
Smeeton, George (1828) *Doings in London*, reproduced in Marriott (ed.), *Unknown London*, vol. 3.
Smith, Adam (1977) [1776] *An Inquiry into the Nature and Causes of the Wealth of Nations*, 2 vols., Everyman.
Sobel, Dava (1998) *Longitude*, New York: Walker.
Spear, Percival (1990) [1965] *A History of Modern India, 1740–1975*, Harmondsworth: Penguin.
Spear, Thomas (1981) 'Oral Tradition: Whose History?', *Journal of Pacific History* 16 (3), pp. 133–48.
Spencer, Herbert (1862) *First Principles*, Williams and Norgate.
Spengler, Oswald (1922) *Decline of the West*, Allen & Unwin.
Spiegelman, Art (2004) *In the Shadow of No Towers*, Viking.
Spivak, Gyatri (2010) [1993] Rosalind C. Morris (ed.) *Can the Subaltern Speak? Reflections on the History of an Idea*, New York: Columbia University Press.
SRG (ed.) (1971) 'Historical Studies Today', Special Issue of *Daedalus* 100 (1).
Stearns, Peter and Carol Stearns (1985) 'Emotionology: Clarifying the History of Emotions and Emotional Standards', *American Historical Review* 90, pp. 813–36.

Stedman Jones, Gareth (1971) *Outcast London: A Study of the Relationship Between Classes in Victorian London*, Oxford: Clarendon Press.
Stedman Jones, Gareth (1983) 'Rethinking Chartism', in idem (ed.), *Languages of Class*, Cambridge: Cambridge University Press.
Stedman Jones, Gareth (2002) 'Introduction', in *Communist Party Manifesto*, Harmondsworth: Penguin.
Stedman Jones, Gareth (2004) *An End to Poverty? An Historical Debate*, Profile Books.
Stedman Jones, Gareth (2016) *Karl Marx: Greatness and Illusion*, Allen Lane.
Steedman, Carolyn (2001) *Dust*, Manchester: Manchester University Press.
Stearns, Peter and Carol Stearns (1986) *Anger: The Struggle for Emotional Control in America's History*, Chicago: University of Chicago Press.
Stiglmayr, Joseph (1909) 'Dionysius the Pseudo-Areopagite', in *The Catholic Encyclopaedia*, vol. 5, New York: Robert Appleton Company [www.newadvent.org/cathen/05013a.htm].
Stoltman, James (1973) 'The Southeastern United States', in Fitting, *Development of North American Archaeology*, pp. 117–37.
Stone, Lawrence (1979) 'The Revival of Narrative: Reflections on a New Old History', *Past & Present* 85, pp. 3–24.
Stone, Lawrence (1990) [1977] *The Family, Sex and Marriage in England, 1500–1800*, Harmondsworth: Penguin.
Strasdin, Kate (2017) *Inside the Royal Wardrobe: A Dress History of Queen Alexandra*, Bloomsbury.
Stryker, Susan (2017) *Transgender History: The Root of Today's Revolution*, New York: Seal Press.
Stubbs, William (1873–1878) *Constitutional History of England*, Oxford: Clarendon Press.
Suetonius (2003) *The Twelve Caesars*, Harmondsworth: Penguin.
Sureda, Joan (2008) *The Golden Age of Spain: Painting, Sculpture, Architecture*, New York: Vendome Press.
Sweet, Rosemary (2004) *Antiquaries*, Hambledon Press.
Tacitus (2008) [1965] *The Annals*, Oxford: Oxford University Press.
Tagg, John (1988) *The Burden of Representation. Essays on Photographies and Histories*, Basingstoke: Macmillan.
Tanner, Duncan (1990) *Political Change and the Labour Party, 1900–1918*, Cambridge: Cambridge University Press.
Taylor, Miles (1996) 'Rethinking the Chartists: Searching for Synthesis in the Historiography of Chartism', *Historical Journal* 39, pp. 479–95.
Tennyson, G. B. (1984) *A Carlyle Reader*, Cambridge: Cambridge University Press.
Thomas, Hugh (1979) *An Unfinished History of the World*, Hamish Hamilton.
Thomas, Keith (1971) *Religion and the Decline of Magic*, New York: Charles Scribner.
Thomas, Robert E. (1952) 'A Reappraisal of Charles A. Beard's *An Economic Interpretation of the Constitution of the United States*', *The American Historical Review* 57 (2), pp. 370–5.
Thompson, Dorothy (1984) *The Chartists: Popular Politics in the Industrial Revolution*, Hounslow: Temple Smith.
Thompson, E. P. (1963) *The Making of the English Working Class*, Harmondsworth: Penguin.
Thompson, E. P. (1975) *Whigs and Hunters: The Origin of the Black Act*, Allen Lane.
Thompson, E. P. (1976) 'Pit-Men, Preachers and Politics: The Effects of Methodism in a Durham Mining Community by Robert Moore', *The British Journal of Sociology* 27 (3), Special Issue. *History and Sociology*, pp. 387–402.
Thompson, E. P. (1978) *The Poverty of Theory and Other Essays*, Merlin Press.
Thompson, E. P. (1991) [1962] 'Time, Work Discipline and Industrial Capitalism', in idem (ed.), *Customs in Common*, Merlin Press.
Thompson, E. P. (1991) [1971] 'The Moral Economy of the Crowd', in idem (ed.), *Customs in Common*, Merlin Press.
Thompson, E. P. (1991) [1972] 'Rough Music', in idem (ed.), *Customs in Common*, Merlin Press.
Thompson, E. P. (1992) 'Theory and Evidence', *History Workshop Journal* 35 (1), pp. 274–5.
Thompson, E. P. (2008) [1965] 'The Peculiarities of the English', in *The Poverty of Theory and Other Essays*, New York: NYU Press.

Thompson, Paul (1978) *The Voice of the Past: Oral History*, Oxford: Oxford University Press.
Thon, Daniel and Jan-Noel Thon (eds.) (2015) *From Comic Strips to Graphic Novels: Contributions to the Theory and History of Graphic Narrative*, Berlin: De Gruyter.
Thucydides (1998) [1972] *The Peloponnesian War*, ed. Walter Blanco and Jennifer Tolbert Roberts, New York: Norton.
Tignor, Robert, et al. (2008) *Worlds Together, Worlds Apart*, New York: Norton.
Tileaga, Cristian and Jovan Byford (eds.) (2014) *Psychology and History: Interdisciplinary Explorations*, Cambridge: Cambridge University Press.
Tilly, Charles (1992) [1990] *Coercion, Capital, and European States, A.D. 990–1990*, Oxford: Basil Blackwell.
Tilly, Louise and Joan W. Scott (1989) *Women, Work and Family*, New York: Routledge.
Timm, Annette F. and Joshua A. Sanborn (2016) *Gender, Sex and the Shaping of Modern Europe. A History from the French Revolution to the Present Day*, Bloomsbury.
Todman, Daniel (2016) *Britain's War: Into Battle 1937–1941*, Allen Lane.
Todman, Daniel (2020) *Britain's War: A New World 1942–1947*, Allen Lane.
Tonkin, Elizabeth (1992) *Narrating Our Pasts: The Social Construction of Oral History*, Cambridge: Cambridge University Press.
Toplin, Robert (ed.) (1997) *Ken Burns's Civil War. Historians Respond*, New York: Oxford University Press.
Tosh, John (2021) [2002] *The Pursuit of History*, Longman.
Tosh, John (2005) *Manliness and Masculinities in Nineteenth-Century Britain*, Harlow: Pearson.
Tosh, John and Robert Shoemaker (eds.) (1991) *Manful Assertions: Masculinities in Britain since 1800*, Routledge.
Tosh, John and Robert Shoemaker (1999) *A Man's Place: Masculinity and the Middle-Class Home in Victorian England*, New Haven: Yale University Press.
Toynbee, Arnold (1933–1961) *A Study of History*, 12 vols., Oxford: Oxford University Press.
Trigger, Bruce (1978) *Gordon Childe. Revolutions in Archaeology*, Thames and Hudson.
Trigger, Bruce (2006) *A History of Archaeological Thought*, Cambridge: Cambridge University Press.
Tristan, Flora (1840) *Promenades Dans Londres*, Paris.
Trouillot, Michel-Rolph (1995) *Silencing the Past: Power and the Production of History*, Boston: Beacon Press.
Tuck, Stephen (2014) *The Night Malcolm X Spoke at the Oxford Union: A Transatlantic Story of Antiracial Protest*, Berkeley: University of California Press.
Turner, Frank (1993) *Contesting Cultural Authority: Essays in Victorian Intellectual Life*, Cambridge: Cambridge University Press.
Turner, Frederick Jackson (1920) [1893] 'The Significance of the Frontier in American History', in Frederick Jackson Turner (ed.), *The Frontier in American History*, New York.
Ucko, Peter (ed.) (1995) *Theory in Archaeology. A World Perspective*, Routledge.
Underdown, David (1971) *Pride's Purge: Politics in the Puritan Revolution*, Oxford: Oxford University Press.
Underdown, David (1985) *Revel, Riot and Rebellion*, Oxford: Oxford University Press.
Upchurch, Charles (2012) 'Full-Text Databases and Historical Research: Cautionary Results from a Ten-Year Study', *Journal of Social History* 46 (1), pp. 89–105.
Usher, Stephen (1985) *The Historians of Greece and Rome*, Hamish Hamilton.
Usner, Daniel H. (2009) *Indian Work: Language and Livelihood in Native American History*, Cambridge, MA: Harvard University Press.
Vansina, Jan (1985) *Oral Tradition as History*, Oxford: Oxford University Press.
Vansina, Jan (1994) *Living in Africa*, Madison: University of Wisconsin Press.
Vansina, Jan (2009) [1961] *Oral Tradition: A Study in Historical Methodology*, New Brunswick: Transaction.
Veeser, Harold (ed.) (1989) *The New Historicism*, New York: Routledge.
Velody, Irving (1998) 'The Archive and the Human Sciences: Notes Towards a Theory of the Archive', *History of the Human Sciences* 11 (4), pp. 1–16.

Venezia, Tony (2009) 'Archive of the Future: Alan Moore's *Watchmen* as Historiographic Novel', *Peer English* 4, pp. 16–31.
Vico, Giambattista (1999) [1744] *Principi di Scienza Nouva (The New Science)*, trans. David March, Harmondsworth: Penguin.
von Ranke, Leopold (1981) *The Secret of World History: Selected Writings on the Art and Science of History*, ed. Roger Wines, New York: Fordham University Press.
Wallas, Graham (1898) *The Life of Francis Place*, Longman.
Wallerstein, Immanuel Maurice (2011) [1974–1989] *The Modern World System*, Academic Press.
Wallis, Patrick (2006) 'A Dreadful Heritage: Interpreting Epidemic Disease at Eyam, 1666–2000', *History Workshop Journal* 61 (1), pp. 31–56.
Walton, Annette (2010) *Oxford Historian*, Vol. VIII.
Ward, Geoffrey, Ken Burns and Ric Burns (1990) *An Illustrated History of the War between the States*, New York: Knopf.
Ward-Perkins, Bryan (2005) *The Fall of Rome and the End of Civilization*, Oxford: Oxford University Press.
Ware, Vron (1992) *Beyond the Pale: White Women, Racism and History*, Verso.
Weber, Eugen (1977) *Peasants into Frenchmen: The Modernization of Rural France*, Chatto and Windus.
Webster, Jim (1989) 'Storming the Bastille: 1789 and All That', *Miniature Wargames* 71.
Webster, Wendy (1998) *Imagining Home: Gender, Race and National Identity, 1945–1964*, University College London Press.
Weis, Charles and Frederick Pottle (1970) *Boswell in Extremes, 1776–1778*, Heinemann.
Weller, Toni (ed.) (2013) *History in the Digital Age*, Routledge.
Wells, H. G. (1920) *The Outline of History*, Cassell.
Wells, H. G. (2005) [1933] *The Shape of Things to Come*, Harmondsworth: Penguin.
White, Hayden (1978) *Tropics of Discourse: Essays in Cultural Criticism*, Baltimore: The Johns Hopkins University Press.
Whitehead, Andrew and Jerry White (eds.) (2013) *London Fictions*, Nottingham: Five Leaves.
Wiener, Martin J. (1981) *English Culture and the Decline of the Industrial Spirit, 1850–1980*, Cambridge: Cambridge University Press.
Wiesner-Hanks, Merry (1993) *Women and Gender in Early Modern Europe*, Cambridge: Cambridge University Press.
Wiesner-Hanks, Merry (2011) *Gender in History. Global Perspectives*, Chichester: Wiley-Blackwell.
Wilcox, D. J. (1987) *The Measure of Times Past: Pre-Newtonian Chronologies and the Rhetoric of Relative Time*, Chicago: University of Chicago Press.
Willey, Gordon and Jeremy Sabloff (1993) *A History of American Archaeology*, San Francisco: Freeman.
Williams, Eric (1966) [1944] *Capitalism and Slavery*, Deutsch.
Williams, Francis (1949) *Fifty Years' March: The Rise of the Labour Party*, Odhams Press.
Williams, Francis (1954) *The Magnificent Journey: The Rise of the Trade Unions*, Odhams Press.
Williams, Jeffrey J. (2009) 'Critical Self-Fashioning: An Interview with Stephen J. Greenblatt', *Minnesota Review* 71–72, pp. 47–61.
Williams, Raymond (2010) *Keywords: A Vocabulary of Culture and Society*, Fontana.
Williamson, Philip (2010) 'Maurice Cowling and Modern British Political History', in Robert Crowcroft (ed.), *The Philosophy, Politics and Religion of British Democracy: Maurice Cowling and Conservatism*, I. B. Taurus.
Wilmer, E. (2000) *Public History Resource Center* [www.publichistory.org/what_is/definition.html].
Wilson, Adrian (1993) *Rethinking Social History: English Society 1570–1920 and Its Interpretation*, Manchester: Manchester University Press.
Wilson, Kathleen (1995) *The Sense of the People. Politics, Culture and Imperialism in England, 1715–1785*, Cambridge: Cambridge University Press.
Wilson, Kathleen (ed.) (2004) *A New Imperial History. Culture, Identity and Modernity in Britain and the Empire, 1660–1840*, Cambridge: Cambridge University Press.
Windscheffel, Alex (2007) *Popular Conservatism in Imperial London*, Royal Historical Society.
Wise, Sarah (2008) *The Blackest Streets: The Life and Death of a Victorian Slum*, Bodley Head.

Wolf, Eric (1997) [1982] *Europe and the People Without History*, Berkeley: University of California Press.
Wood, Marcus (1994) *Radical Satire and Print Culture, 1790–1822*, Oxford: Oxford University Press.
Wood, Marcus (2000) *Blind Memory: Visual Representations of Slavery in England and America, 1780–1865*, Manchester: Manchester University Press.
Woodward, W. E. (1936) *A New American History*, Faber & Faber.
Woolf, D. R. (2000) *Reading History in Early Modern England*, Cambridge: Cambridge University Press.
Woolf, Virginia (2002) [1985] *Moments of Being*, ed. Jeanne Schulkind, Pimlico Press.
Woolfson, Jonathan (ed.) (2005) *Renaissance Historiography*, Basingstoke: Macmillan.
Worster, Donald (1993) *The Wealth of Nature: Environmental History and the Ecological Imagination*, New York: Oxford University Press.
Wright, Patrick (1998) *On Living in an Old Country: The National Past in Contemporary Britain*, Verso.
Wrigley, E. A. (1990) *Continuity, Chance and Change*, Cambridge: Cambridge University Press.
Wrigley, E. A., R. S. Davies, J. E. Oeppen and R. S. Schofield (1989) *English Population History from Family Reconstitution, 1580–1837*, Cambridge: Cambridge University Press.
Wrigley, E. A., David Eversley and Peter Laslett (1966) *An Introduction to English Historical Demography: From the Sixteenth to Nineteenth Centuries*, Weidenfeld and Nicolson.
Wrigley, E. A. and R. S. Schofield (1981) *The Population History of England, 1541–1871: A Reconstruction*, Cambridge: Cambridge University Press.
Wu, Duncan (1994) *Romanticism: An Anthology*, Oxford: Blackwell.
Yeo, Stephen (1977) 'A New Life. The Religion of Socialism in Britain 1883–1896', *History Workshop Journal* 4 (1), pp. 5–56.
Yonge, C. M. (1988) [1876] 'On Woman and the Church', in James Moore (ed.), *Religion in Victorian Britain*, Manchester: Manchester University Press.
Young, Michael and Peter Willmott (1957) *Family and Kinship in East London*, Routledge and Kegan Paul.
Young, Robert (1990) *White Mythologies: Writing, History and the West*, Routledge.
Young, Robert (2001) *Postcolonialism: An Historical Introduction*, Oxford: Oxford University Press.
Zangwill, Israel (1998) [1892] *Children of the Ghetto*, ed. Meri-Jane Rochelson, Detroit, MI: Wayne State University Press.
Zemon Davis, Natalie (1987) *Fiction in the Archives: Pardon Tales and Their Tellers in Sixteenth-Century France*, Cambridge: Polity Press.
Zemon Davis, Natalie (2007) *Trickster Travels: A Sixteenth-Century Muslim between Worlds*, Faber.

Index

Adorno, Theodore 114
Afghanistan 67, 233, 304, 430
Africa 5, 9, 28, 44, 53, 115, 117, 186, 271, 272, 317, 405; ancient 54, 57, 77, 104, 209, 316, 331, 411, 413; anthropology 322, 324, 328; archaeology 304, 308; environment 291; geography 363, 365; global history 268, 273, 274, 275, 276, 287, 294, 297; historiography 267, 426, 427; literature 341; oral histories 441, 446–8, 454; slave trade 82, 86–8, 91, 117, 178, 246, 264, 266, 273, 293, 394, 429
AIDS 211, 213–15, 219, 278
Albert, Prince Consort 227–9
Alexander the Great 9, 257
Alexander, Sally 203–5
Althusser, Louis, *For Marx* 108
American Anthropological Association 323
American Historical Association 73–4
America, United States of 9, 42, 43, 53, 55, 60, 67, 68, 77, 83, 96, 101, 114, 117, 118, 124, 131, 150, 169, 170, 175, 182, 185, 192, 193, 195, 212, 238, 239, 240, 243, 255, 256, 258, 259, 266, 280, 289, 317, 394, 397, 412, 422, 423, 456; anthropology 323, 329–30, 331; archaeology 305–6, 308–10, 312, 320; archives 421, 427–8, 430, 432, 435–6; Civil Rights Movement 89, 90, 412, 437; Civil War 82, 84, 86, 238, 240–3, 245, 428, 430; consensus historians 71, 80–3, 84, 85; Declaration of Independence 35, 86, 93, 305; environment 91, 292, 293, 296; frontier thesis 71, 75–6, 79; global history 264, 267, 270, 273, 274, 297; historiography 71–89, 91–2, 98–9, 135, 157, 164; literature 347–51; oral history 442, 449, 450, 454; progressive historians 71, 76–80, 82, 84–5, 91; public history 225, 226; race 83–91, 238, 246, 259, 346–7; radicalism 83–6, 89, 97; Revolution/War of Independence 28, 54, 59, 60, 65, 67, 78–9, 82, 87, 88, 93, 94, 98, 113, 124, 141, 152, 187, 251, 252, 257, 387, 396, 411

Amerindians 87, 305, *306*, 308–10
Anderson, Benedict 165, 216
Anderson, Hans Christian 455
Anderson, Perry 110–11, 131–2, 134–5
Anglo-Saxon England 32, 228, 233, 234, 429
Annales School 121, 164, 182, 274, 292, 310, 361, 394
anthropology 322–37; definition 323; development 323–4; ethnohistory 331–4; functionalism 326–8; microhistory 334–6; myth 329–31; structuralism 238–9
antiquarianism 33–4, 36
apartheid 426, 447–8; South African History Online 446–7
Apocalypse Now see Coppola, Francis Ford
Arabs/Arab world 22, 27, 28, 122, 268–70, 287, 310, 316–19, 331, 349, 411, 422; Arabic 28, 35, 43, 264, 404
archaeology 303–21; artefacts 305–7; definition 304–6; development 306–9; empire 309–10; historical 313–15; Jerusalem 315–20; popularity 303–4; theoretical 310–12
architecture 4, 28, 41, 47, 174, 229, 257, 259, 315, 361, 380, 430
archives 8, 9, 25, 190, 207, 216, 239, 241, 244, 379, 389, 391, 405, 415, 452, 453; anthropology 324, 328, 331; archaeology 311; business history 157, 158–60; community 422–7; definition 417–20; digitization 427–34; environmental history 296–7; Jewish (YIVO) 420–2; oral history 443, 445, 451; professionalization 425–6; public history 223, 225, 226, 227, 230, 232–3; social media. 434–8; state 422–7
aristocracy 98, 107, 111, 129, 130, 132, 170, 195, 228, 389; visual imagery 245, 255
Ark of the Covenant 417
army 7, 151, 202, 238, 243, 304, 381–3, 402, 417
art; City 359–61; industrialization 155, 248–50; painting 11, 63, 65, 71–2, 100, 155, 207, 237, 245–50, 253–5, 260, 296, 343, 348, 354, 360, 362–3, 368–9, 407, 421, 444
Ashton, T.S. 154–5

Asia 5, 114, 169, 264, 266, 268, 271, 272, 274, 287, 294; anthropology 322; archaeology 309, 317; environment 297; geography 362, 365
Astell, Mary 202
atheism 173, 176
Athens 5, 7, 330
atomic bomb 81, 120, 126, 240
Augustine of Hippo 19, 406
Augustus, Roman emperor 10–12
Australia 225, 291, 410; and public history 225, 226
authority 58, 68, 96, 169, 171, 195, 214, 245, 272, 291, 381, 401; imperial 118, 122, 123, 188, 209, 281, 383; religious 22, 31, 35, 72, 96, 187; social 115, 131, 163, 165–8, 182, 186–7, 188, 327, 412, 446

Bacon, Francis 33, 38, 52, 295
Bakhtin, Mikhail, *Rabelais and his World* 187–8, 196
Baldwin, James 90
Baldwin, Stanley 139
Bancroft, George 73–5, 86, 98, 272
banking 58, 77, 130–1, 157, 201, 264–5, 359, 429
Barbauld, Anna Laetitia 96, 202
Bartok, Bela 456
Battle of the Books 31
Battle of Cable Street 221–4
Bayly, Christopher 275
Beard, Charles 77–80, 82, 84–5
Beard, Mary Ritter 204
Beauvoir, Simone De, *The Second Sex* 208
Bede, Venerable 405; *Ecclesiastical History of the English People* 19
Bell-Smith, Frederic Marlett, *The Heart of Empire* 360
Belot, Octavie 202
Beloved see Morrison, Toni
Bengry, Justin 219
Benjamin, Walter 254, 348, 434
Bentham, Jeremy 142, 387
Berg, Maxine 153–4, 202
Berger, John, *Ways of Seeing* 254
Berlin Wall 104, 108, 114
Berman, Marshall, *All That is Solid Melts into Air* 116
Bhabha, Homi 122, 124
the Bible 13–15, 17–18, 35, 43–4, 84, 201, 248, 270, 286, 307, 350, 364, 417; Christianity 13, 15, 18, 35, 405; Hebrew 17, 18; history 13–15, 17, 19, 21, 22, 26, 32, 43, 44
biographies/autobiographies 27, 33, 186, 267, 341, 356, 392, 393, 414, 420, 431, 451, 452–3, 454; ancient history 11, 22; Carlyle 51; Chartist 388, 389, 390; criminal 428, 452; Islam 27; politics 136, 140, 233–4; public history 23; slave 346; Whig 64–5

Black Death 147, 149, 151, 278–9
Black Lives Matter 89–91, 436–7, 439; and colonialism/postcolonialism 91; and democracy 90; Europe 91; Floyd, George 89, 436; heritage 90–1
Blake, William 98, 379
Bloch, Marc 164, 274
Blythe, Ronald 449
Booth, Charles 152, 368–72, 453; poverty mapping 369–72
Booth, William, *Darkest England* 175, 363
Boswell, James 41–2
Boudicca 202
Boyle, Robert 38, 52
Braudel, Fernand 121, 164, 184, 273–4, 292, 312, 361, 372; *The Mediterranean World in the Era of Philip II* 184, 273–4, 292, 361
Brewer, John 134, 141, 152
Britain: Act of Union (1707) 35, 39, 63, 67; Albion and medieval Chroniclers 32–3; architecture 174, 229, 361, 380, 430; business history 156–8; City of London 129–31, 132, 141–5, 326–7, 338–9, 357, 359–63, 436; Conservative Party 130, 131, 137, 140, 143, 452; empire (*see* British Empire); 'four nations' 66, 137; heritage 228–30, 235, 426; historiography 31, 33–6, 54–69, 58, 162; Labour Party 77, 111, 129, 131, 136–40, 142, 144, 145, 176, 237, 388; Liberal Party 137–8; parliament 35, 56, 60, 61, 64, 67, 93, 137, 138, 139–40, 141–2, 145, 159, 191, 198, 199, 200, 251, 354, 386, 387, 401, 425, 431; working class 77, 110, 130, 132, 136, 138, 154, 165–6, 175, 176, 201, 205, 215, 239, 252, 355, 357, 360, 361, 369, 387, 389, 443
British Library 427–8
Bruni, Leonardo, *History of Florence* 29
Buddhism 404
Burckhardt, Jacob, *Civilization of the Renaissance in Italy* 18–12, 28–30
bureaucracies 68, 115, 136, 151, 163, 178, 179, 195, 265, 354, 424
Burke, Edmund 54–61, 67, 69, 94, 99–100, 202; French Revolution 54–60, 94, 99–100; India 59–60; Whig history 56–7, 60, 61, 67, 69
Burke, Peter 29, 31, 74; anthropology 325–6; cultural history 180, 182, 186; social theory 163; visual evidence 245, 255
Burns, Ken, *The Civil War* 240–3
Burton, Antoinette 209, 418–19
business history 146, 155–60
Butler, Judith 213
Butterfield, Herbert 60–3
Bynum, Caroline 20–8, 207
Byzantine Empire 13, 26, 150, 232, 317

calendar 21, 22, 318, 339, 399, 400, 405–9, 424–5; Gregorian 408
Camden, William: *Britannia* 33–4
Cannadine, David 54, 64–5, 69, 142
capitalism 37, 39, 40–1, 53, 77, 81–4, 90–1, 115, 117, 122, 155, 157, 168, 171, 190, 191, 281, 295, 340, 361, 388, 390, 393, 399; female labour 154, 199–202, 203, 205–6; gentlemanly 129–36, 143; global 149, 266–7, 271, 294–5, 334; Marx 83, 105–13, 266, 271, 394, 411; religion 173; slavery 86–7, 266, 273; time 397, 399–402, 415
Caribbean 88, 91, 186, 264, 266, 288, 365
Carlyle, Thomas 45, 48, 50–3, 100–2, *103*; French Revolution 100–1, 102
Carr, E.H. 377–8, 380–1, 384, 396; *What is History?* 378
cartography 276, 365, 367, 368, 370, 372, 373
Catholicism 22, 42, 49, 50, 60, 61, 62–3, 66, 175, 182, 188, 207, 221, 248, 329, 335, 365, 388, 408, 411; Catholic emancipation 58, 62, 67, 130, 141
causality *see* historiography
cave paintings 245
Caxton, William 22, 437
Chakravarti, Dipesh 276–7
Chamberlain, Mary 450
Charles I 34, 61
Chartism 386–91
Chauncey, George 218
Childe, V. Gordon 304–5, 312
children 74, 89, 105, 148, 200, 208, 217, 218, 222, 225, 232–3, 298, 329, 333, 336, 346, 357, 381, 386, 393, 421, 435–6; family 169, 171–2, 192; labour 154, 198, 202, 257; nation 67–8; oral history 442, 444, 445–7, 452–3; slum 254, 363, 372, 397; time 398
China 22, 53, 122, 278, 280, 281, 365, 394, 421; environmental 287, 289, 294–6; global history 117, 264, 268, 275, 276; travel 268, 287, 364
Chou En Lai 262
Christianity 3, 48, 50, 95, 108, 130, 150, 173, 174–5, 176, 177, 278, 286, 307, 316, 317; and cartography 365–7; empire 323–4, 331; global history 268, 271; historiography 3, 13–15, 17, 18–22, 26–7, 28, 30, 31, 35, 41–3, 62; myth 95–6, 329, 334–6; nonconformity 117, 136, 177, 334; radicalism 55, 166–7, 176–7; secularization 27–8, 41, 44–5, 173–6, 275, 412; slavery 83–4, 86; time 404–9, 411; women 199
chronology 132, 134, 137, 160, 171, 241, 256, 404, 407, 450, 453; archaeology 303, 315, 316, 317, 336, 344, 390; Christian 14, 405–9; historiography 9, 10, 15, 17, 19, 27, 33, 34, 43; periodization 412–16; time 398–9, 404

Cicero, Marcus Tullius 5, 7, 29
cities 14, 91, 93, 94, 175, 176, 178, 265, 268, 270, 280, 316–20, 361–2, 373, 379, 406, 418, 439, 443, 448, 450, 455; ancient 5, 6, 23, 278, 285, 304; City of London 129–31, 132, 141–5, 326–7, 338–9, 357, 359–63, 436; modernity 48, 252, 258–9, 361, 400; representation 252, 338, 351, 352, 354, 355, 362, 363–4; sexuality 211, 218
citizenship 5, 23, 48, 67–8, 93, 115, 121, 133, 136, 143, 150, 191, 209, 217, 225–6, 262, 277, 347–8, 368, 371, 425, 436
Civil War 294; American 82, 84, 86, 238, 240–3, 245, 428, 430; English 31, 32, 34, 35, 60, 61, 62, 63, 94, 160, 182, 231, 294; Spanish 222
Clarendon, Edward Hyde, First Earl of, *History of the Rebellion and Civil War in England* 33–4
Clark, Alice 204
Clark, Anne 205
Clarke, Peter 137–8
Clashfern, Lord Mackay of 423–5
class 17, 31, 44, 77, 79, 115, 116, 129, 130, 131, 134, 137, 143, 144, 151, 171, 250, 387, 402; authority 165–8; culture 182, 183; gender 162, 194, 198, 199–206, 209, 214–16, 219, 398, 411; historiography 59, 65, 67, 71, 78, 80, 82, 83–4, 85, 108–13, 135, 167–8, 177–9, 191, 192, 212, 225, 228–9, 380, 388–90, 394; identity 140; Marx 105–13, 132, 162, 167, 168, 173; metropolis 252, 352, 354–7, 360–1, 369–71; middle 83, 111, 122, 130, 136, 147, 155, 165, 170, 191, 193, 214–15, 245, 357, 362, 368, 379; oral history 443–6, 449, 450; race 87, 162, 194, 219, 281; religion 108, 173–7; working 45, 64, 66–7, 77, 107, 109–12, 132, 136, 137–8, 142, 154, 165, 166–8, 170, 173, 176, 239, 245, 354, 355, 357, 360–1, 368, 369, 387, 388–90, 400, 443–6, 450
classics 17, 29–30, 31, 32, 310
Claude glasses 45–6
Cleghorn, Hugh 289–91
Cobbett, William, *Rural Rides* 142, 379, 387
Cocks, H. G. 213
Cole, G.D.H., *Chartist Portraits* 388; and Postgate, Raymond, *The Common People* 108
Cole, Thomas 71–2, 75
Colley, Linda 251
Collingwood, R.G.: archaeology 310–12, 320; historiography 3, 4, 74, 139, 345, 347, 392, 410
colonialism/postcolonialism 114, 117, 122–6, 188, 267, 340; environment 287–91; identity 91, 196, 209; sexuality 217–18, 219

Columbus, Christopher 76, 318, 365, 401
comics 209, 349–51, 384
commerce/commercialization 31, 33, 39–40, 42, 48, 49, 53, 117, 120, 130–1, 142, 144, 157, 184, 227, 256, 266, 271, 272, 273, 275, 285, 287, 291, 294, 336, 352, 400, 401, 410, 429, 430, 431, 444, 456
Common Era (CE) 3, 23
Communism 107–9, 112, 351, 394
Communist Party 110, 452; Historians Group 110, 155
Comte, Auguste 163, 392, 410
Conan Doyle, Sir Arthur: *The Man with the Twisted Lip* 338–40
Condorcet, Nicholas 123
Confucius 22
Connell, Raewyn 215
Conrad, Joseph, *Heart of Darkness* 243, 340, 363
Conservatism 45, 54, 140, 167, 229, 297; Burke 55, 59, 99
Constantine the Great 13, 19
constitution/constitutionalism 41, 45, 103, 105; American 9, 71, 76, 77, 78, 79, 81, 82, 83, 91, 350, 423; British 54–9, 99–100, 137–9, 141, 144, 228–9, 368, 388; Whig historiography 35, 60–9, 108, 110
consumption 81, 115, 152–3, 155, 156, 172, 181, 188, 196, 207, 265, 277, 293, 320; conspicuous 186; public history 227–30, 232, 235
Cook, Captain James 322, 331–4
Cook, Matt 213, 219
Coppola, Francis Ford, *Apocalypse Now* 243–5
Cowling, Maurice 138–40, 145
Croce, Benedetto 74, 311
Cromwell, Oliver *32*, 51, 231
Cromwell, Thomas 341
Crosby, Alfred, *Columbian Exchange* and *Ecological Imperialism.* 293–4
Cruikshank, George 250, 352–5
Cubism 254
Culloden, Battle of (1746) 65, 108
Cullwick, Hannah 215
culture 98, 172, 193, 379, 380; and anthropology 181, 322, 324–6, 329–35; archaeology 304, 305–14, 320, 347; archives 420–2, 426; carnival 186–8; empire 122, 125, 140, 188–92, 362, 363; environment 284–5, 287, 293; gender 140, 203, 205, 208, 217, 219; global 263, 266, 267, 268, 270, 272, 275, 276, 279, 281; history 5, 6, 15, 17, 22, 23, 25, 26, 29, 30, 33, 39, 56, 68, 74–5, 77, 81–2, 84, 89, 103, 104, 106, 107, 111, 115, 119, 131, 148, 155, 170, 175, 177, 180–97, 196, 210, 225, 228, 229, 338, 344, 392; and oral history 441, 448, 450, 451, 454–7; political 56, 93–6, 98, 111, 113, 118, 130, 132, 140, 145, 351; sexuality 218; time 397–402, 407; visual 238, 239–40, 245, 250–3, 257, 260; working class 165–8, 205, 354–7, 361, 369, 390–1
Cunningham, Alexander 309
Curie, Marie 202
Curti, Merle 84

Dangerfield, George, *The Strange Death of Liberal England* 137
Darwin, Charles 43–4, 307, 392, 400
Davidoff, Leonore and Hall, Catherine, *Family Fortunes* 165, 201, 210, 214–15
Davin, Anna 203
Davis, David Brion 88, 107, 275
Dawson, Graham 209
democracy 42, 90, 96, 104, 109, 112, 116, 133, 136, 171, 262; American 75, 81, 83–4, 90, 92; archives 433; British 51, 60, 69, 143–4; public history
Descartes, René 38–9
determinism 106–8, 137, 259–60, 286, 350, 411
DeVun, Leah 213
diaries 41, 104, 139, 193, 194, 215, 218, 222, 225, 227, 234, 296, 324, 421, 428
Dickens, Charles 51, 101, 237, 340, 343, 352, 354–6, 363, 379; *Bleak House* 238, 340, 354; *Hard Times* 51; *Oliver Twist* 237, 344, 354, 363; *Pickwick Papers* 354, 355; *Sketches of Boz* 354; *Tale of Two Cities* 101
Diderot, Denis 38, 270
digital/digitization 225, 254, 260, 417, 427–39
Dixon, John, *The Oracle* 251
documentary sources 126, 158, 185, 237–45, 271, 272, 273, 296, 314, 320, 324, 343, 391, 454, 458
Domesday Book 314, 422–3
Douglas, Mary 196
Douglass, Frederick 90, 241
Drake, Barbara 204
Driver, Felix 363–4
Du Bois, W. E. 83–4, 429
Duffy, Eamon, *The Stripping of the Altars* 62–3
Durkheim, Emile 164–5, 169, 173, 177, 327, 400–1

East Anglia, oral histories of 449–50, 455
East India Company 118, 123, 156, 192, 263, 288, 381–3, 392, 431
East Midlands Oral History Archive 443, 445
economic history 146–61; business 155–60; development 147–50; industrial revolution 150, 153–5, 160; population 148–9, 150, 160; poverty 152; Roman Empire 150–2
Egan, Pierce, *Life in London* 352–4
Egypt 122, 152, 264, 266, 308, 309, 310, 317, 362, 436; ancient 5, 9, 20, 23, 25, 32, 257, 268, 269, 270, 274, 276, 278, 285, 303, 308, 418

Einstein, Albert 372, 408, 410
Elizabeth I 31, 33, 202, 245, 246–7
Elton, Geoffrey 42, 64, 341, 377–81, 384–5, 391, 396; *The Practice of History* 378; *Return to Essentials* 378
emotions 192, 340, 342, 358, 385; affective history 192, 194–7, 216; anger 193, 195, 385; emotionology 194; fear 193; linguistic turn 195; love 65, 148; 171, 193, 194, 195, 207, 385, 428; and revolution 196; Victorian 193
End of Days 13, 18, 26
Engels, Friedrich 105, 113
Englishness 55, 130, 379
English village, image of the 379–80
Enlightenment 75, 103, 106, 112, 114, 126, 202, 212, 213, 305, 361, 372, 455; English 34, 37–45; France 37, 38, 44; historiography 267, 270–2, 377, 379, 391, 392; modernity 114–22; postcolonialism 122–5, 218; religion 41–5; response to 46, 53, 54–60, 73–4, 379; revolution 44, 93, 94, 152; Romanticism 37, 45–52; Scottish 37, 43, 48, 307; the sublime 48, 379; time 406–9
environment/environmentalism 283–99, 361, 411; ancient 3, 7, 34, 283, 284–6, 298; built 3, 34, 229, 252, 255, 315, 347, 352, 418, 430, 439; climate 88, 258, 279–80, 283–6, 288, 291–6, 298, 359, 361, 364, 415; definition 283–4; desiccation 289–91, 292, 297; empire 284, 287–91, 293–4; forest/ deforestation 289–91; global history 265, 266, 274, 279; medieval 286–7; modern 48, 75–6, 291–8
ethnohistory 331
ethnomusicology 456
Eusebius of Caesarea 13, 19
evidence 17, 129, 131, 134, 148, 155, 158, 163, 177, 273, 275, 296, 343–4, 357; American historians 98; ancient historians 3, 6–8, 9, 11, 12, 14, 15, 24, 27; anthropology 324, 325; archaeology 305, 310, 311, 313, 314, 317, 320; and causality 391–5; digitisation 432, 433–4, 439; early modern 17, 30, 31, 34; Enlightenment 39, 43, 44; interpretation 313, 386–91; medieval historians 17, 19, 35; modern 104, 118, 271, 377–9, 380, 384–5, 395–6, 414, 418, 429; oral history 441, 442, 451, 453, 454; postcolonial 124; public history 222, 223, 227, 230, 233; visual history 237–8, 242, 245, 246, 255; Whig historians 60, 61, 64, 65, 69
Eyam as a plague village 146, 148, 150

Fabian historiography 109–11, 338
family 22, 48, 58, 108, 178, 179, 362; emotions 192, 195; gender 200, 202, 208, 214, 217, 219, 445; history of 74, 159, 162, 164, 165, 168–72, 221, 233–4, 235, 427; records 12, 169, 225, 227, 232; representation of 254, 255, 348, 357; time 398, 399
Fascism 28, 109, 185, 221, 225, 232, 412; and Battle of Cable Steet 221–4, 232, 233, 235
Febvre, Lucien 164, 292
feminism 110, 177, 198–211; class 199–200, 203; first-wave 200; historiography 199, 204–7, 219; Industrial Revolution 172, 198–9, 201, 205, 219; liberalism 200; Marxism 200–2, 205, 219; Renaissance 206–7; second-wave 203–7, 210, 211; separate spheres 200, 201, 207, 214, 219; witchcraft 209–10, 219, 404–5, 429
Ferguson, Niall 64, 411
feudalism 81, 107, 110, 131, 295
Figes, Orlando 342
film 120, 253, 255, 258, 303, 434; *Apocalypse Now* 243–5; *The Civil War* 240–3; as history 181, 186, 223, 225, 234, 237–45, 260, 421
First World War 118–19, 137, 205, 258, 272, 318, 341, 350, 394, 414, 420, 425, 430; archives 425, 430
Flavius Josephus 23, *24*
Florence 29, 30, 182
Fogel, Robert and Stanley Engerman, *Time on the Cross* 85, 427
folk culture/folklore 5, 6, 48, 49, 62, 74, 182, 187, 191, 221, 238, 330, 331, 333, 334, 336, 346, 362, 442, 448, 450, 454, 455–7; music 455–6; tales 15, 85, 119, 455, 457
Foucault, Michel 120–1, 184, 213–19, 419
France 26, 28, 37, 44, 55–6, 63, 65, 81, 94, 99–101, 105, 110, 142, 182, 256, 258–9, 326, 329, 336, 349, 351, 380, 396, 421; Enlightenment 37, 38, 115; peasant culture 100, 169, 181, 182; Revolution 28, 44, 48, 54–60, 68, 74, 93, 94–5, 99–103, 112–13, 141, 173, 252, 257, 262, 387, 388, 389
France, David, *The Death and Life of Marsha P. Johnson* 212
Franklin, Rosalind 202
Freud, Sigmund/Freudian 208, 217, 393
Fry, Stephen 229
Fukuyama, Francis, *The End of History and the Last Man* 104
functionalism 313; anthropology 324, 326, 327–8, 337, 454; sociology 337

Gacon-Dufour, Marie-Armande 202
Gandhi, Mahatma 90, 107, 144
Gay, Peter 193
Gay Power 212
Geertz, Clifford 196, 293, 324–5

gender 29, 111, 162, 168, 194, 195, 198, 199, 201, 203, 205–10, 211, 213–15, 219, 222, 313, 373, 380, 398; and class 112, 203, 205, 206; femininity 200, 208, 219; masculinity 209, 215, 219; and psychology 208, 219; and race 209
General Global Crisis 283, 294–5
Geoffrey of Monmouth 32–3
geography 359–73; ancient 4, 5, 285, 287; empire 363–7; historiography 33, 79, 116, 177, 215, 222, 274, 276, 289, 292, 294, 359–73; maps 260, 364–72; urban space 218, 352, 359–63, 368–72
George, M. Dorothy 204
Germany/German 37–8, 43, 49, 63, 98, 102, 103–5, 107, 117, 131, 168–9, 174, 228, 258, 259, 304, 318, 329, 351, 394, 421–2, 437, 455, 457; Enlightenment 37, 38, 43; Nazism 28, 117, 120, 186, 216–17, 222, 233, 239, 240, 259, 304, 330, 348, 351, 384, 393–4, 420–1; Romanticism 28–9, 48, 52, 72, 73, 75, 103
Gibbon, Edward 7, 37, 42–3; *Decline and Fall of the Roman Empire* 42, 96, 118, 163
Gillray, James 252–3; *John Bull and the Sinking Fund* 253
Ginzburg, Carlo 334–6
Glacken, Clarence, *Traces on the Rhodian Shore* 293
global history/globalization 262–99; empire 264, 265, 268, 275, 278, 279, 281; environmental 265, 266, 274, 279; historical 264–7; historiography 270–3; pandemics 277–81
Glorious Revolution (1688) 54–6, 59, 61–3, 99
Goethe, Johann Wolfgang von 46, 52, 98, 100
gothic 48–9, 174–5, 339, 380–1; architecture 47, 147, 174, 381; literature 48, 49
Greece/Greek 49, 150, 257, 330; anthropology 323, 330; archaeology 303, 305, 309, 313, 315, 318; environmentalism 76, 278, 283, 284, 285, 298; historiography 3–15, 22–8, 103, 104, 212, 228, 267, 270, 273, 276, 339, 400, 418, 428; Renaissance 29, 30, 31, 35; Romans 3, 7, 9, 31, 35, 270, 410
Greenwich Mean Time (GMT) 400, 415
Gregorian calendar 408
Grimm, Jakob and Wilhelm 455–6
Guha, Ranajit 107, 124–5
Guicciardini, Francesco 30, 270

Habermas, Jürgen 121, 347
Hall, Catherine 165, 190, 201, 205, 214–15
Hammond, J.L. and Hammond, Barbara 388
Hanisch, Carol 204
Hannam, June 210
Harding, Arthur, and the East End underworld 452–3

Harrison, John 401, 403
Harvey, David 401–2, 415
Harvey, William 38, 52
Hawaiian culture and ethnohistory 332–4
Hegel, G.W.F. 75, 98, 102–4, 113, 271; Marx 105–6, 112
Held, David 265
Henry VIII 33, 341, 422
Herder, Johann Gottfried von 271
heritage and the heritage industry 159, 221, 225, 227, 228–30, 235, 351, 426
hero, and Romanticism 37, 42, 48, 49–52
Herodotus 3–15, 285, 339, 406, 418
Hill, Christopher 34, 107, 110, 125, 182, 186–7
historical materialism 104, 105–12, 134, 312
Historiography; causation 391–5; evidence 386–90; nature of 377–81; truth 381–6
History Workshop Movement 110
Hitler, Adolf 107, 233, 239, 259, 393
Hobbes, Thomas 202
Hobsbawm, Eric 110–11, 125, 142, 155, 164–5, 201, 203, 294, 330, 414
Hodgkin, Dorothy 202
Hodgson, Marshall 275, 276
Hofstadter, Richard 80, 82, 85
Holmes, Sherlock 338–9
Holocaust 120, 238, 316, 347–8, 350, 386, 421; and YIVO archive 417, 420–2
Homer 4–6, 8
Hudson River School of Art 71, 73, 75, 89
humanism 132; and Renaissance 29, 35–6
Hume, David 34, 37, 39, 41–3, 153
Hutchins, Barbara 204

Ibn Battuta 268–9
Ibn Khaldun 286
identity 178, 179, 184, 186, 194, 196, 246, 338; class 140, 167, 339; empire 122, 190, 191–2; gender 205, 207–10, 219; national 5, 48–9, 63, 68, 75, 81, 98, 185, 225, 229, 251, 255, 359; sexuality 211–19
The Iliad 3–4
imperialism 89, 110, 150, 238, 334; British empire 69, 124, 251, 275, 291, 292, 331, 400; environment 284, 287–91, 293–4; geography 359, 361, 363–7; historiography 122, 130, 131, 132, 144, 217, 394, 402; postcolonialism 91, 114, 122–6, 162, 188, 267, 359, 362, 364
India; ancient 270; anthropology 324, 329, 336; archaeology 309–10, 315; British Empire 60, 91, 107, 117–18, 190–2, 209, 309, 336, 362, 396, 431; East India Company 118, 123, 156, 192, 263, 288, 381, 382, 383, 392, 431; environmentalism 283, 285–6, 287, 288–91, 294, 298; global 264, 266, 270, 271, 273, 276, 278, 280, 281, 365;

historiography 43, 53, 107, 122, 168, 189; 'mutiny' 105, 377, 381–4, 394, 396; postcolonialism 124–5, 188, 191, 202, 209
individualism 28–9, 73, 76, 81–2, 115, 143–5, 170–1, 173, 177, 181, 184, 407
industrialization 50, 51, 53, 116, 119, 131, 132, 142, 146, 153, 160, 165, 263, 266, 272, 275, 276, 297, 392, 444, 454; class 154–5, 205, 389, 390; gender 172, 199, 201–2, 203, 205; religion 173, 175; representation 49, 248–9, 252, 379; time 398, 399–402
industrial revolution 132, 156, 160, 182, 198, 199, 219, 248, 266, 273, 293, 297, 344; labour 205, 248–50; standard of living 150, 152–4, 155
internet 225, 227, 415, 428, 430, 435, 437, 457; archives 428, 430; oral history 457; public history 225, 227, 435–7
interpretation 189, 237–8, 285–6, 334, 344, 358, 368, 377, 384, 391, 406, 443, 456; American historians 77, 78–9, 85; ancient historians 7, 9, 14; anthropology 325, 329; archaeology 311–13, 320; postmodernism 121, 126; revolution 98, 99; Whig historiography 35, 60–3, 69, 405, 415, 452
Ireland/Irish 233, 251; in Britain 58, 59, 66, 67, 137; migration 178, 222; race 51, 65, 250, 371; radicalism 97, 137; Rebellion (1641) 34, 233
Islam/Islamic 288, 304, 318, 319; global 270, 275–6, 279; hadeeth (oral) 27–8; historiography 17, 18, 22, 26–8, 35, 63, 131, 404, 406; Jerusalem 319; travel 268, 276, 286–7
Italy 22, 133, 150, 291, 296, 313, 397, 405, 413; fascism 185, 221; nationalism 49, 131; peasant culture 182, 334; Renaissance 28–30, 38, 181–2, 206, 257, 270; Rome 7, 9–13, 19, 22, 24, 28–30, 43, 96, 151, 228, 246, 267, 270, 276, 303, 339, 400, 405, 407, 408, 411

Jacobs, Jane 361–2
Jakobson, Roman 183
Japan 276, 296, 349, 365, 394, 413, 429
Jefferson, Thomas 28, 46, 98; American independence 86, 433; archaeology 305–6, 308–9
Jerusalem 23–5, 108, 365; archaeology 315–19, 320
Jesus 43, 45, 316, 329, 334, 404, 406, 409; gender identity 207–8; historiography 3, 13, 26
Jew/Jewish 35, 42, 67, 68, 96, 108, 120, 130, 216, 234, 239, 256, 270, 279, 316–19, 335, 336, 347, 351, 388, 393–4, 417, 420–2; ancient 10, 13–14, 318; Blood Libel 322, 329–31; East London 221, 222–4, 357, 363, 371, 452; historiography 17, 18, 19, 21, 22–6, 30, 35, 81; migration 50, 178, 268; time 40, 402, 405–6; *see also* Holocaust, YIVO archive; Jerusalem
Jewish Chronicle 429
Joan of Arc 202
Johnson, Marsha P. 211–12
Jones, Gareth Stedman 112, 168, 206, 389, 396
Judaism 17, 18, 22, 23, 27, 317, 329, 422; Hebrew 17, 18, 23, 25, 319, 357, 421

Kant, Immanuel 37, 123, 310
Kean, Hilda 227
Kelley, Robert 222
Kelly, Joan 206
Kenya, oral history and the 1914 rebellion 454
Kern, Stephen 346, 392–4, 402
King, Martin Luther 90–1, 436, 437
King's Cross Voices 443–4
Kipling, Rudyard 281, 331
Klingender, Francis, *Art and the Industrial Revolution* 248
Kristeva, Julia 208

labour 111, 255, 257, 264, 340; American 83, 86, 87, 88; British Labour Party 77, 111, 129, 131, 136–40, 142, 144, 145, 176, 237, 388; capitalism 106–7, 266; division of 40, 51, 115, 271, 340; economy 40, 149, 150, 151, 172; gender 112, 115, 143, 153–4, 172, 201–2, 205–6, 208, 340, 445; historians 74, 110, 111–12, 157, 160, 203; metropolitan 355, 369; movement 77, 110, 132, 176–7, 388; poor 40, 117, 355, 410; rural 248, 250, 279, 280, 445, 449, 450; time 400, 415; working-class 111–12, 140, 168, 203–6, 369
landscape 5, 6, 17, 31, 185, 260, 289, 291, 314, 373, 418; American tradition 71, 72, 74, 305; Romanticism 45, 50; rural 249, 250, 379–80; urban 175, 218, 248, 252, 255, 363, 379
language 52, 281, 307, 323; American 74–5, 246, 308, 309; historiography 12, 23, 95–6, 104, 111, 112, 118, 122, 137, 190, 208, 219, 240, 344, 347, 381; identity 49, 67, 111, 420; political 139–40, 205, 389, 390; popular culture 162, 164, 180, 181, 183–4, 186, 188, 198, 222, 353, 355, 363, 393, 449, 455; structuralism 328, 331, 337, 419
Laslett, Peter 165, 170, 399
Le Roy Ladurie, Emmanuel 182, 186, 325
Lévi-Strauss, Claude 184, 328, 333
liberal/liberalism 49, 51, 129, 135, 141, 144, 145, 155, 176, 177, 238, 277, 392, 415, 418; American 79, 80, 81, 82, 85, 91, 435, 437; feminism 198, 200; historians 42, 55, 62, 104, 109, 111, 119, 126, 142–3; neo- 149, 150, 212

Liberal/Liberalism 62, 133, 137, 138, 165, 166, 176, 388, 390; British Liberal Party 137–8
libraries 19–20, 22, 23, 31, 43, 190, 215, 223, 276, 331, 418, 421, 427–8, 430–2, 434; Bodleian Library 430, 432; British Library 155, 156, 231, 388, 427, 429, 430–1; Library of Congress 331, 428
Light, Alison 344
literature; fiction 49, 96, 97, 148, 338, 339–43, 347, 355–8, 368, 393; graphic novel 347–51; historicism 344–7; as history 338–43; and metropolis 351–7
Livy, Titus 10, 29–30, 42
Locke, John 52, 81, 94, 202, 270–1
London 22, 148, 149, 174, 186, 230, 238, 239, 254, 255, 257, 265, 280, 308, 317, 323, 330, 367, 379, 397, 400, 402, 421, 428–9; business history 156; Charles Booth 368–73; City of 129–31, 132, 141–5, 326–7, 338–9, 357, 359–63, 436; East London 193, 218, 221–4, 371–2; and empire 142, 144, 147, 156, 190, 191, 192, 363–4, 431; literary representation 252, 338–9, 350, 351–7, 363; Lord Mayor's Show 326–9; oral history 443–4, 452; politics 140, 142–4, 177; poor 117, 355–7, 410; radicalism 93, 96, 99, 141, 368
London School of Economics 147, 157, 453
longitude 225, 401; search for 401–3
Lorrain, Claude 45–6, 250
Lund, Niels Moeller, *Heart of the Empire* 359–61
luxury goods, and economic history 146, 151
Lyell, Charles 307

Macaulay, Thomas Babington, *History of England* 54, 64, 67, 96, 98, 123, 272
MacDonald, James Ramsay 136–8, 177
Macfarlane, Alan. 322, 324, 327
Machiavelli, Niccolo 9, 30, 257, 270
Madness. 120–1, 184, 243, 244
Magna Carta 35, 54, 66–7, 423
Maimonides, Rabbi Moses ben 26
Malinowski, Bronislaw, *Sexual Life of Savages* 327–8
Malthus, Thomas, *An Essay on the Principles of Population* 40, 149
Mandeville, Bernard, *Fable of the Bees* 153, 286
Mantel, Hilary, *Wolf Hall* 341
Maps *see* cartography
Marat, Jean-Paul 100–2
Marco Polo 268, 286
marriage 10, 40, 149, 165, 169–72, 193–8, 211, 216, 240, 428
Marwick, Arthur 13, 166, 412–14
Marx, Karl/ Marxism 266; American historiography 77, 79, 83–5; Class 125, 162, 165–8, 388–9, 391; colonialism 266, 273; feminism 198–200, 205, 208, 219; historical materialism 104–7; historiography 44, 103, 108–12, 160; modernization 116–17, 132–3, 173; revolution 111–13; stages theory 106–7, 294, 394, 410–11; twentieth century 108–12, 181
masculinity 200, 207–10, 215, 226, 245
Mass Observation 239, 432
Mayhew, Henry 152, 352, 355–6, 368
McCullin, Don, *Sleeping with Ghosts* 255
McNeill, William 272
Mediterranean 5, 76, 270, 274, 278–9, 285, 287, 291, 313, 365, 409, 422; *see also* Braudel, Fernand
memory 82, 104, 402, 418, 422, 426, 432; ancient historiography 8–9, 12, 27, 287, 406; historiography 185–6, 208–11, 232; oral history 441–3, 449–57; public history 326, 347, 350, 362
Mesopotamia 276, 310
Methodism 166–7, 175, 445, 480
Michelet, Jules 28, 30, 73, 292; *History of the French Revolution* 74, 101, 271
microhistories 322, 325, 334, 336
Middle Ages/ medieval 13, 18–35, 49, 63, 80, 108, 121, 147, 149–50, 157, 169, 172, 180, 182; carnival 180–7; gender 192, 207–8; global 262, 276, 283; heritage 228–9, 235, 329; travel 268–70, 286, 364
migration 14, 50, 149–50, 168, 178, 181, 263, 266, 279, 285, 295, 313, 431, 450, 454, 457
millenarian movements 14, 68
Mill, John Stuart 123, 200
modernity 27, 43, 48, 88, 116–18, 123, 129, 131, 147, 177, 189, 213, 252, 277, 351, 360–2, 413; Enlightenment 114, 117; Renaissance 28–31; time 397, 401–2
Mohammad, Prophet 26, 51
Momigliano, Arnaldo, *Classical Foundations of Modern Historiography* 22–3, 25
Morrison, Arthur, *Child of the Jago* 357, 371
Morrison, Toni, *Beloved* 346–7
Moses 14, 18–19, 22, 26, 317, 357, 404
Mosley, Oswald 221–2, 452
Mumford, Lewis 133, 272–3, 362
museums 222–3, 225, 227, 234, 418, 438; British Museum 233; Chicago Museum 309; London Museum 157; National Museum, Copenhagen 307; Natural History Museum 174–5; Pitt Rivers 308
music 11, 41, 85, 122, 180–2, 234, 240–1, 355, 412; archive 417, 421, 428–30; carnival 186–7, 326, 390; emotion 194; oral history 448, 450, 455–6; religion 175–6; video games 259
Muslim *see* Islam/Islamic

myths/mythology 43–4, 136, 148, 184–5, 204, 216, 221, 238, 247–9, 252, 267, 286, 323, 332, 337, 350, 363, 436, 454; American 74–5, 305, 308, 438; ancient 3–8, 12, 14–15, 18, 32–3, 95–6, 339; Jewish, Blood Libel 316, 329–31; narrative 119–20, 124; nationalism 49, 51, 53; outcast London 356–7

Namier, Lewis 65, 139, 145
Napoleon/Napoleonic Wars 28, 51, 65, 103, 109, 122, 308, 362, 409
narrative 30, 131–2, 140, 142, 148, 150, 153, 184–5, 192, 196, 215, 296–7, 322, 327, 331, 380–1, 383–4, 392–6, 410–11, 413–15, 453–4; American 71, 74, 79–81, 85, 90–2, 241–2, 243, 245, 252, 449; ancient 10–11, 14–15, 17, 21; archaeological 304, 316–17; archives 428–30, 437; Biblical 26, 286; gender 201, 205, 209, 216; global 273, 276, 292–4; Jewish 17, 23, 26; literary 338, 341, 343–6, 349–50, 353–4; national 31–6, 100, 109, 262, 266, 272; and postmodernism 114–16, 118–25; public history 221–3, 228–9, 232; time 397–8, 402, 404, 406–7; travel 268; video games 256–7, 260; Whig 60–5, 68–9
nation/national/nationalism 50, 52, 60, 63–71, 98, 103, 110–11, 116, 122–5, 132–8, 143, 150, 163, 191, 225; American 72–6, 79–85, 91; character/identity 45, 48–9, 55–6, 214–17, 251, 343, 359; histories 17, 25, 28–33, 37, 42, 43–4, 206, 209, 228, 262, 265–6, 326, 394; Romanticism 45, 48–9, 50–2; Whig historiography 60–9
The National Archives 417, 422–3, 425–7, 429, 431–2
National Convention 1858 386
National Trust 229
newspapers 93–4, 159, 190, 222, 231, 254, 296, 349, 354, 368, 390; archives 428–33
Newton Burgoland (Leicestershire), oral history of 443–5
Newton, Sir Isaac: empiricism 38–9, 52; time 404–10

objectivity 42–3, 47, 69, 74, 104, 368, 379–81, 407
The Odyssey 4
online technologies *see* digital/digitization
Opie, Robert 231–2
oral history; Arthur Harding 452–4; folk sources 455–7; historiography 448–50; Kings Cross Voices 443–4; Newton Burgoland 445–6; potential 442–3; South African History Online 446–8
Orientalism 122, 126, 189, 217, 331, 362

Paine, Thomas 60, 94–100, 152, 187; *Age of Reason* 94–5; *Common Sense* 42, 118; *Rights of Man* 99
paintings *see* art: painting
Parker, Geoffrey: *Global Crisis* 294–6
Passerini, Luisa 450–1; *Fascism in Popular Memory* 187
Pathé News 238
Patriarchy 201–2, 206
Peasants' Revolt (1381) 149–50, 279–80, 424
periodization 412–15
Persia/Persian 4–5, 22, 25, 28, 257, 264, 270, 278, 317
Peterloo Massacre (1819) 142, 205, 386–7
Petrie, William Flinders 308
philosophy, of history: 14, 42, 51–2, 112, 289, 310, 385; Hegel 103–6, 271
photography 239, 245, 253–5, 258, 434
Pitt-Rivers, Augustus 307, 309
plague 146–51, 213, 265, 278–80, 399, 407–8; Black Death 278–80
Plumb, J.H. 54, 63–9
political history 129–45; civil society 141–3; nation state 129–36; *see also* Britain, Labour Party; Britain, Liberal Party
Polybius 8–9, 29
population 40, 51, 88, 133, 154, 169; environment 264, 276–82; social change 146–50, 164, 172
Portelli, Alessandro, *The Death of Luigi Trastulli and Other Stories* 185
Porter, Roy 38–9, 54–5, 64, 66; *Enlightenment: Britain and the Creation of the Modern World* 38; Edward Gibbon 42–3; visual history 250
Portugal/Portuguese 186, 264, 296, 304, 365, 422
postcolonialism 122–5, 267
postmodernism 118–22, 320, 362, 378
poverty 90, 110, 135, 164, 170, 209–10, 213, 233–5, 297, 389; metropolitan 48, 140, 176–7, 180, 190–1, 216, 222, 252, 291, 349, 353–6, 363–4, 373, 452
Price, Richard 55–6, 59, 99
Primitive Methodism 166–7, 175
progress 19, 55, 63–4, 68, 90, 92, 97–8, 103–4, 124, 126, 137, 143, 213, 229, 250, 258, 270, 272–3, 275, 289, 315, 348, 353, 380, 392, 395, 402, 406, 409–11, 428, 474; Burke 54, 56, 58, 61, 69; Enlightenment 38, 58, 106, 117–18, 120–3; Marx 103, 106–7, 271, 410; modernity 117–18, 213; time 38, 48, 79, 117, 372, 415; Whig 58, 61, 63–4, 68–9, 415
propaganda 33, 141, 233, 239–40, 255, 342, 385, 391
prosopography 22, 27

Protestant/Protestantism 43, 54, 61–2, 66, 69, 72, 83, 171, 175, 388, 408, 468; Protestant Ethic 117, 164, 173; Whig historiography 60, 63
Ptolemy 165
public history 159, 228, 234, 236, 438; academy 221–3, 226–7, 229–30, 235; archive 223, 225–7, 230, 232–3, 426; consumption 223, 227, 229–30, 232; heritage 221, 225, 227–30, 235, 426
Public Record Office *see* The National Archives

Rabelais, Francois, *Gargantua* 246–7
railways 291; business history 156–7, 159
Ranke, Leopold von 100, 104, 121, 163, 237, 312, 384, 392
the Reformation 28, 62–3, 175, 210, 248, 411
religion 26, 33, 37, 41, 44–5, 58, 63, 84, 95, 106, 116, 119, 122, 124, 168, 173–6, 178–80, 183, 196, 201, 234, 272, 324, 384, 399, 445; ancient 12–13, 43, 62, 108, 284, 336; empire 13, 42, 66–7, 188–9, 191, 217–18, 265; modernity 43, 116, 177, 189, 402; radicalism 95–6, 108
Renaissance 17–18, 33, 38, 74, 174, 181–2, 198, 206–7, 248, 257, 267, 270, 274, 344, 365, 380, 407, 414; ancients 15, 22, 28, 30–1, 35; humanism 28–9, 35–6; women 198, 206–7, 213
Riefenstahl, Leni, *Triumph of the Will* 239
Robertson, William 34, 37, 53, 62; *History of America* 43
Romantic/Romanticism 29, 37, 42, 45–9, 51–3, 59; American historiography 72–5; Enlightenment 45–6; German 29, 37, 48, 52, 72–3, 75, 100, 103, 174, 422; literature 42, 46, 52, 97, 345; radicalism 142; sublime 46–8, 59, 379
Rome/Roman: cartography; empire 276, 365; historiography 9–13, 28–31
Roper, Lyndal, *Oedipus and the Devil* 210
Rowbotham, Sheila: *Hidden from History* 203–5, 220
Russia/Russian 109, 233, 264, 277, 280, 296, 382, 474; Revolution 342, 420, 466

Sahlins, Marshall 332–3, 335, 337, 478
Said, Edward: *Orientalism* 122–4, 126
Sallust 59, 61, 79–80
Samuel, Raphael 176, 222, 230, 236, 391, 450; *East End Underworld* 452–3; *Theatres of Memory* 185
Sarkar, Sumit 107, 168, 179
Saussure, Ferdinand de 183, 188
Schama, Simon 54, 64–5, 227–8, 343; *Citizens* 68; *Dead Certainties* 342; *History of Britain* 68, 225; *Landscape and Memory* 69, 185; *Rembrandt's Eyes* 69

science 3, 7, 38, 46, 50–1, 65, 83, 99, 103–4, 118, 120, 122, 139, 147, 152, 163, 172, 193, 202, 217, 248, 257, 270, 276–7, 283, 286, 288–9, 304, 309, 323–4, 359, 361, 368–71, 377, 379, 391–2, 394, 396, 407–8, 414, 431; historiography 27, 39, 44, 52, 60, 64, 74, 77, 108, 124, 162, 200, 218, 273, 346, 378, 396, 410; religion 41, 43–5, 116, 124, 173–4, 176–7, 189, 234, 272
Scotland/Scottish 55, 63, 67, 108, 231, 251, 296, 367, 404, 408, 429, 456–7; Enlightenment 34, 37–9, 43, 45, 48–9, 52, 66, 115, 455; Romanticism 37, 49, 52
Scott, Joan Wallach 206, 213, 395
Scott, Sir Walter 45, 48, 53, 63, 97, 455–6
Second World War 71, 80, 122, 124, 135–6, 170, 174, 184, 209, 232, 239, 256, 265, 273, 330, 394, 414; modernity 114, 116, 118, 126, 351
secularization 44–5, 173–5, 275, 412
Sellar, W.C. and Yeatman, R.J.: *1066 and All That* 63, 68
semiotics 328
Seven Years War 38, 65
Shakespeare, William 12, 51, 190–1, 341, 397, 406
the 'sixties' 84–5, 211–12, 239–40, 412–14
slavery: abolition 86–8, 117–18, 264, 394; American 83–7; archives 428–9; capitalism 86–7; historiography 88, 107, 275; race 87; representation 246
Smith, Adam 37–42, 94, 98, 117–18, 123, 143, 271; slavery 117, 123; stages theory 268, 407; *Wealth of Nations* 42, 118, 287
social history 162–79; class 165–8; emergence 162–5; family 168–72; religion 173–7
socialism/socialist: American 77, 79, 81; British 132, 139, 176, 390; feminism 201–3, 205–6
socialist historiography/Marx 105–8, 112
sociology 79, 163–4, 166–7, 173, 177–9, 274; electoral 129, 136, 139; historical sociology 164–5
Somme, Battle of 118, 258, 318, 402
South African History Online 446–8
South Sea Bubble (1720) 156
Soviet Union 80–1, 85, 109–10, 114, 350, 397, 420–1
Spain/Spanish 10, 131, 274, 296, 313; ancient 9, 405, 408; Civil War 222; Islam 26–7; Jews 268, 422
Spear, Percival, *A History of India* 382–6
Spengler, Oswald; *Decline of the West* 272
Spielgelman, Art: *Maus: A Survivor's Tale* 347; *In the Shadow of No Towers* 347–50
Spivak, Gayatri 124–5
stages theory of development 53, 83, 103, 106–7, 115, 134, 267, 271, 303, 307, 394, 410–11

standard of living debate 153–6, 172
the state 67, 98, 103–5, 111–18, 136–8, 171, 176, 190; ancient 5, 23, 25–6, 285–6; archive 422–7; civil society 141–4; modernity 49, 115, 121; theories of 103–7, 129–36; Whig 116–19, 121
Stedman Jones, Gareth 168; Chartism 206, 389–90; Marxism 112
Stoker, Bran, *Dracula* 49–50, 393
Stowe, Harriet Beecher, *Uncle Tom's Cabin* 246
Strabo 365–6
structuralism 132, 326–8; anthropology 183–5, 322, 333, 337
Subaltern Studies 124–6
subjectivity 204, 208, 210, 219, 340, 370–1, 385, 425; Romanticism 46–7, 52, 74
Suetonius: *Lives of the Twelve Caesars* 11–12, 15
Swift, Jonathan 34–5, 352; *Tale of the Tub* 31
symbolism 18, 174, 248, 324–5, 336, 380

Tacitus 10–12, 15, 23, 28–9
the Talmud 25–6
technology 106, 146, 152, 157–60, 241, 266, 276, 279, 305, 362, 384, 434; information 190, 372, 427, 432
teleology 14, 62, 267, 395
television 12, 64, 68, 121, 186, 209, 225, 227, 234, 237–8, 240, 245, 254, 260, 264, 303, 341, 347, 395
terrorism 67; America (9/11) 91, 264, 347–51, 411–12, 442
Thomas, Keith: *Religion and the Decline of Magic* 324, 328
Thomason Tracts 34, 231
Thompson, Dorothy 389
Thompson, E.P. 67, 109–10, 125, 132, 142, 160, 165–8, 177, 186–7, 203, 340, 368, 399–400; *Making of the English Working Class* 109, 142, 160, 167, 203; plebeian culture 94, 165–6, 182, 187, 390–1
Thucydides 3, 6–11, 15, 29, 285; *History of the Peloponnesian War* 7
time 397–416; Christianity 3, 13–14, 18–19, 22, 26–7, 30, 41–5, 48, 50, 95, 173, 175–6, 324, 335, 404–7, 409; family 398; Greenwich Mean Time 276, 400–1; Industrial 146, 150, 152–6, 160, 198–9, 205, 219, 248, 266, 273, 297, 344, 399–401; Islamic 22, 26–7, 35, 275–6, 404; Jewish 17, 23–5, 267, 316, 329–30, 402, 406, 420–2; Newton 404–7; railways 156, 159, 291; rural 250, 279, 444–8; *see also* chronology; periodization
the Torah 14, 18, 25, 32, 35
Toynbee, Arnold 123, 147, 272–3, 275; *A Study of History* 272

travel accounts 262, 270, 286, 364; ancient 15, 268–70, 283, 286–7; global 268–70; urban 352–6, 359, 361, 363
Trevelyan, George Macaulay 54, 60, 63–6
Trevor-Roper, Hugh (Lord Dacre) 267, 295
truth 7, 15, 21, 25, 242, 378, 381–6, 396; in literature 52, 340, 342, 345–7; and maps 368–9, 371; and modernity 118, 126; and visual evidence 237, 245–6, 255

Underdown, David 107, 182
urbanization 44, 48, 53, 154, 173, 272, 344, 393, 400, 444, 454
urban spaces 359, 363; *see also* cities

Vansina, Jan 441, 454–5
Vaughan Williams, Ralph 456–7
Vergil, Polydore 30, 33
Vico, Giambattista 73–5
Victorian 23, 44, 51, 77, 144, 148, 157, 168, 173–5, 193, 198, 200, 215–16, 227–9, 254, 257, 326, 350, 363, 368–9, 371–2, 397, 400, 411–15, 425; metropolis 218, 352–4, 363, 367, 370–2; periodization 30, 257, 262, 265, 276, 294, 390, 412–13
Victoria, Queen 66, 227–8, 383, 414
video games 237, 256–7, 258–60
Vietnam War 238, 243–4, 255, 258, 293; *Apocalypse Now* 238, 243–5
Vincent, John 54, 64
Visual history 242–6, 250; archive 239–41, 244; comics 209, 243, 347–51; film/television 237–40, 242–5, 248, 253–4, 255, 258; paintings 245–51, 253–4; prints and photographs 241–2, 245–6, 250–6; video games 256–60
Voltaire 38, 42, 53, 55

wages 10, 111, 149, 153–5, 172, 201, 216, 279
Ward-Perkins, Bryan, *The Fall of Rome and the End of Civilization* 151–2
Waterhouse, Alfred 174–5
Weber, Max: religion 83, 135, 164, 167, 173, 325; social theory 85, 107–8, 132, 135, 164, 173–4
Wells, H.G. 272–3, 408–11 -; *Outline of History* 272
Whig historiography 46, 83–4, 105, 109, 111, 112–15, 162–3; American 125–6; 'new Whig' 115–21
White, Hayden 119, 345
Wikipedia 433–4
Wilkes, John 93, 141–2, 187, 386, 389
Wilkie, Sir David, *Chelsea Pensioners Reading the Gazette of the Battle of Waterloo* 63, 65, 66

Williams, Eric: *Capitalism and Slavery* 86–7, 273–4
Williams, Raymond 109–10
witchcraft 62, 74, 335, 404–5, 429, 434;
　　anthropology 324, 326, 328; feminism
　　198, 210, 219
Wolf, Eric: *Europe and a People without History*
　　263–4, 276, 294, 314, 364
Wolfe, General James 342
Wollstonecraft, Mary 96–8, 100, 202
women's history 93, 96–8, 115, 121, 142–3, 177,
　　198–203, 204–11, 269, 324, 332, 372, 398,
　　422, 429; anthropology 438–9; archive
　　422, 428–30, 437, 447; carnival 183;
　　family 153, 172; identity 211–14; labour
　　109–10, 154; oral history 450–2, 457;
　　politics 137–8; sexuality 214–19; *see also*
　　feminism; witchcraft

Woolf, Virginia 413–14
Wordsworth, William 44, 47, 97
working class 76–9, 107–12, 164, 223, 226–7;
　　culture 164, 222–5; feminism 201–6, 209,
　　215; industrial 154–5, 160; metropolitan
　　354–7, 360–1, 369–70, 388–90; oral
　　history 443–5, 449; politics 67, 96, 132–3,
　　136–44, 166–73, 387; religion 45–6,
　　173–6
world history *see* global history/globalization
Wright, Patrick 229–30
Wrigley, E.A. 150, 153, 169

YIVO Institute 420–2

Zangwill, Israel 357
Zemon Davis, Natalie 268, 322, 325

9780367740955